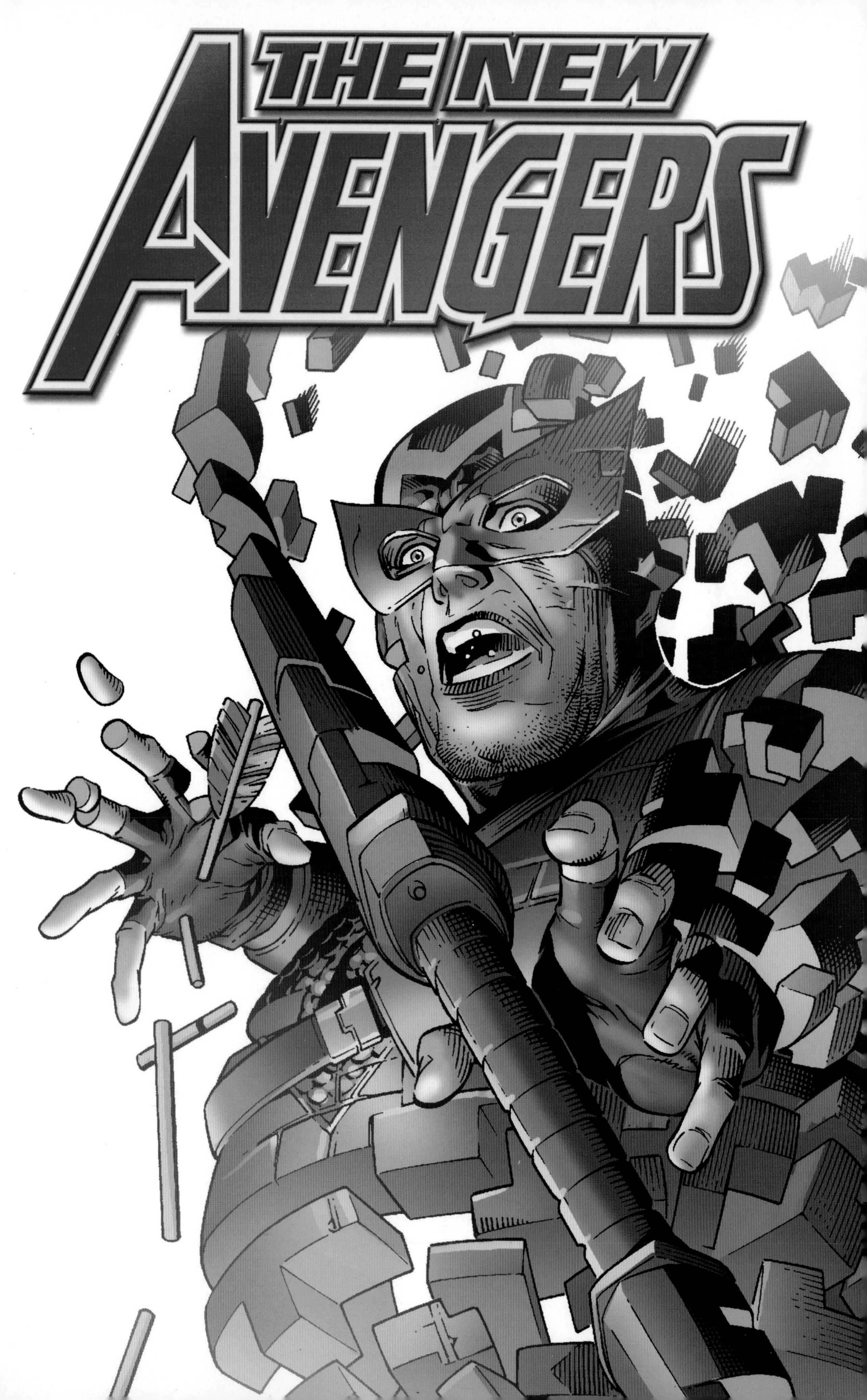
THE NEW AVENGERS

THE NEW AVENGERS

WRITER: **Brian Michael Bendis**

NEW AVENGERS #38 & 47

ARTIST: **Michael Gaydos**

COLOR ART: *Jose Villarrubia*

COVER ARTIST: *Marko Djurdjevic*

NEW AVENGERS #39

ARTIST: **David Mack**

COLOR ART: *Jose Villarrubia*

COVER ARTIST: *David Mack*

NEW AVENGERS #40, 42 & 45

PENCILS: **Jim Cheung**

INKERS: *John Dell & Jay Leisten*

COLORIST: *Justin Ponsor*

COVER ARTIST: *Aleksi Briclot*

NEW AVENGERS #41, 43-44 & 46

PENCILS: **Billy Tan**

INKERS: *Billy Tan, Danny Miki & Matt Banning*

COLORIST: *Justin Ponsor*

COVER ARTIST: *Aleksi Briclot*

LETTERER: *RS & Comicraft's Albert Deschesne*

ASSOCIATE EDITORS: *Molly Lazer & Jeanine Schaefer*

EDITOR: *Tom Brevoort*

NEW AVENGERS VOL. 5. Contains material originally published in magazine form as NEW AVENGERS #38-47. First printing 2010. ISBN# 978-0-7851-4579-0. Published by MARVEL WORLDWIDE, INC., a subsidiary of MARVEL ENTERTAINMENT, LLC. OFFICE OF PUBLICATION: 417 5th Avenue, New York, NY 10016. Copyright © 2008 and 2010 Marvel Characters, Inc. All rights reserved. $29.99 per copy in the U.S. (GST #R127032852); Canadian Agreement #40668537. All characters featured in this issue and the distinctive names and likenesses thereof, and all related indicia are trademarks of Marvel Characters, Inc. No similarity between of any of the names, characters, persons, and/or institutions in this magazine with those of any living or dead person or institution is intended, and any such similarity which may exist is purely coincidental. **Printed in China.** ALAN FINE, EVP - Office of the President, Marvel Worldwide, Inc. and EVP & CMO Marvel Characters B.V.; DAN BUCKLEY, Chief Executive Officer and Publisher - Print, Animation & Digital Media; JIM SOKOLOWSKI, Chief Operating Officer; DAVID GABRIEL, SVP of Publishing Sales & Circulation; DAVID BOGART, SVP of Business Affairs & Talent Management; MICHAEL PASCIULLO, VP Merchandising & Communications; JIM O'KEEFE, VP of Operations & Logistics; DAN CARR, Executive Director of Publishing Technology; JUSTIN F. GABRIE, Director of Publishing & Editorial Operations; SUSAN CRESPI, Editorial Operations Manager; ALEX MORALES, Publishing Operations Manager; STAN LEE, Chairman Emeritus. For information regarding advertising in Marvel Comics or on Marvel.com, please contact Ron Stern, VP of Business Development, at rstern@marvel.com. For Marvel subscription inquiries, please call 800-217-9158. Manufactured between 3/10/210 and 4/14/10 by R.R. DONNELLEY ASIA PRINTING SOLUTIONS, DONGGUAN, GUANGDONG, CHINA.

10 9 8 7 6 5 4 3 2 1

COLLECTION EDITOR: *Mark D. Beazley*
ASSISTANT EDITOR: *Alex Starbuck*
ASSOCIATE EDITOR: *John Denning*
EDITOR, SPECIAL PROJECTS: *Jennifer Grünwald*
SENIOR EDITOR, SPECIAL PROJECTS: *Jeff Youngquist*
SENIOR VICE PRESIDENT OF SALES: *David Gabriel*
PRODUCTION: *Jerry Kalinowski*
DESIGNER: *Jeff Powell*

EDITOR IN CHIEF: *Joe Quesada*
PUBLISHER: *Dan Buckley*
EXECUTIVE PRODUCER: *Alan Fine*

PREVIOUSLY...

The New Avengers know that the shape-shifting aliens known as the Skrulls have invaded the Earth. And, since they cannot tell who is really a Skrull, they cannot trust anyone to be who they seem to be, including each other. This has sent the Avengers into a tailspin of mistrust.

Recently, the Avengers stopped the Hood's newly-organized gang of super-villains, but the Hood broke his cohorts out of S.H.I.E.L.D. custody and took them right back to the Avengers. The attack at the Sanctum Sanctorum was fierce, and though the Avengers won the day, they did so at the cost of Doctor Strange, who lost both his mastery of the mystic arts and his home. Luke Cage's wife, Jessica Jones, fled the battle in mortal fear for their child's safety. Jessica has found asylum with the registered Mighty Avengers, even though she betrayed her husband's beliefs by doing so...

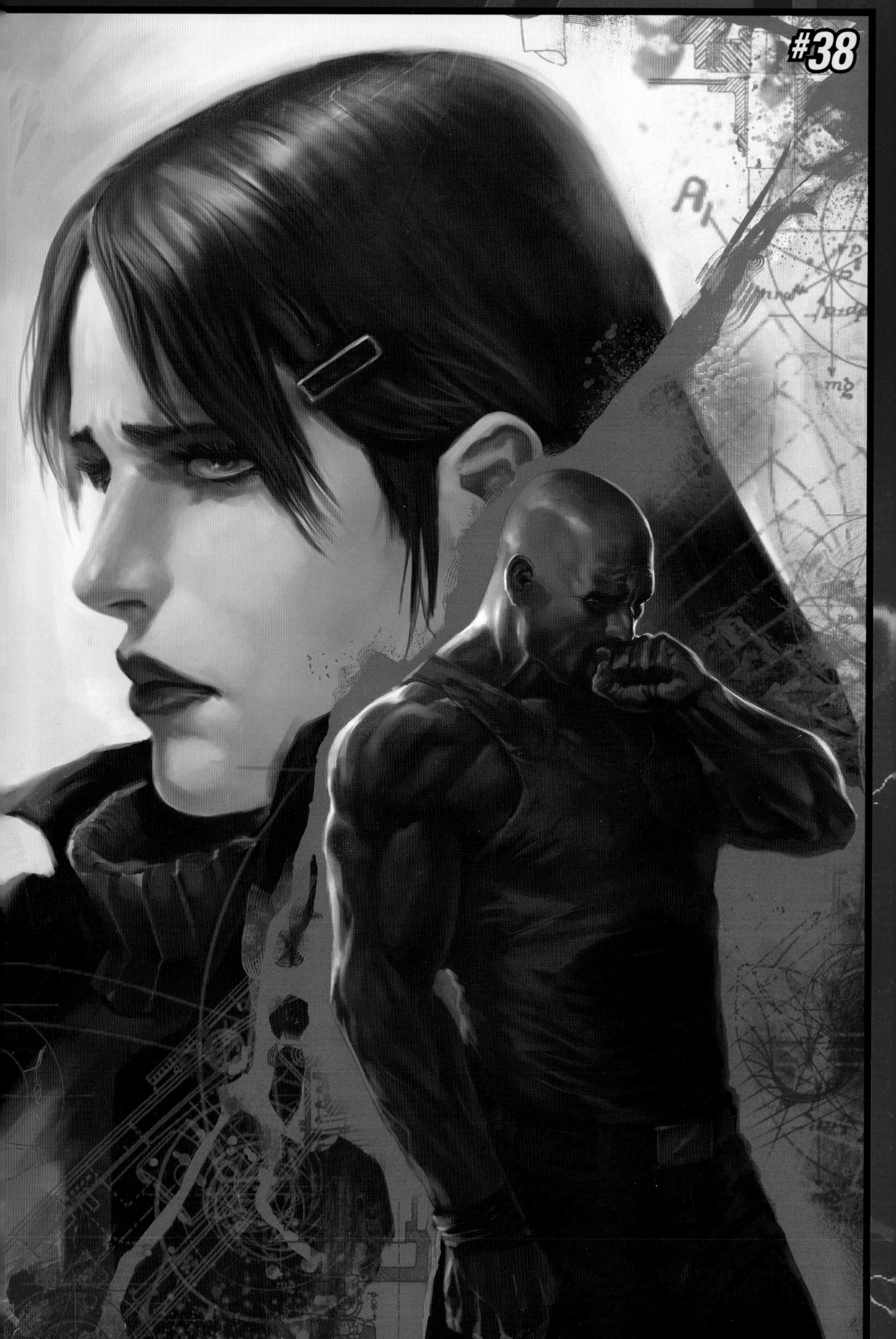
#38

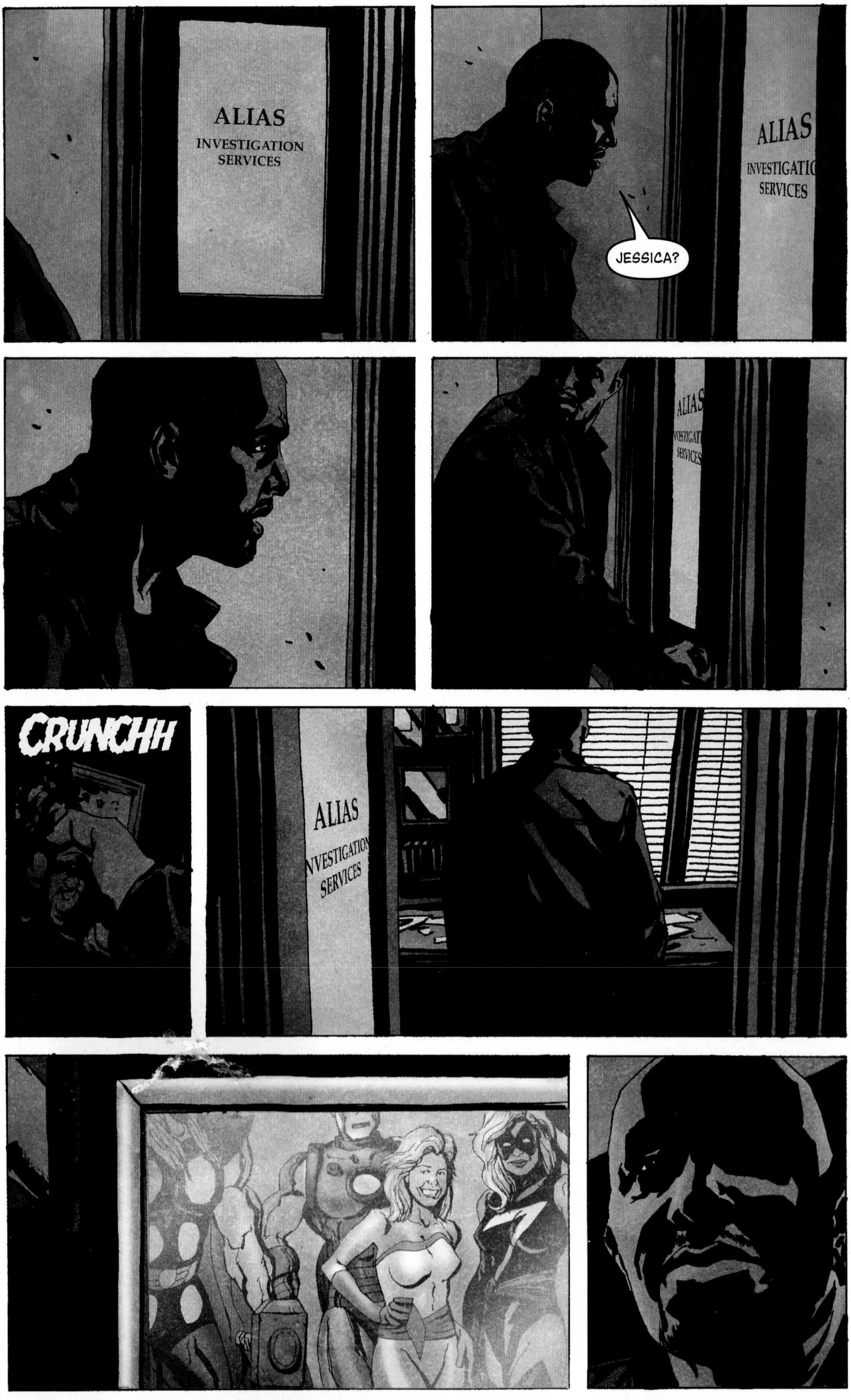
ALIAS
INVESTIGATION
SERVICES
JESSICA?
CRUNCHH

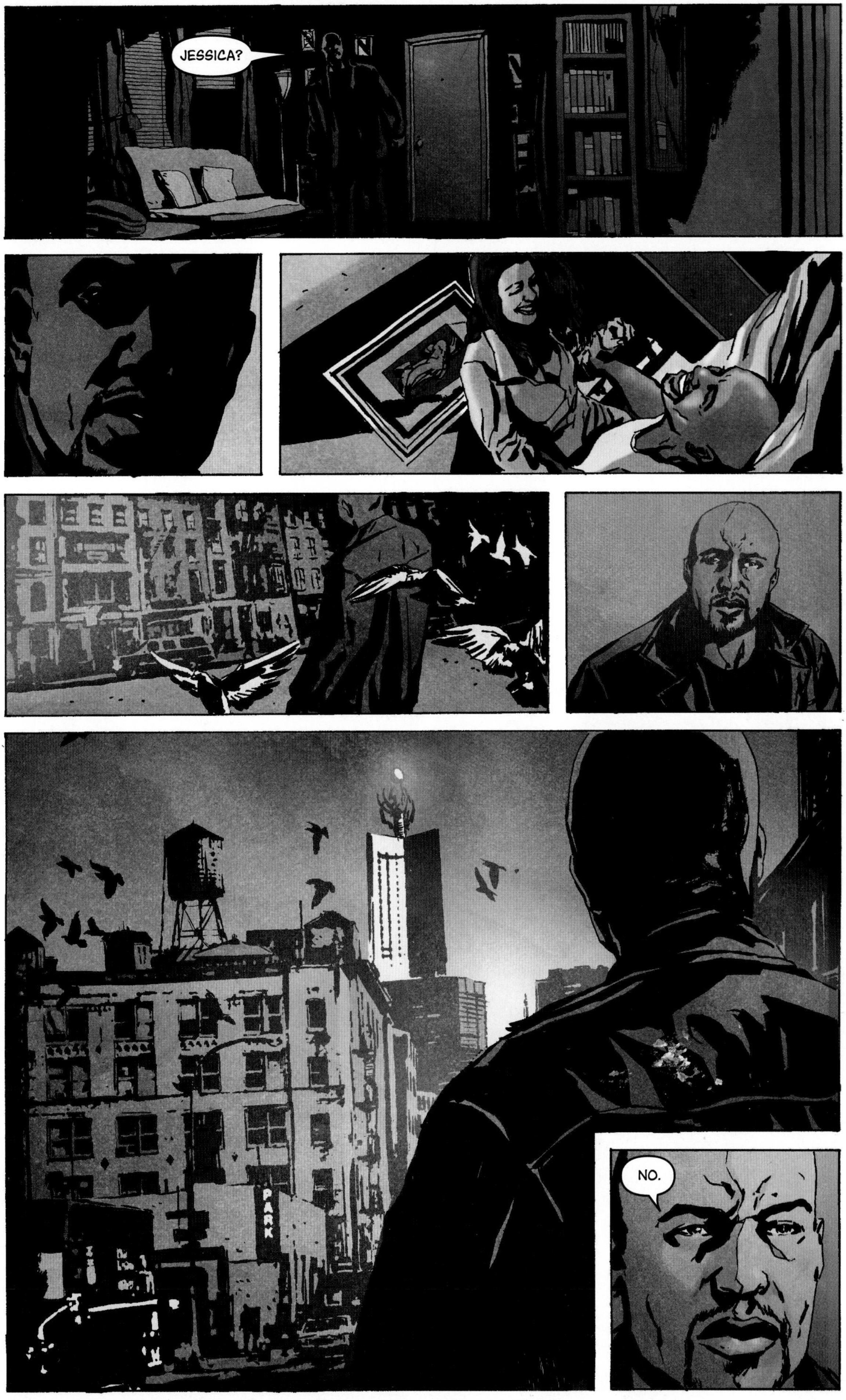
JESSICA?
NO.

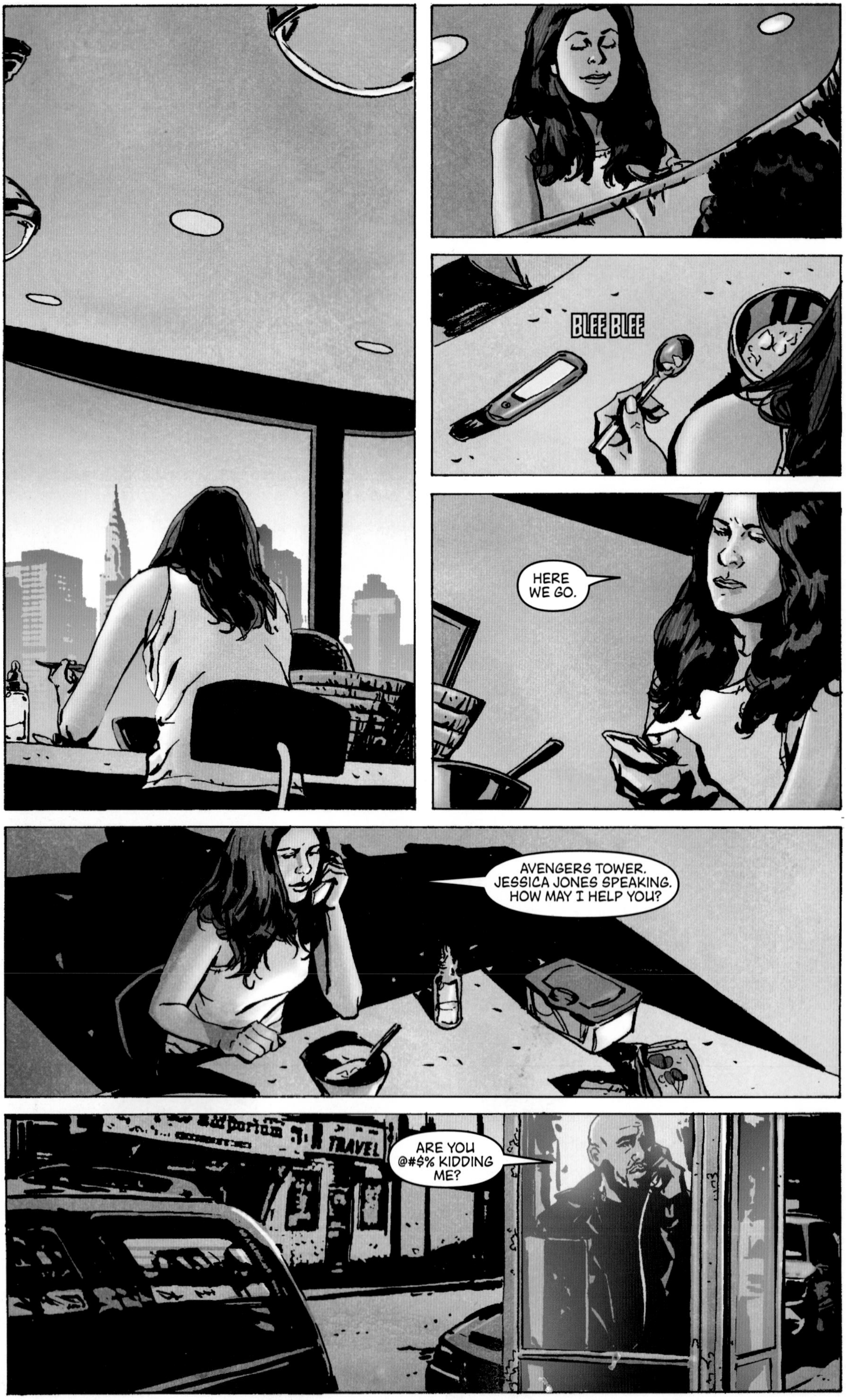
BLEE BLEE
HERE WE GO.
AVENGERS TOWER. JESSICA JONES SPEAKING. HOW MAY I HELP YOU?
TRAVEL
ARE YOU @#$% KIDDING ME?

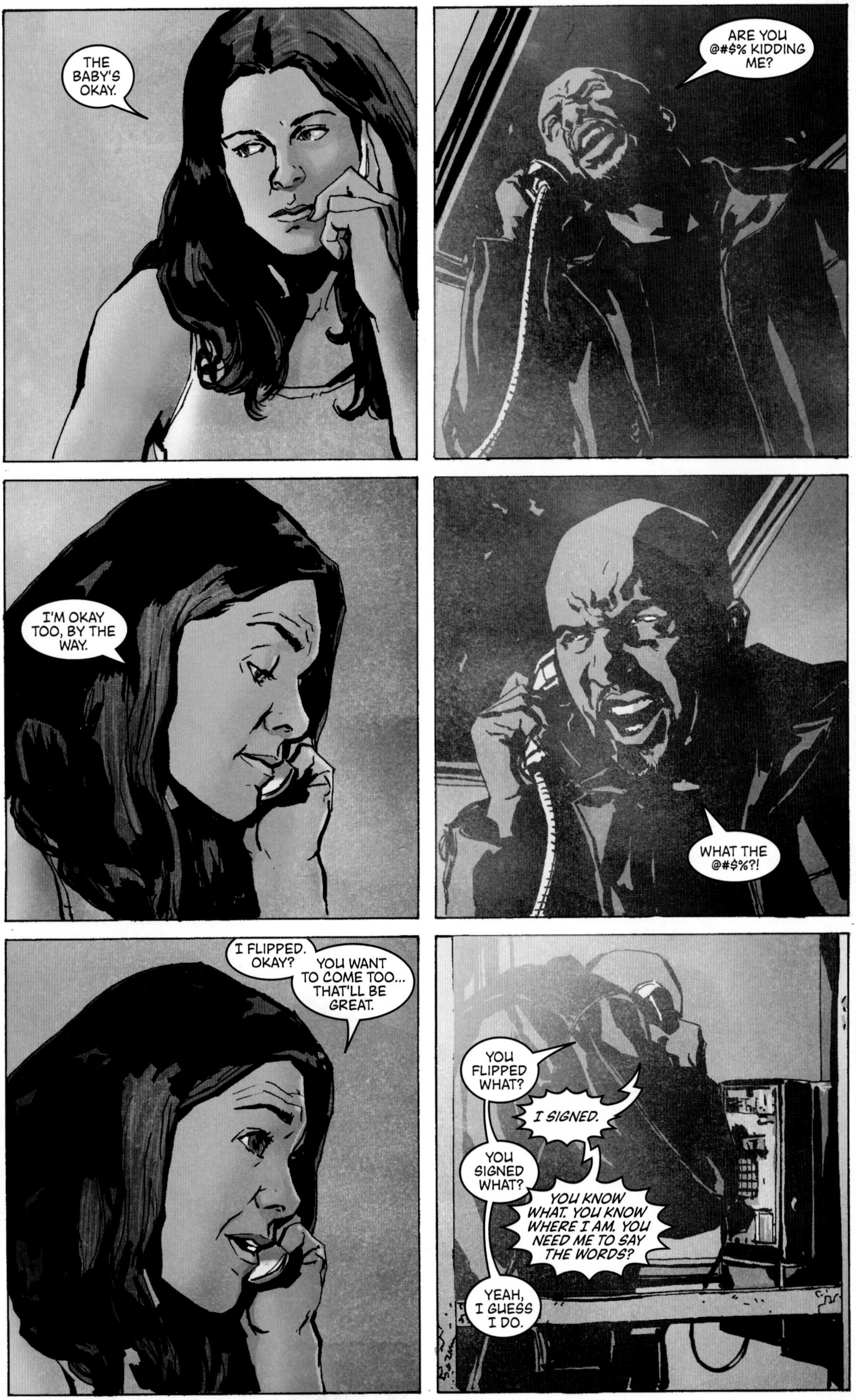
THE BABY'S OKAY.
ARE YOU @#$% KIDDING ME?
I'M OKAY TOO, BY THE WAY.
WHAT THE @#$%?!
I FLIPPED. OKAY?
YOU WANT TO COME TOO... THAT'LL BE GREAT.
YOU FLIPPED WHAT?
I SIGNED.
YOU SIGNED WHAT?
YOU KNOW WHAT. YOU KNOW WHERE I AM. YOU NEED ME TO SAY THE WORDS?
YEAH, I GUESS I DO.

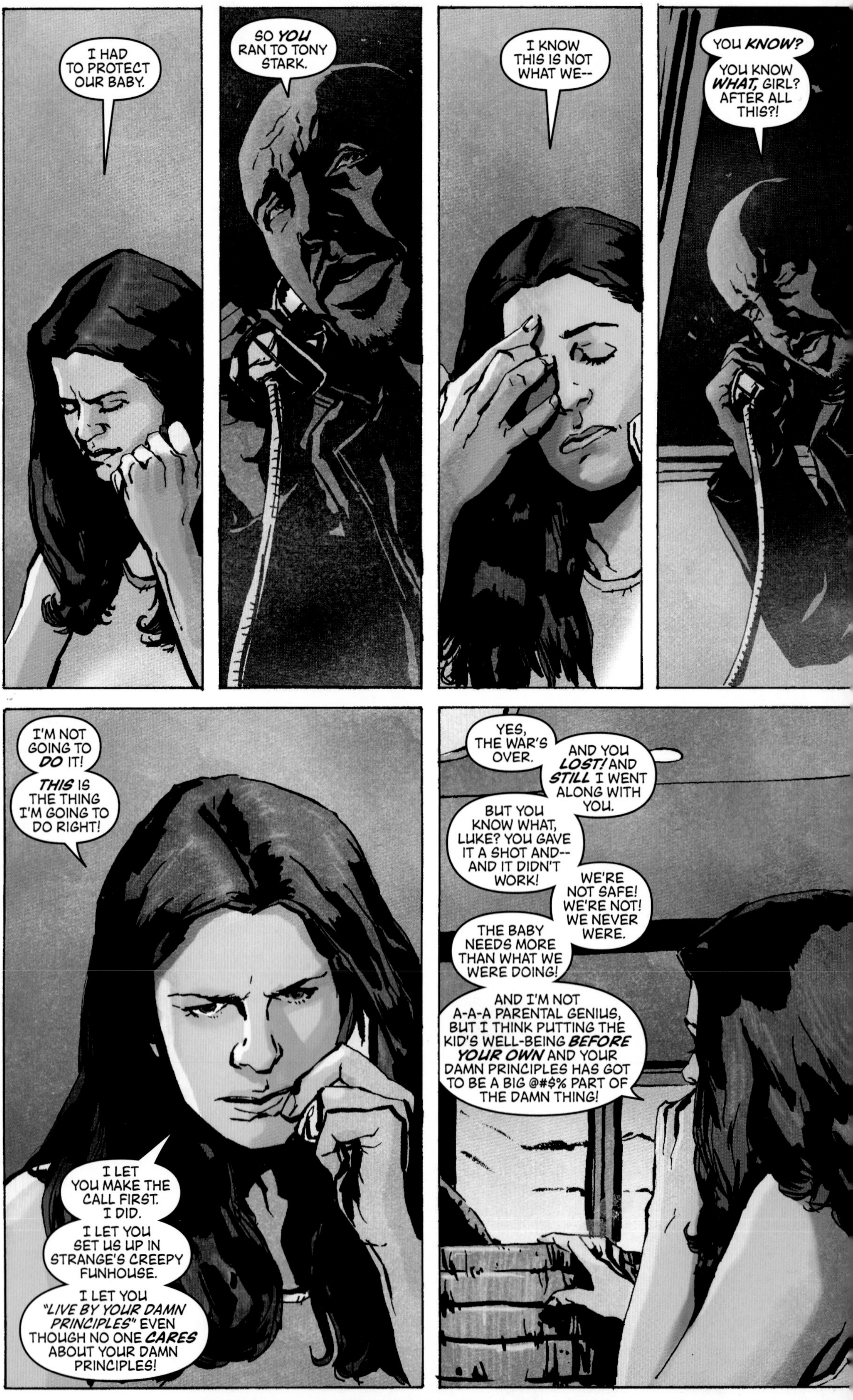
I HAD TO PROTECT OUR BABY.
SO *YOU* RAN TO TONY STARK.
I KNOW THIS IS NOT WHAT WE--
YOU *KNOW?*
YOU KNOW *WHAT,* GIRL? AFTER ALL THIS?!
I'M NOT GOING TO *DO* IT!
THIS IS THE THING I'M GOING TO DO RIGHT!
I LET YOU MAKE THE CALL FIRST. I DID.
I LET YOU SET US UP IN STRANGE'S CREEPY FUNHOUSE.
I LET YOU *"LIVE BY YOUR DAMN PRINCIPLES"* EVEN THOUGH NO ONE *CARES* ABOUT YOUR DAMN PRINCIPLES!
YES, THE WAR'S OVER.
AND YOU *LOST!* AND *STILL* I WENT ALONG WITH YOU.
BUT YOU KNOW WHAT, LUKE? YOU GAVE IT A SHOT AND-- AND IT DIDN'T WORK!
WE'RE NOT SAFE! WE'RE NOT! WE NEVER WERE.
THE BABY NEEDS MORE THAN WHAT WE WERE DOING!
AND I'M NOT A-A-A PARENTAL GENIUS, BUT I THINK PUTTING THE KID'S WELL-BEING *BEFORE YOUR OWN* AND YOUR DAMN PRINCIPLES HAS GOT TO BE A BIG @#$% PART OF THE DAMN THING!

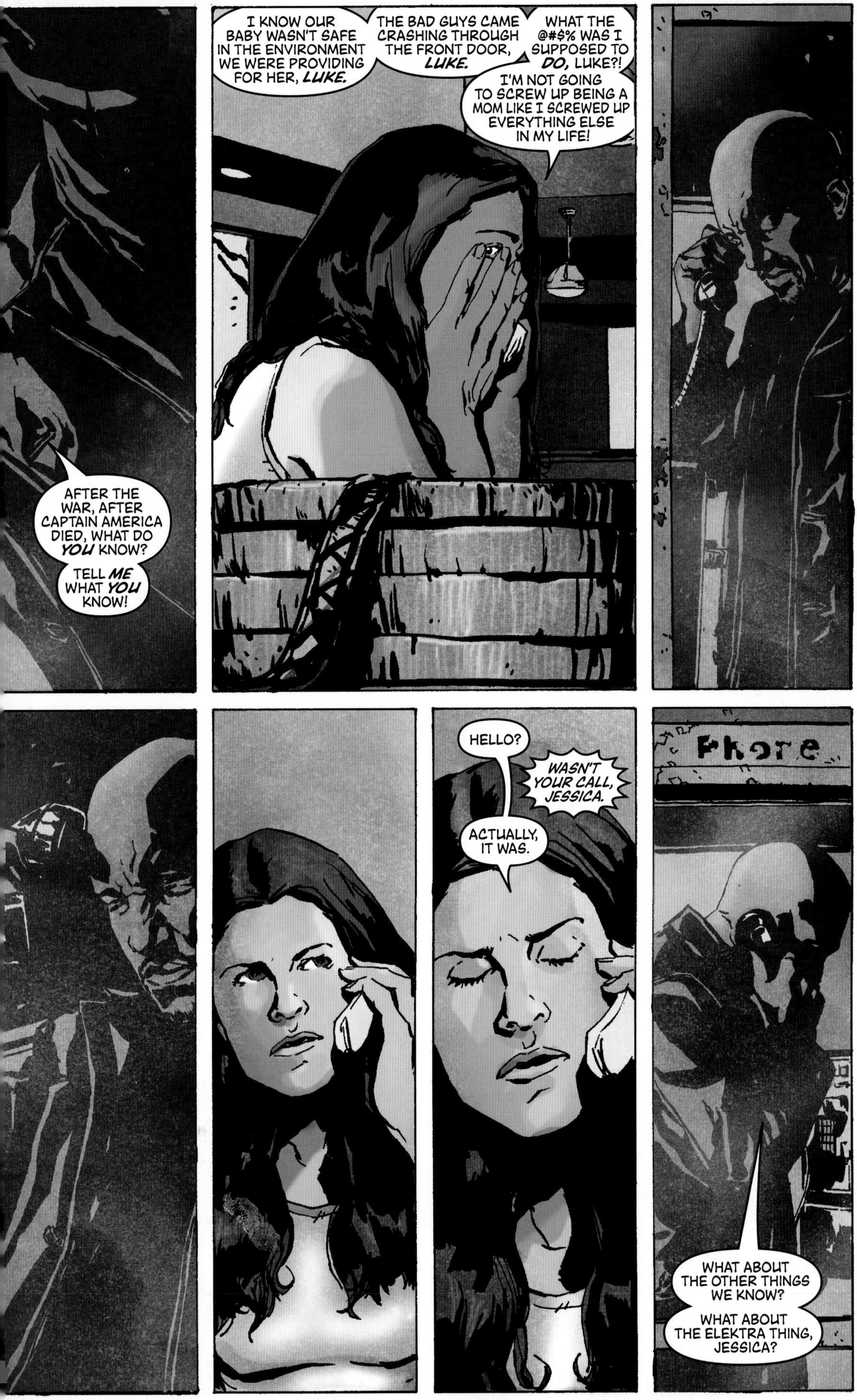

I KNOW OUR BABY WASN'T SAFE IN THE ENVIRONMENT WE WERE PROVIDING FOR HER, LUKE.
THE BAD GUYS CAME CRASHING THROUGH THE FRONT DOOR, LUKE.
WHAT THE @#$% WAS I SUPPOSED TO DO, LUKE?!
I'M NOT GOING TO SCREW UP BEING A MOM LIKE I SCREWED UP EVERYTHING ELSE IN MY LIFE!
AFTER THE WAR, AFTER CAPTAIN AMERICA DIED, WHAT DO YOU KNOW?
TELL ME WHAT YOU KNOW!
HELLO?
WASN'T YOUR CALL, JESSICA.
ACTUALLY, IT WAS.
Phone
WHAT ABOUT THE OTHER THINGS WE KNOW?
WHAT ABOUT THE ELEKTRA THING, JESSICA?

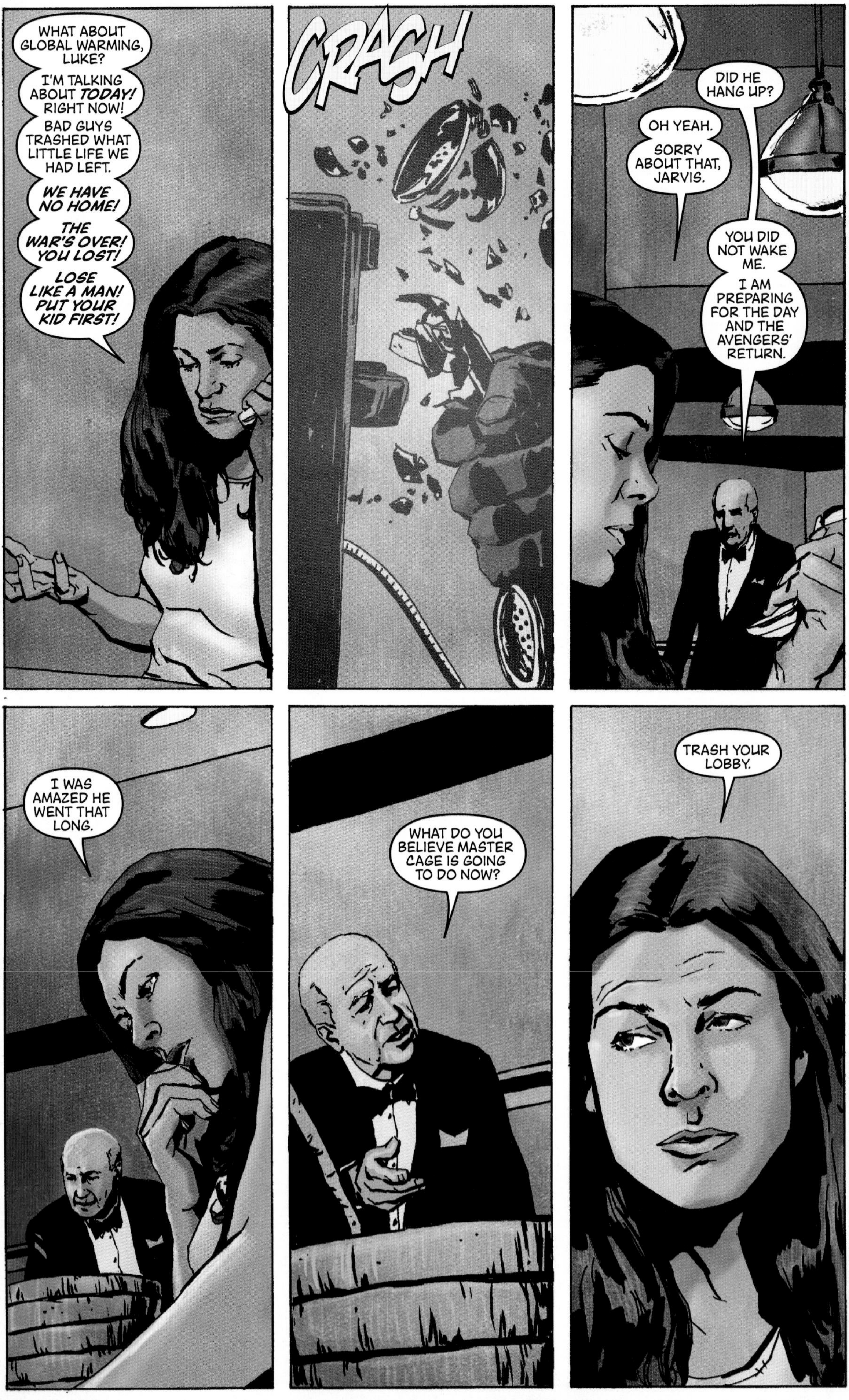
WHAT ABOUT GLOBAL WARMING, LUKE?
I'M TALKING ABOUT *TODAY!* RIGHT NOW!
BAD GUYS TRASHED WHAT LITTLE LIFE WE HAD LEFT.
WE HAVE NO HOME!
THE WAR'S OVER! YOU LOST!
LOSE LIKE A MAN! PUT YOUR KID FIRST!
CRASH
DID HE HANG UP?
OH YEAH.
SORRY ABOUT THAT, JARVIS.
YOU DID NOT WAKE ME.
I AM PREPARING FOR THE DAY AND THE AVENGERS' RETURN.
I WAS AMAZED HE WENT THAT LONG.
WHAT DO YOU BELIEVE MASTER CAGE IS GOING TO DO NOW?
TRASH YOUR LOBBY.

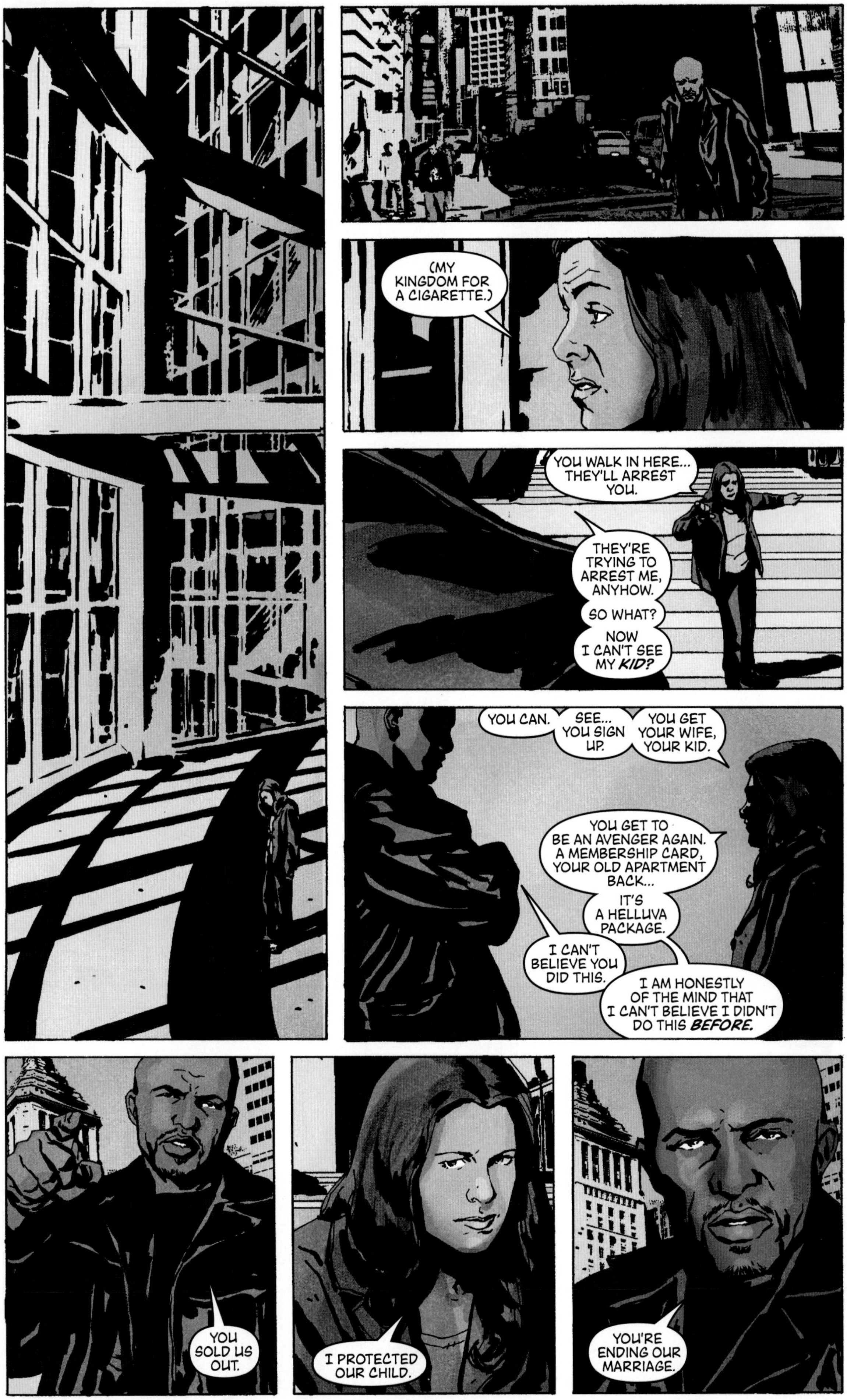
(MY KINGDOM FOR A CIGARETTE.)
YOU WALK IN HERE... THEY'LL ARREST YOU.
THEY'RE TRYING TO ARREST ME, ANYHOW.
SO WHAT?
NOW I CAN'T SEE MY *KID?*
YOU CAN.
SEE... YOU SIGN UP.
YOU GET YOUR WIFE, YOUR KID.
YOU GET TO BE AN AVENGER AGAIN. A MEMBERSHIP CARD, YOUR OLD APARTMENT BACK...
IT'S A HELLUVA PACKAGE.
I CAN'T BELIEVE YOU DID THIS.
I AM HONESTLY OF THE MIND THAT I CAN'T BELIEVE I DIDN'T DO THIS *BEFORE.*
YOU SOLD US OUT.
I PROTECTED OUR CHILD.
YOU'RE ENDING OUR MARRIAGE.

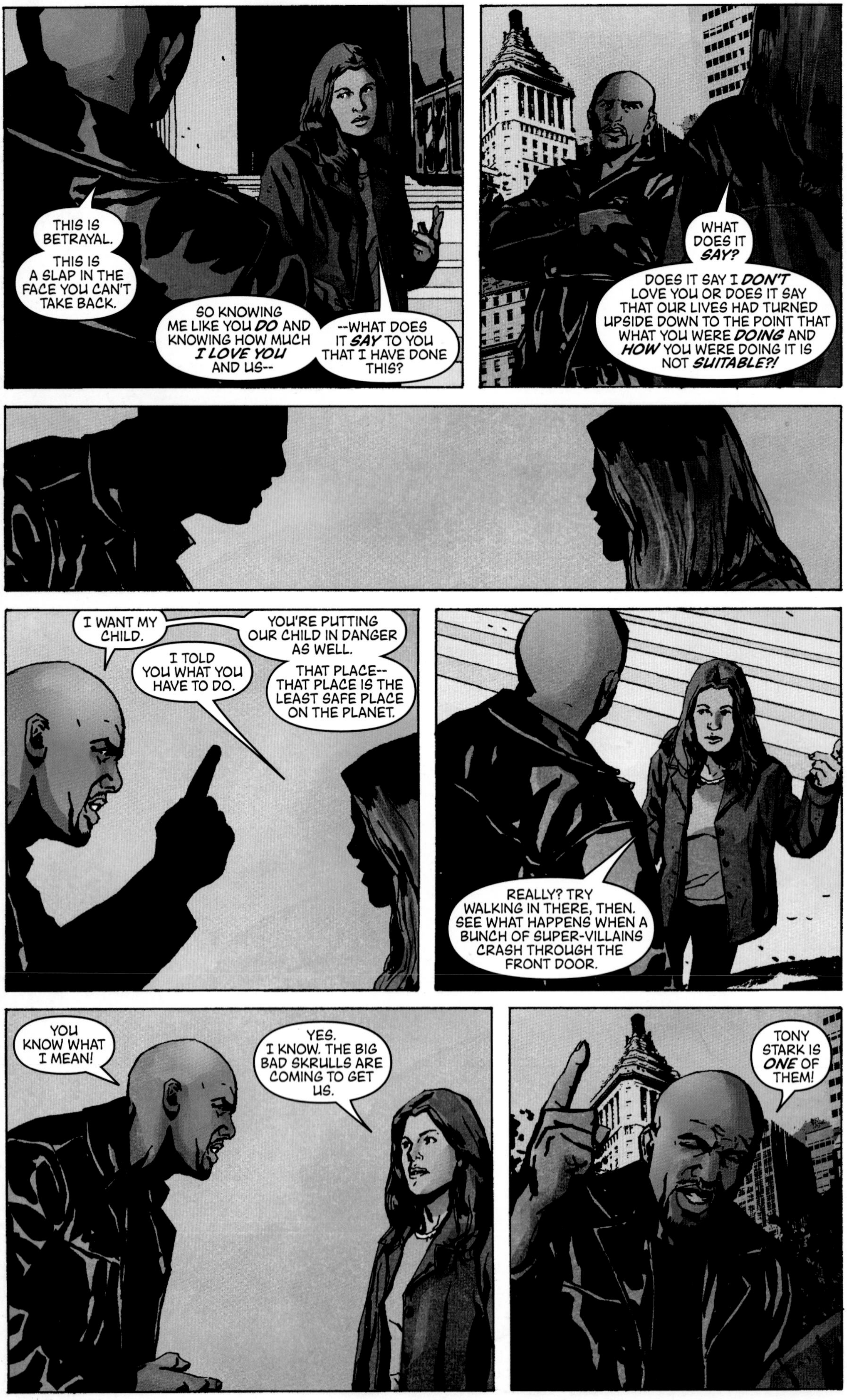
THIS IS BETRAYAL.
THIS IS A SLAP IN THE FACE YOU CAN'T TAKE BACK.
SO KNOWING ME LIKE YOU DO AND KNOWING HOW MUCH I LOVE YOU AND US--
--WHAT DOES IT SAY TO YOU THAT I HAVE DONE THIS?
WHAT DOES IT SAY?
DOES IT SAY I DON'T LOVE YOU OR DOES IT SAY THAT OUR LIVES HAD TURNED UPSIDE DOWN TO THE POINT THAT WHAT YOU WERE DOING AND HOW YOU WERE DOING IT IS NOT SUITABLE?!
I WANT MY CHILD.
YOU'RE PUTTING OUR CHILD IN DANGER AS WELL.
I TOLD YOU WHAT YOU HAVE TO DO.
THAT PLACE-- THAT PLACE IS THE LEAST SAFE PLACE ON THE PLANET.
REALLY? TRY WALKING IN THERE, THEN. SEE WHAT HAPPENS WHEN A BUNCH OF SUPER-VILLAINS CRASH THROUGH THE FRONT DOOR.
YOU KNOW WHAT I MEAN!
YES. I KNOW. THE BIG BAD SKRULLS ARE COMING TO GET US.
TONY STARK IS ONE OF THEM!

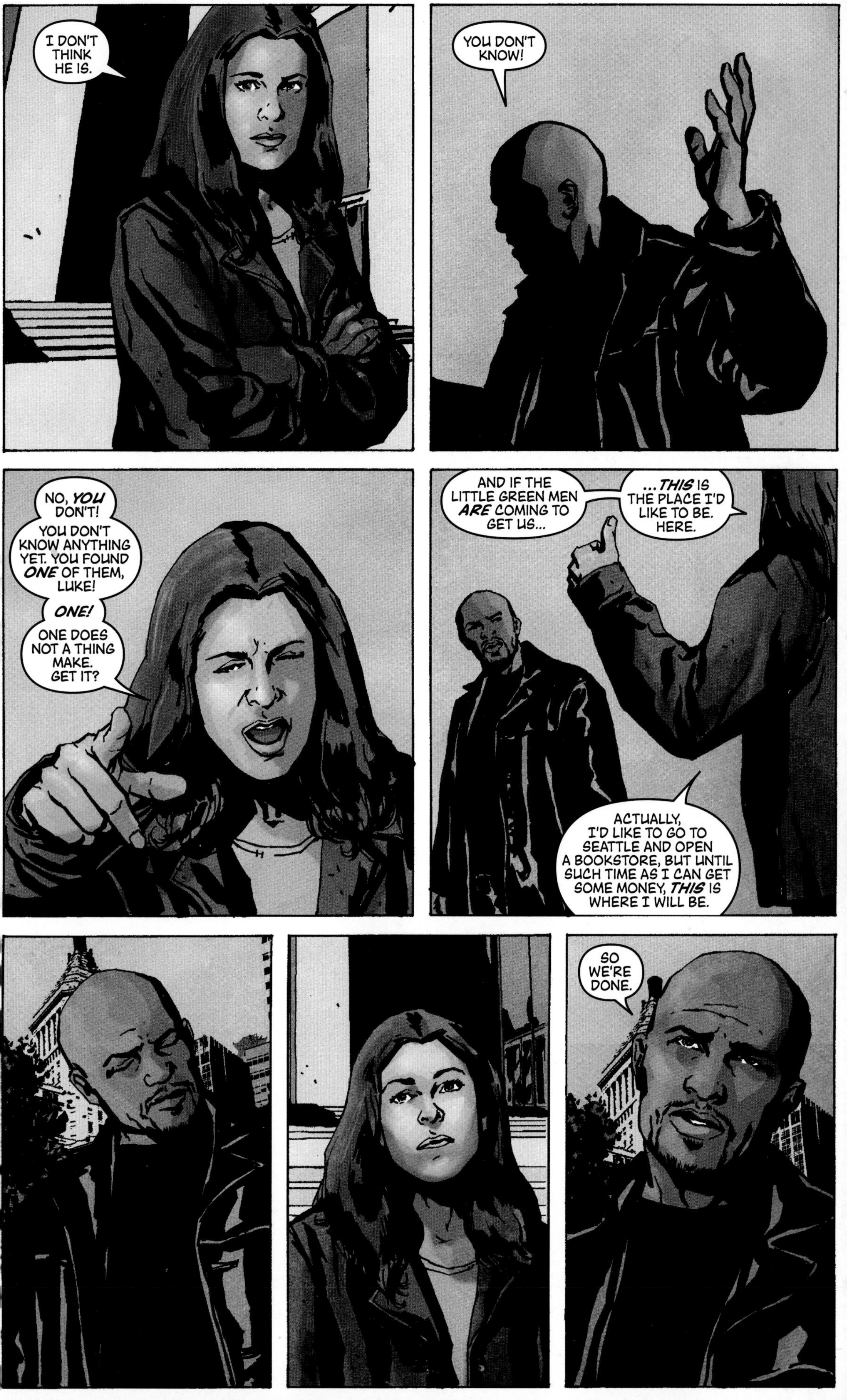
I DON'T THINK HE IS.
YOU DON'T KNOW!
NO, YOU DON'T!
YOU DON'T KNOW ANYTHING YET. YOU FOUND ONE OF THEM, LUKE!
ONE!
ONE DOES NOT A THING MAKE. GET IT?
AND IF THE LITTLE GREEN MEN ARE COMING TO GET US...
...THIS IS THE PLACE I'D LIKE TO BE. HERE.
ACTUALLY, I'D LIKE TO GO TO SEATTLE AND OPEN A BOOKSTORE, BUT UNTIL SUCH TIME AS I CAN GET SOME MONEY, THIS IS WHERE I WILL BE.
SO WE'RE DONE.

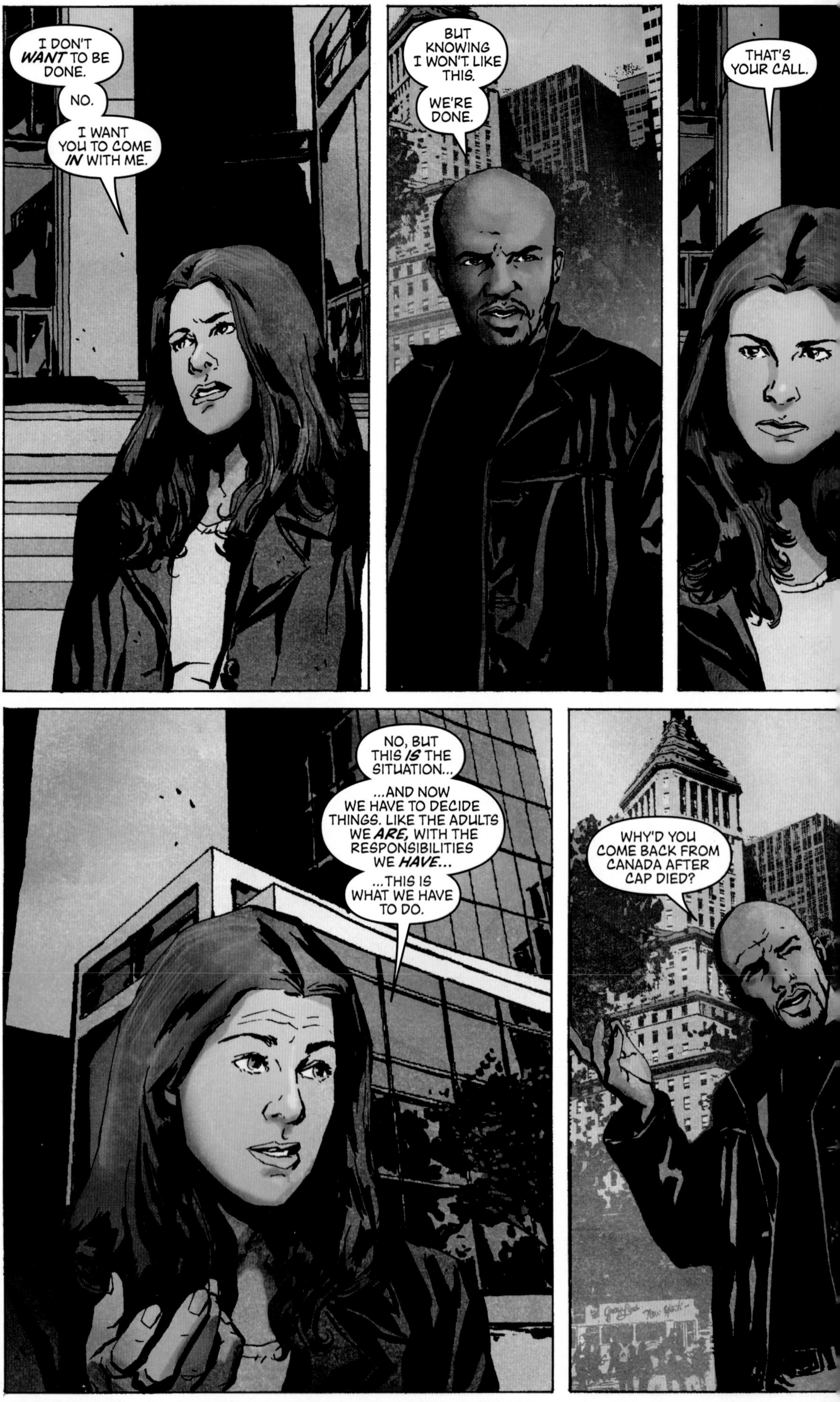

I DON'T *WANT* TO BE DONE.
NO.
I WANT YOU TO COME *IN* WITH ME.
BUT KNOWING I WON'T LIKE THIS.
WE'RE DONE.
THAT'S YOUR CALL.
NO, BUT THIS *IS* THE SITUATION...
...AND NOW WE HAVE TO DECIDE THINGS. LIKE THE ADULTS WE *ARE,* WITH THE RESPONSIBILITIES WE *HAVE...*
...THIS IS WHAT WE HAVE TO DO.
WHY'D YOU COME BACK FROM CANADA AFTER CAP DIED?

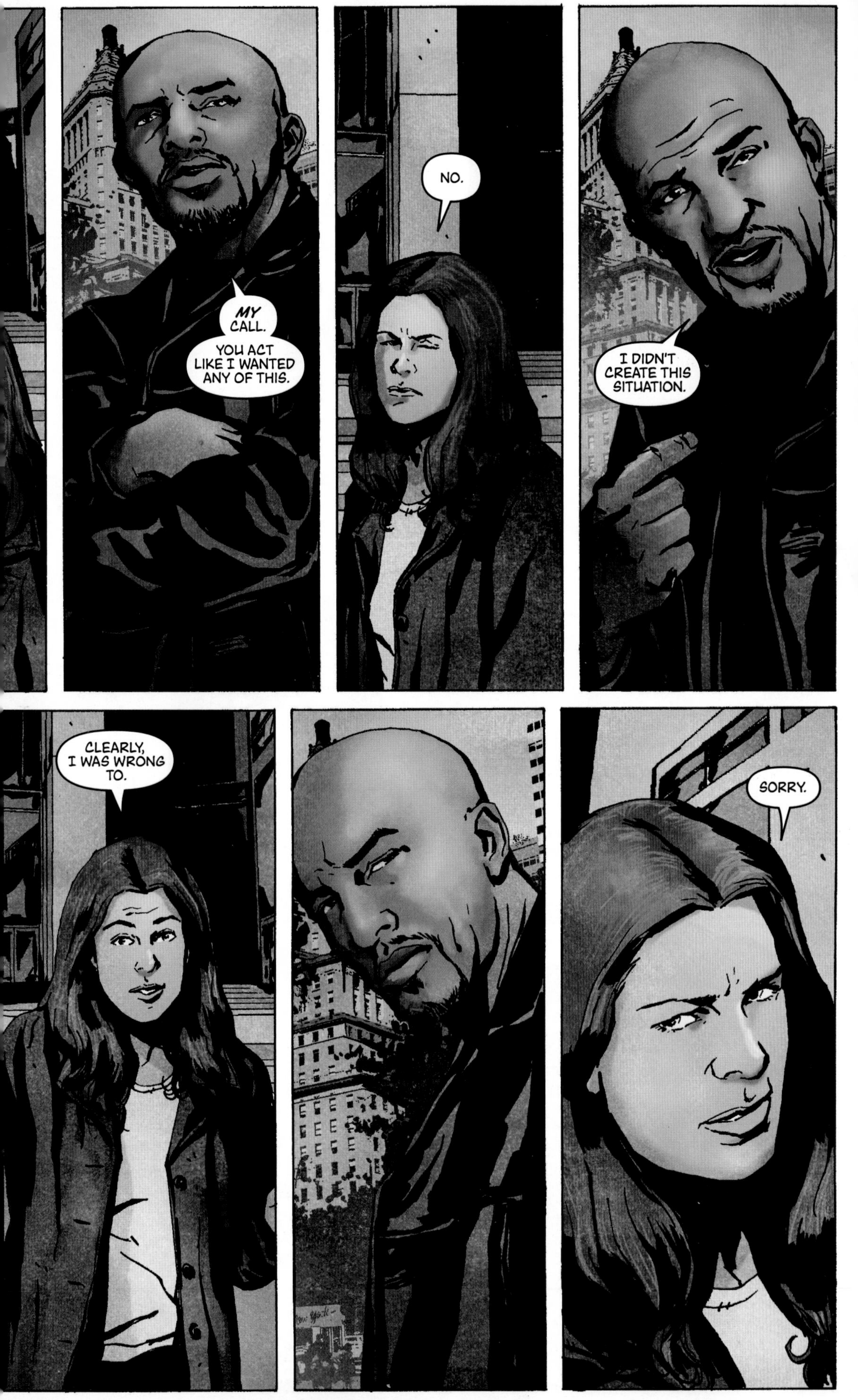
MY CALL.
YOU ACT LIKE I WANTED ANY OF THIS.
NO.
I DIDN'T CREATE THIS SITUATION.
CLEARLY, I WAS WRONG TO.
SORRY.

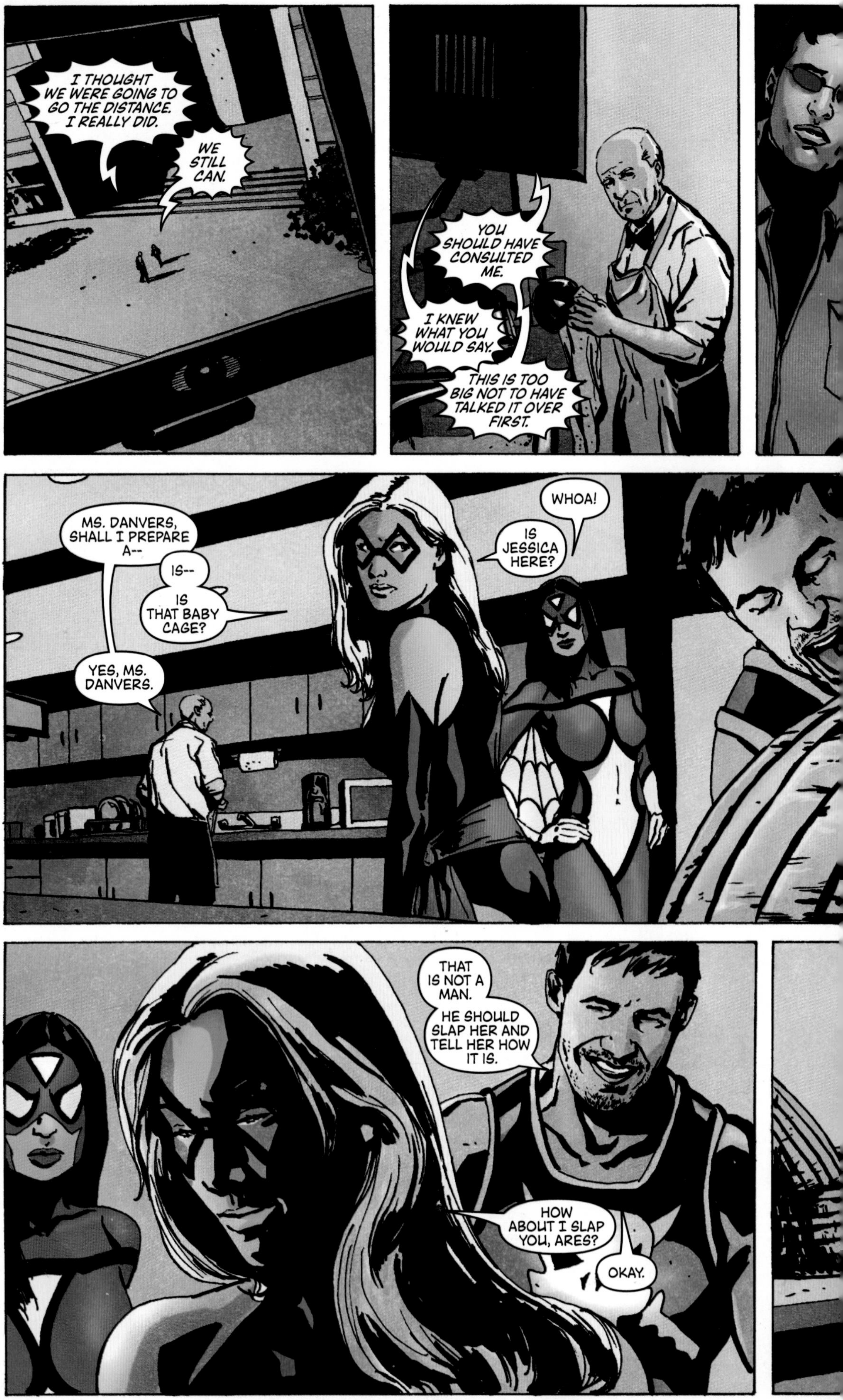
I THOUGHT WE WERE GOING TO GO THE DISTANCE. I REALLY DID.
WE STILL CAN.
YOU SHOULD HAVE CONSULTED ME.
I KNEW WHAT YOU WOULD SAY.
THIS IS TOO BIG NOT TO HAVE TALKED IT OVER FIRST.
MS. DANVERS, SHALL I PREPARE A--
IS--
IS THAT BABY CAGE?
YES, MS. DANVERS.
WHOA!
IS JESSICA HERE?
THAT IS NOT A MAN.
HE SHOULD SLAP HER AND TELL HER HOW IT IS.
HOW ABOUT I SLAP YOU, ARES?
OKAY.

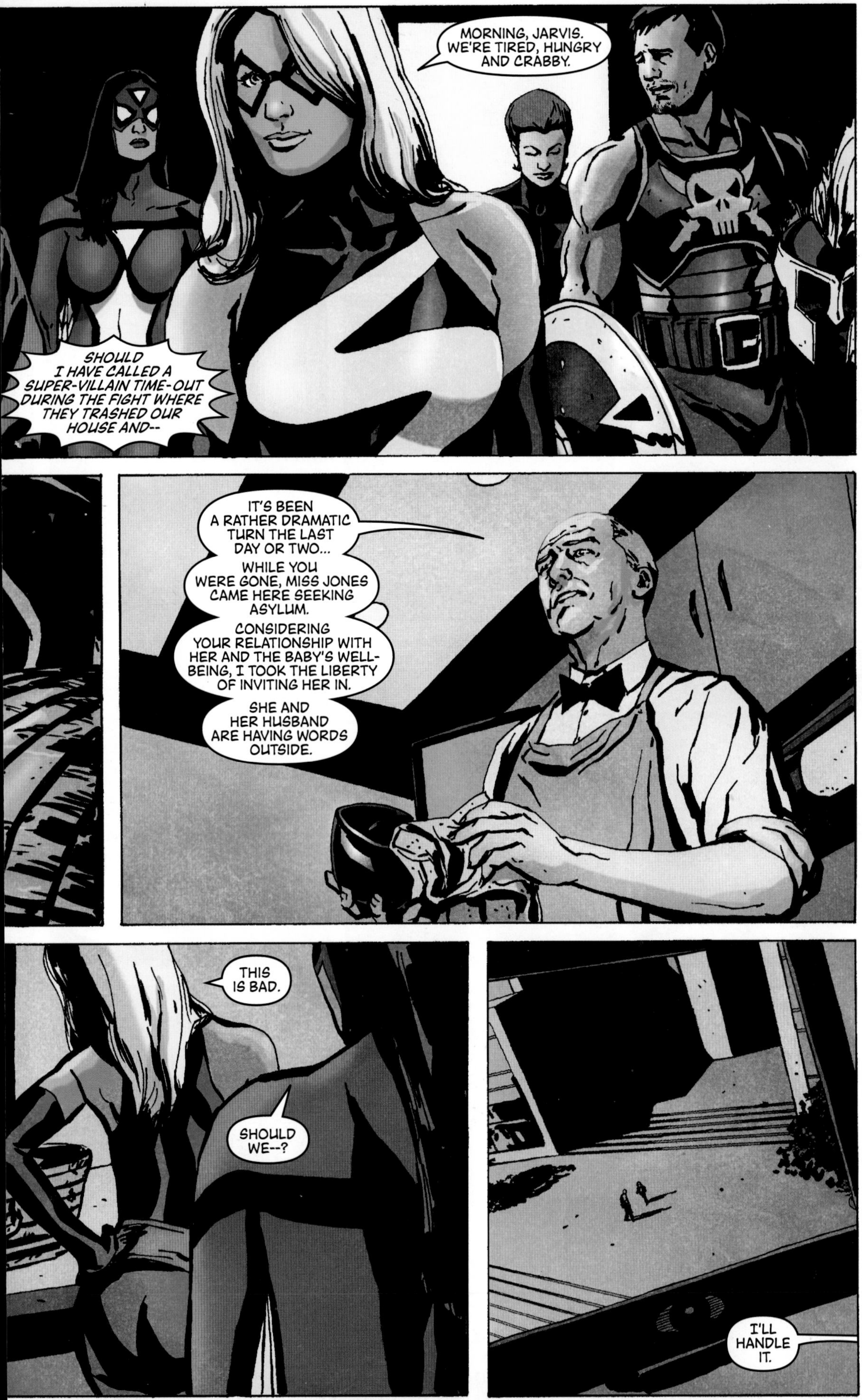
MORNING, JARVIS. WE'RE TIRED, HUNGRY AND CRABBY.
SHOULD I HAVE CALLED A SUPER-VILLAIN TIME-OUT DURING THE FIGHT WHERE THEY TRASHED OUR HOUSE AND--
IT'S BEEN A RATHER DRAMATIC TURN THE LAST DAY OR TWO...
WHILE YOU WERE GONE, MISS JONES CAME HERE SEEKING ASYLUM.
CONSIDERING YOUR RELATIONSHIP WITH HER AND THE BABY'S WELL-BEING, I TOOK THE LIBERTY OF INVITING HER IN.
SHE AND HER HUSBAND ARE HAVING WORDS OUTSIDE.
THIS IS BAD.
SHOULD WE--?
I'LL HANDLE IT.

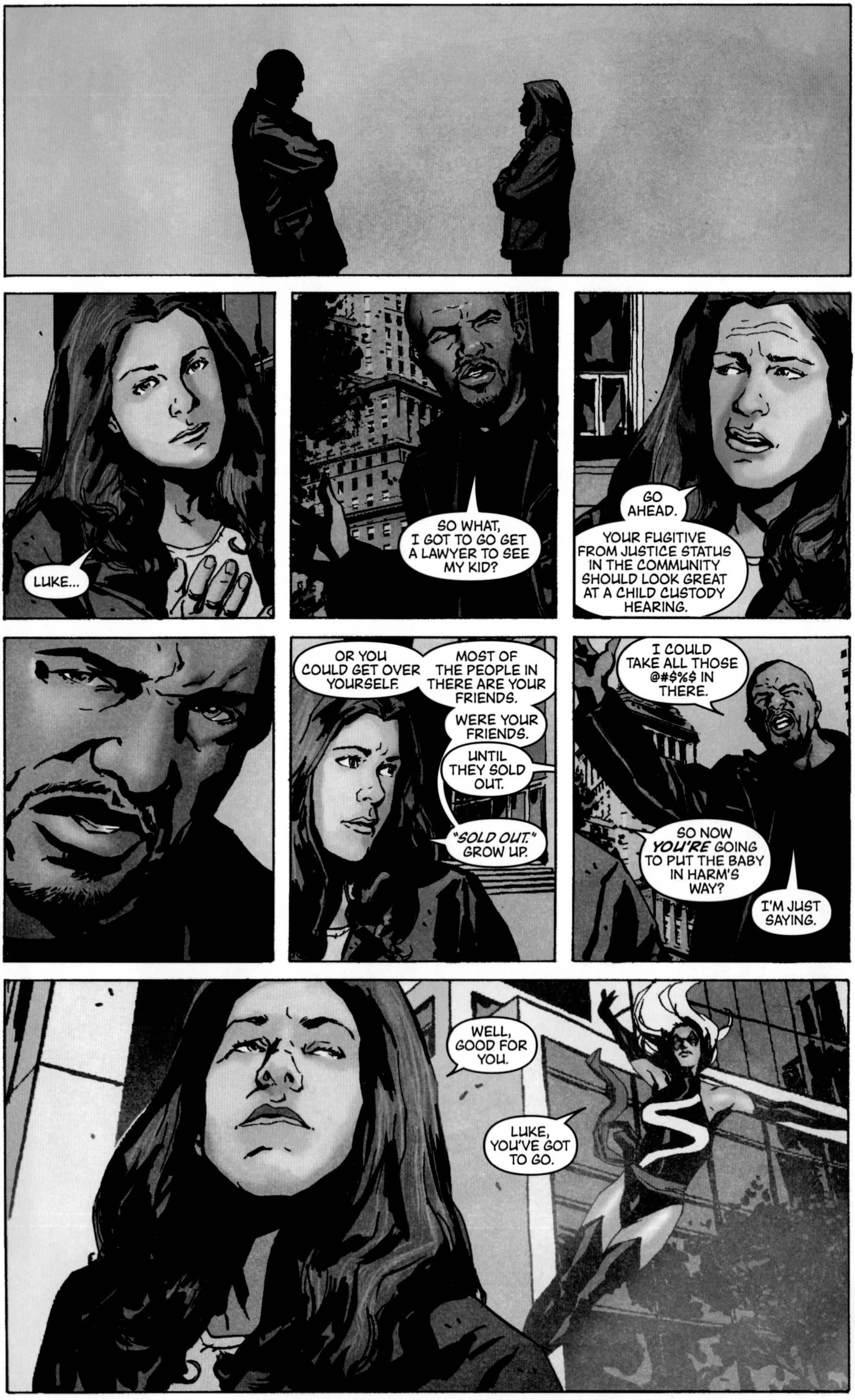
LUKE...
SO WHAT, I GOT TO GO GET A LAWYER TO SEE MY KID?
GO AHEAD.
YOUR FUGITIVE FROM JUSTICE STATUS IN THE COMMUNITY SHOULD LOOK GREAT AT A CHILD CUSTODY HEARING.
OR YOU COULD GET OVER YOURSELF.
MOST OF THE PEOPLE IN THERE ARE YOUR FRIENDS.
WERE YOUR FRIENDS.
UNTIL THEY SOLD OUT.
"SOLD OUT." GROW UP.
I COULD TAKE ALL THOSE @#$%$ IN THERE.
SO NOW YOU'RE GOING TO PUT THE BABY IN HARM'S WAY?
I'M JUST SAYING.
WELL, GOOD FOR YOU.
LUKE, YOU'VE GOT TO GO.

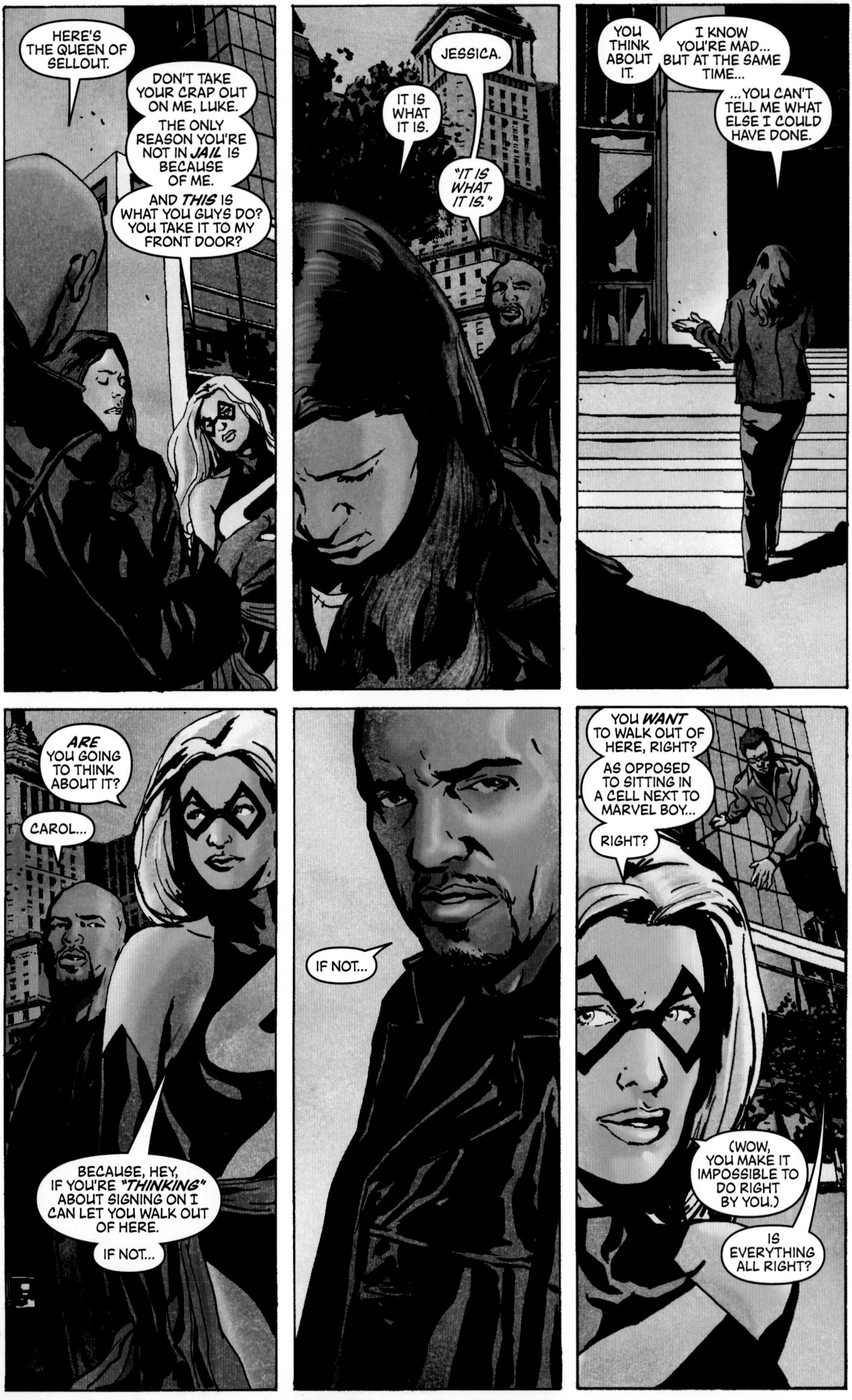
HERE'S THE QUEEN OF SELLOUT.
DON'T TAKE YOUR CRAP OUT ON ME, LUKE.
THE ONLY REASON YOU'RE NOT IN JAIL IS BECAUSE OF ME.
AND THIS IS WHAT YOU GUYS DO? YOU TAKE IT TO MY FRONT DOOR?
JESSICA.
IT IS WHAT IT IS.
"IT IS WHAT IT IS."
YOU THINK ABOUT IT.
I KNOW YOU'RE MAD... BUT AT THE SAME TIME...
...YOU CAN'T TELL ME WHAT ELSE I COULD HAVE DONE.
ARE YOU GOING TO THINK ABOUT IT?
CAROL...
BECAUSE, HEY, IF YOU'RE "THINKING" ABOUT SIGNING ON I CAN LET YOU WALK OUT OF HERE.
IF NOT...
IF NOT...
YOU WANT TO WALK OUT OF HERE, RIGHT?
AS OPPOSED TO SITTING IN A CELL NEXT TO MARVEL BOY...
RIGHT?
(WOW, YOU MAKE IT IMPOSSIBLE TO DO RIGHT BY YOU.)
IS EVERYTHING ALL RIGHT?

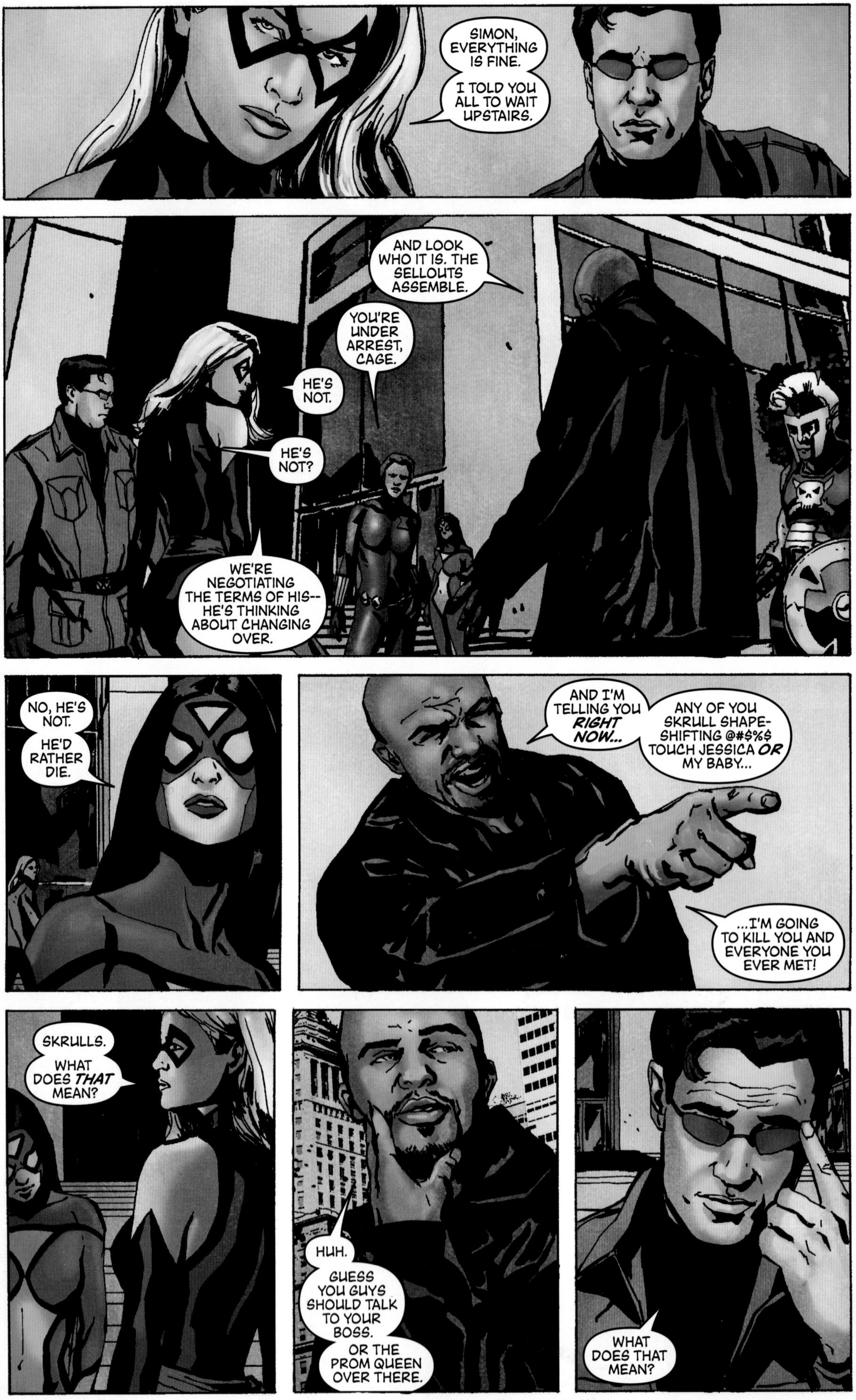
SIMON, EVERYTHING IS FINE.
I TOLD YOU ALL TO WAIT UPSTAIRS.
AND LOOK WHO IT IS. THE SELLOUTS ASSEMBLE.
YOU'RE UNDER ARREST, CAGE.
HE'S NOT.
HE'S NOT?
WE'RE NEGOTIATING THE TERMS OF HIS-- HE'S THINKING ABOUT CHANGING OVER.
NO, HE'S NOT.
HE'D RATHER DIE.
AND I'M TELLING YOU *RIGHT NOW...*
ANY OF YOU SKRULL SHAPE-SHIFTING @#$%$ TOUCH JESSICA *OR* MY BABY...
...I'M GOING TO KILL YOU AND EVERYONE YOU EVER MET!
SKRULLS.
WHAT DOES *THAT* MEAN?
HUH.
GUESS YOU GUYS SHOULD TALK TO YOUR BOSS.
OR THE PROM QUEEN OVER THERE.
WHAT DOES THAT MEAN?

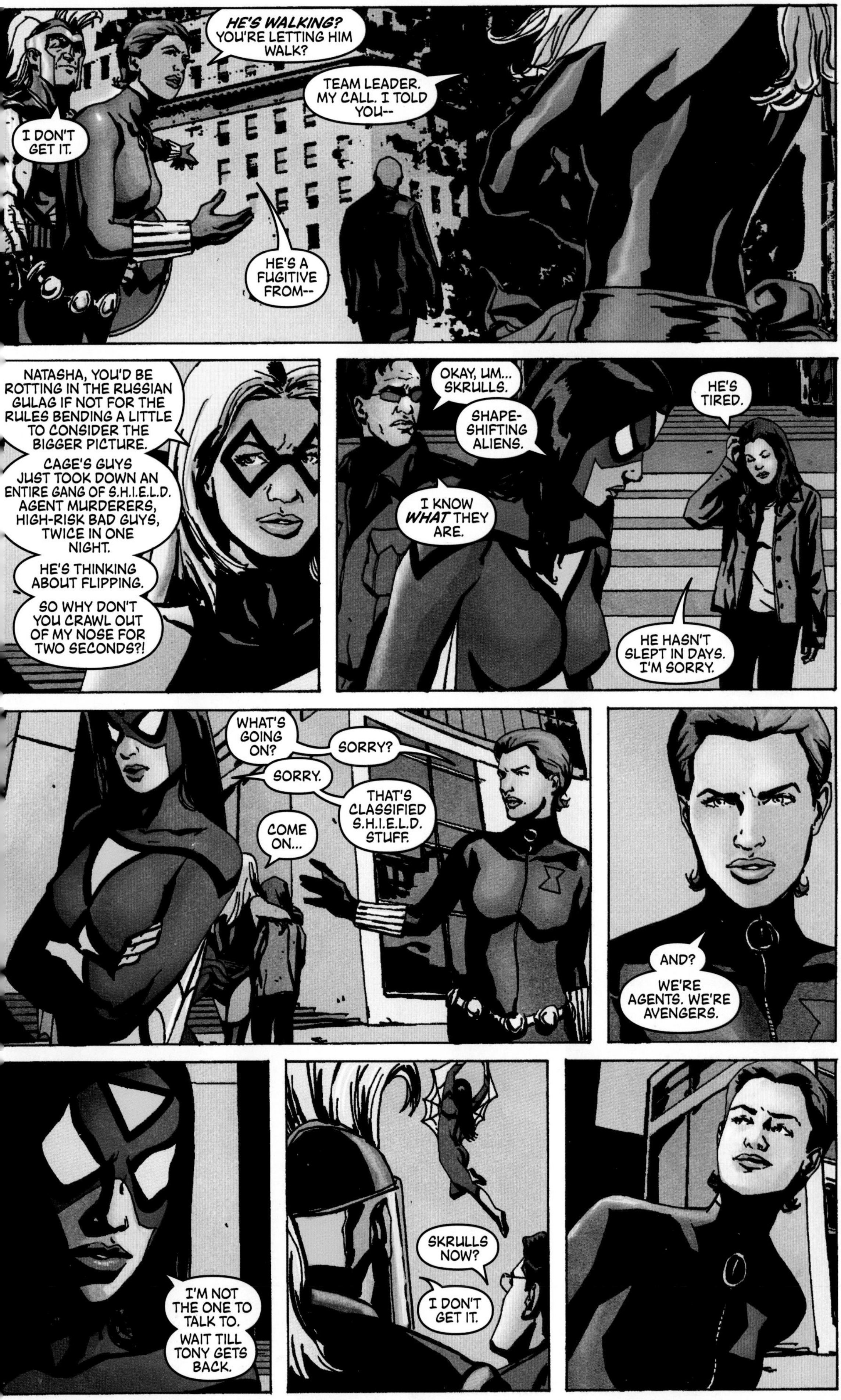
HE'S WALKING? YOU'RE LETTING HIM WALK?
I DON'T GET IT.
TEAM LEADER. MY CALL. I TOLD YOU--
HE'S A FUGITIVE FROM--
NATASHA, YOU'D BE ROTTING IN THE RUSSIAN GULAG IF NOT FOR THE RULES BENDING A LITTLE TO CONSIDER THE BIGGER PICTURE.
CAGE'S GUYS JUST TOOK DOWN AN ENTIRE GANG OF S.H.I.E.L.D. AGENT MURDERERS, HIGH-RISK BAD GUYS, TWICE IN ONE NIGHT.
HE'S THINKING ABOUT FLIPPING.
SO WHY DON'T YOU CRAWL OUT OF MY NOSE FOR TWO SECONDS?!
OKAY, UM... SKRULLS.
SHAPE-SHIFTING ALIENS.
I KNOW WHAT THEY ARE.
HE'S TIRED.
HE HASN'T SLEPT IN DAYS. I'M SORRY.
WHAT'S GOING ON?
SORRY?
SORRY.
THAT'S CLASSIFIED S.H.I.E.L.D. STUFF.
COME ON...
AND?
WE'RE AGENTS. WE'RE AVENGERS.
I'M NOT THE ONE TO TALK TO.
WAIT TILL TONY GETS BACK.
SKRULLS NOW?
I DON'T GET IT.

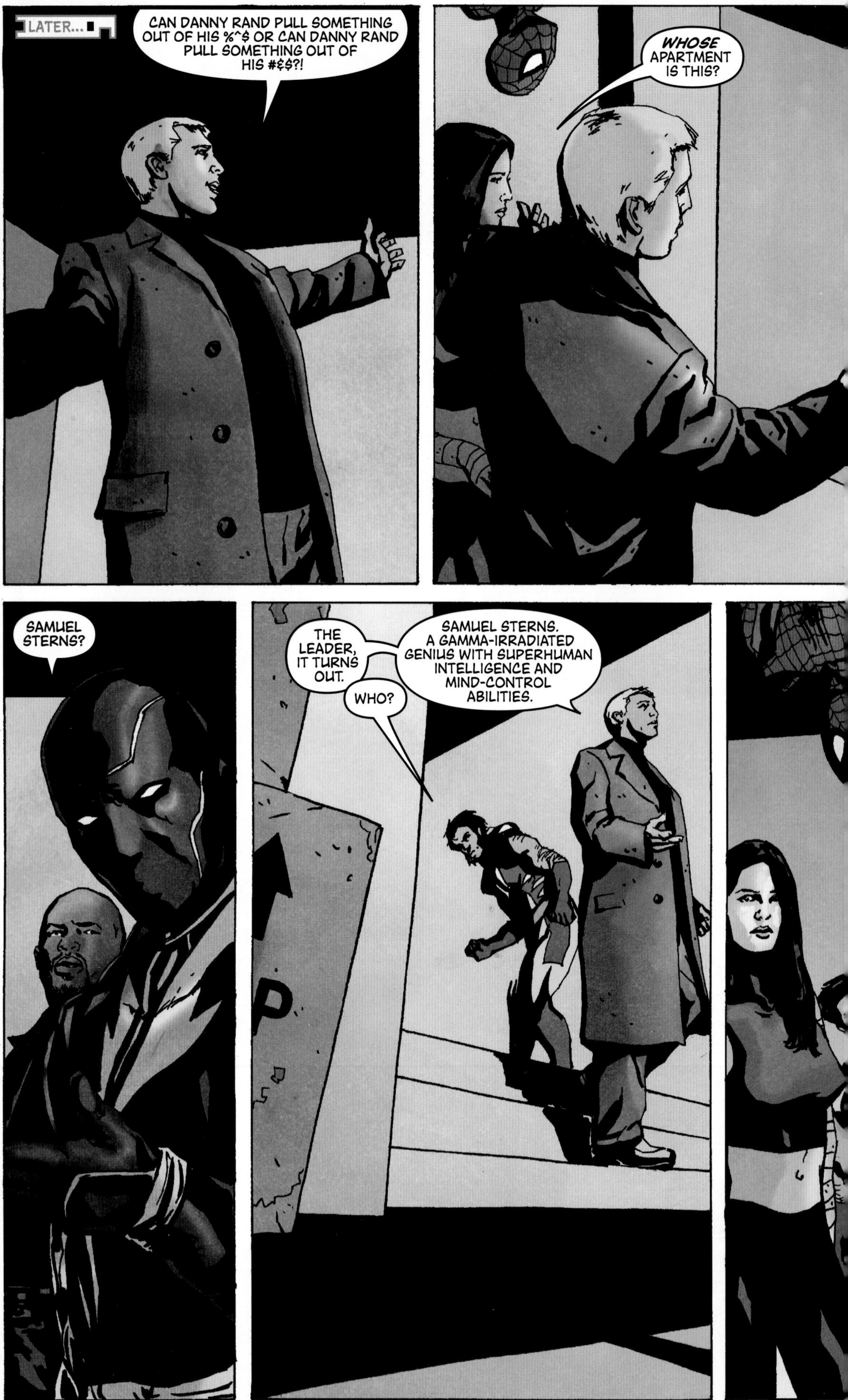
LATER...
CAN DANNY RAND PULL SOMETHING OUT OF HIS %^$ OR CAN DANNY RAND PULL SOMETHING OUT OF HIS #&$?!
WHOSE APARTMENT IS THIS?
SAMUEL STERNS?
SAMUEL STERNS. A GAMMA-IRRADIATED GENIUS WITH SUPERHUMAN INTELLIGENCE AND MIND-CONTROL ABILITIES.
THE LEADER, IT TURNS OUT.
WHO?

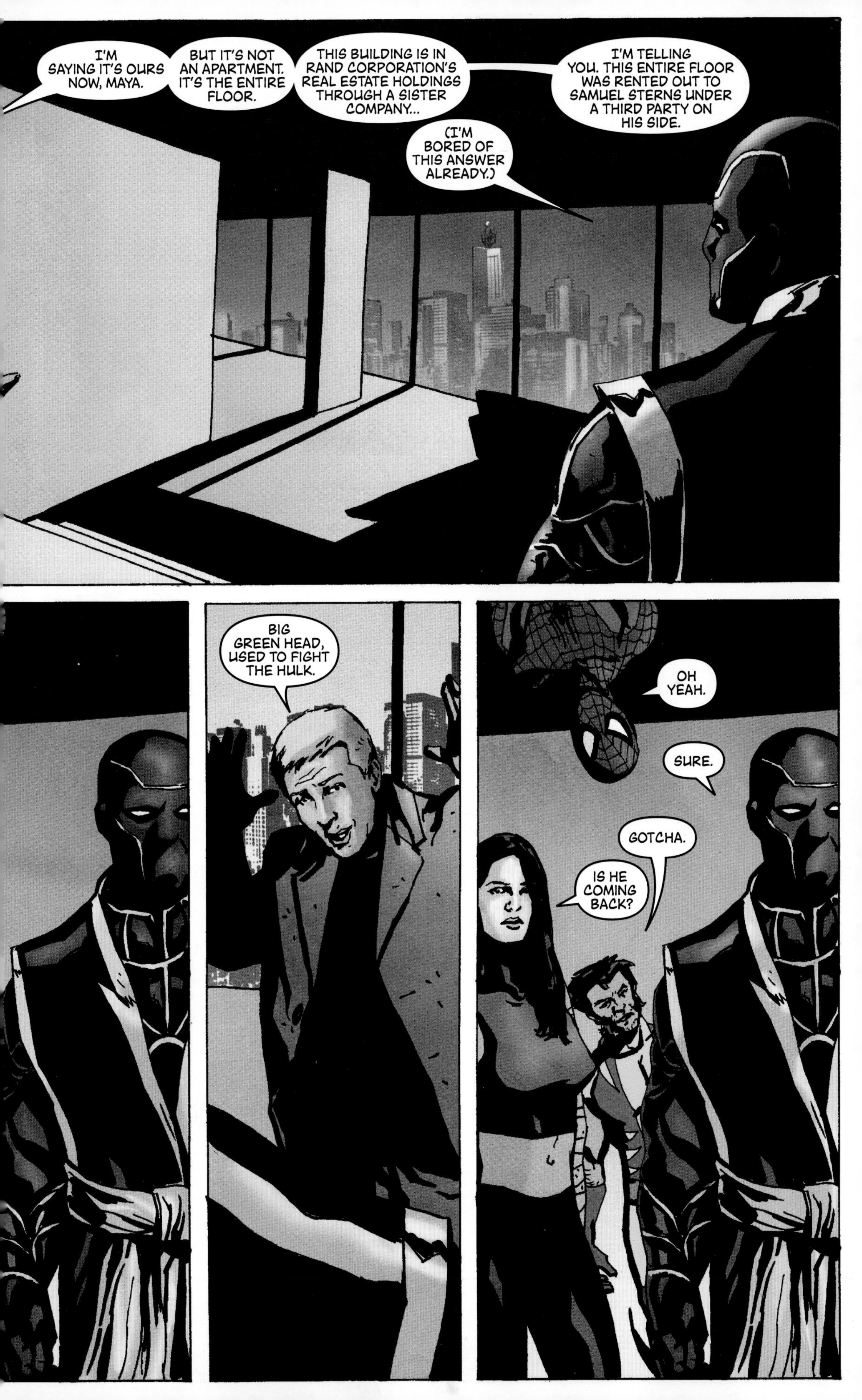
I'M SAYING IT'S OURS NOW, MAYA.
BUT IT'S NOT AN APARTMENT. IT'S THE ENTIRE FLOOR.
THIS BUILDING IS IN RAND CORPORATION'S REAL ESTATE HOLDINGS THROUGH A SISTER COMPANY...
I'M TELLING YOU. THIS ENTIRE FLOOR WAS RENTED OUT TO SAMUEL STERNS UNDER A THIRD PARTY ON HIS SIDE.
(I'M BORED OF THIS ANSWER ALREADY.)
BIG GREEN HEAD, USED TO FIGHT THE HULK.
OH YEAH.
SURE.
GOTCHA.
IS HE COMING BACK?

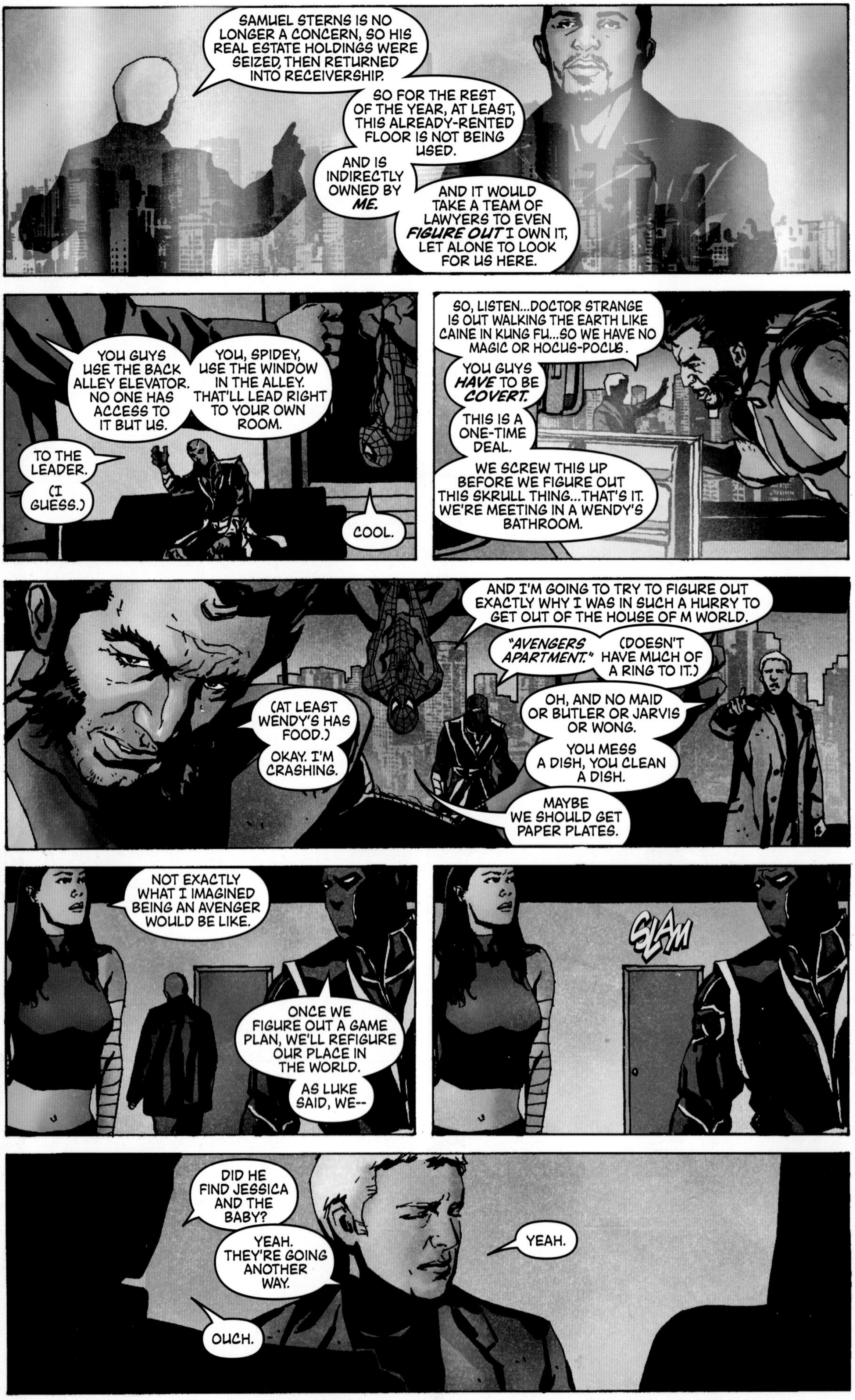
SAMUEL STERNS IS NO LONGER A CONCERN, SO HIS REAL ESTATE HOLDINGS WERE SEIZED, THEN RETURNED INTO RECEIVERSHIP.
SO FOR THE REST OF THE YEAR, AT LEAST, THIS ALREADY-RENTED FLOOR IS NOT BEING USED.
AND IS INDIRECTLY OWNED BY *ME.*
AND IT WOULD TAKE A TEAM OF LAWYERS TO EVEN *FIGURE OUT* I OWN IT, LET ALONE TO LOOK FOR US HERE.
YOU GUYS USE THE BACK ALLEY ELEVATOR. NO ONE HAS ACCESS TO IT BUT US.
YOU, SPIDEY, USE THE WINDOW IN THE ALLEY. THAT'LL LEAD RIGHT TO YOUR OWN ROOM.
TO THE LEADER.
(I GUESS.)
COOL.
SO, LISTEN...DOCTOR STRANGE IS OUT WALKING THE EARTH LIKE CAINE IN KUNG FU...SO WE HAVE NO MAGIC OR HOCUS-POCUS.
YOU GUYS *HAVE* TO BE *COVERT.*
THIS IS A ONE-TIME DEAL.
WE SCREW THIS UP BEFORE WE FIGURE OUT THIS SKRULL THING...THAT'S IT. WE'RE MEETING IN A WENDY'S BATHROOM.
AND I'M GOING TO TRY TO FIGURE OUT EXACTLY WHY I WAS IN SUCH A HURRY TO GET OUT OF THE HOUSE OF M WORLD.
"AVENGERS APARTMENT."
(DOESN'T HAVE MUCH OF A RING TO IT.)
(AT LEAST WENDY'S HAS FOOD.)
OKAY. I'M CRASHING.
OH, AND NO MAID OR BUTLER OR JARVIS OR WONG.
YOU MESS A DISH, YOU CLEAN A DISH.
MAYBE WE SHOULD GET PAPER PLATES.
NOT EXACTLY WHAT I IMAGINED BEING AN AVENGER WOULD BE LIKE.
ONCE WE FIGURE OUT A GAME PLAN, WE'LL REFIGURE OUR PLACE IN THE WORLD.
AS LUKE SAID, WE--
SLAM
DID HE FIND JESSICA AND THE BABY?
YEAH.
YEAH. THEY'RE GOING ANOTHER WAY.
OUCH.

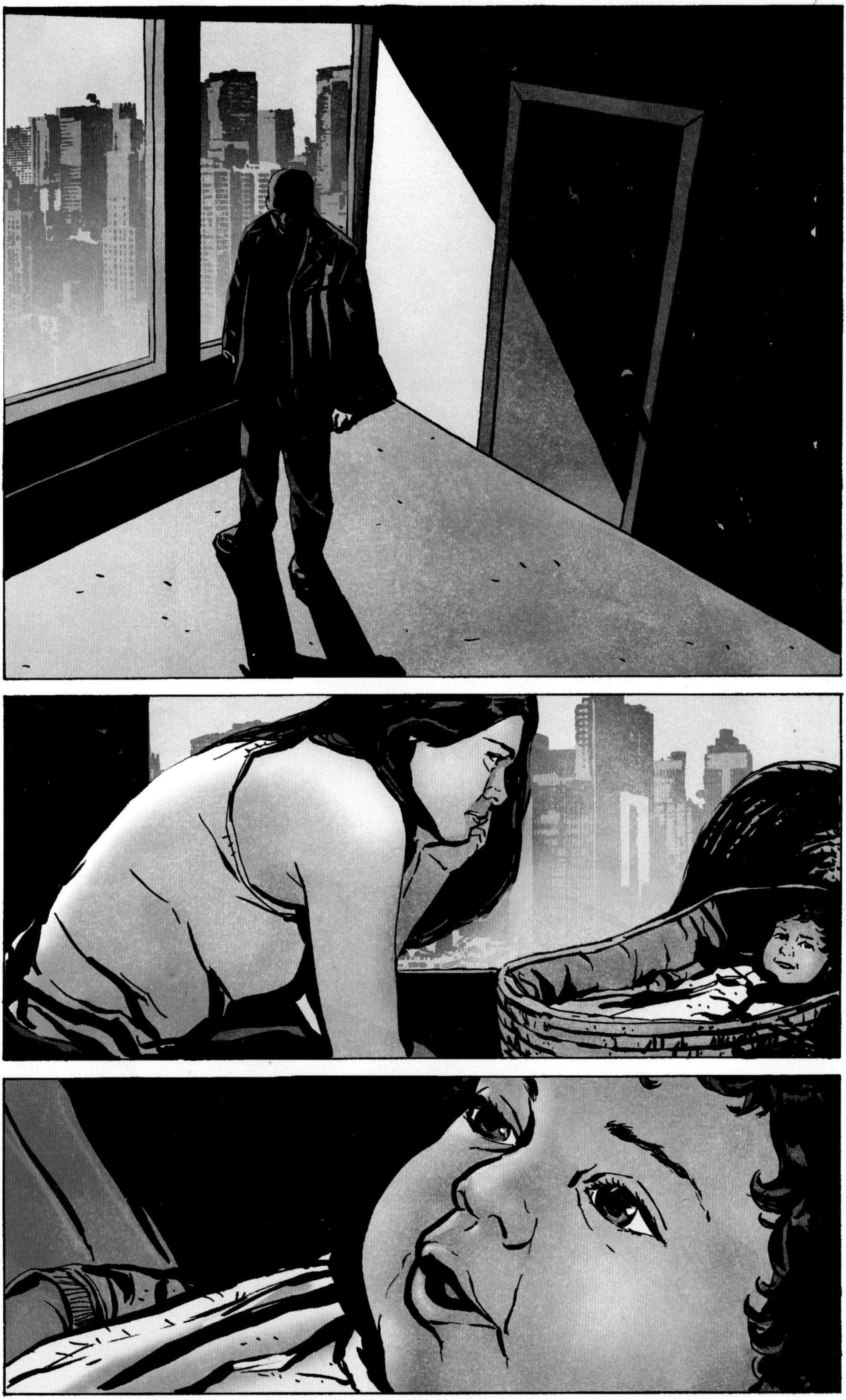

#39

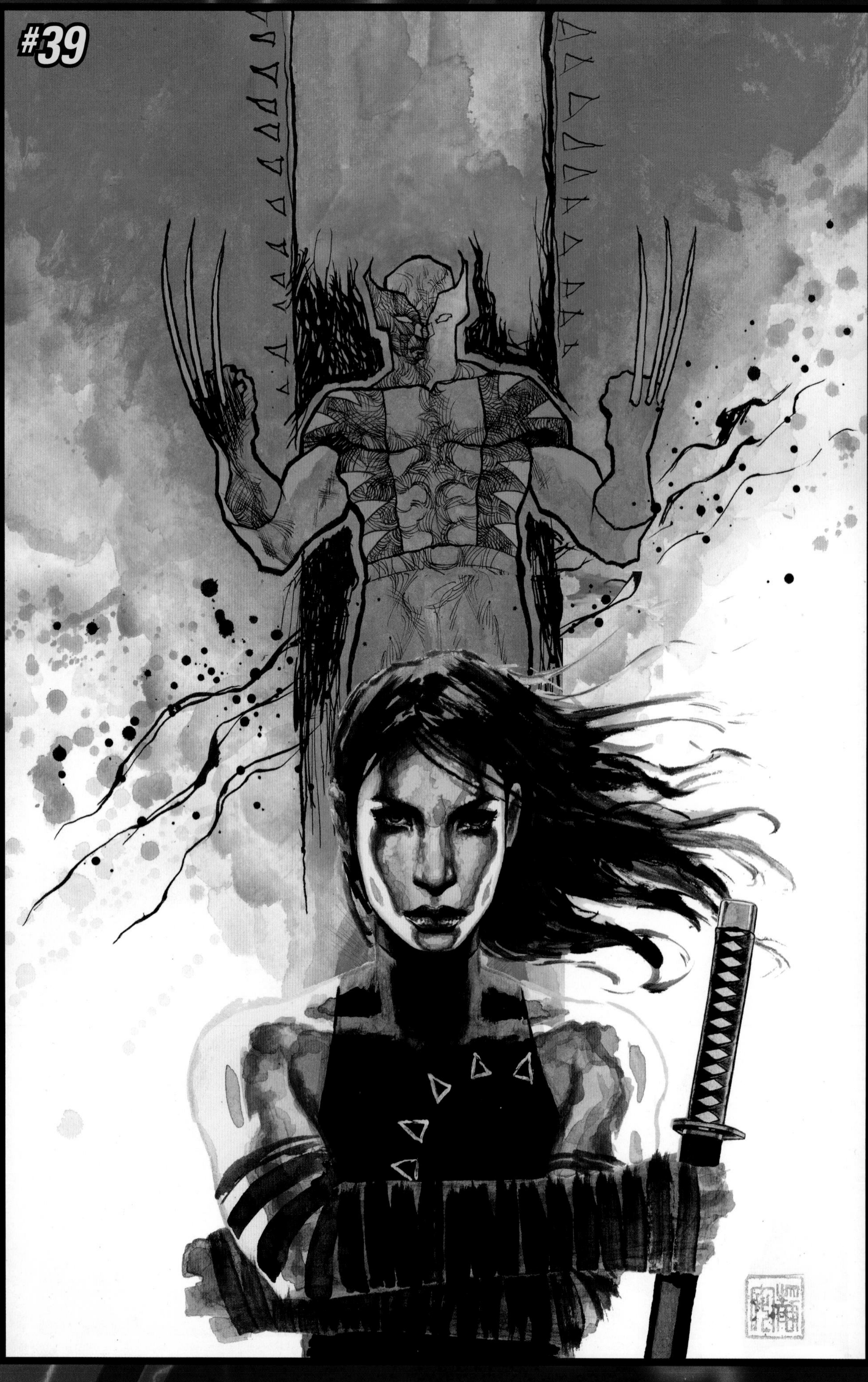

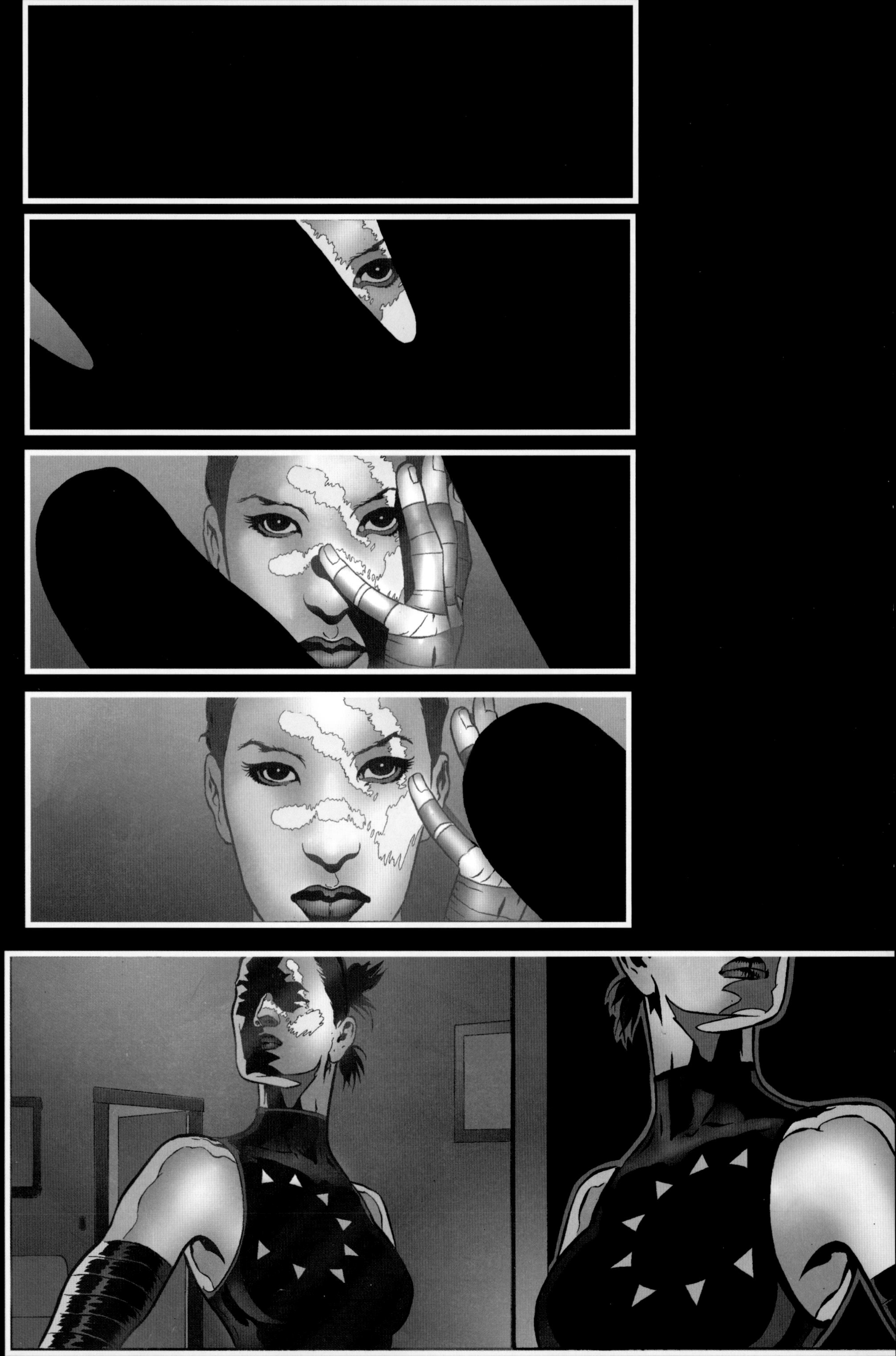

I AIN'T A SKRULL, MAYA.

I DIDN'T SAY YOU WERE.

YOU'RE THINKING...

...HE'S NEVER EVEN ONCE MENTIONED OUR PAST.

DOES HE KNOW ABOUT OUR PAST? IS THAT WHY HE HASN'T MENTIONED IT?

IS IT REALLY HIM?

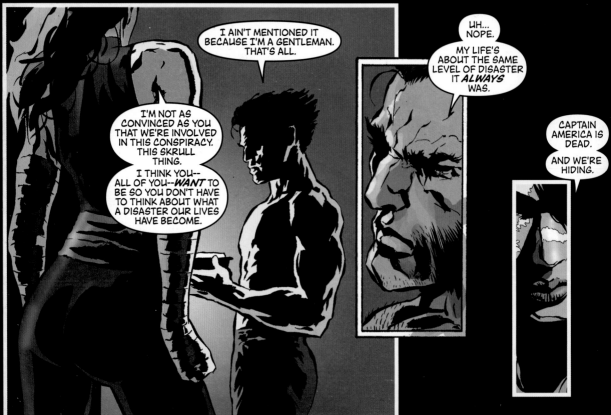

I AIN'T MENTIONED IT BECAUSE I'M A GENTLEMAN. THAT'S ALL.

I'M NOT AS CONVINCED AS YOU THAT WE'RE INVOLVED IN THIS CONSPIRACY. THIS SKRULL THING.

I THINK YOU-- ALL OF YOU--WANT TO BE SO YOU DON'T HAVE TO THINK ABOUT WHAT A DISASTER OUR LIVES HAVE BECOME.

UH... NOPE.

MY LIFE'S ABOUT THE SAME LEVEL OF DISASTER IT ALWAYS WAS.

CAPTAIN AMERICA IS DEAD.

AND WE'RE HIDING.

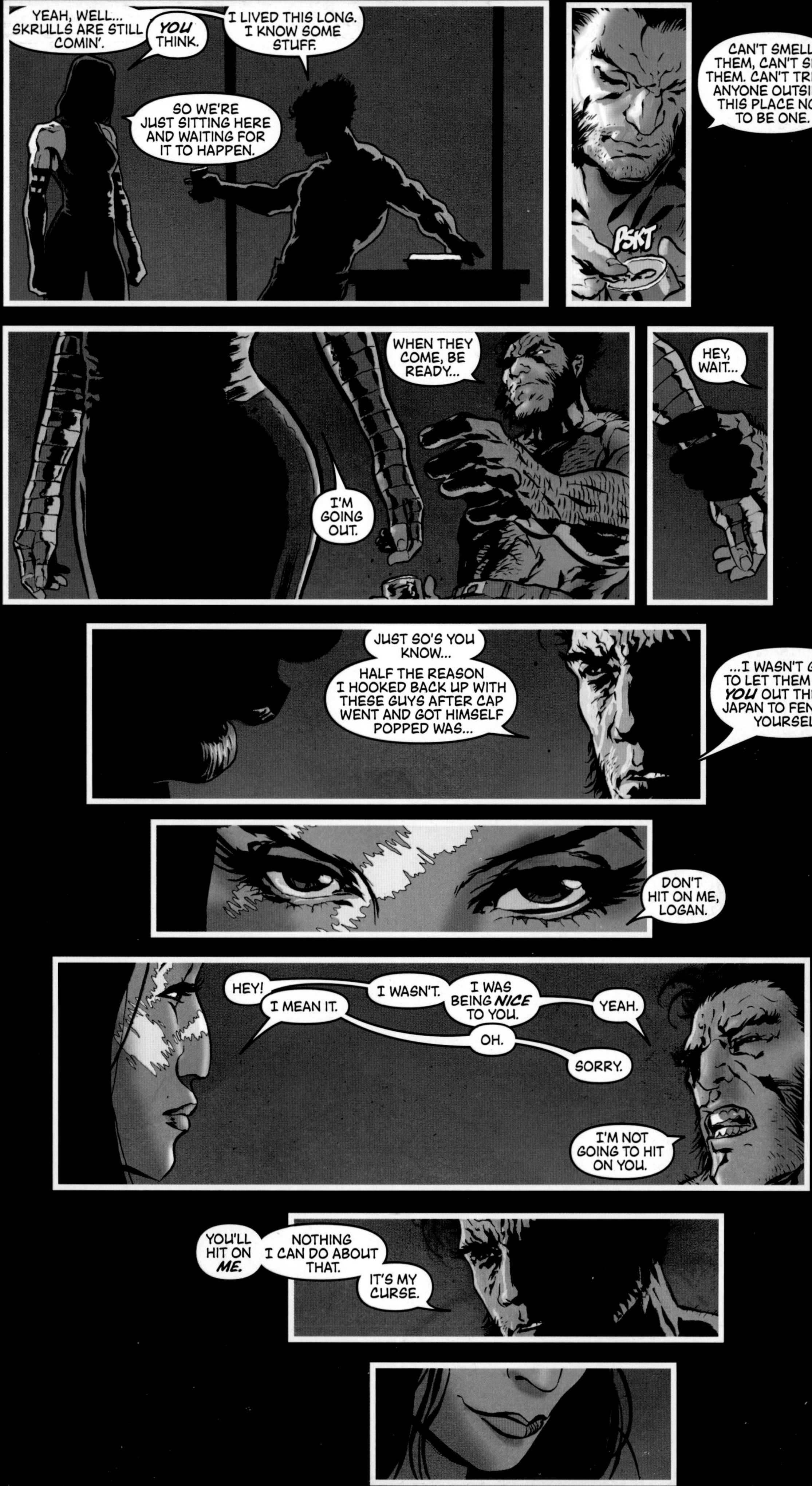
YEAH, WELL... SKRULLS ARE STILL COMIN'.
YOU THINK.
I LIVED THIS LONG. I KNOW SOME STUFF.
SO WE'RE JUST SITTING HERE AND WAITING FOR IT TO HAPPEN.
CAN'T SMELL THEM, CAN'T SEE THEM. CAN'T TRUST ANYONE OUTSIDE THIS PLACE NOT TO BE ONE.
PSKT
WHEN THEY COME, BE READY...
I'M GOING OUT.
HEY, WAIT...
JUST SO'S YOU KNOW...
HALF THE REASON I HOOKED BACK UP WITH THESE GUYS AFTER CAP WENT AND GOT HIMSELF POPPED WAS...
...I WASN'T GOING TO LET THEM LEAVE YOU OUT THERE IN JAPAN TO FEND FOR YOURSELF.
DON'T HIT ON ME, LOGAN.
HEY!
I WASN'T.
I WAS BEING NICE TO YOU.
I MEAN IT.
YEAH.
OH.
SORRY.
I'M NOT GOING TO HIT ON YOU.
YOU'LL HIT ON ME.
NOTHING I CAN DO ABOUT THAT.
IT'S MY CURSE.

NELSON
MURDOC
& BLAKI
ATTORNEYS
AT LAW

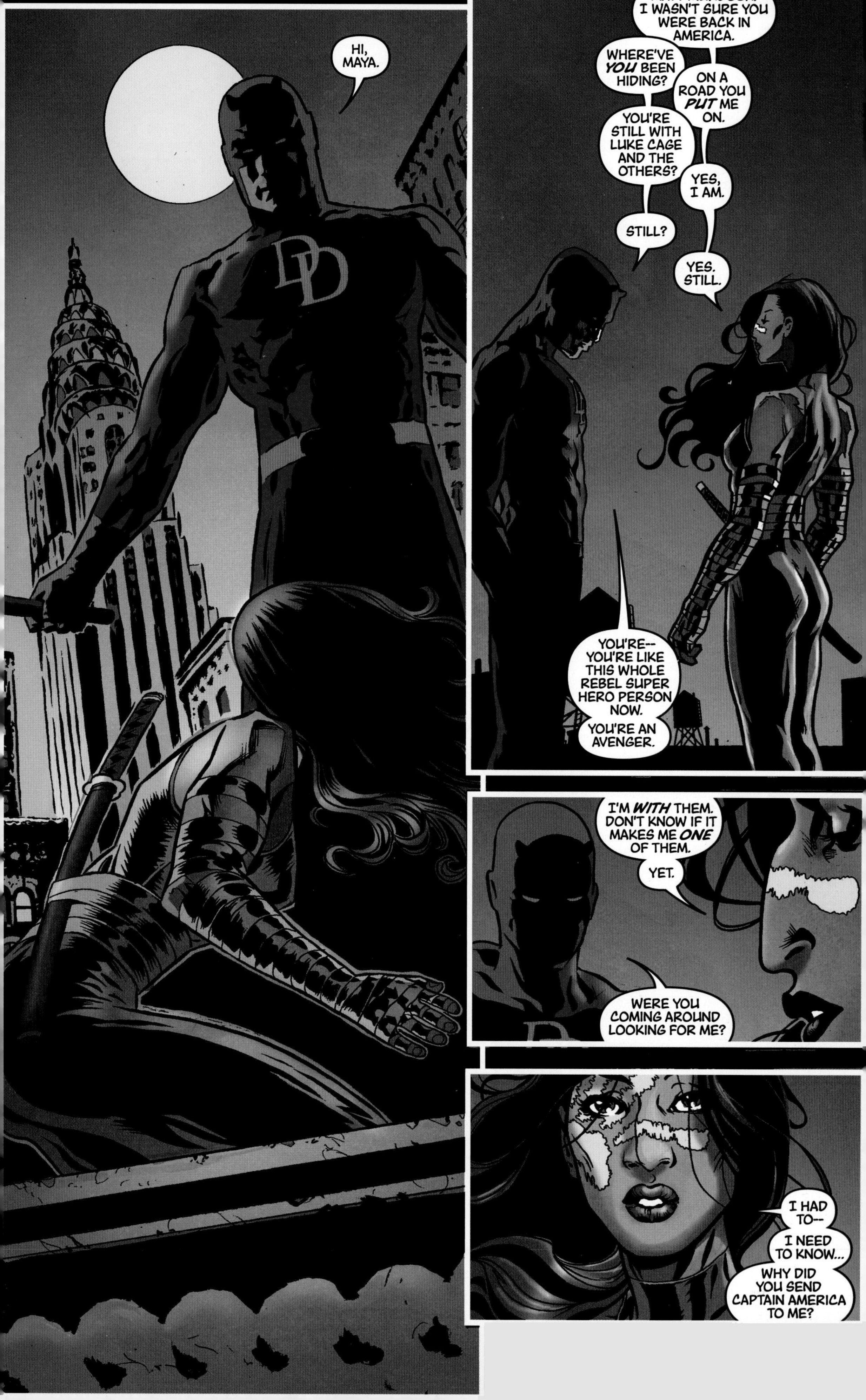
HI, MAYA.
I WASN'T SURE YOU WERE BACK IN AMERICA.
WHERE'VE YOU BEEN HIDING?
ON A ROAD YOU PUT ME ON.
YOU'RE STILL WITH LUKE CAGE AND THE OTHERS?
YES, I AM.
STILL?
YES. STILL.
YOU'RE-- YOU'RE LIKE THIS WHOLE REBEL SUPER HERO PERSON NOW.
YOU'RE AN AVENGER.
I'M WITH THEM. DON'T KNOW IF IT MAKES ME ONE OF THEM.
YET.
WERE YOU COMING AROUND LOOKING FOR ME?
I HAD TO--
I NEED TO KNOW...
WHY DID YOU SEND CAPTAIN AMERICA TO ME?

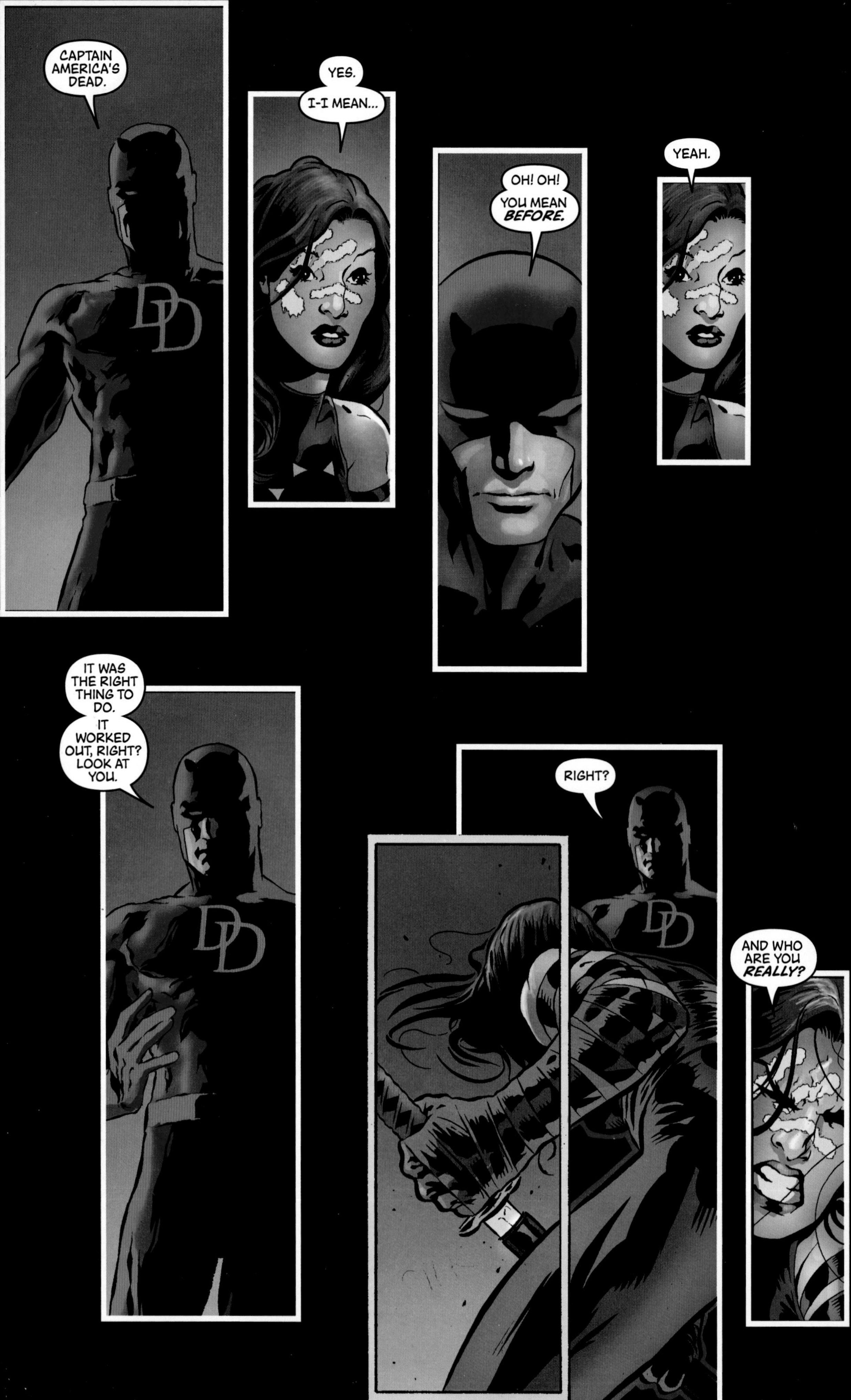
CAPTAIN AMERICA'S DEAD.
YES.
I-I MEAN...
OH! OH!
YOU MEAN *BEFORE.*
YEAH.
IT WAS THE RIGHT THING TO DO.
IT WORKED OUT, RIGHT? LOOK AT YOU.
RIGHT?
AND WHO ARE YOU *REALLY?*

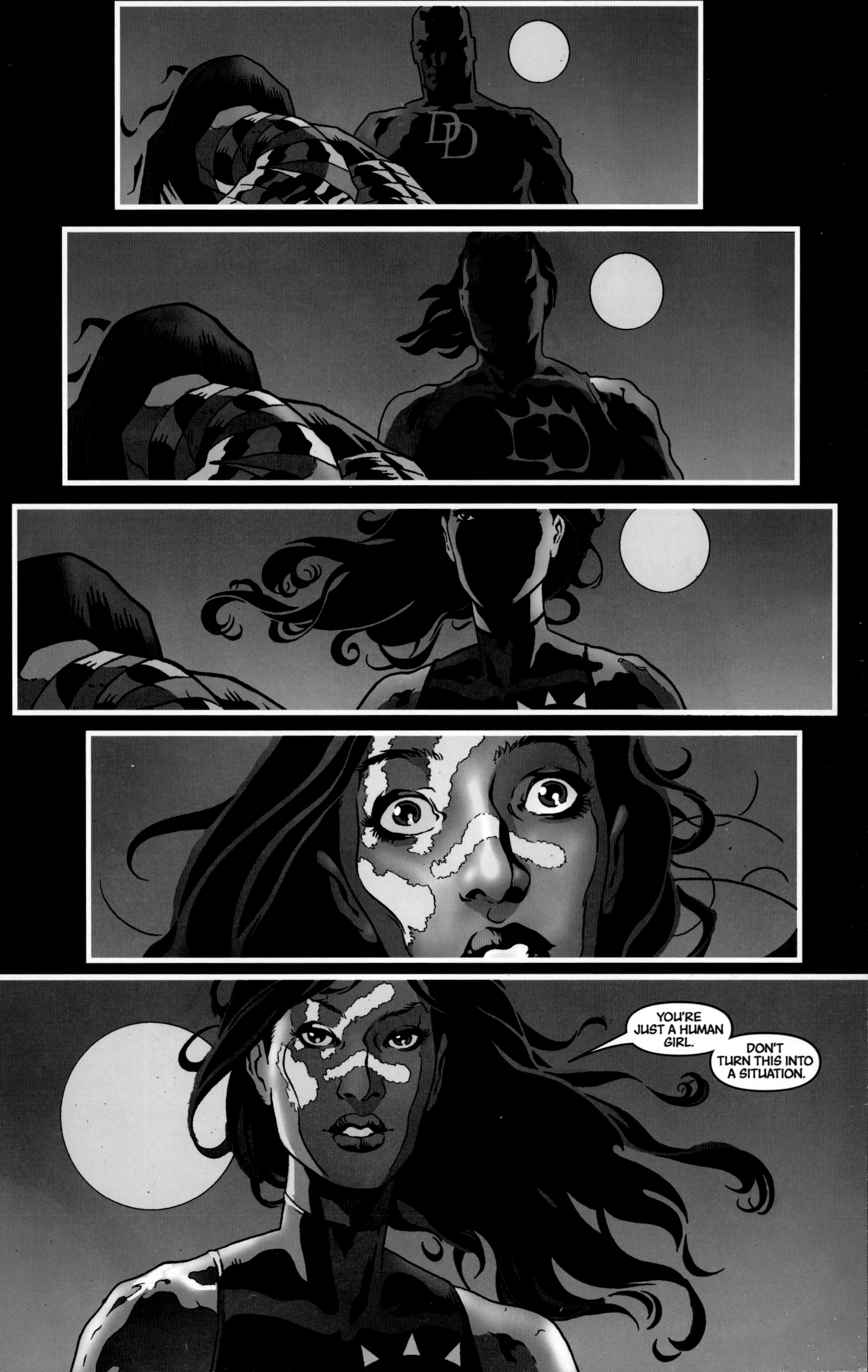
YOU'RE JUST A HUMAN GIRL.
DON'T TURN THIS INTO A SITUATION.

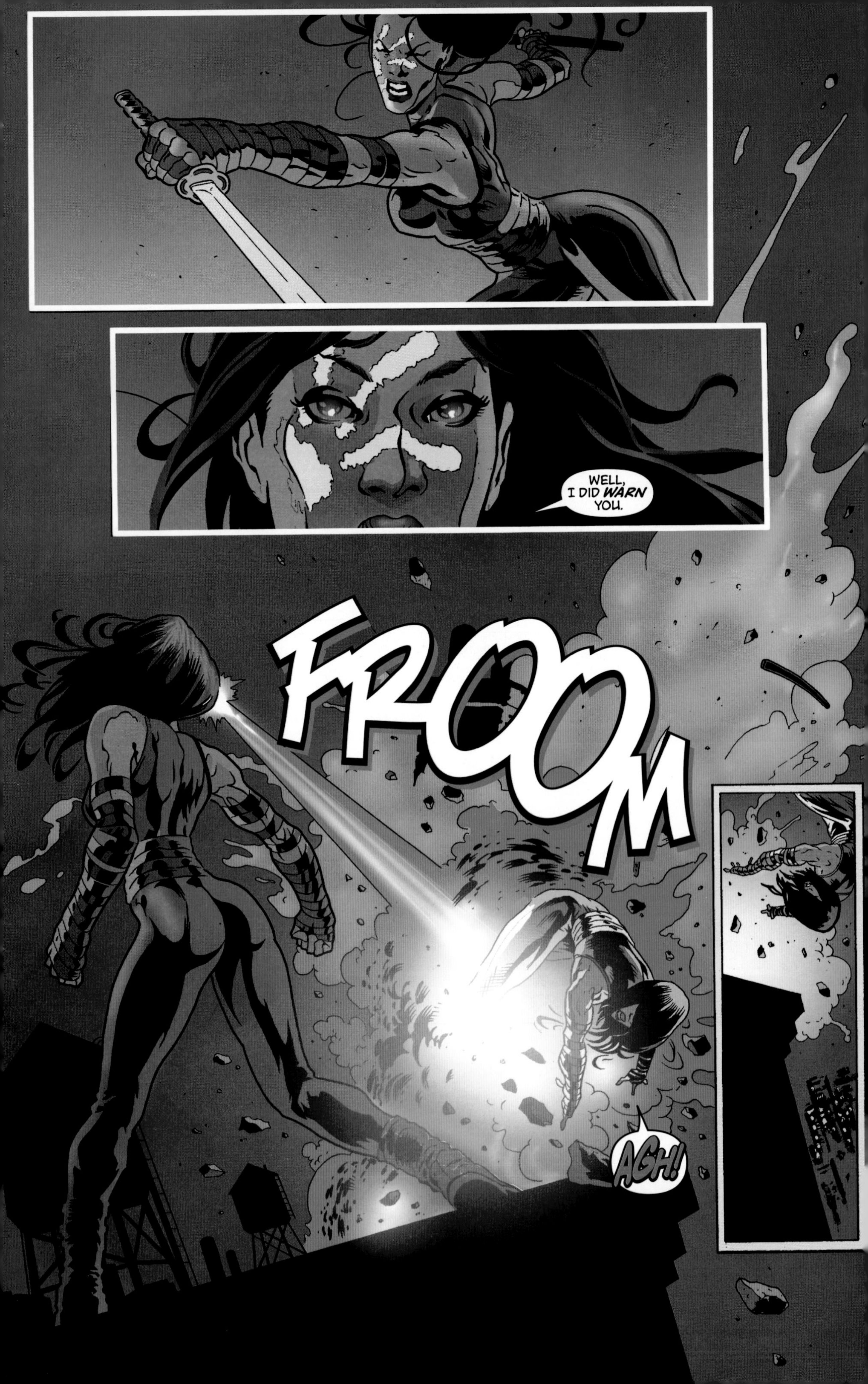
WELL, I DID WARN YOU.
FROOM
AGH!

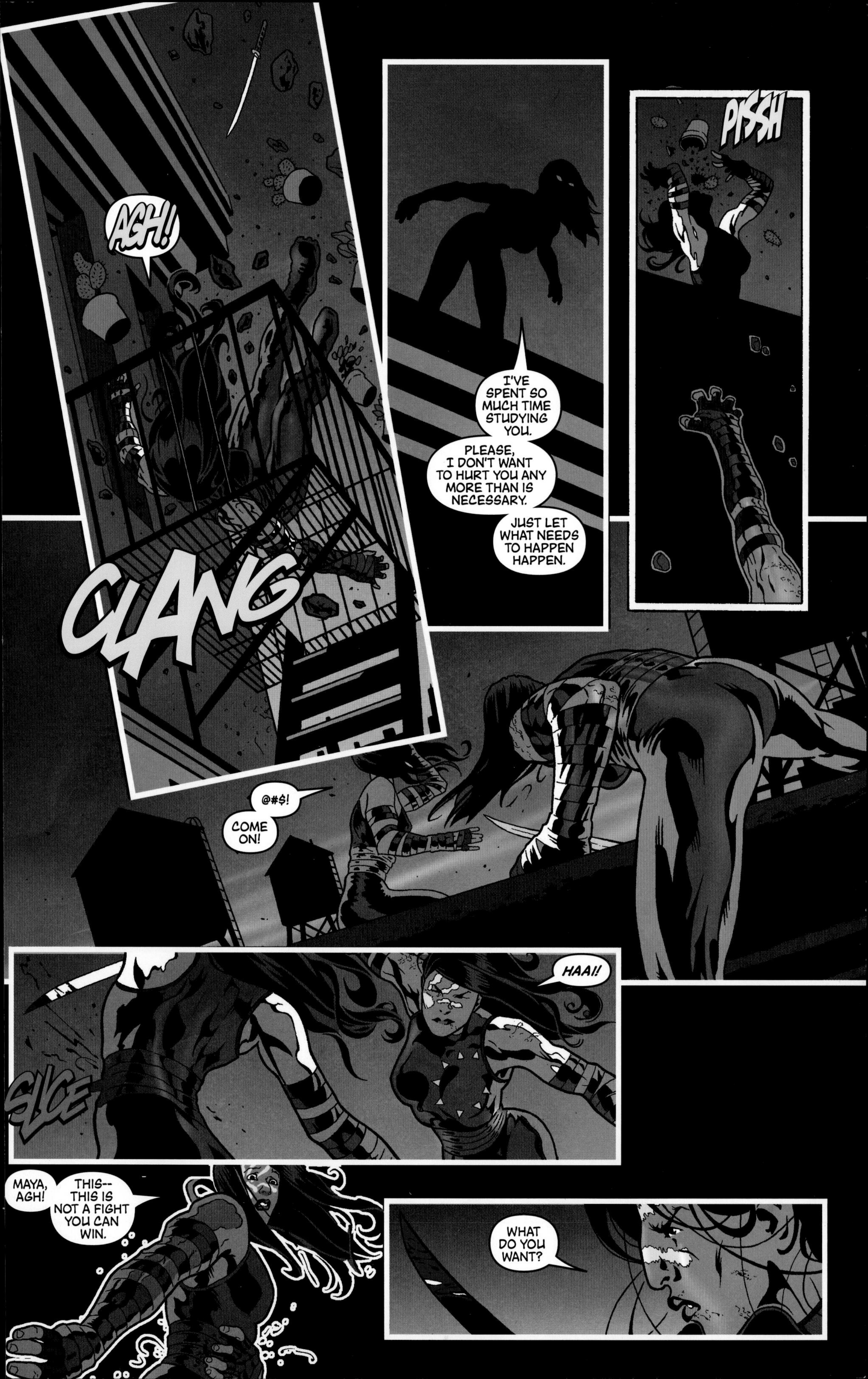
AGH!
CLANG
I'VE SPENT SO MUCH TIME STUDYING YOU.
PLEASE, I DON'T WANT TO HURT YOU ANY MORE THAN IS NECESSARY.
JUST LET WHAT NEEDS TO HAPPEN HAPPEN.
PISSH
@#$!
COME ON!
HAAI!
SLICE
MAYA, AGH!
THIS-- THIS IS NOT A FIGHT YOU CAN WIN.
WHAT DO YOU WANT?

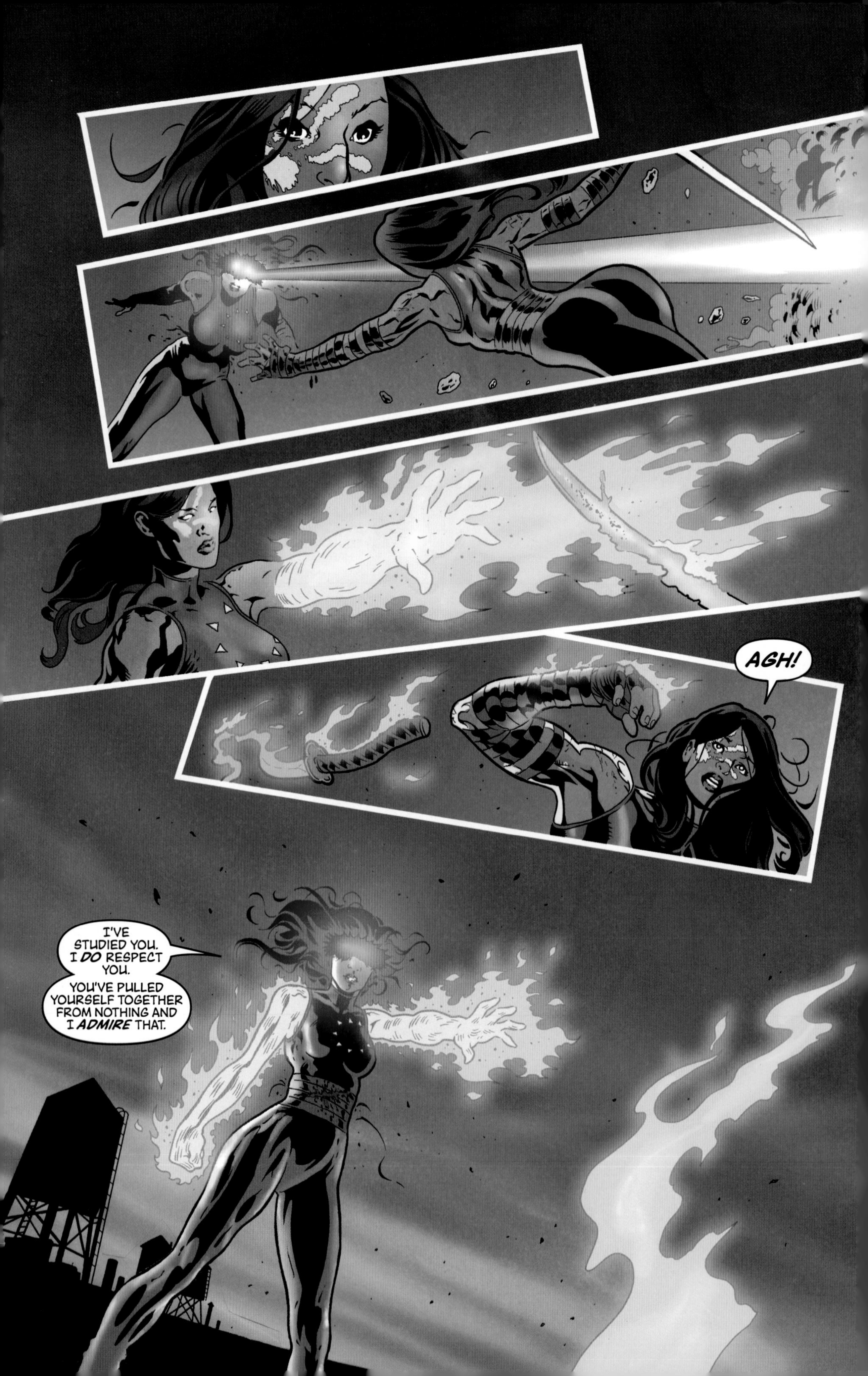
AGH!
I'VE STUDIED YOU. I *DO* RESPECT YOU. YOU'VE PULLED YOURSELF TOGETHER FROM NOTHING AND I *ADMIRE* THAT.

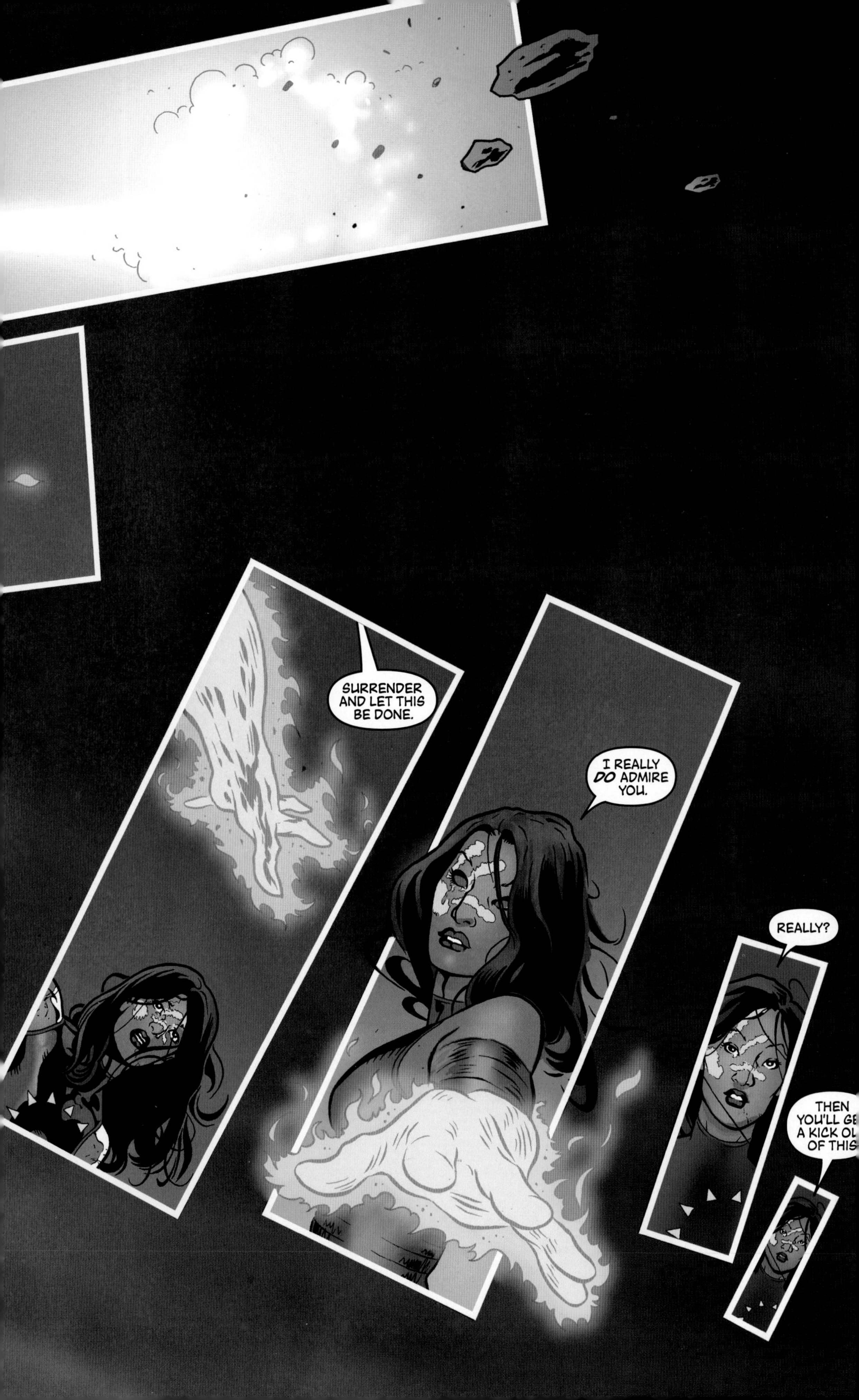
SURRENDER AND LET THIS BE DONE.
I REALLY *DO* ADMIRE YOU.
REALLY?
THEN YOU'LL GE A KICK OU OF THIS

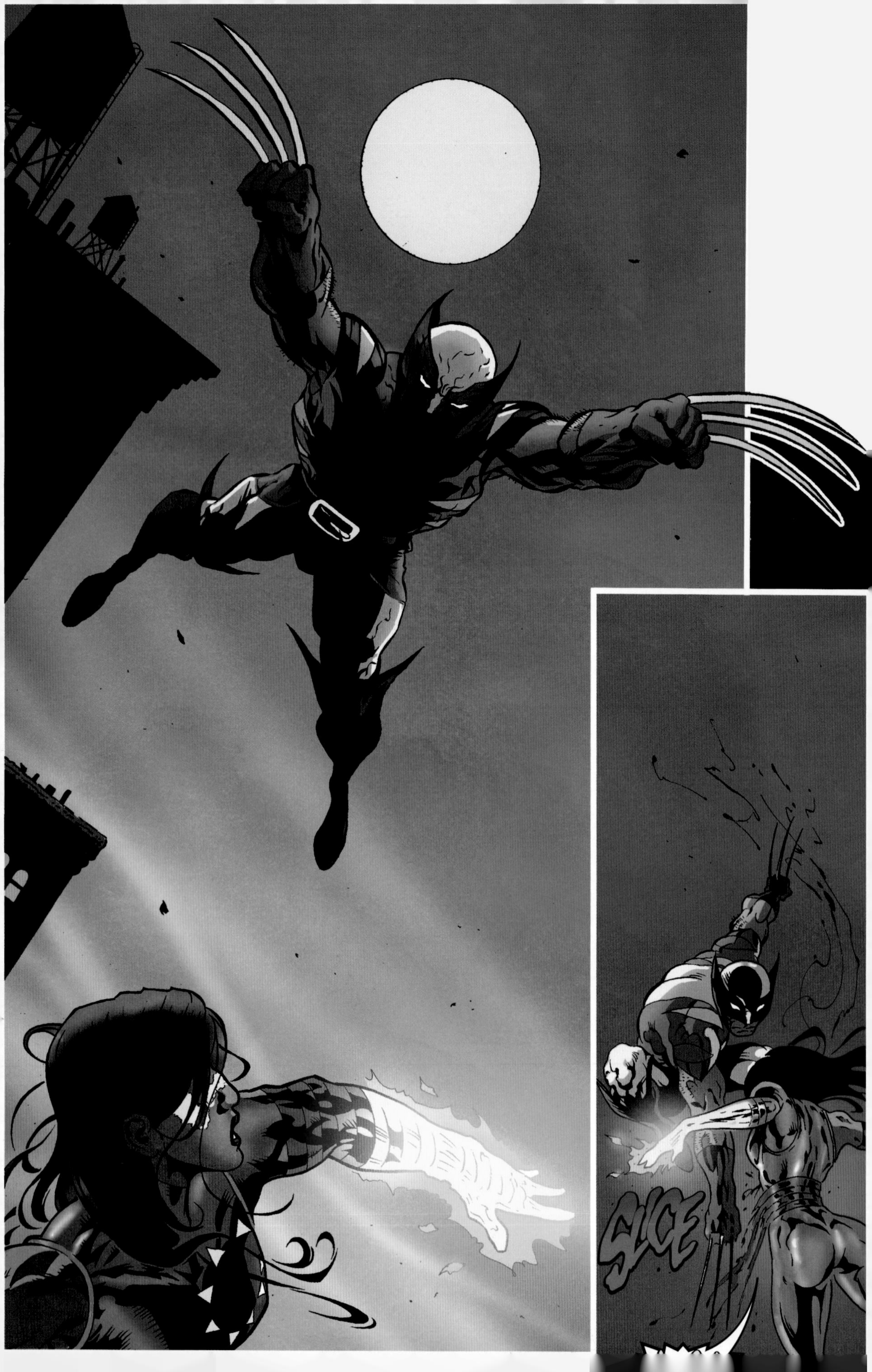
SLICE

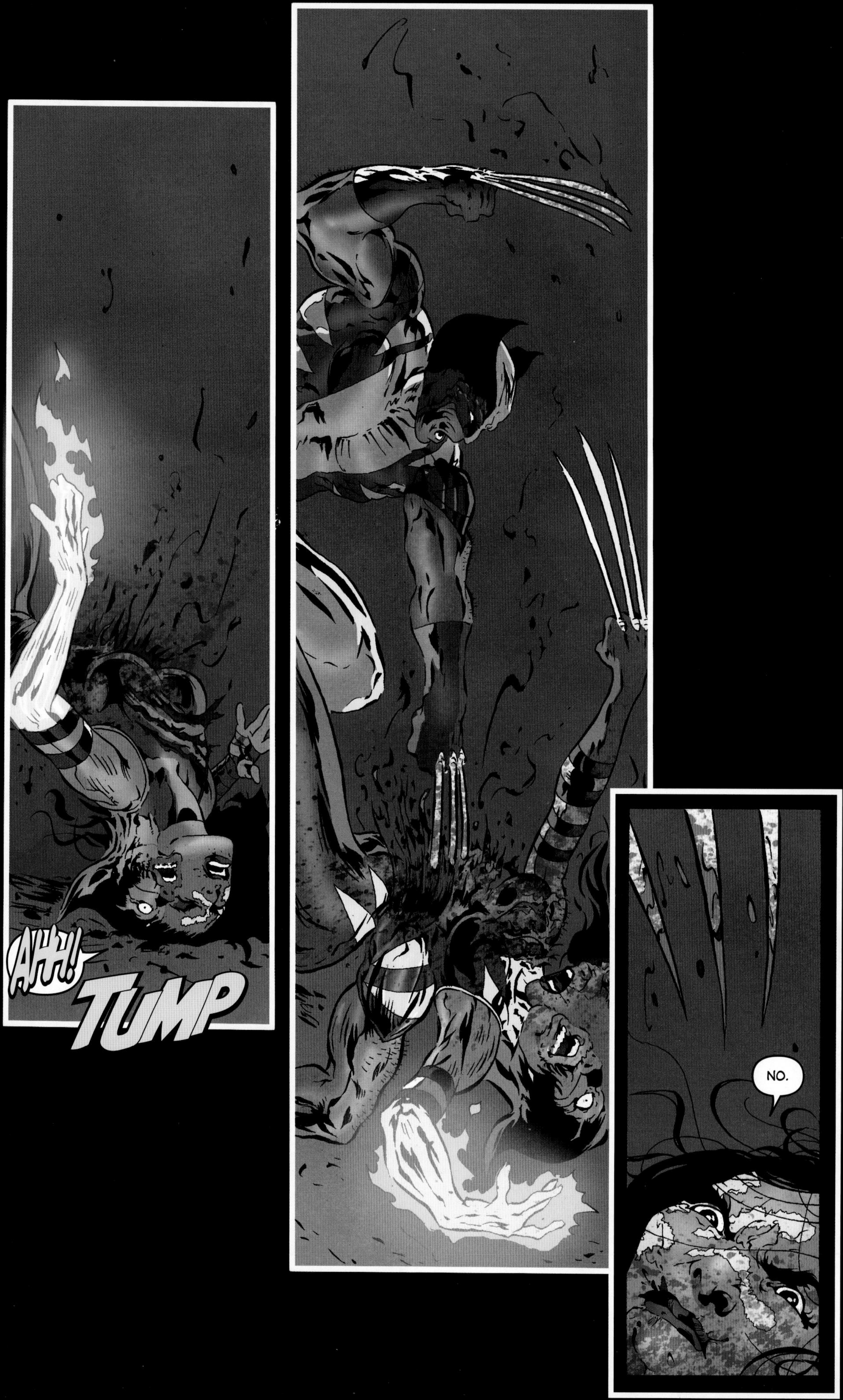
AHH!
TUMP
NO.

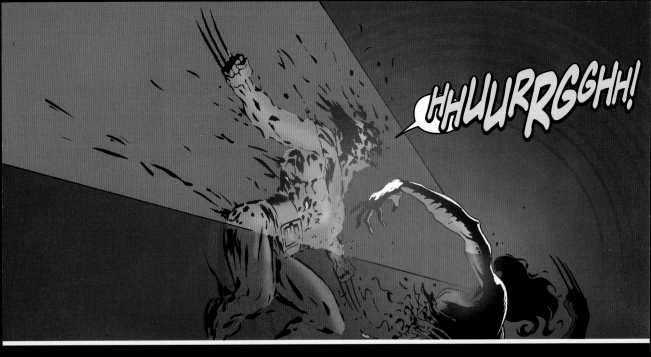

HHUURRGGHH!

NO!

YOU DON'T EVEN KNOW WHAT YOU'RE FIGHTING FOR! YOU DON'T KNOW--

WE'RE TRAINED TO DIE.

BAMF

AGH!

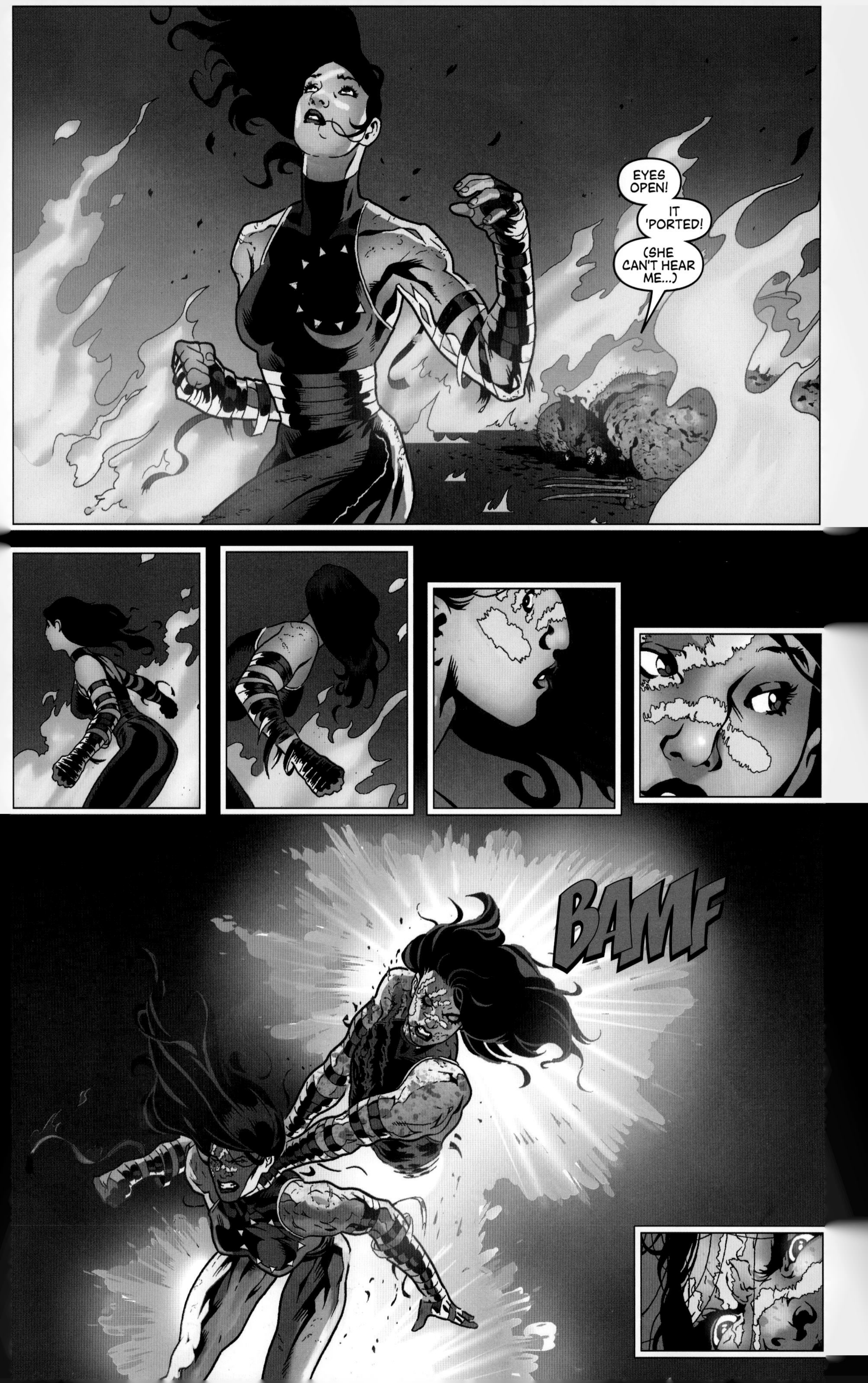
EYES OPEN!
IT 'PORTED!
(SHE CAN'T HEAR ME...)
BAMF

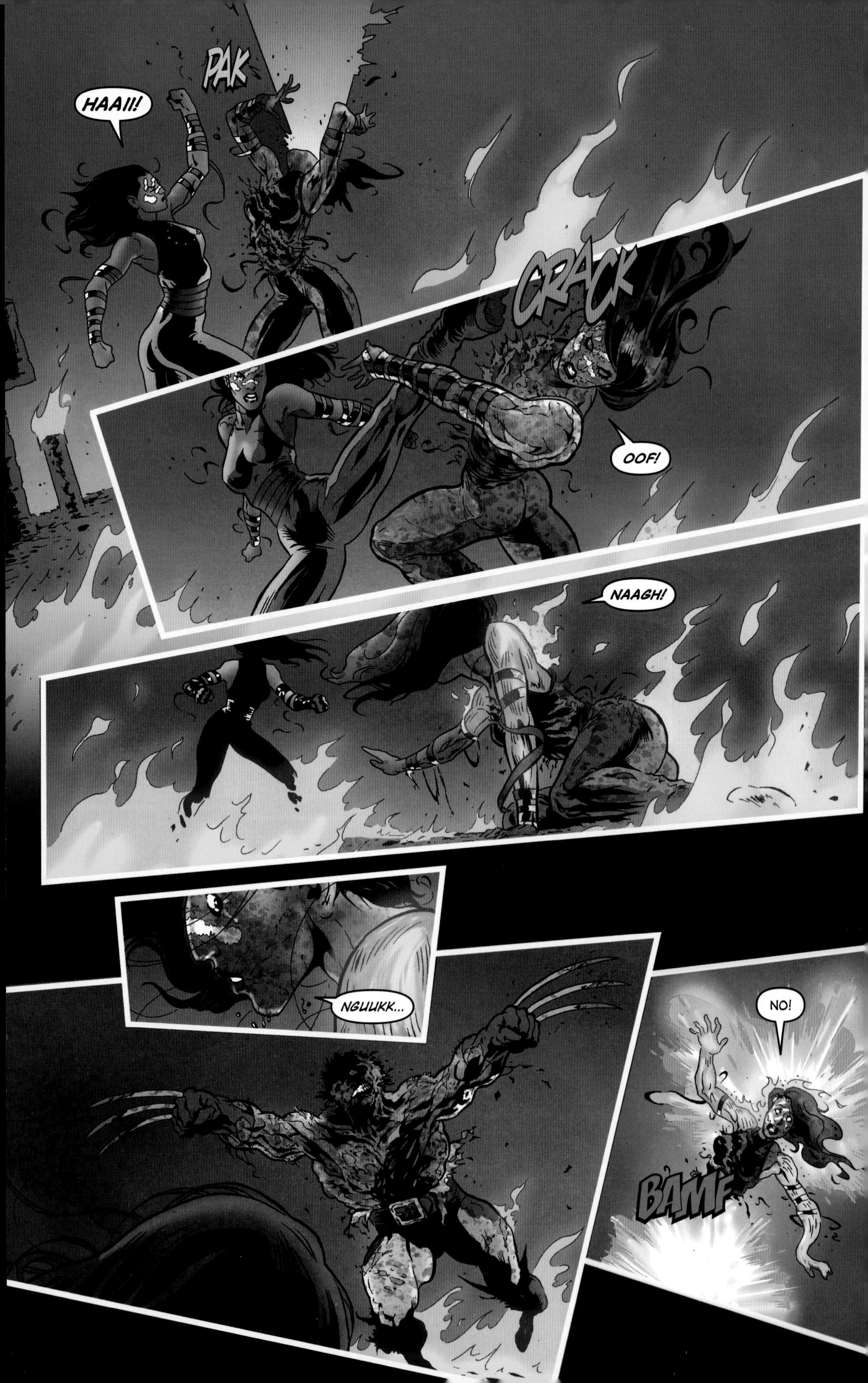
HAAII!
PAK
CRACK
OOF!
NAAGH!
NGUUKK...
NO!
BAMF

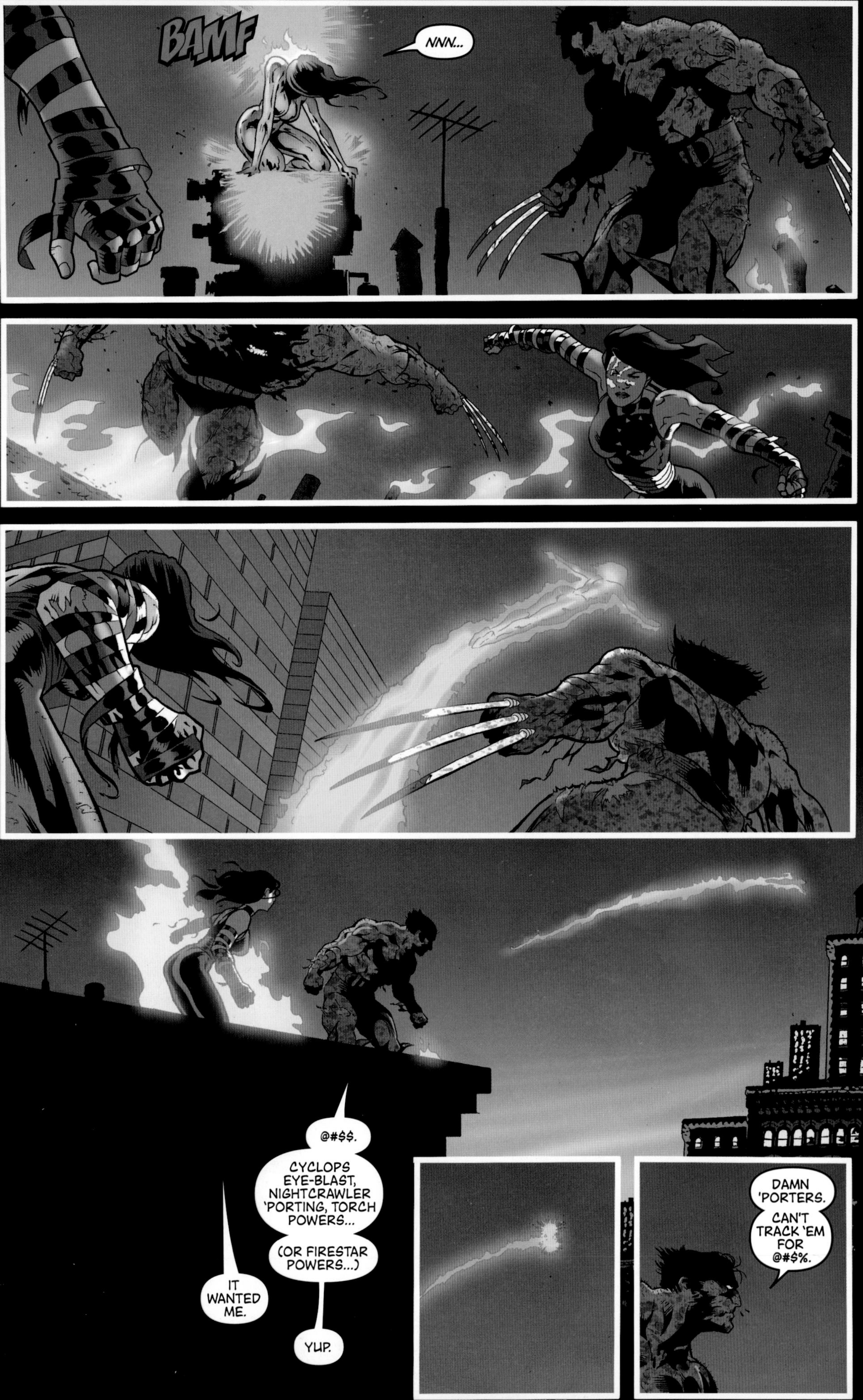

BAMF
NNN...
@#$$.
CYCLOPS EYE-BLAST, NIGHTCRAWLER 'PORTING, TORCH POWERS...
(OR FIRESTAR POWERS...)
IT WANTED ME.
YUP.
DAMN 'PORTERS.
CAN'T TRACK 'EM FOR @#$%.

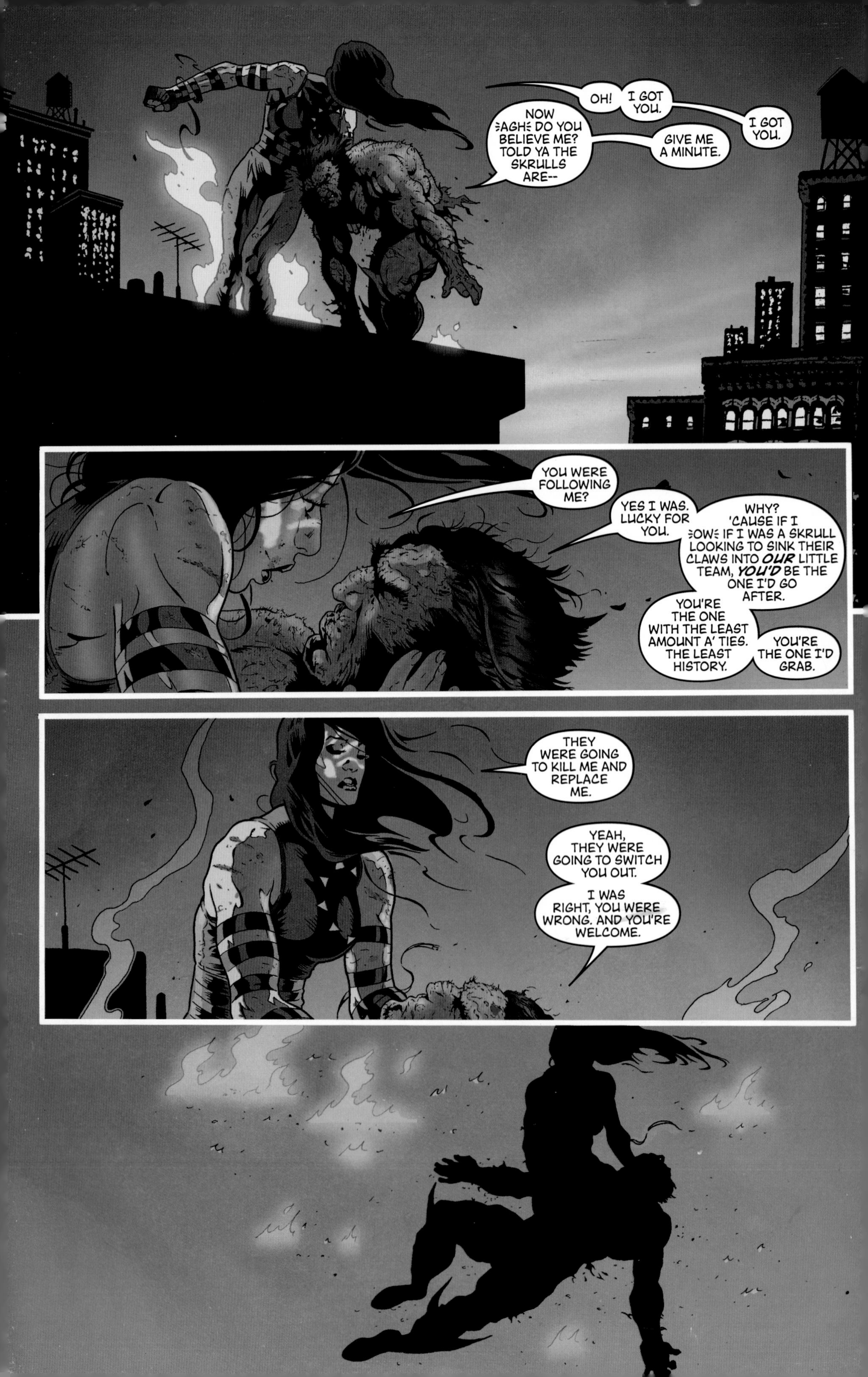

NOW ≶AGH≶ DO YOU BELIEVE ME? TOLD YA THE SKRULLS ARE--
OH!
I GOT YOU.
I GOT YOU.
GIVE ME A MINUTE.
YOU WERE FOLLOWING ME?
YES I WAS. LUCKY FOR YOU.
WHY? 'CAUSE IF I ≶OW≶ IF I WAS A SKRULL LOOKING TO SINK THEIR CLAWS INTO ***OUR*** LITTLE TEAM, ***YOU'D*** BE THE ONE I'D GO AFTER.
YOU'RE THE ONE WITH THE LEAST AMOUNT A' TIES. THE LEAST HISTORY.
YOU'RE THE ONE I'D GRAB.
THEY WERE GOING TO KILL ME AND REPLACE ME.
YEAH, THEY WERE GOING TO SWITCH YOU OUT.
I WAS RIGHT, YOU WERE WRONG. AND YOU'RE WELCOME.

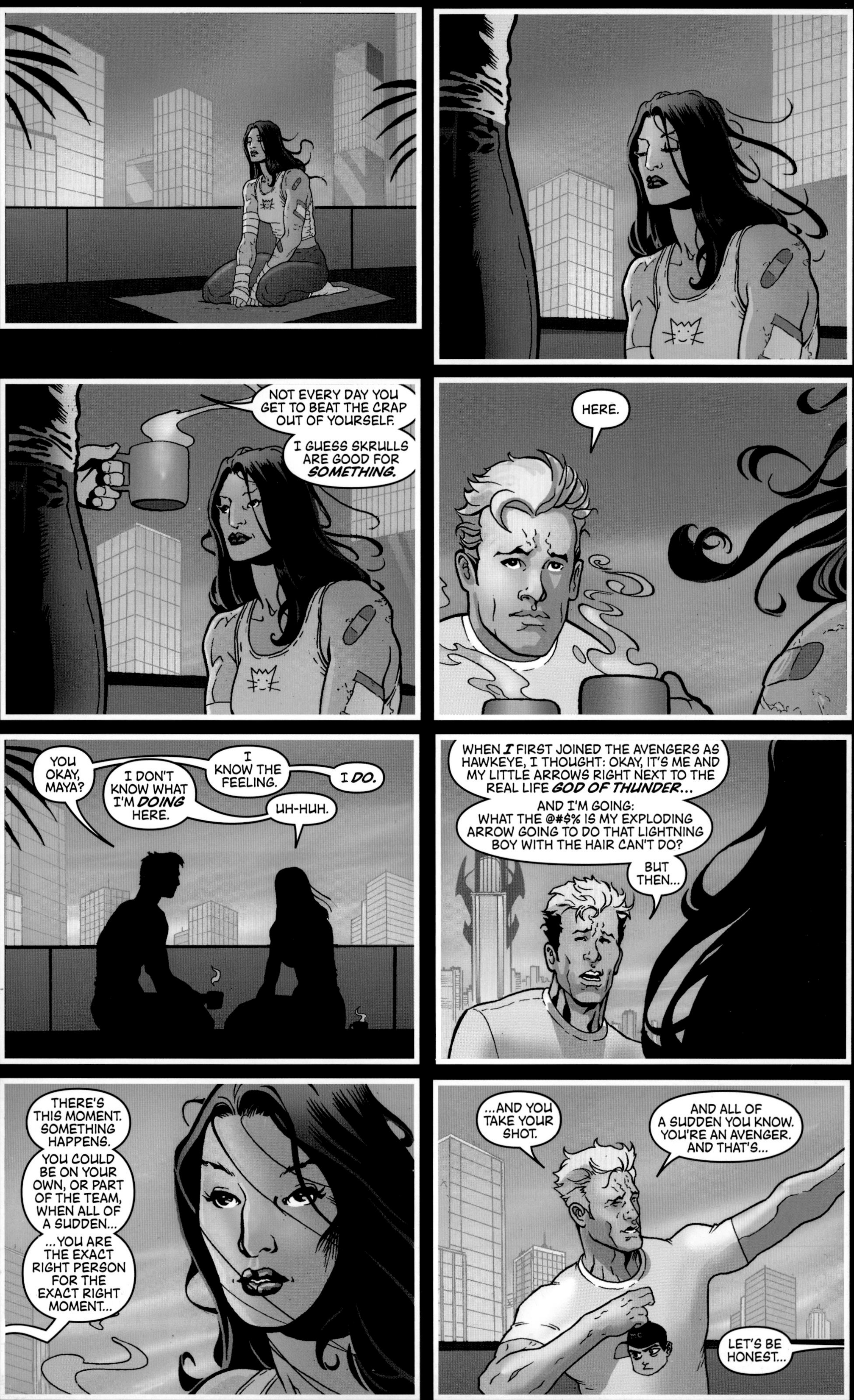
NOT EVERY DAY YOU GET TO BEAT THE CRAP OUT OF YOURSELF.
I GUESS SKRULLS ARE GOOD FOR *SOMETHING.*
HERE.
YOU OKAY, MAYA?
I DON'T KNOW WHAT I'M *DOING* HERE.
I KNOW THE FEELING.
UH-HUH.
I *DO.*
WHEN *I* FIRST JOINED THE AVENGERS AS HAWKEYE, I THOUGHT: OKAY, IT'S ME AND MY LITTLE ARROWS RIGHT NEXT TO THE REAL LIFE *GOD OF THUNDER...*
AND I'M GOING: WHAT THE @#$% IS MY EXPLODING ARROW GOING TO DO THAT LIGHTNING BOY WITH THE HAIR CAN'T DO?
BUT THEN...
THERE'S THIS MOMENT. SOMETHING HAPPENS.
YOU COULD BE ON YOUR OWN, OR PART OF THE TEAM, WHEN ALL OF A SUDDEN...
...YOU ARE THE EXACT RIGHT PERSON FOR THE EXACT RIGHT MOMENT...
...AND YOU TAKE YOUR SHOT.
AND ALL OF A SUDDEN YOU KNOW. YOU'RE AN AVENGER. AND THAT'S...
LET'S BE HONEST...

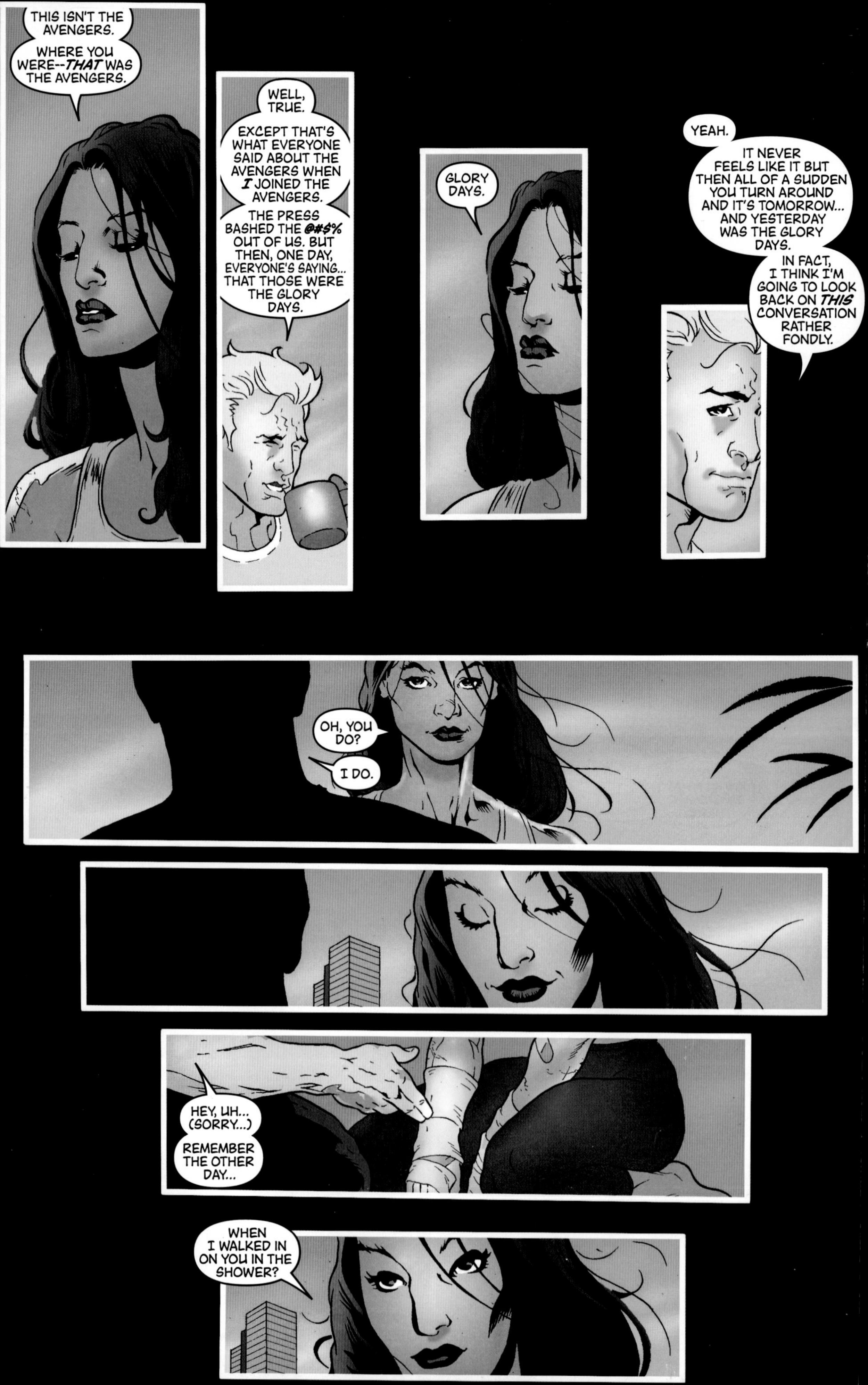

THIS ISN'T THE AVENGERS.
WHERE YOU WERE--*THAT* WAS THE AVENGERS.
WELL, TRUE.
EXCEPT THAT'S WHAT EVERYONE SAID ABOUT THE AVENGERS WHEN *I* JOINED THE AVENGERS.
THE PRESS BASHED THE @#$% OUT OF US. BUT THEN, ONE DAY, EVERYONE'S SAYING... THAT THOSE WERE THE GLORY DAYS.
GLORY DAYS.
YEAH.
IT NEVER FEELS LIKE IT BUT THEN ALL OF A SUDDEN YOU TURN AROUND AND IT'S TOMORROW... AND YESTERDAY WAS THE GLORY DAYS.
IN FACT, I THINK I'M GOING TO LOOK BACK ON *THIS* CONVERSATION RATHER FONDLY.
OH, YOU DO?
I DO.
HEY, UH... (SORRY...)
REMEMBER THE OTHER DAY...
WHEN I WALKED IN ON YOU IN THE SHOWER?

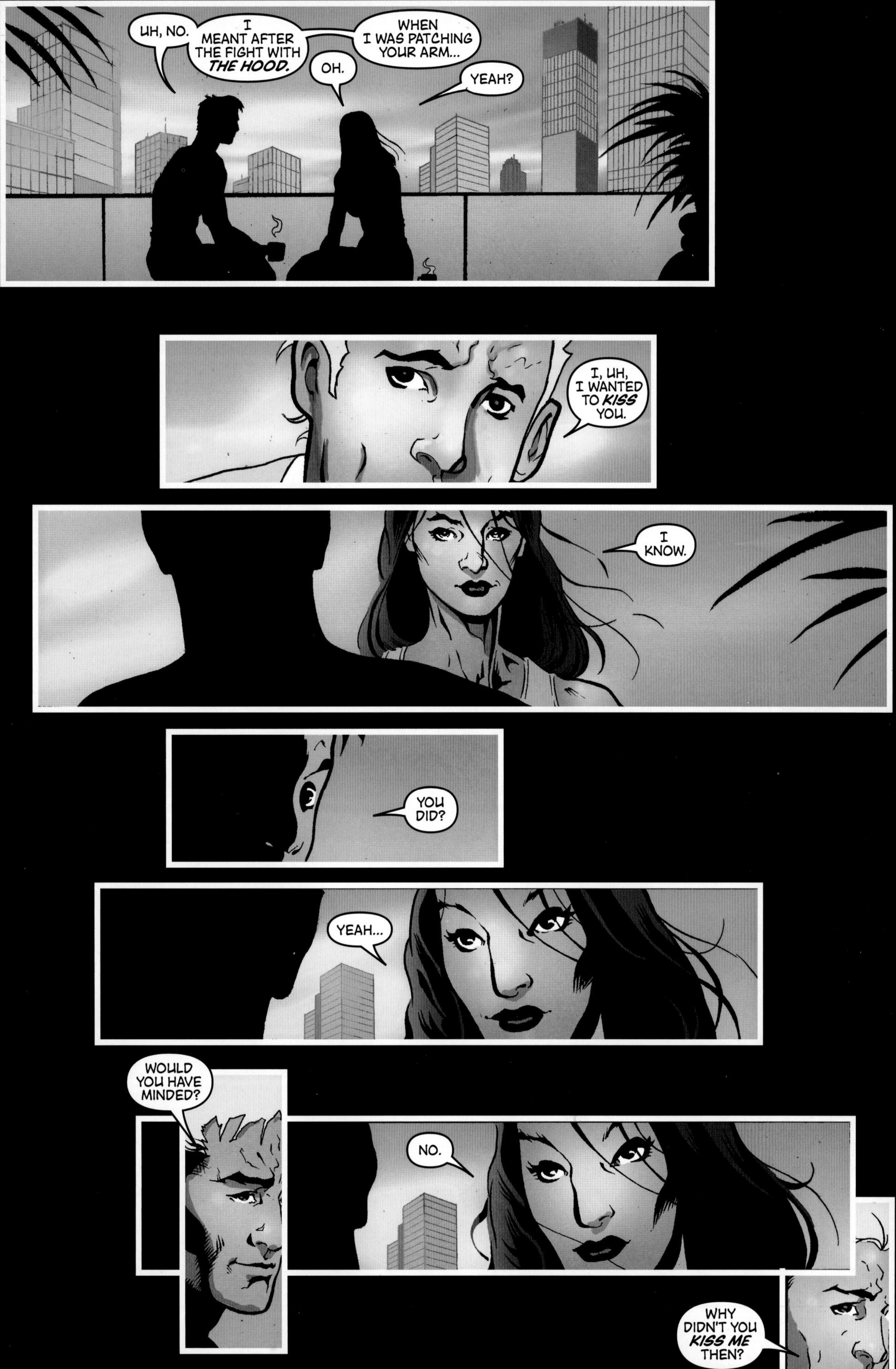
UH, NO.
I MEANT AFTER THE FIGHT WITH *THE HOOD.*
OH.
WHEN I WAS PATCHING YOUR ARM...
YEAH?
I, UH, I WANTED TO *KISS* YOU.
I KNOW.
YOU DID?
YEAH...
WOULD YOU HAVE MINDED?
NO.
WHY DIDN'T YOU *KISS ME* THEN?

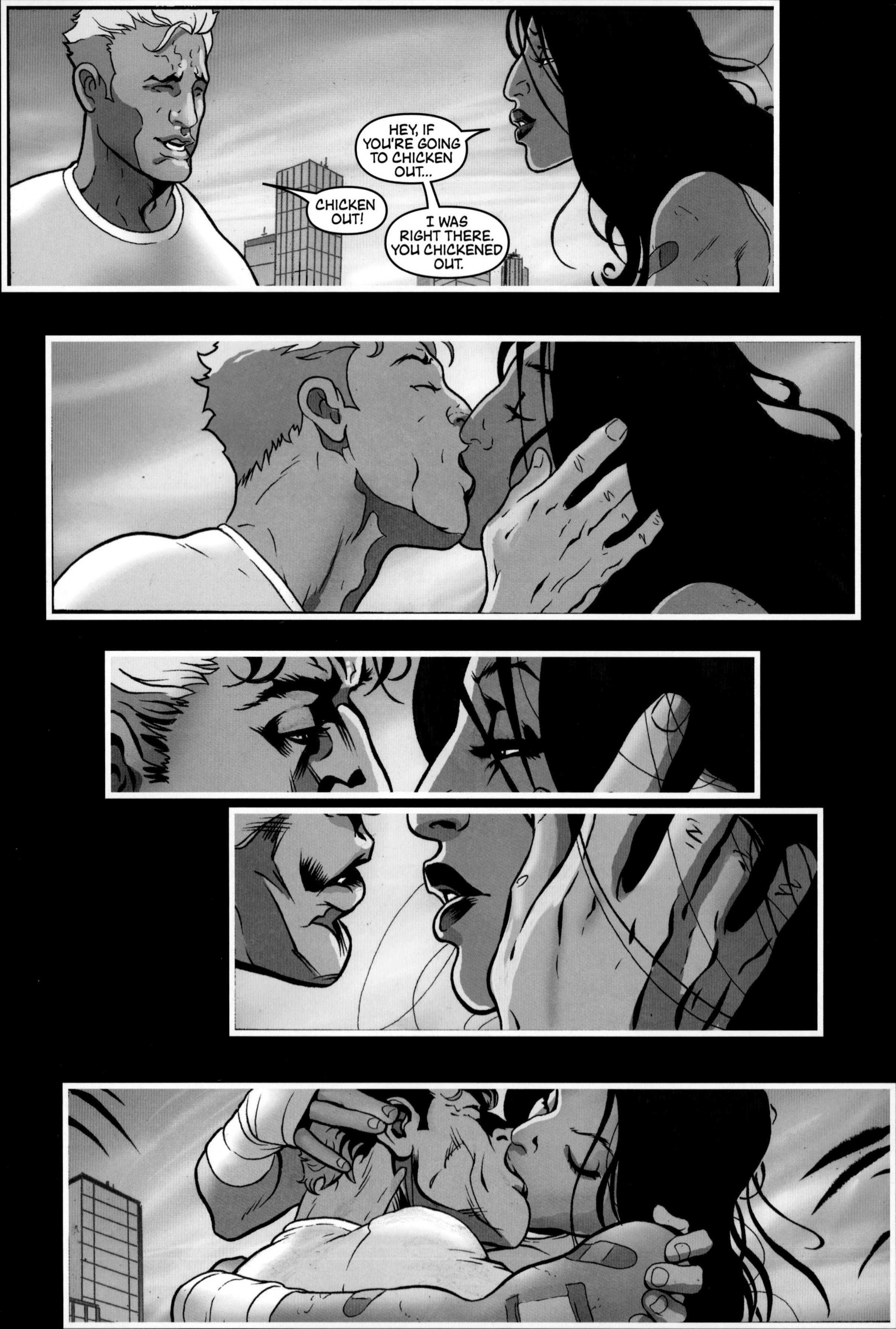
HEY, IF YOU'RE GOING TO CHICKEN OUT...
CHICKEN OUT!
I WAS RIGHT THERE. YOU CHICKENED OUT.

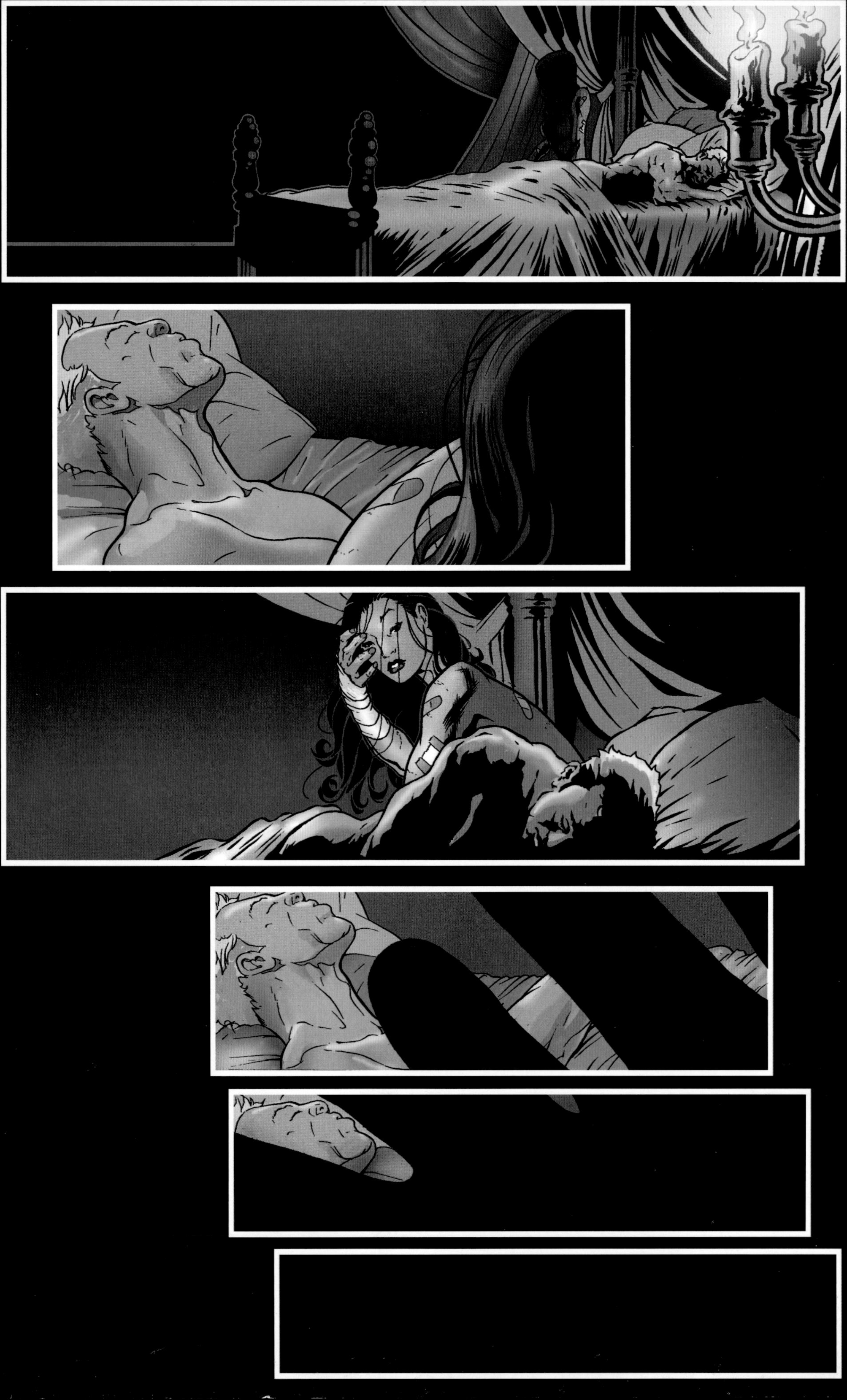

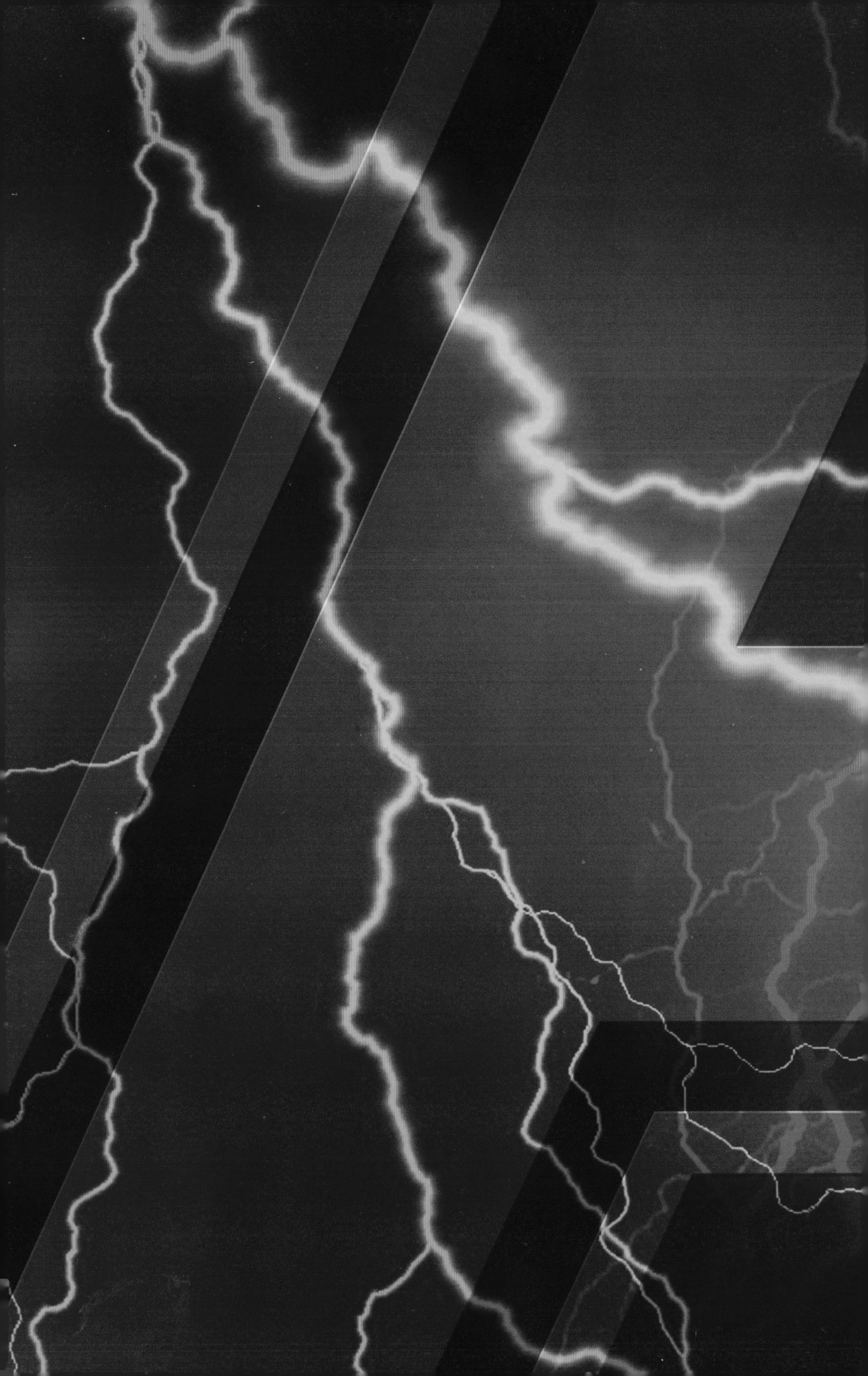

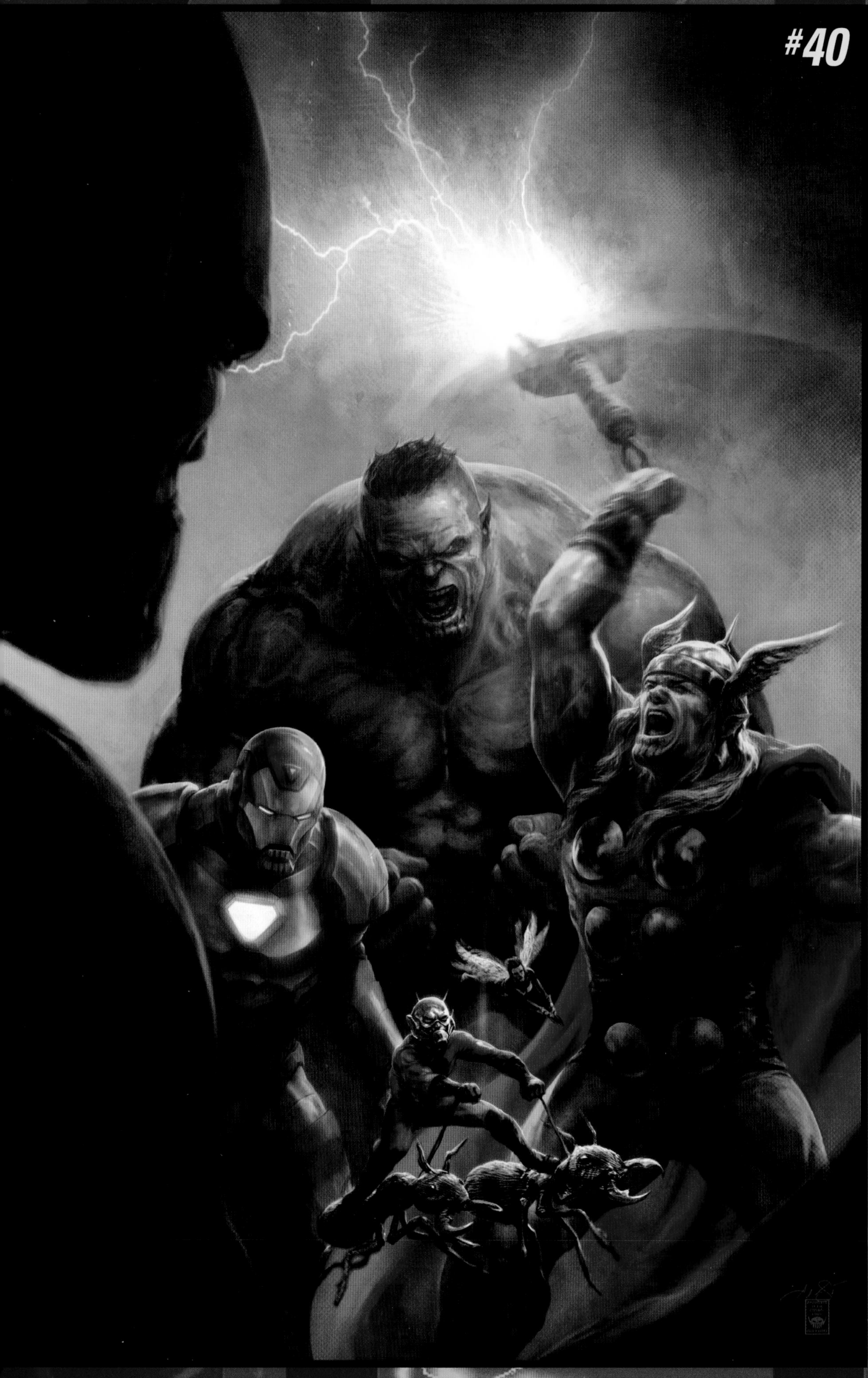
#40

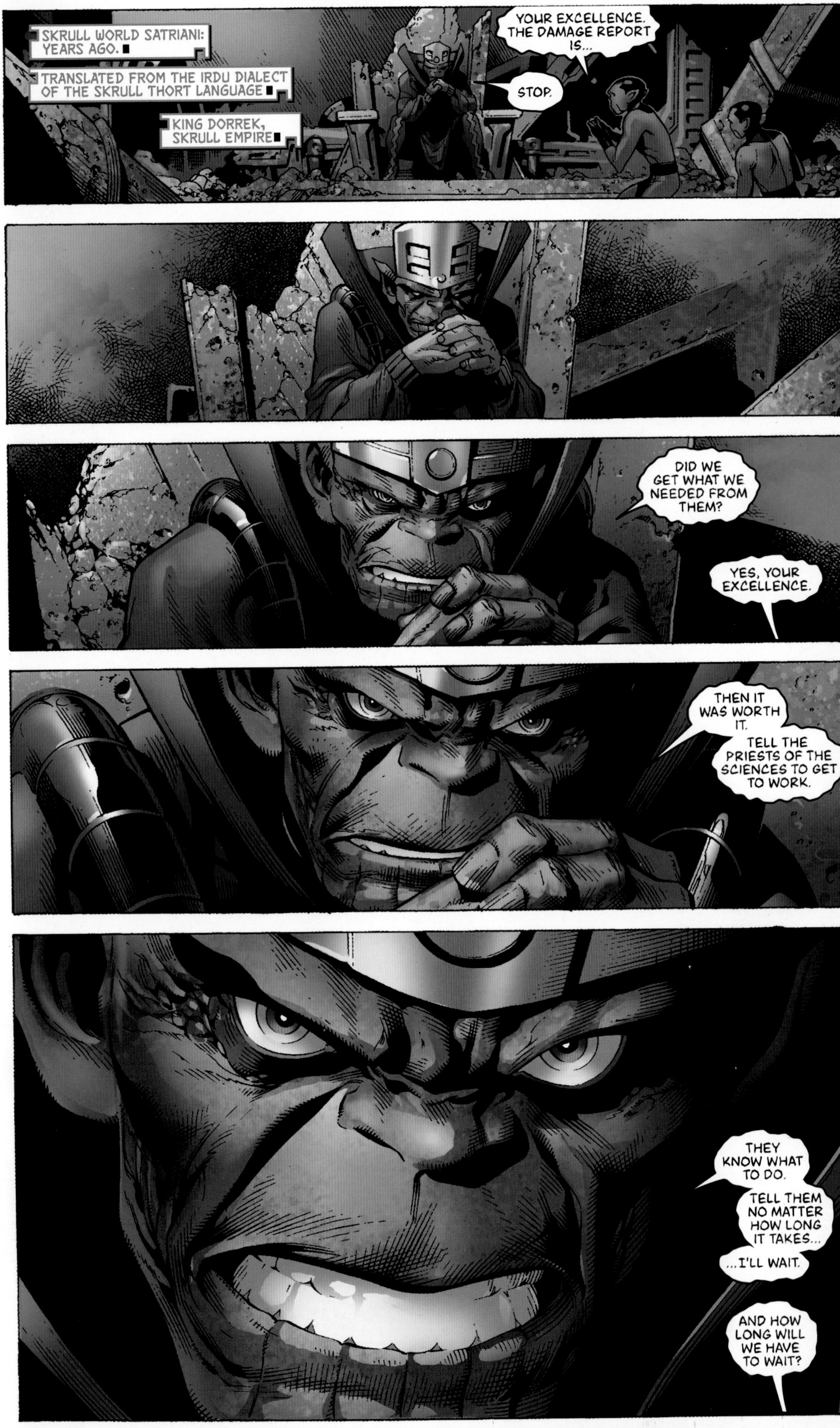
SKRULL WORLD SATRIANI: YEARS AGO.
TRANSLATED FROM THE IRDU DIALECT OF THE SKRULL THORT LANGUAGE
KING DORREK, SKRULL EMPIRE
YOUR EXCELLENCE. THE DAMAGE REPORT IS...
STOP.
DID WE GET WHAT WE NEEDED FROM THEM?
YES, YOUR EXCELLENCE.
THEN IT WAS WORTH IT.
TELL THE PRIESTS OF THE SCIENCES TO GET TO WORK.
THEY KNOW WHAT TO DO.
TELL THEM NO MATTER HOW LONG IT TAKES...
...I'LL WAIT.
AND HOW LONG WILL WE HAVE TO WAIT?

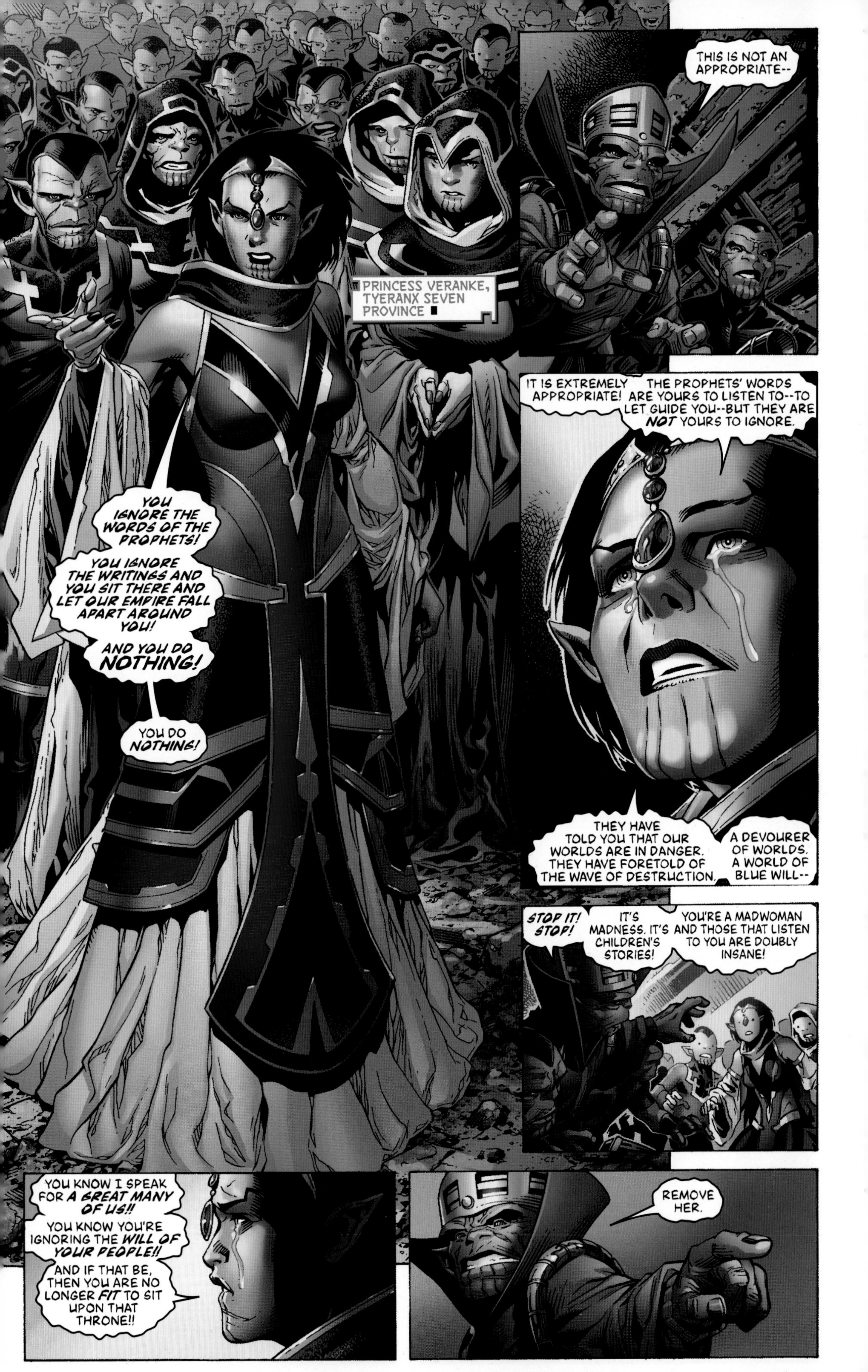

PRINCESS VERANKE, TYERANX SEVEN PROVINCE
YOU IGNORE THE WORDS OF THE PROPHETS!
YOU IGNORE THE WRITINGS AND YOU SIT THERE AND LET OUR EMPIRE FALL APART AROUND YOU!
AND YOU DO NOTHING!
YOU DO NOTHING!
THIS IS NOT AN APPROPRIATE--
IT IS EXTREMELY APPROPRIATE!
THE PROPHETS' WORDS ARE YOURS TO LISTEN TO--TO LET GUIDE YOU--BUT THEY ARE NOT YOURS TO IGNORE.
THEY HAVE TOLD YOU THAT OUR WORLDS ARE IN DANGER. THEY HAVE FORETOLD OF THE WAVE OF DESTRUCTION.
A DEVOURER OF WORLDS. A WORLD OF BLUE WILL--
STOP IT! STOP!
IT'S MADNESS. IT'S CHILDREN'S STORIES!
YOU'RE A MADWOMAN AND THOSE THAT LISTEN TO YOU ARE DOUBLY INSANE!
YOU KNOW I SPEAK FOR A GREAT MANY OF US!!
YOU KNOW YOU'RE IGNORING THE WILL OF YOUR PEOPLE!!
AND IF THAT BE, THEN YOU ARE NO LONGER FIT TO SIT UPON THAT THRONE!!
REMOVE HER.

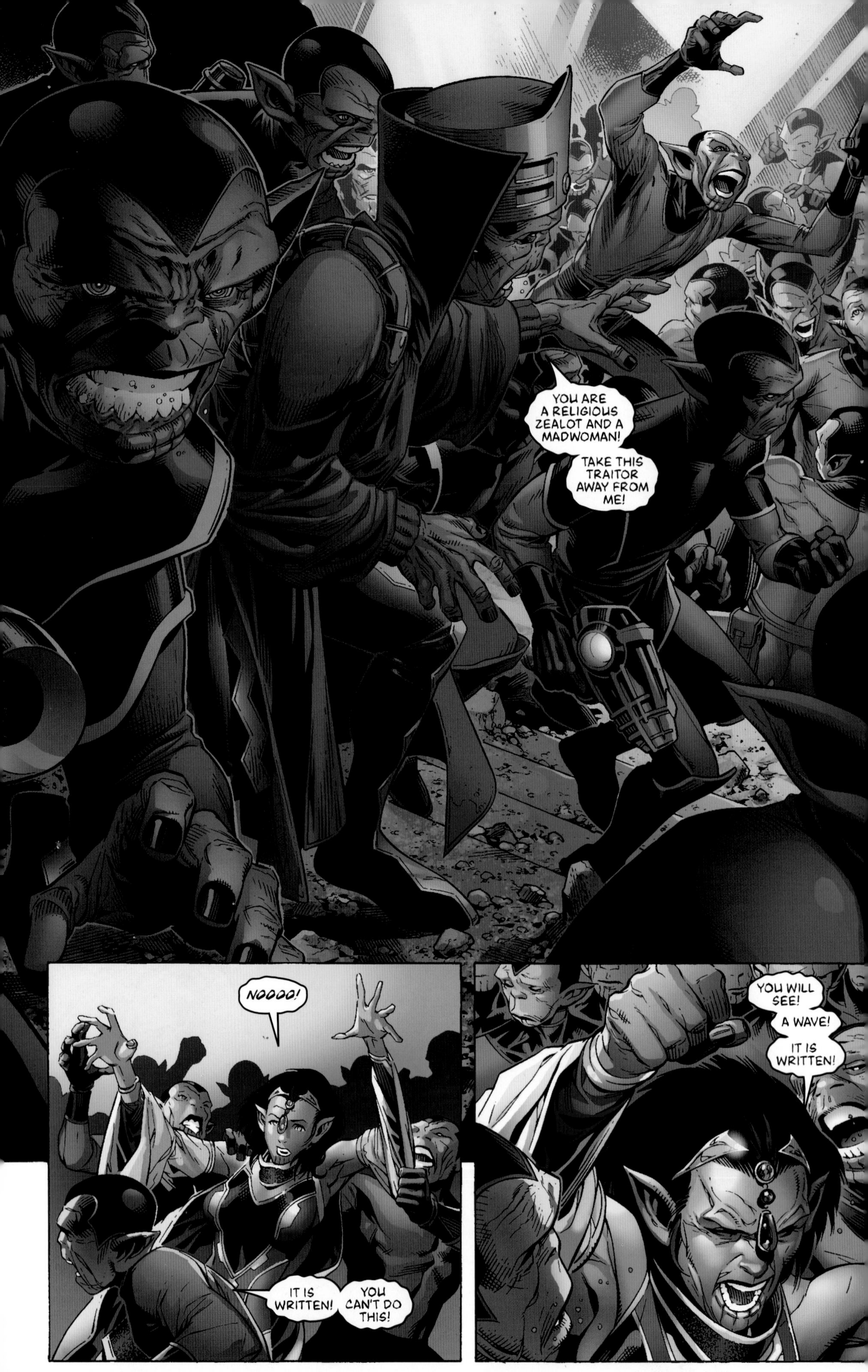
YOU ARE A RELIGIOUS ZEALOT AND A MADWOMAN!
TAKE THIS TRAITOR AWAY FROM ME!
NOOOO!
IT IS WRITTEN!
YOU CAN'T DO THIS!
YOU WILL SEE!
A WAVE!
IT IS WRITTEN!

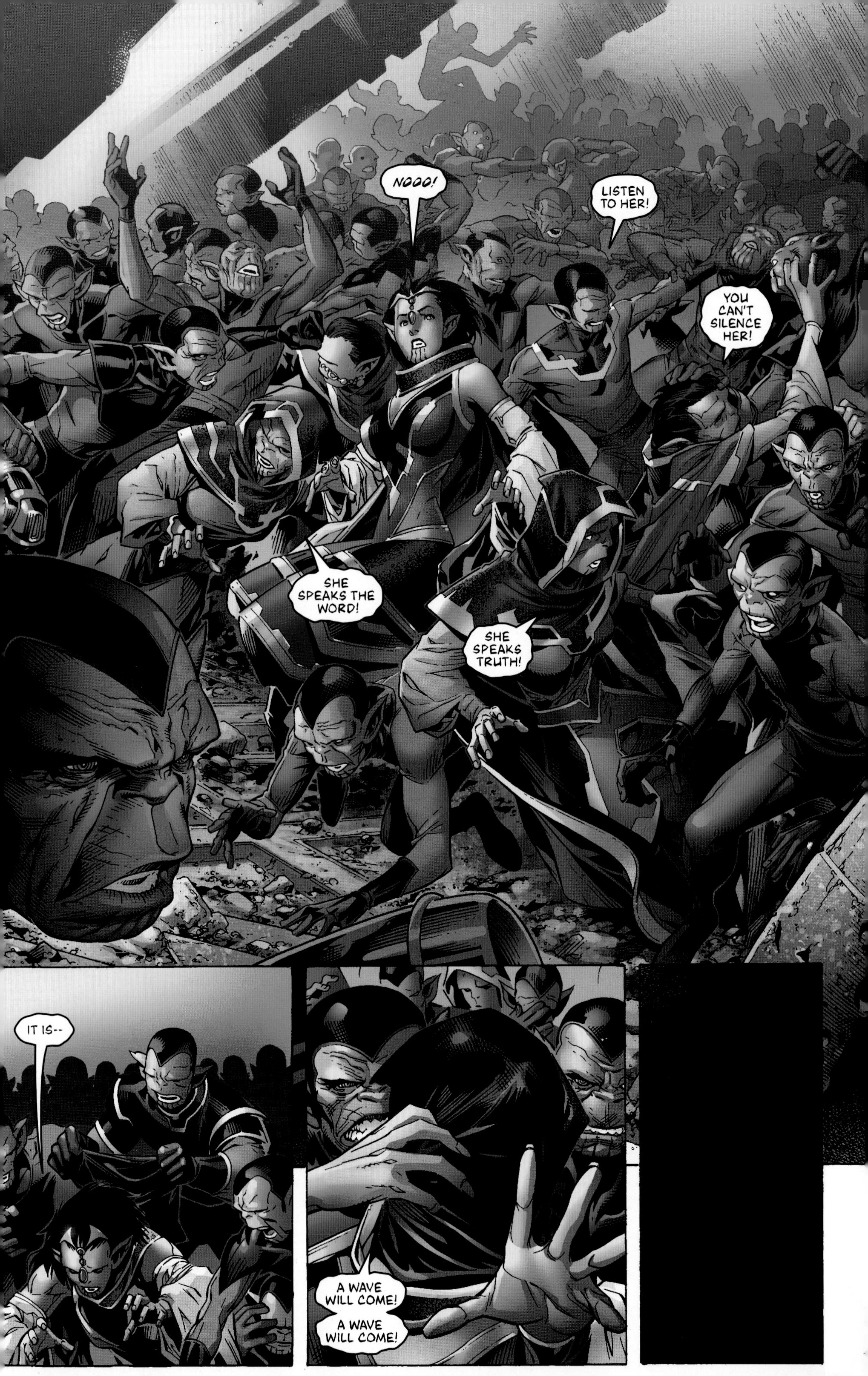
NOOO!
LISTEN TO HER!
YOU CAN'T SILENCE HER!
SHE SPEAKS THE WORD!
SHE SPEAKS TRUTH!
IT IS--
A WAVE WILL COME!
A WAVE WILL COME!

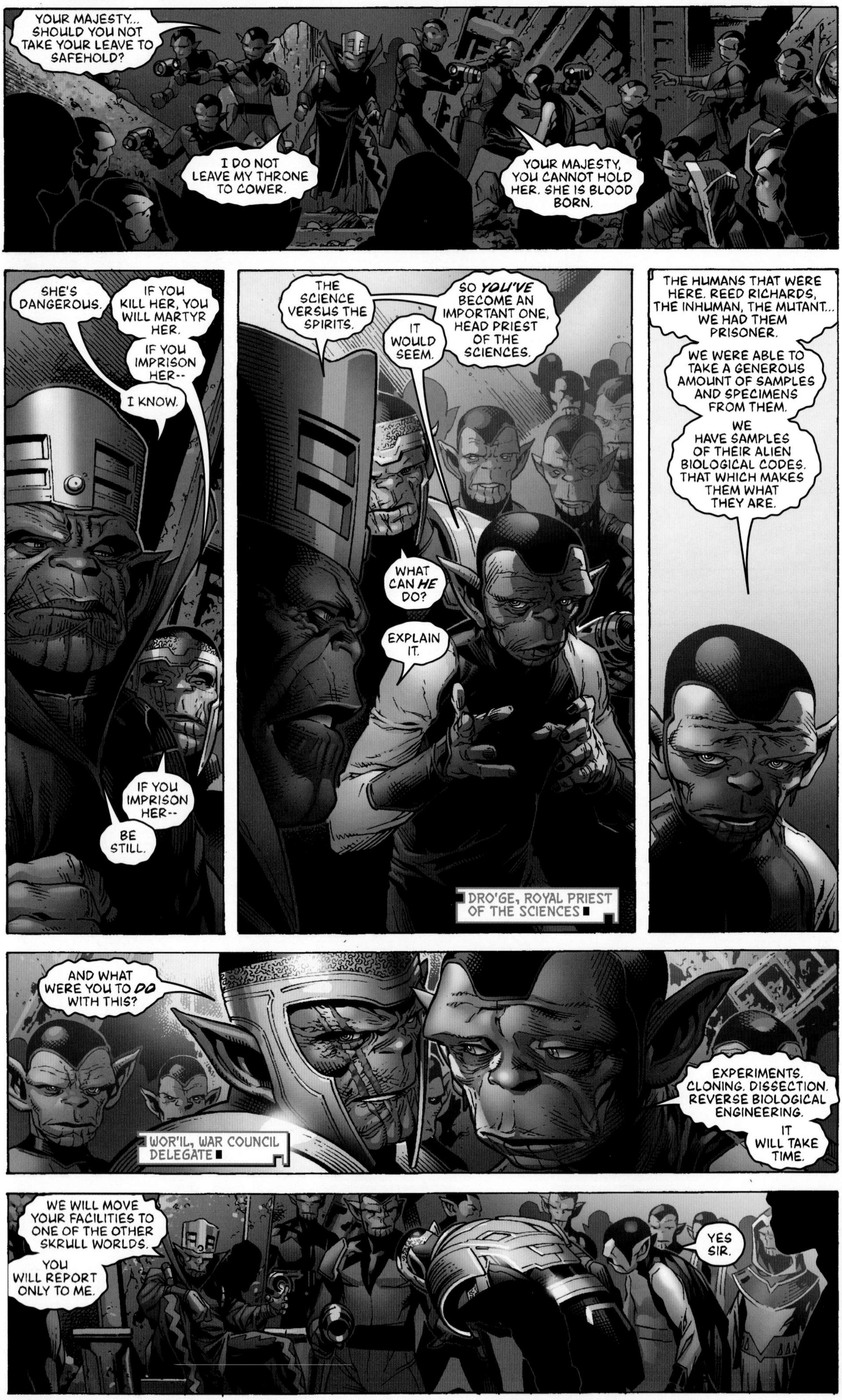
YOUR MAJESTY... SHOULD YOU NOT TAKE YOUR LEAVE TO SAFEHOLD?
I DO NOT LEAVE MY THRONE TO COWER.
YOUR MAJESTY, YOU CANNOT HOLD HER. SHE IS BLOOD BORN.
SHE'S DANGEROUS.
IF YOU KILL HER, YOU WILL MARTYR HER.
IF YOU IMPRISON HER--
I KNOW.
IF YOU IMPRISON HER--
BE STILL.
THE SCIENCE VERSUS THE SPIRITS.
SO YOU'VE BECOME AN IMPORTANT ONE, HEAD PRIEST OF THE SCIENCES.
IT WOULD SEEM.
WHAT CAN HE DO?
EXPLAIN IT.
DRO'GE, ROYAL PRIEST OF THE SCIENCES
THE HUMANS THAT WERE HERE. REED RICHARDS, THE INHUMAN, THE MUTANT... WE HAD THEM PRISONER.
WE WERE ABLE TO TAKE A GENEROUS AMOUNT OF SAMPLES AND SPECIMENS FROM THEM.
WE HAVE SAMPLES OF THEIR ALIEN BIOLOGICAL CODES. THAT WHICH MAKES THEM WHAT THEY ARE.
AND WHAT WERE YOU TO DO WITH THIS?
WOR'IL, WAR COUNCIL DELEGATE
EXPERIMENTS. CLONING. DISSECTION. REVERSE BIOLOGICAL ENGINEERING.
IT WILL TAKE TIME.
WE WILL MOVE YOUR FACILITIES TO ONE OF THE OTHER SKRULL WORLDS.
YOU WILL REPORT ONLY TO ME.
YES SIR.

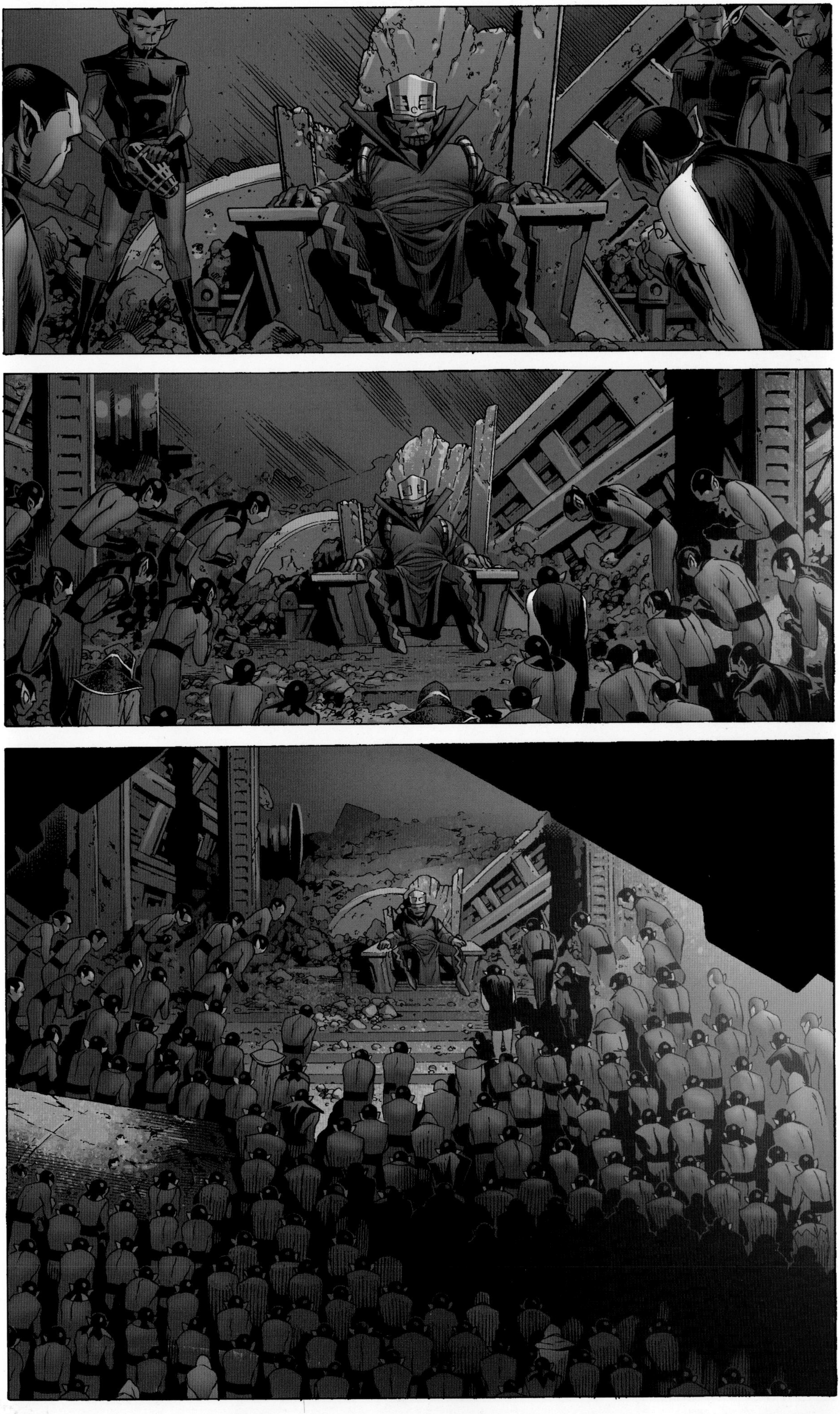

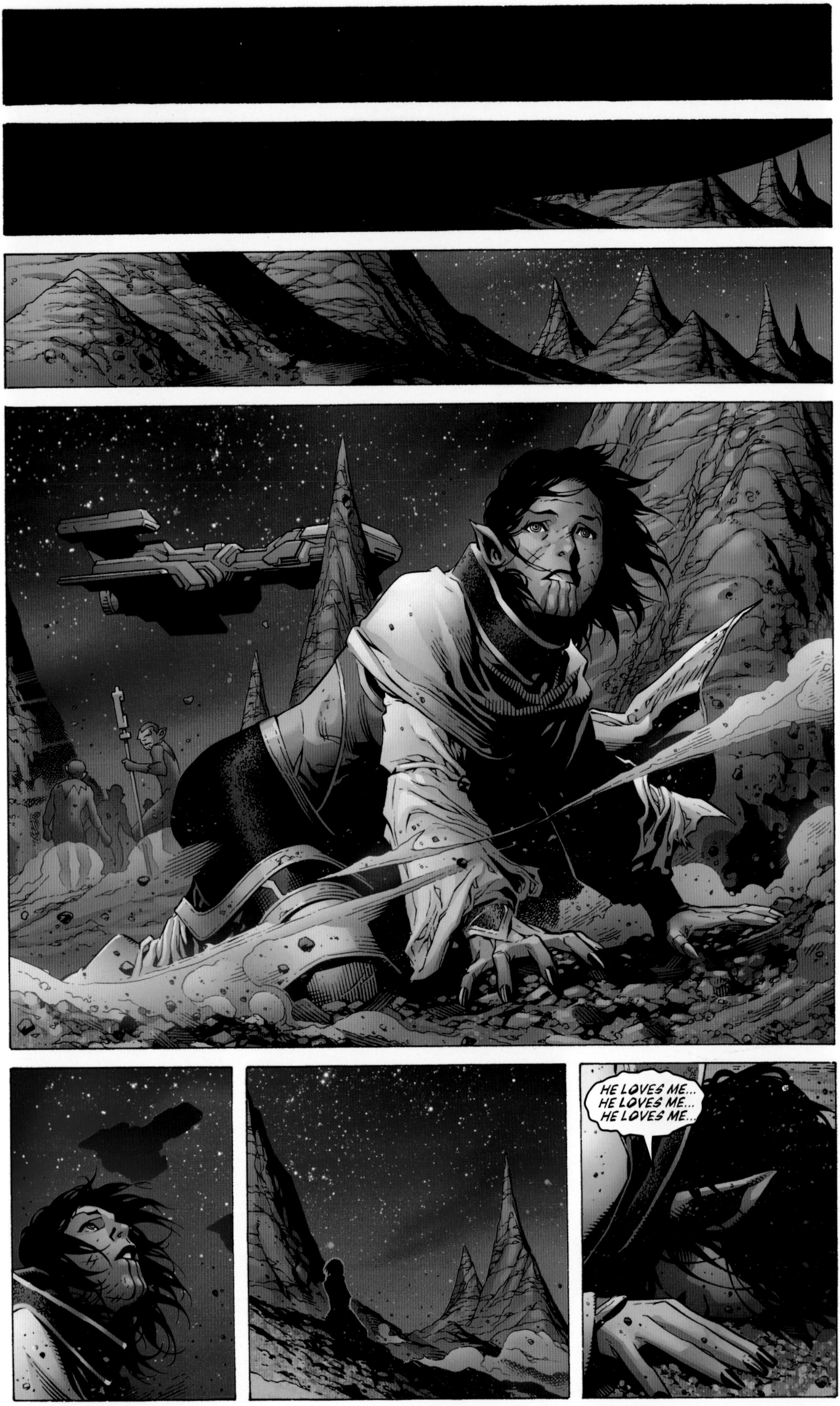
HE LOVES ME...
HE LOVES ME...
HE LOVES ME...

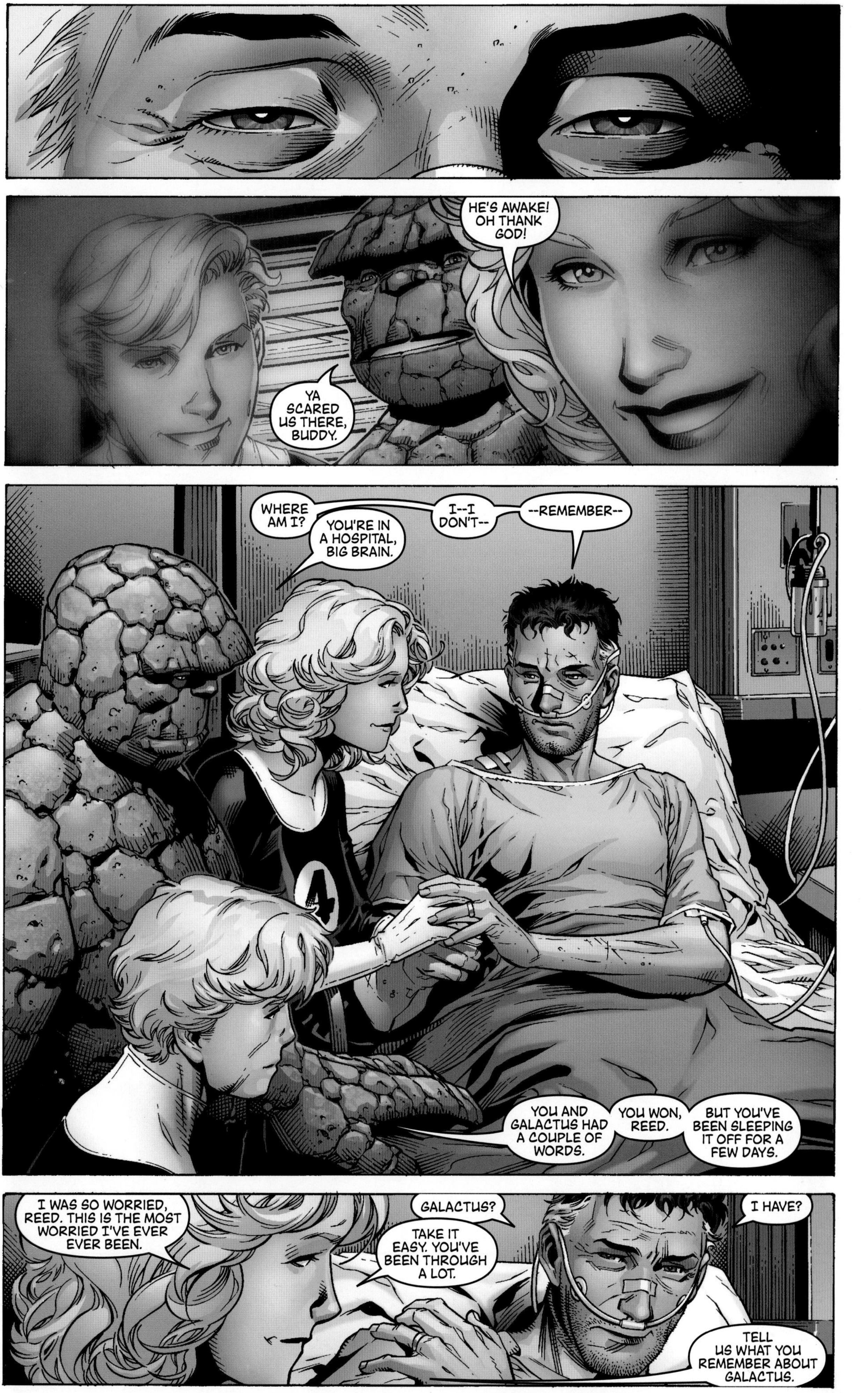

HE'S AWAKE! OH THANK GOD!
YA SCARED US THERE, BUDDY.
WHERE AM I?
YOU'RE IN A HOSPITAL, BIG BRAIN.
I--I DON'T--
--REMEMBER--
YOU AND GALACTUS HAD A COUPLE OF WORDS.
YOU WON, REED.
BUT YOU'VE BEEN SLEEPING IT OFF FOR A FEW DAYS.
I WAS SO WORRIED, REED. THIS IS THE MOST WORRIED I'VE EVER EVER BEEN.
GALACTUS?
TAKE IT EASY. YOU'VE BEEN THROUGH A LOT.
I HAVE?
TELL US WHAT YOU REMEMBER ABOUT GALACTUS.

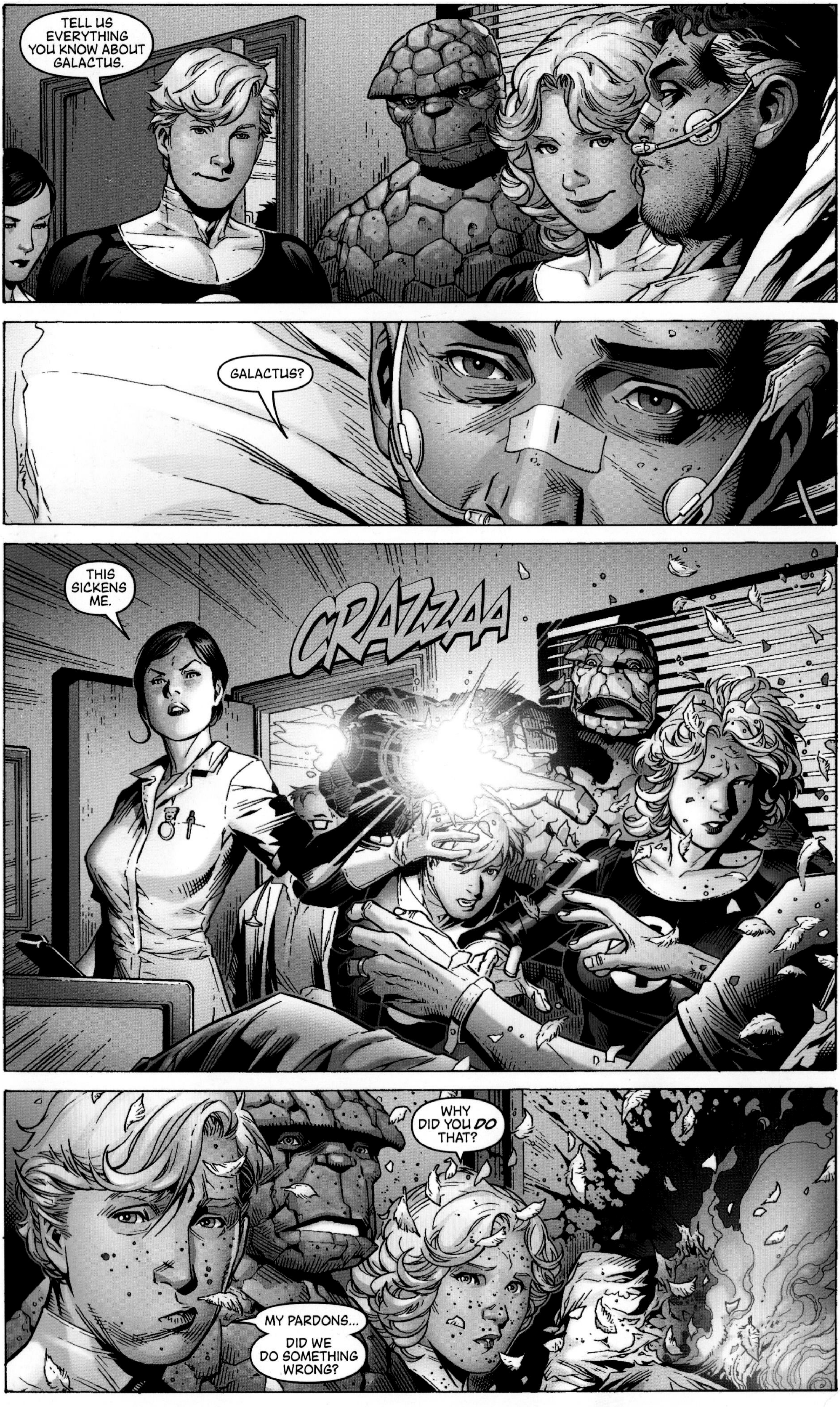
TELL US EVERYTHING YOU KNOW ABOUT GALACTUS.
GALACTUS?
THIS SICKENS ME.
CRAZZAA
WHY DID YOU DO THAT?
MY PARDONS...
DID WE DO SOMETHING WRONG?

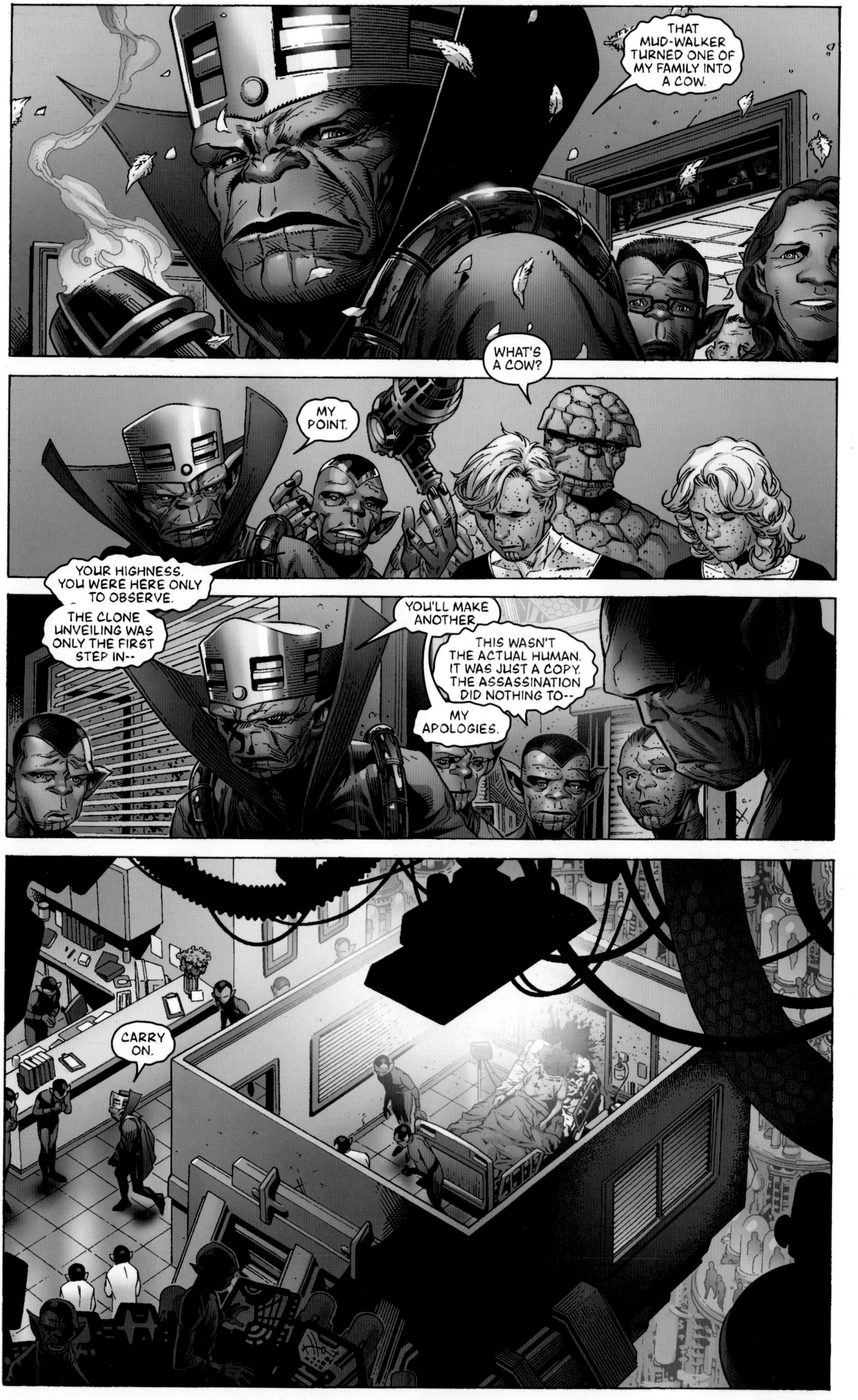
THAT MUD-WALKER TURNED ONE OF MY FAMILY INTO A COW.
WHAT'S A COW?
MY POINT.
YOUR HIGHNESS. YOU WERE HERE ONLY TO OBSERVE.
THE CLONE UNVEILING WAS ONLY THE FIRST STEP IN--
YOU'LL MAKE ANOTHER.
THIS WASN'T THE ACTUAL HUMAN. IT WAS JUST A COPY. THE ASSASSINATION DID NOTHING TO--
MY APOLOGIES.
CARRY ON.

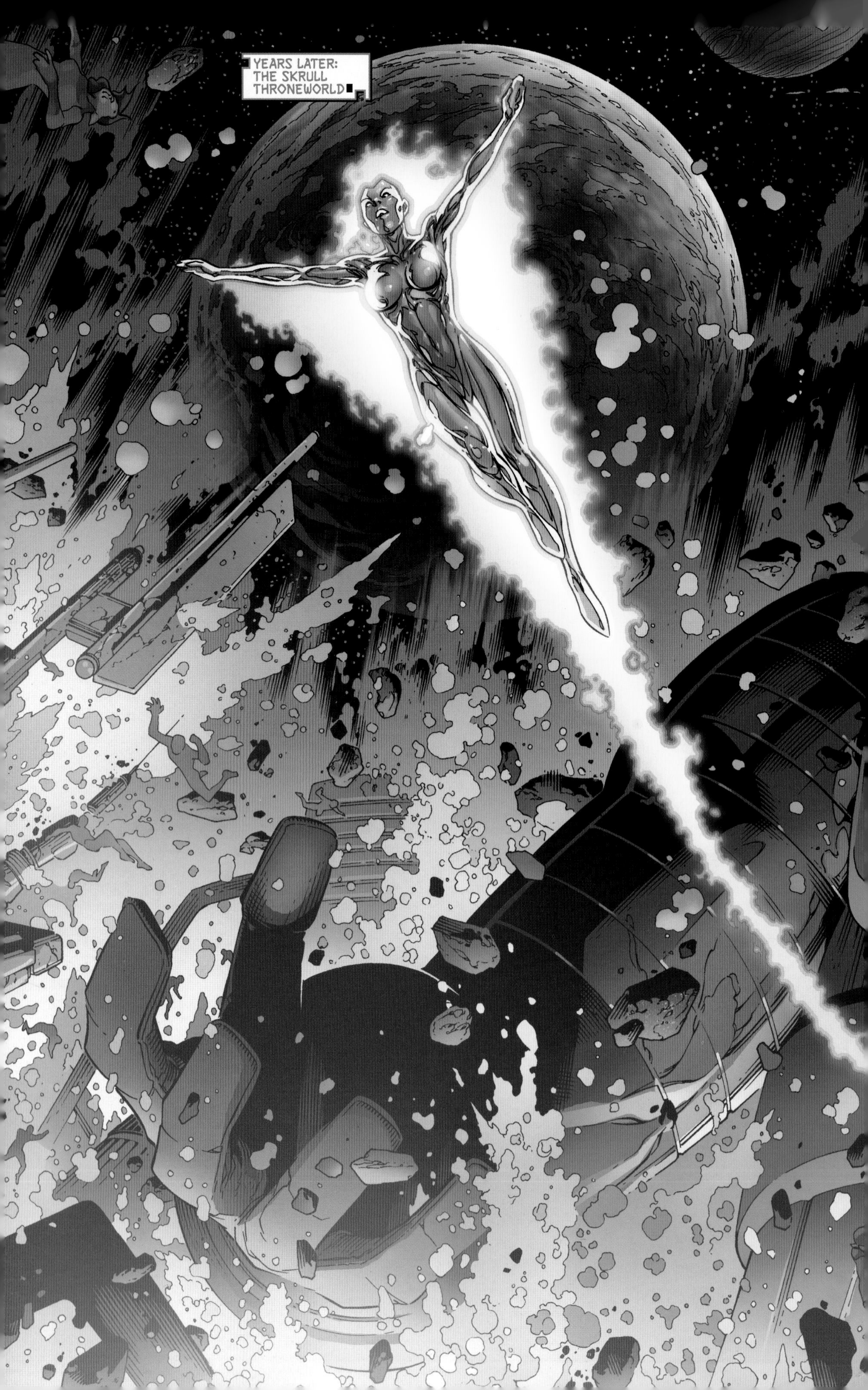
YEARS LATER:
THE SKRULL
THRONEWORLD

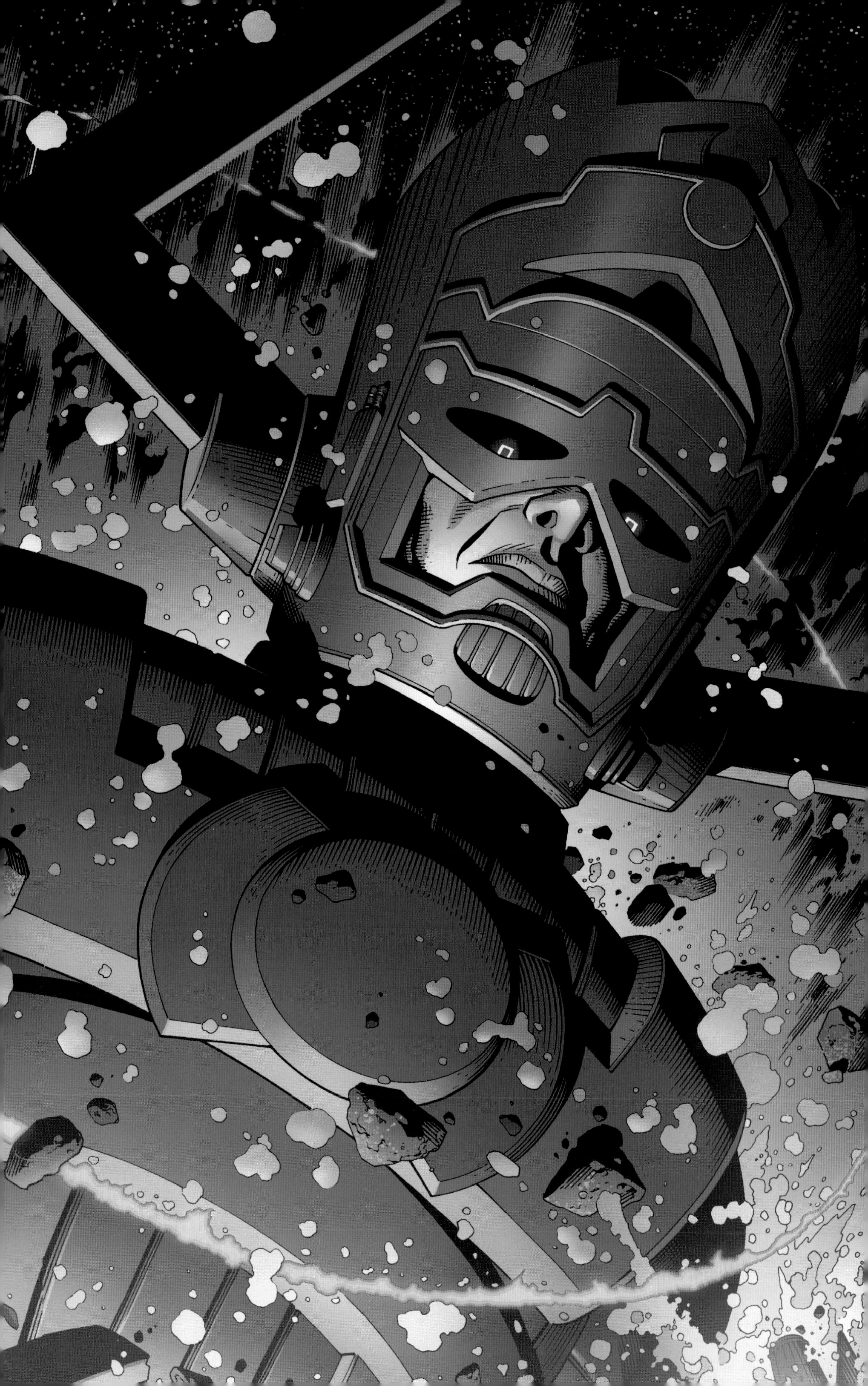

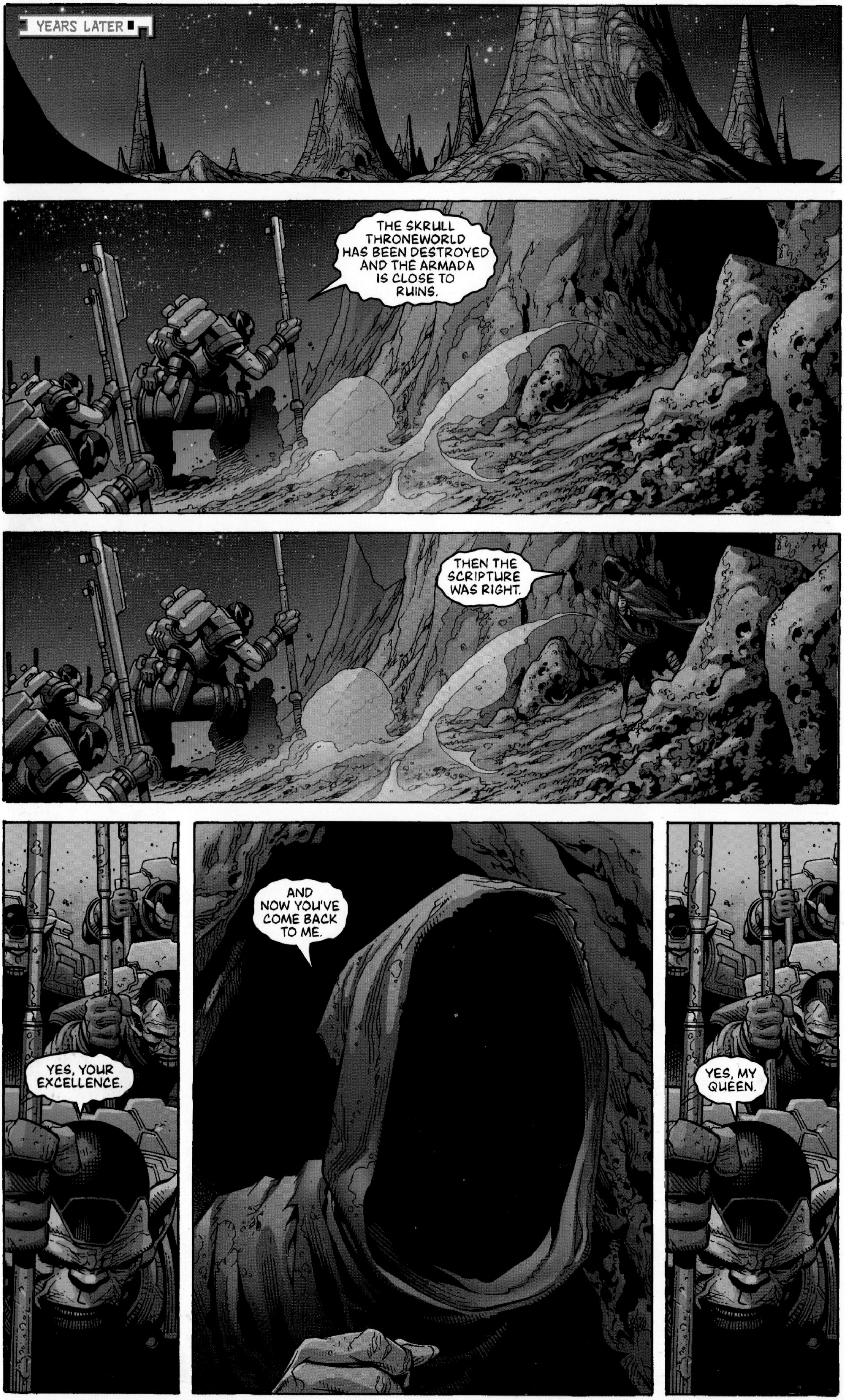
YEARS LATER
THE SKRULL THRONEWORLD HAS BEEN DESTROYED AND THE ARMADA IS CLOSE TO RUINS.
THEN THE SCRIPTURE WAS RIGHT.
YES, YOUR EXCELLENCE.
AND NOW YOU'VE COME BACK TO ME.
YES, MY QUEEN.

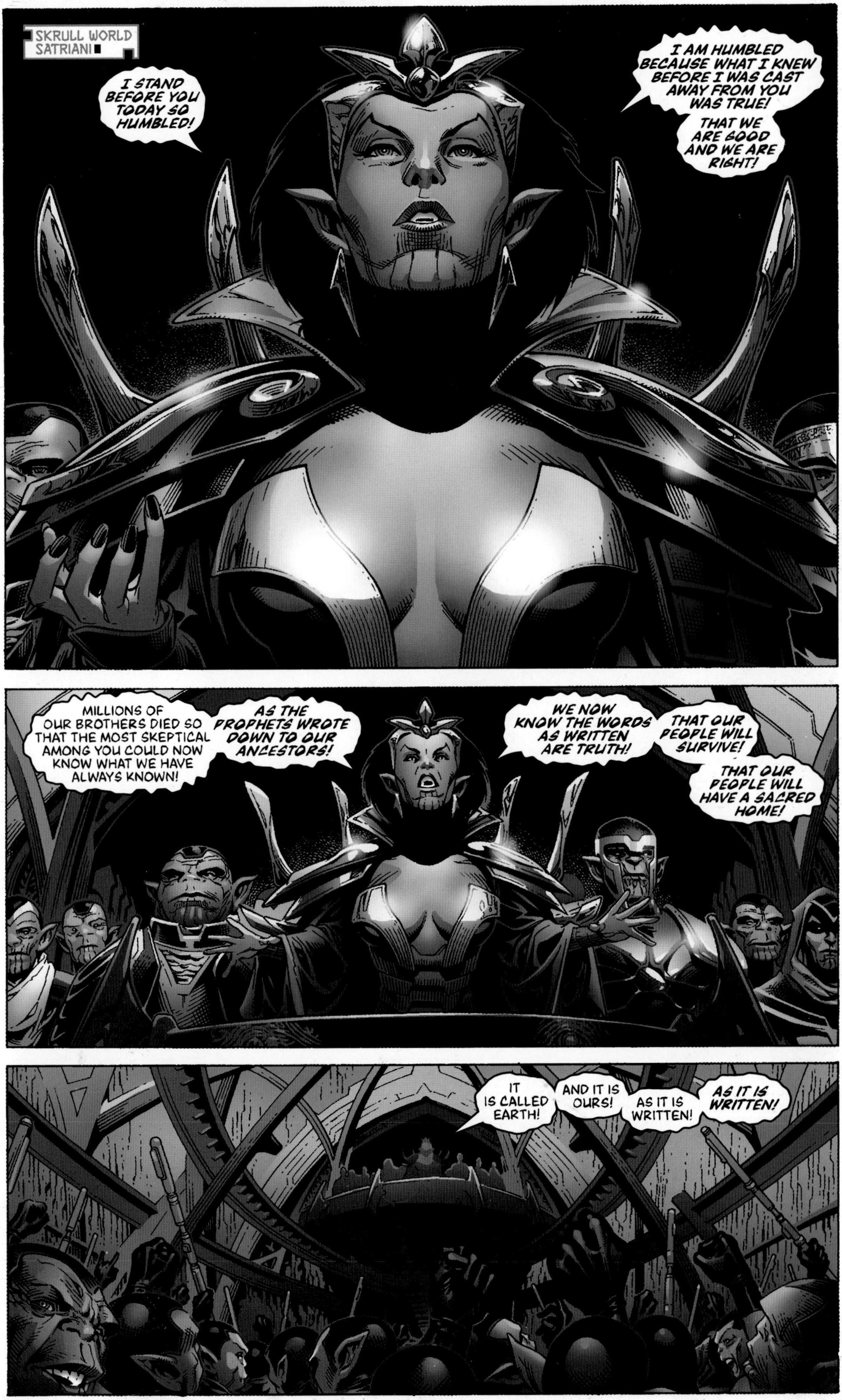
SKRULL WORLD SATRIANI
I STAND BEFORE YOU TODAY SO HUMBLED!
I AM HUMBLED BECAUSE WHAT I KNEW BEFORE I WAS CAST AWAY FROM YOU WAS TRUE!
THAT WE ARE GOOD AND WE ARE RIGHT!
MILLIONS OF OUR BROTHERS DIED SO THAT THE MOST SKEPTICAL AMONG YOU COULD NOW KNOW WHAT WE HAVE ALWAYS KNOWN!
AS THE PROPHETS WROTE DOWN TO OUR ANCESTORS!
WE NOW KNOW THE WORDS AS WRITTEN ARE TRUTH!
THAT OUR PEOPLE WILL SURVIVE!
THAT OUR PEOPLE WILL HAVE A SACRED HOME!
IT IS CALLED EARTH!
AND IT IS OURS!
AS IT IS WRITTEN!
AS IT IS WRITTEN!

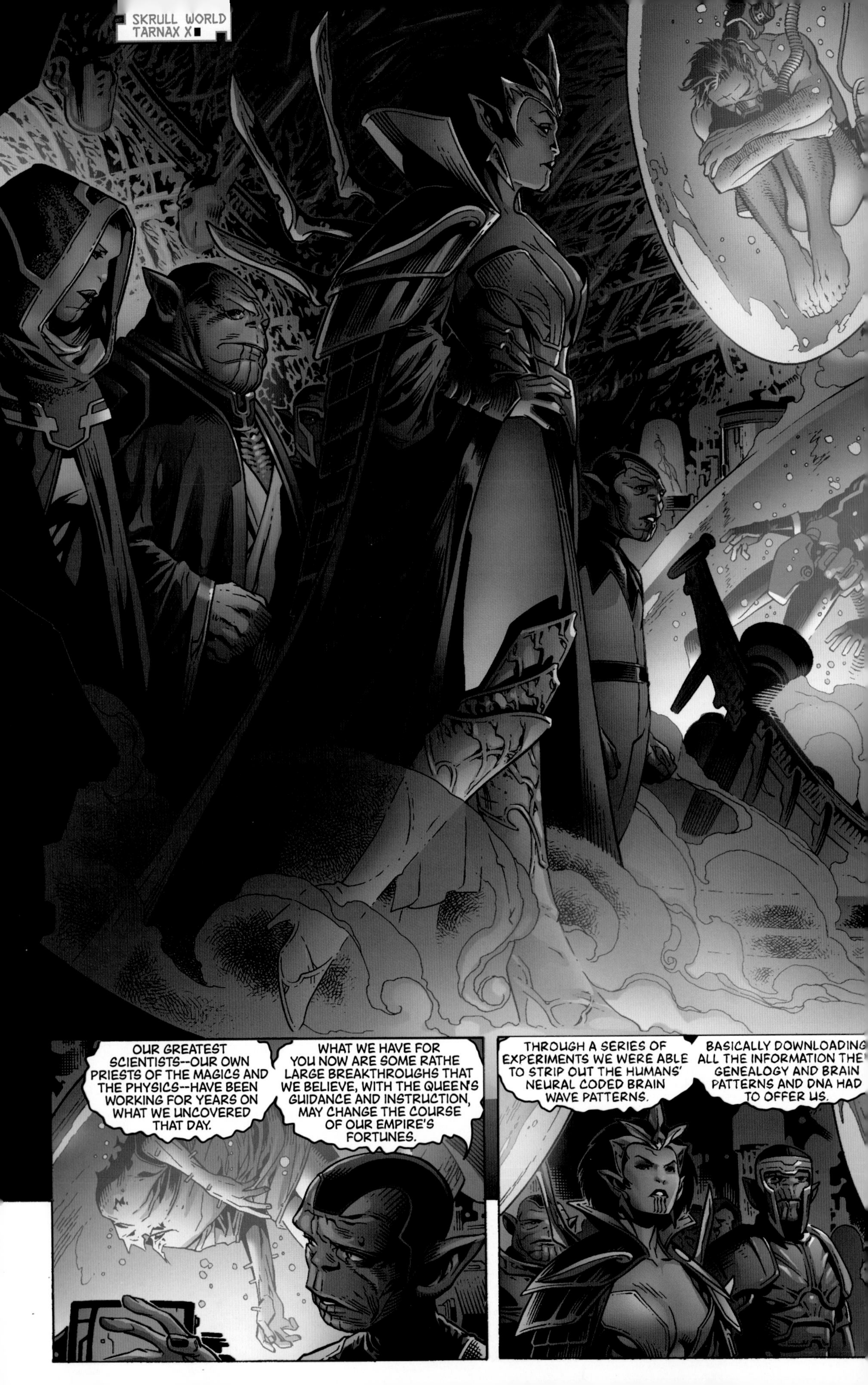

SKRULL WORLD TARNAX X
OUR GREATEST SCIENTISTS--OUR OWN PRIESTS OF THE MAGICS AND THE PHYSICS--HAVE BEEN WORKING FOR YEARS ON WHAT WE UNCOVERED THAT DAY.
WHAT WE HAVE FOR YOU NOW ARE SOME RATHE LARGE BREAKTHROUGHS THAT WE BELIEVE, WITH THE QUEEN'S GUIDANCE AND INSTRUCTION, MAY CHANGE THE COURSE OF OUR EMPIRE'S FORTUNES.
THROUGH A SERIES OF EXPERIMENTS WE WERE ABLE TO STRIP OUT THE HUMANS' NEURAL CODED BRAIN WAVE PATTERNS.
BASICALLY DOWNLOADING ALL THE INFORMATION THE GENEALOGY AND BRAIN PATTERNS AND DNA HAD TO OFFER US.

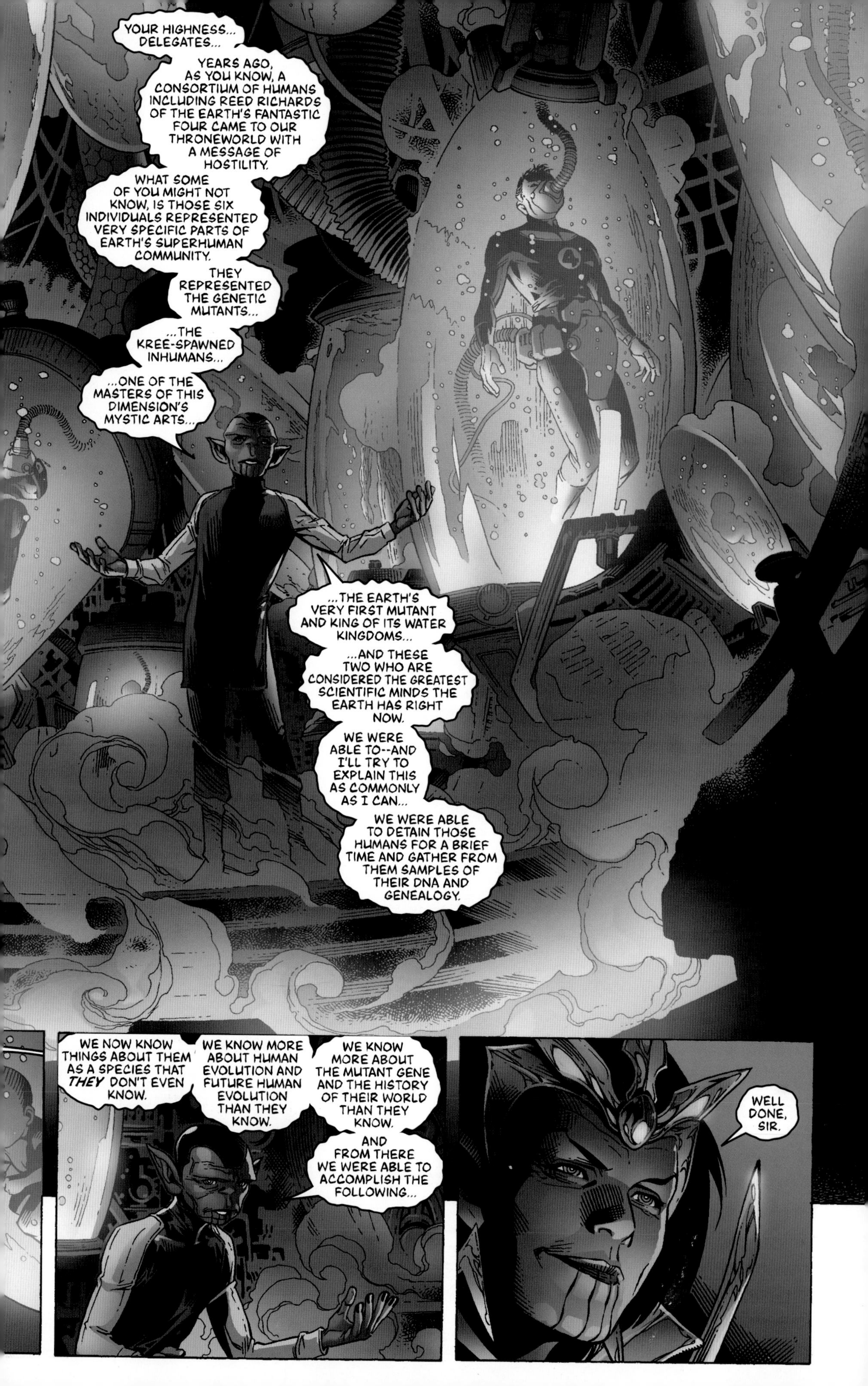
YOUR HIGHNESS... DELEGATES...
YEARS AGO, AS YOU KNOW, A CONSORTIUM OF HUMANS INCLUDING REED RICHARDS OF THE EARTH'S FANTASTIC FOUR CAME TO OUR THRONEWORLD WITH A MESSAGE OF HOSTILITY.
WHAT SOME OF YOU MIGHT NOT KNOW, IS THOSE SIX INDIVIDUALS REPRESENTED VERY SPECIFIC PARTS OF EARTH'S SUPERHUMAN COMMUNITY.
THEY REPRESENTED THE GENETIC MUTANTS...
...THE KREE-SPAWNED INHUMANS...
...ONE OF THE MASTERS OF THIS DIMENSION'S MYSTIC ARTS...
...THE EARTH'S VERY FIRST MUTANT AND KING OF ITS WATER KINGDOMS...
...AND THESE TWO WHO ARE CONSIDERED THE GREATEST SCIENTIFIC MINDS THE EARTH HAS RIGHT NOW.
WE WERE ABLE TO--AND I'LL TRY TO EXPLAIN THIS AS COMMONLY AS I CAN...
WE WERE ABLE TO DETAIN THOSE HUMANS FOR A BRIEF TIME AND GATHER FROM THEM SAMPLES OF THEIR DNA AND GENEALOGY.
WE NOW KNOW THINGS ABOUT THEM AS A SPECIES THAT *THEY* DON'T EVEN KNOW.
WE KNOW MORE ABOUT HUMAN EVOLUTION AND FUTURE HUMAN EVOLUTION THAN THEY KNOW.
WE KNOW MORE ABOUT THE MUTANT GENE AND THE HISTORY OF THEIR WORLD THAN THEY KNOW.
AND FROM THERE WE WERE ABLE TO ACCOMPLISH THE FOLLOWING...
WELL DONE, SIR.

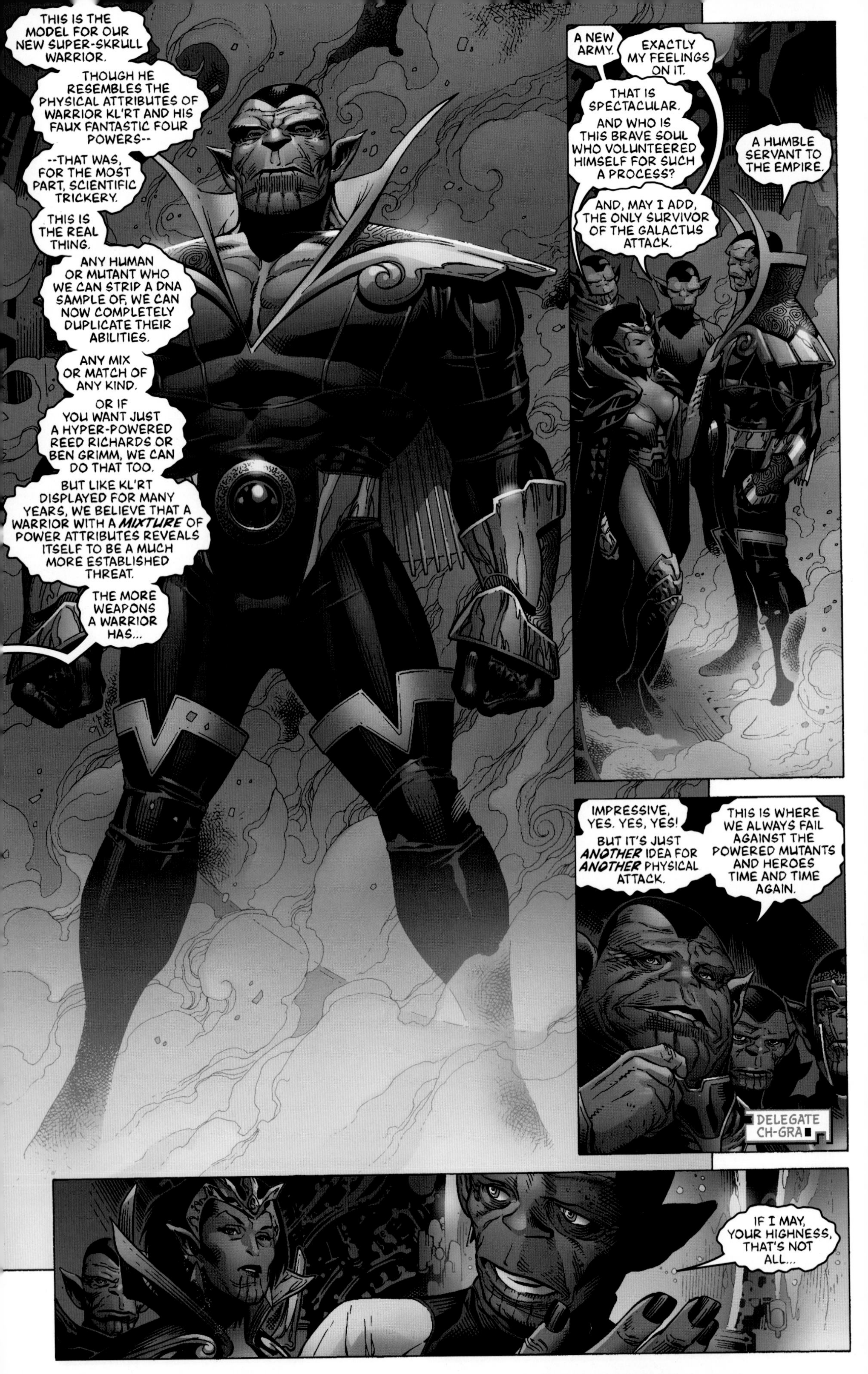
THIS IS THE MODEL FOR OUR NEW SUPER-SKRULL WARRIOR.
THOUGH HE RESEMBLES THE PHYSICAL ATTRIBUTES OF WARRIOR KL'RT AND HIS FAUX FANTASTIC FOUR POWERS--
--THAT WAS, FOR THE MOST PART, SCIENTIFIC TRICKERY.
THIS IS THE REAL THING.
ANY HUMAN OR MUTANT WHO WE CAN STRIP A DNA SAMPLE OF, WE CAN NOW COMPLETELY DUPLICATE THEIR ABILITIES.
ANY MIX OR MATCH OF ANY KIND.
OR IF YOU WANT JUST A HYPER-POWERED REED RICHARDS OR BEN GRIMM, WE CAN DO THAT TOO.
BUT LIKE KL'RT DISPLAYED FOR MANY YEARS, WE BELIEVE THAT A WARRIOR WITH A *MIXTURE* OF POWER ATTRIBUTES REVEALS ITSELF TO BE A MUCH MORE ESTABLISHED THREAT.
THE MORE WEAPONS A WARRIOR HAS...
A NEW ARMY.
EXACTLY MY FEELINGS ON IT.
THAT IS SPECTACULAR.
AND WHO IS THIS BRAVE SOUL WHO VOLUNTEERED HIMSELF FOR SUCH A PROCESS?
A HUMBLE SERVANT TO THE EMPIRE.
AND, MAY I ADD, THE ONLY SURVIVOR OF THE GALACTUS ATTACK.
IMPRESSIVE, YES. YES, YES! BUT IT'S JUST ***ANOTHER*** IDEA FOR ***ANOTHER*** PHYSICAL ATTACK.
THIS IS WHERE WE ALWAYS FAIL AGAINST THE POWERED MUTANTS AND HEROES TIME AND TIME AGAIN.
DELEGATE CH-GRA
IF I MAY, YOUR HIGHNESS, THAT'S NOT ALL...

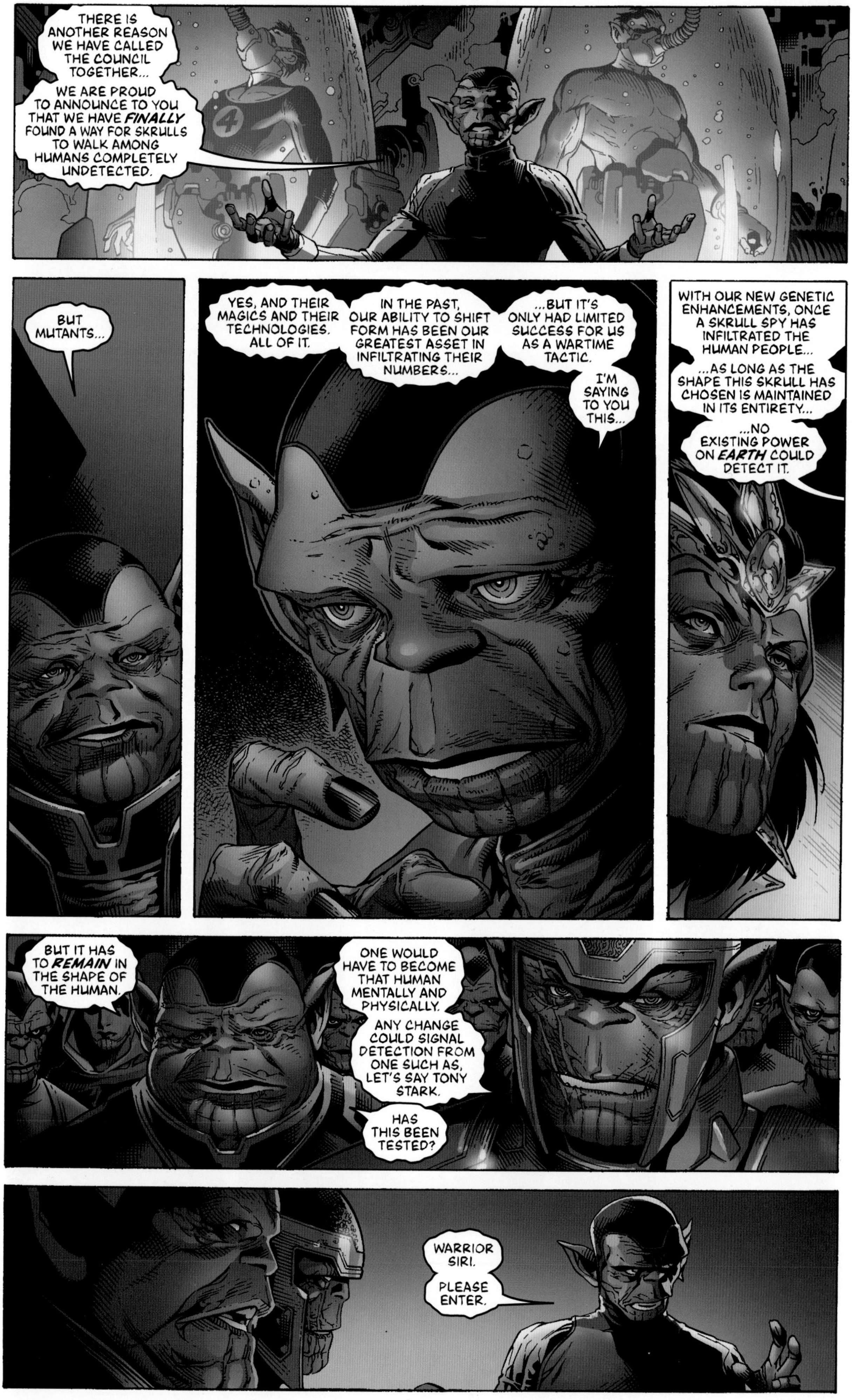
THERE IS ANOTHER REASON WE HAVE CALLED THE COUNCIL TOGETHER...
WE ARE PROUD TO ANNOUNCE TO YOU THAT WE HAVE *FINALLY* FOUND A WAY FOR SKRULLS TO WALK AMONG HUMANS COMPLETELY UNDETECTED.
BUT MUTANTS...
YES, AND THEIR MAGICS AND THEIR TECHNOLOGIES. ALL OF IT.
IN THE PAST, OUR ABILITY TO SHIFT FORM HAS BEEN OUR GREATEST ASSET IN INFILTRATING THEIR NUMBERS...
...BUT IT'S ONLY HAD LIMITED SUCCESS FOR US AS A WARTIME TACTIC.
I'M SAYING TO YOU THIS...
WITH OUR NEW GENETIC ENHANCEMENTS, ONCE A SKRULL SPY HAS INFILTRATED THE HUMAN PEOPLE...
...AS LONG AS THE SHAPE THIS SKRULL HAS CHOSEN IS MAINTAINED IN ITS ENTIRETY...
...NO EXISTING POWER ON *EARTH* COULD DETECT IT.
BUT IT HAS TO *REMAIN* IN THE SHAPE OF THE HUMAN.
ONE WOULD HAVE TO BECOME THAT HUMAN MENTALLY AND PHYSICALLY.
ANY CHANGE COULD SIGNAL DETECTION FROM ONE SUCH AS, LET'S SAY TONY STARK.
HAS THIS BEEN TESTED?
WARRIOR SIRI.
PLEASE ENTER.

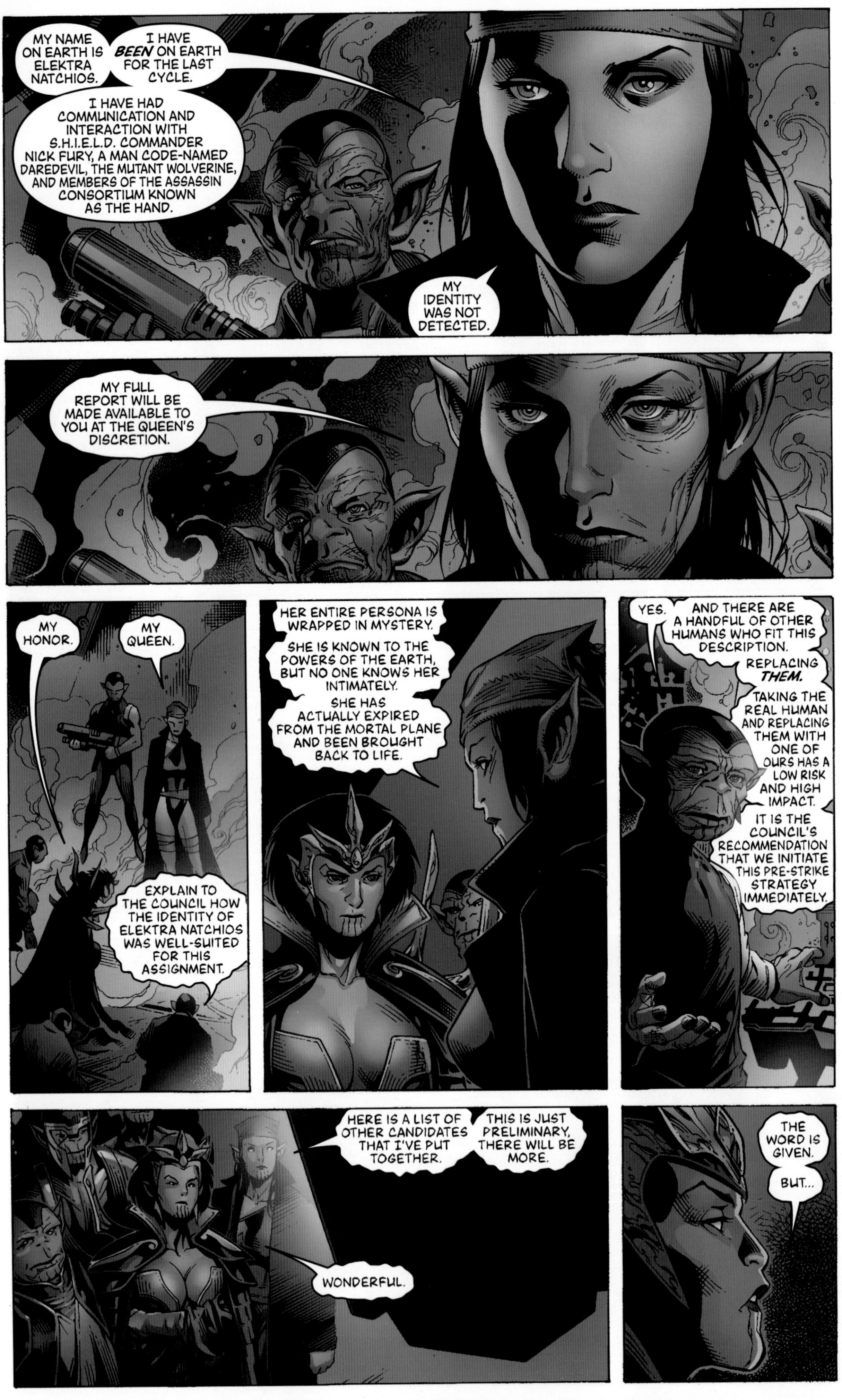
MY NAME ON EARTH IS ELEKTRA NATCHIOS.
I HAVE *BEEN* ON EARTH FOR THE LAST CYCLE.
I HAVE HAD COMMUNICATION AND INTERACTION WITH S.H.I.E.L.D. COMMANDER NICK FURY, A MAN CODE-NAMED DAREDEVIL, THE MUTANT WOLVERINE, AND MEMBERS OF THE ASSASSIN CONSORTIUM KNOWN AS THE HAND.
MY IDENTITY WAS NOT DETECTED.
MY FULL REPORT WILL BE MADE AVAILABLE TO YOU AT THE QUEEN'S DISCRETION.
MY HONOR.
MY QUEEN.
EXPLAIN TO THE COUNCIL HOW THE IDENTITY OF ELEKTRA NATCHIOS WAS WELL-SUITED FOR THIS ASSIGNMENT.
HER ENTIRE PERSONA IS WRAPPED IN MYSTERY.
SHE IS KNOWN TO THE POWERS OF THE EARTH, BUT NO ONE KNOWS HER INTIMATELY.
SHE HAS ACTUALLY EXPIRED FROM THE MORTAL PLANE AND BEEN BROUGHT BACK TO LIFE.
YES.
AND THERE ARE A HANDFUL OF OTHER HUMANS WHO FIT THIS DESCRIPTION.
REPLACING *THEM.*
TAKING THE REAL HUMAN AND REPLACING THEM WITH ONE OF OURS HAS A LOW RISK AND HIGH IMPACT.
IT IS THE COUNCIL'S RECOMMENDATION THAT WE INITIATE THIS PRE-STRIKE STRATEGY IMMEDIATELY.
HERE IS A LIST OF OTHER CANDIDATES THAT I'VE PUT TOGETHER.
THIS IS JUST PRELIMINARY, THERE WILL BE MORE.
WONDERFUL.
THE WORD IS GIVEN.
BUT...

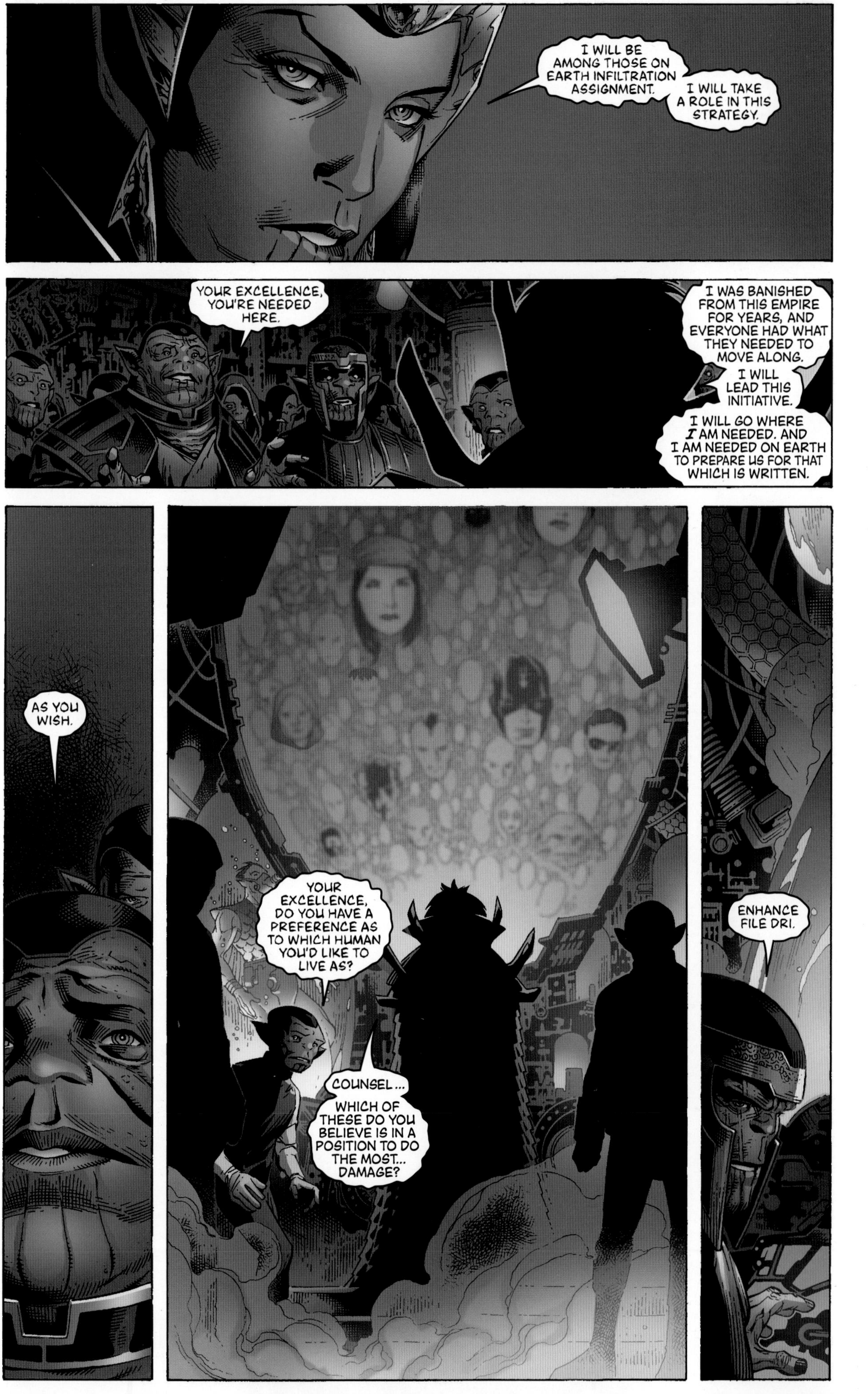

I WILL BE AMONG THOSE ON EARTH INFILTRATION ASSIGNMENT.
I WILL TAKE A ROLE IN THIS STRATEGY.
YOUR EXCELLENCE, YOU'RE NEEDED HERE.
I WAS BANISHED FROM THIS EMPIRE FOR YEARS, AND EVERYONE HAD WHAT THEY NEEDED TO MOVE ALONG.
I WILL LEAD THIS INITIATIVE.
I WILL GO WHERE I AM NEEDED. AND I AM NEEDED ON EARTH TO PREPARE US FOR THAT WHICH IS WRITTEN.
AS YOU WISH.
YOUR EXCELLENCE, DO YOU HAVE A PREFERENCE AS TO WHICH HUMAN YOU'D LIKE TO LIVE AS?
COUNSEL...
WHICH OF THESE DO YOU BELIEVE IS IN A POSITION TO DO THE MOST... DAMAGE?
ENHANCE FILE DRI.

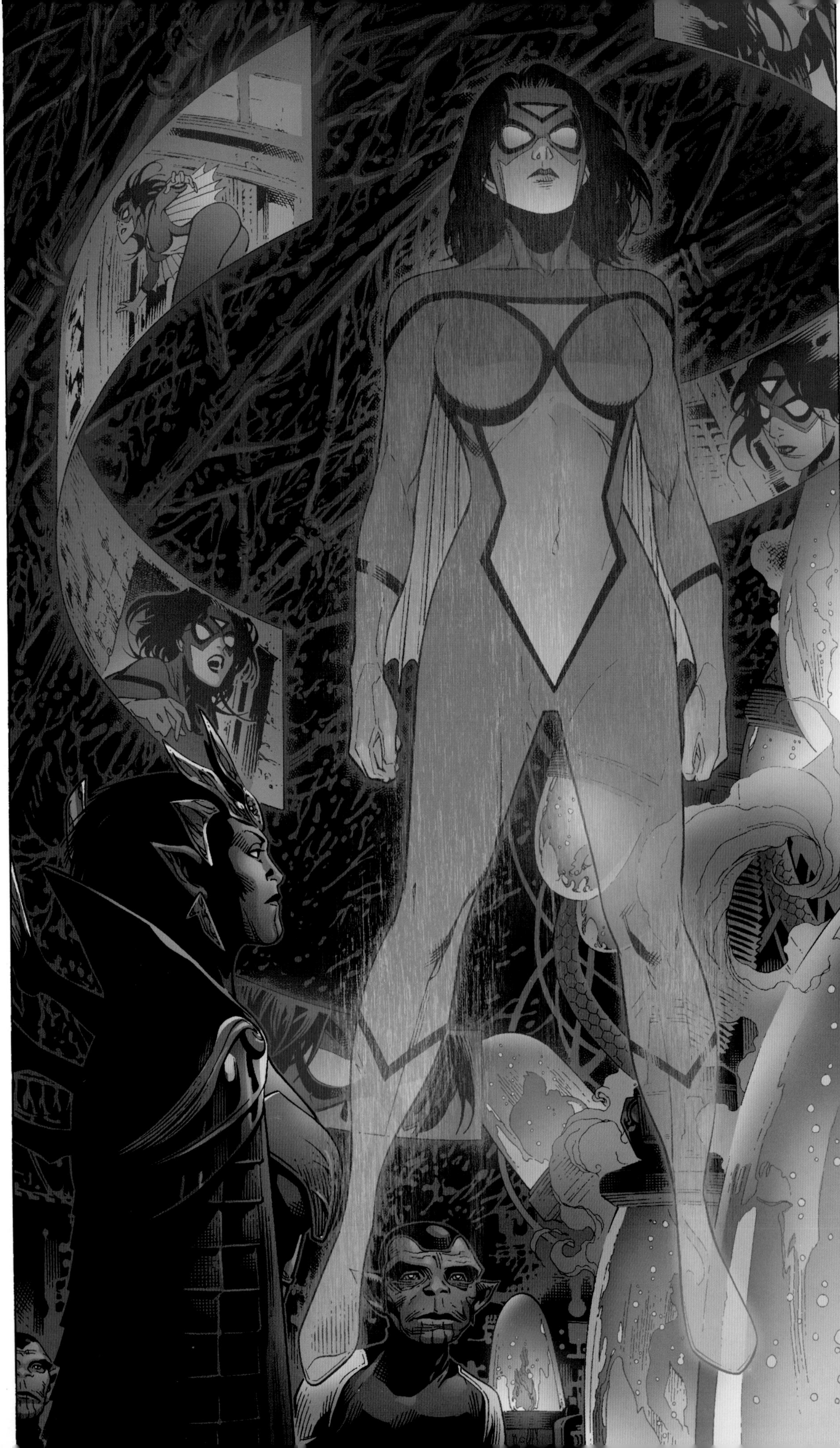

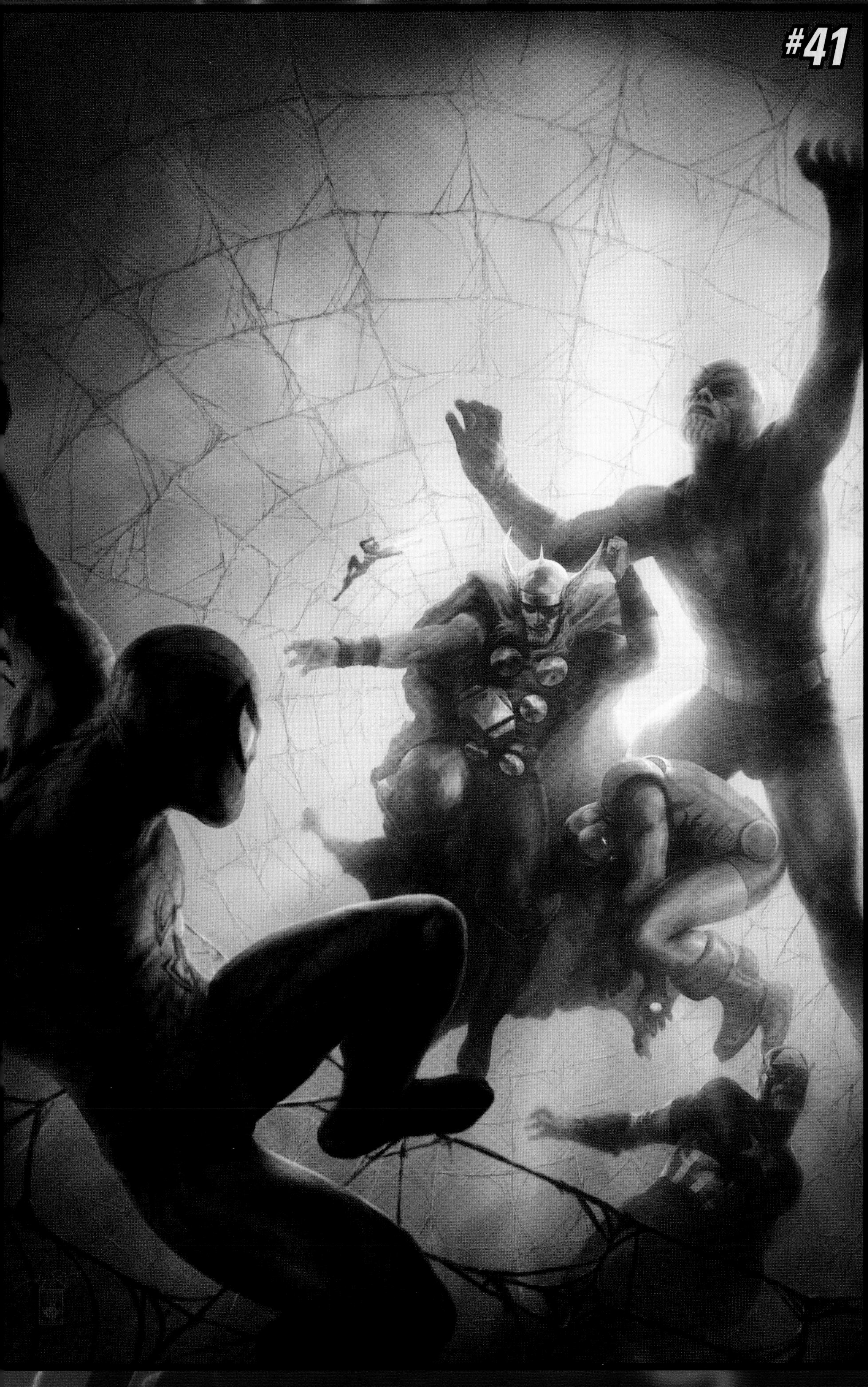
#41

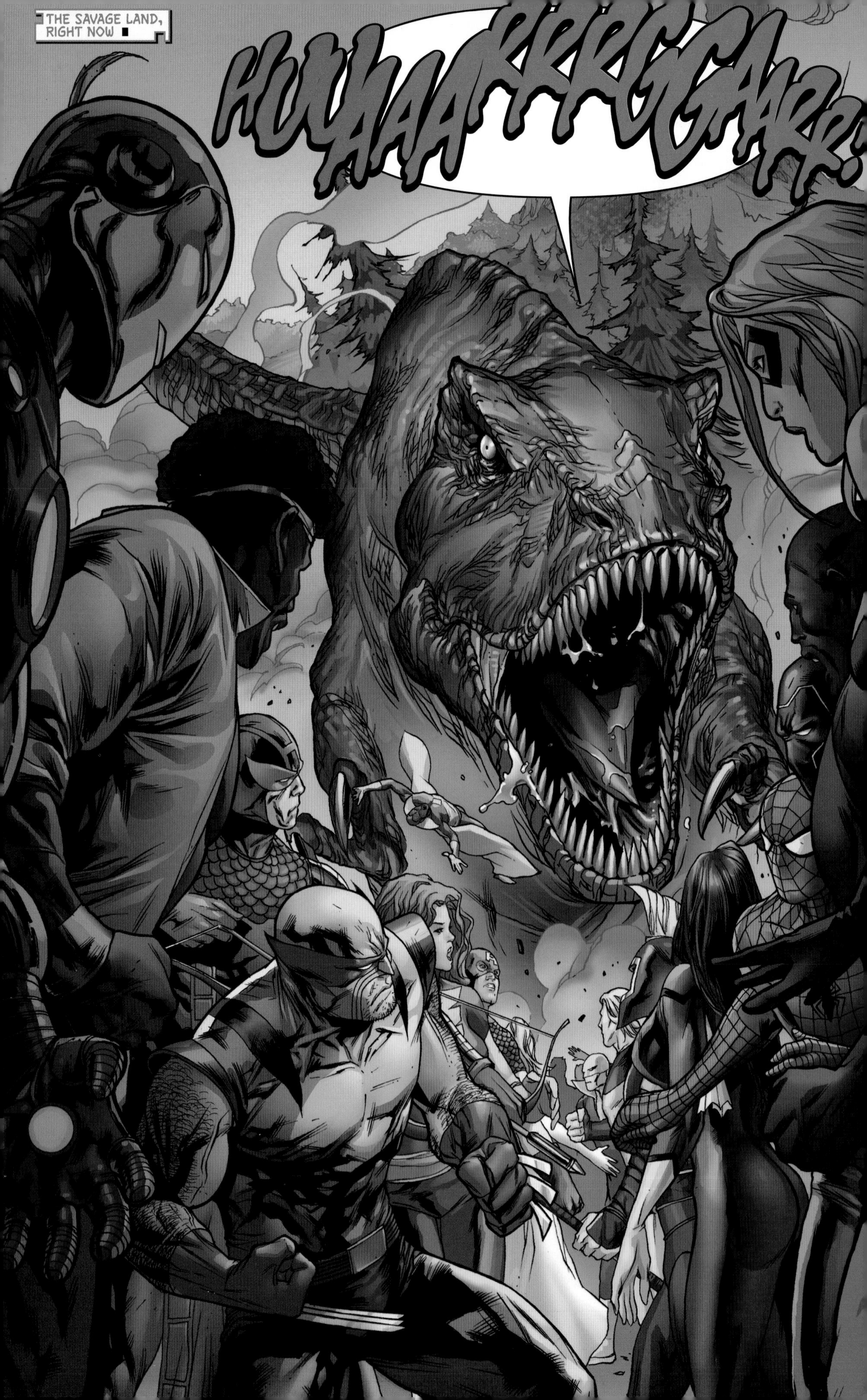
THE SAVAGE LAND, RIGHT NOW
HUUAAARRRGGARR!

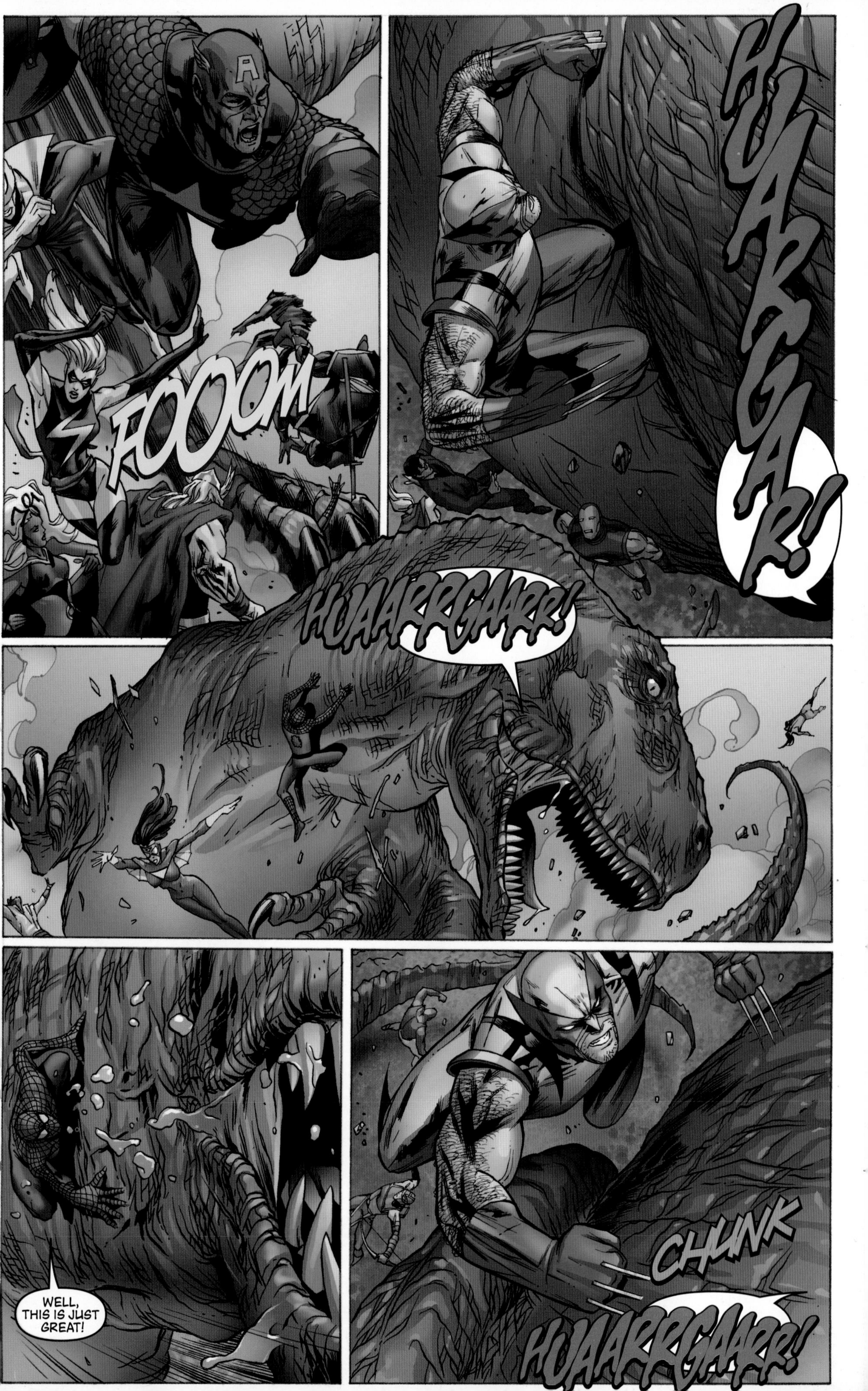
FOOOM
HUAARGAAR!
HUAARRGAARR!
WELL, THIS IS JUST GREAT!
CHUNK
HUAARRGAARR!

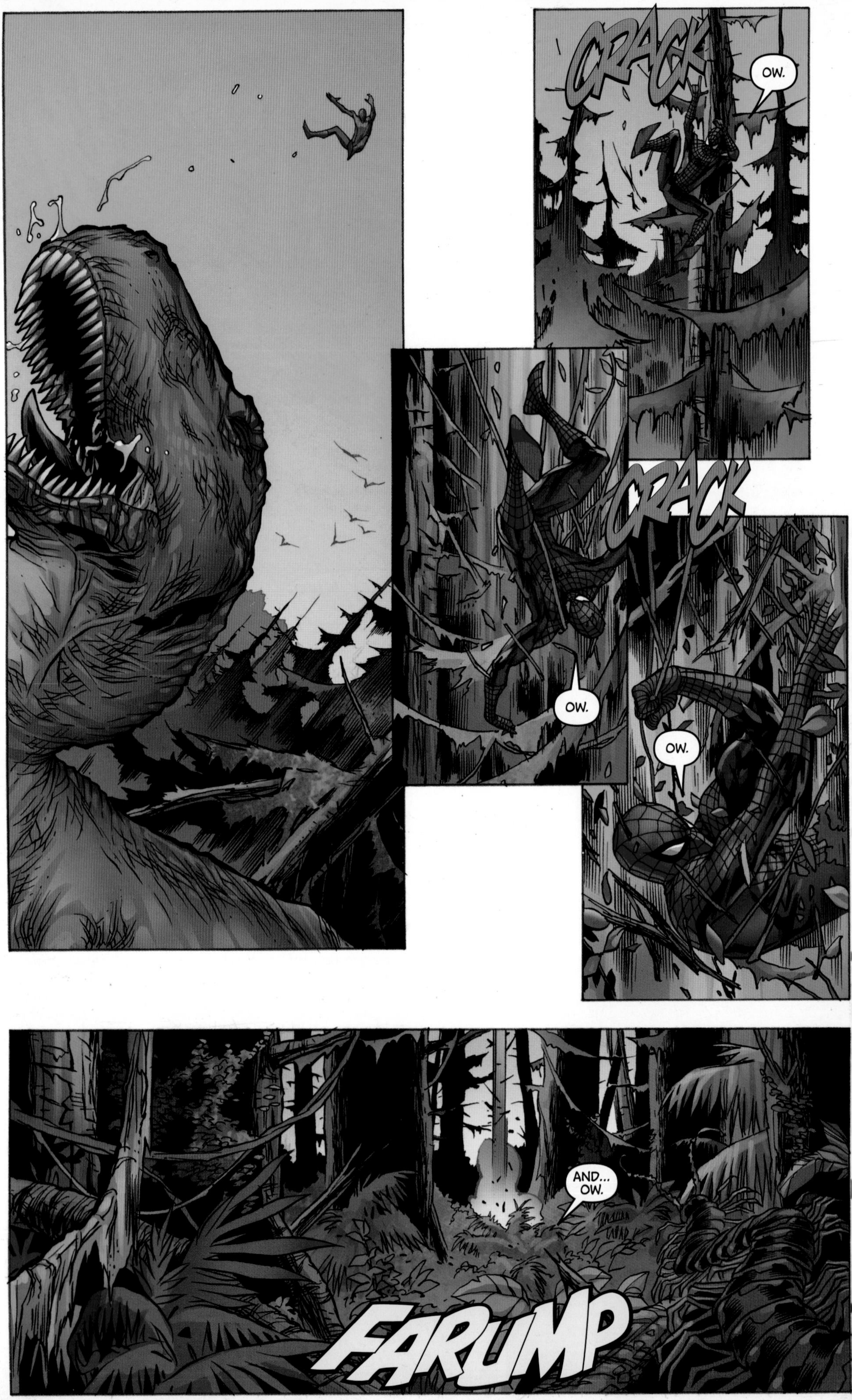
CRACK
OW.
OW.
CRACK
OW.
AND... OW.
FARUMP

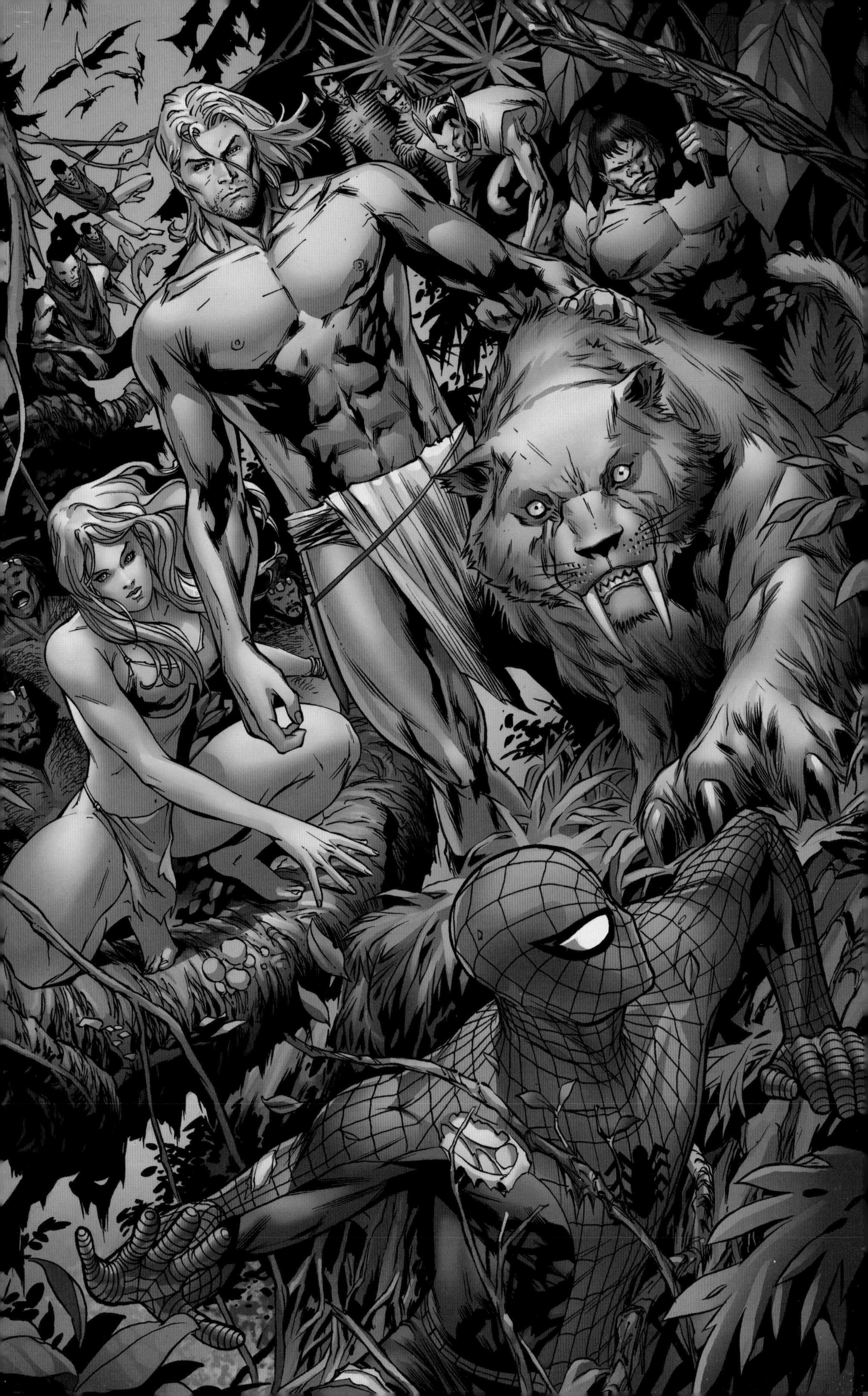

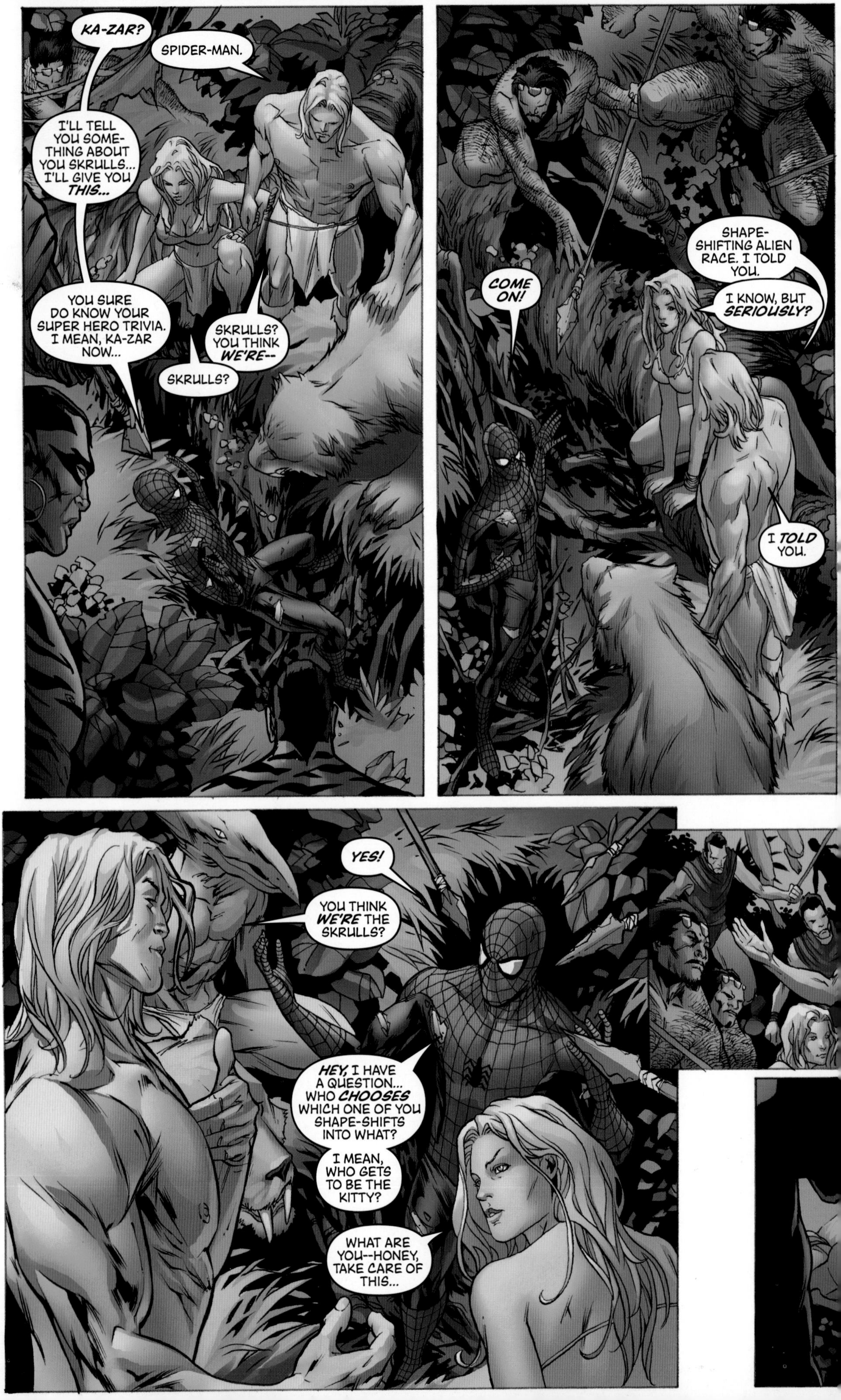
KA-ZAR?
SPIDER-MAN.
I'LL TELL YOU SOMETHING ABOUT YOU SKRULLS... I'LL GIVE YOU THIS...
YOU SURE DO KNOW YOUR SUPER HERO TRIVIA. I MEAN, KA-ZAR NOW...
SKRULLS?
SKRULLS? YOU THINK WE'RE--
COME ON!
SHAPE-SHIFTING ALIEN RACE. I TOLD YOU.
I KNOW, BUT SERIOUSLY?
I TOLD YOU.
YES!
YOU THINK WE'RE THE SKRULLS?
HEY, I HAVE A QUESTION... WHO CHOOSES WHICH ONE OF YOU SHAPE-SHIFTS INTO WHAT?
I MEAN, WHO GETS TO BE THE KITTY?
WHAT ARE YOU--HONEY, TAKE CARE OF THIS...

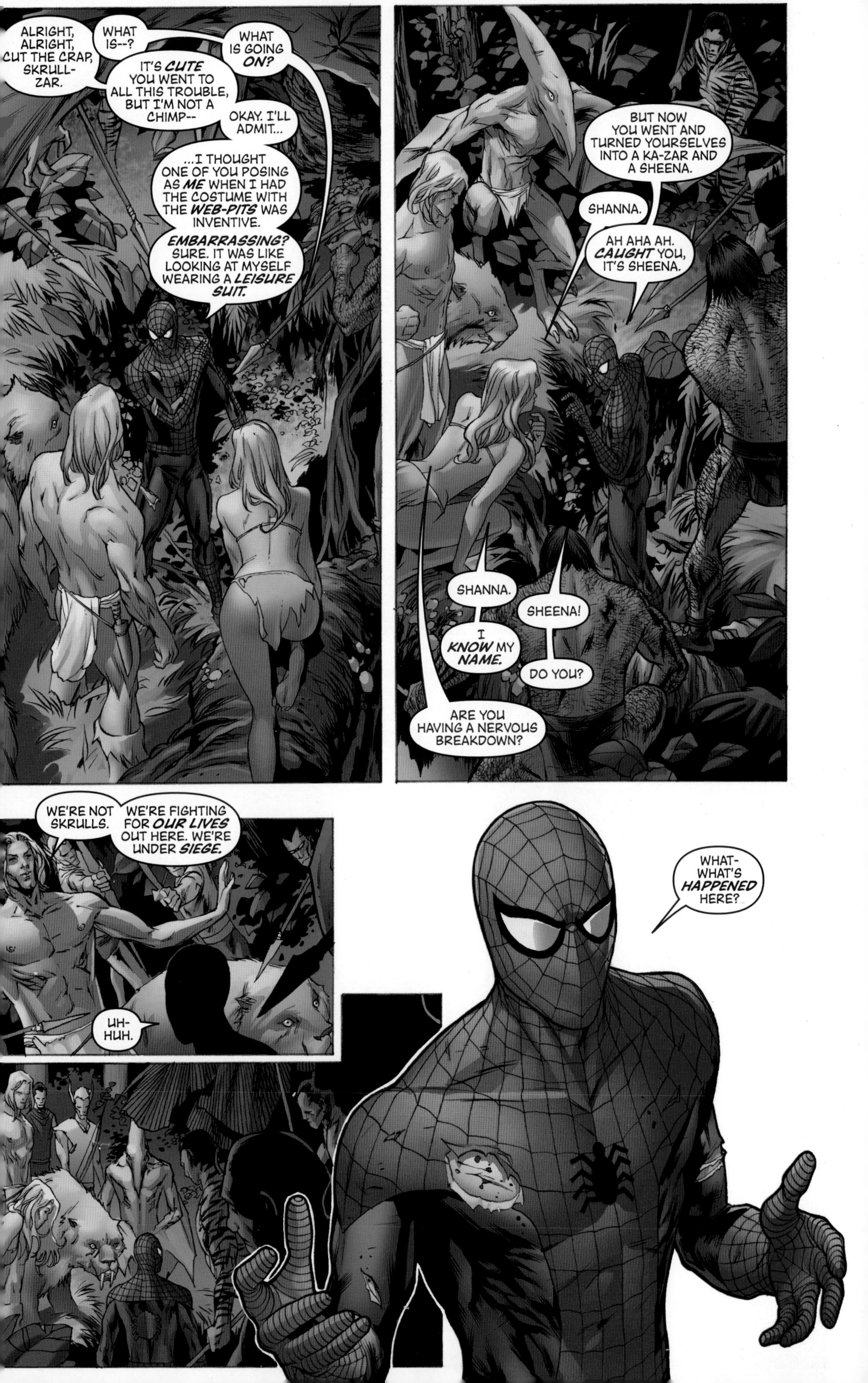
ALRIGHT, ALRIGHT, CUT THE CRAP, SKRULL-ZAR.
WHAT IS--?
WHAT IS GOING ON?
IT'S CUTE YOU WENT TO ALL THIS TROUBLE, BUT I'M NOT A CHIMP--
OKAY. I'LL ADMIT...
...I THOUGHT ONE OF YOU POSING AS ME WHEN I HAD THE COSTUME WITH THE WEB-PITS WAS INVENTIVE.
EMBARRASSING? SURE. IT WAS LIKE LOOKING AT MYSELF WEARING A LEISURE SUIT.
BUT NOW YOU WENT AND TURNED YOURSELVES INTO A KA-ZAR AND A SHEENA.
SHANNA.
AH AHA AH. CAUGHT YOU, IT'S SHEENA.
SHANNA.
SHEENA!
I KNOW MY NAME.
DO YOU?
ARE YOU HAVING A NERVOUS BREAKDOWN?
WE'RE NOT SKRULLS.
WE'RE FIGHTING FOR OUR LIVES OUT HERE. WE'RE UNDER SIEGE.
UH-HUH.
WHAT-WHAT'S HAPPENED HERE?

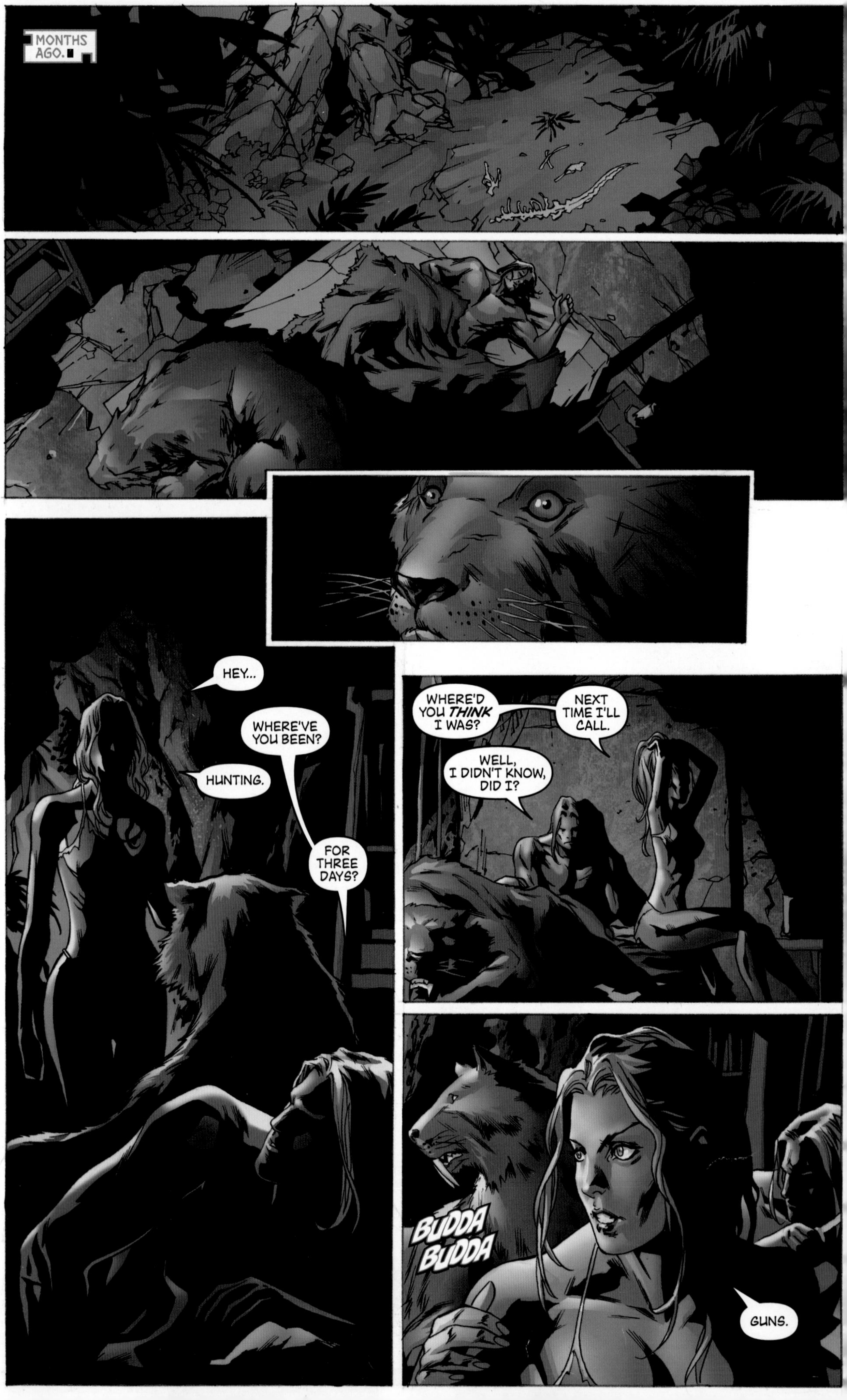
MONTHS AGO.
HEY...
WHERE'VE YOU BEEN?
HUNTING.
FOR THREE DAYS?
WHERE'D YOU *THINK* I WAS?
NEXT TIME I'LL CALL.
WELL, I DIDN'T KNOW, DID I?
BUDDA BUDDA
GUNS.

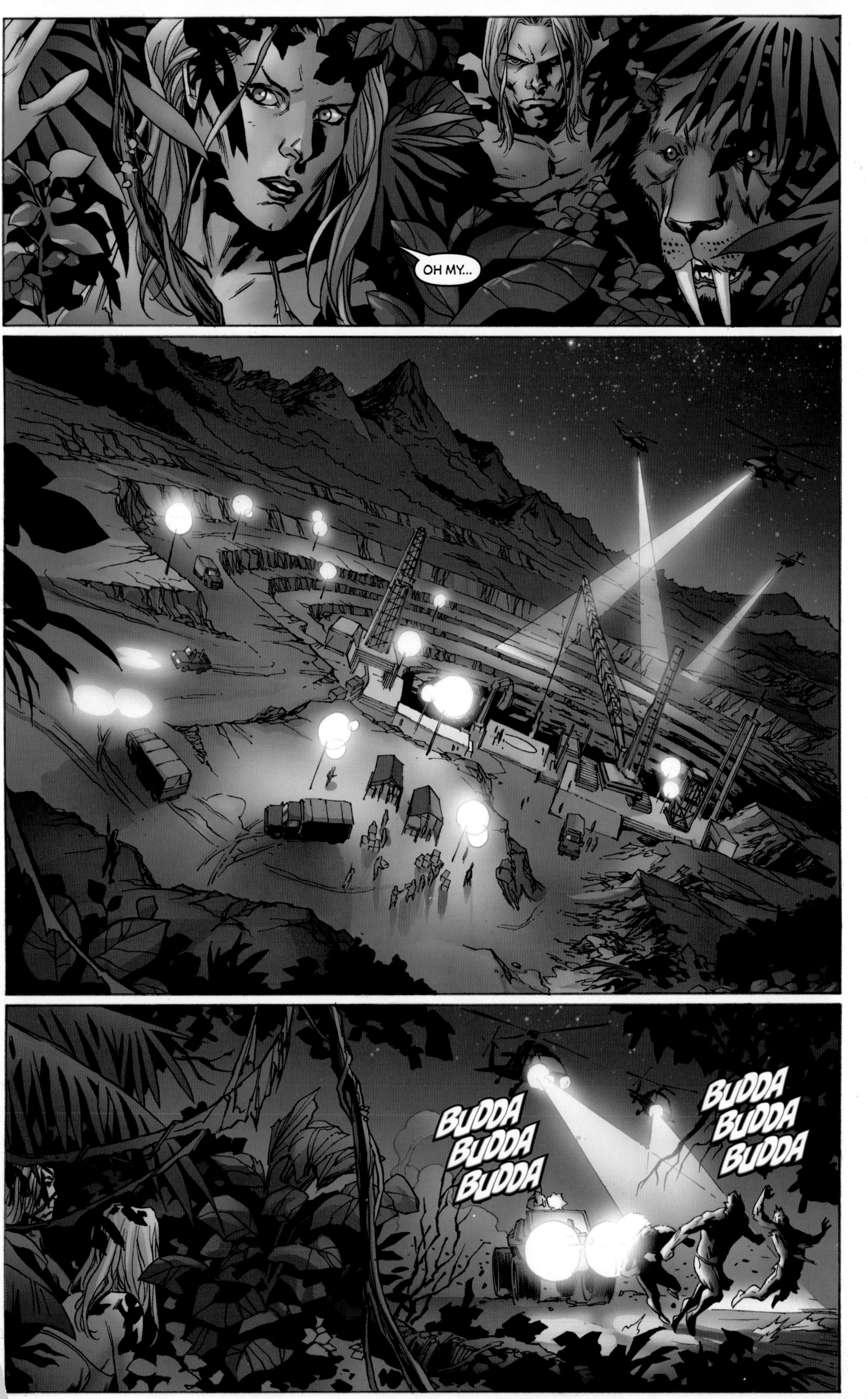
OH MY...
BUDDA BUDDA BUDDA
BUDDA BUDDA BUDDA

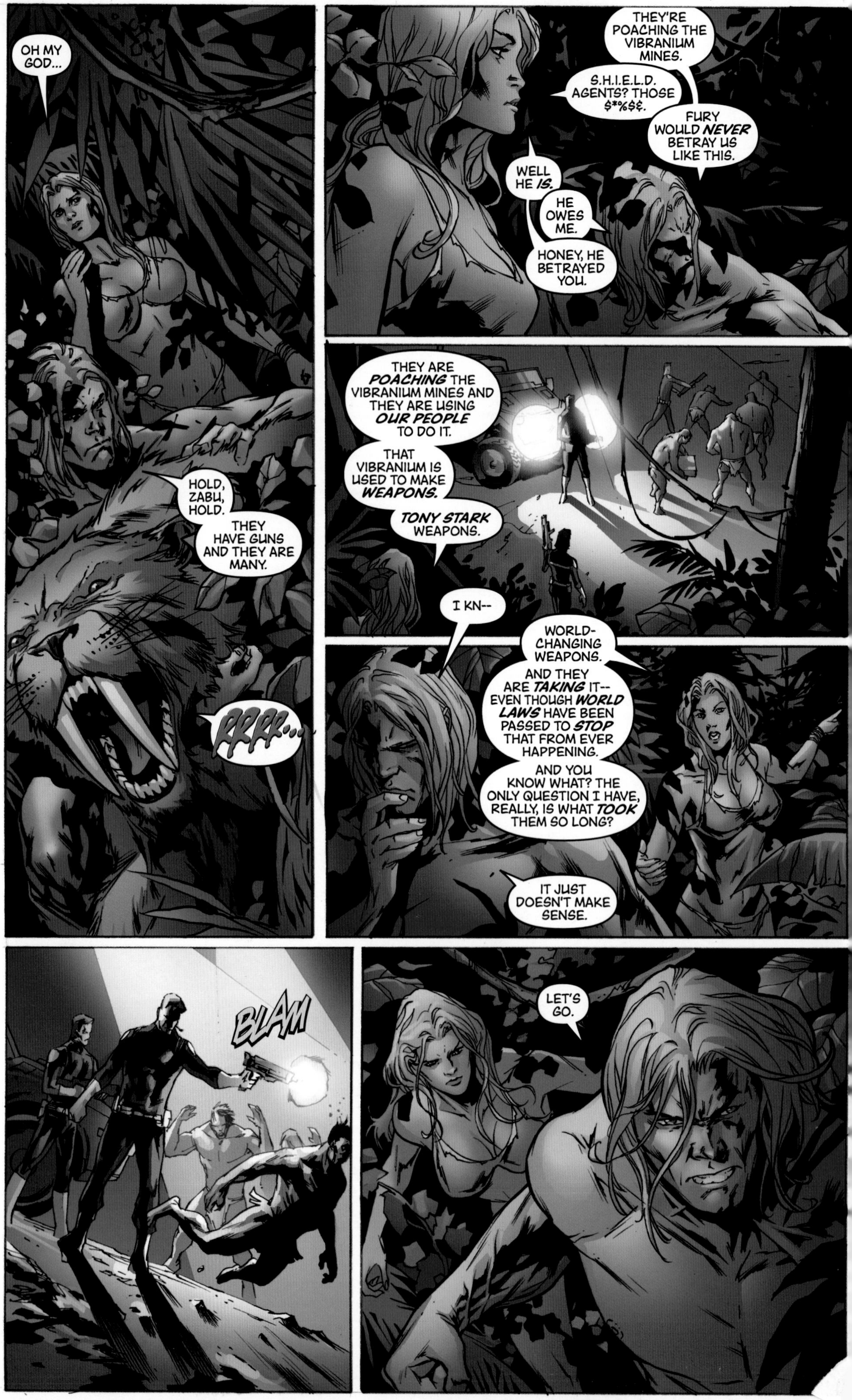
OH MY GOD...
HOLD, ZABU, HOLD.
THEY HAVE GUNS AND THEY ARE MANY.
RRRR...
THEY'RE POACHING THE VIBRANIUM MINES.
S.H.I.E.L.D. AGENTS? THOSE $*%$$.
FURY WOULD NEVER BETRAY US LIKE THIS.
WELL HE IS.
HE OWES ME.
HONEY, HE BETRAYED YOU.
THEY ARE POACHING THE VIBRANIUM MINES AND THEY ARE USING OUR PEOPLE TO DO IT.
THAT VIBRANIUM IS USED TO MAKE WEAPONS.
TONY STARK WEAPONS.
I KN--
WORLD-CHANGING WEAPONS.
AND THEY ARE TAKING IT-- EVEN THOUGH WORLD LAWS HAVE BEEN PASSED TO STOP THAT FROM EVER HAPPENING.
AND YOU KNOW WHAT? THE ONLY QUESTION I HAVE, REALLY, IS WHAT TOOK THEM SO LONG?
IT JUST DOESN'T MAKE SENSE.
BLAM
LET'S GO.

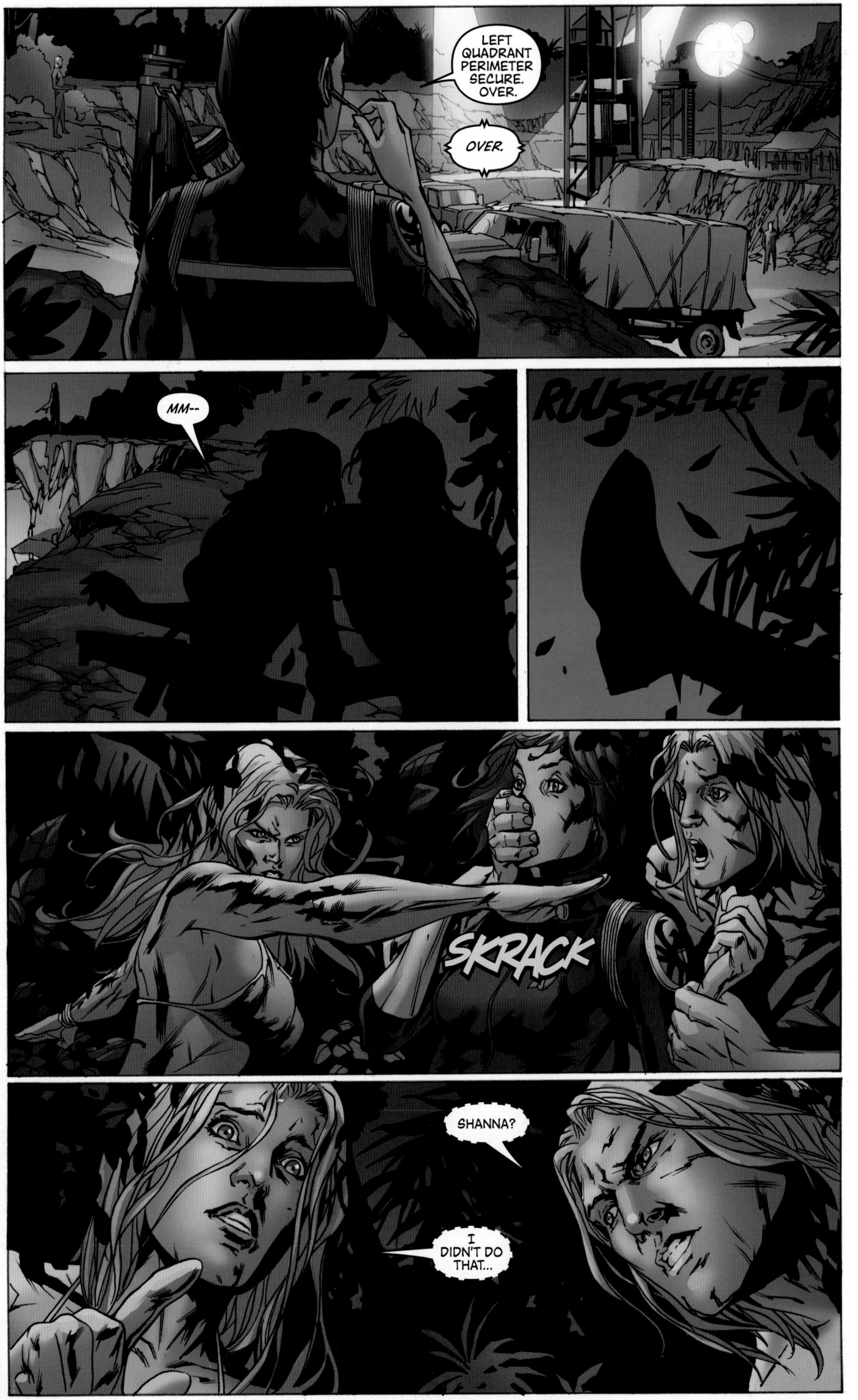
LEFT QUADRANT PERIMETER SECURE. OVER.
OVER.
MM--
RUUSSSLLLEE
SKRACK
SHANNA?
I DIDN'T DO THAT...

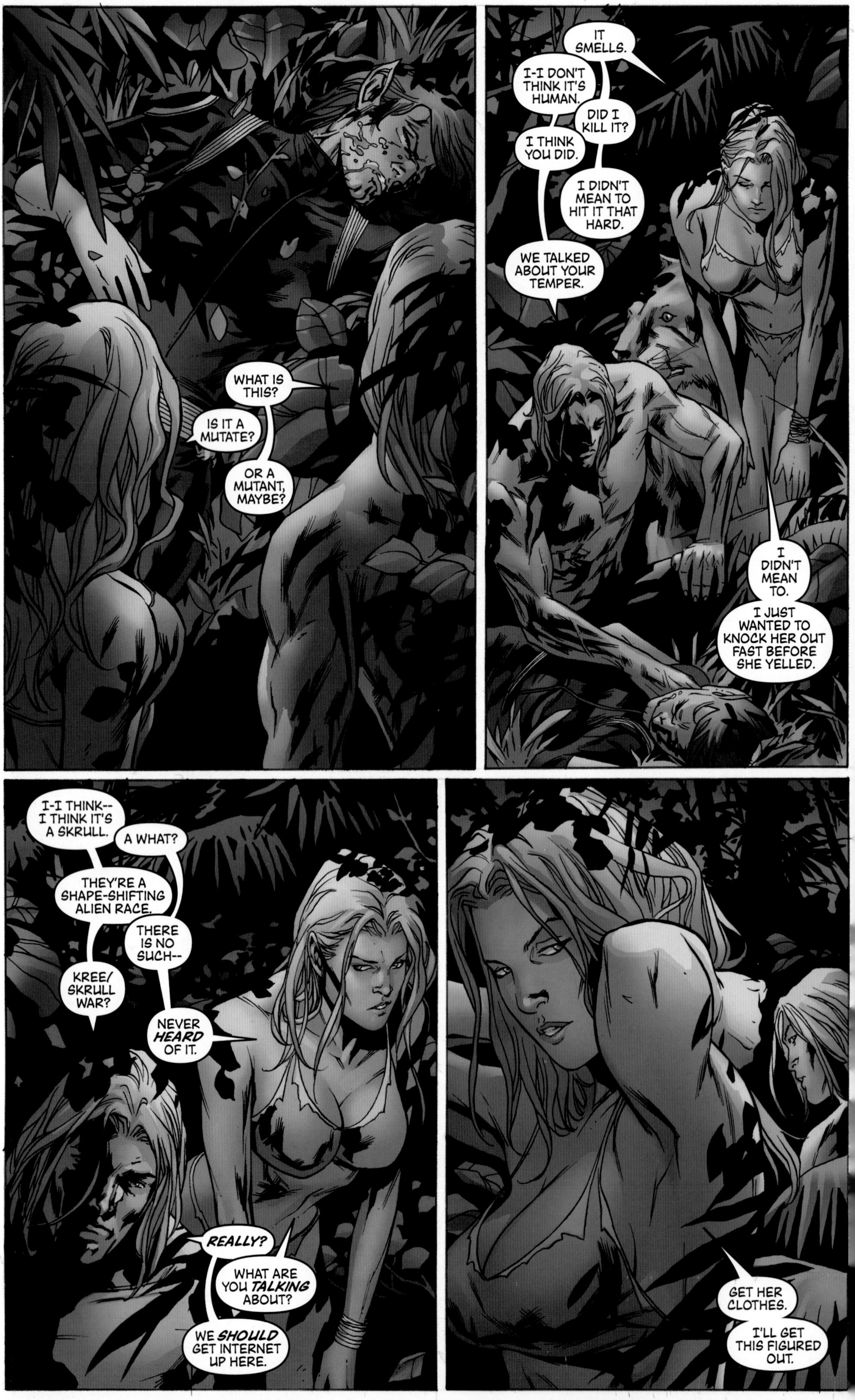
WHAT IS THIS?
IS IT A MUTATE?
OR A MUTANT, MAYBE?
IT SMELLS.
I-I DON'T THINK IT'S HUMAN.
DID I KILL IT?
I THINK YOU DID.
I DIDN'T MEAN TO HIT IT THAT HARD.
WE TALKED ABOUT YOUR TEMPER.
I DIDN'T MEAN TO.
I JUST WANTED TO KNOCK HER OUT FAST BEFORE SHE YELLED.
I-I THINK-- I THINK IT'S A SKRULL.
A WHAT?
THEY'RE A SHAPE-SHIFTING ALIEN RACE.
THERE IS NO SUCH--
KREE/ SKRULL WAR?
NEVER *HEARD* OF IT.
REALLY?
WHAT ARE YOU *TALKING* ABOUT?
WE *SHOULD* GET INTERNET UP HERE.
GET HER CLOTHES.
I'LL GET THIS FIGURED OUT.

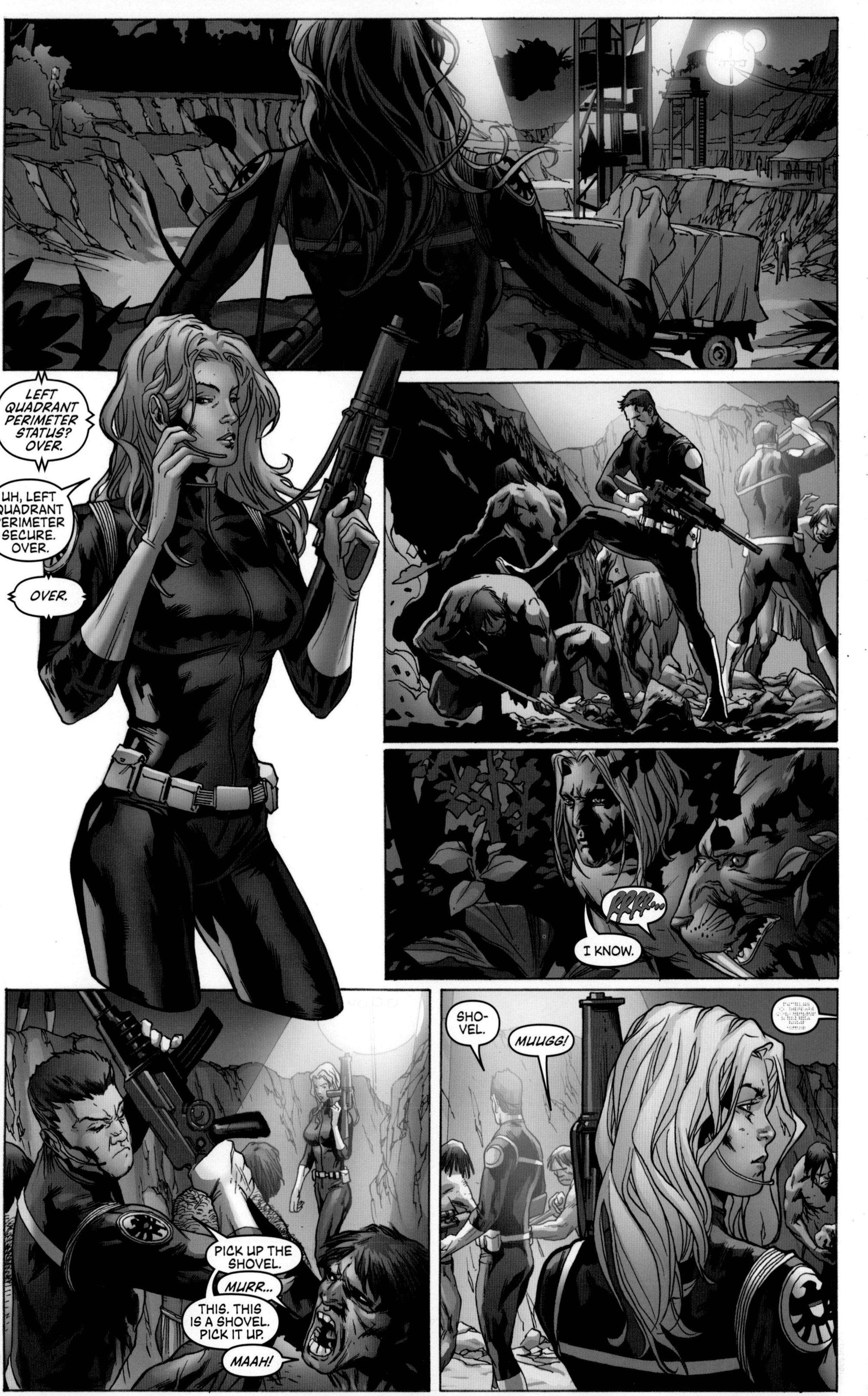
LEFT QUADRANT PERIMETER STATUS? OVER.
UH, LEFT QUADRANT PERIMETER SECURE. OVER.
OVER.
RRRR...
I KNOW.
PICK UP THE SHOVEL.
MURR...
THIS. THIS IS A SHOVEL. PICK IT UP.
MAAH!
SHO-VEL.
MUUGG!

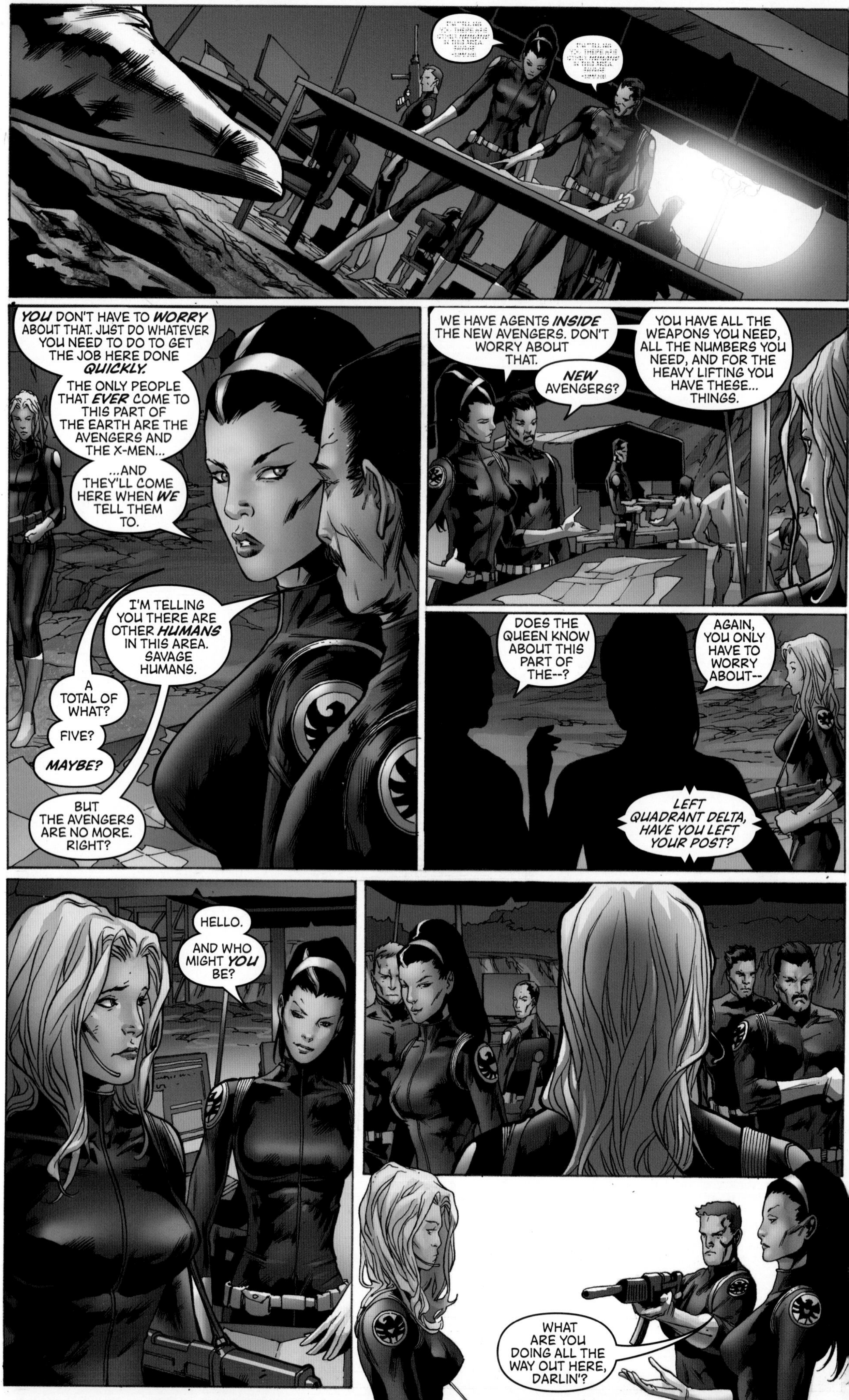

YOU DON'T HAVE TO WORRY ABOUT THAT. JUST DO WHATEVER YOU NEED TO DO TO GET THE JOB HERE DONE QUICKLY.
THE ONLY PEOPLE THAT EVER COME TO THIS PART OF THE EARTH ARE THE AVENGERS AND THE X-MEN...
...AND THEY'LL COME HERE WHEN WE TELL THEM TO.
I'M TELLING YOU THERE ARE OTHER HUMANS IN THIS AREA. SAVAGE HUMANS.
A TOTAL OF WHAT?
FIVE?
MAYBE?
BUT THE AVENGERS ARE NO MORE. RIGHT?
WE HAVE AGENTS INSIDE THE NEW AVENGERS. DON'T WORRY ABOUT THAT.
NEW AVENGERS?
YOU HAVE ALL THE WEAPONS YOU NEED, ALL THE NUMBERS YOU NEED, AND FOR THE HEAVY LIFTING YOU HAVE THESE... THINGS.
DOES THE QUEEN KNOW ABOUT THIS PART OF THE--?
AGAIN, YOU ONLY HAVE TO WORRY ABOUT--
LEFT QUADRANT DELTA, HAVE YOU LEFT YOUR POST?
HELLO.
AND WHO MIGHT YOU BE?
WHAT ARE YOU DOING ALL THE WAY OUT HERE, DARLIN'?

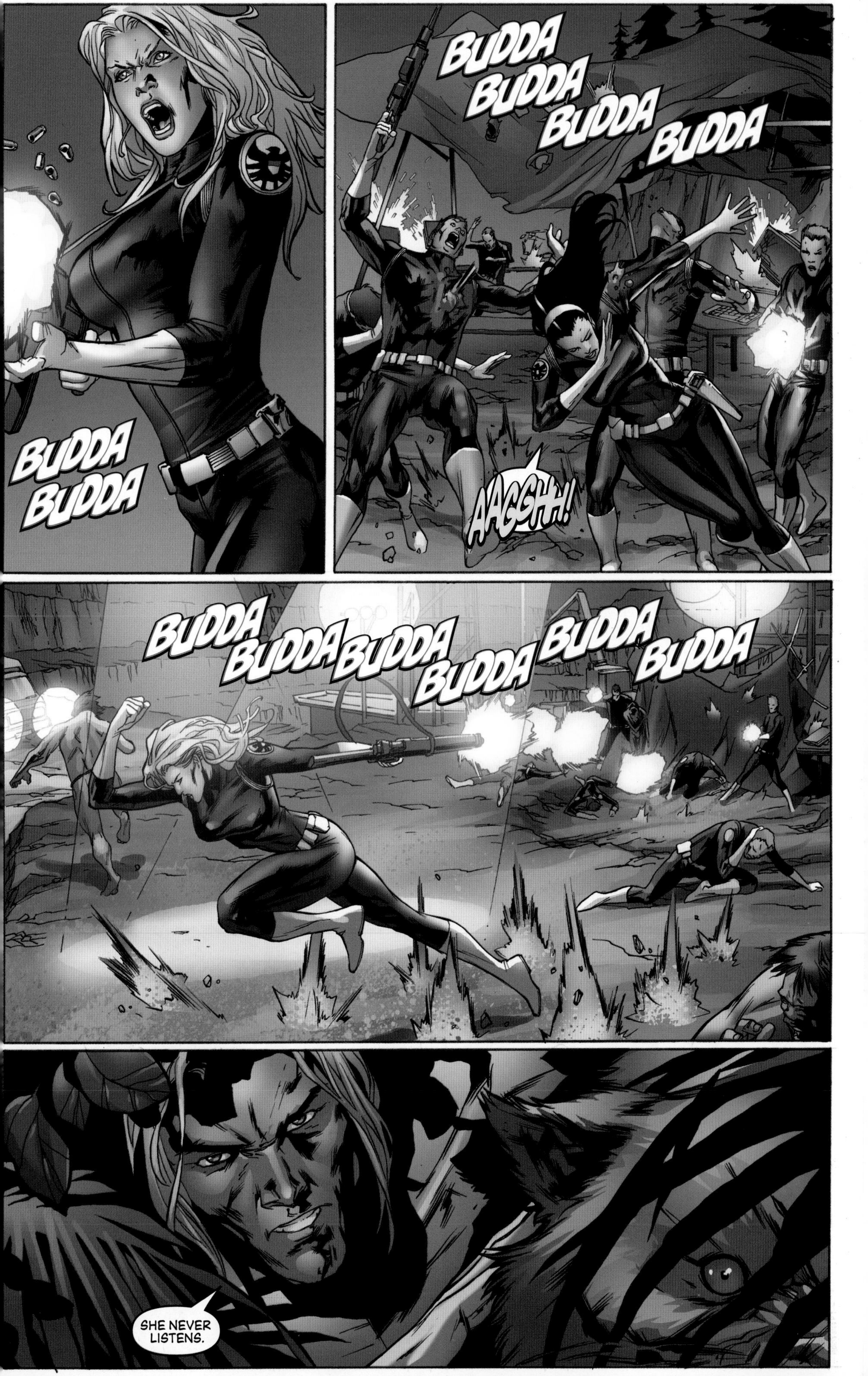
BUDDA
BUDDA
BUDDA
BUDDA
BUDDA
BUDDA
AAGGHH!
BUDDA
BUDDA
BUDDA
BUDDA
BUDDA
BUDDA
SHE NEVER LISTENS.

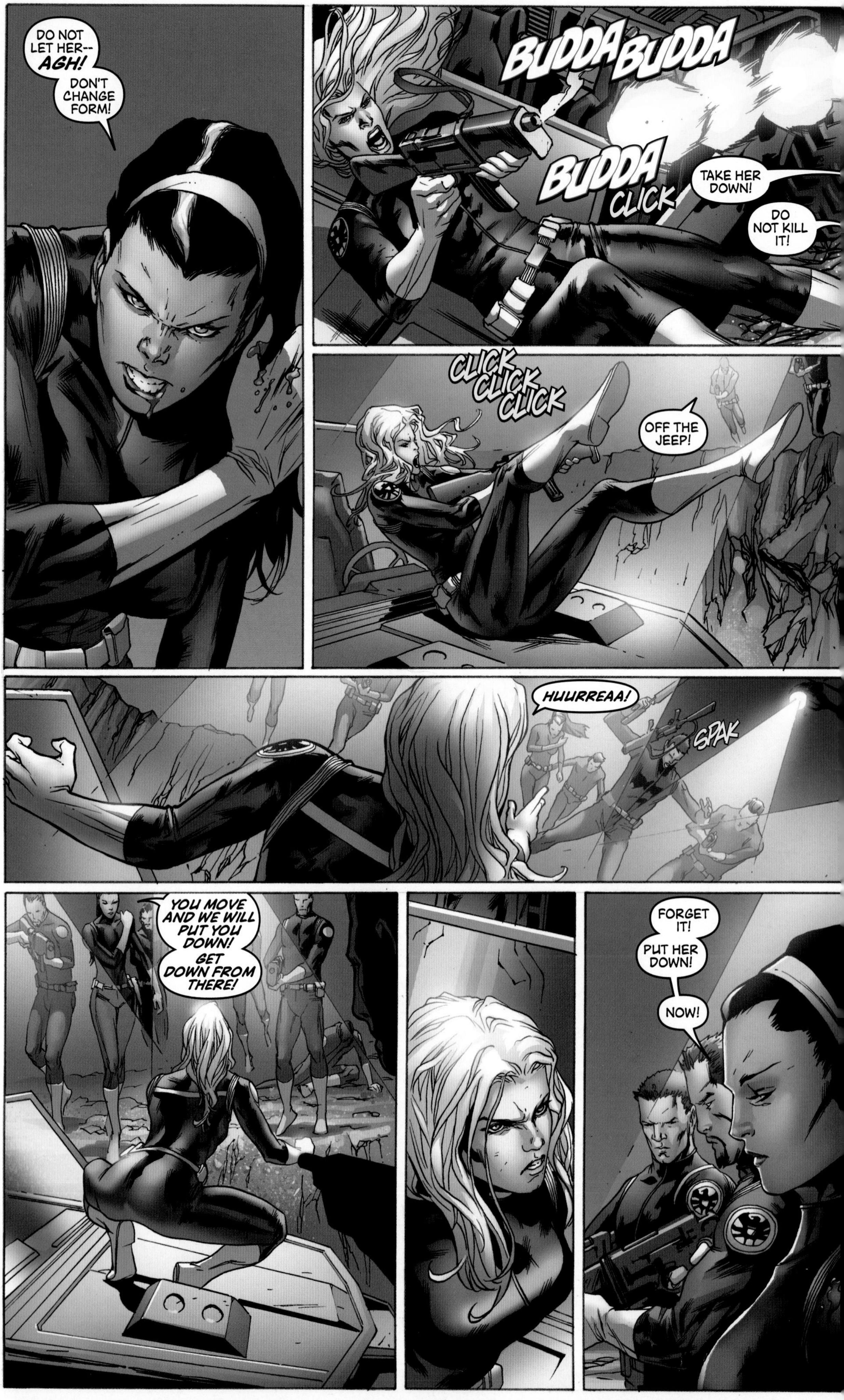
DO NOT LET HER-- AGH!
DON'T CHANGE FORM!
BUDDA BUDDA
BUDDA
CLICK
TAKE HER DOWN!
DO NOT KILL IT!
CLICK CLICK CLICK
OFF THE JEEP!
HUURREAA!
SPAK
YOU MOVE AND WE WILL PUT YOU DOWN! GET DOWN FROM THERE!
FORGET IT!
PUT HER DOWN!
NOW!

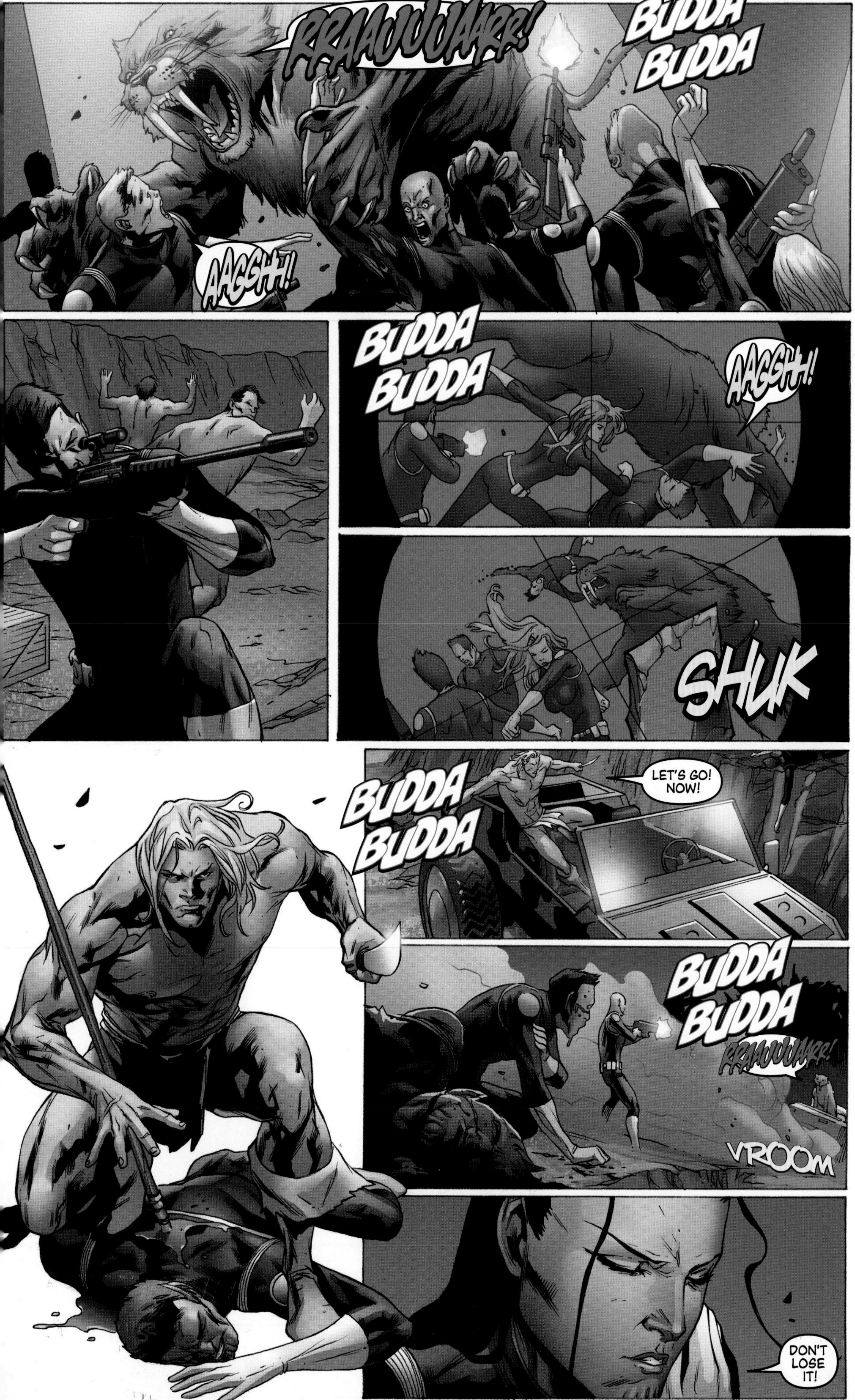
RRAAUUUWARR!
BUDDA BUDDA
AAGGHH!
BUDDA BUDDA
AAGGHH!
SHUK
BUDDA BUDDA
LET'S GO! NOW!
BUDDA BUDDA
RRAAUUUWARR!
VROOM
DON'T LOSE IT!

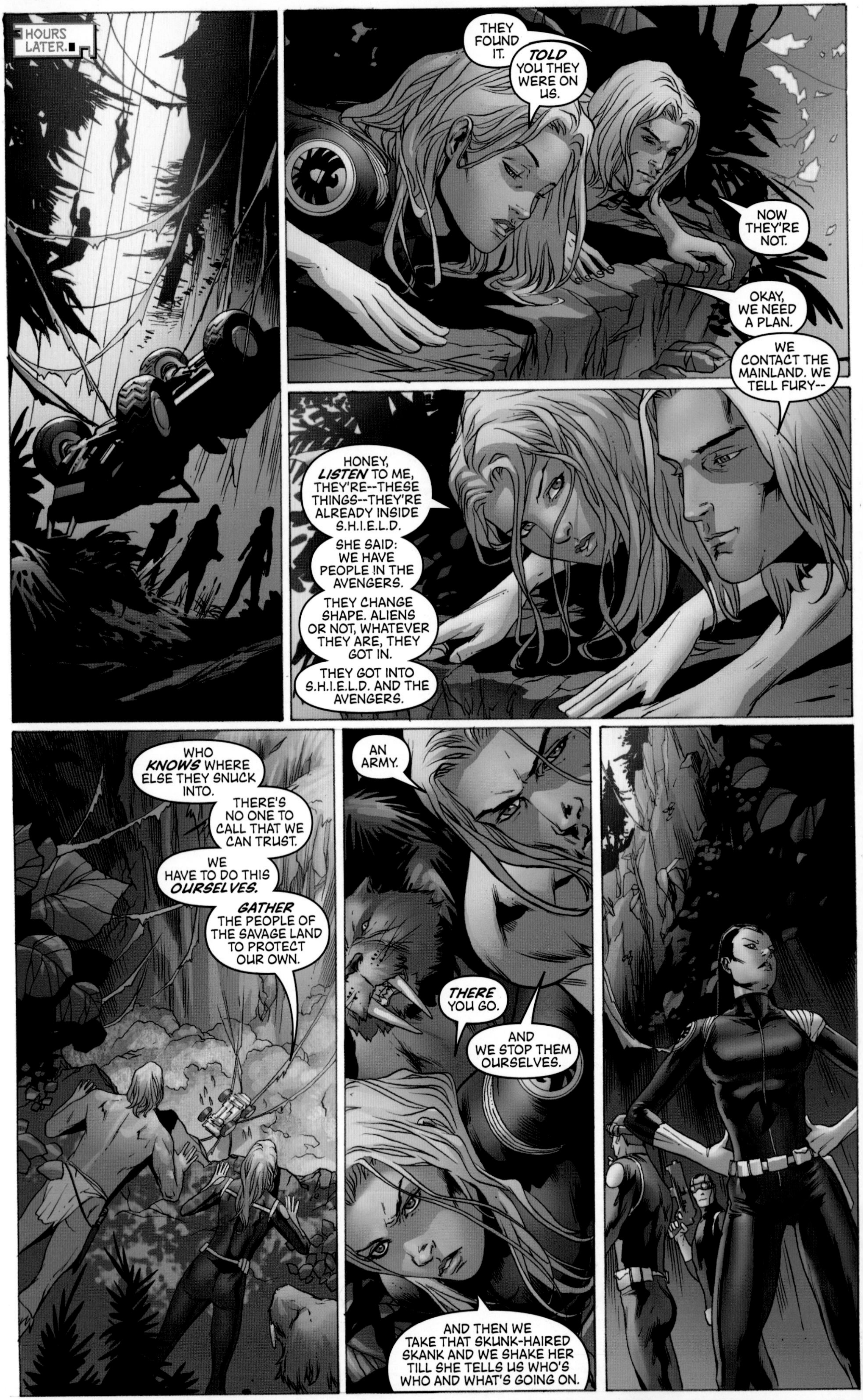
HOURS LATER.
THEY FOUND IT.
TOLD YOU THEY WERE ON US.
NOW THEY'RE NOT.
OKAY, WE NEED A PLAN.
WE CONTACT THE MAINLAND. WE TELL FURY--
HONEY, LISTEN TO ME, THEY'RE--THESE THINGS--THEY'RE ALREADY INSIDE S.H.I.E.L.D.
SHE SAID: WE HAVE PEOPLE IN THE AVENGERS.
THEY CHANGE SHAPE. ALIENS OR NOT, WHATEVER THEY ARE, THEY GOT IN.
THEY GOT INTO S.H.I.E.L.D. AND THE AVENGERS.
WHO KNOWS WHERE ELSE THEY SNUCK INTO.
THERE'S NO ONE TO CALL THAT WE CAN TRUST.
WE HAVE TO DO THIS OURSELVES.
GATHER THE PEOPLE OF THE SAVAGE LAND TO PROTECT OUR OWN.
AN ARMY.
THERE YOU GO.
AND WE STOP THEM OURSELVES.
AND THEN WE TAKE THAT SKUNK-HAIRED SKANK AND WE SHAKE HER TILL SHE TELLS US WHO'S WHO AND WHAT'S GOING ON.

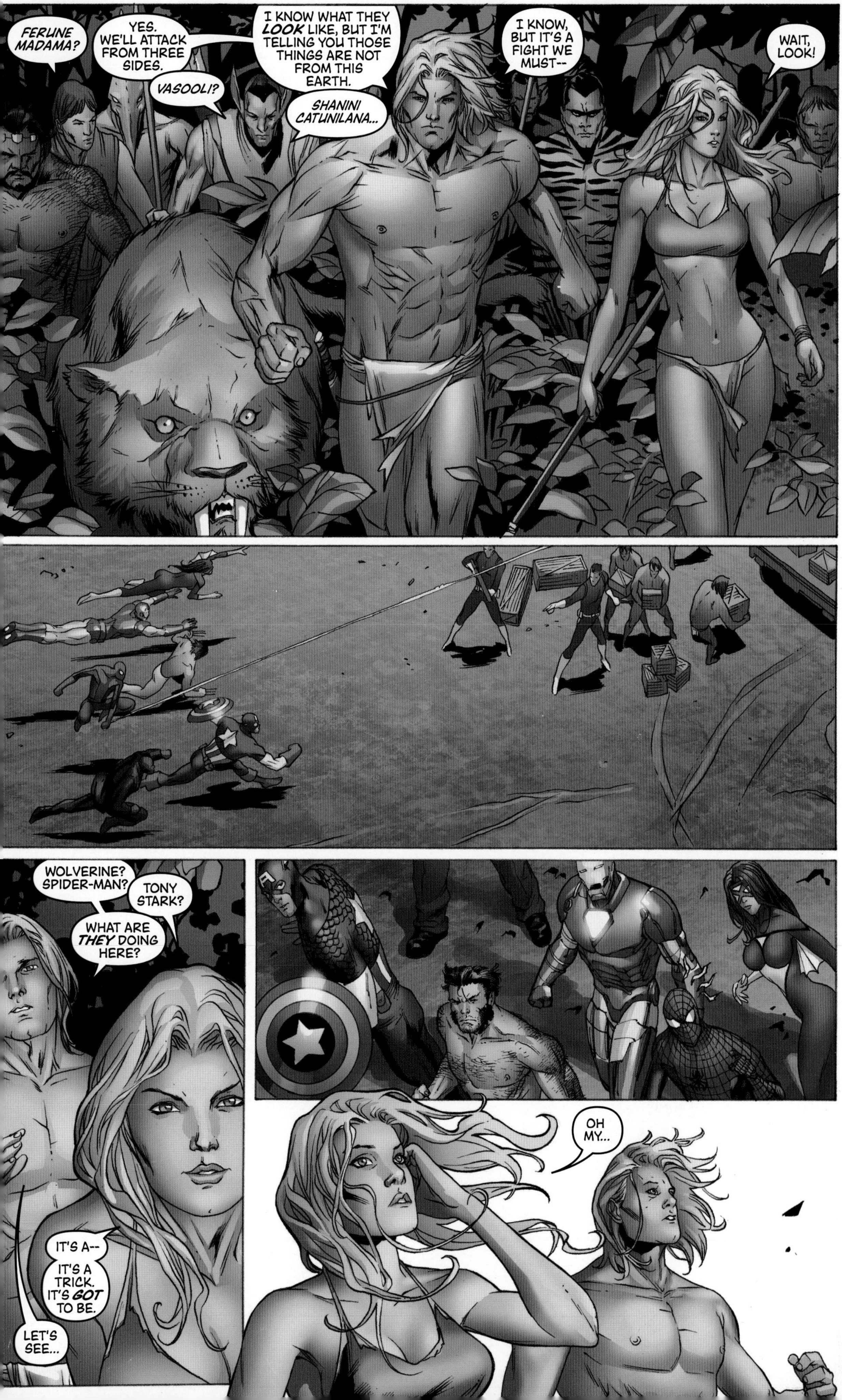

FERUNE MADAMA?
YES. WE'LL ATTACK FROM THREE SIDES.
VASOOLI?
I KNOW WHAT THEY LOOK LIKE, BUT I'M TELLING YOU THOSE THINGS ARE NOT FROM THIS EARTH.
SHANINI CATUNILANA...
I KNOW, BUT IT'S A FIGHT WE MUST--
WAIT, LOOK!
WOLVERINE? SPIDER-MAN?
TONY STARK?
WHAT ARE THEY DOING HERE?
IT'S A--
IT'S A TRICK. IT'S GOT TO BE.
LET'S SEE...
OH MY...

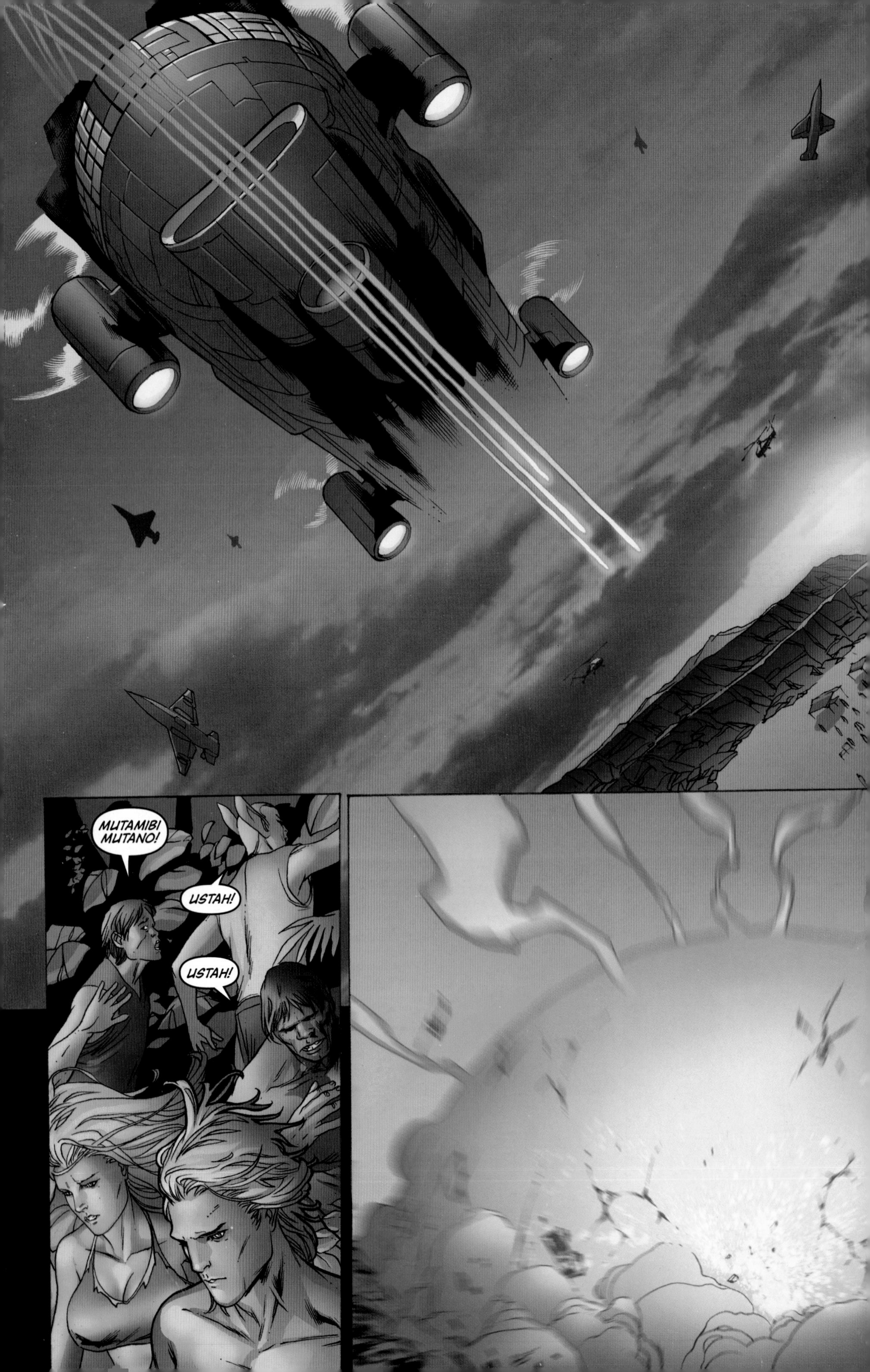
MUTAMIBI MUTANO!
USTAH!
USTAH!

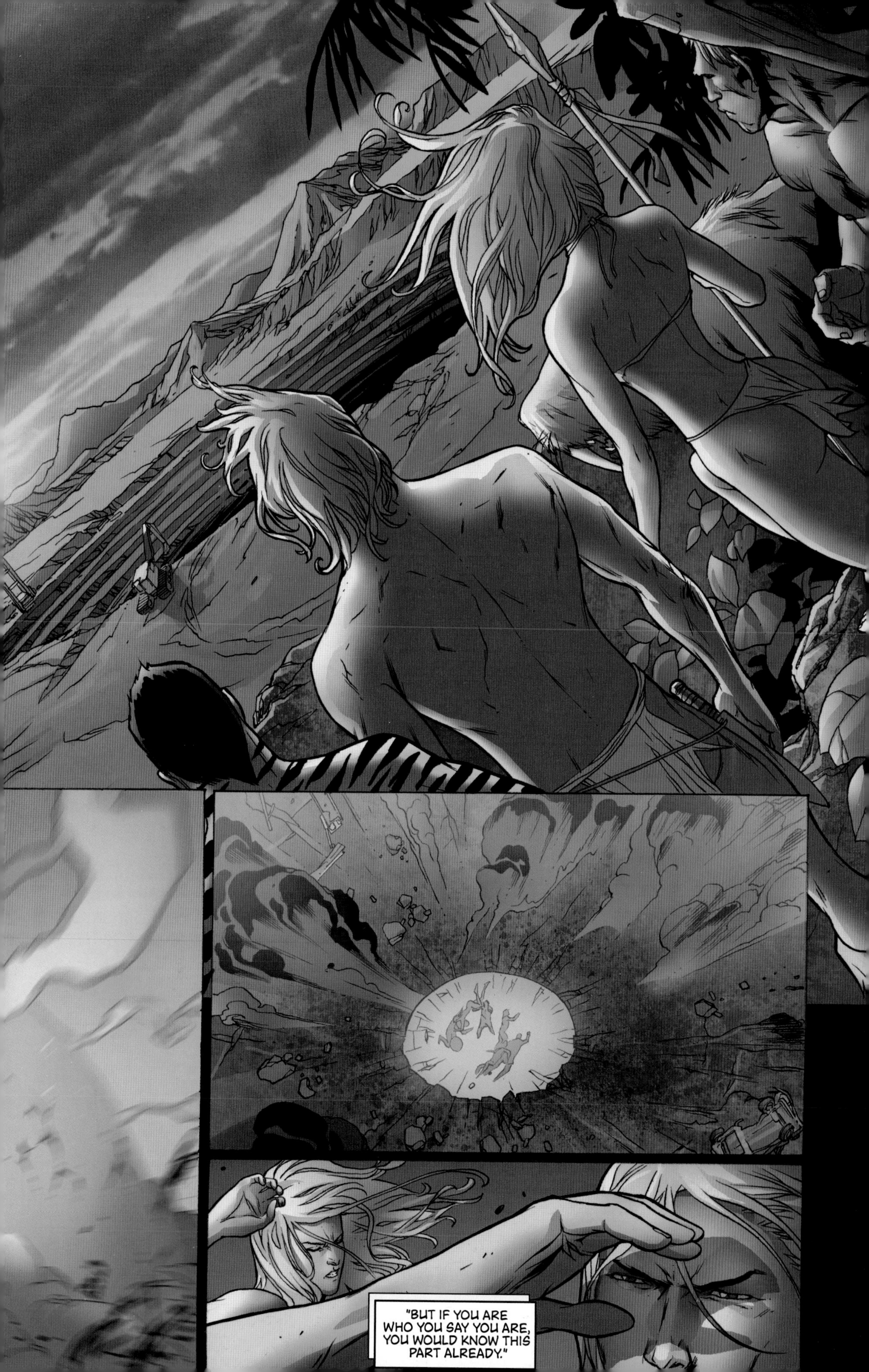
"BUT IF YOU ARE WHO YOU SAY YOU ARE, YOU WOULD KNOW THIS PART ALREADY."

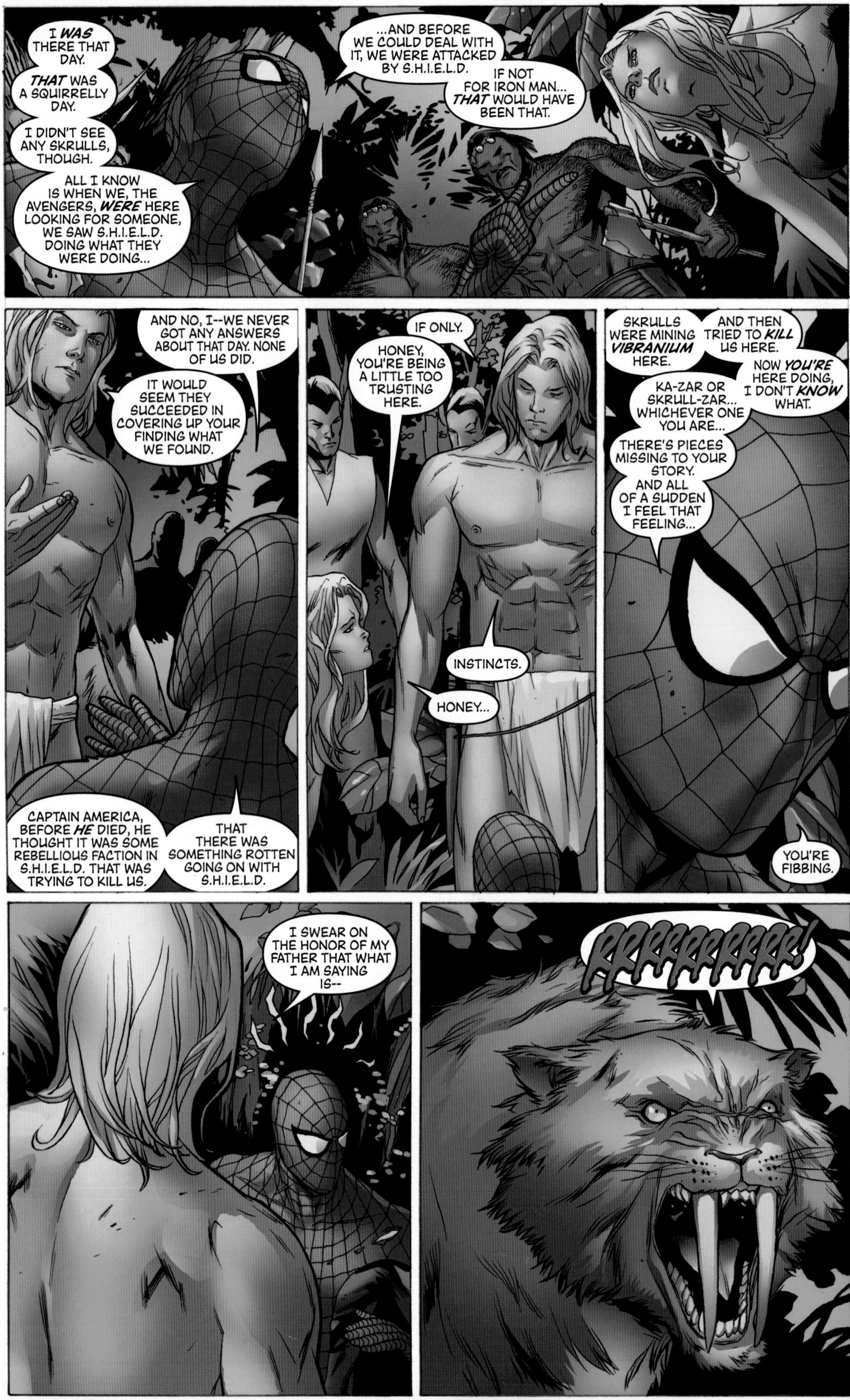
I WAS THERE THAT DAY.
THAT WAS A SQUIRRELLY DAY.
I DIDN'T SEE ANY SKRULLS, THOUGH.
ALL I KNOW IS WHEN WE, THE AVENGERS, WERE HERE LOOKING FOR SOMEONE, WE SAW S.H.I.E.L.D. DOING WHAT THEY WERE DOING...
...AND BEFORE WE COULD DEAL WITH IT, WE WERE ATTACKED BY S.H.I.E.L.D.
IF NOT FOR IRON MAN... THAT WOULD HAVE BEEN THAT.
AND NO, I--WE NEVER GOT ANY ANSWERS ABOUT THAT DAY. NONE OF US DID.
IT WOULD SEEM THEY SUCCEEDED IN COVERING UP YOUR FINDING WHAT WE FOUND.
CAPTAIN AMERICA, BEFORE HE DIED, HE THOUGHT IT WAS SOME REBELLIOUS FACTION IN S.H.I.E.L.D. THAT WAS TRYING TO KILL US.
THAT THERE WAS SOMETHING ROTTEN GOING ON WITH S.H.I.E.L.D.
IF ONLY.
HONEY, YOU'RE BEING A LITTLE TOO TRUSTING HERE.
INSTINCTS.
HONEY...
SKRULLS WERE MINING VIBRANIUM HERE.
AND THEN TRIED TO KILL US HERE.
NOW YOU'RE HERE DOING, I DON'T KNOW WHAT.
KA-ZAR OR SKRULL-ZAR... WHICHEVER ONE YOU ARE...
THERE'S PIECES MISSING TO YOUR STORY.
AND ALL OF A SUDDEN I FEEL THAT FEELING...
YOU'RE FIBBING.
I SWEAR ON THE HONOR OF MY FATHER THAT WHAT I AM SAYING IS--
RRRRRRRRRRR!

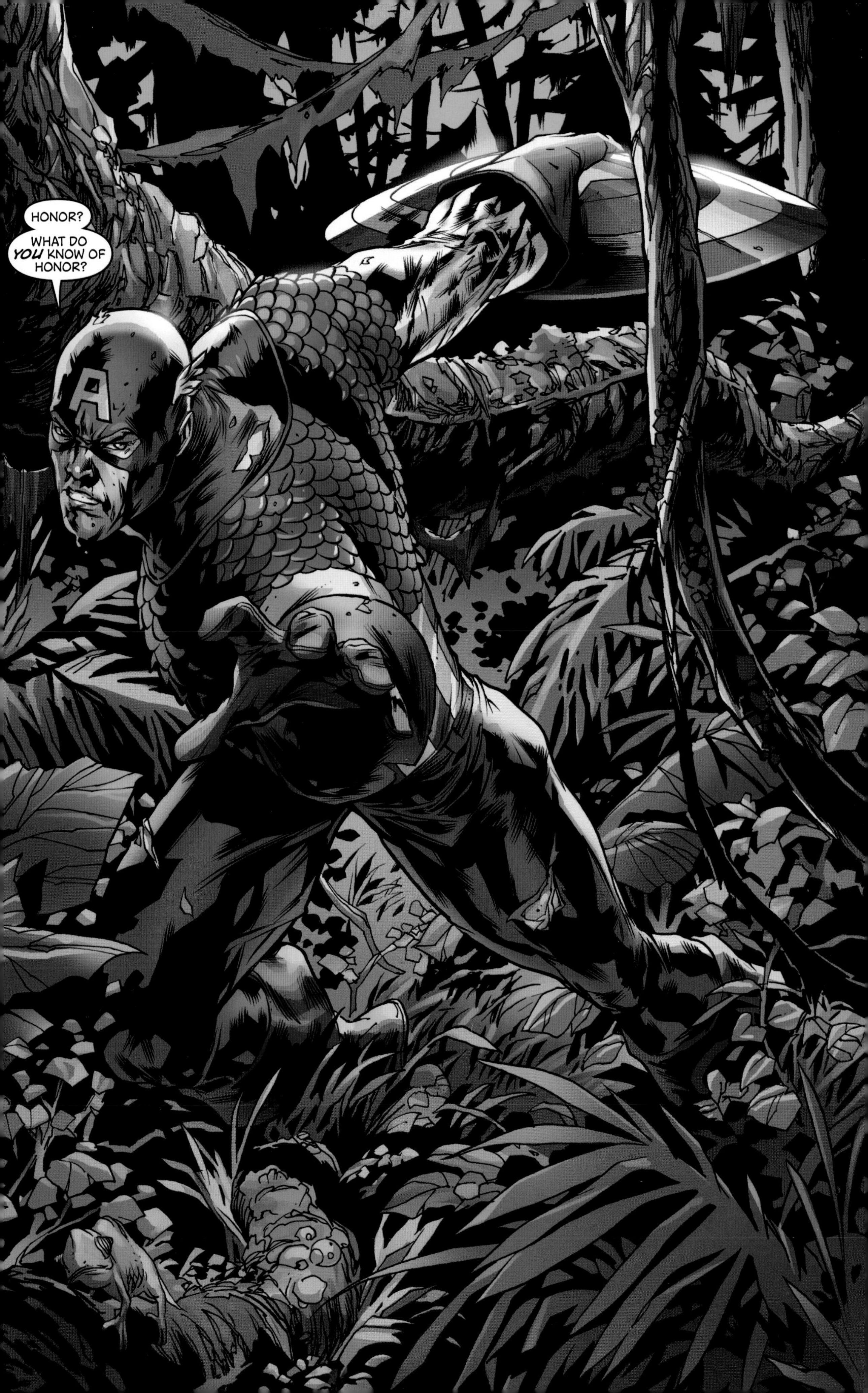
HONOR?
WHAT DO *YOU* KNOW OF HONOR?

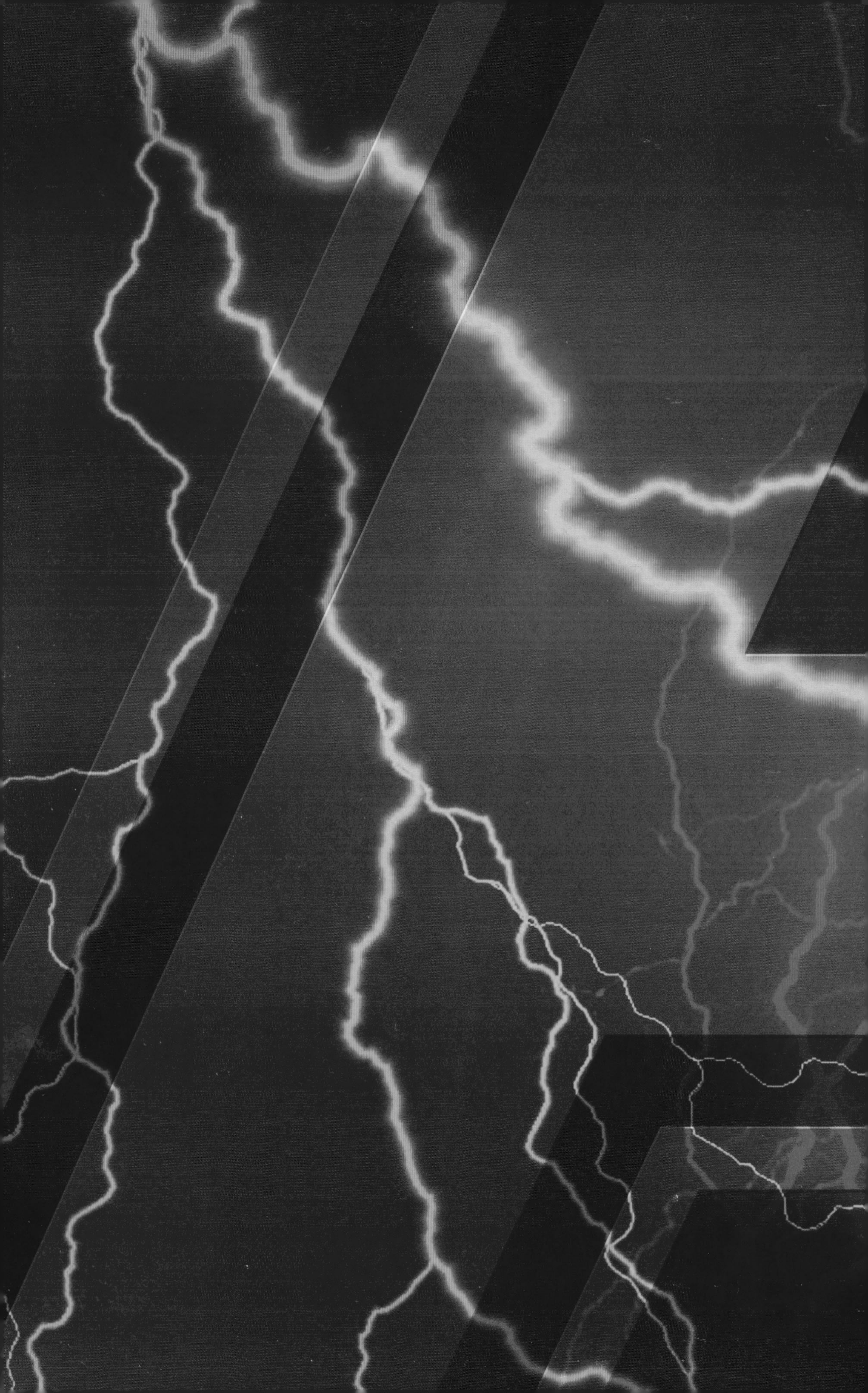

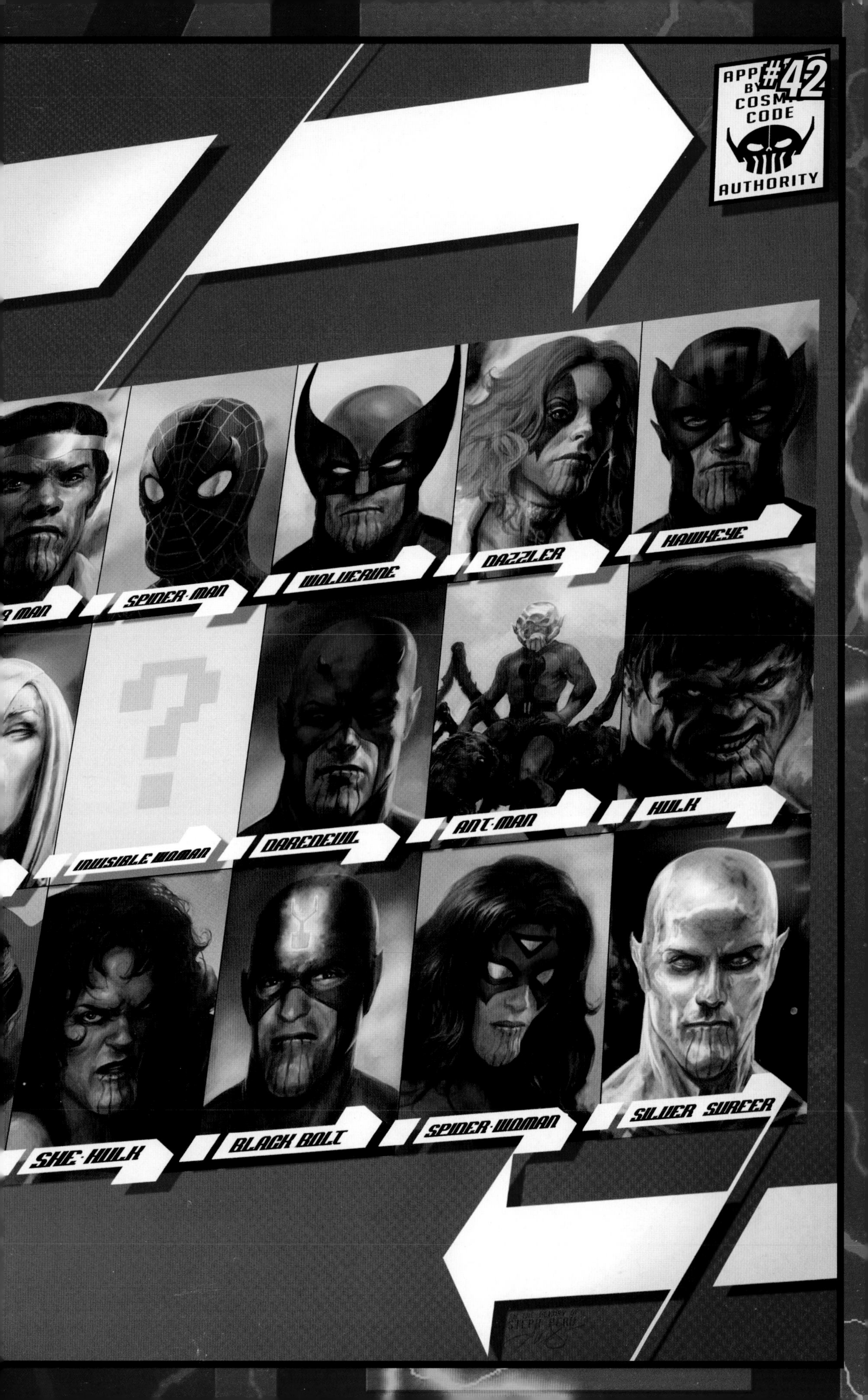
#42
APP
BY
COSM
CODE
AUTHORITY
SPIDER-MAN
WOLVERINE
DAZZLER
HAWKEYE
INVISIBLE WOMAN
DAREDEVIL
ANT-MAN
HULK
SHE-HULK
BLACK BOLT
SPIDER-WOMAN
SILVER SURFER

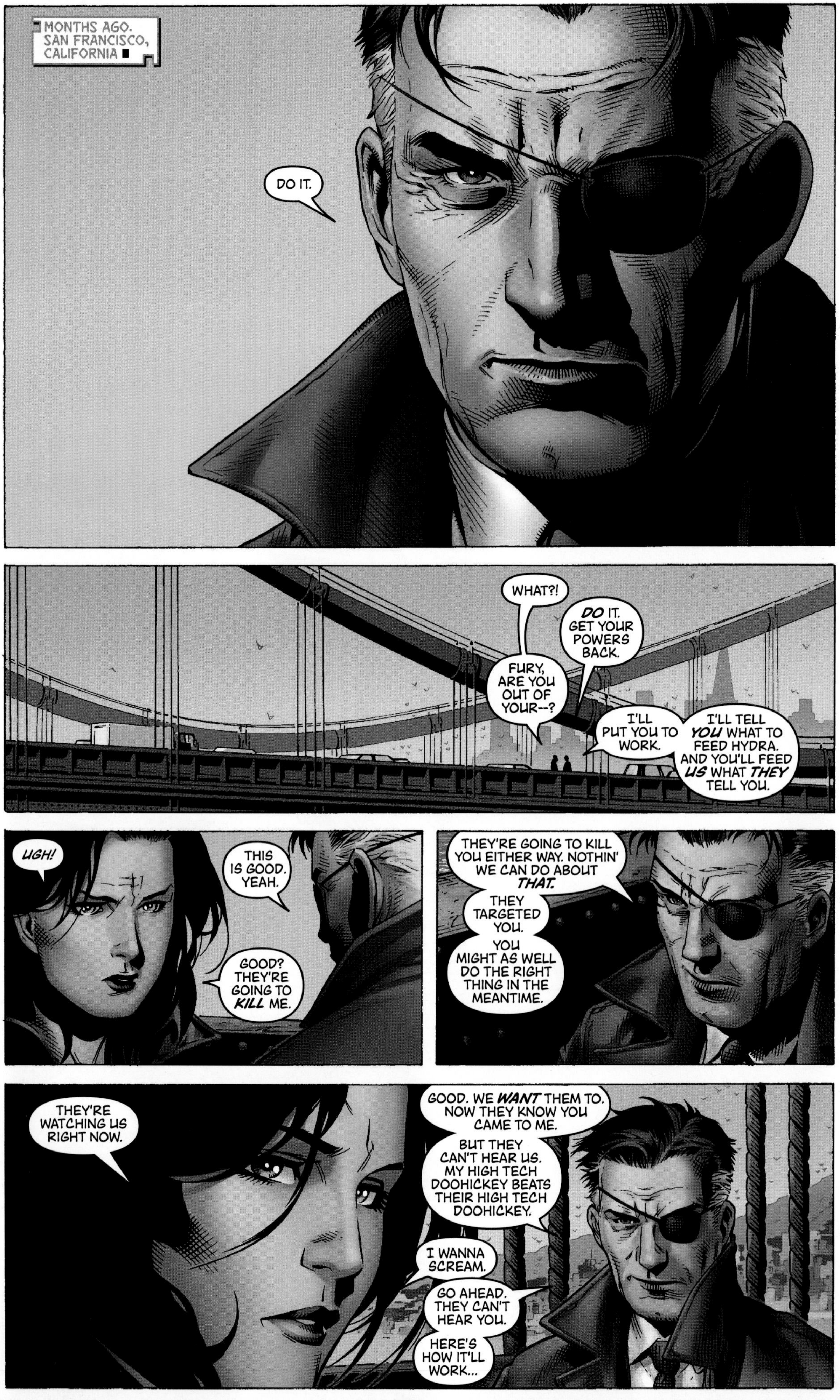
MONTHS AGO. SAN FRANCISCO, CALIFORNIA
DO IT.
WHAT?!
FURY, ARE YOU OUT OF YOUR--?
DO IT. GET YOUR POWERS BACK.
I'LL PUT YOU TO WORK.
I'LL TELL YOU WHAT TO FEED HYDRA. AND YOU'LL FEED US WHAT THEY TELL YOU.
UGH!
THIS IS GOOD. YEAH.
GOOD? THEY'RE GOING TO KILL ME.
THEY'RE GOING TO KILL YOU EITHER WAY. NOTHIN' WE CAN DO ABOUT THAT.
THEY TARGETED YOU.
YOU MIGHT AS WELL DO THE RIGHT THING IN THE MEANTIME.
THEY'RE WATCHING US RIGHT NOW.
GOOD. WE WANT THEM TO. NOW THEY KNOW YOU CAME TO ME.
BUT THEY CAN'T HEAR US. MY HIGH TECH DOOHICKEY BEATS THEIR HIGH TECH DOOHICKEY.
I WANNA SCREAM.
GO AHEAD. THEY CAN'T HEAR YOU.
HERE'S HOW IT'LL WORK...

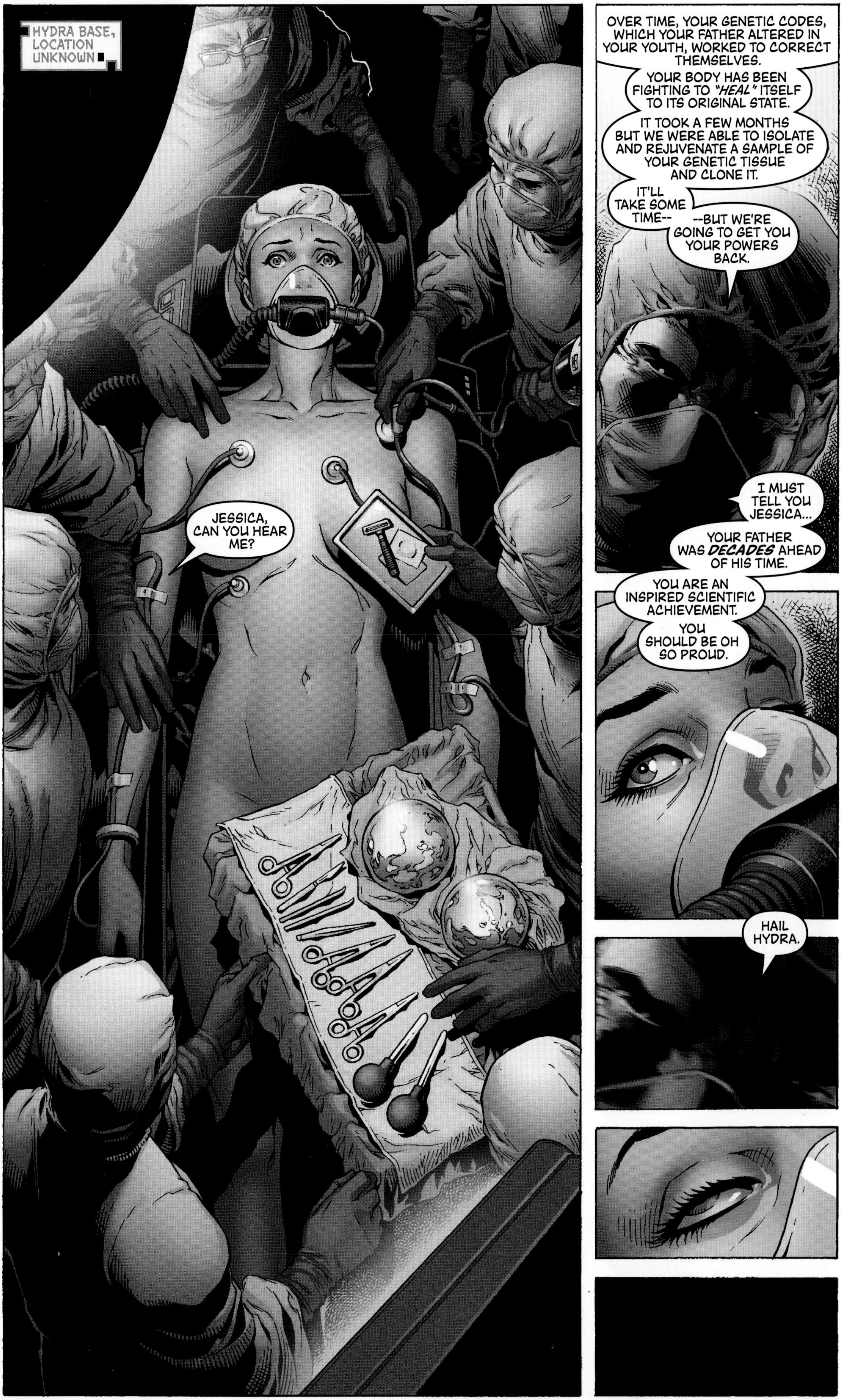
HYDRA BASE, LOCATION UNKNOWN
JESSICA, CAN YOU HEAR ME?
OVER TIME, YOUR GENETIC CODES, WHICH YOUR FATHER ALTERED IN YOUR YOUTH, WORKED TO CORRECT THEMSELVES.
YOUR BODY HAS BEEN FIGHTING TO "HEAL" ITSELF TO ITS ORIGINAL STATE.
IT TOOK A FEW MONTHS BUT WE WERE ABLE TO ISOLATE AND REJUVENATE A SAMPLE OF YOUR GENETIC TISSUE AND CLONE IT.
IT'LL TAKE SOME TIME--
--BUT WE'RE GOING TO GET YOU YOUR POWERS BACK.
I MUST TELL YOU JESSICA...
YOUR FATHER WAS DECADES AHEAD OF HIS TIME.
YOU ARE AN INSPIRED SCIENTIFIC ACHIEVEMENT.
YOU SHOULD BE OH SO PROUD.
HAIL HYDRA.

SHE'S OUT.

LET'S.

SHALL WE PROCEED, MY QUEEN?

FOR THE GLORY.

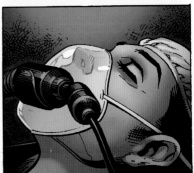

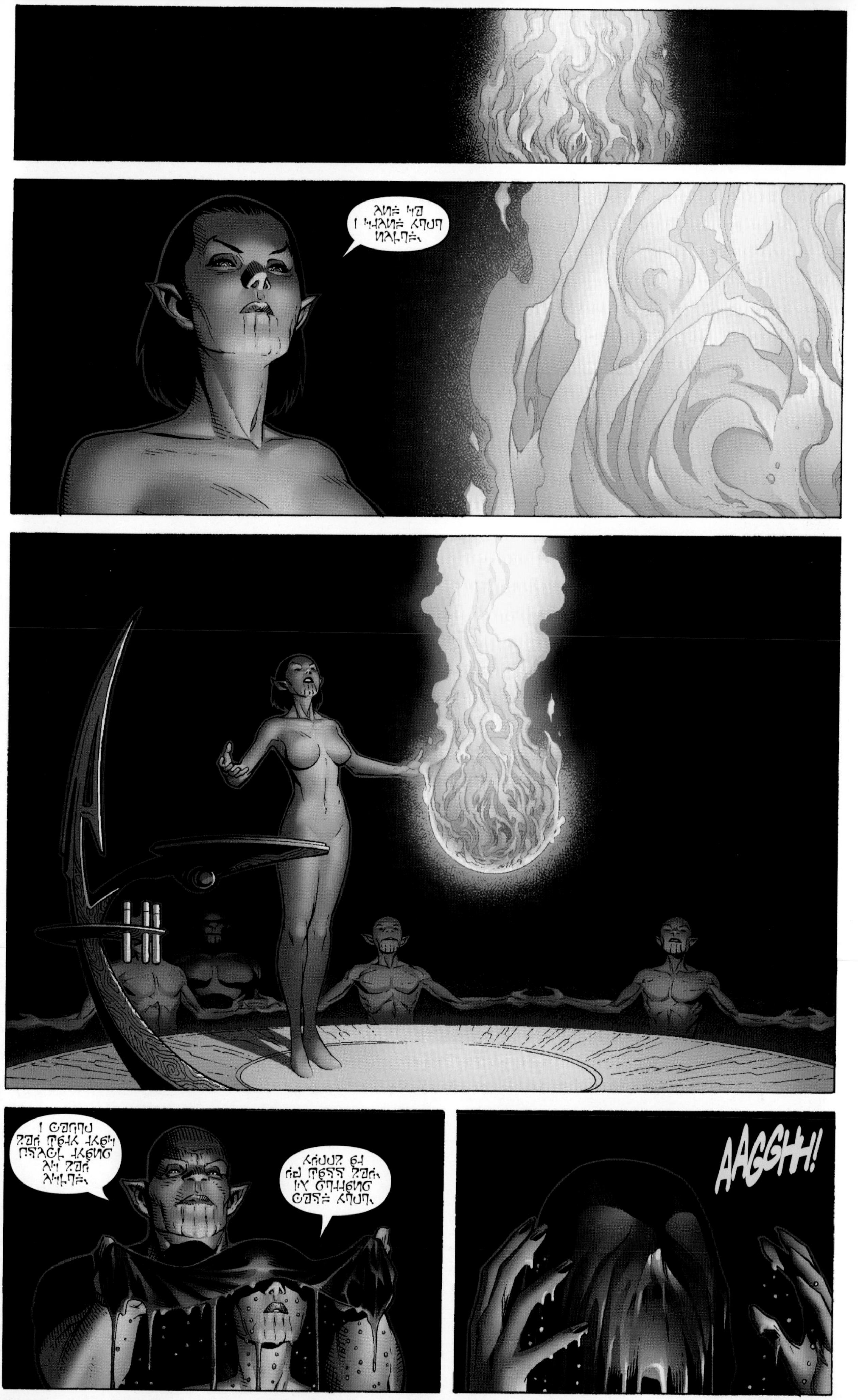
AAGGHH!

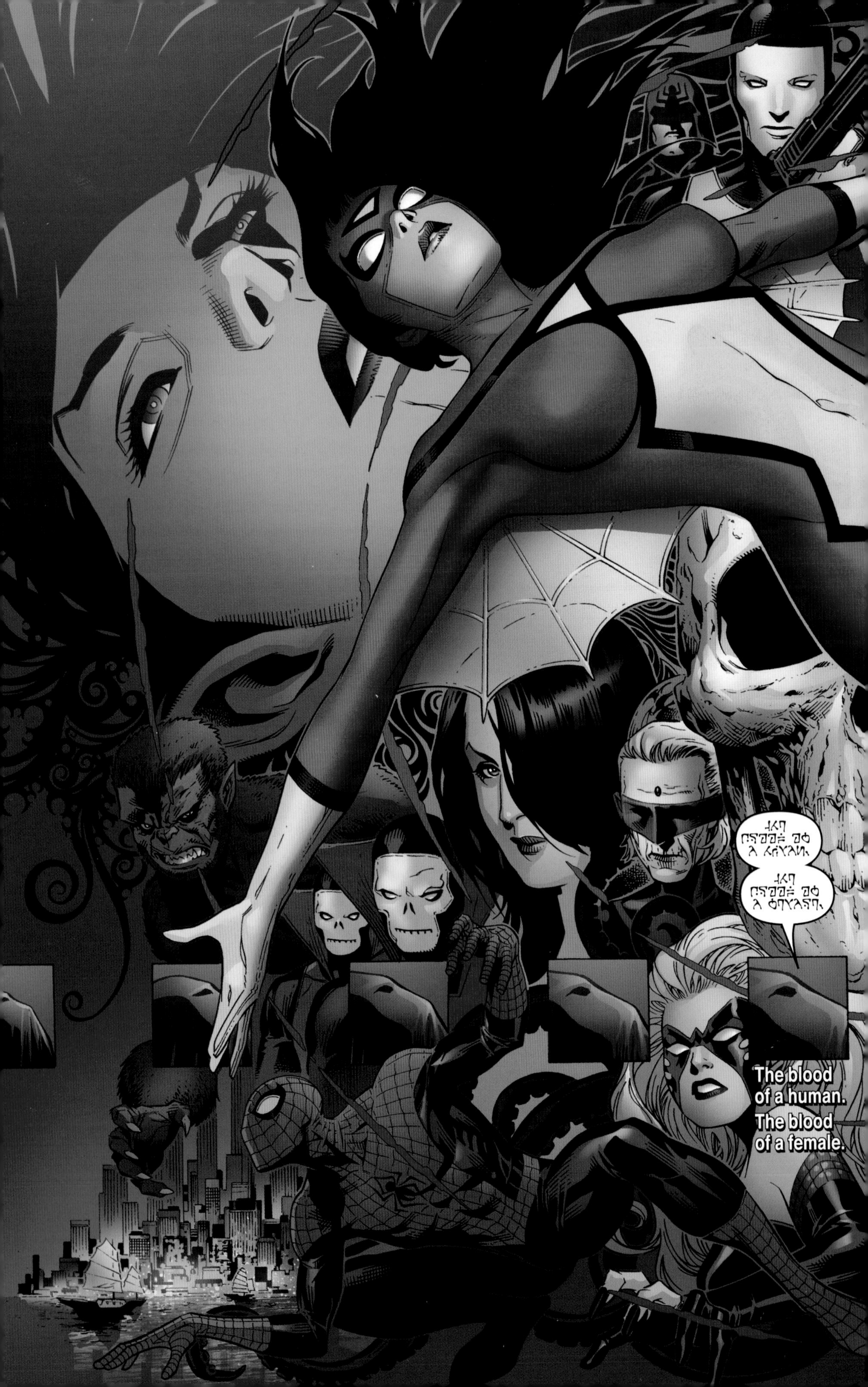
The blood of a human.
The blood of a female.

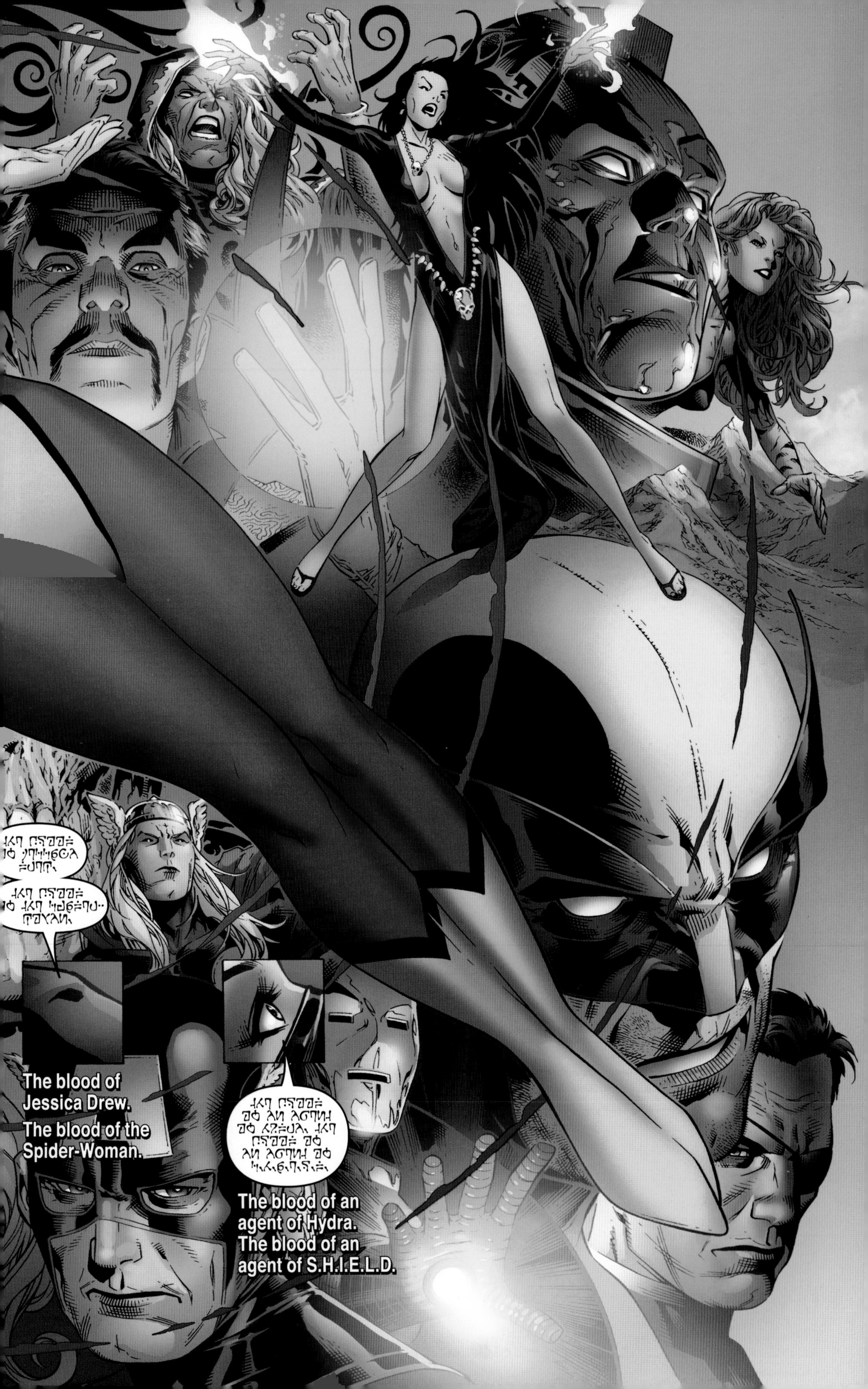
The blood of
Jessica Drew.
The blood of the
Spider-Woman.
The blood of an
agent of Hydra.
The blood of an
agent of S.H.I.E.L.D.

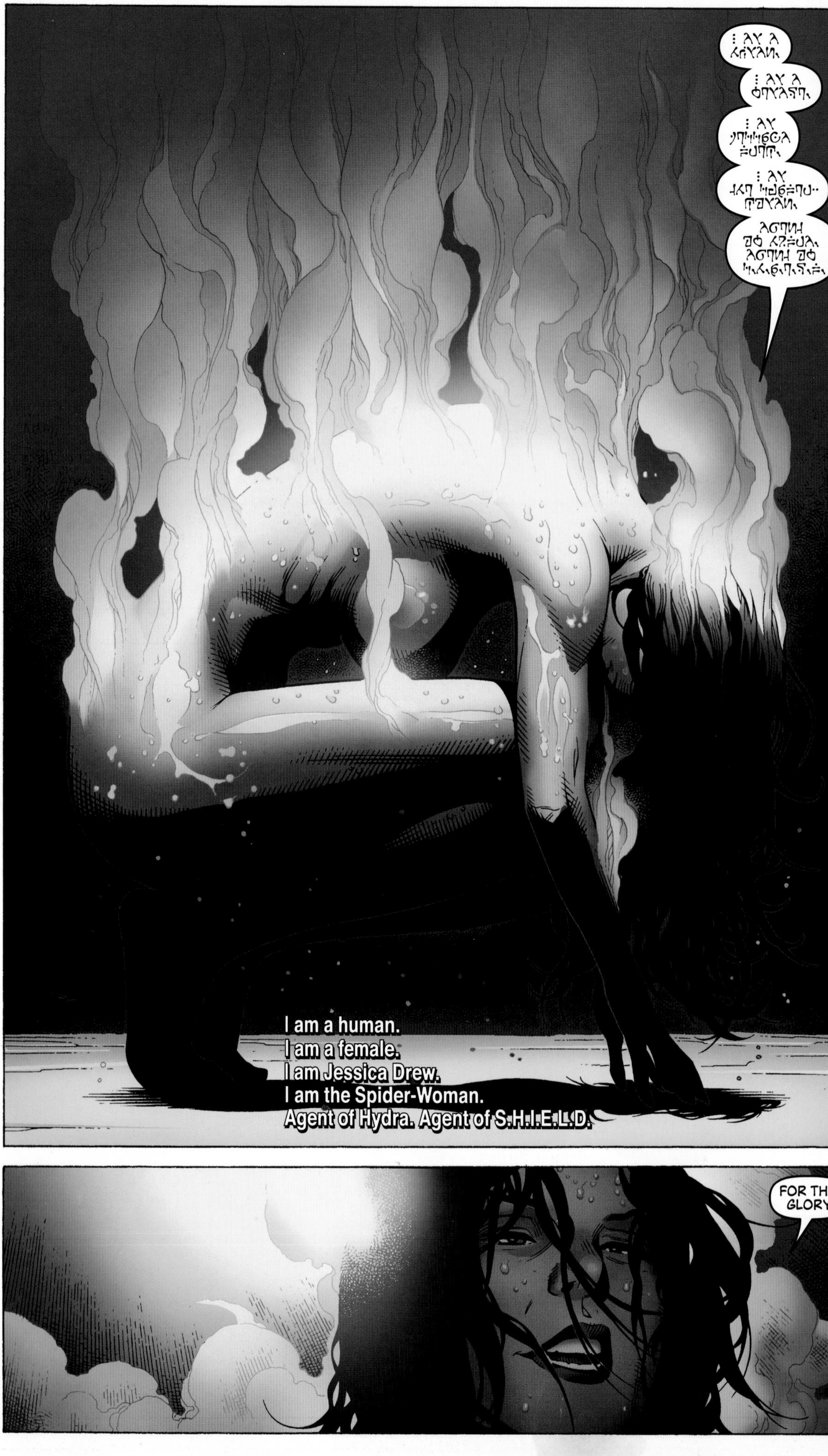
I am a human.
I am a female.
I am Jessica Drew.
I am the Spider-Woman.
Agent of Hydra. Agent of S.H.I.E.L.D.
FOR THE GLORY.

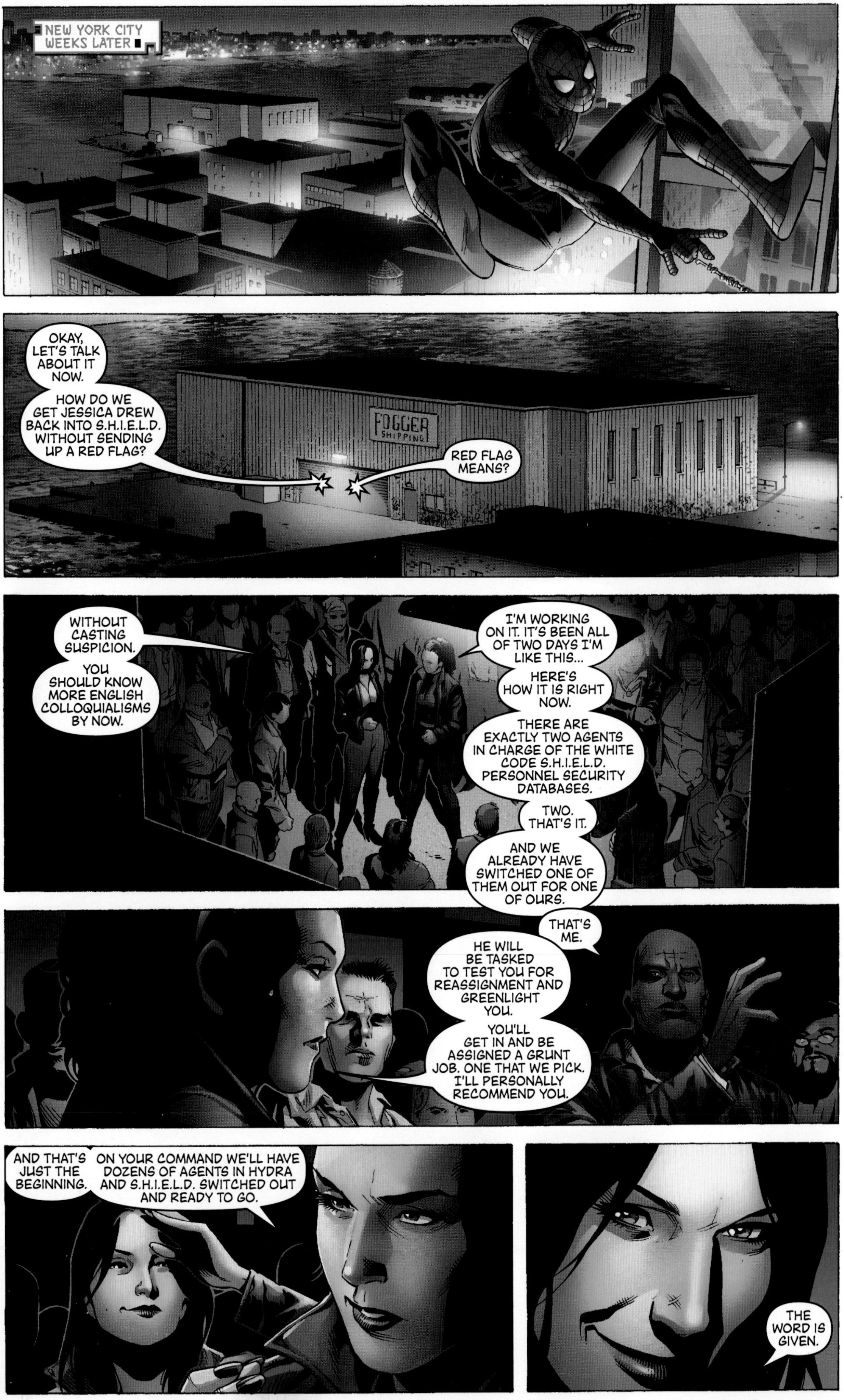
NEW YORK CITY WEEKS LATER
OKAY, LET'S TALK ABOUT IT NOW.
HOW DO WE GET JESSICA DREW BACK INTO S.H.I.E.L.D. WITHOUT SENDING UP A RED FLAG?
RED FLAG MEANS?
FOGGER SHIPPING
WITHOUT CASTING SUSPICION.
YOU SHOULD KNOW MORE ENGLISH COLLOQUIALISMS BY NOW.
I'M WORKING ON IT. IT'S BEEN ALL OF TWO DAYS I'M LIKE THIS...
HERE'S HOW IT IS RIGHT NOW.
THERE ARE EXACTLY TWO AGENTS IN CHARGE OF THE WHITE CODE S.H.I.E.L.D. PERSONNEL SECURITY DATABASES.
TWO. THAT'S IT.
AND WE ALREADY HAVE SWITCHED ONE OF THEM OUT FOR ONE OF OURS.
THAT'S ME.
HE WILL BE TASKED TO TEST YOU FOR REASSIGNMENT AND GREENLIGHT YOU.
YOU'LL GET IN AND BE ASSIGNED A GRUNT JOB. ONE THAT WE PICK. I'LL PERSONALLY RECOMMEND YOU.
AND THAT'S JUST THE BEGINNING.
ON YOUR COMMAND WE'LL HAVE DOZENS OF AGENTS IN HYDRA AND S.H.I.E.L.D. SWITCHED OUT AND READY TO GO.
THE WORD IS GIVEN.

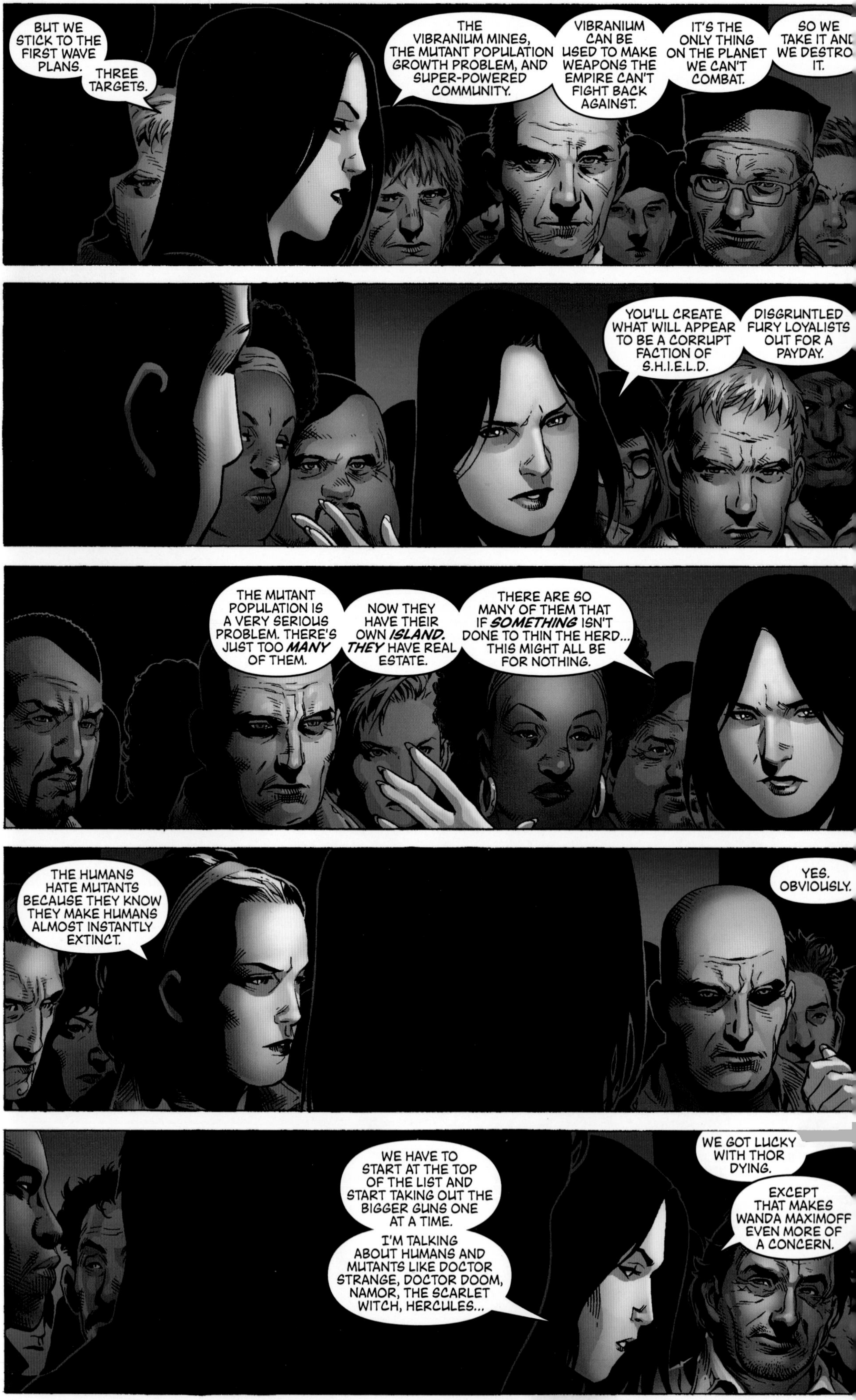
BUT WE STICK TO THE FIRST WAVE PLANS.
THREE TARGETS.
THE VIBRANIUM MINES, THE MUTANT POPULATION GROWTH PROBLEM, AND SUPER-POWERED COMMUNITY.
VIBRANIUM CAN BE USED TO MAKE WEAPONS THE EMPIRE CAN'T FIGHT BACK AGAINST.
IT'S THE ONLY THING ON THE PLANET WE CAN'T COMBAT.
SO WE TAKE IT AND WE DESTRO IT.
YOU'LL CREATE WHAT WILL APPEAR TO BE A CORRUPT FACTION OF S.H.I.E.L.D.
DISGRUNTLED FURY LOYALISTS OUT FOR A PAYDAY.
THE MUTANT POPULATION IS A VERY SERIOUS PROBLEM. THERE'S JUST TOO MANY OF THEM.
NOW THEY HAVE THEIR OWN ISLAND. THEY HAVE REAL ESTATE.
THERE ARE SO MANY OF THEM THAT IF SOMETHING ISN'T DONE TO THIN THE HERD... THIS MIGHT ALL BE FOR NOTHING.
THE HUMANS HATE MUTANTS BECAUSE THEY KNOW THEY MAKE HUMANS ALMOST INSTANTLY EXTINCT.
YES. OBVIOUSLY.
WE HAVE TO START AT THE TOP OF THE LIST AND START TAKING OUT THE BIGGER GUNS ONE AT A TIME.
I'M TALKING ABOUT HUMANS AND MUTANTS LIKE DOCTOR STRANGE, DOCTOR DOOM, NAMOR, THE SCARLET WITCH, HERCULES...
WE GOT LUCKY WITH THOR DYING.
EXCEPT THAT MAKES WANDA MAXIMOFF EVEN MORE OF A CONCERN.

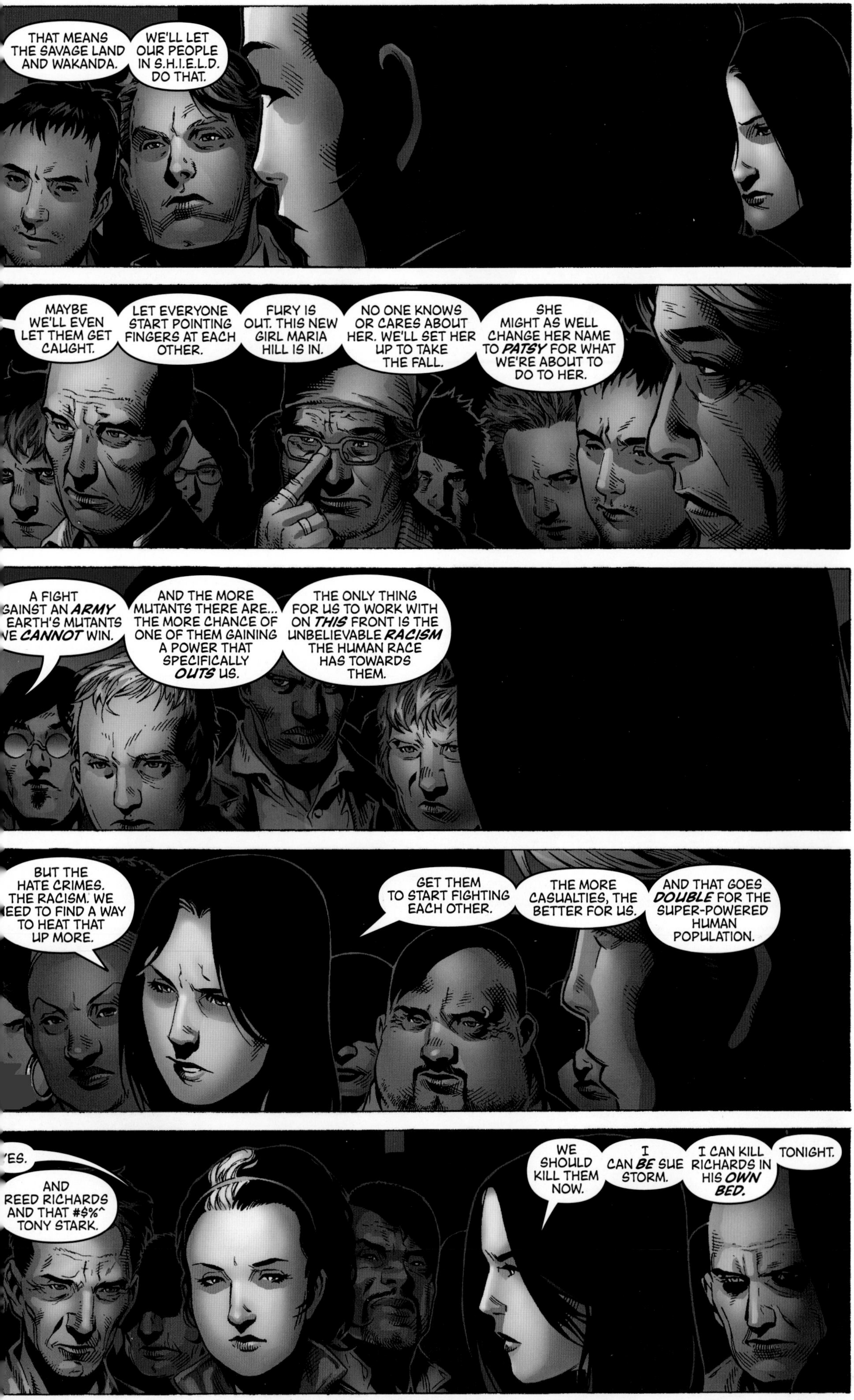
THAT MEANS THE SAVAGE LAND AND WAKANDA.
WE'LL LET OUR PEOPLE IN S.H.I.E.L.D. DO THAT.
MAYBE WE'LL EVEN LET THEM GET CAUGHT.
LET EVERYONE START POINTING FINGERS AT EACH OTHER.
FURY IS OUT. THIS NEW GIRL MARIA HILL IS IN.
NO ONE KNOWS OR CARES ABOUT HER. WE'LL SET HER UP TO TAKE THE FALL.
SHE MIGHT AS WELL CHANGE HER NAME TO PATSY FOR WHAT WE'RE ABOUT TO DO TO HER.
A FIGHT GAINST AN ARMY EARTH'S MUTANTS VE CANNOT WIN.
AND THE MORE MUTANTS THERE ARE... THE MORE CHANCE OF ONE OF THEM GAINING A POWER THAT SPECIFICALLY OUTS US.
THE ONLY THING FOR US TO WORK WITH ON THIS FRONT IS THE UNBELIEVABLE RACISM THE HUMAN RACE HAS TOWARDS THEM.
BUT THE HATE CRIMES. THE RACISM. WE EED TO FIND A WAY TO HEAT THAT UP MORE.
GET THEM TO START FIGHTING EACH OTHER.
THE MORE CASUALTIES, THE BETTER FOR US.
AND THAT GOES DOUBLE FOR THE SUPER-POWERED HUMAN POPULATION.
YES.
AND REED RICHARDS AND THAT #$%^ TONY STARK.
WE SHOULD KILL THEM NOW.
I CAN BE SUE STORM.
I CAN KILL RICHARDS IN HIS OWN BED.
TONIGHT.

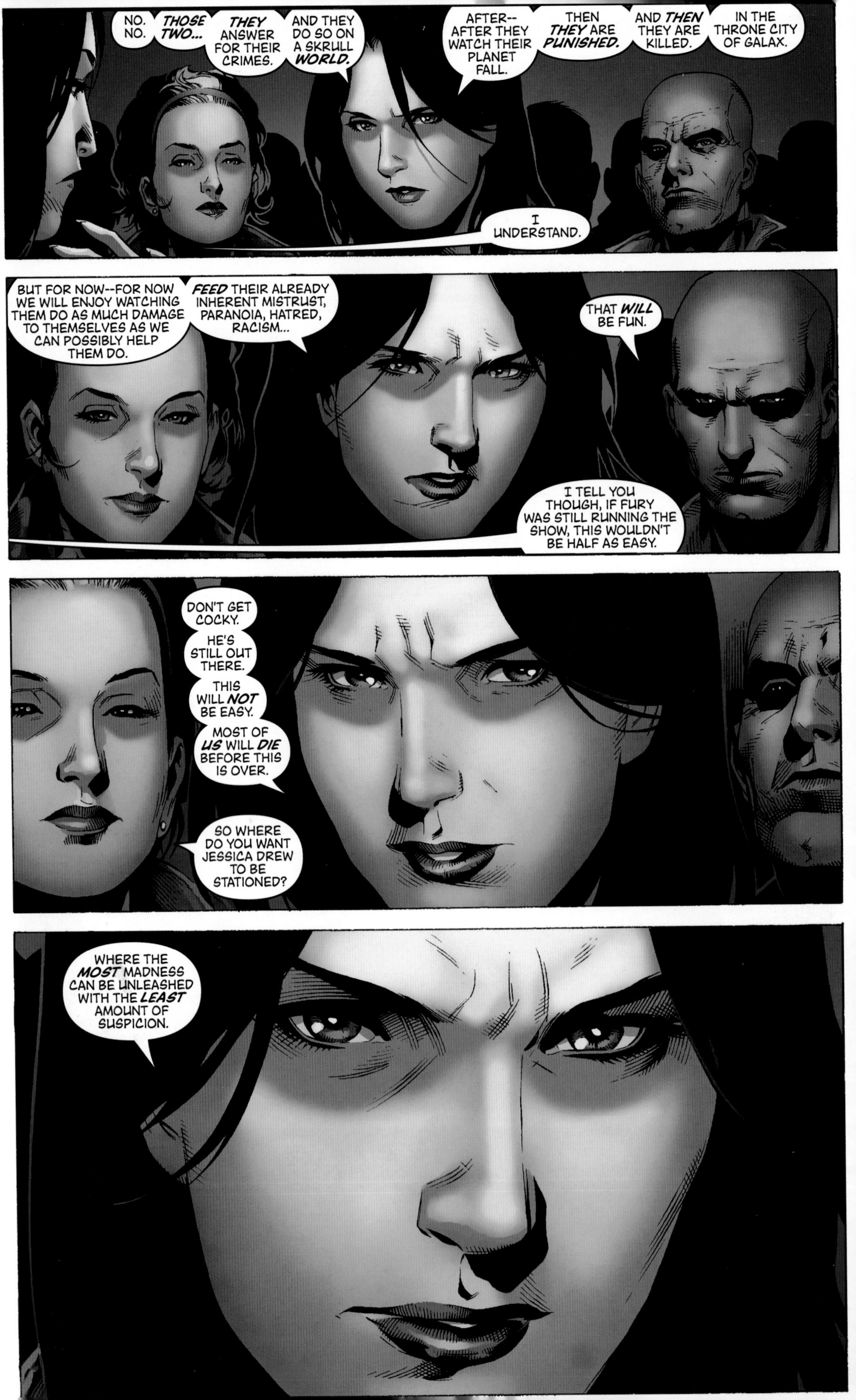
NO. NO.
THOSE TWO...
THEY ANSWER FOR THEIR CRIMES.
AND THEY DO SO ON A SKRULL WORLD.
AFTER-- AFTER THEY WATCH THEIR PLANET FALL.
THEN THEY ARE PUNISHED.
AND THEN THEY ARE KILLED.
IN THE THRONE CITY OF GALAX.
I UNDERSTAND.
BUT FOR NOW--FOR NOW WE WILL ENJOY WATCHING THEM DO AS MUCH DAMAGE TO THEMSELVES AS WE CAN POSSIBLY HELP THEM DO.
FEED THEIR ALREADY INHERENT MISTRUST, PARANOIA, HATRED, RACISM...
THAT WILL BE FUN.
I TELL YOU THOUGH, IF FURY WAS STILL RUNNING THE SHOW, THIS WOULDN'T BE HALF AS EASY.
DON'T GET COCKY.
HE'S STILL OUT THERE.
THIS WILL NOT BE EASY.
MOST OF US WILL DIE BEFORE THIS IS OVER.
SO WHERE DO YOU WANT JESSICA DREW TO BE STATIONED?
WHERE THE MOST MADNESS CAN BE UNLEASHED WITH THE LEAST AMOUNT OF SUSPICION.

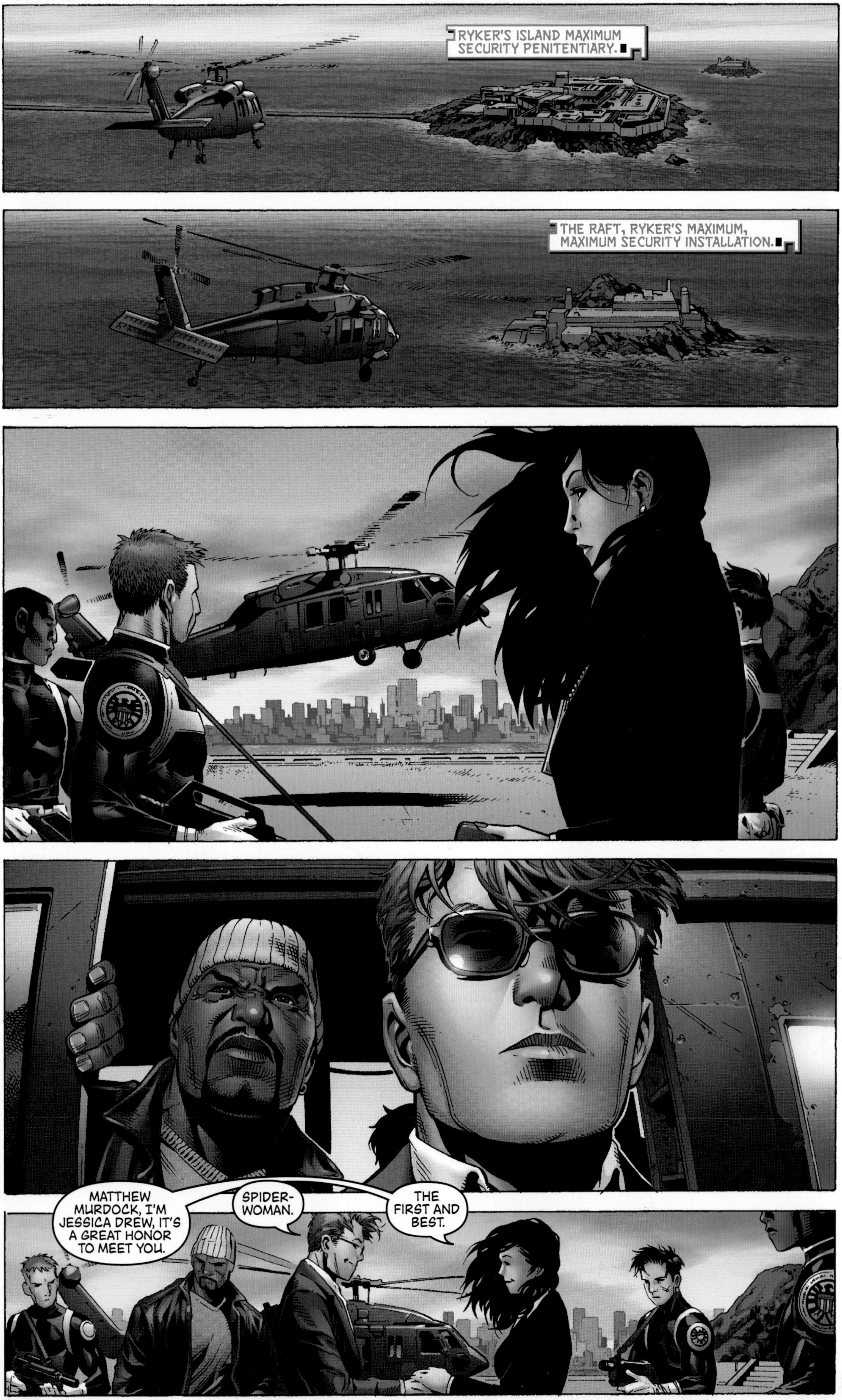
RYKER'S ISLAND MAXIMUM SECURITY PENITENTIARY.
THE RAFT, RYKER'S MAXIMUM, MAXIMUM SECURITY INSTALLATION.
MATTHEW MURDOCK, I'M JESSICA DREW, IT'S A GREAT HONOR TO MEET YOU.
SPIDER-WOMAN.
THE FIRST AND BEST.

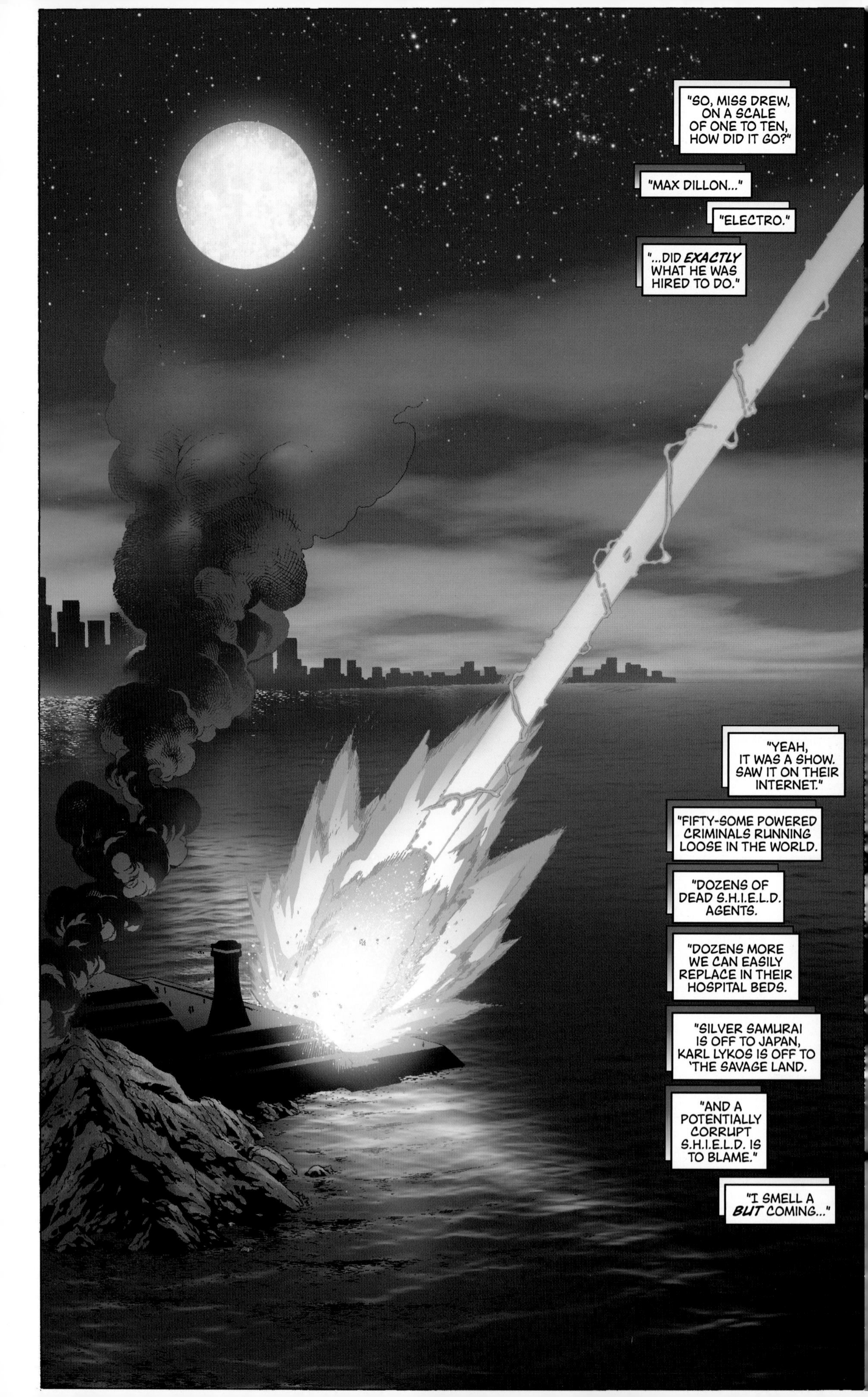
"SO, MISS DREW, ON A SCALE OF ONE TO TEN, HOW DID IT GO?"
"MAX DILLON..."
"ELECTRO."
"...DID *EXACTLY* WHAT HE WAS HIRED TO DO."
"YEAH, IT WAS A SHOW. SAW IT ON THEIR INTERNET."
"FIFTY-SOME POWERED CRIMINALS RUNNING LOOSE IN THE WORLD.
"DOZENS OF DEAD S.H.I.E.L.D. AGENTS.
"DOZENS MORE WE CAN EASILY REPLACE IN THEIR HOSPITAL BEDS.
"SILVER SAMURAI IS OFF TO JAPAN, KARL LYKOS IS OFF TO 'THE SAVAGE LAND.
"AND A POTENTIALLY CORRUPT S.H.I.E.L.D. IS TO BLAME."
"I SMELL A *BUT* COMING..."

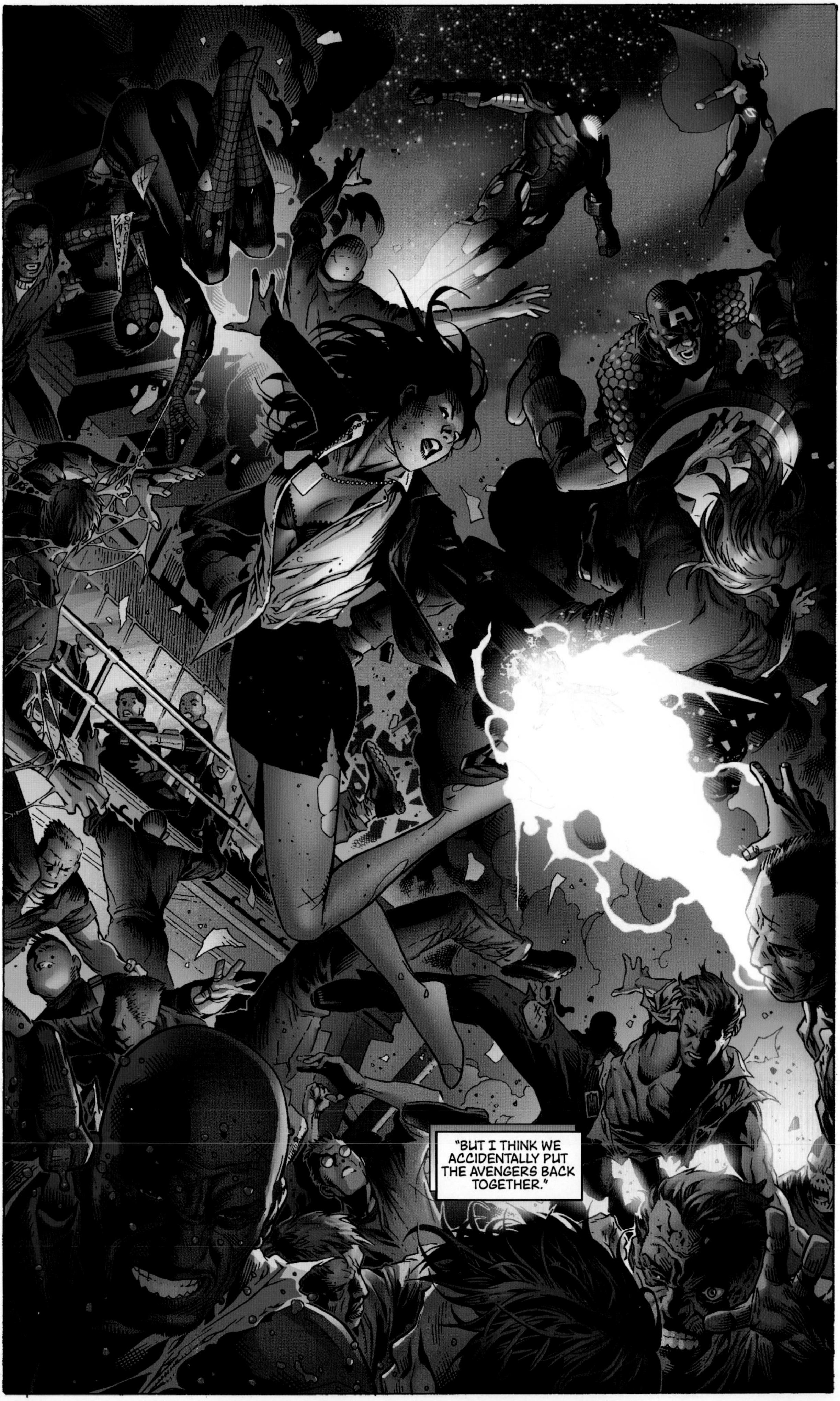
"BUT I THINK WE ACCIDENTALLY PUT THE AVENGERS BACK TOGETHER."

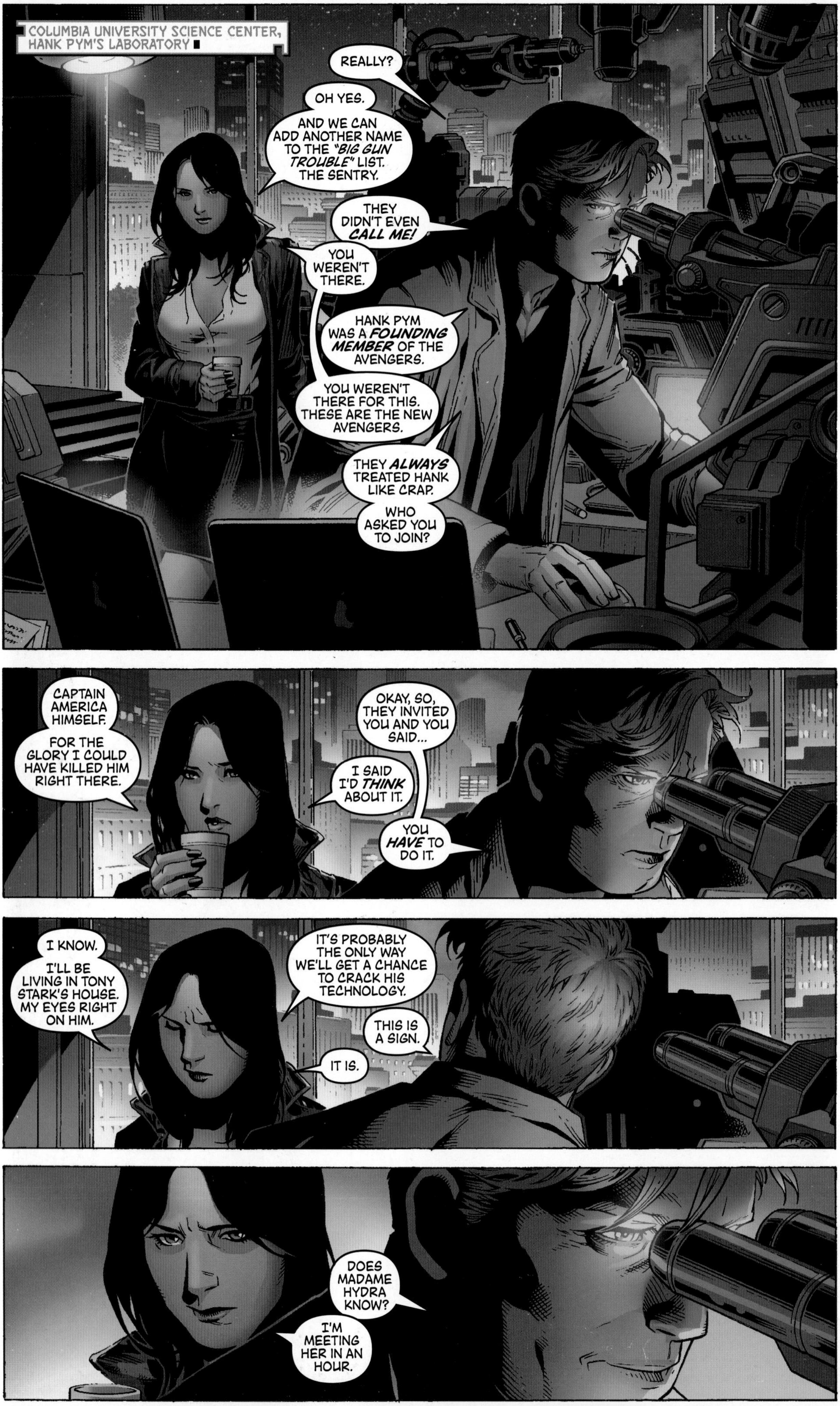
COLUMBIA UNIVERSITY SCIENCE CENTER, HANK PYM'S LABORATORY
REALLY?
OH YES.
AND WE CAN ADD ANOTHER NAME TO THE "BIG GUN TROUBLE" LIST. THE SENTRY.
THEY DIDN'T EVEN CALL ME!
YOU WEREN'T THERE.
HANK PYM WAS A FOUNDING MEMBER OF THE AVENGERS.
YOU WEREN'T THERE FOR THIS. THESE ARE THE NEW AVENGERS.
THEY ALWAYS TREATED HANK LIKE CRAP.
WHO ASKED YOU TO JOIN?
CAPTAIN AMERICA HIMSELF.
FOR THE GLORY I COULD HAVE KILLED HIM RIGHT THERE.
OKAY, SO, THEY INVITED YOU AND YOU SAID...
I SAID I'D THINK ABOUT IT.
YOU HAVE TO DO IT.
I KNOW.
I'LL BE LIVING IN TONY STARK'S HOUSE. MY EYES RIGHT ON HIM.
IT'S PROBABLY THE ONLY WAY WE'LL GET A CHANCE TO CRACK HIS TECHNOLOGY.
THIS IS A SIGN.
IT IS.
DOES MADAME HYDRA KNOW?
I'M MEETING HER IN AN HOUR.

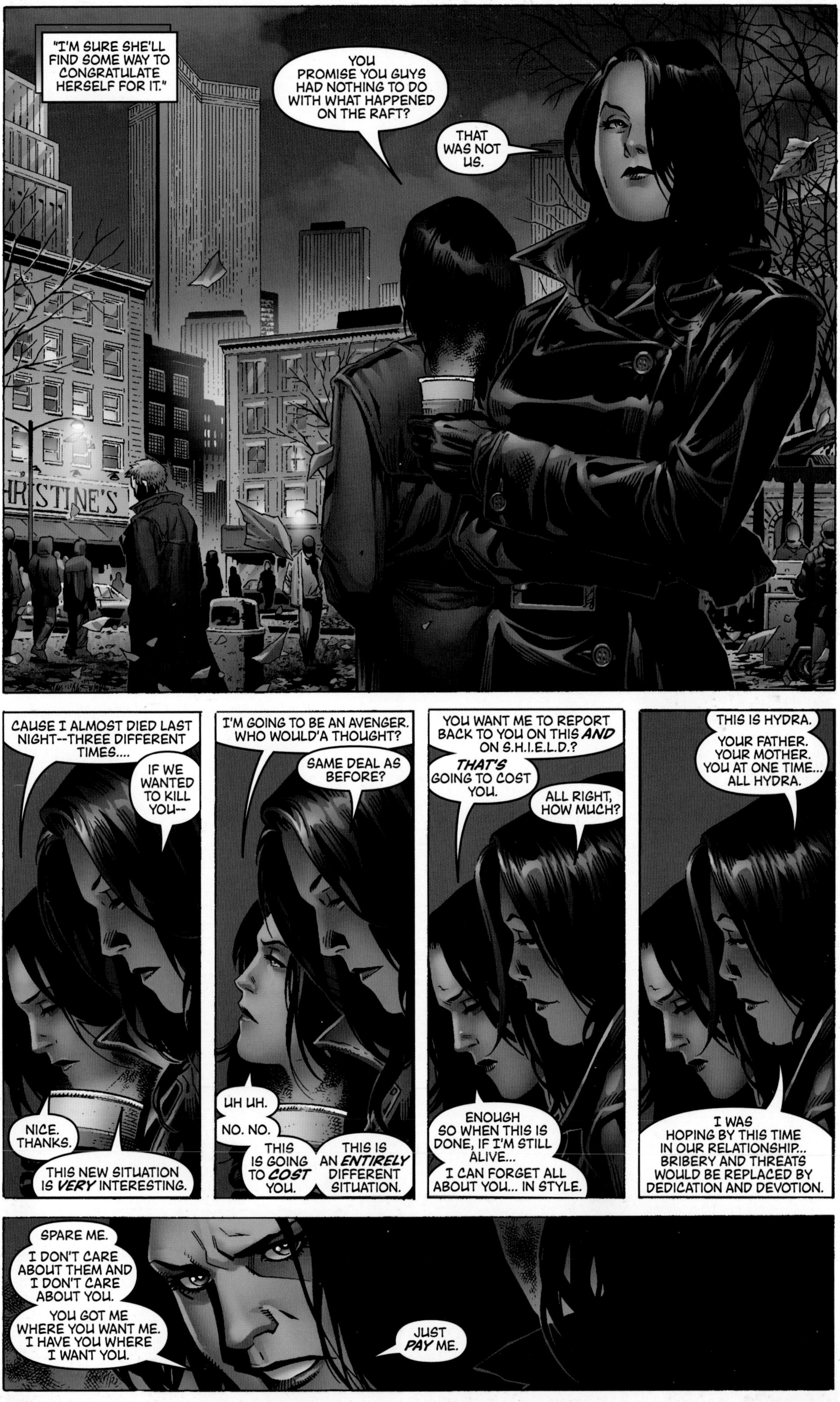
"I'M SURE SHE'LL FIND SOME WAY TO CONGRATULATE HERSELF FOR IT."
YOU PROMISE YOU GUYS HAD NOTHING TO DO WITH WHAT HAPPENED ON THE RAFT?
THAT WAS NOT US.
RISTINE'S
CAUSE I ALMOST DIED LAST NIGHT--THREE DIFFERENT TIMES....
IF WE WANTED TO KILL YOU--
NICE. THANKS.
THIS NEW SITUATION IS *VERY* INTERESTING.
I'M GOING TO BE AN AVENGER. WHO WOULD'A THOUGHT?
SAME DEAL AS BEFORE?
UH UH.
NO. NO.
THIS IS GOING TO *COST* YOU.
THIS IS AN *ENTIRELY* DIFFERENT SITUATION.
YOU WANT ME TO REPORT BACK TO YOU ON THIS *AND* ON S.H.I.E.L.D.?
THAT'S GOING TO COST YOU.
ALL RIGHT, HOW MUCH?
ENOUGH SO WHEN THIS IS DONE, IF I'M STILL ALIVE...
I CAN FORGET ALL ABOUT YOU... IN STYLE.
THIS IS HYDRA.
YOUR FATHER. YOUR MOTHER. YOU AT ONE TIME... ALL HYDRA.
I WAS HOPING BY THIS TIME IN OUR RELATIONSHIP... BRIBERY AND THREATS WOULD BE REPLACED BY DEDICATION AND DEVOTION.
SPARE ME.
I DON'T CARE ABOUT THEM AND I DON'T CARE ABOUT YOU.
YOU GOT ME WHERE YOU WANT ME. I HAVE YOU WHERE I WANT YOU.
JUST *PAY* ME.

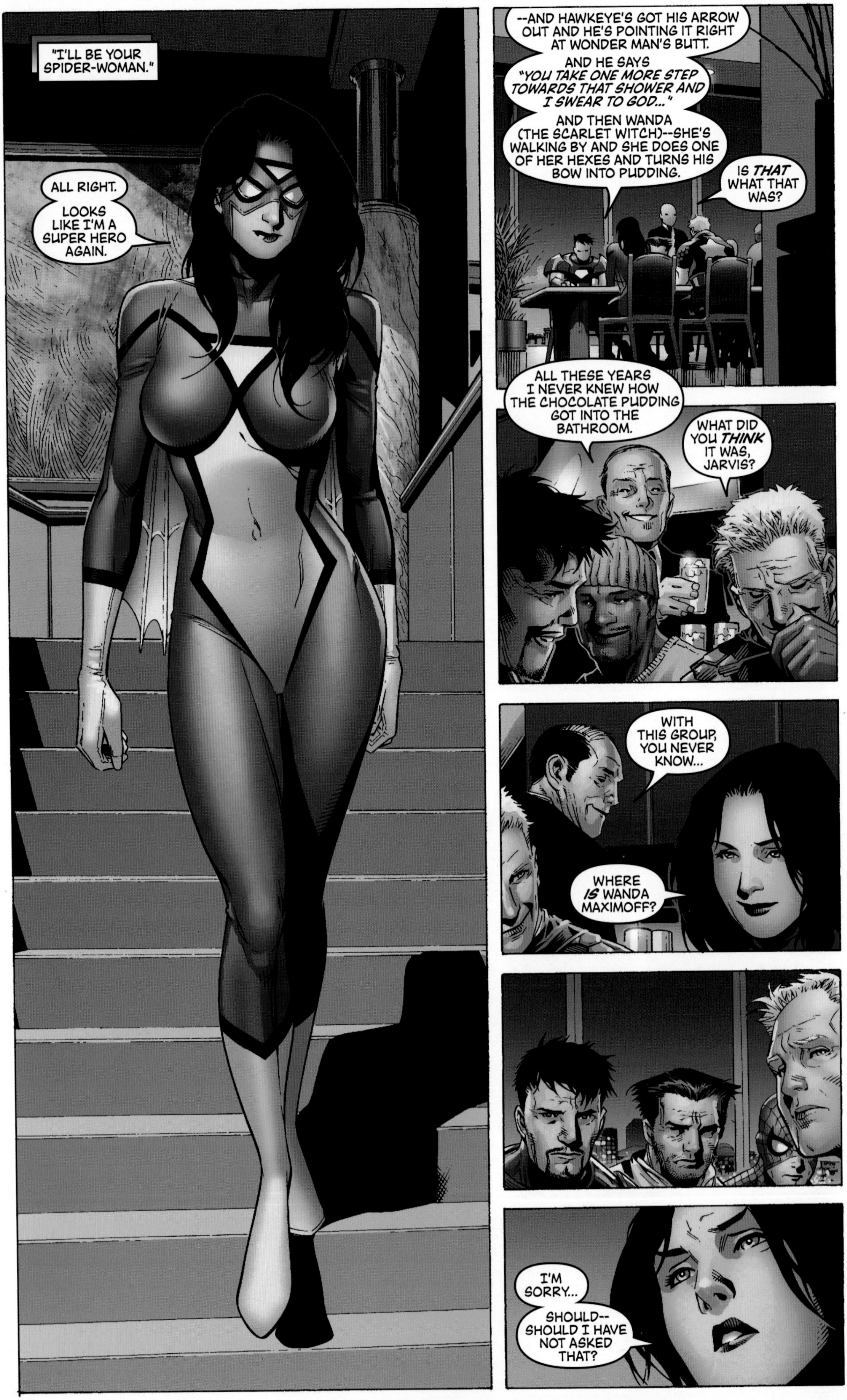
"I'LL BE YOUR SPIDER-WOMAN."
ALL RIGHT.
LOOKS LIKE I'M A SUPER HERO AGAIN.
--AND HAWKEYE'S GOT HIS ARROW OUT AND HE'S POINTING IT RIGHT AT WONDER MAN'S BUTT.
AND HE SAYS "YOU TAKE ONE MORE STEP TOWARDS THAT SHOWER AND I SWEAR TO GOD..."
AND THEN WANDA (THE SCARLET WITCH)--SHE'S WALKING BY AND SHE DOES ONE OF HER HEXES AND TURNS HIS BOW INTO PUDDING.
IS THAT WHAT THAT WAS?
ALL THESE YEARS I NEVER KNEW HOW THE CHOCOLATE PUDDING GOT INTO THE BATHROOM.
WHAT DID YOU THINK IT WAS, JARVIS?
WITH THIS GROUP, YOU NEVER KNOW...
WHERE IS WANDA MAXIMOFF?
I'M SORRY...
SHOULD--SHOULD I HAVE NOT ASKED THAT?

SHE, UM, SHE HAD A BREAK-DOWN.

THAT DAY AT THE MANSION. WHEN IT ALL WENT TO HELL... THAT WAS HER.

THAT WAS *HER?*

OH MAN.

WELL, WHEN YOUR FATHER'S MAGNETO...

SHE'S NOT A BAD PERSON, LOGAN, SHE'S A *SICK* PERSON.

SORRY I--

YEAH, WITH A TERRORIST FOR A DAD, STARK. I'M SURE IT DOES A NUMBER ON A KID.

IT'S OKAY. YOU DIDN'T KNOW.

I HOPE SO. SHE'S WITH HER FAMILY NOW.

IS SHE OKAY?

SHE'S WITH *MAGNETO?*

IT'S HER FAMILY.

WELL, I'M SURE AIN'T NOTHING BAD WILL COME A THAT.

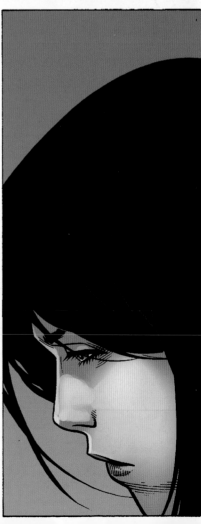

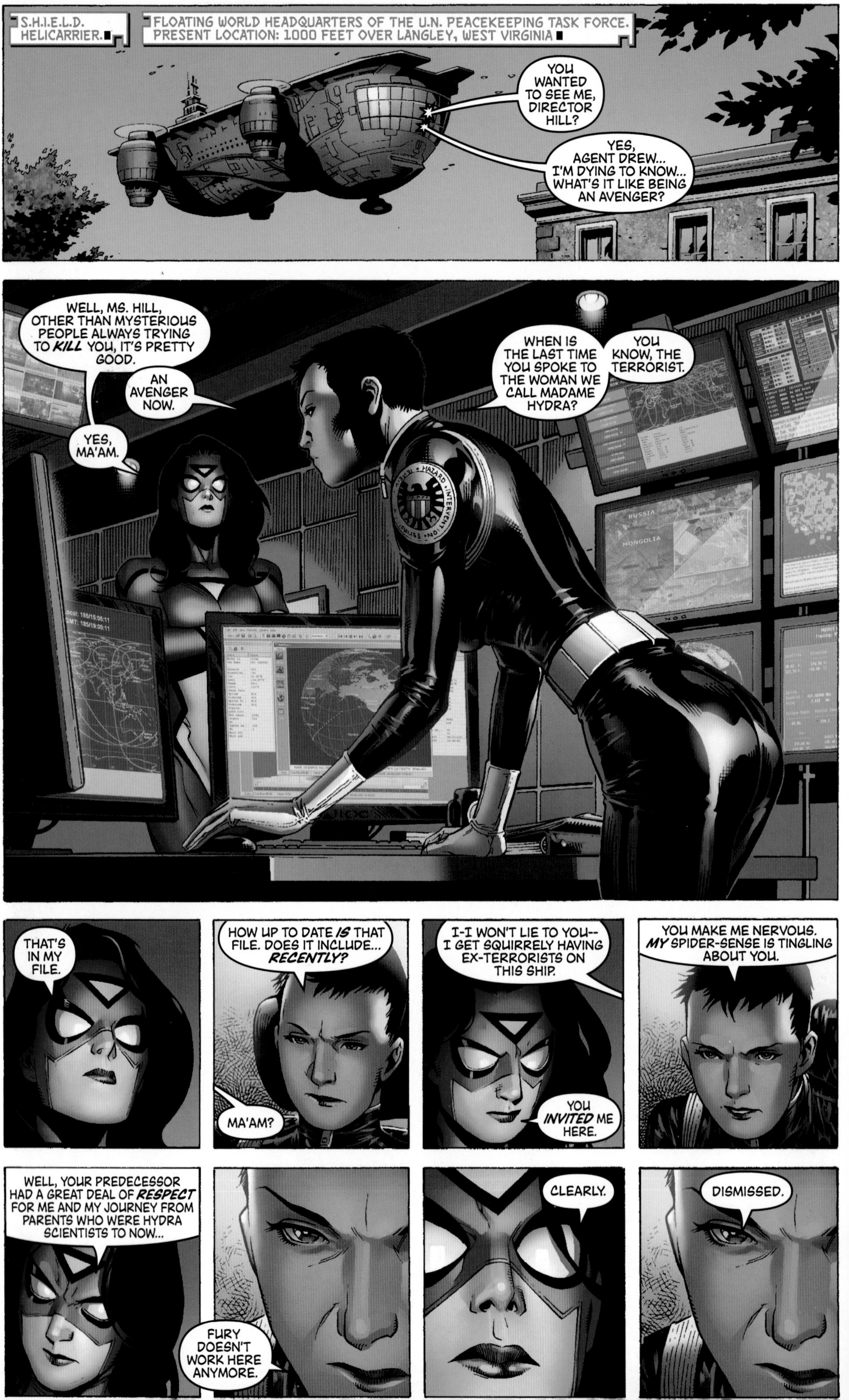
S.H.I.E.L.D. HELICARRIER.
FLOATING WORLD HEADQUARTERS OF THE U.N. PEACEKEEPING TASK FORCE. PRESENT LOCATION: 1000 FEET OVER LANGLEY, WEST VIRGINIA
YOU WANTED TO SEE ME, DIRECTOR HILL?
YES, AGENT DREW... I'M DYING TO KNOW... WHAT'S IT LIKE BEING AN AVENGER?
WELL, MS. HILL, OTHER THAN MYSTERIOUS PEOPLE ALWAYS TRYING TO KILL YOU, IT'S PRETTY GOOD.
AN AVENGER NOW.
YES, MA'AM.
WHEN IS THE LAST TIME YOU SPOKE TO THE WOMAN WE CALL MADAME HYDRA?
YOU KNOW, THE TERRORIST.
THAT'S IN MY FILE.
HOW UP TO DATE IS THAT FILE. DOES IT INCLUDE... RECENTLY?
MA'AM?
I-I WON'T LIE TO YOU-- I GET SQUIRRELY HAVING EX-TERRORISTS ON THIS SHIP.
YOU INVITED ME HERE.
YOU MAKE ME NERVOUS. MY SPIDER-SENSE IS TINGLING ABOUT YOU.
WELL, YOUR PREDECESSOR HAD A GREAT DEAL OF RESPECT FOR ME AND MY JOURNEY FROM PARENTS WHO WERE HYDRA SCIENTISTS TO NOW...
FURY DOESN'T WORK HERE ANYMORE.
CLEARLY.
DISMISSED.

IS THERE ANYTHING I CAN DO TO MAKE YOU, LET'S SAY, *LESS* SUSPICIOUS OF ME?

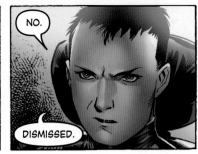

NO.

DISMISSED.

YOU KNOW...

I BET A LOT MORE PEOPLE DON'T TRUST *YOU* THAN DON'T TRUST *ME.*

IN FACT, I'D BE A WHOLE LOT MORE WORRIED BY THE FACT THAT MOST OF THIS SHIP AND MOST OF S.H.I.E.L.D. AND THOSE RENEGADE AGENTS WE FOUND IN THE SAVAGE LAND...

...HATE YOUR GUTS.

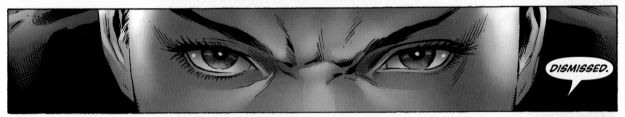

DISMISSED.

MAYBE YOU SHOULD TRY WEARING AN EYEPATCH.

GLEE GLEE

YES.

WHY AREN'T YOU HERE?

WHERE ARE YOU?

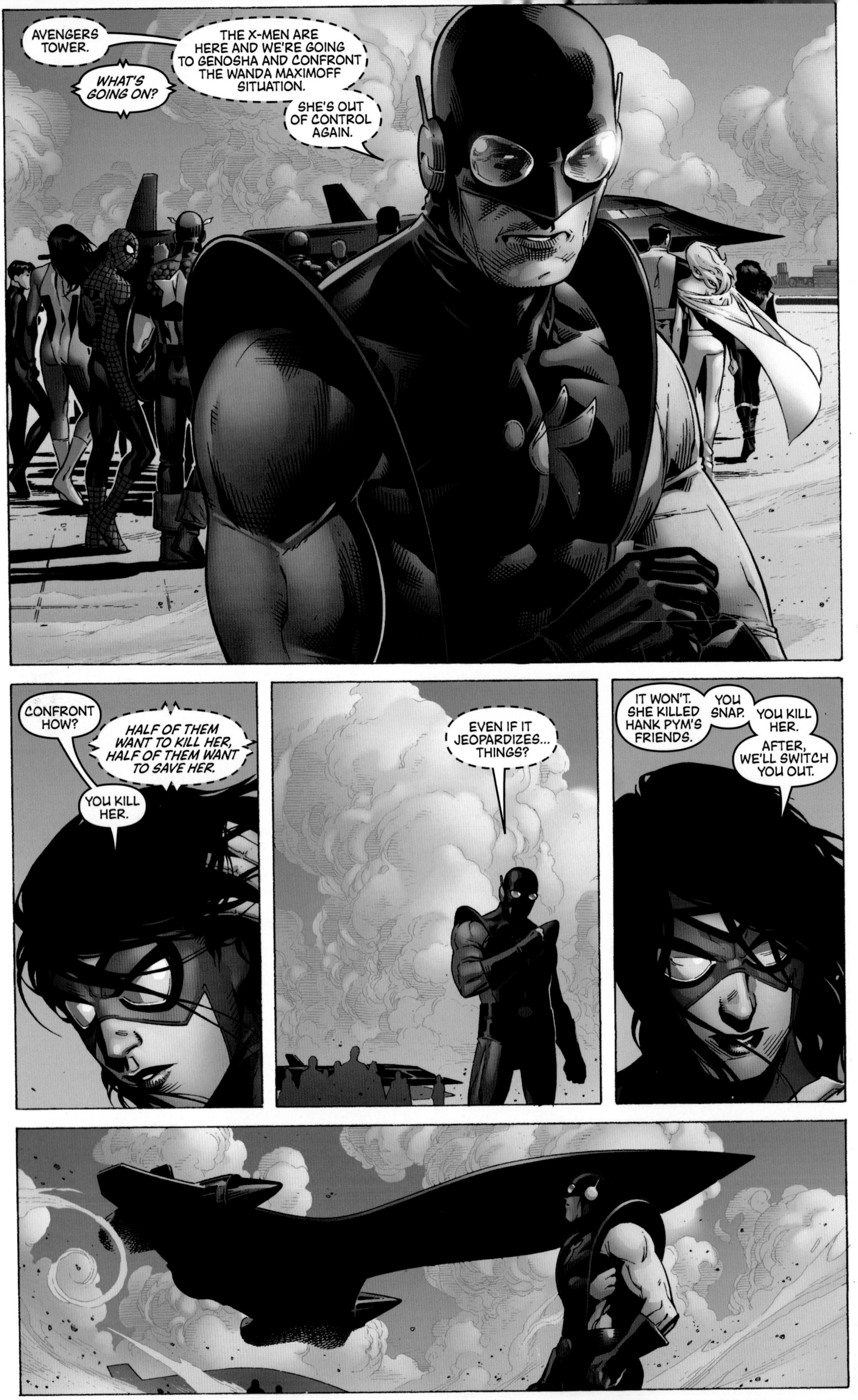
AVENGERS TOWER.
WHAT'S GOING ON?
THE X-MEN ARE HERE AND WE'RE GOING TO GENOSHA AND CONFRONT THE WANDA MAXIMOFF SITUATION.
SHE'S OUT OF CONTROL AGAIN.
CONFRONT HOW?
HALF OF THEM WANT TO KILL HER, HALF OF THEM WANT TO SAVE HER.
YOU KILL HER.
EVEN IF IT JEOPARDIZES... THINGS?
IT WON'T. SHE KILLED HANK PYM'S FRIENDS.
YOU SNAP.
YOU KILL HER.
AFTER, WE'LL SWITCH YOU OUT.

GENOSHA. HOURS LATER.

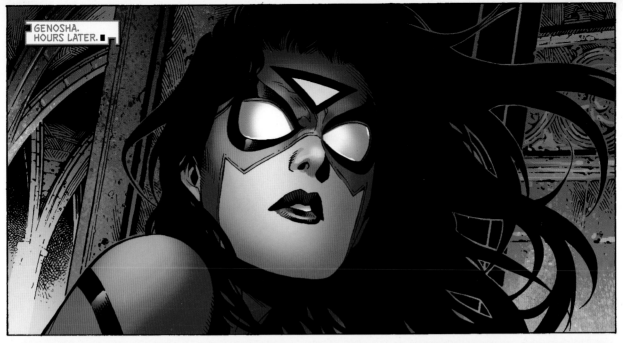

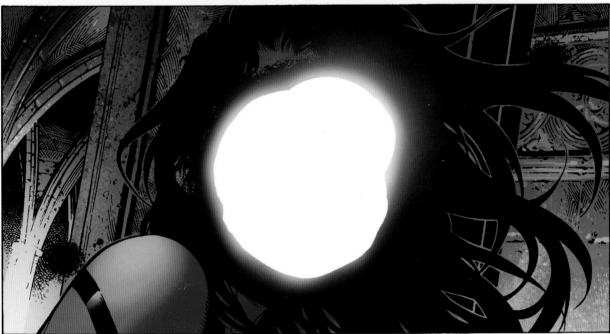

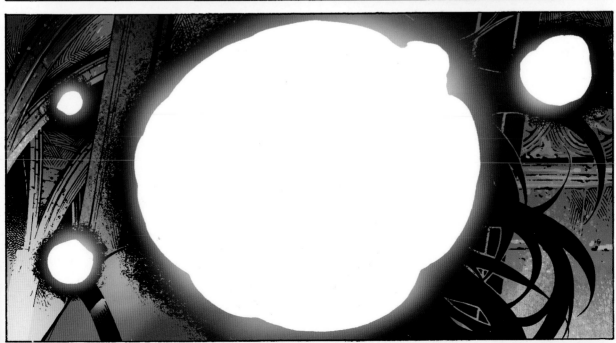

#43

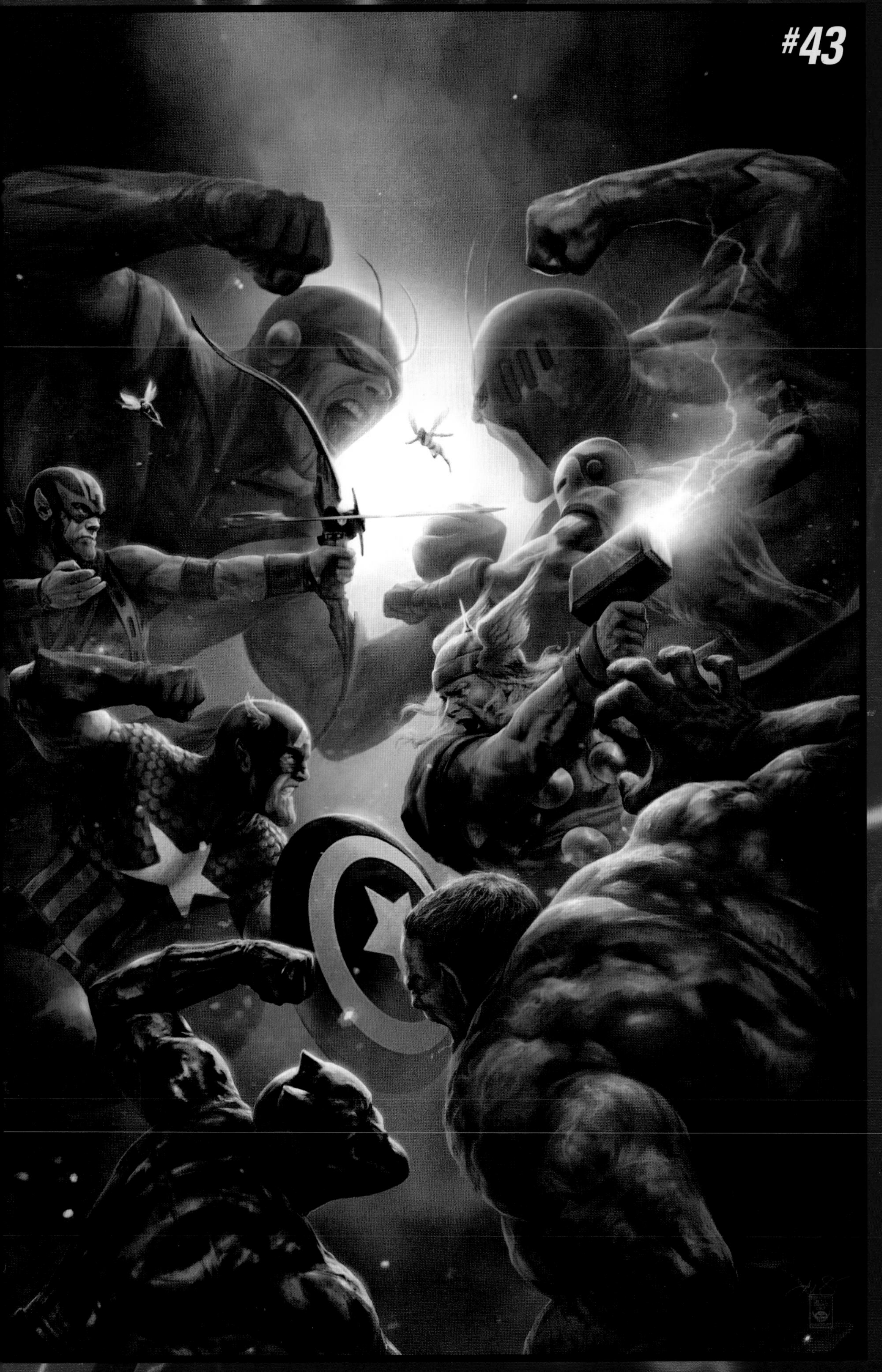

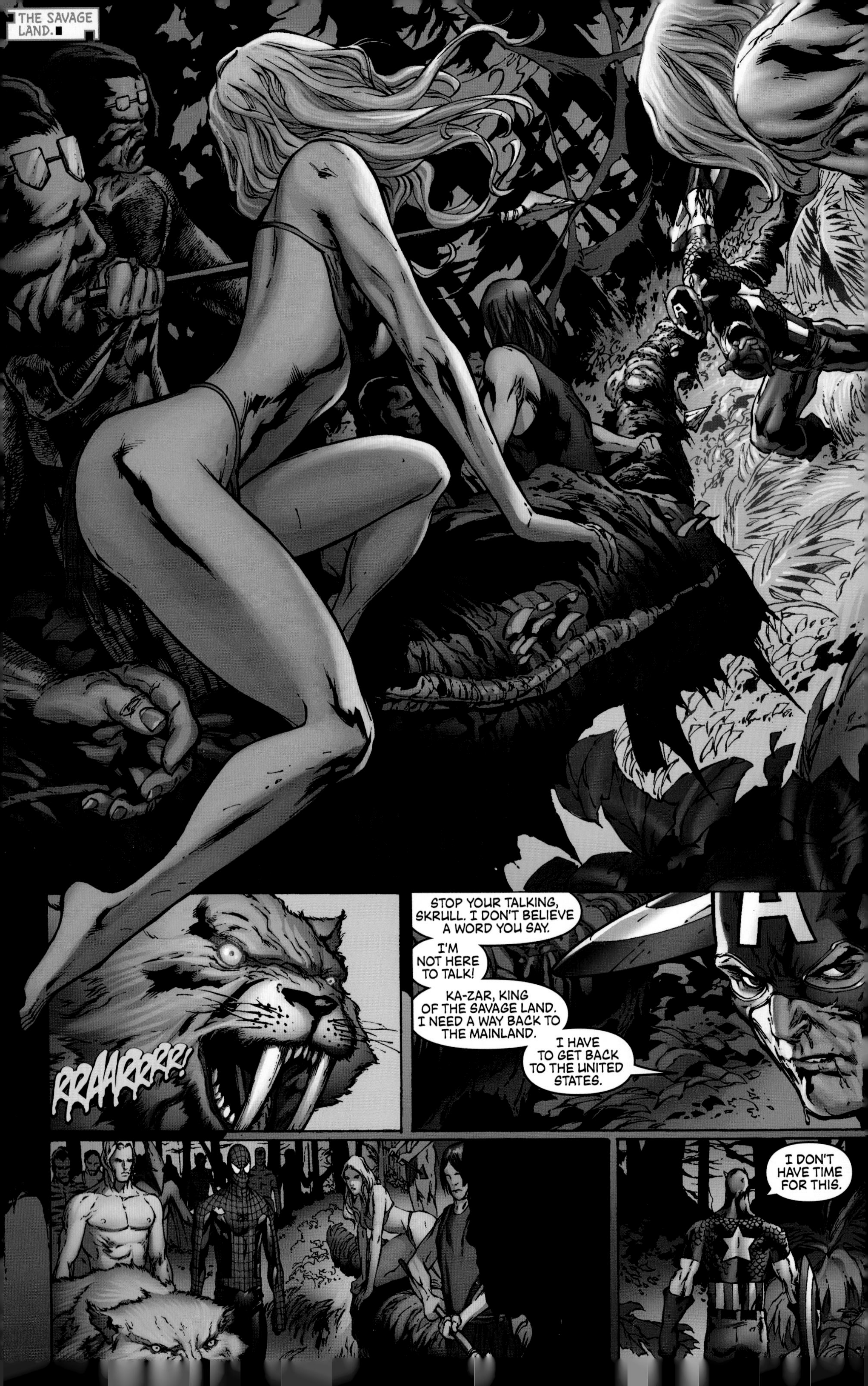
THE SAVAGE LAND.
RRAARRRR!
STOP YOUR TALKING, SKRULL. I DON'T BELIEVE A WORD YOU SAY.
I'M NOT HERE TO TALK!
KA-ZAR, KING OF THE SAVAGE LAND. I NEED A WAY BACK TO THE MAINLAND.
I HAVE TO GET BACK TO THE UNITED STATES.
I DON'T HAVE TIME FOR THIS.

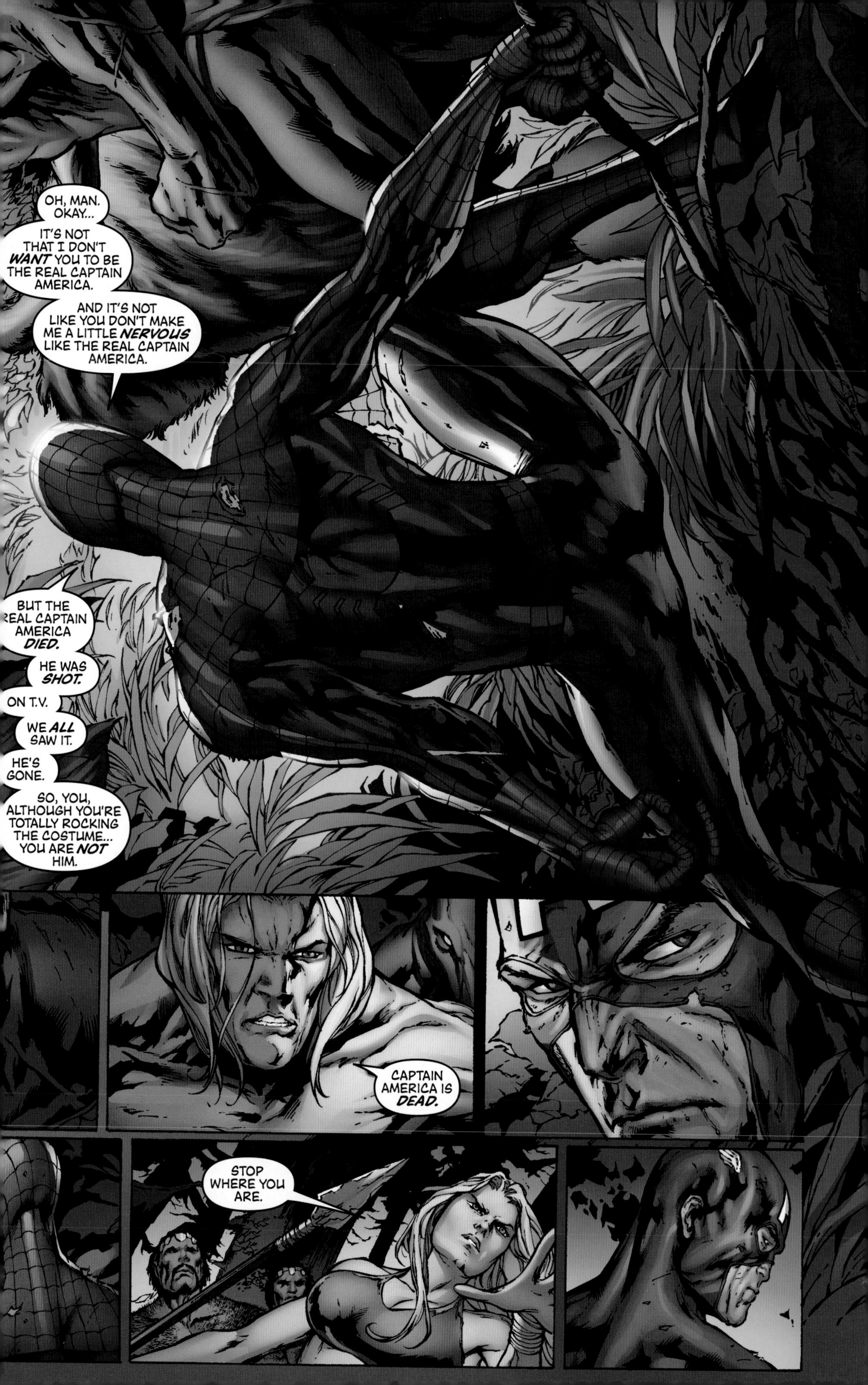

OH, MAN. OKAY...
IT'S NOT THAT I DON'T *WANT* YOU TO BE THE REAL CAPTAIN AMERICA.
AND IT'S NOT LIKE YOU DON'T MAKE ME A LITTLE *NERVOUS* LIKE THE REAL CAPTAIN AMERICA.
BUT THE REAL CAPTAIN AMERICA *DIED.*
HE WAS *SHOT.*
ON T.V.
WE *ALL* SAW IT.
HE'S GONE.
SO, YOU, ALTHOUGH YOU'RE TOTALLY ROCKING THE COSTUME... YOU ARE *NOT* HIM.
CAPTAIN AMERICA IS *DEAD.*
STOP WHERE YOU ARE.

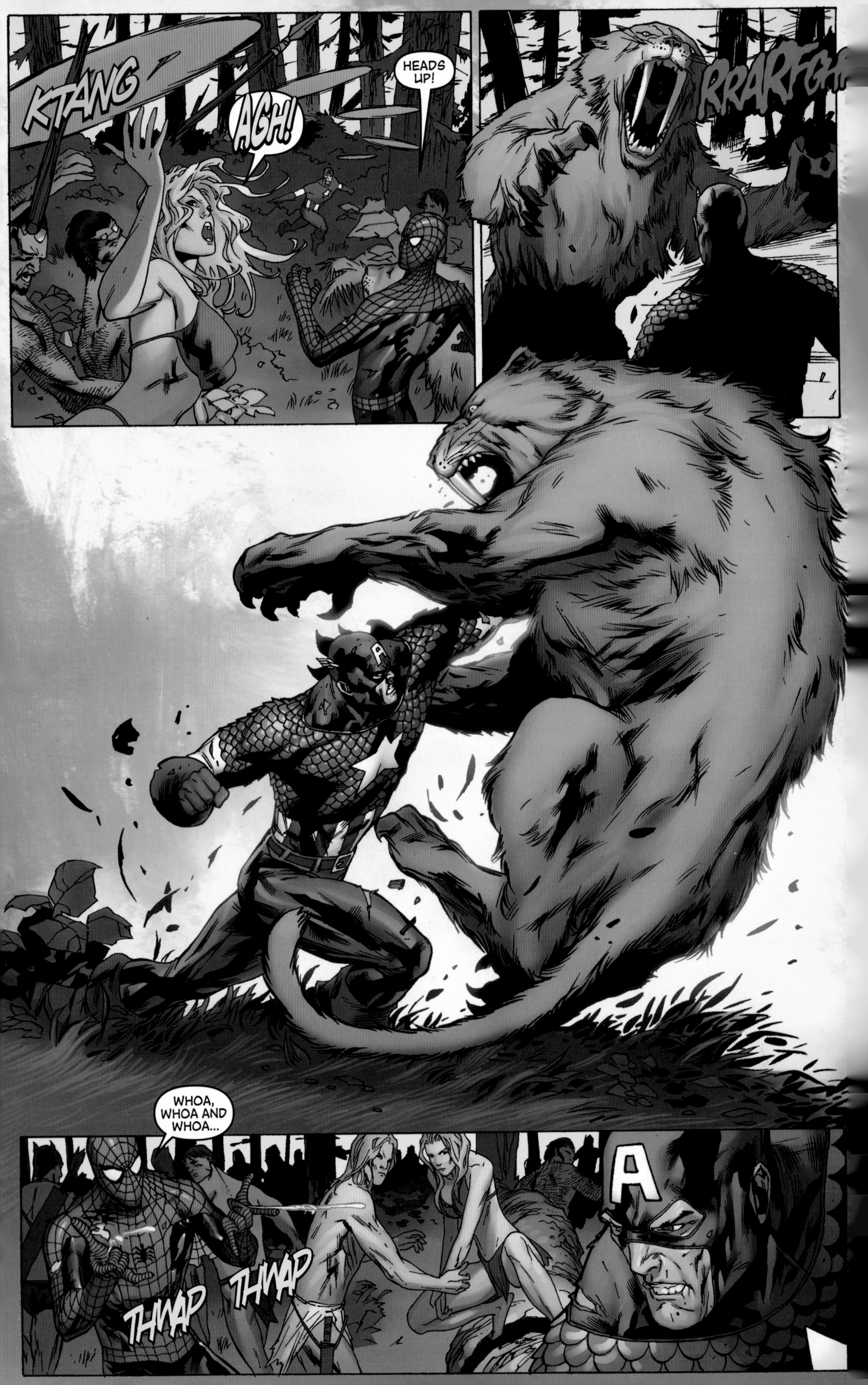
KTANG
AGH!
HEADS UP!
RRARFGH
WHOA, WHOA AND WHOA...
THWAP
THWAP

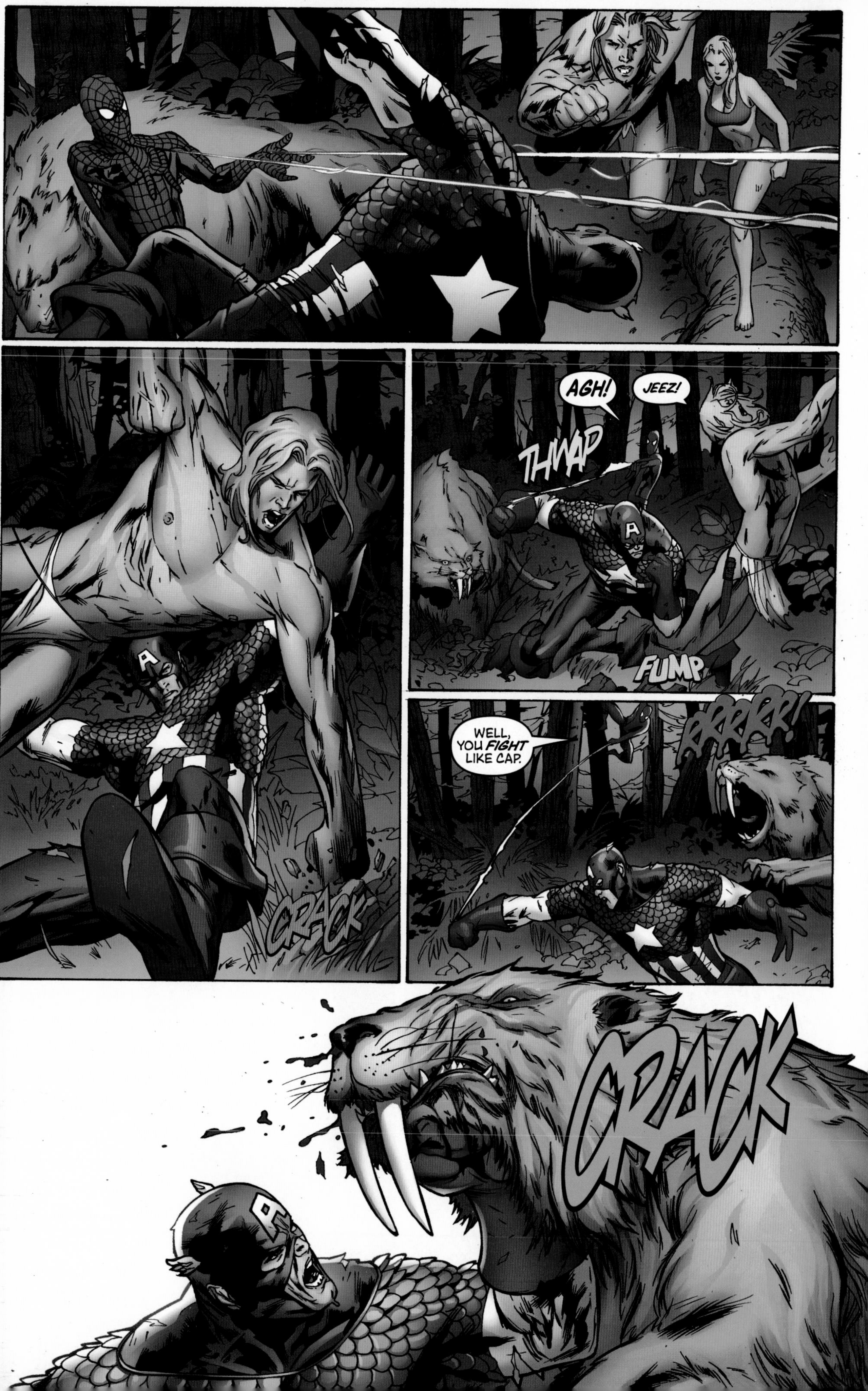
AGH!
JEEZ!
THWAP
FUMP
CRACK
WELL, YOU FIGHT LIKE CAP.
RRRRR!
CRACK

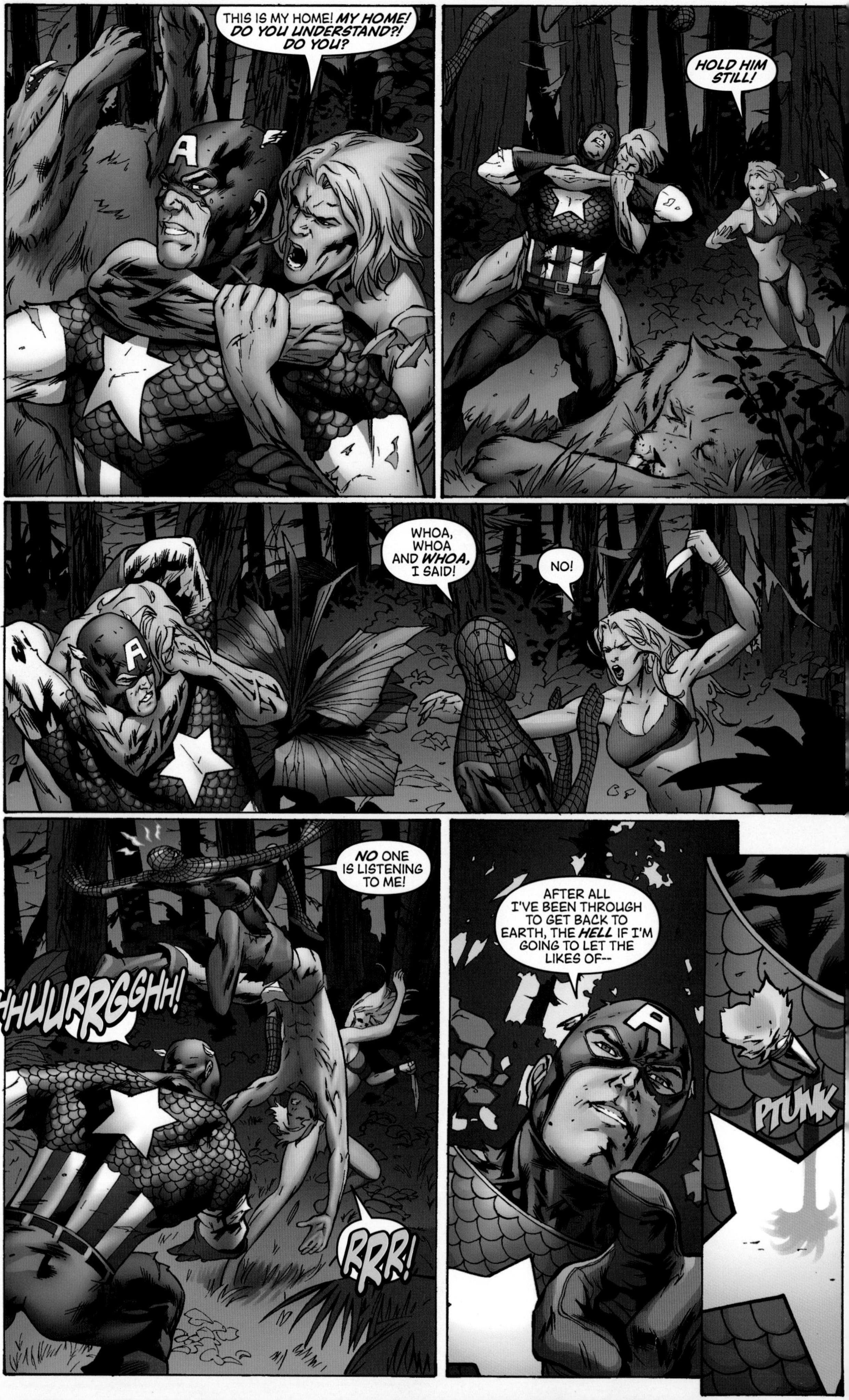
THIS IS MY HOME! MY HOME! DO YOU UNDERSTAND?! DO YOU?
HOLD HIM STILL!
WHOA, WHOA AND WHOA, I SAID!
NO!
NO ONE IS LISTENING TO ME!
HHUURRGGHH!
RRR!
AFTER ALL I'VE BEEN THROUGH TO GET BACK TO EARTH, THE HELL IF I'M GOING TO LET THE LIKES OF--
PTUNK

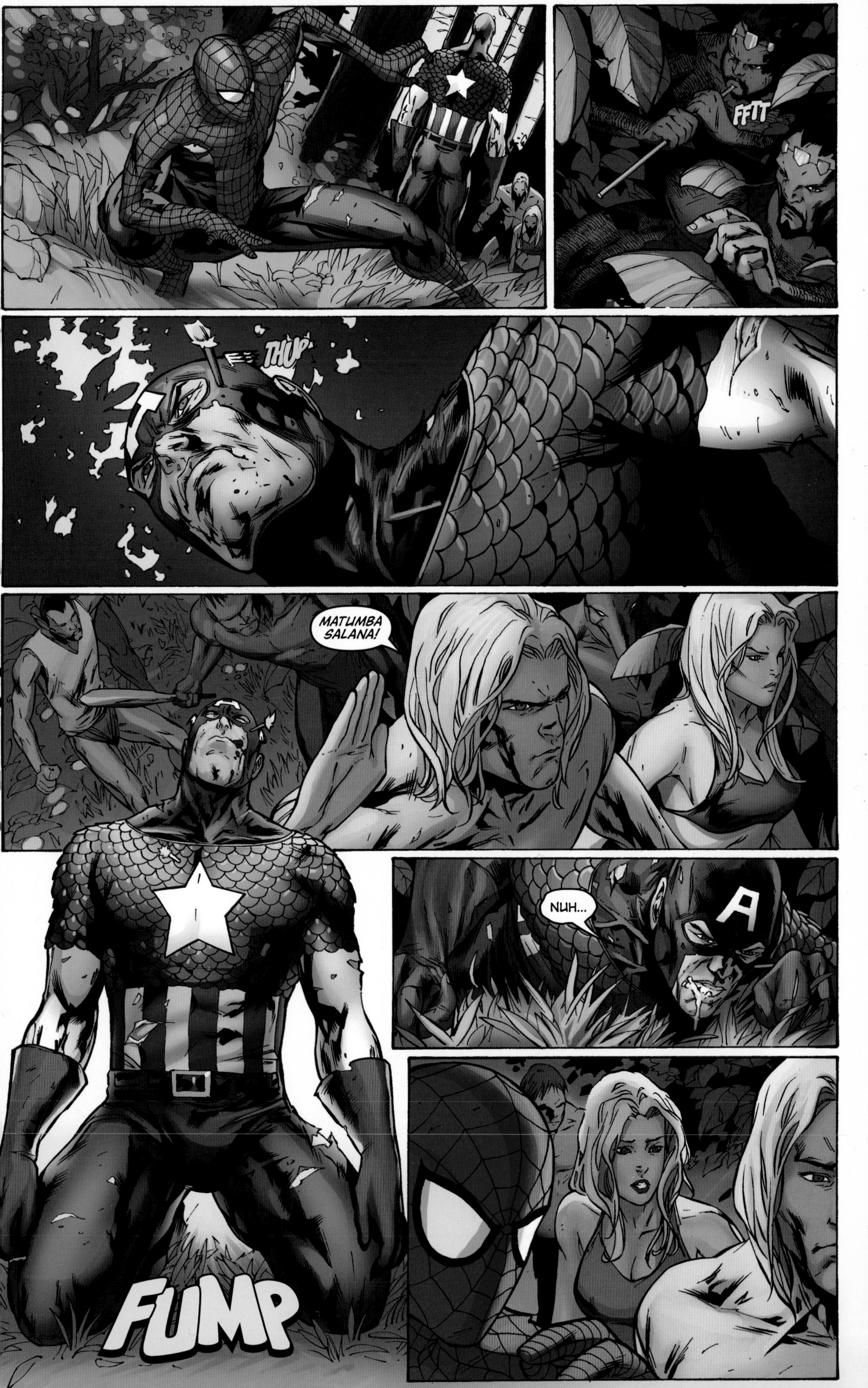
FFTT
THUP
MATUMBA SALANA!
NUH...
FUMP

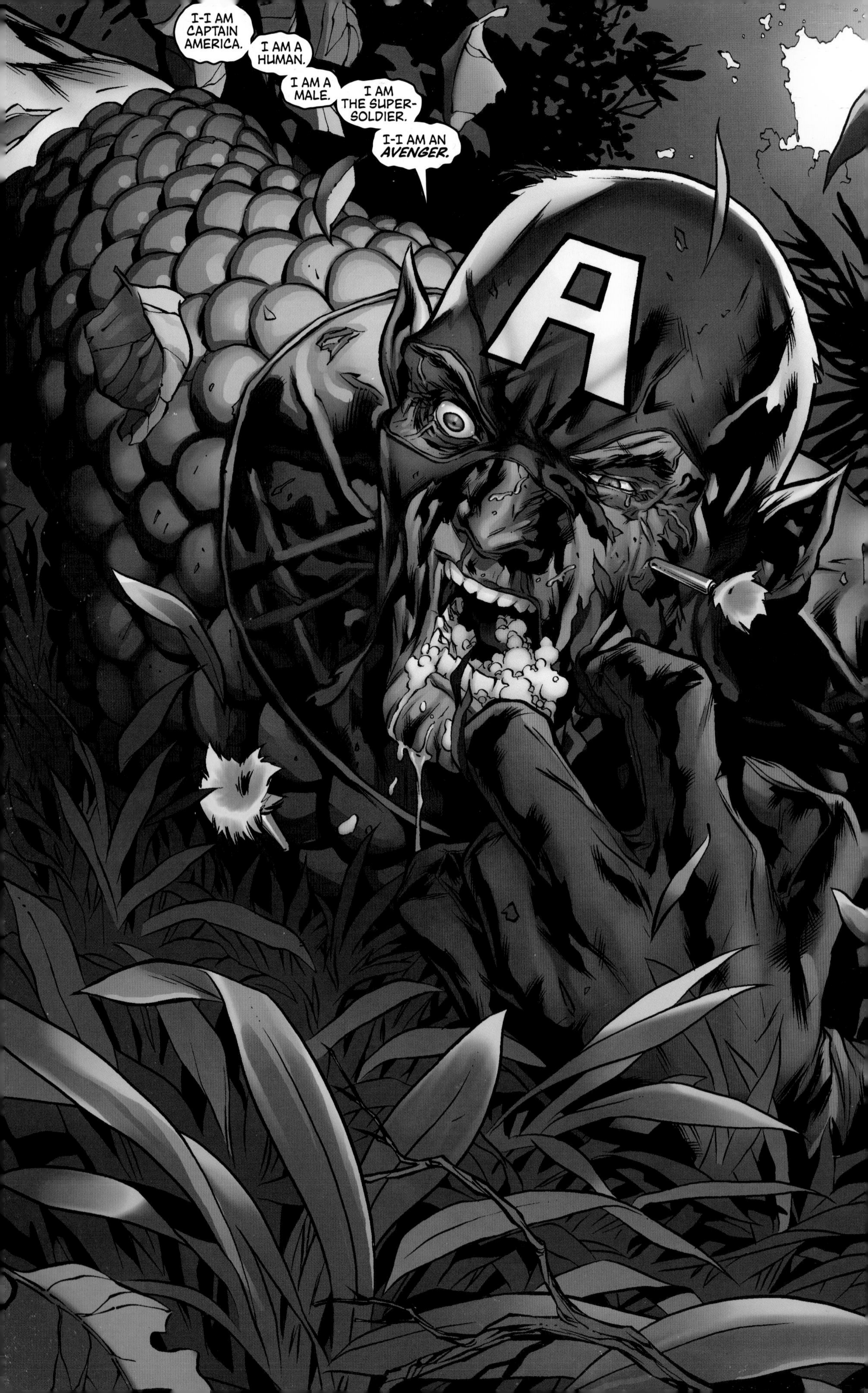
I-I AM CAPTAIN AMERICA.
I AM A HUMAN.
I AM A MALE.
I AM THE SUPER-SOLDIER.
I-I AM AN *AVENGER.*

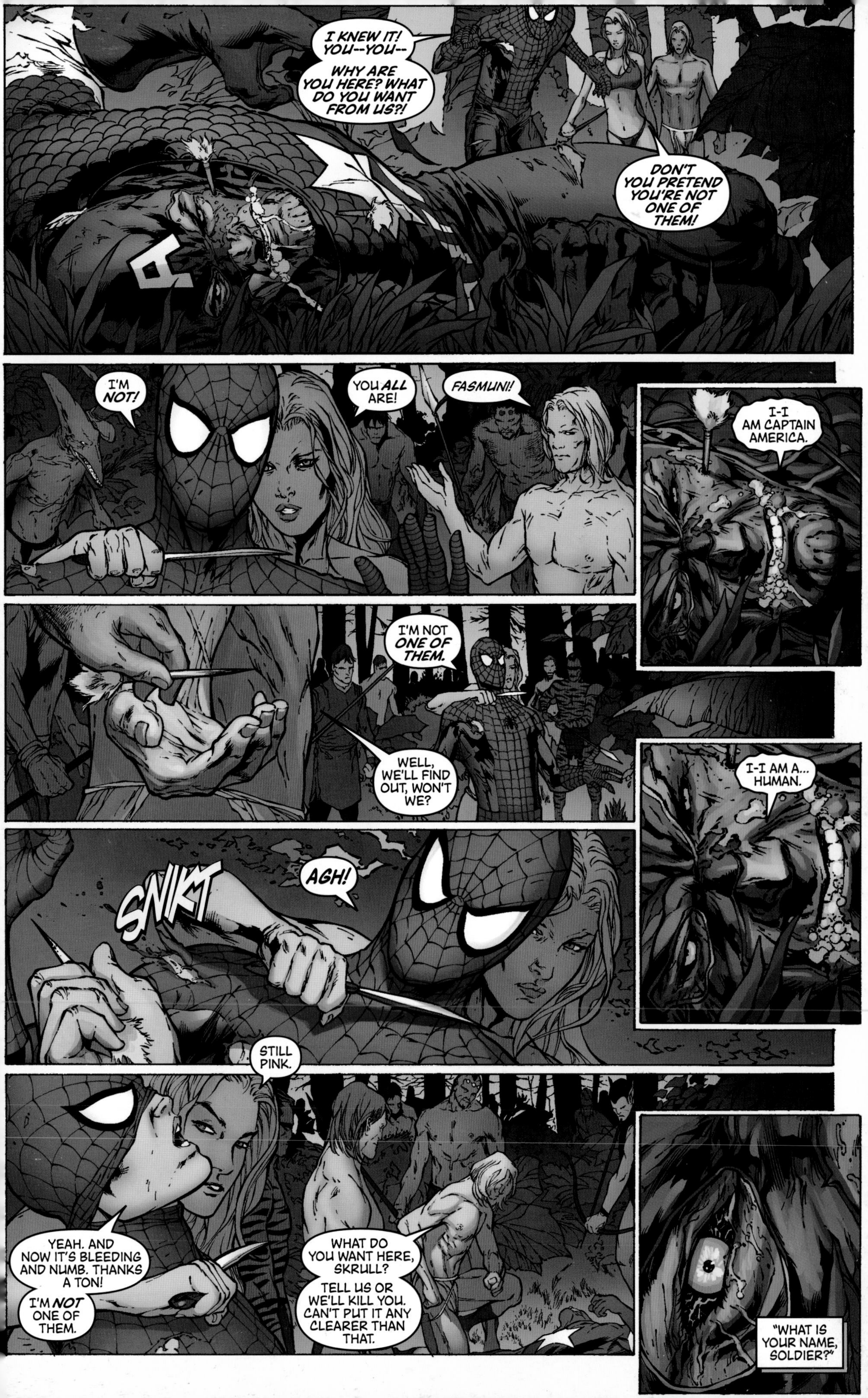
I KNEW IT! YOU--YOU--
WHY ARE YOU HERE? WHAT DO YOU WANT FROM US?!
DON'T YOU PRETEND YOU'RE NOT ONE OF THEM!
I'M NOT!
YOU ALL ARE!
FASMUNI!
I-I AM CAPTAIN AMERICA.
I'M NOT ONE OF THEM.
WELL, WE'LL FIND OUT, WON'T WE?
I-I AM A... HUMAN.
SNIKT
AGH!
STILL PINK.
YEAH. AND NOW IT'S BLEEDING AND NUMB. THANKS A TON!
I'M NOT ONE OF THEM.
WHAT DO YOU WANT HERE, SKRULL?
TELL US OR WE'LL KILL YOU. CAN'T PUT IT ANY CLEARER THAN THAT.
"WHAT IS YOUR NAME, SOLDIER?"

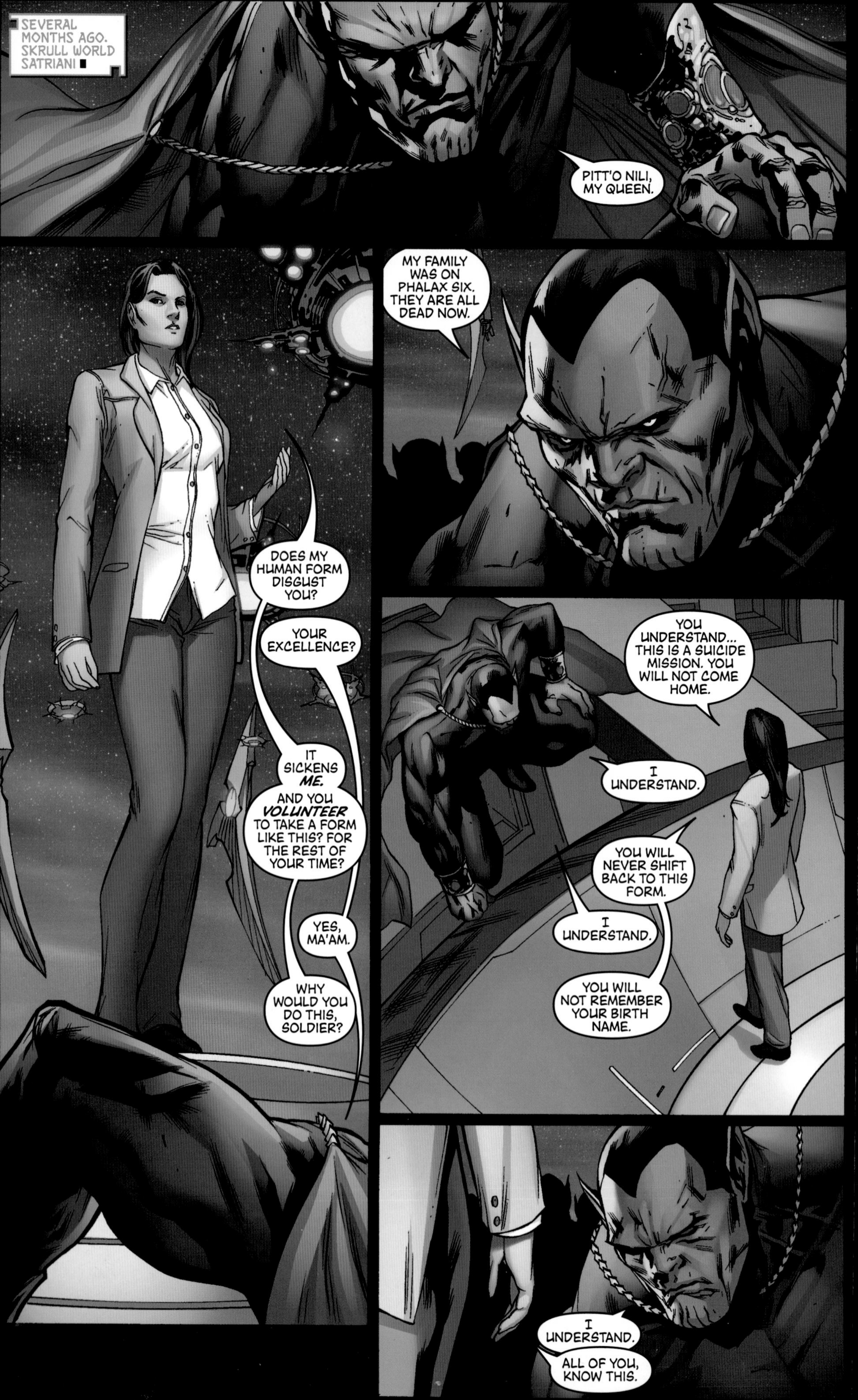
SEVERAL MONTHS AGO. SKRULL WORLD SATRIANI
PITT'O NILI, MY QUEEN.
MY FAMILY WAS ON PHALAX SIX. THEY ARE ALL DEAD NOW.
DOES MY HUMAN FORM DISGUST YOU?
YOUR EXCELLENCE?
IT SICKENS *ME.*
AND YOU *VOLUNTEER* TO TAKE A FORM LIKE THIS? FOR THE REST OF YOUR TIME?
YES, MA'AM.
WHY WOULD YOU DO THIS, SOLDIER?
YOU UNDERSTAND... THIS IS A SUICIDE MISSION. YOU WILL NOT COME HOME.
I UNDERSTAND.
YOU WILL NEVER SHIFT BACK TO THIS FORM.
I UNDERSTAND.
YOU WILL NOT REMEMBER YOUR BIRTH NAME.
I UNDERSTAND.
ALL OF YOU, KNOW THIS.

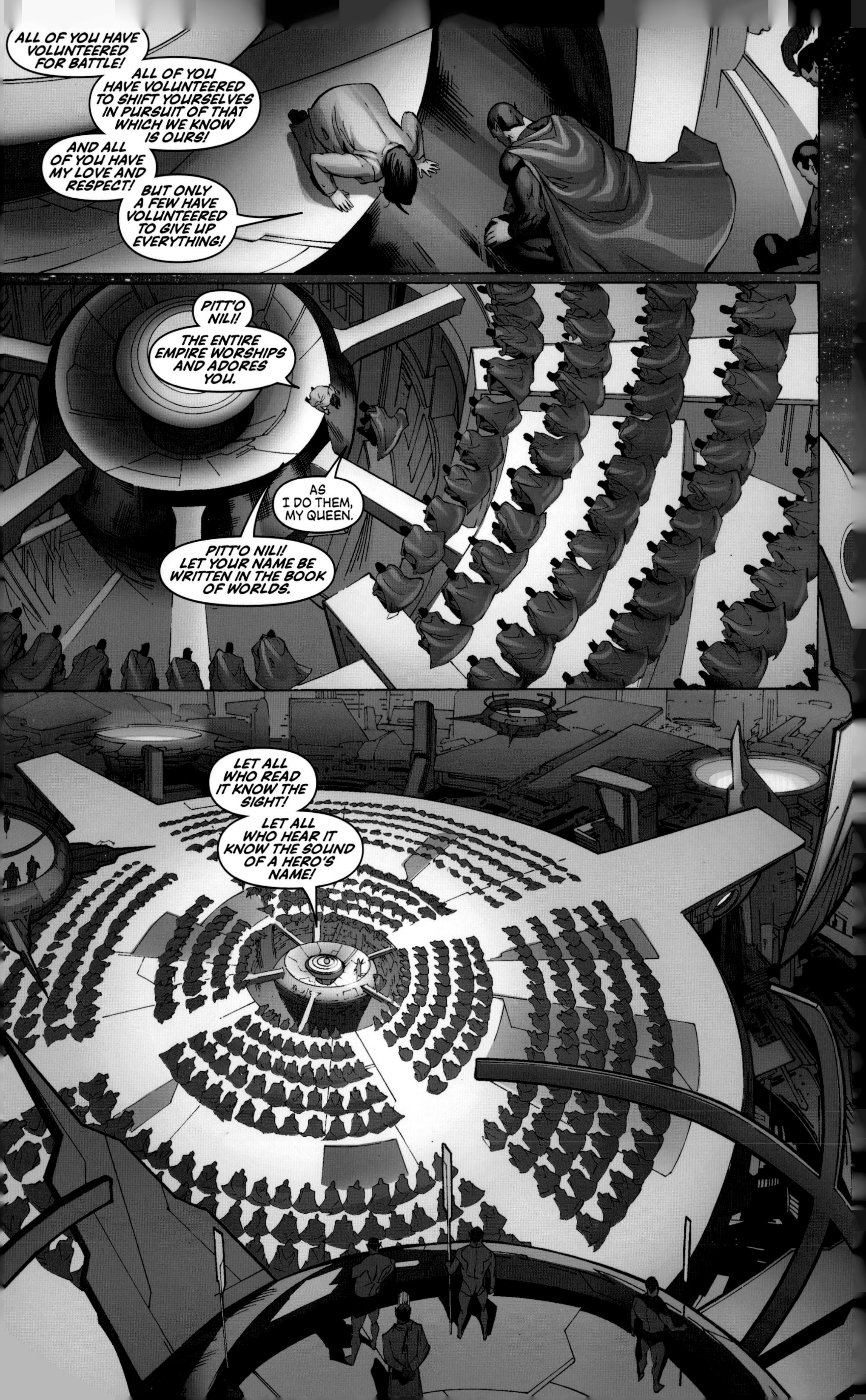
ALL OF YOU HAVE VOLUNTEERED FOR BATTLE!
ALL OF YOU HAVE VOLUNTEERED TO SHIFT YOURSELVES IN PURSUIT OF THAT WHICH WE KNOW IS OURS!
AND ALL OF YOU HAVE MY LOVE AND RESPECT!
BUT ONLY A FEW HAVE VOLUNTEERED TO GIVE UP EVERYTHING!
PITT'O NILI!
THE ENTIRE EMPIRE WORSHIPS AND ADORES YOU.
AS I DO THEM, MY QUEEN.
PITT'O NILI! LET YOUR NAME BE WRITTEN IN THE BOOK OF WORLDS.
LET ALL WHO READ IT KNOW THE SIGHT!
LET ALL WHO HEAR IT KNOW THE SOUND OF A HERO'S NAME!

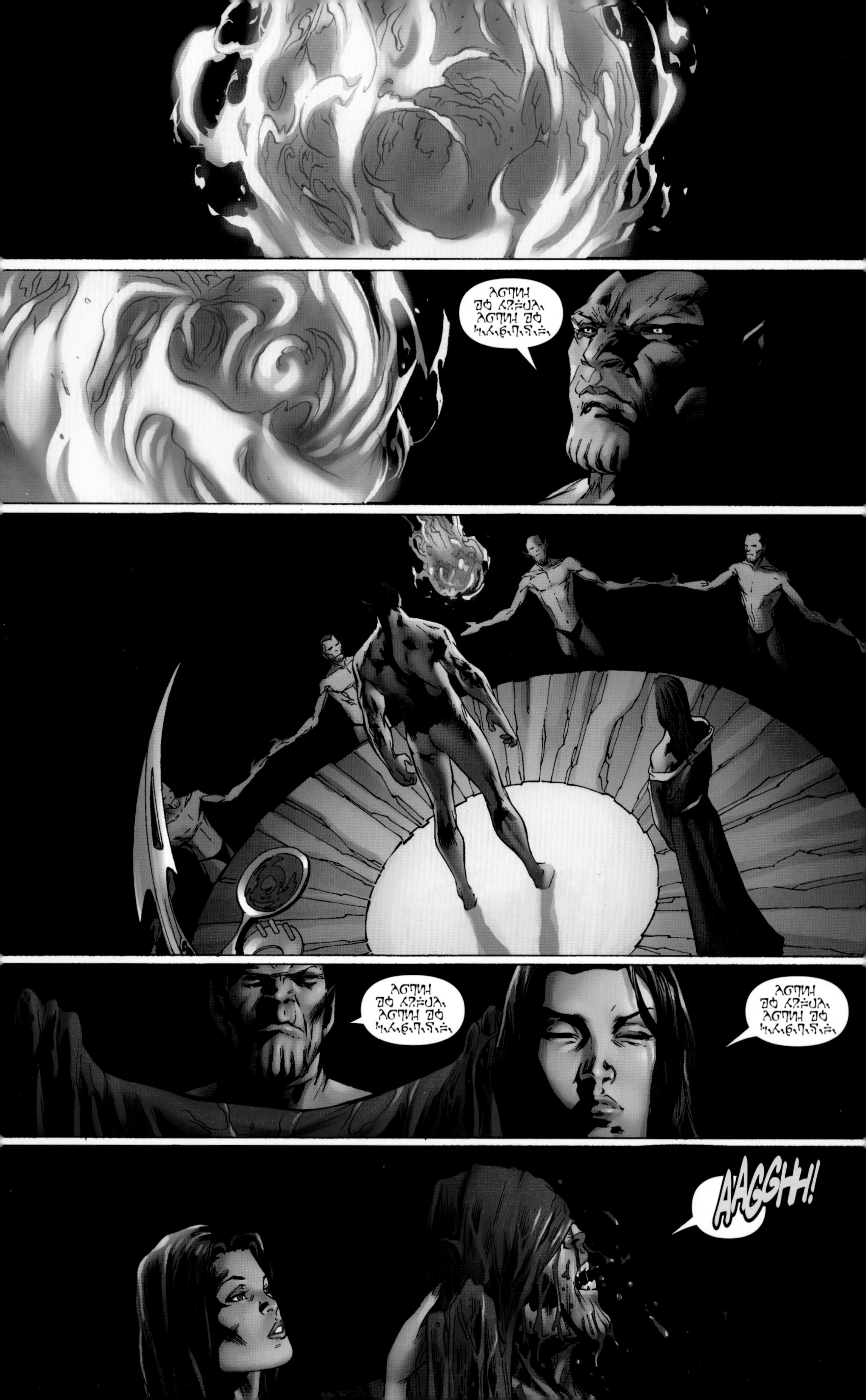
AAGGH!

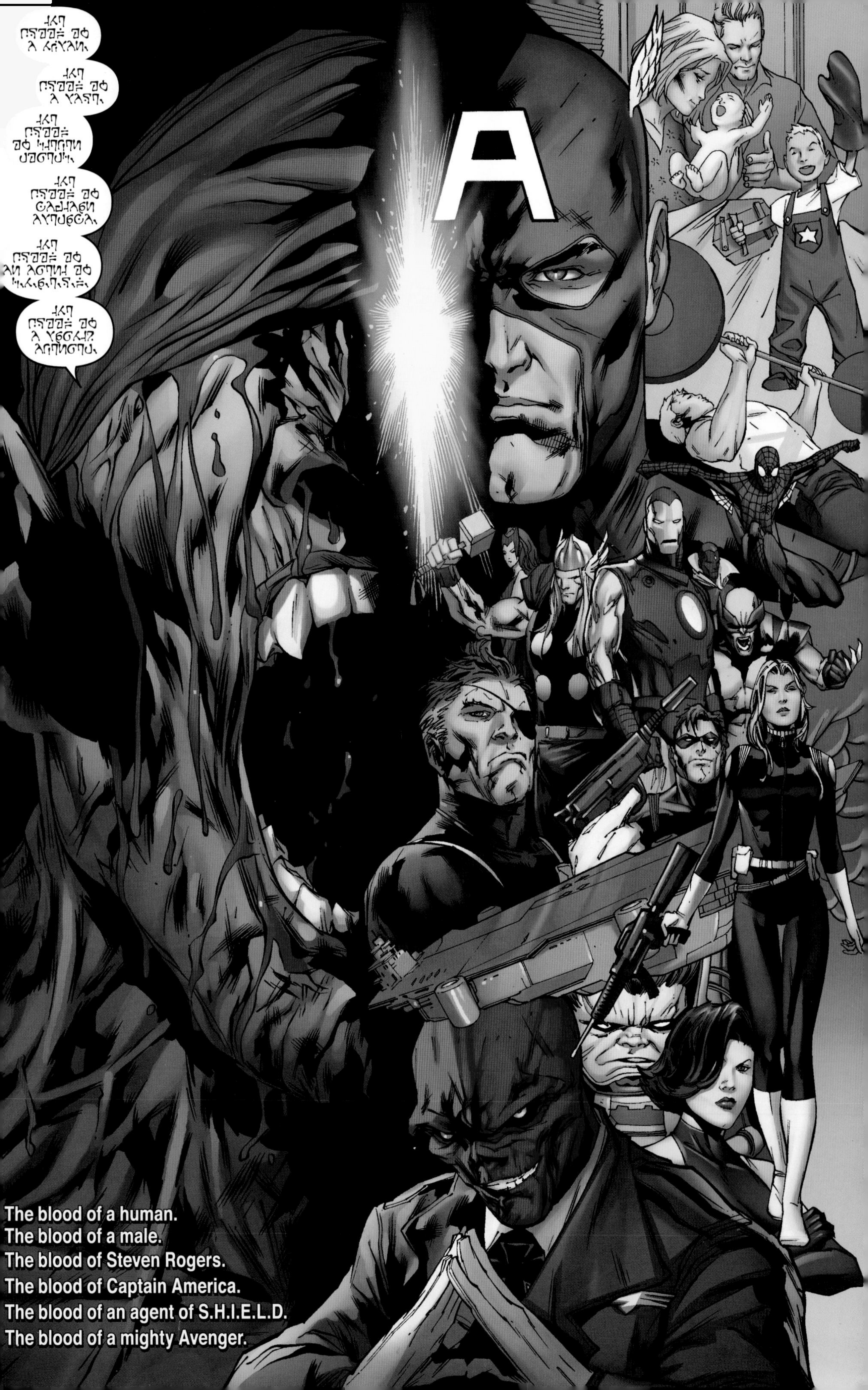
The blood of a human.
The blood of a male.
The blood of Steven Rogers.
The blood of Captain America.
The blood of an agent of S.H.I.E.L.D.
The blood of a mighty Avenger.

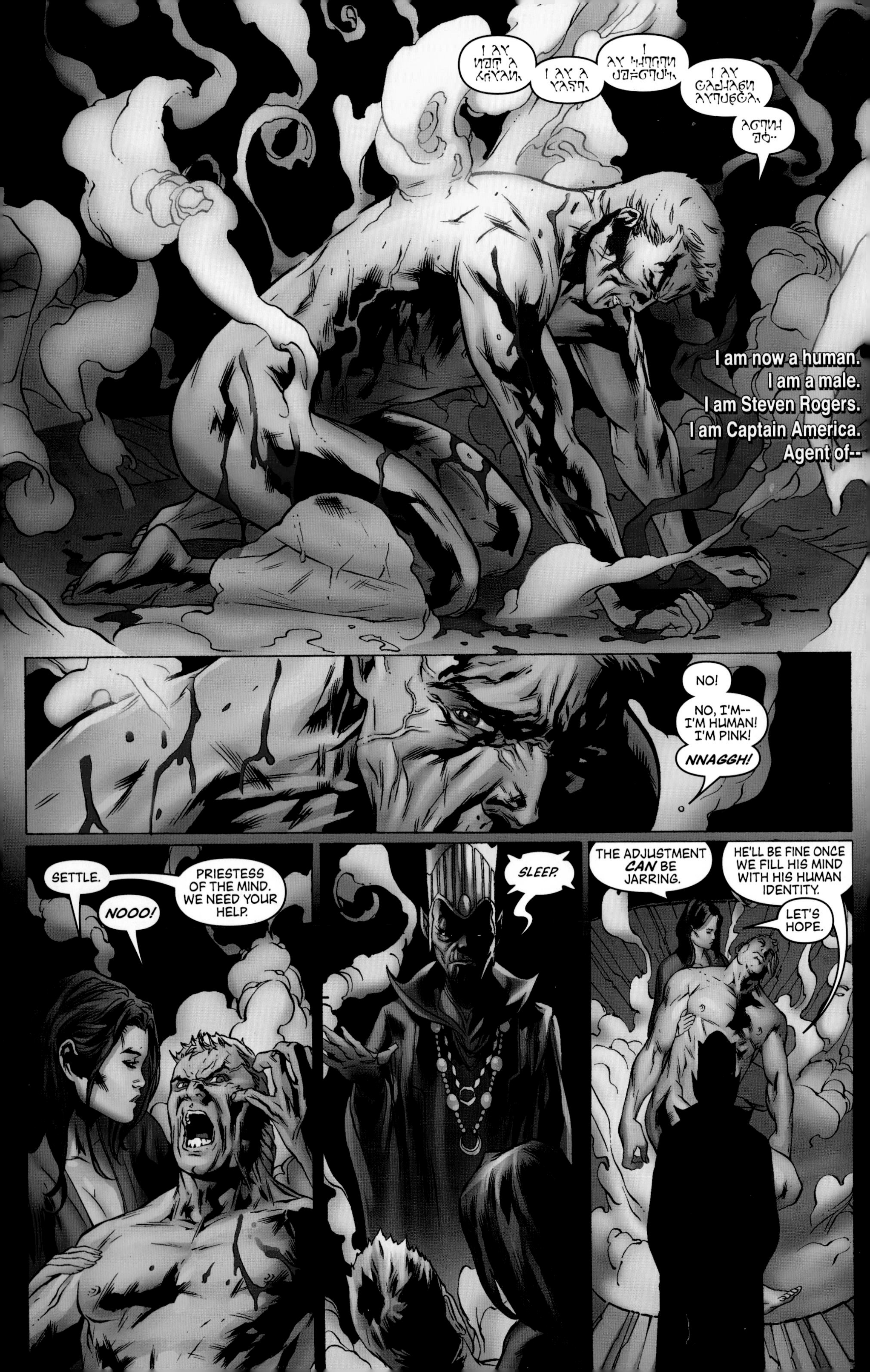
I am now a human.
I am a male.
I am Steven Rogers.
I am Captain America.
Agent of--
NO!
NO, I'M-- I'M HUMAN! I'M PINK!
NNAGGH!
SETTLE.
PRIESTESS OF THE MIND. WE NEED YOUR HELP.
NOOO!
SLEEP.
THE ADJUSTMENT CAN BE JARRING.
HE'LL BE FINE ONCE WE FILL HIS MIND WITH HIS HUMAN IDENTITY.
LET'S HOPE.

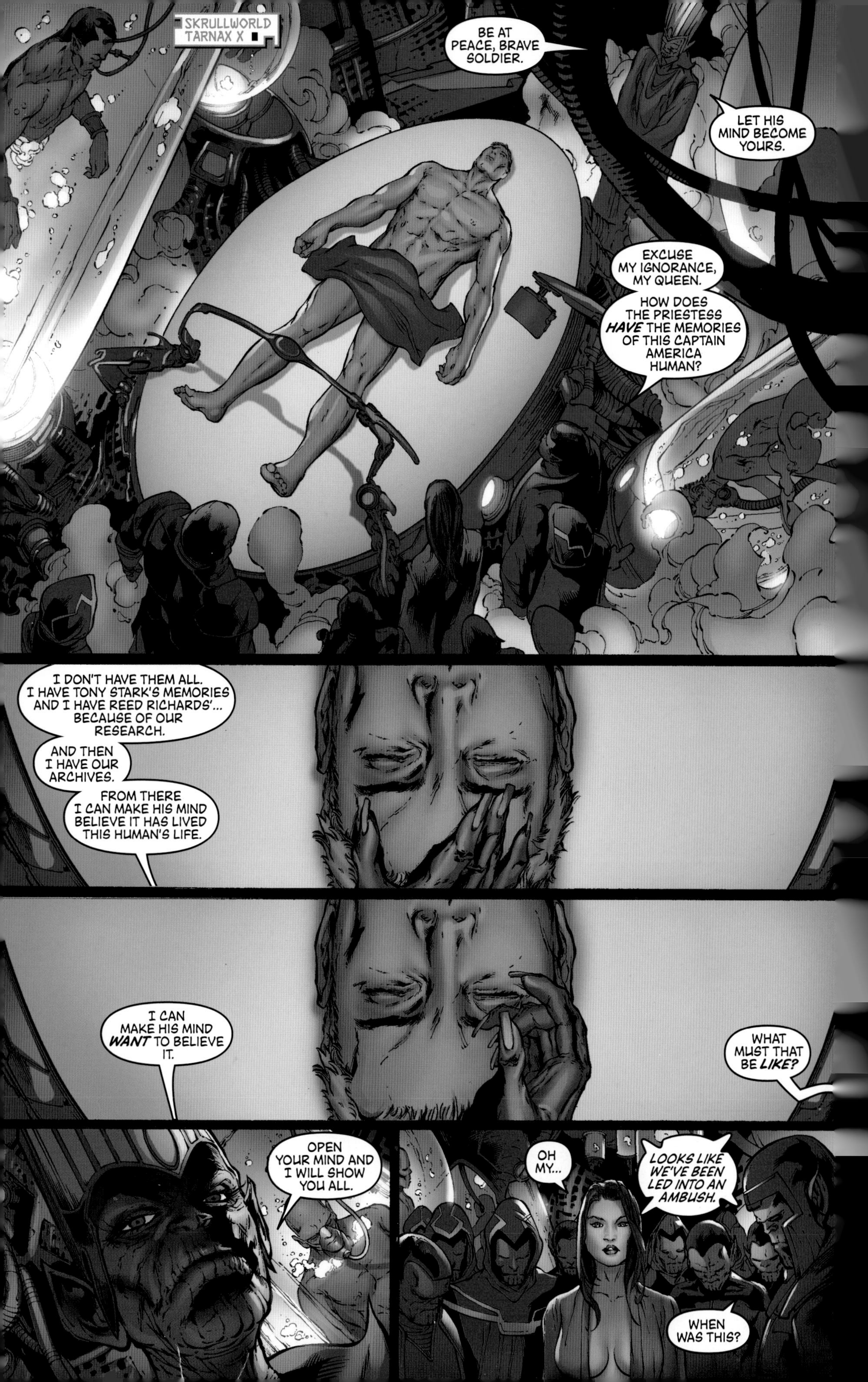
SKRULLWORLD TARNAX X
BE AT PEACE, BRAVE SOLDIER.
LET HIS MIND BECOME YOURS.
EXCUSE MY IGNORANCE, MY QUEEN.
HOW DOES THE PRIESTESS HAVE THE MEMORIES OF THIS CAPTAIN AMERICA HUMAN?
I DON'T HAVE THEM ALL. I HAVE TONY STARK'S MEMORIES AND I HAVE REED RICHARDS'... BECAUSE OF OUR RESEARCH.
AND THEN I HAVE OUR ARCHIVES.
FROM THERE I CAN MAKE HIS MIND BELIEVE IT HAS LIVED THIS HUMAN'S LIFE.
I CAN MAKE HIS MIND WANT TO BELIEVE IT.
WHAT MUST THAT BE LIKE?
OPEN YOUR MIND AND I WILL SHOW YOU ALL.
OH MY...
LOOKS LIKE WE'VE BEEN LED INTO AN AMBUSH.
WHEN WAS THIS?

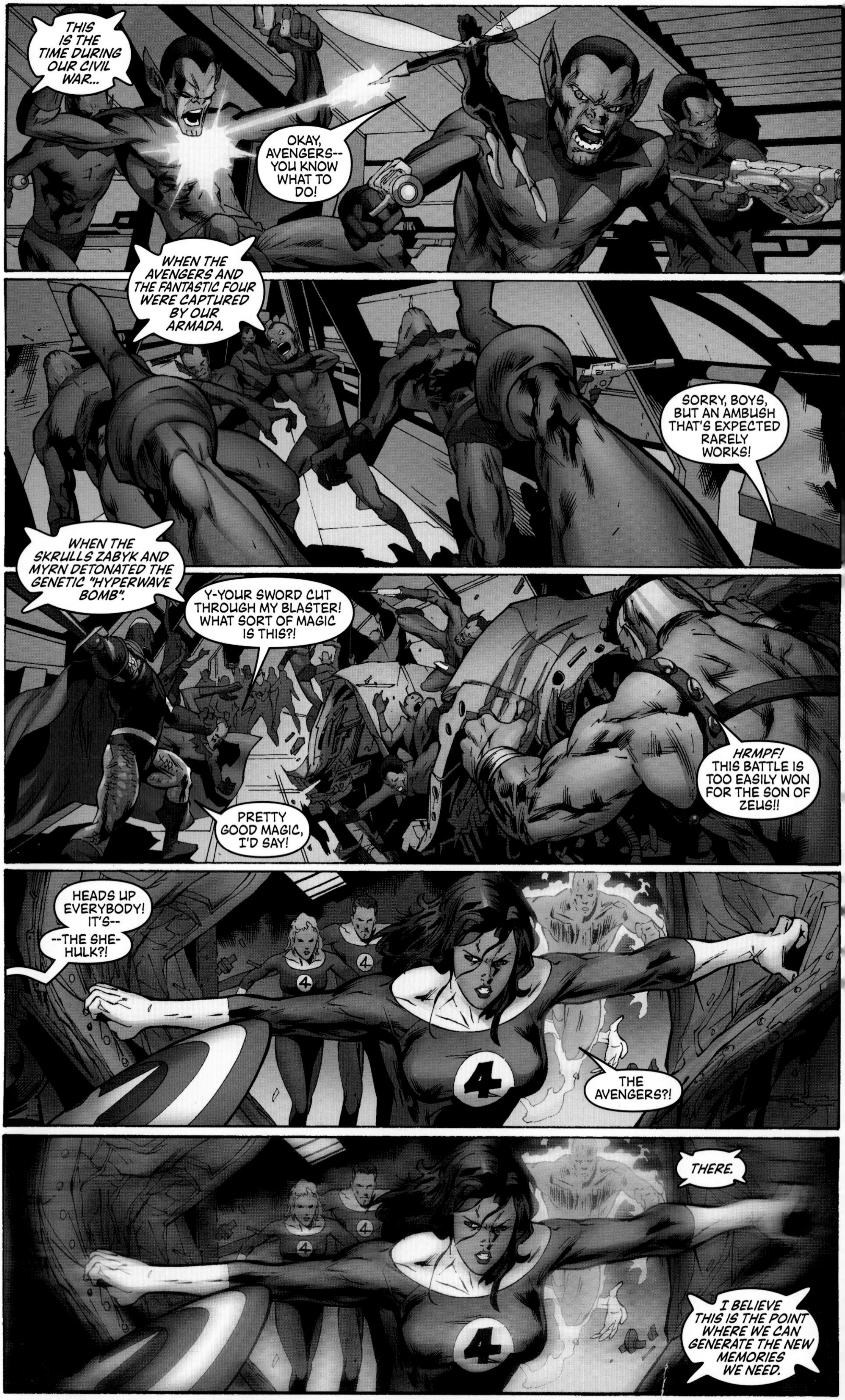
THIS IS THE TIME DURING OUR CIVIL WAR...
OKAY, AVENGERS-- YOU KNOW WHAT TO DO!
WHEN THE AVENGERS AND THE FANTASTIC FOUR WERE CAPTURED BY OUR ARMADA.
SORRY, BOYS, BUT AN AMBUSH THAT'S EXPECTED RARELY WORKS!
WHEN THE SKRULLS ZABYK AND MYRN DETONATED THE GENETIC "HYPERWAVE BOMB".
Y-YOUR SWORD CUT THROUGH MY BLASTER! WHAT SORT OF MAGIC IS THIS?!
PRETTY GOOD MAGIC, I'D SAY!
HRMPF! THIS BATTLE IS TOO EASILY WON FOR THE SON OF ZEUS!!
HEADS UP EVERYBODY! IT'S--
--THE SHE-HULK?!
THE AVENGERS?!
THERE.
I BELIEVE THIS IS THE POINT WHERE WE CAN GENERATE THE NEW MEMORIES WE NEED.

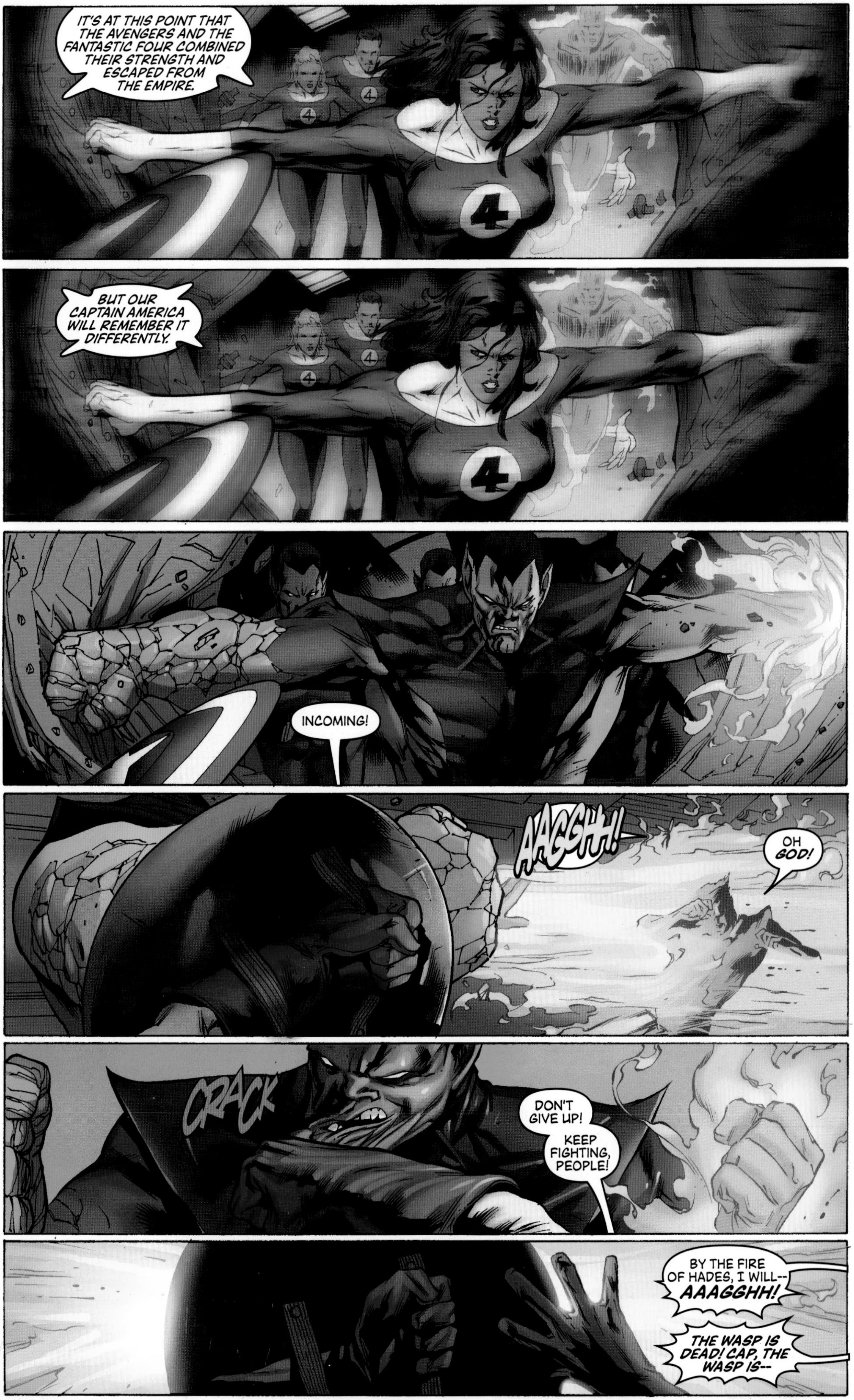
IT'S AT THIS POINT THAT THE AVENGERS AND THE FANTASTIC FOUR COMBINED THEIR STRENGTH AND ESCAPED FROM THE EMPIRE.
BUT OUR CAPTAIN AMERICA WILL REMEMBER IT DIFFERENTLY.
INCOMING!
AAGGHH!
OH GOD!
CRACK
DON'T GIVE UP!
KEEP FIGHTING, PEOPLE!
BY THE FIRE OF HADES, I WILL-- AAAGGHH!
THE WASP IS DEAD! CAP, THE WASP IS--

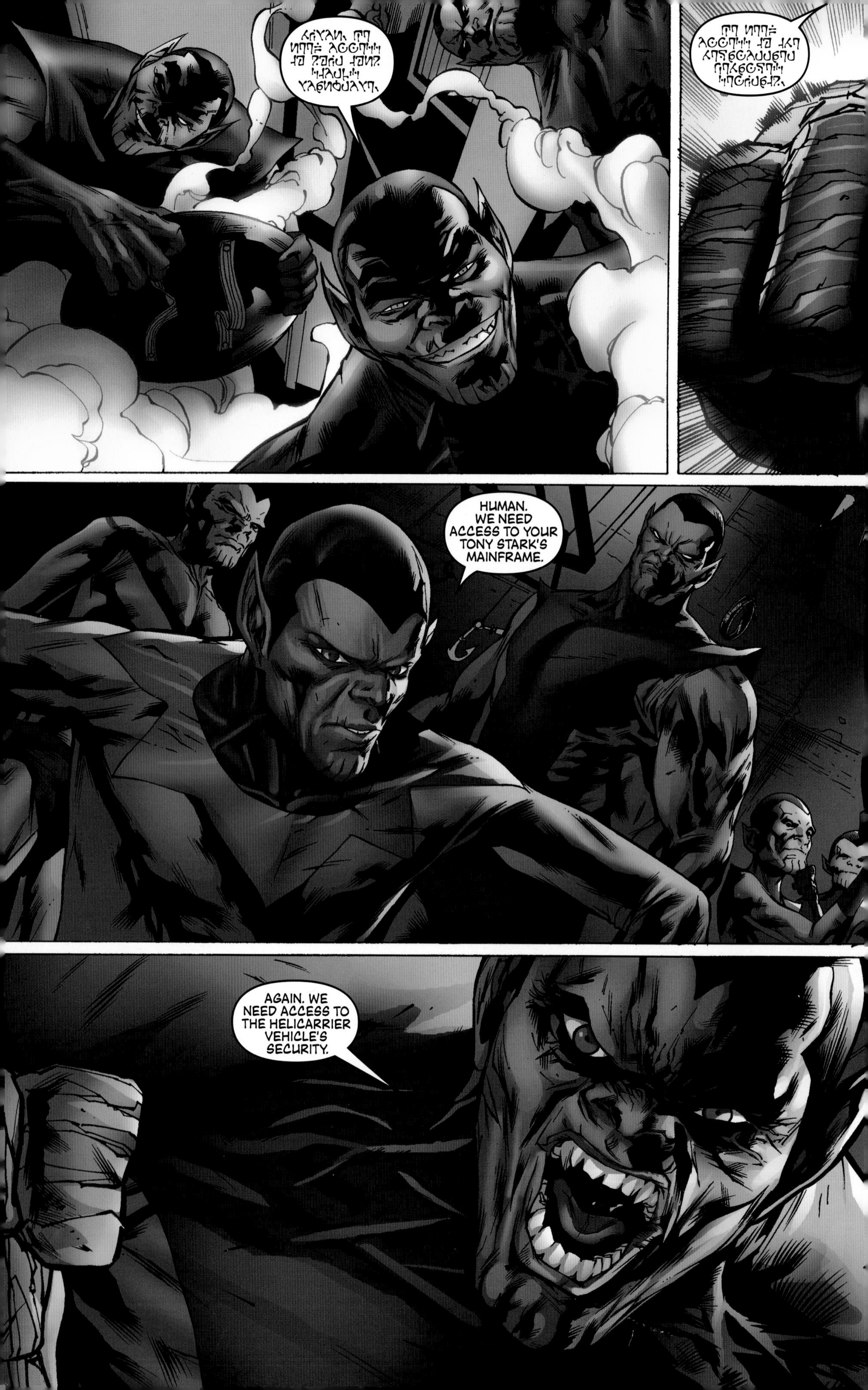
HUMAN. WE NEED ACCESS TO YOUR TONY STARK'S MAINFRAME.
AGAIN. WE NEED ACCESS TO THE HELICARRIER VEHICLE'S SECURITY.

ᐱᕐᐱᕐᐸᖕ ᒥᑎ ᐱᑎᑎᕐ ᐱᕐᕐᒥᑎᕐ ᒥᑎ ᒪᑎᑎ ᐱᑎᑎᕐ ᕐᐱᕐᐱᑎ ᕐᑎᑎᒥᑎᕐᐱᕐᑎᑎ

ᒥᑎ ᐱᑎᑎᕐ ᐱᕐᕐᒥᑎᕐ ᒥᑎ ᒪᑎᑎ ᕐᑎᒥᐱᕐᐱᑎᑎᑎ ᕐᑎᐱᕐᕐᒥᑎᕐ ᒪᑎᑎᕐᒥᑎ

WELL, YOU CAN GO STRAIGHT TO HELL, YOU GREEN PIECE OF—

CRACK

YEAH? DROP D—

SMACK

AND THAT'S HOW OUR CAPTAIN AMERICA WILL BELIEVE HE WAS CAPTURED AND HELD BY THE SKRULL EMPIRE.

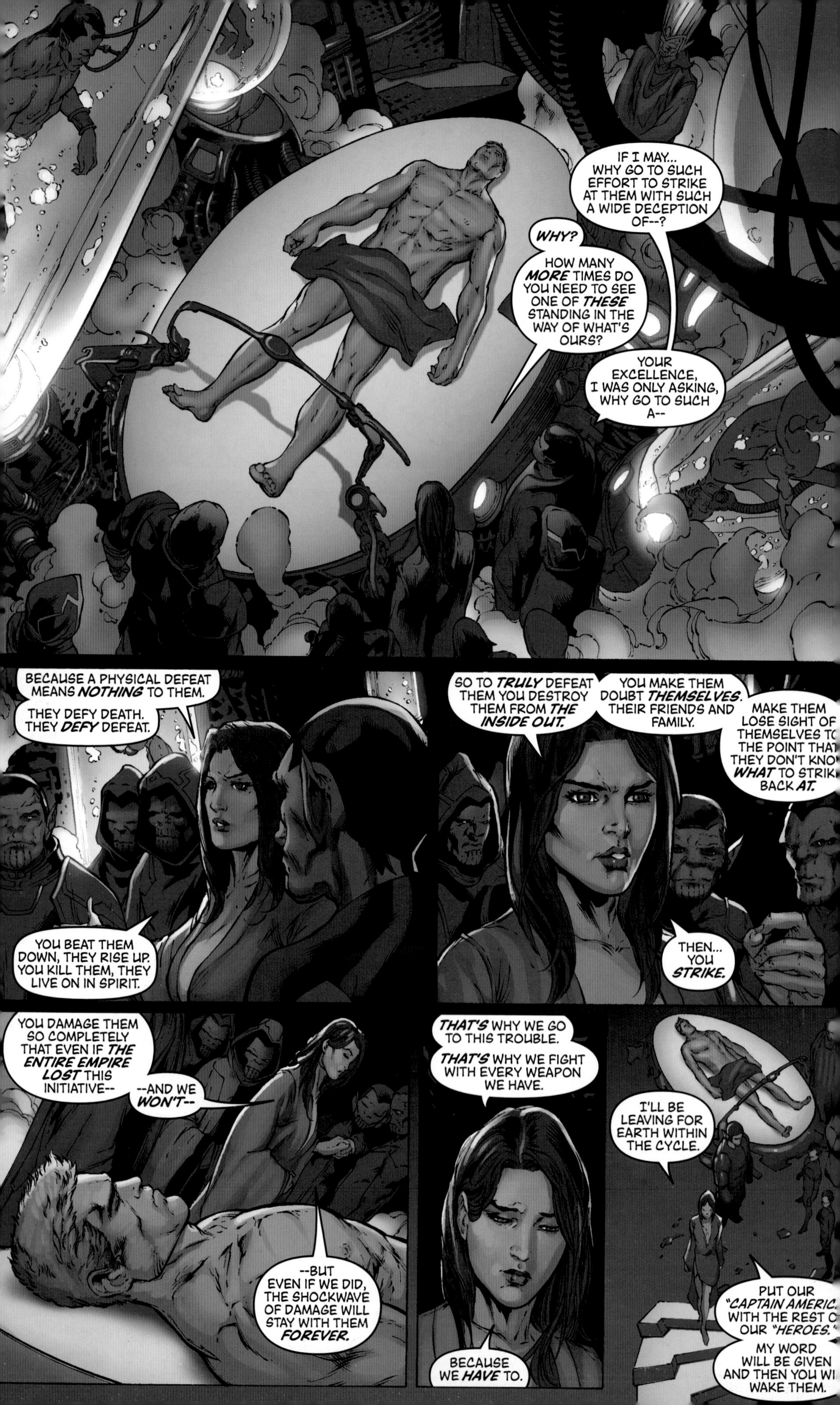
IF I MAY... WHY GO TO SUCH EFFORT TO STRIKE AT THEM WITH SUCH A WIDE DECEPTION OF--?
WHY?
HOW MANY MORE TIMES DO YOU NEED TO SEE ONE OF THESE STANDING IN THE WAY OF WHAT'S OURS?
YOUR EXCELLENCE, I WAS ONLY ASKING, WHY GO TO SUCH A--
BECAUSE A PHYSICAL DEFEAT MEANS NOTHING TO THEM.
THEY DEFY DEATH. THEY DEFY DEFEAT.
YOU BEAT THEM DOWN, THEY RISE UP. YOU KILL THEM, THEY LIVE ON IN SPIRIT.
SO TO TRULY DEFEAT THEM YOU DESTROY THEM FROM THE INSIDE OUT.
YOU MAKE THEM DOUBT THEMSELVES. THEIR FRIENDS AND FAMILY.
THEN... YOU STRIKE.
YOU DAMAGE THEM SO COMPLETELY THAT EVEN IF THE ENTIRE EMPIRE LOST THIS INITIATIVE--
--AND WE WON'T--
--BUT EVEN IF WE DID, THE SHOCKWAVE OF DAMAGE WILL STAY WITH THEM FOREVER.
THAT'S WHY WE GO TO THIS TROUBLE.
THAT'S WHY WE FIGHT WITH EVERY WEAPON WE HAVE.
BECAUSE WE HAVE TO.
I'LL BE LEAVING FOR EARTH WITHIN THE CYCLE.
MY WORD WILL BE GIVEN

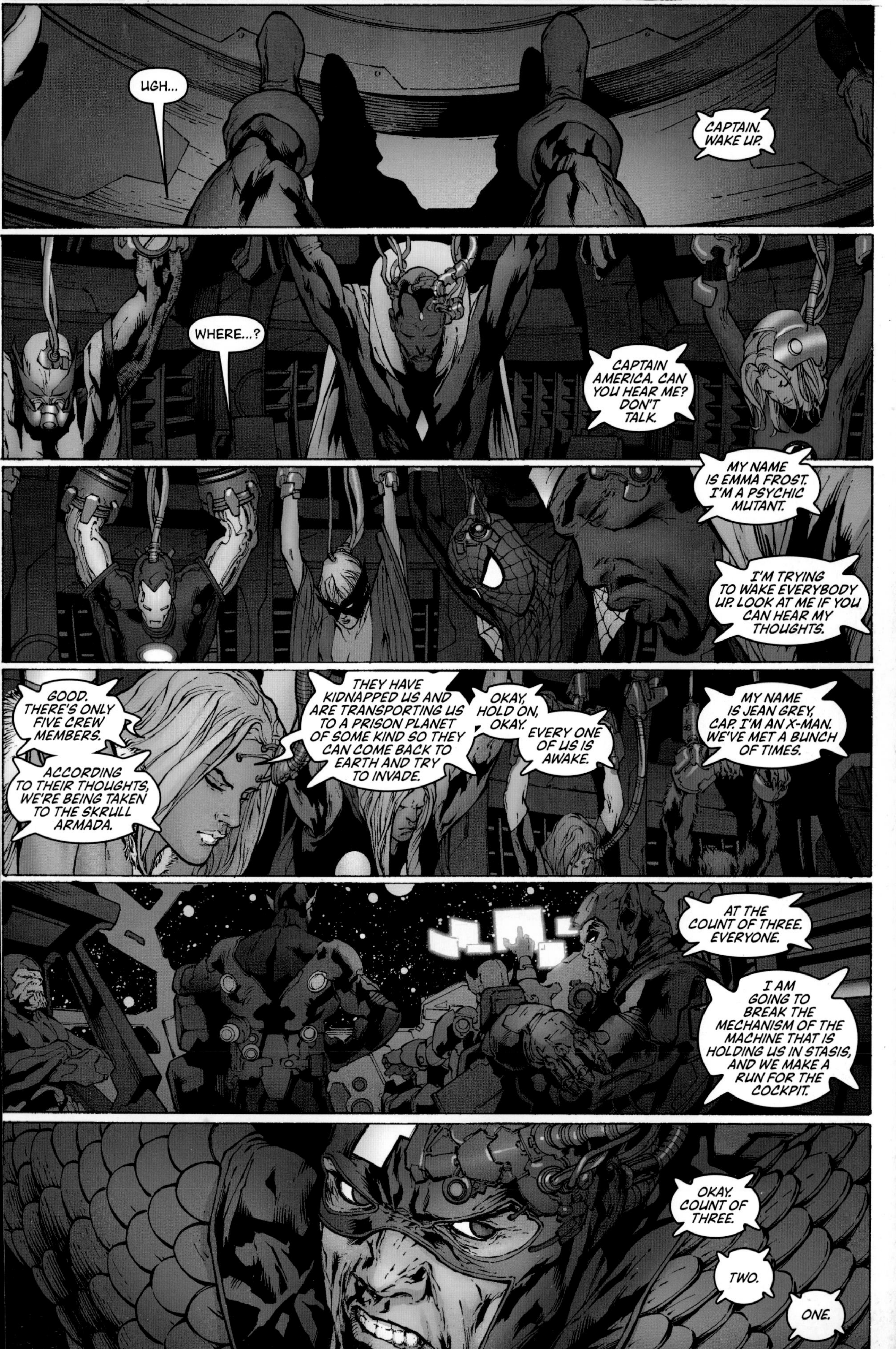
UGH...
CAPTAIN. WAKE UP.
WHERE...?
CAPTAIN AMERICA. CAN YOU HEAR ME? DON'T TALK.
MY NAME IS EMMA FROST. I'M A PSYCHIC MUTANT.
I'M TRYING TO WAKE EVERYBODY UP. LOOK AT ME IF YOU CAN HEAR MY THOUGHTS.
GOOD. THERE'S ONLY FIVE CREW MEMBERS.
ACCORDING TO THEIR THOUGHTS, WE'RE BEING TAKEN TO THE SKRULL ARMADA.
THEY HAVE KIDNAPPED US AND ARE TRANSPORTING US TO A PRISON PLANET OF SOME KIND SO THEY CAN COME BACK TO EARTH AND TRY TO INVADE.
OKAY, HOLD ON, OKAY.
EVERY ONE OF US IS AWAKE.
MY NAME IS JEAN GREY, CAP. I'M AN X-MAN. WE'VE MET A BUNCH OF TIMES.
AT THE COUNT OF THREE. EVERYONE.
I AM GOING TO BREAK THE MECHANISM OF THE MACHINE THAT IS HOLDING US IN STASIS, AND WE MAKE A RUN FOR THE COCKPIT.
OKAY. COUNT OF THREE.
TWO.
ONE.

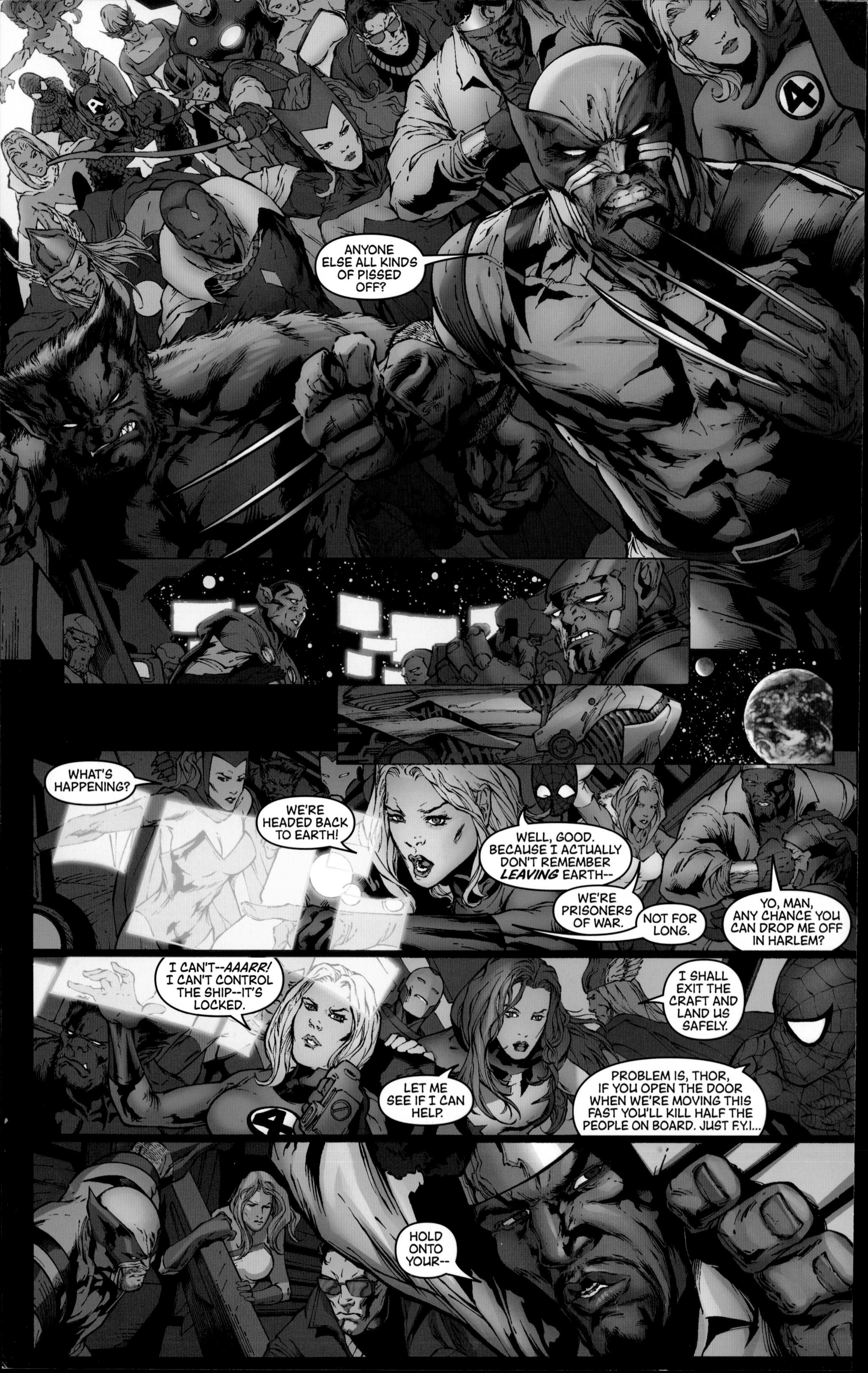
ANYONE ELSE ALL KINDS OF PISSED OFF?
WHAT'S HAPPENING?
WE'RE HEADED BACK TO EARTH!
WELL, GOOD. BECAUSE I ACTUALLY DON'T REMEMBER *LEAVING* EARTH--
WE'RE PRISONERS OF WAR.
NOT FOR LONG.
YO, MAN, ANY CHANCE YOU CAN DROP ME OFF IN HARLEM?
I CAN'T--*AAARR!* I CAN'T CONTROL THE SHIP--IT'S LOCKED.
I SHALL EXIT THE CRAFT AND LAND US SAFELY.
LET ME SEE IF I CAN HELP.
PROBLEM IS, THOR, IF YOU OPEN THE DOOR WHEN WE'RE MOVING THIS FAST YOU'LL KILL HALF THE PEOPLE ON BOARD. JUST F.Y.I...
HOLD ONTO YOUR--

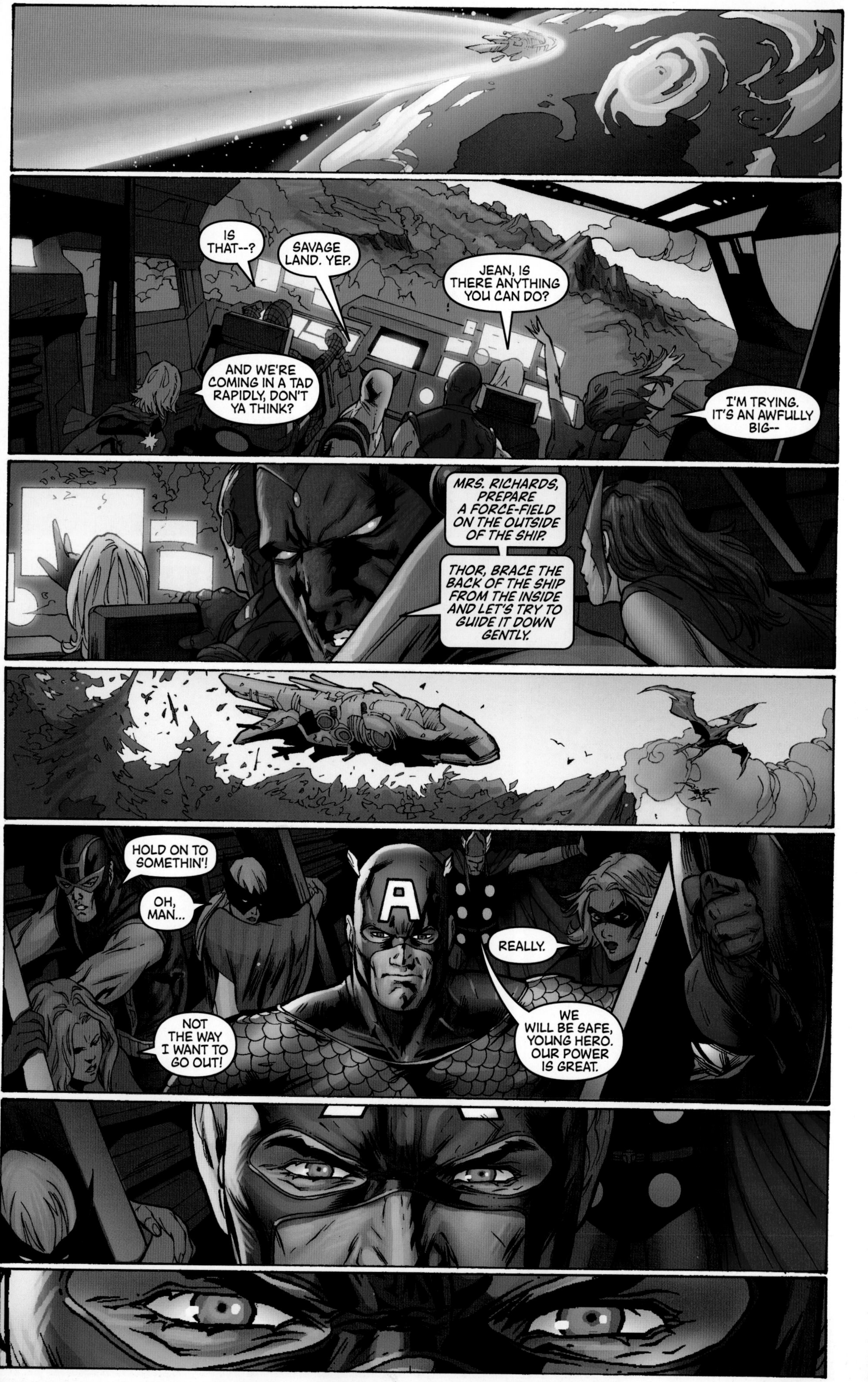
IS THAT--?
SAVAGE LAND. YEP.
AND WE'RE COMING IN A TAD RAPIDLY, DON'T YA THINK?
JEAN, IS THERE ANYTHING YOU CAN DO?
I'M TRYING. IT'S AN AWFULLY BIG--
MRS. RICHARDS, PREPARE A FORCE-FIELD ON THE OUTSIDE OF THE SHIP.
THOR, BRACE THE BACK OF THE SHIP FROM THE INSIDE AND LET'S TRY TO GUIDE IT DOWN GENTLY.
HOLD ON TO SOMETHIN'!
OH, MAN...
NOT THE WAY I WANT TO GO OUT!
REALLY.
WE WILL BE SAFE, YOUNG HERO. OUR POWER IS GREAT.

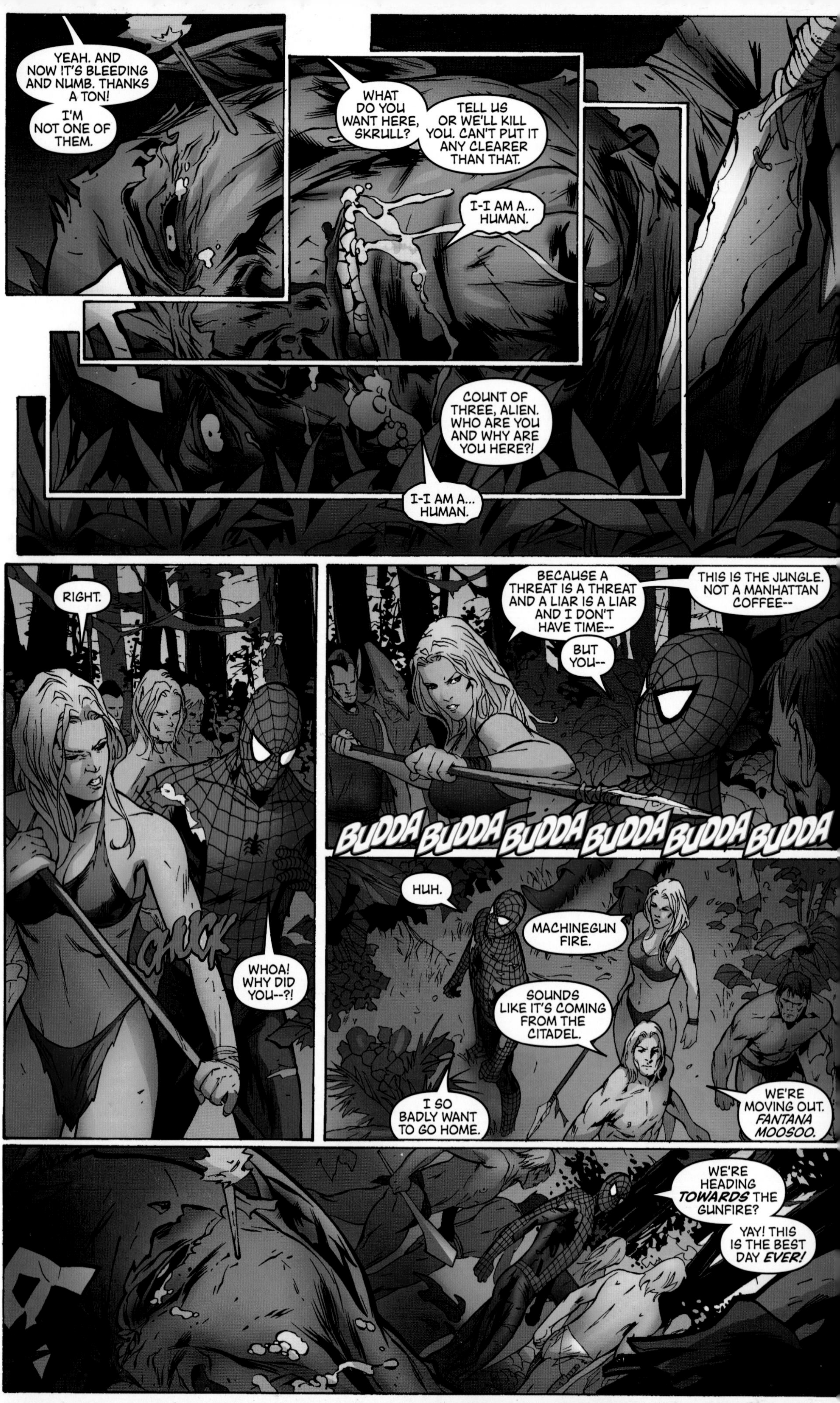
YEAH. AND NOW IT'S BLEEDING AND NUMB. THANKS A TON!
I'M NOT ONE OF THEM.
WHAT DO YOU WANT HERE, SKRULL?
TELL US OR WE'LL KILL YOU. CAN'T PUT IT ANY CLEARER THAN THAT.
I-I AM A... HUMAN.
COUNT OF THREE, ALIEN. WHO ARE YOU AND WHY ARE YOU HERE?!
I-I AM A... HUMAN.
RIGHT.
CHUCK
WHOA! WHY DID YOU--?!
BECAUSE A THREAT IS A THREAT AND A LIAR IS A LIAR AND I DON'T HAVE TIME--
THIS IS THE JUNGLE. NOT A MANHATTAN COFFEE--
BUT YOU--
BUDDA BUDDA BUDDA BUDDA BUDDA BUDDA
HUH.
MACHINEGUN FIRE.
SOUNDS LIKE IT'S COMING FROM THE CITADEL.
I SO BADLY WANT TO GO HOME.
WE'RE MOVING OUT. *FANTANA MOOSOO.*
WE'RE HEADING *TOWARDS* THE GUNFIRE?
YAY! THIS IS THE BEST DAY *EVER!*

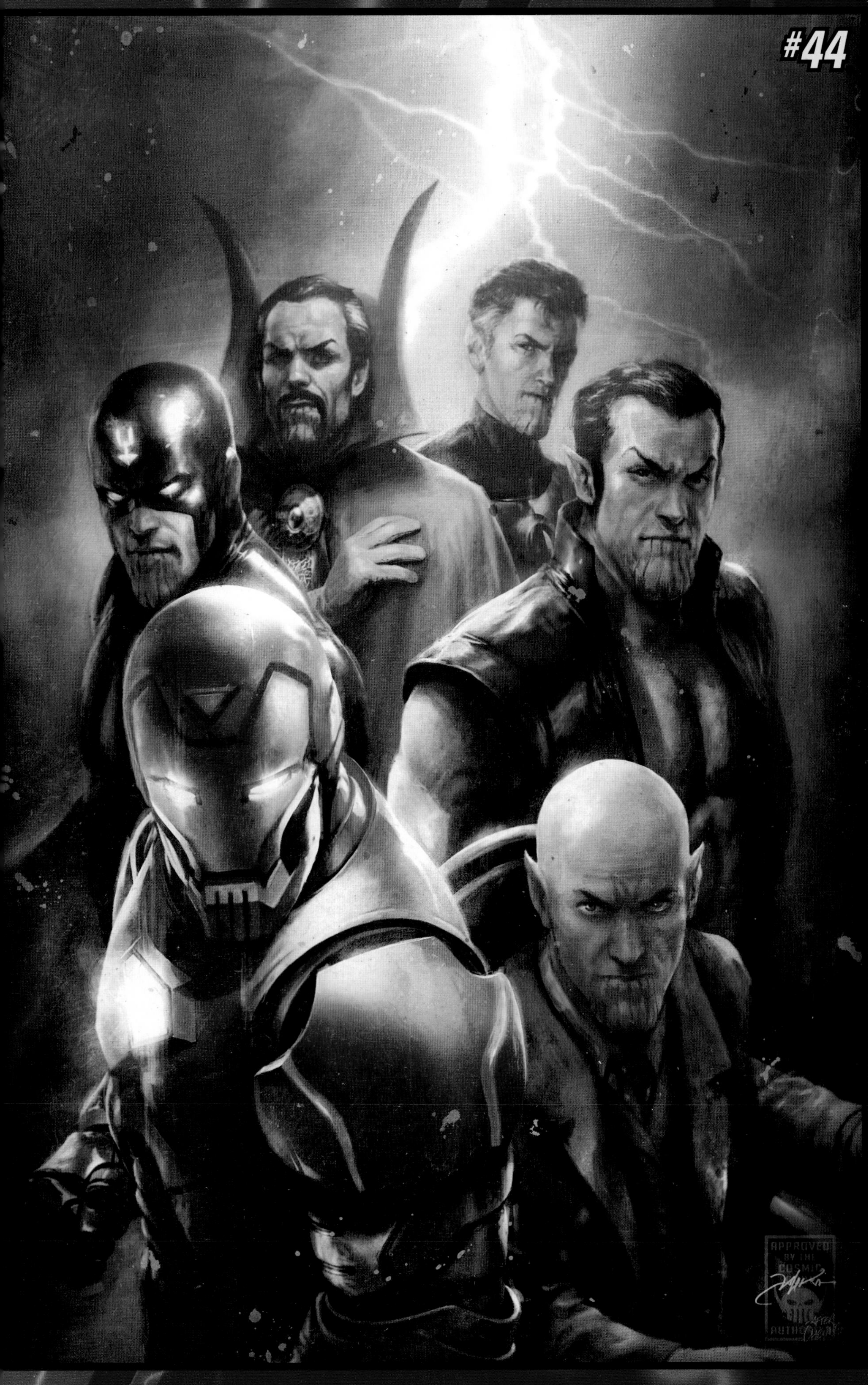
#44
APPROVED BY THE COSMIC

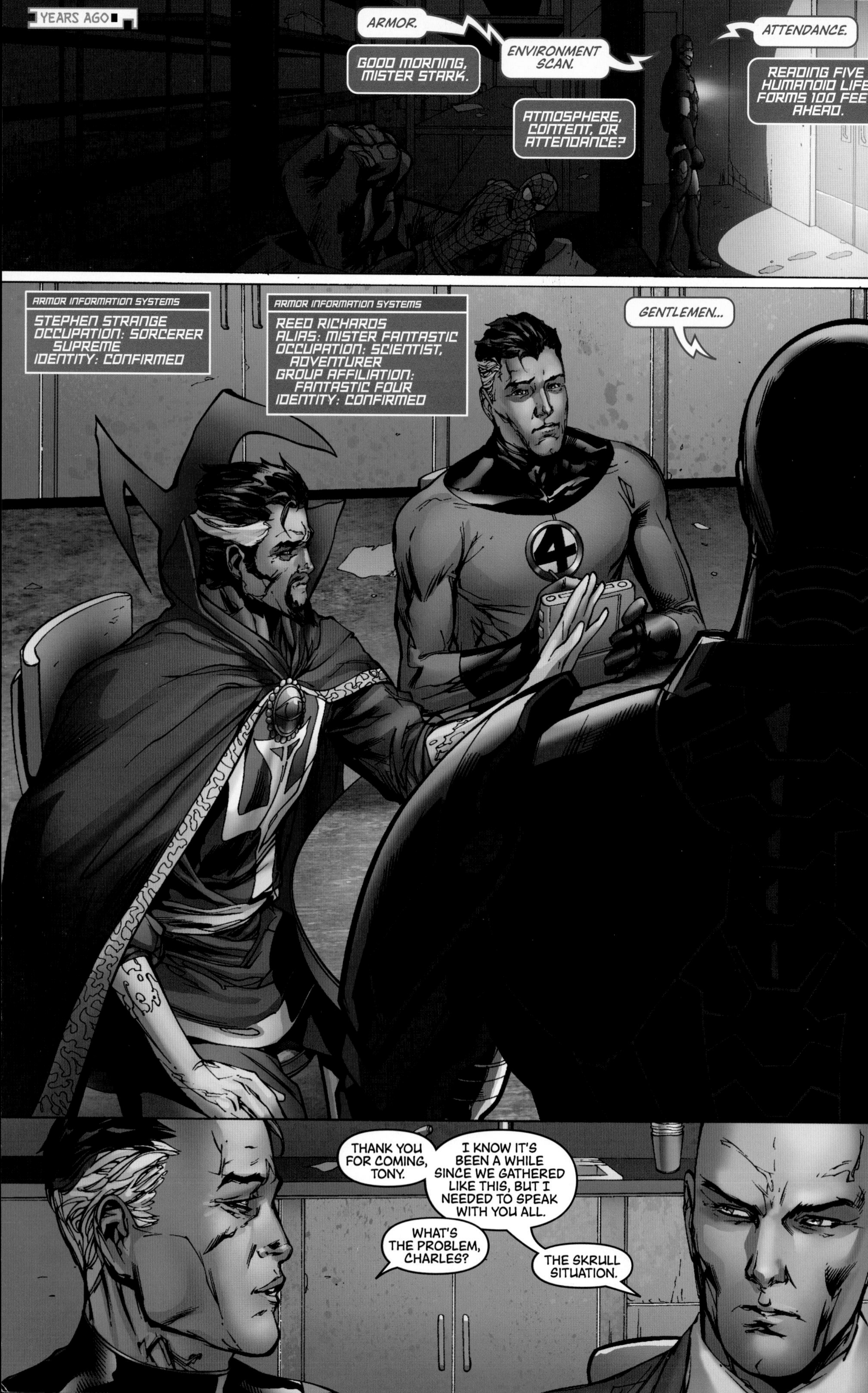
YEARS AGO
ARMOR.
GOOD MORNING, MISTER STARK.
ENVIRONMENT SCAN.
ATMOSPHERE, CONTENT, OR ATTENDANCE?
ATTENDANCE.
READING FIVE HUMANOID LIFE FORMS 100 FEE AHEAD.
ARMOR INFORMATION SYSTEMS
STEPHEN STRANGE
OCCUPATION: SORCERER SUPREME
IDENTITY: CONFIRMED
ARMOR INFORMATION SYSTEMS
REED RICHARDS
ALIAS: MISTER FANTASTIC
OCCUPATION: SCIENTIST, ADVENTURER
GROUP AFFILIATION: FANTASTIC FOUR
IDENTITY: CONFIRMED
GENTLEMEN...
THANK YOU FOR COMING, TONY.
I KNOW IT'S BEEN A WHILE SINCE WE GATHERED LIKE THIS, BUT I NEEDED TO SPEAK WITH YOU ALL.
WHAT'S THE PROBLEM, CHARLES?
THE SKRULL SITUATION.

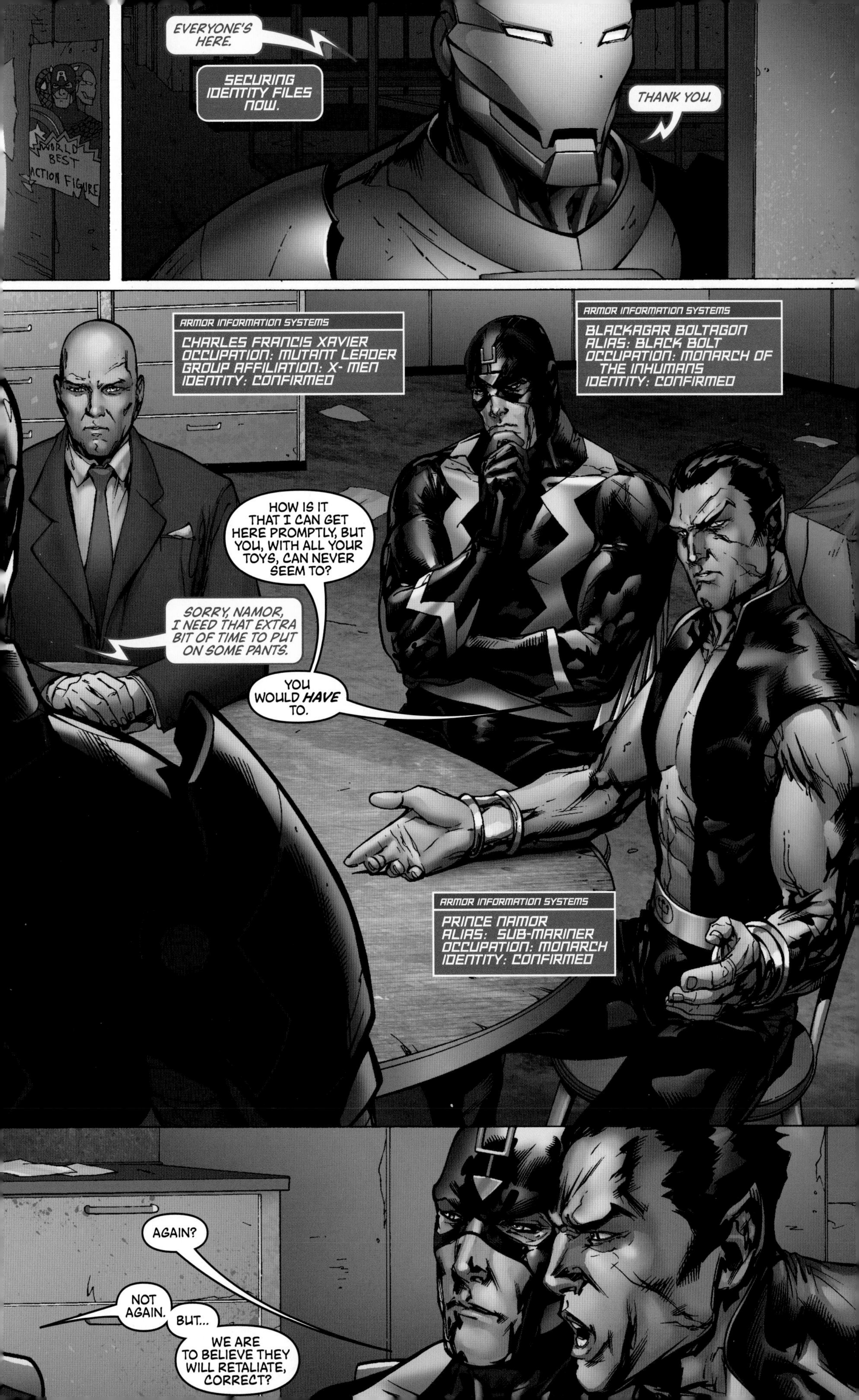
EVERYONE'S HERE.
SECURING IDENTITY FILES NOW.
THANK YOU.
WORLD BEST ACTION FIGURE
ARMOR INFORMATION SYSTEMS
CHARLES FRANCIS XAVIER
OCCUPATION: MUTANT LEADER
GROUP AFFILIATION: X- MEN
IDENTITY: CONFIRMED
ARMOR INFORMATION SYSTEMS
BLACKAGAR BOLTAGON
ALIAS: BLACK BOLT
OCCUPATION: MONARCH OF THE INHUMANS
IDENTITY: CONFIRMED
HOW IS IT THAT I CAN GET HERE PROMPTLY, BUT YOU, WITH ALL YOUR TOYS, CAN NEVER SEEM TO?
SORRY, NAMOR, I NEED THAT EXTRA BIT OF TIME TO PUT ON SOME PANTS.
YOU WOULD HAVE TO.
ARMOR INFORMATION SYSTEMS
PRINCE NAMOR
ALIAS: SUB-MARINER
OCCUPATION: MONARCH
IDENTITY: CONFIRMED
AGAIN?
NOT AGAIN.
BUT...
WE ARE TO BELIEVE THEY WILL RETALIATE, CORRECT?

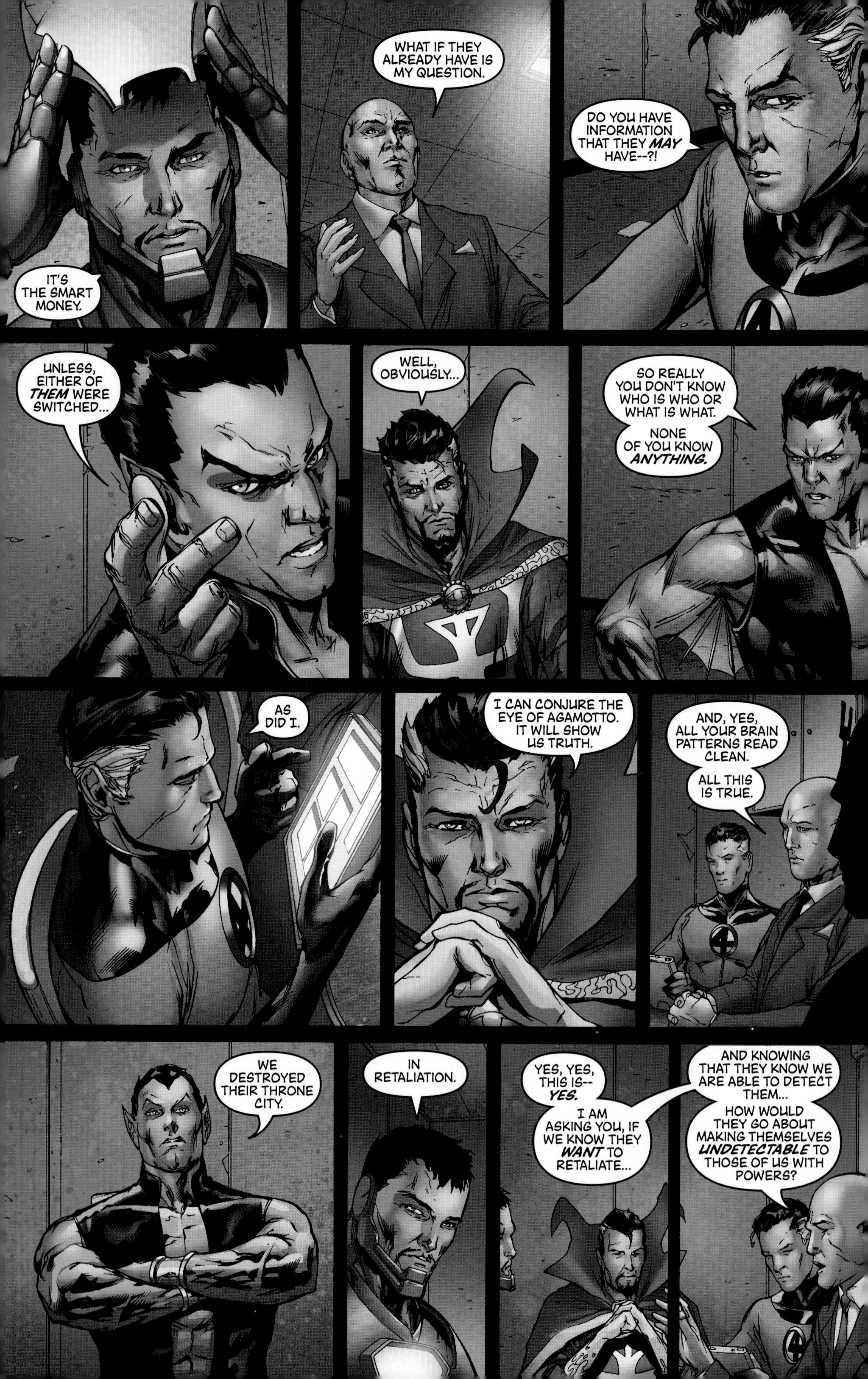
IT'S THE SMART MONEY.
WHAT IF THEY ALREADY HAVE IS MY QUESTION.
DO YOU HAVE INFORMATION THAT THEY *MAY* HAVE--?!
UNLESS, EITHER OF *THEM* WERE SWITCHED...
WELL, OBVIOUSLY...
SO REALLY YOU DON'T KNOW WHO IS WHO OR WHAT IS WHAT.
NONE OF YOU KNOW *ANYTHING.*
AS DID I.
I CAN CONJURE THE EYE OF AGAMOTTO. IT WILL SHOW US TRUTH.
AND, YES, ALL YOUR BRAIN PATTERNS READ CLEAN.
ALL THIS IS TRUE.
WE DESTROYED THEIR THRONE CITY.
IN RETALIATION.
YES, YES, THIS IS-- *YES.*
I AM ASKING YOU, IF WE KNOW THEY *WANT* TO RETALIATE...
AND KNOWING THAT THEY KNOW WE ARE ABLE TO DETECT THEM...
HOW WOULD THEY GO ABOUT MAKING THEMSELVES *UNDETECTABLE* TO THOSE OF US WITH POWERS?

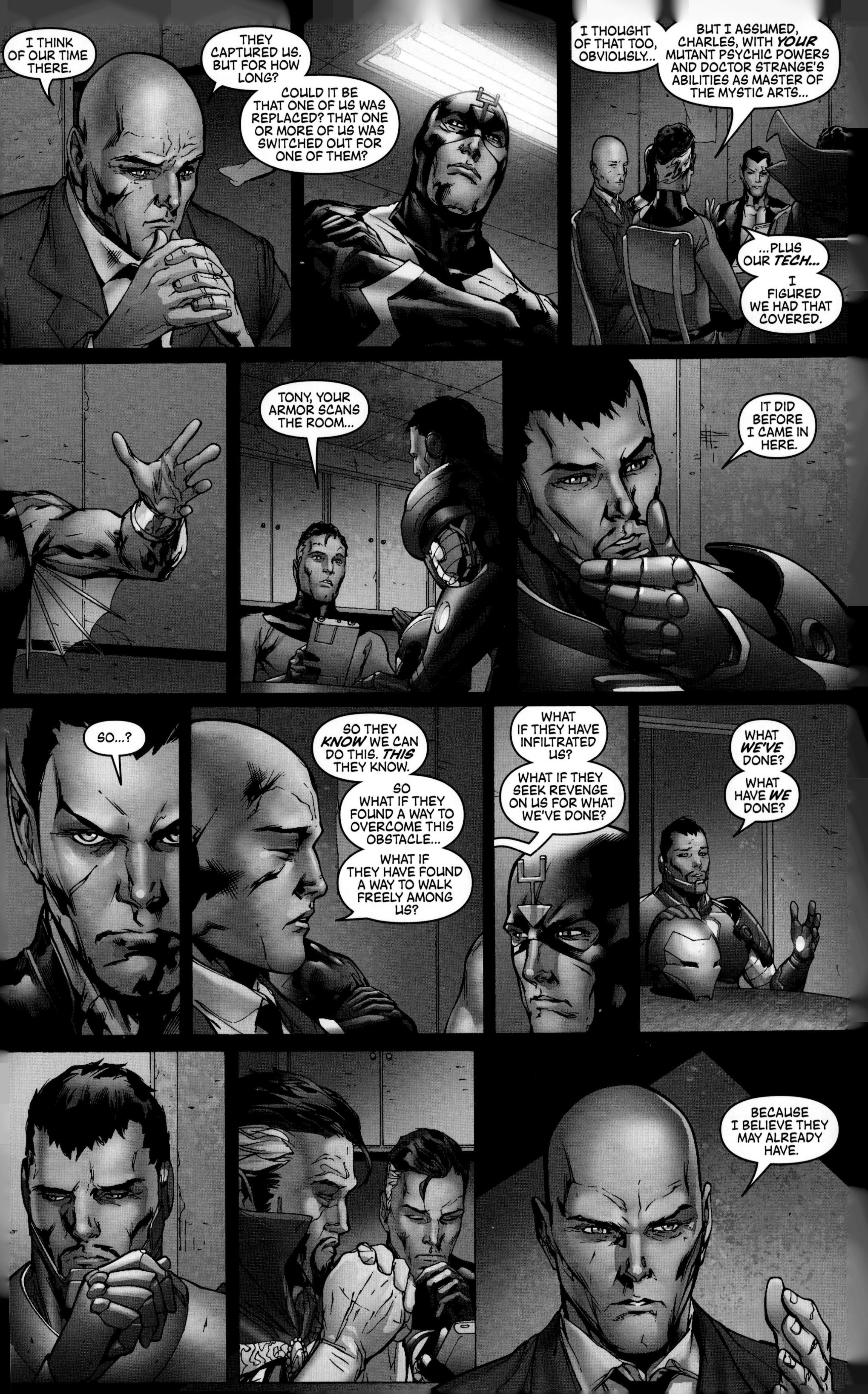
I THINK OF OUR TIME THERE.
THEY CAPTURED US. BUT FOR HOW LONG?
COULD IT BE THAT ONE OF US WAS REPLACED? THAT ONE OR MORE OF US WAS SWITCHED OUT FOR ONE OF THEM?
I THOUGHT OF THAT TOO, OBVIOUSLY...
BUT I ASSUMED, CHARLES, WITH *YOUR* MUTANT PSYCHIC POWERS AND DOCTOR STRANGE'S ABILITIES AS MASTER OF THE MYSTIC ARTS...
...PLUS OUR *TECH...*
I *FIGURED* WE HAD THAT COVERED.
TONY, YOUR ARMOR SCANS THE ROOM...
IT DID BEFORE I CAME IN HERE.
SO...?
SO THEY *KNOW* WE CAN DO THIS. *THIS* THEY KNOW.
SO WHAT IF THEY FOUND A WAY TO OVERCOME THIS OBSTACLE...
WHAT IF THEY HAVE FOUND A WAY TO WALK FREELY AMONG US?
WHAT IF THEY HAVE INFILTRATED US?
WHAT IF THEY SEEK REVENGE ON US FOR WHAT WE'VE DONE?
WHAT *WE'VE* DONE?
WHAT HAVE *WE* DONE?
BECAUSE I BELIEVE THEY MAY ALREADY HAVE.

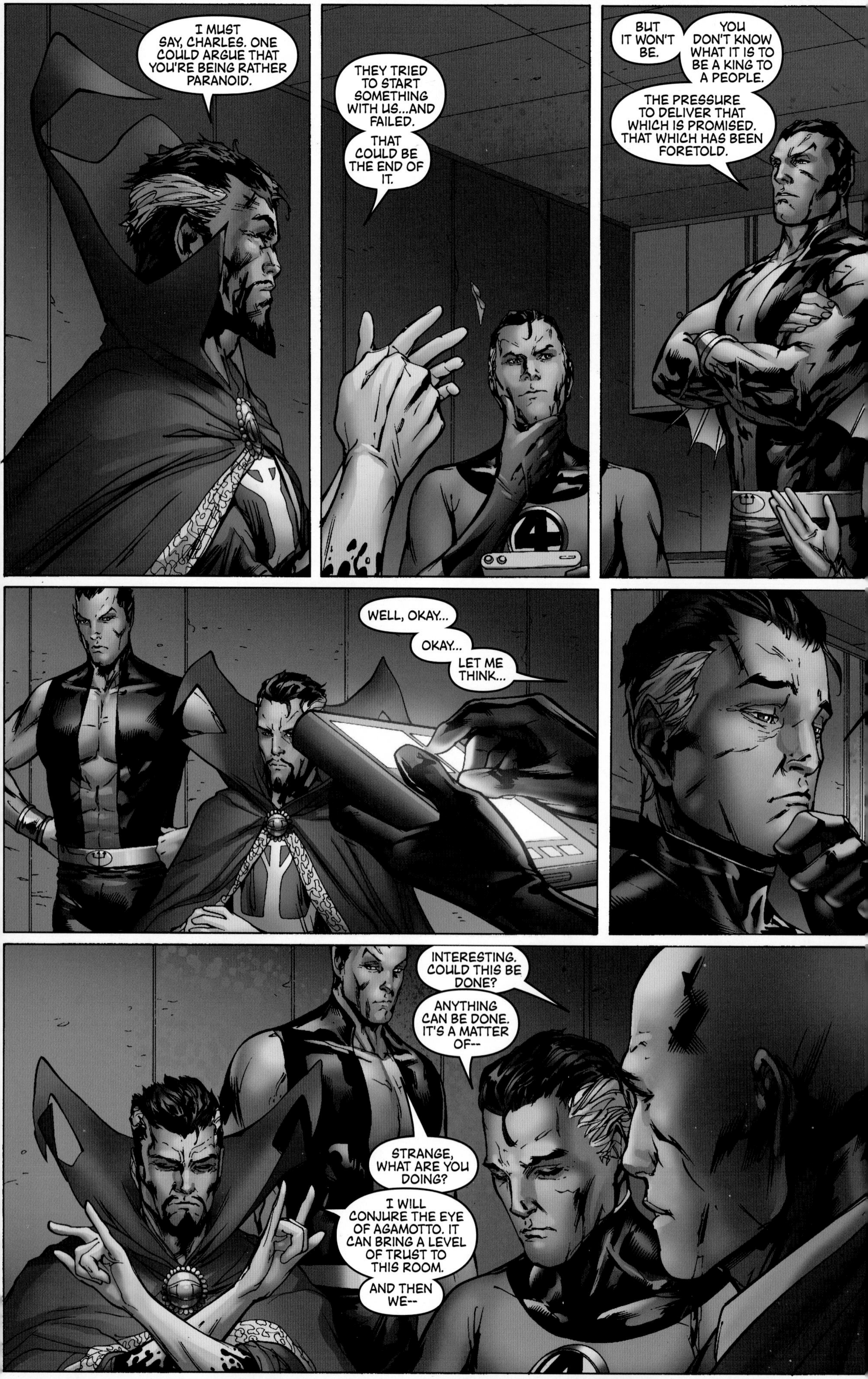

I MUST SAY, CHARLES. ONE COULD ARGUE THAT YOU'RE BEING RATHER PARANOID.
THEY TRIED TO START SOMETHING WITH US...AND FAILED.
THAT COULD BE THE END OF IT.
BUT IT WON'T BE.
YOU DON'T KNOW WHAT IT IS TO BE A KING TO A PEOPLE.
THE PRESSURE TO DELIVER THAT WHICH IS PROMISED. THAT WHICH HAS BEEN FORETOLD.
WELL, OKAY...
OKAY...
LET ME THINK...
INTERESTING. COULD THIS BE DONE?
ANYTHING CAN BE DONE. IT'S A MATTER OF--
STRANGE, WHAT ARE YOU DOING?
I WILL CONJURE THE EYE OF AGAMOTTO. IT CAN BRING A LEVEL OF TRUST TO THIS ROOM.
AND THEN WE--

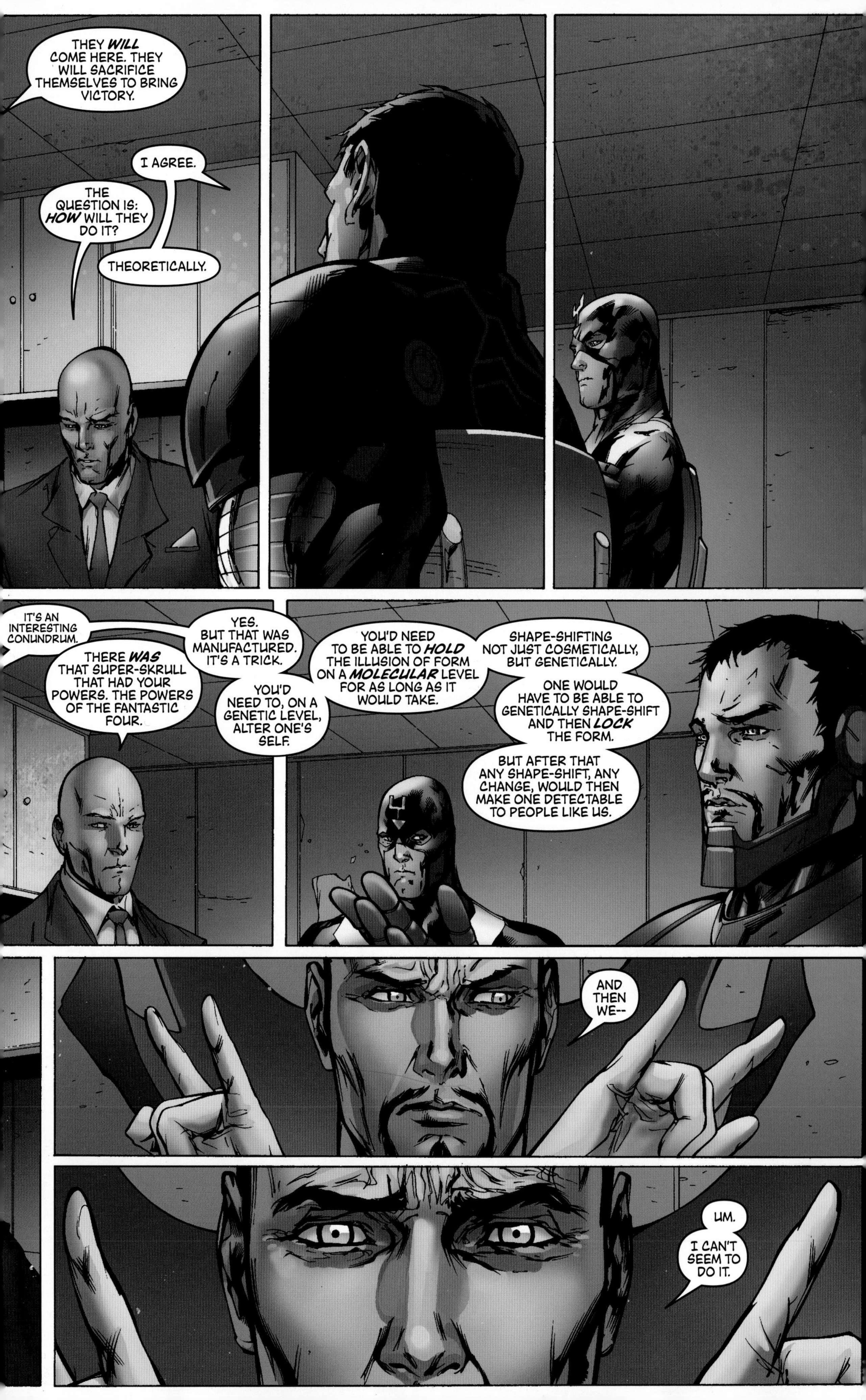
THEY *WILL* COME HERE. THEY WILL SACRIFICE THEMSELVES TO BRING VICTORY.
I AGREE.
THE QUESTION IS: *HOW* WILL THEY DO IT?
THEORETICALLY.
IT'S AN INTERESTING CONUNDRUM.
THERE *WAS* THAT SUPER-SKRULL THAT HAD YOUR POWERS. THE POWERS OF THE FANTASTIC FOUR.
YES. BUT THAT WAS MANUFACTURED. IT'S A TRICK.
YOU'D NEED TO, ON A GENETIC LEVEL, ALTER ONE'S SELF.
YOU'D NEED TO BE ABLE TO *HOLD* THE ILLUSION OF FORM ON A *MOLECULAR* LEVEL FOR AS LONG AS IT WOULD TAKE.
SHAPE-SHIFTING NOT JUST COSMETICALLY, BUT GENETICALLY.
ONE WOULD HAVE TO BE ABLE TO GENETICALLY SHAPE-SHIFT AND THEN *LOCK* THE FORM.
BUT AFTER THAT ANY SHAPE-SHIFT, ANY CHANGE, WOULD THEN MAKE ONE DETECTABLE TO PEOPLE LIKE US.
AND THEN WE--
UM.
I CAN'T SEEM TO DO IT.

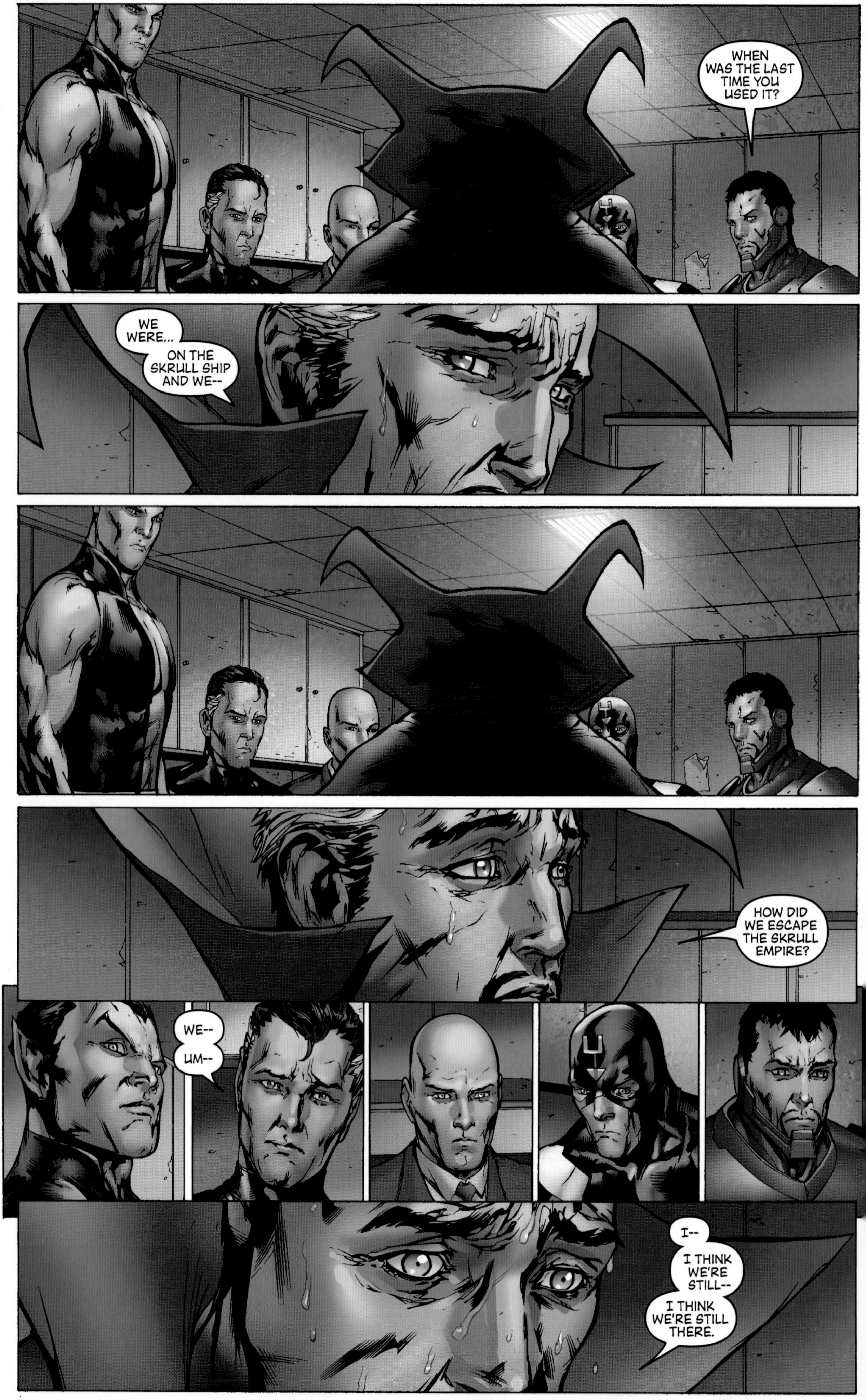
WHEN WAS THE LAST TIME YOU USED IT?
WE WERE...
ON THE SKRULL SHIP AND WE--
HOW DID WE ESCAPE THE SKRULL EMPIRE?
WE--
UM--
I--
I THINK WE'RE STILL--
I THINK WE'RE STILL THERE.

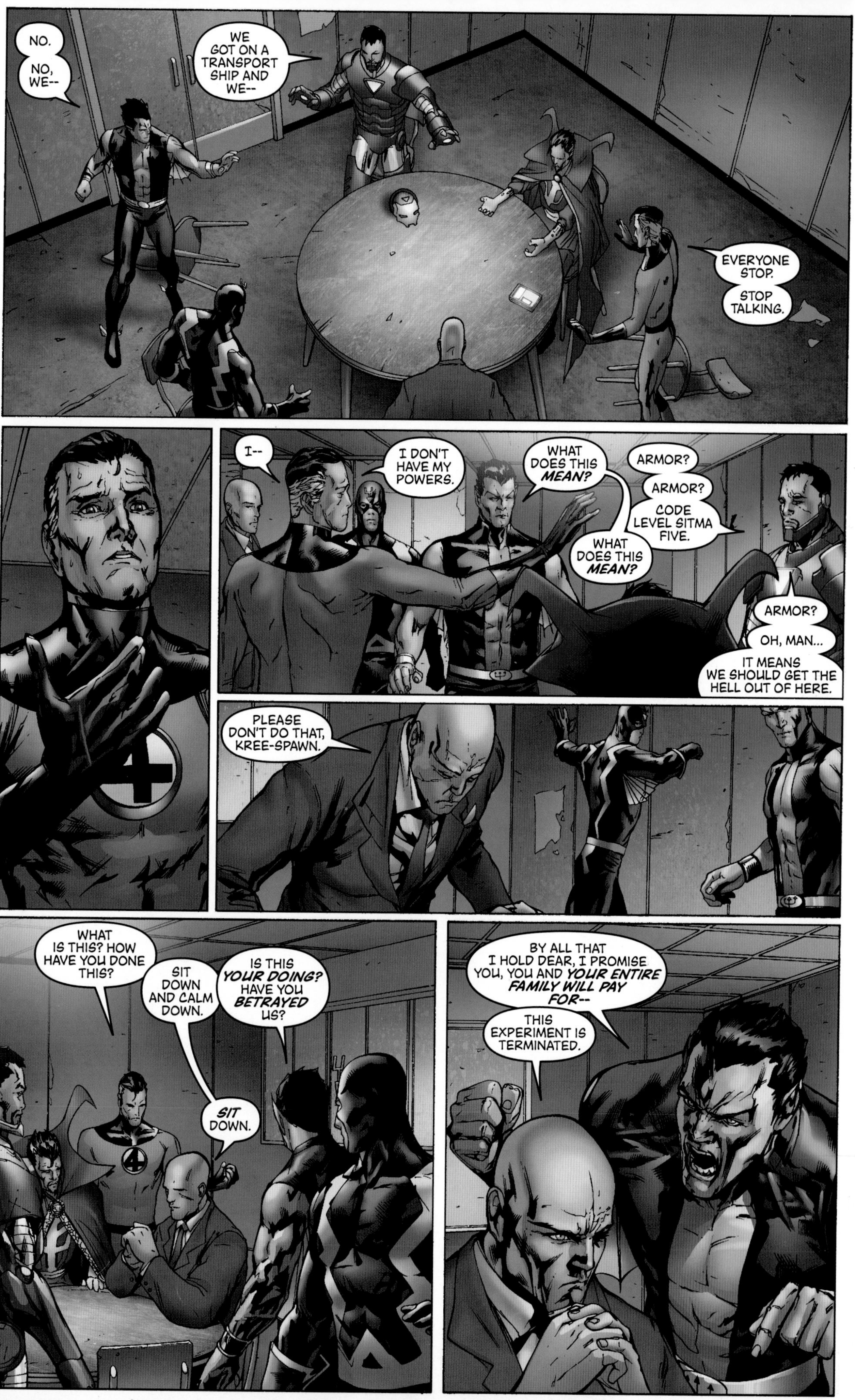
NO.
NO, WE--
WE GOT ON A TRANSPORT SHIP AND WE--
EVERYONE STOP.
STOP TALKING.
I--
I DON'T HAVE MY POWERS.
WHAT DOES THIS *MEAN?*
WHAT DOES THIS *MEAN?*
ARMOR?
ARMOR?
CODE LEVEL SITMA FIVE.
ARMOR?
OH, MAN...
IT MEANS WE SHOULD GET THE HELL OUT OF HERE.
PLEASE DON'T DO THAT, KREE-SPAWN.
WHAT IS THIS? HOW HAVE YOU DONE THIS?
SIT DOWN AND CALM DOWN.
IS THIS *YOUR DOING?* HAVE YOU *BETRAYED* US?
SIT DOWN.
BY ALL THAT I HOLD DEAR, I PROMISE YOU, YOU AND *YOUR ENTIRE FAMILY WILL PAY FOR--*
THIS EXPERIMENT IS TERMINATED.

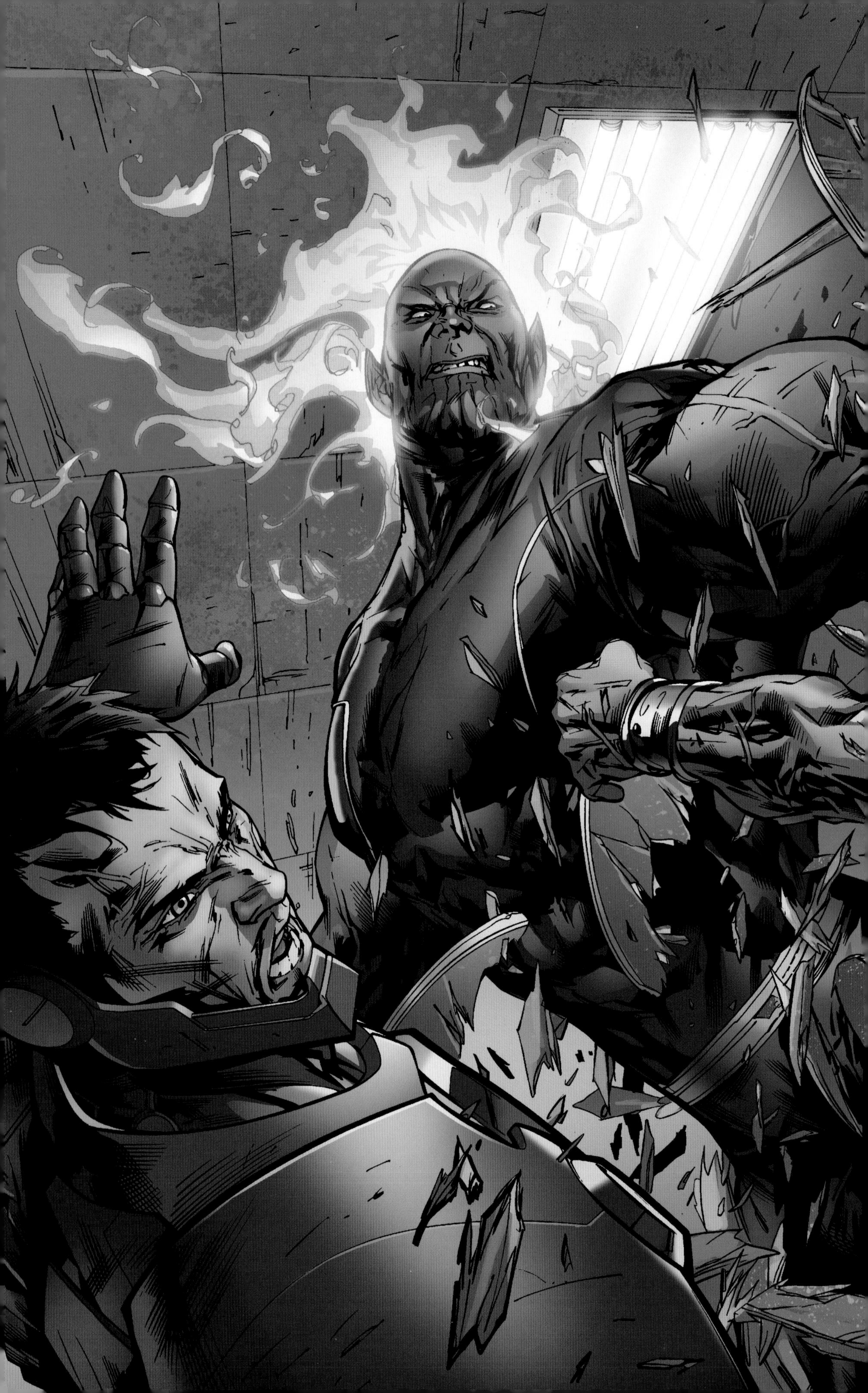

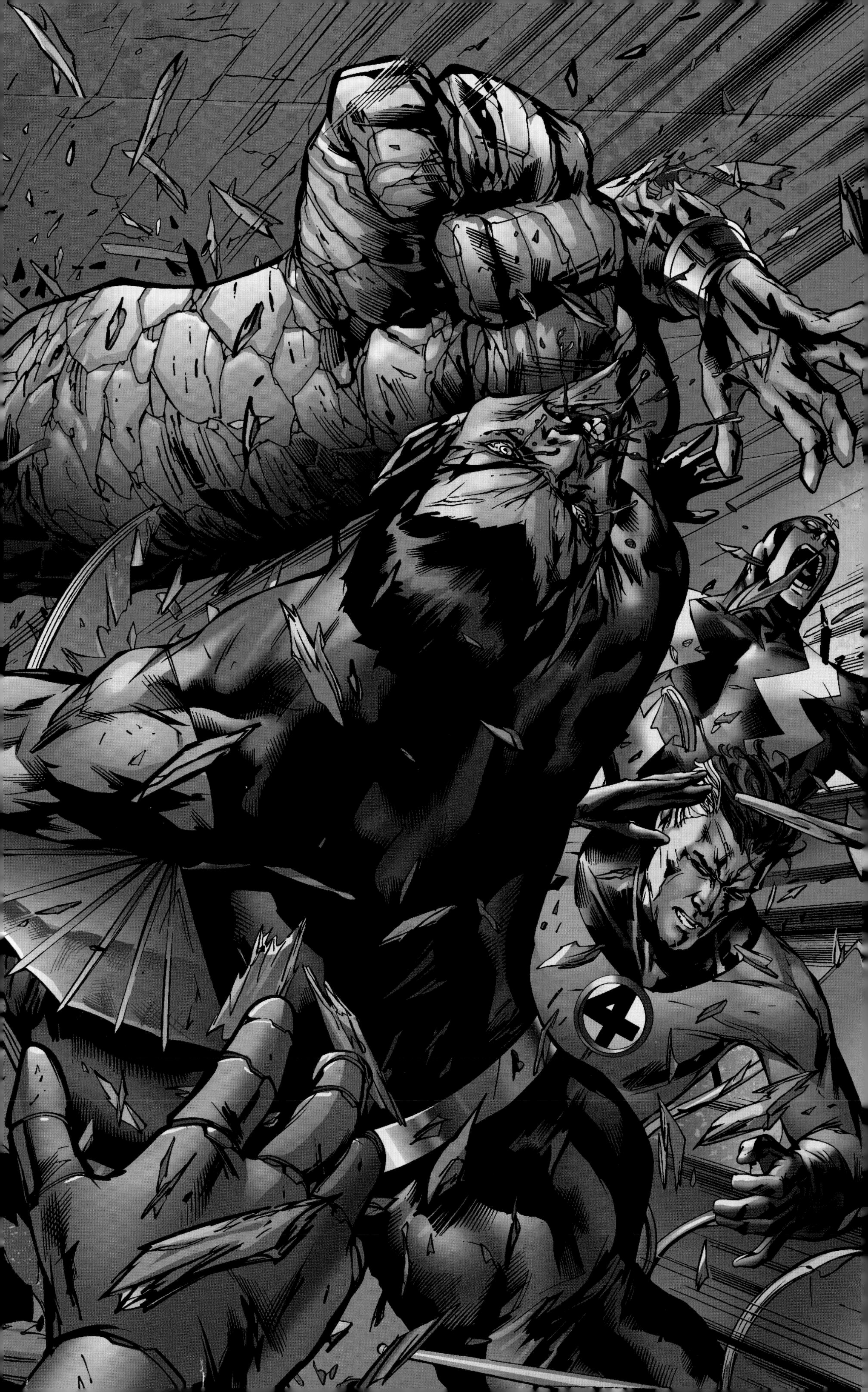

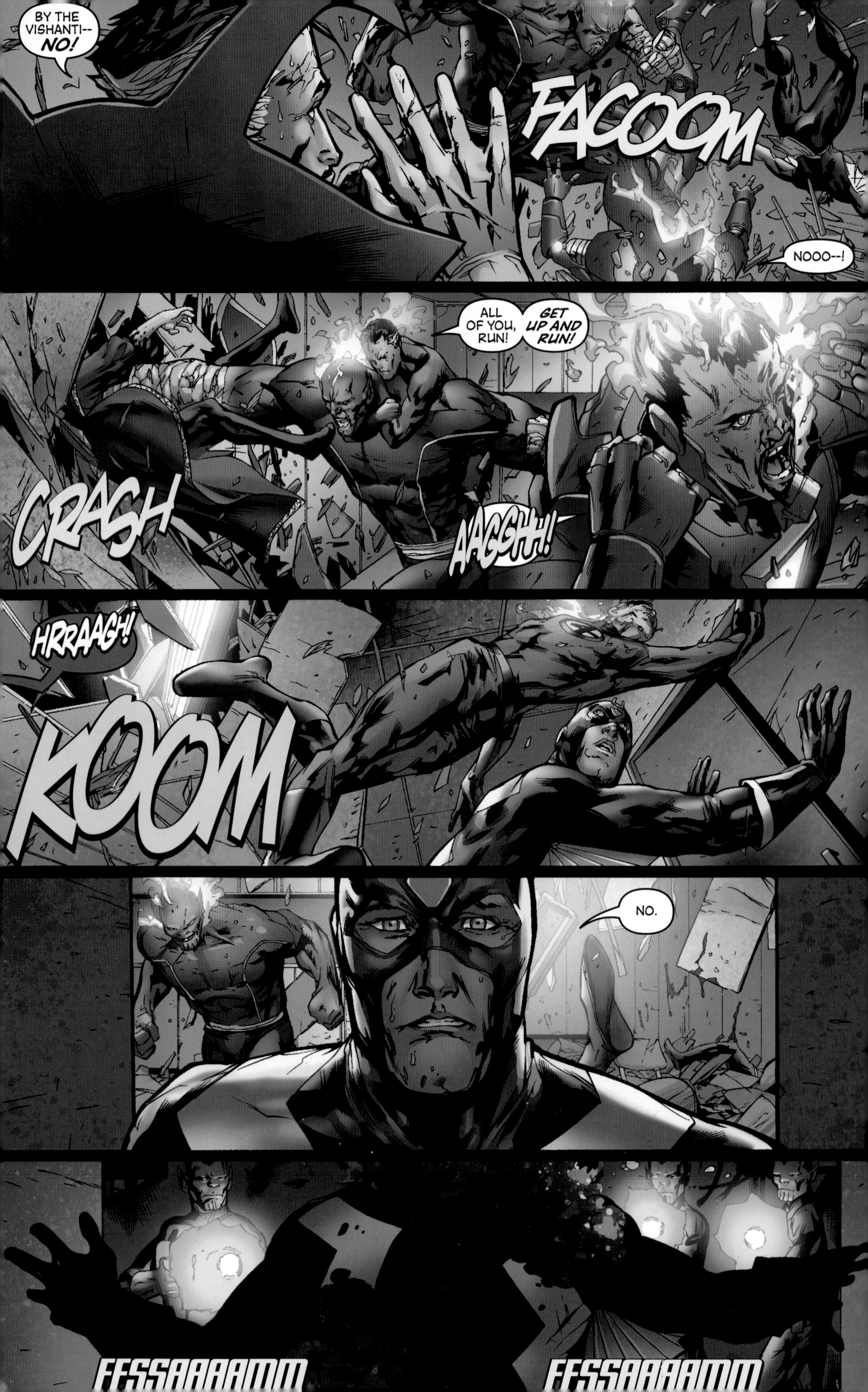

BY THE VISHANTI-- NO!
FACOOM
NOOO--!
ALL OF YOU, RUN!
GET UP AND RUN!
CRASH
AAGGHH!
HRRAAGH!
KOOM
NO.
FFSSAAAAAMM
FFSSAAAAAMM

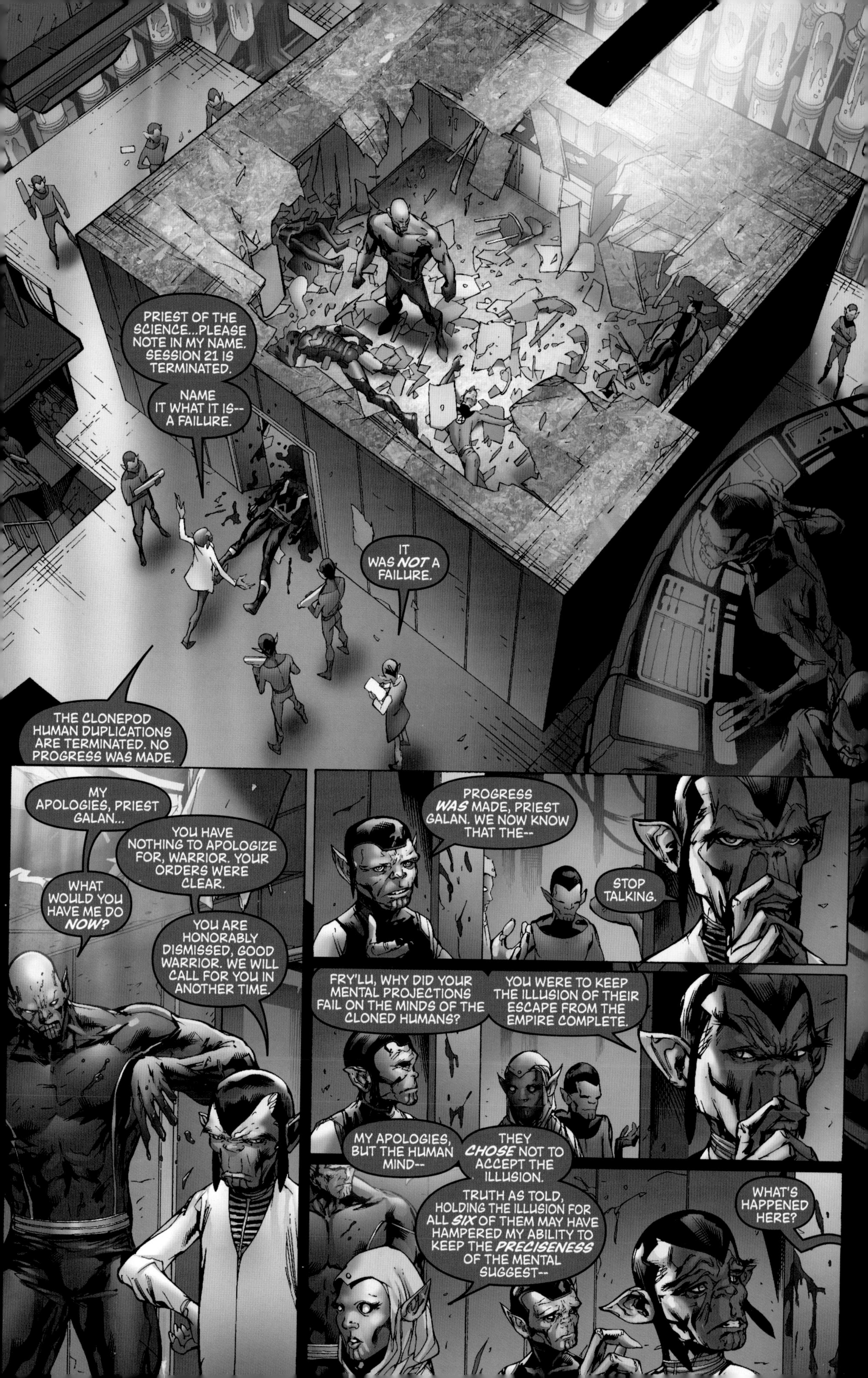
PRIEST OF THE SCIENCE...PLEASE NOTE IN MY NAME. SESSION 21 IS TERMINATED.
NAME IT WHAT IT IS-- A FAILURE.
IT WAS NOT A FAILURE.
THE CLONEPOD HUMAN DUPLICATIONS ARE TERMINATED. NO PROGRESS WAS MADE.
MY APOLOGIES, PRIEST GALAN...
WHAT WOULD YOU HAVE ME DO NOW?
YOU HAVE NOTHING TO APOLOGIZE FOR, WARRIOR. YOUR ORDERS WERE CLEAR.
YOU ARE HONORABLY DISMISSED, GOOD WARRIOR. WE WILL CALL FOR YOU IN ANOTHER TIME.
PROGRESS WAS MADE, PRIEST GALAN. WE NOW KNOW THAT THE--
STOP TALKING.
FRY'LU, WHY DID YOUR MENTAL PROJECTIONS FAIL ON THE MINDS OF THE CLONED HUMANS?
YOU WERE TO KEEP THE ILLUSION OF THEIR ESCAPE FROM THE EMPIRE COMPLETE.
MY APOLOGIES, BUT THE HUMAN MIND--
THEY CHOSE NOT TO ACCEPT THE ILLUSION.
TRUTH AS TOLD, HOLDING THE ILLUSION FOR ALL SIX OF THEM MAY HAVE HAMPERED MY ABILITY TO KEEP THE PRECISENESS OF THE MENTAL SUGGEST--
WHAT'S HAPPENED HERE?

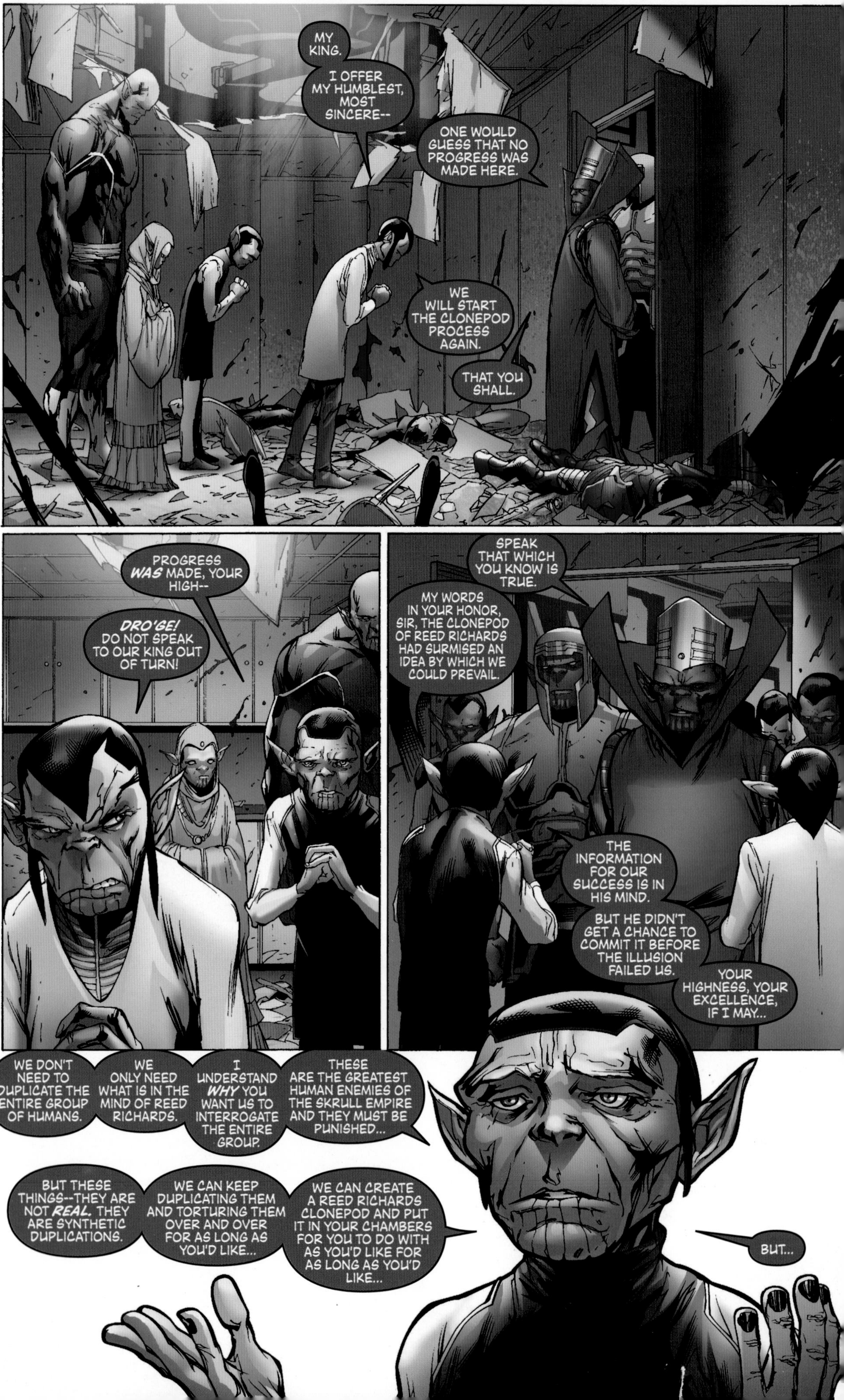
MY KING.
I OFFER MY HUMBLEST, MOST SINCERE--
ONE WOULD GUESS THAT NO PROGRESS WAS MADE HERE.
WE WILL START THE CLONEPOD PROCESS AGAIN.
THAT YOU SHALL.
PROGRESS *WAS* MADE, YOUR HIGH--
DRO'GE! DO NOT SPEAK TO OUR KING OUT OF TURN!
SPEAK THAT WHICH YOU KNOW IS TRUE.
MY WORDS IN YOUR HONOR, SIR, THE CLONEPOD OF REED RICHARDS HAD SURMISED AN IDEA BY WHICH WE COULD PREVAIL.
THE INFORMATION FOR OUR SUCCESS IS IN HIS MIND.
BUT HE DIDN'T GET A CHANCE TO COMMIT IT BEFORE THE ILLUSION FAILED US.
YOUR HIGHNESS, YOUR EXCELLENCE, IF I MAY...
WE DON'T NEED TO DUPLICATE THE ENTIRE GROUP OF HUMANS.
WE ONLY NEED WHAT IS IN THE MIND OF REED RICHARDS.
I UNDERSTAND *WHY* YOU WANT US TO INTERROGATE THE ENTIRE GROUP.
THESE ARE THE GREATEST HUMAN ENEMIES OF THE SKRULL EMPIRE AND THEY MUST BE PUNISHED...
BUT THESE THINGS--THEY ARE NOT *REAL.* THEY ARE SYNTHETIC DUPLICATIONS.
WE CAN KEEP DUPLICATING THEM AND TORTURING THEM OVER AND OVER FOR AS LONG AS YOU'D LIKE...
WE CAN CREATE A REED RICHARDS CLONEPOD AND PUT IT IN YOUR CHAMBERS FOR YOU TO DO WITH AS YOU'D LIKE FOR AS LONG AS YOU'D LIKE...
BUT...

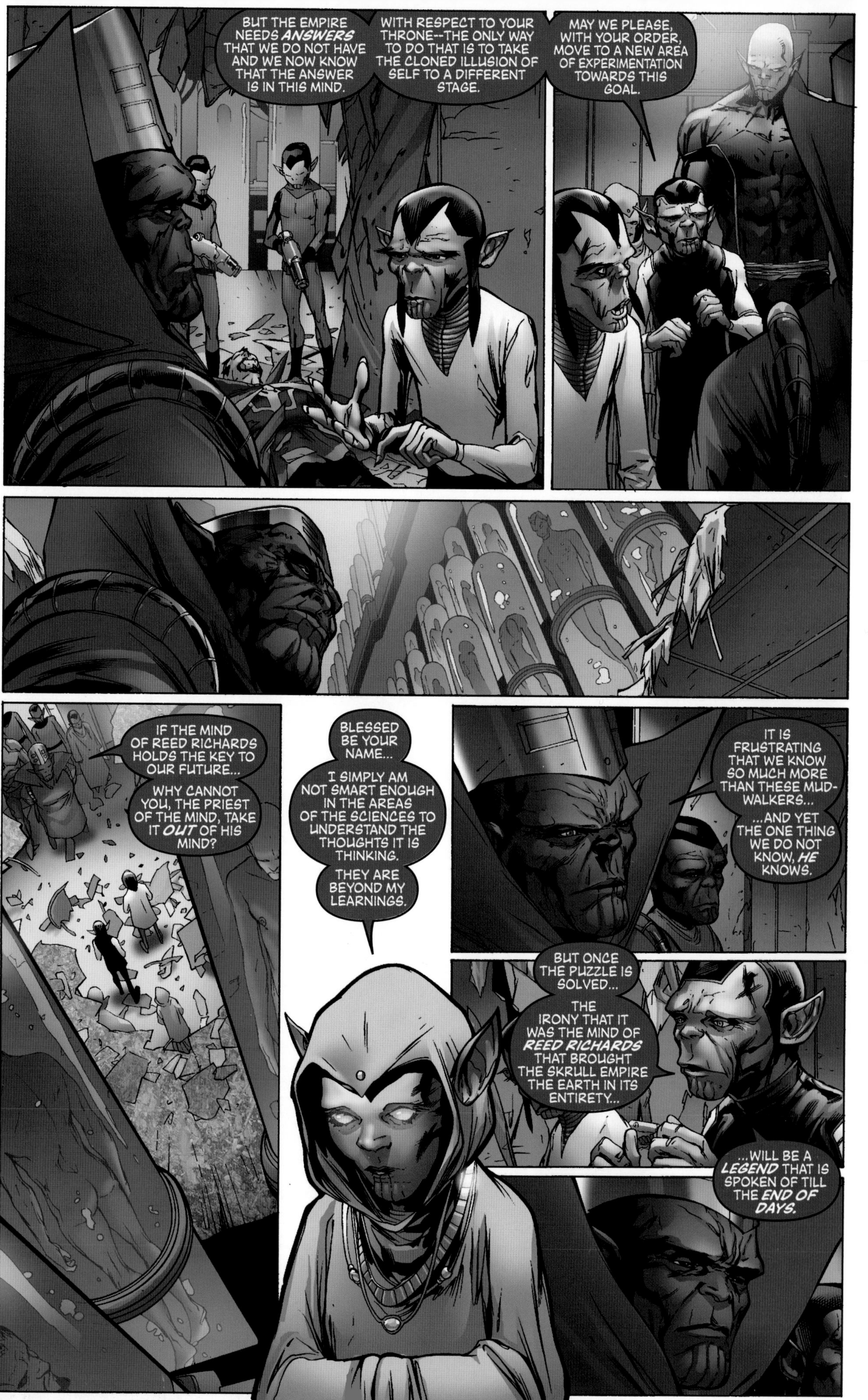
BUT THE EMPIRE NEEDS ANSWERS THAT WE DO NOT HAVE AND WE NOW KNOW THAT THE ANSWER IS IN THIS MIND.
WITH RESPECT TO YOUR THRONE--THE ONLY WAY TO DO THAT IS TO TAKE THE CLONED ILLUSION OF SELF TO A DIFFERENT STAGE.
MAY WE PLEASE, WITH YOUR ORDER, MOVE TO A NEW AREA OF EXPERIMENTATION TOWARDS THIS GOAL.
IF THE MIND OF REED RICHARDS HOLDS THE KEY TO OUR FUTURE...
WHY CANNOT YOU, THE PRIEST OF THE MIND, TAKE IT OUT OF HIS MIND?
BLESSED BE YOUR NAME...
I SIMPLY AM NOT SMART ENOUGH IN THE AREAS OF THE SCIENCES TO UNDERSTAND THE THOUGHTS IT IS THINKING.
THEY ARE BEYOND MY LEARNINGS.
IT IS FRUSTRATING THAT WE KNOW SO MUCH MORE THAN THESE MUD-WALKERS...
...AND YET THE ONE THING WE DO NOT KNOW, HE KNOWS.
BUT ONCE THE PUZZLE IS SOLVED...
THE IRONY THAT IT WAS THE MIND OF REED RICHARDS THAT BROUGHT THE SKRULL EMPIRE THE EARTH IN ITS ENTIRETY...
...WILL BE A LEGEND THAT IS SPOKEN OF TILL THE END OF DAYS.

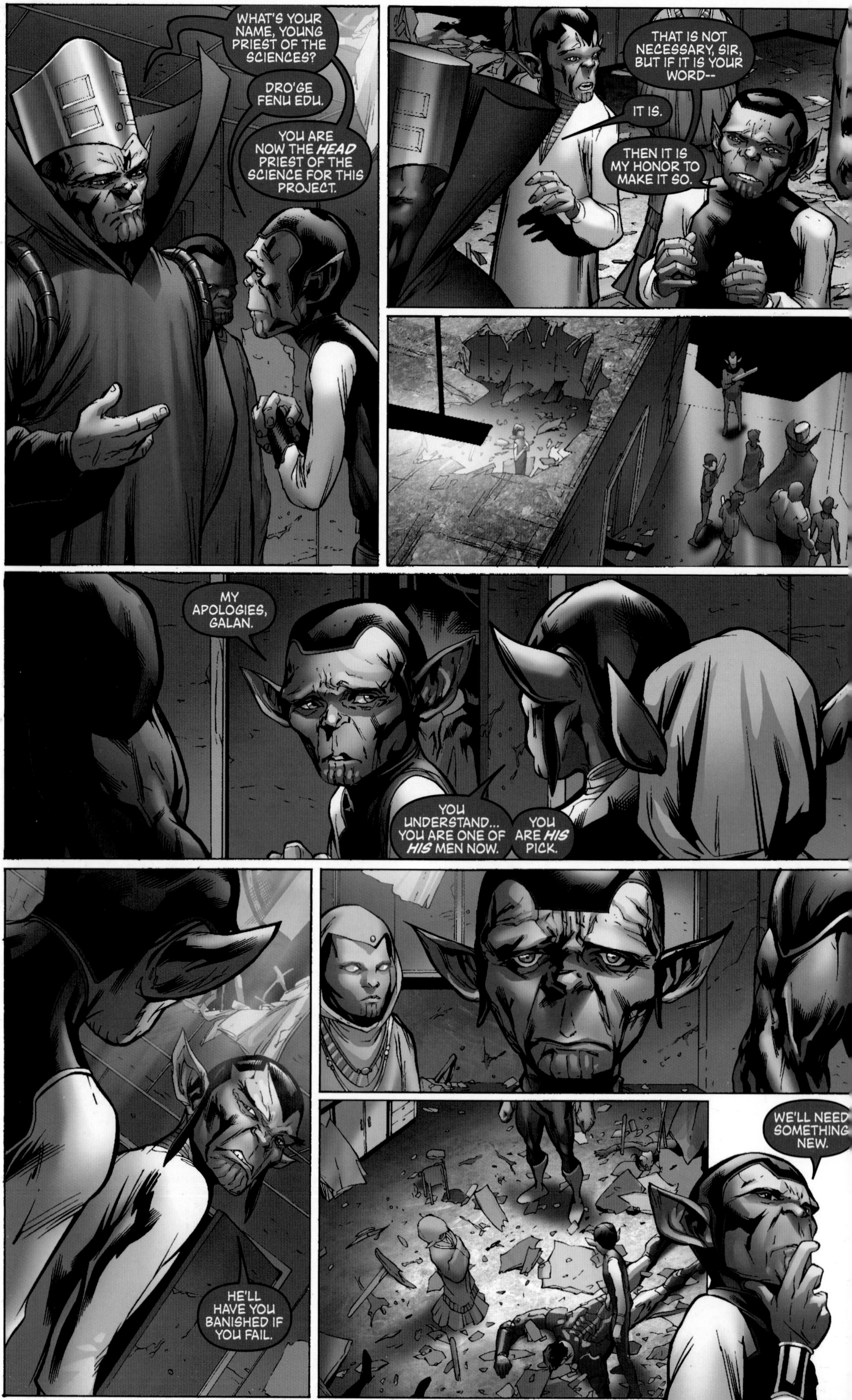
WHAT'S YOUR NAME, YOUNG PRIEST OF THE SCIENCES?
DRO'GE FENU EDU.
YOU ARE NOW THE *HEAD* PRIEST OF THE SCIENCE FOR THIS PROJECT.
THAT IS NOT NECESSARY, SIR, BUT IF IT IS YOUR WORD--
IT IS.
THEN IT IS MY HONOR TO MAKE IT SO.
MY APOLOGIES, GALAN.
YOU UNDERSTAND... YOU ARE ONE OF *HIS* MEN NOW.
YOU ARE *HIS* PICK.
HE'LL HAVE YOU BANISHED IF YOU FAIL.
WE'LL NEED SOMETHING NEW.

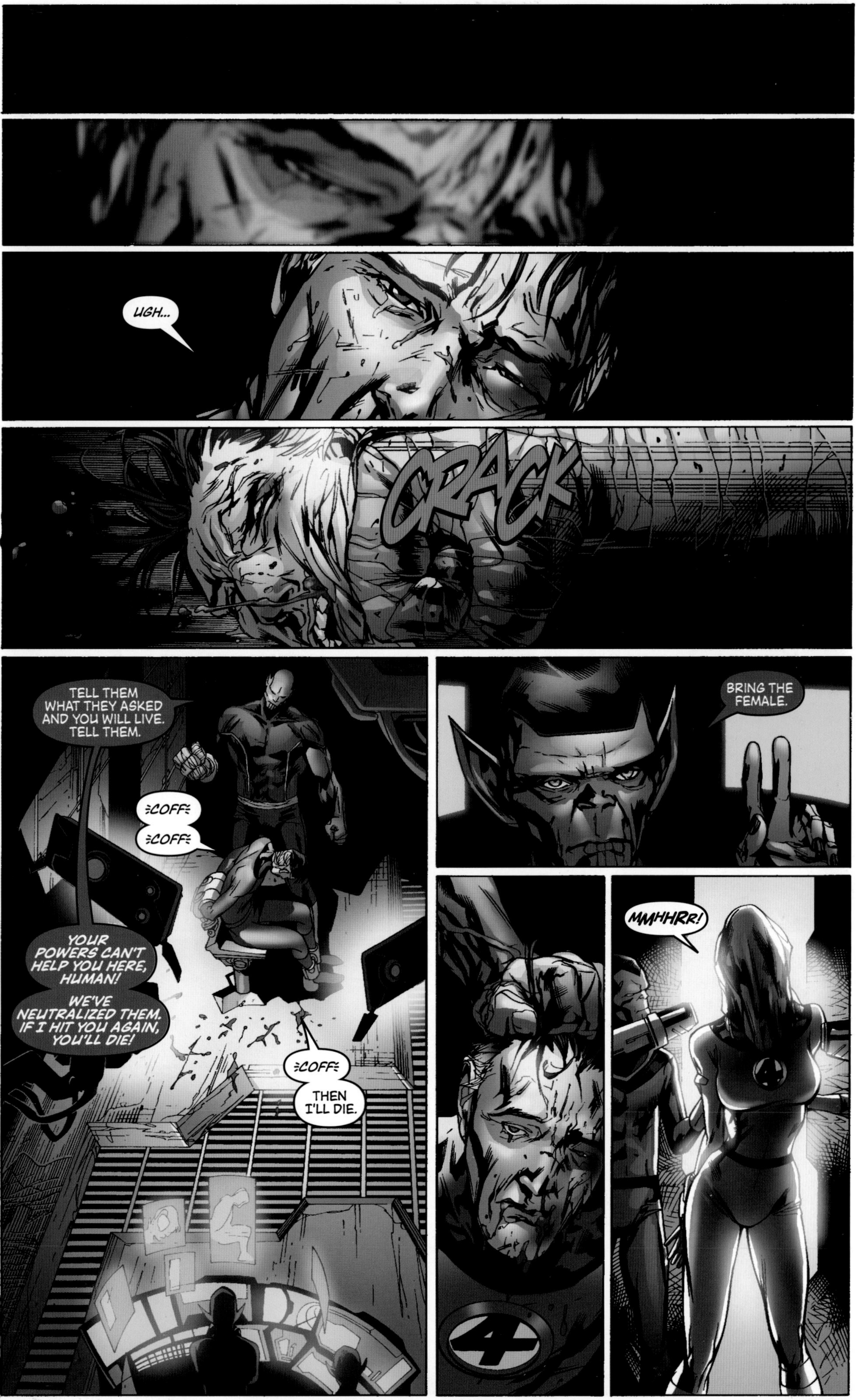
UGH...
CRACK
TELL THEM WHAT THEY ASKED AND YOU WILL LIVE. TELL THEM.
COFF
COFF
YOUR POWERS CAN'T HELP YOU HERE, HUMAN!
WE'VE NEUTRALIZED THEM. IF I HIT YOU AGAIN, YOU'LL DIE!
COFF
THEN I'LL DIE.
BRING THE FEMALE.
MMHHRr!

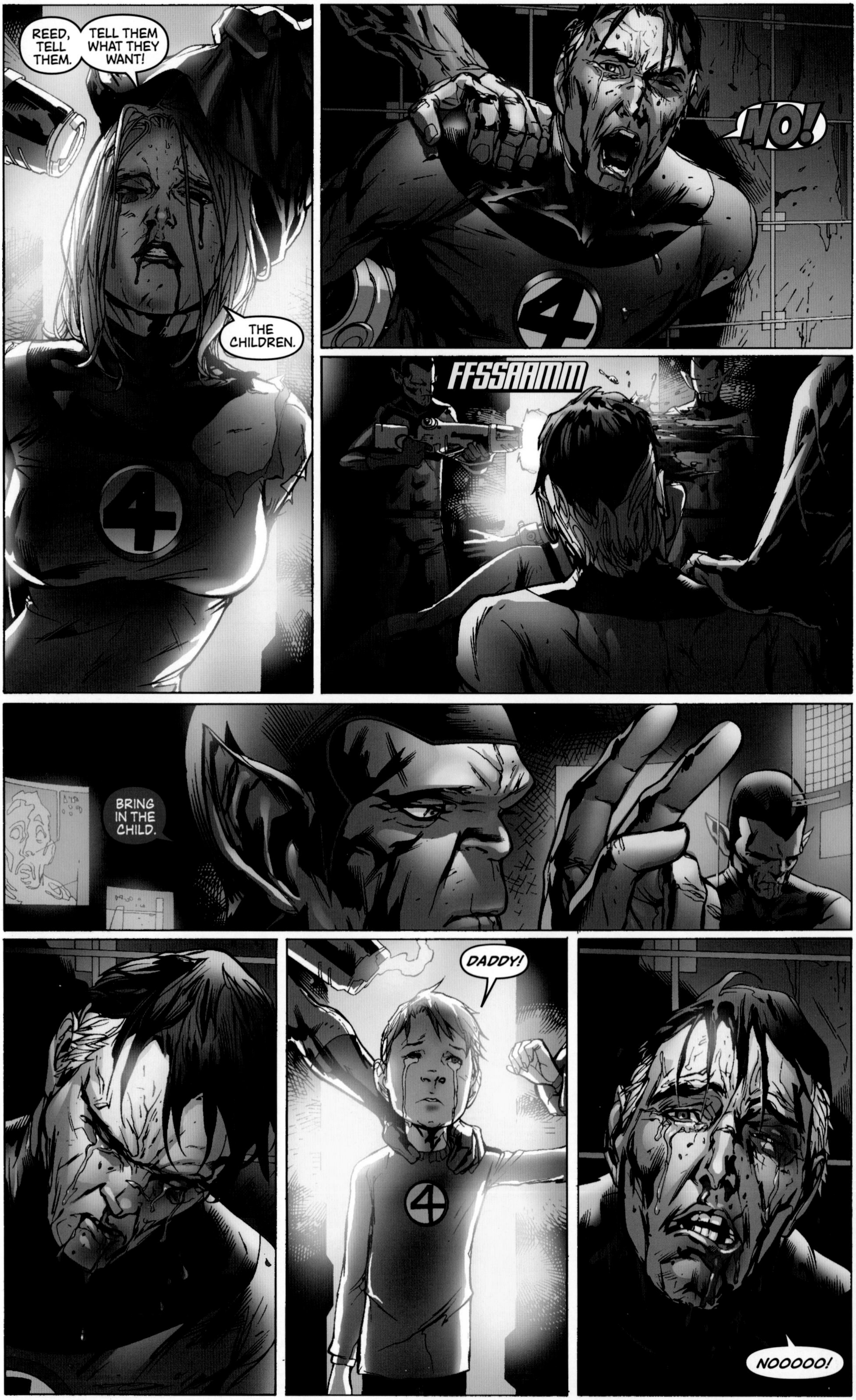
REED, TELL THEM.
TELL THEM WHAT THEY WANT!
THE CHILDREN.
NO!
FFSSAAMM
BRING IN THE CHILD.
DADDY!
NOOOOO!

DADDY!

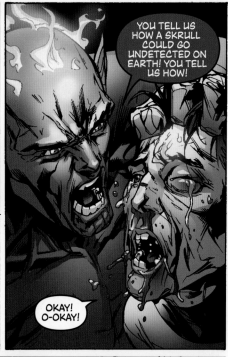

YOU TELL US HOW A SKRULL COULD GO UNDETECTED ON EARTH! YOU TELL US HOW!

OKAY! O-OKAY!

I'LL T-TELL YOU. I'LL TELL YOU ANYTHING. BUT YOU LET MY CHILD GO!

HE IS TELLING A FALSEHOOD.

HE IS ALREADY PLANNING TO RELEASE A CHEMICAL-BASED WEAPON THAT WILL INSTANTLY KILL EVERYONE HERE.

YOU LEAVE MY CHILD ALONE!

END THIS.

THERE IS ANOTHER WAY. IT WILL REQUIRE SOMETHING SUBTLE.

BY YOUR WORD.

WILL NOTHING BREAK HIM?

I'M AT A LOSS TO UNDERSTAND THIS SPECIES' MOTIVATIONS.

SMACK

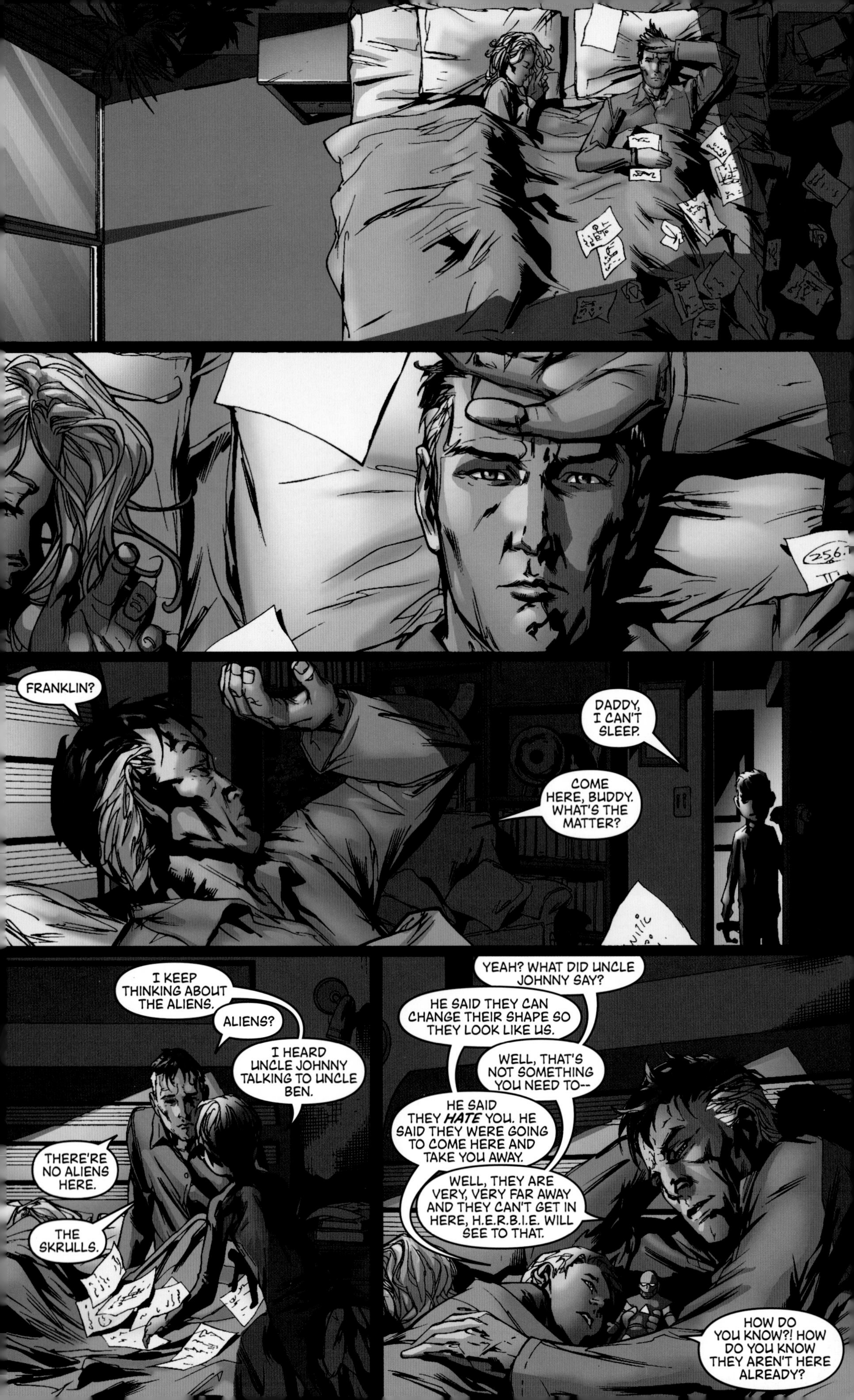
FRANKLIN?
DADDY, I CAN'T SLEEP.
COME HERE, BUDDY. WHAT'S THE MATTER?
I KEEP THINKING ABOUT THE ALIENS.
ALIENS?
I HEARD UNCLE JOHNNY TALKING TO UNCLE BEN.
THERE'RE NO ALIENS HERE.
THE SKRULLS.
YEAH? WHAT DID UNCLE JOHNNY SAY?
HE SAID THEY CAN CHANGE THEIR SHAPE SO THEY LOOK LIKE US.
WELL, THAT'S NOT SOMETHING YOU NEED TO--
HE SAID THEY *HATE* YOU. HE SAID THEY WERE GOING TO COME HERE AND TAKE YOU AWAY.
WELL, THEY ARE VERY, VERY FAR AWAY AND THEY CAN'T GET IN HERE, H.E.R.B.I.E. WILL SEE TO THAT.
HOW DO YOU KNOW?! HOW DO YOU KNOW THEY AREN'T HERE ALREADY?

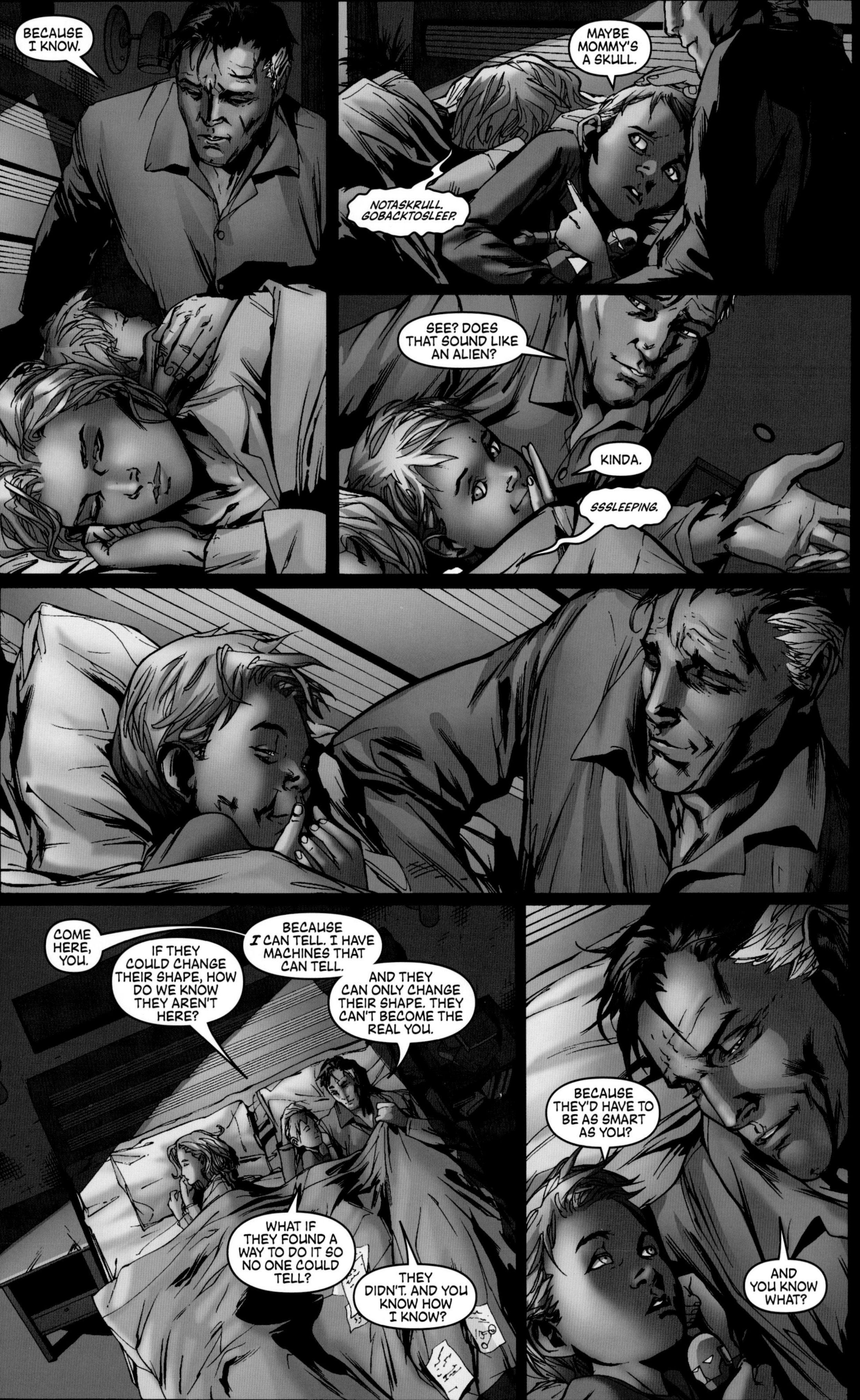
BECAUSE I KNOW.
MAYBE MOMMY'S A SKULL.
NOTASKRULL. GOBACKTOSLEEP.
SEE? DOES THAT SOUND LIKE AN ALIEN?
KINDA.
SSSLEEPING.
COME HERE, YOU.
IF THEY COULD CHANGE THEIR SHAPE, HOW DO WE KNOW THEY AREN'T HERE?
BECAUSE I CAN TELL. I HAVE MACHINES THAT CAN TELL.
AND THEY CAN ONLY CHANGE THEIR SHAPE. THEY CAN'T BECOME THE REAL YOU.
WHAT IF THEY FOUND A WAY TO DO IT SO NO ONE COULD TELL?
THEY DIDN'T. AND YOU KNOW HOW I KNOW?
BECAUSE THEY'D HAVE TO BE AS SMART AS YOU?
AND YOU KNOW WHAT?

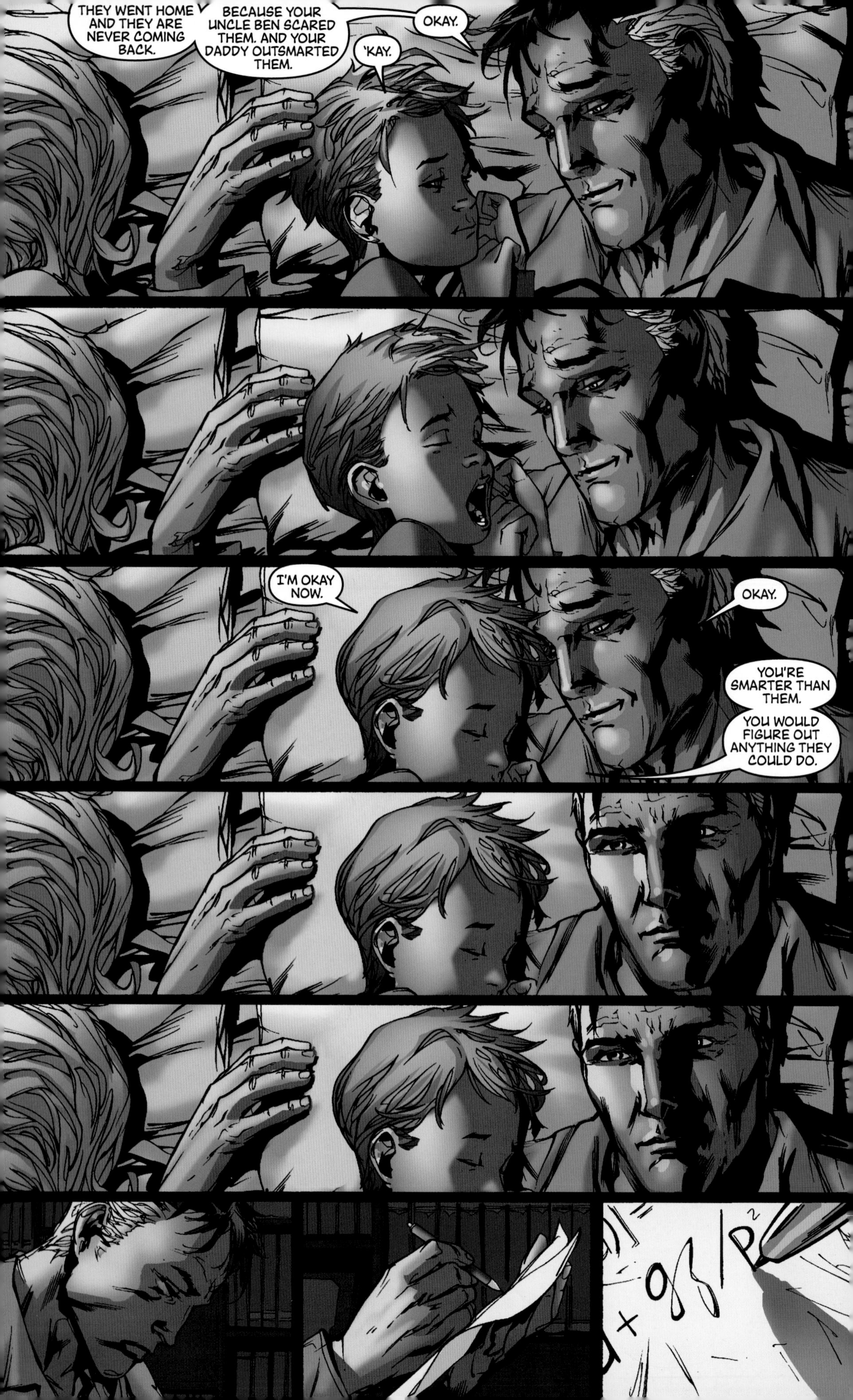
THEY WENT HOME AND THEY ARE NEVER COMING BACK.
BECAUSE YOUR UNCLE BEN SCARED THEM. AND YOUR DADDY OUTSMARTED THEM.
OKAY.
'KAY.
I'M OKAY NOW.
OKAY.
YOU'RE SMARTER THAN THEM.
YOU WOULD FIGURE OUT ANYTHING THEY COULD DO.

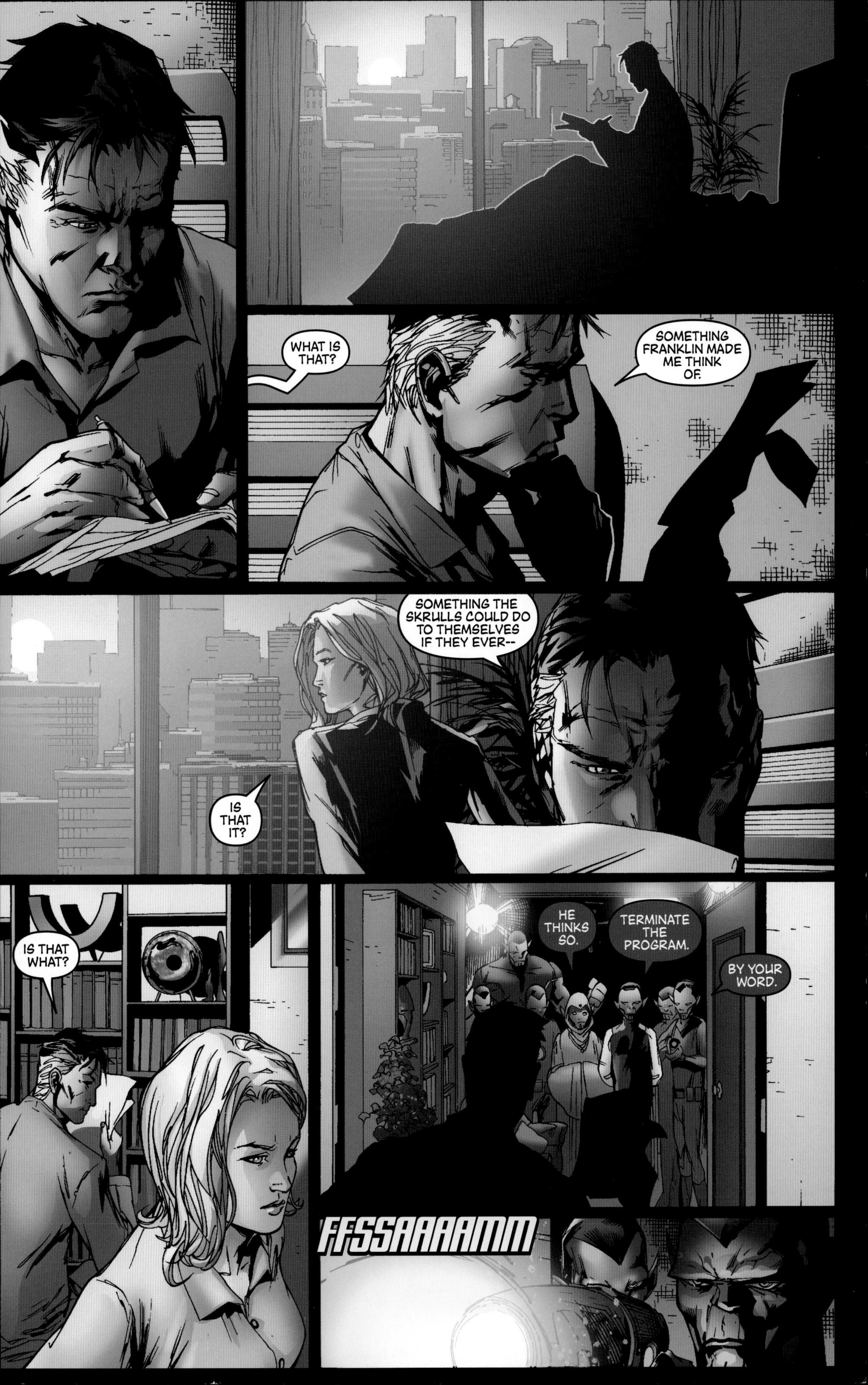
WHAT IS THAT?
SOMETHING FRANKLIN MADE ME THINK OF.
SOMETHING THE SKRULLS COULD DO TO THEMSELVES IF THEY EVER--
IS THAT IT?
IS THAT WHAT?
HE THINKS SO.
TERMINATE THE PROGRAM.
BY YOUR WORD.
FFSSAAAAAMM

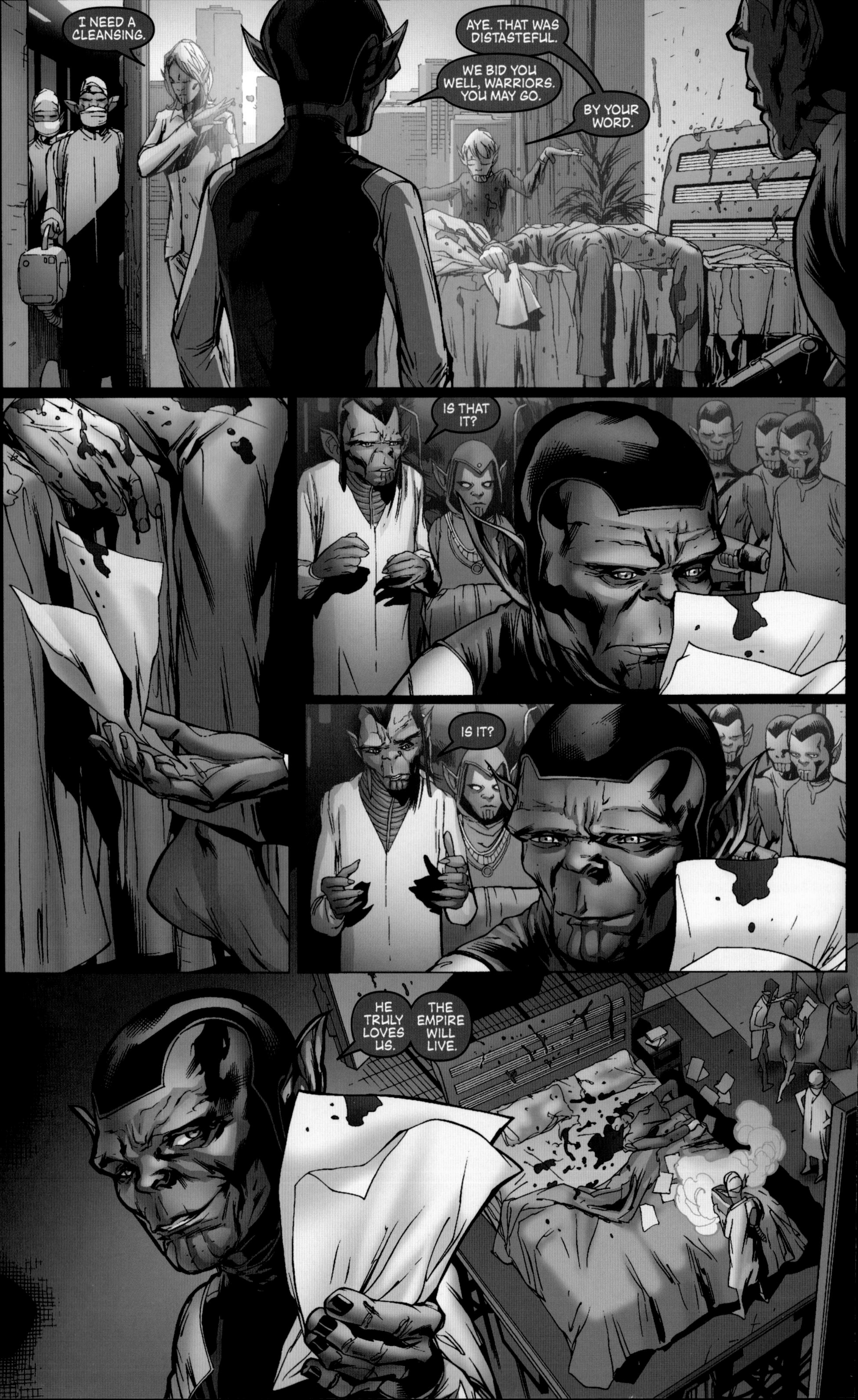
I NEED A CLEANSING.
AYE. THAT WAS DISTASTEFUL.
WE BID YOU WELL, WARRIORS. YOU MAY GO.
BY YOUR WORD.
IS THAT IT?
IS IT?
HE TRULY LOVES US.
THE EMPIRE WILL LIVE.

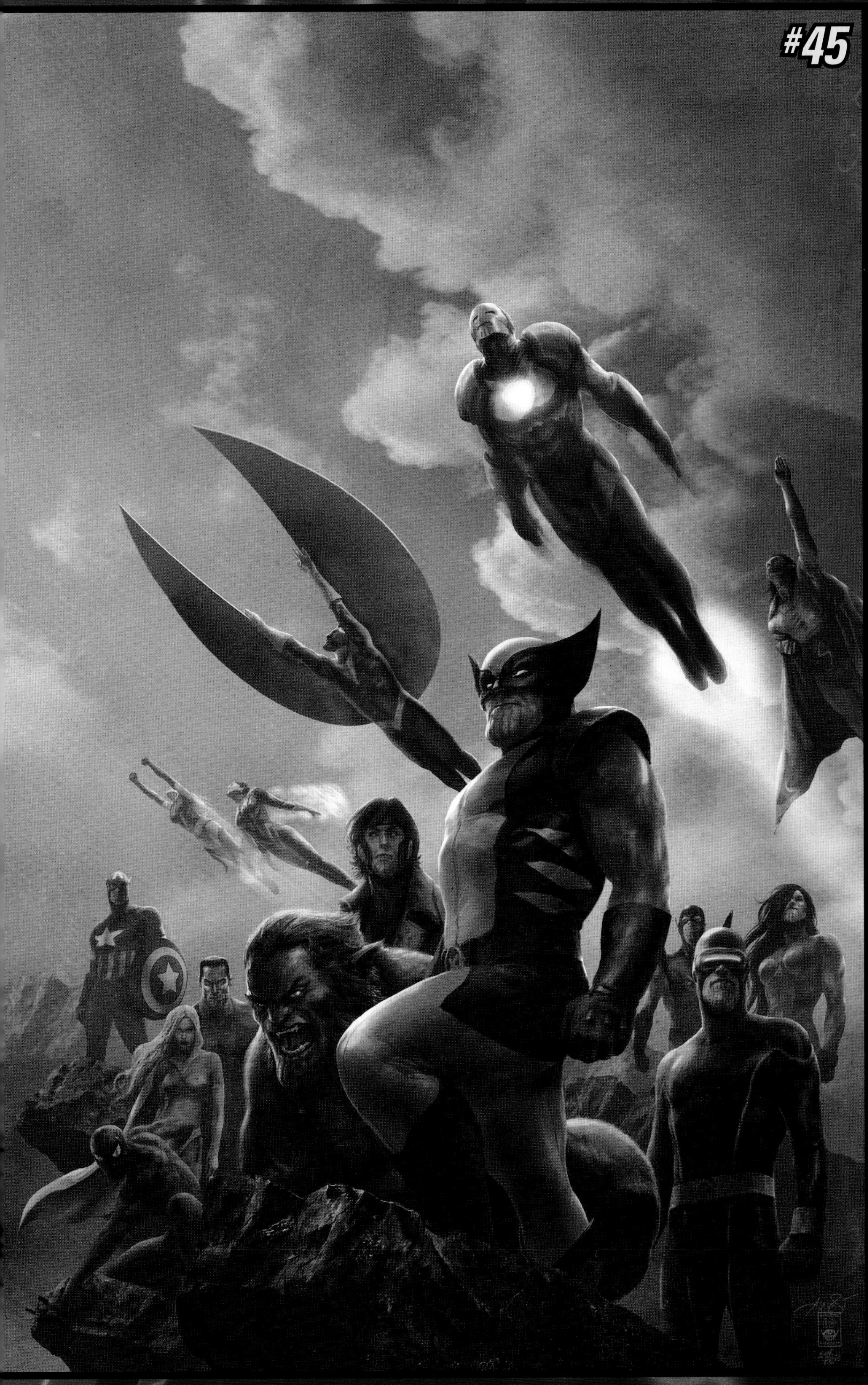
#45

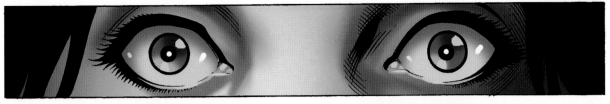

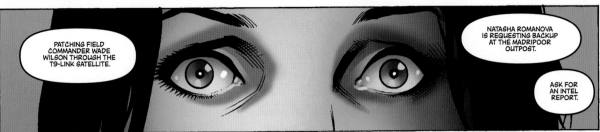

PATCHING FIELD COMMANDER WADE WILSON THROUGH THE T9-LINK SATELLITE.

NATASHA ROMANOVA IS REQUESTING BACKUP AT THE MADRIPOOR OUTPOST.

ASK FOR AN INTEL REPORT.

DIRECTOR SHAW HASN'T REPORTED IN YET.

SEND A B-TEAM OUT TO THE SAVAGE LAND AND SEE WHAT IS WHAT.

ANY WORD ON WEAPON XXXC?

SOME KIND OF FLUCTUATION.

LATVERIA HAS NO AMBASSADOR, HE'S LYING.

LATVERIA HAS NO AMBASSADOR? SINCE WHEN?

AGENT SITWELL IS CALLING IN?

THE BROOD SIGNAL IS STILL OFFLINE. SEE WHAT YOU CAN DO WITH IT.

SERIOUSLY, SINCE WHEN?

HAVE WE GOTTEN AN UPDATE FROM GENOSHA'S OUTPOST?

GENOSHA, THIS IS HELICARRIER FIVE.

YOU'RE LATE WITH THE SCHEDULED UPDATE.

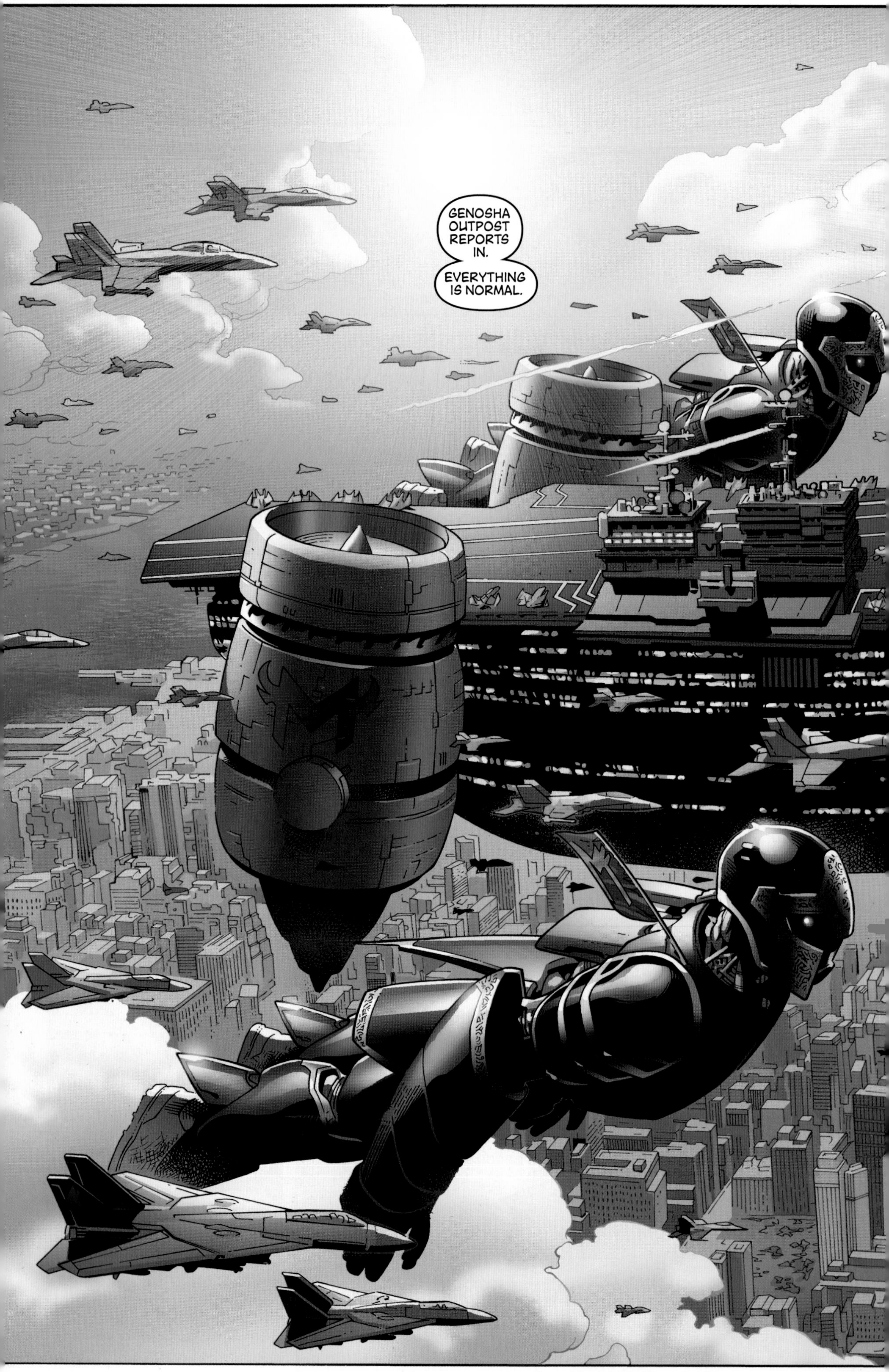
GENOSHA OUTPOST REPORTS IN.
EVERYTHING IS NORMAL.

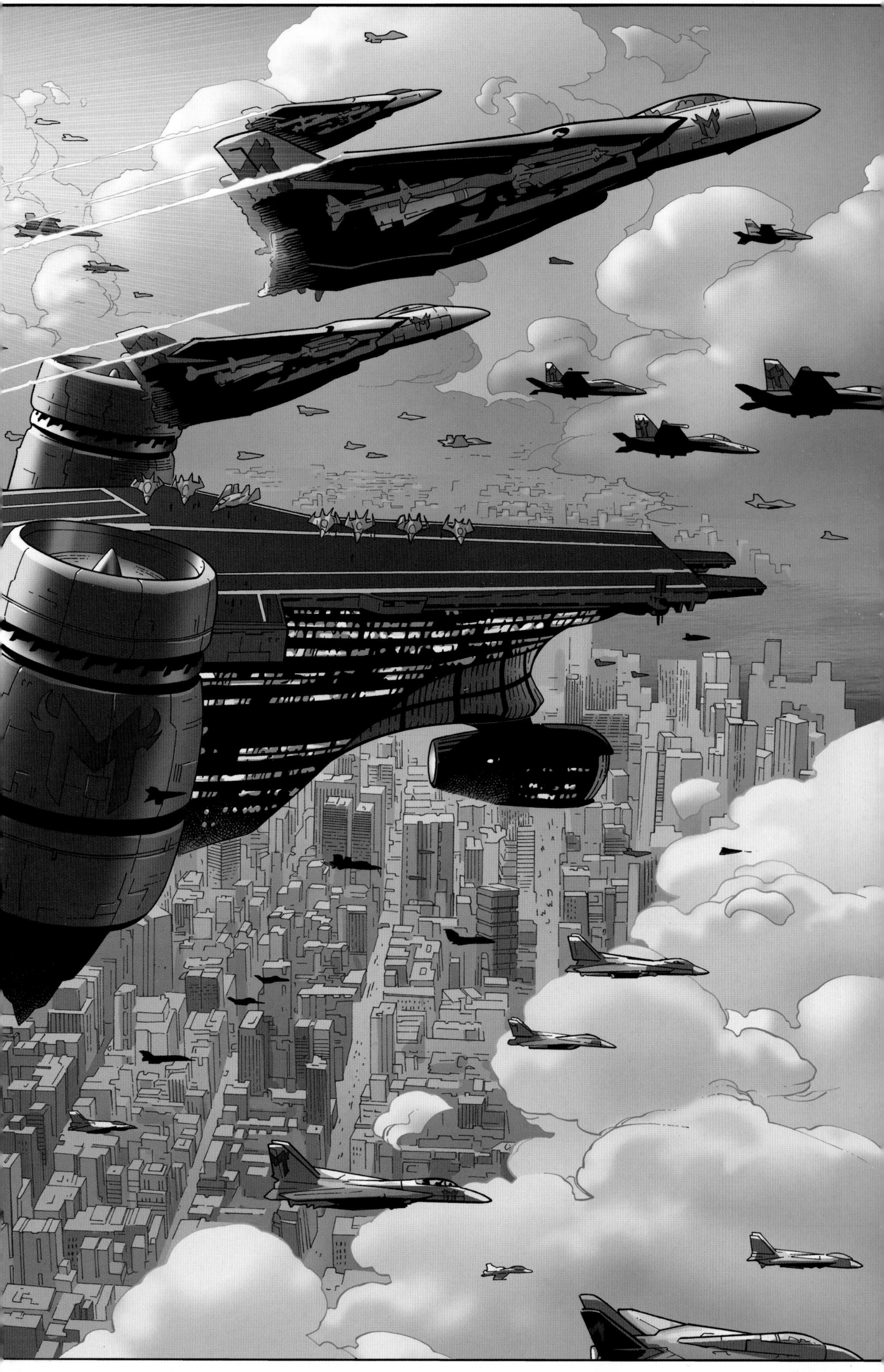

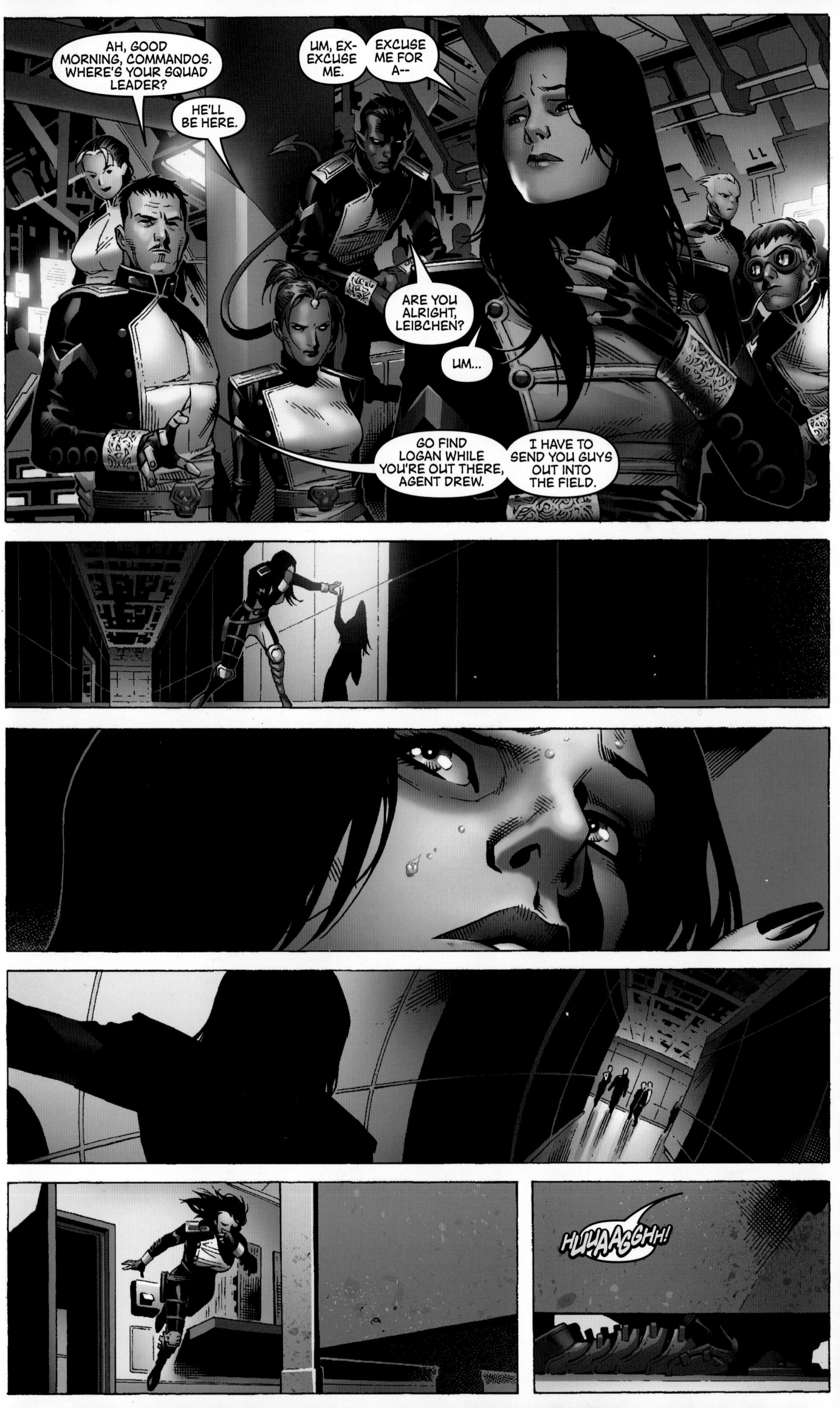
AH, GOOD MORNING, COMMANDOS. WHERE'S YOUR SQUAD LEADER?
HE'LL BE HERE.
UM, EX- EXCUSE ME.
EXCUSE ME FOR A--
ARE YOU ALRIGHT, LEIBCHEN?
UM...
I HAVE TO SEND YOU GUYS OUT INTO THE FIELD.
GO FIND LOGAN WHILE YOU'RE OUT THERE, AGENT DREW.
HUUAAGGHH!

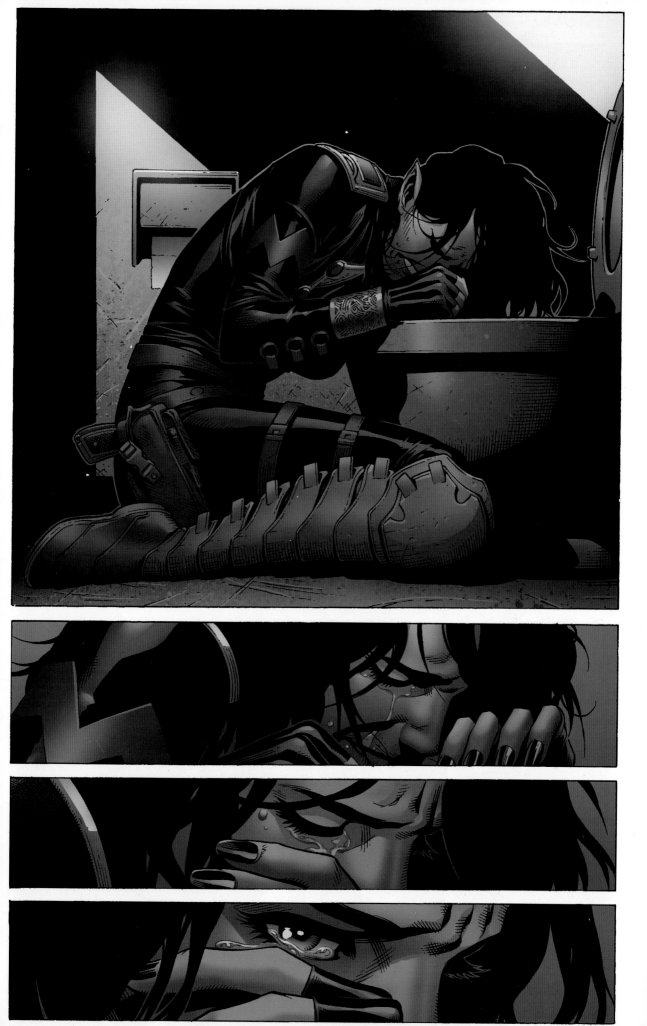

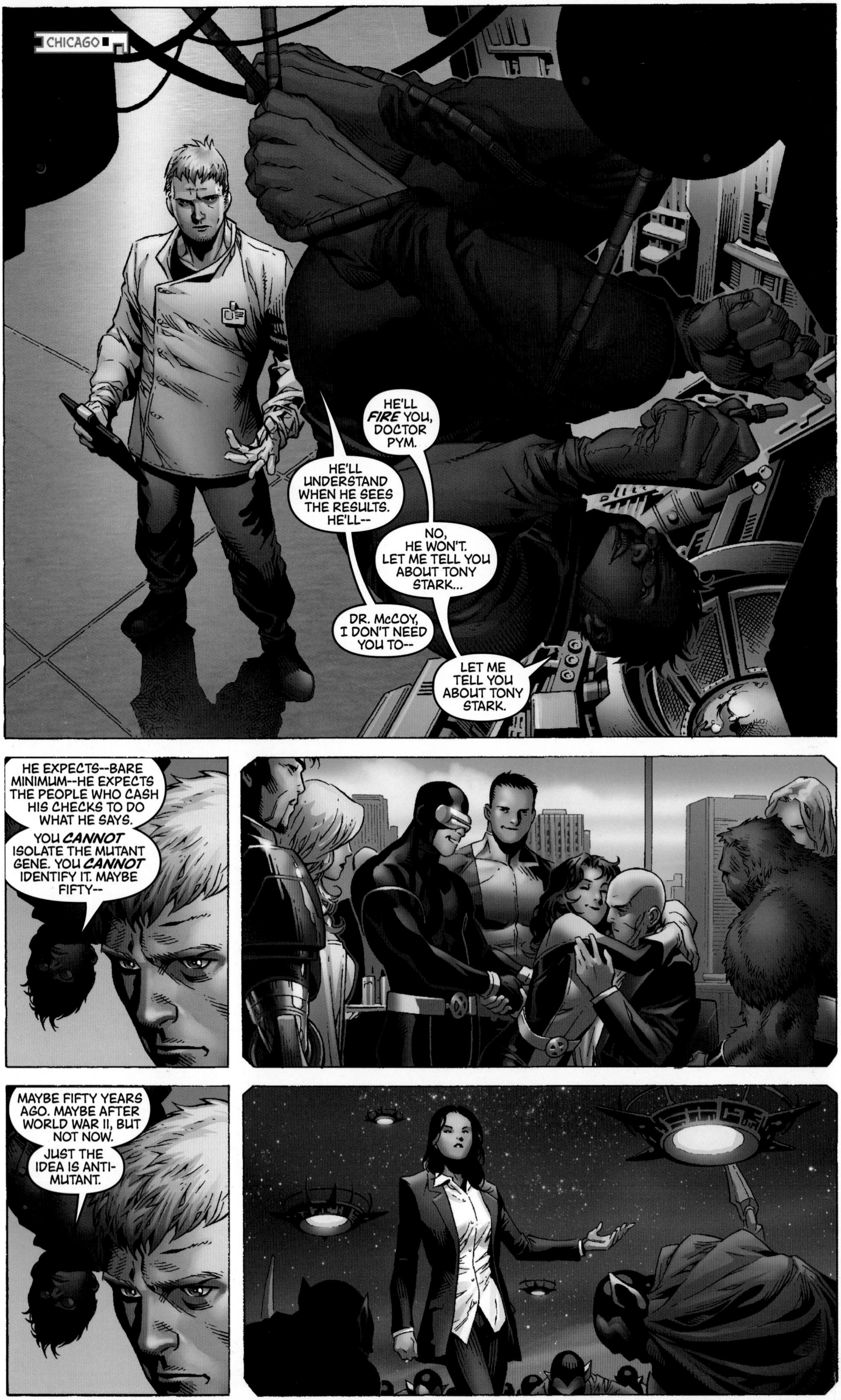
CHICAGO
HE'LL *FIRE* YOU, DOCTOR PYM.
HE'LL UNDERSTAND WHEN HE SEES THE RESULTS. HE'LL--
NO, HE WON'T. LET ME TELL YOU ABOUT TONY STARK...
DR. McCOY, I DON'T NEED YOU TO--
LET ME TELL YOU ABOUT TONY STARK.
HE EXPECTS--BARE MINIMUM--HE EXPECTS THE PEOPLE WHO CASH HIS CHECKS TO DO WHAT HE SAYS.
YOU *CANNOT* ISOLATE THE MUTANT GENE. YOU *CANNOT* IDENTIFY IT. MAYBE FIFTY--
MAYBE FIFTY YEARS AGO. MAYBE AFTER WORLD WAR II, BUT NOT NOW.
JUST THE IDEA IS ANTI-MUTANT.

I LIKE YOU, HENRY. WE'VE KNOWN EACH OTHER A GOOD LONG TIME...

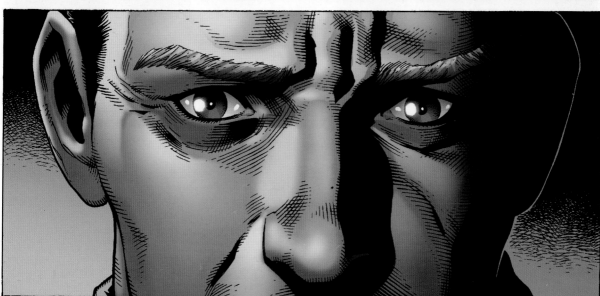

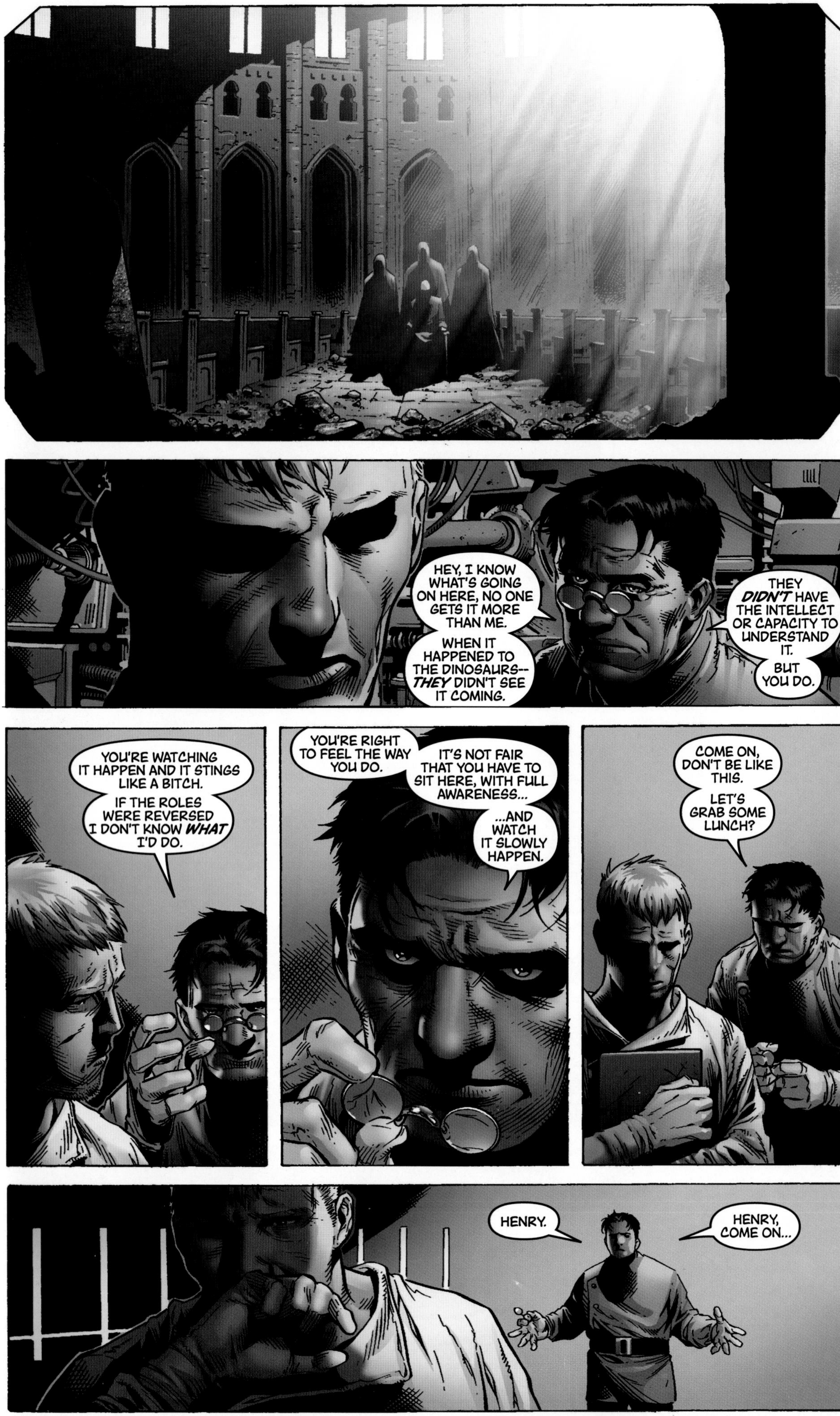
HEY, I KNOW WHAT'S GOING ON HERE, NO ONE GETS IT MORE THAN ME.
WHEN IT HAPPENED TO THE DINOSAURS-- *THEY* DIDN'T SEE IT COMING.
THEY *DIDN'T* HAVE THE INTELLECT OR CAPACITY TO UNDERSTAND IT.
BUT YOU DO.
YOU'RE WATCHING IT HAPPEN AND IT STINGS LIKE A BITCH.
IF THE ROLES WERE REVERSED I DON'T KNOW *WHAT* I'D DO.
YOU'RE RIGHT TO FEEL THE WAY YOU DO.
IT'S NOT FAIR THAT YOU HAVE TO SIT HERE, WITH FULL AWARENESS...
...AND WATCH IT SLOWLY HAPPEN.
COME ON, DON'T BE LIKE THIS.
LET'S GRAB SOME LUNCH?
HENRY.
HENRY, COME ON...

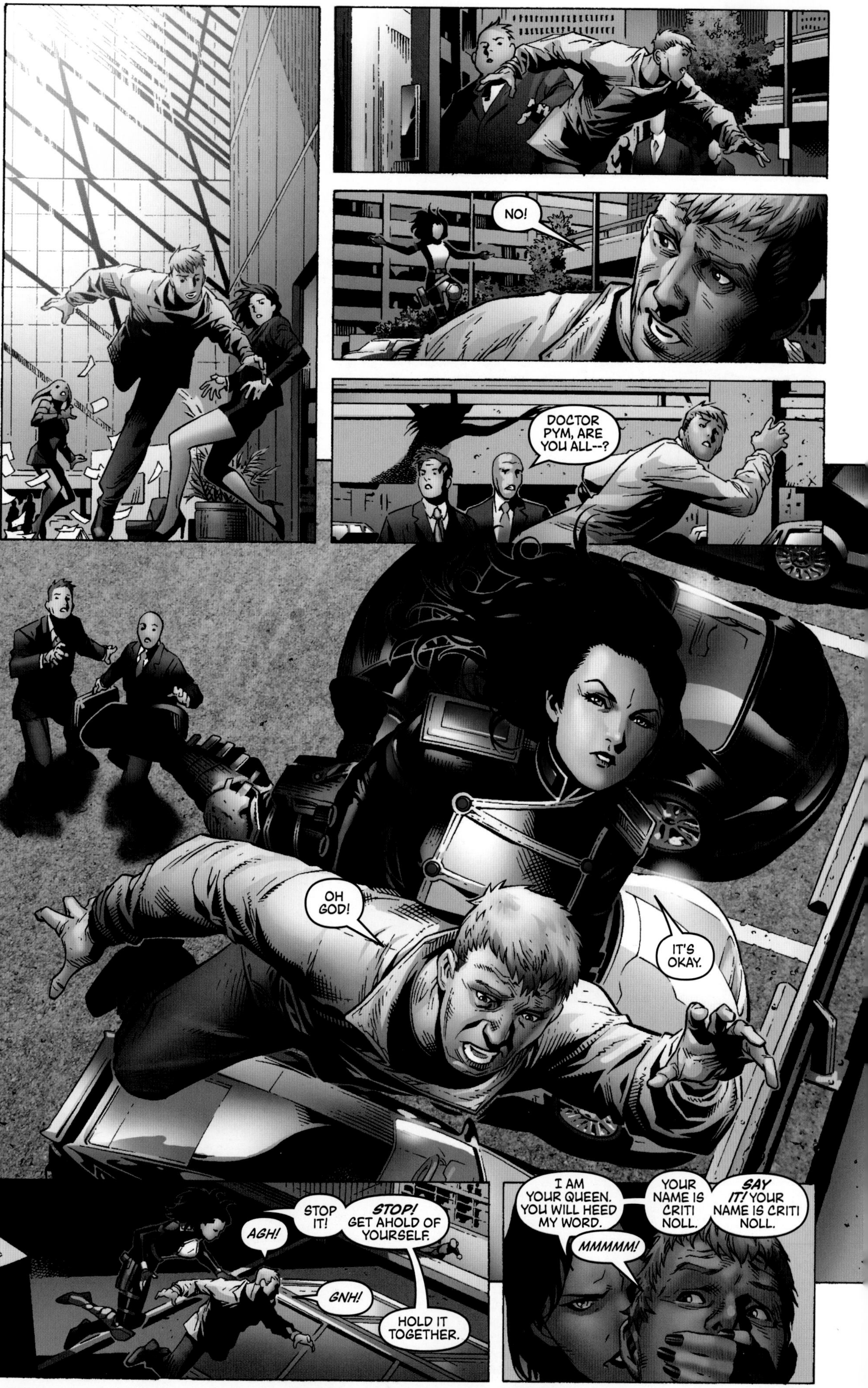
NO!
DOCTOR PYM, ARE YOU ALL--?
OH GOD!
IT'S OKAY.
STOP IT!
STOP! GET AHOLD OF YOURSELF.
AGH!
GNH!
HOLD IT TOGETHER.
I AM YOUR QUEEN. YOU WILL HEED MY WORD.
YOUR NAME IS CRITI NOLL.
SAY IT! YOUR NAME IS CRITI NOLL.
MMMMM!

I AM YOUR QUEEN.

MY NAME IS VERANKE.

YOU HAVE SWORN YOUR ALLEGIANCE. SAY YOUR NAME.

CRITI.

YES.

I DON'T UNDERSTAND... EVERYTHING IS--EVERYTHING IS *WRONG*.

YES. YOU CALLED ME AND YOU SAID YOU WERE GOING TO GO WITH THE AVENGERS AND THE X-MEN AND DEAL WITH THE SCARLET WITCH.

YOU CALLED ME. DO YOU REMEMBER?

I DID. I CALLED YOU.

YOU WENT TO THE SCARLET WITCH. AND THEN THE WORLD WENT WHITE.

THE WORLD WENT WHITE.

DID YOU KILL HER?

WHITE.

NO. NO. WE NEVER GOT TO HER.

WE CAME TO GENOSHA AND--

OH MY GOD.

SHE DID *THIS*?

HOW? SHE--SHE ISN'T *THIS* POWERFUL. SHE ISN'T A GOD.

SHE *IS* POWERFUL.

THAT'S WHY SHE WAS ON OUR *LIST*. WE COULDN'T POSSIBLY TAKE THE PLANET WITH HER *ON IT*.

SHE'S ONE OF THE REASONS WE ARE *HERE*. HIDING.

WHY--BUT WHY ISN'T THE WORLD IN *CHAOS* OVER THIS? WHY ISN'T THE WORLD *REACTING*?

DO THEY NOT KNOW?

FALL 200

Alison on 4

WILL

only on

Sarah & Almando Show

Weekday Mornings
Starting This Fall

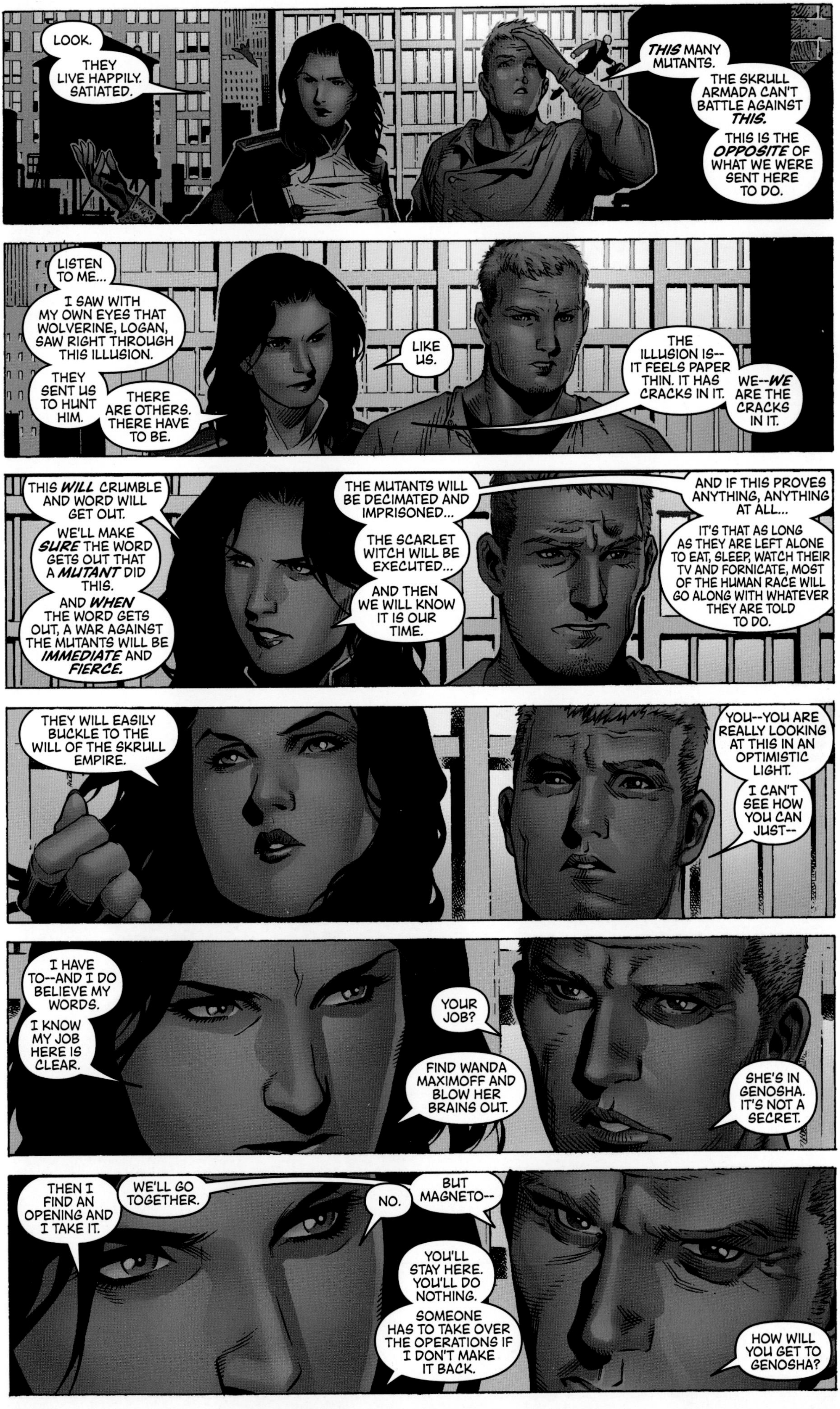
LOOK.
THEY LIVE HAPPILY. SATIATED.
THIS MANY MUTANTS.
THE SKRULL ARMADA CAN'T BATTLE AGAINST THIS.
THIS IS THE OPPOSITE OF WHAT WE WERE SENT HERE TO DO.
LISTEN TO ME...
I SAW WITH MY OWN EYES THAT WOLVERINE, LOGAN, SAW RIGHT THROUGH THIS ILLUSION.
THEY SENT US TO HUNT HIM.
THERE ARE OTHERS. THERE HAVE TO BE.
LIKE US.
THE ILLUSION IS-- IT FEELS PAPER THIN. IT HAS CRACKS IN IT.
WE--WE ARE THE CRACKS IN IT.
THIS WILL CRUMBLE AND WORD WILL GET OUT.
WE'LL MAKE SURE THE WORD GETS OUT THAT A MUTANT DID THIS.
AND WHEN THE WORD GETS OUT, A WAR AGAINST THE MUTANTS WILL BE IMMEDIATE AND FIERCE.
THE MUTANTS WILL BE DECIMATED AND IMPRISONED...
THE SCARLET WITCH WILL BE EXECUTED...
AND THEN WE WILL KNOW IT IS OUR TIME.
AND IF THIS PROVES ANYTHING, ANYTHING AT ALL...
IT'S THAT AS LONG AS THEY ARE LEFT ALONE TO EAT, SLEEP, WATCH THEIR TV AND FORNICATE, MOST OF THE HUMAN RACE WILL GO ALONG WITH WHATEVER THEY ARE TOLD TO DO.
THEY WILL EASILY BUCKLE TO THE WILL OF THE SKRULL EMPIRE.
YOU--YOU ARE REALLY LOOKING AT THIS IN AN OPTIMISTIC LIGHT.
I CAN'T SEE HOW YOU CAN JUST--
I HAVE TO--AND I DO BELIEVE MY WORDS.
I KNOW MY JOB HERE IS CLEAR.
YOUR JOB?
FIND WANDA MAXIMOFF AND BLOW HER BRAINS OUT.
SHE'S IN GENOSHA. IT'S NOT A SECRET.
THEN I FIND AN OPENING AND I TAKE IT.
WE'LL GO TOGETHER.
NO.
BUT MAGNETO--
YOU'LL STAY HERE. YOU'LL DO NOTHING.
SOMEONE HAS TO TAKE OVER THE OPERATIONS IF I DON'T MAKE IT BACK.
HOW WILL YOU GET TO GENOSHA?

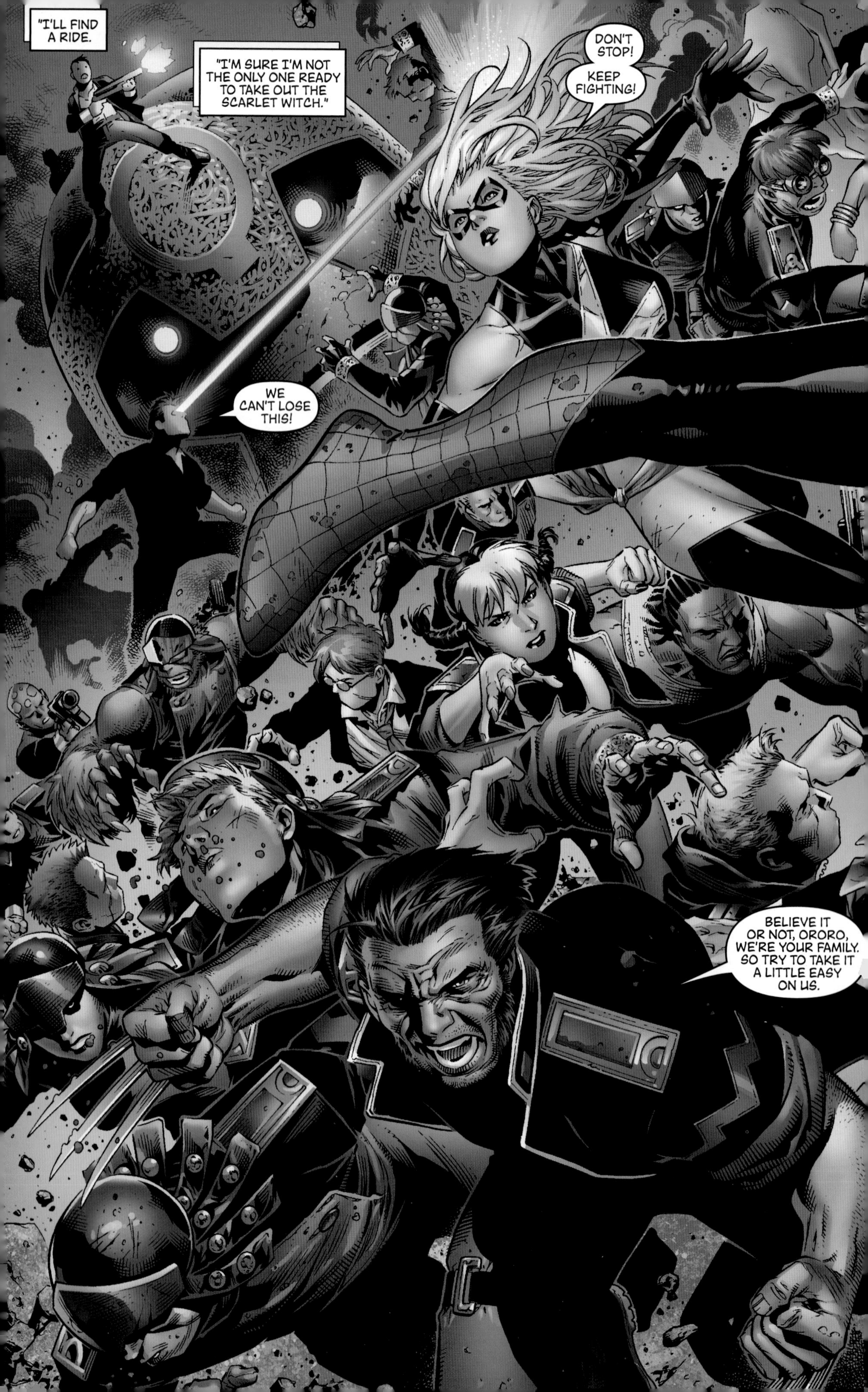
"I'LL FIND A RIDE.
"I'M SURE I'M NOT THE ONLY ONE READY TO TAKE OUT THE SCARLET WITCH."
DON'T STOP!
KEEP FIGHTING!
WE CAN'T LOSE THIS!
BELIEVE IT OR NOT, ORORO, WE'RE YOUR FAMILY. SO TRY TO TAKE IT A LITTLE EASY ON US.

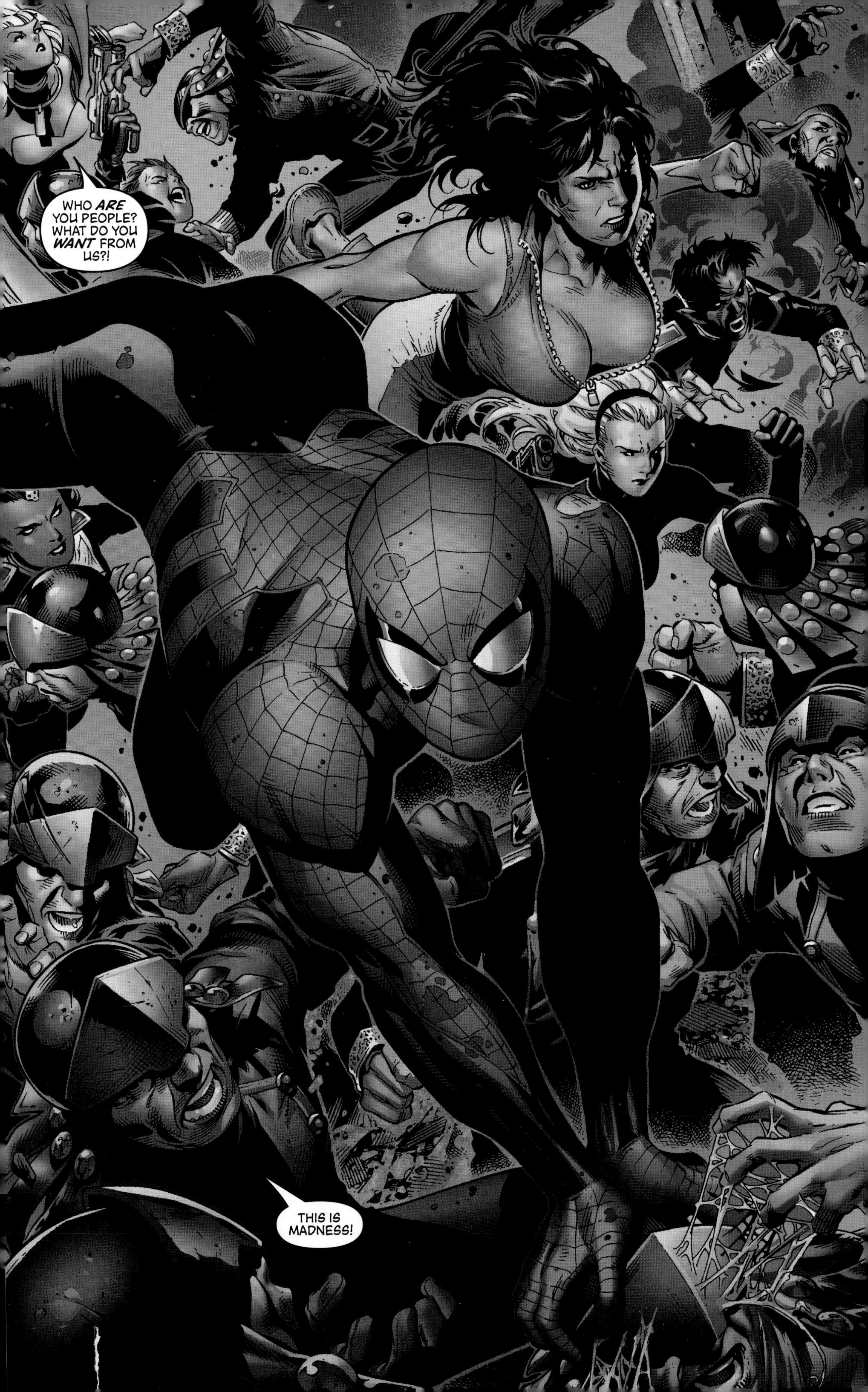
WHO ARE YOU PEOPLE? WHAT DO YOU WANT FROM US?!
THIS IS MADNESS!

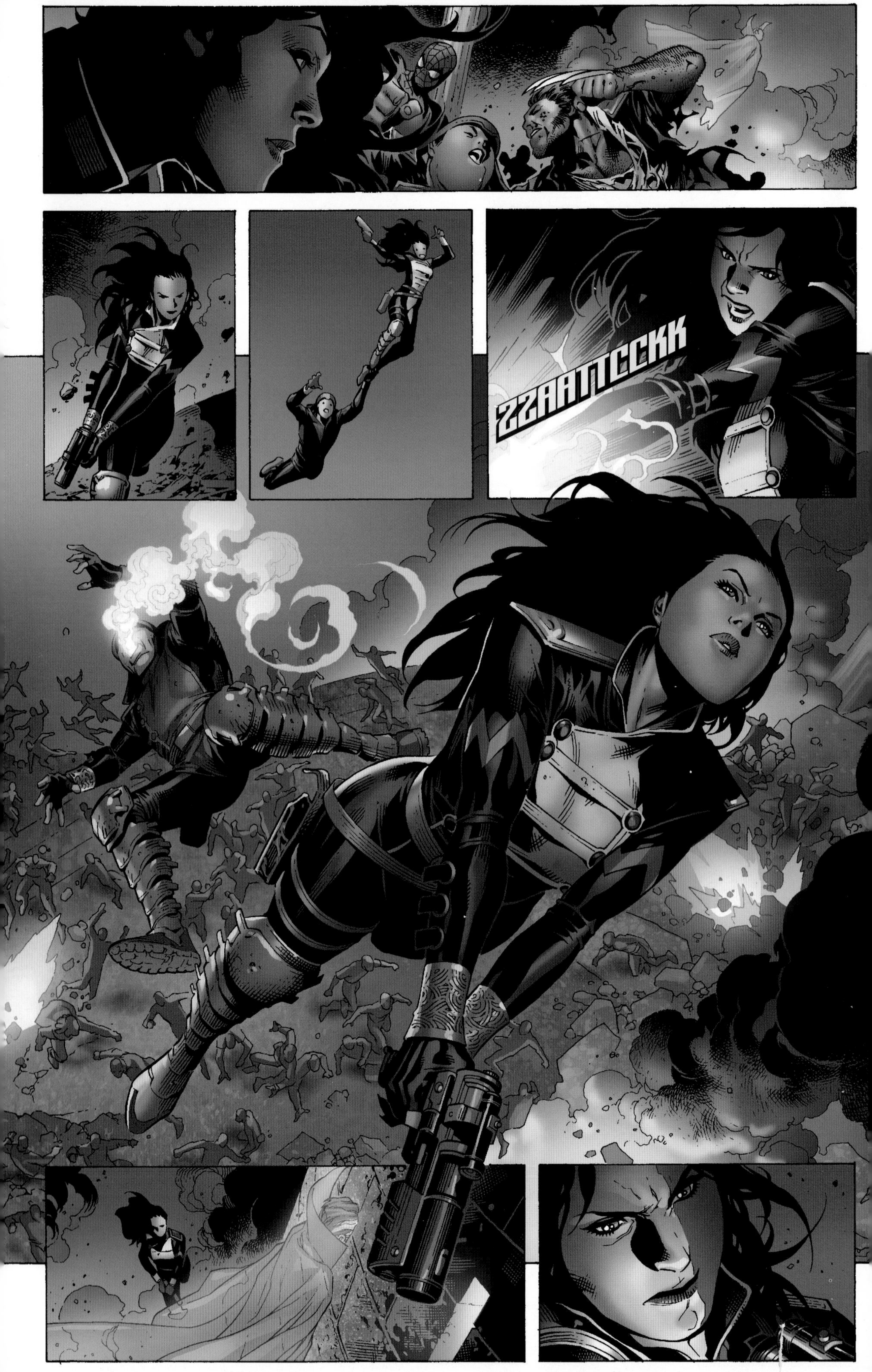
ZZAATTCCKK

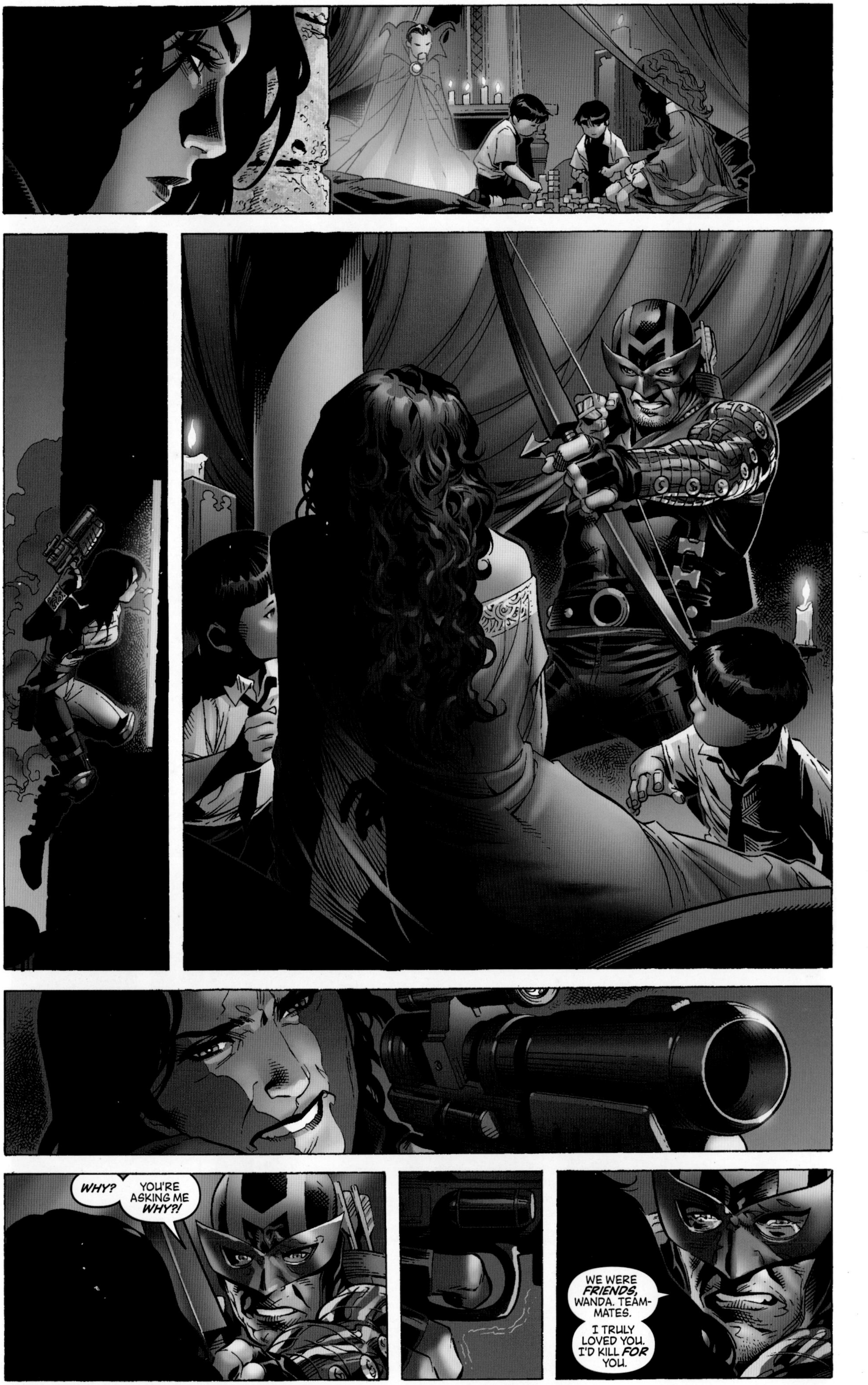
WHY?
YOU'RE ASKING ME WHY?!
WE WERE FRIENDS, WANDA. TEAM-MATES.
I TRULY LOVED YOU. I'D KILL FOR YOU.

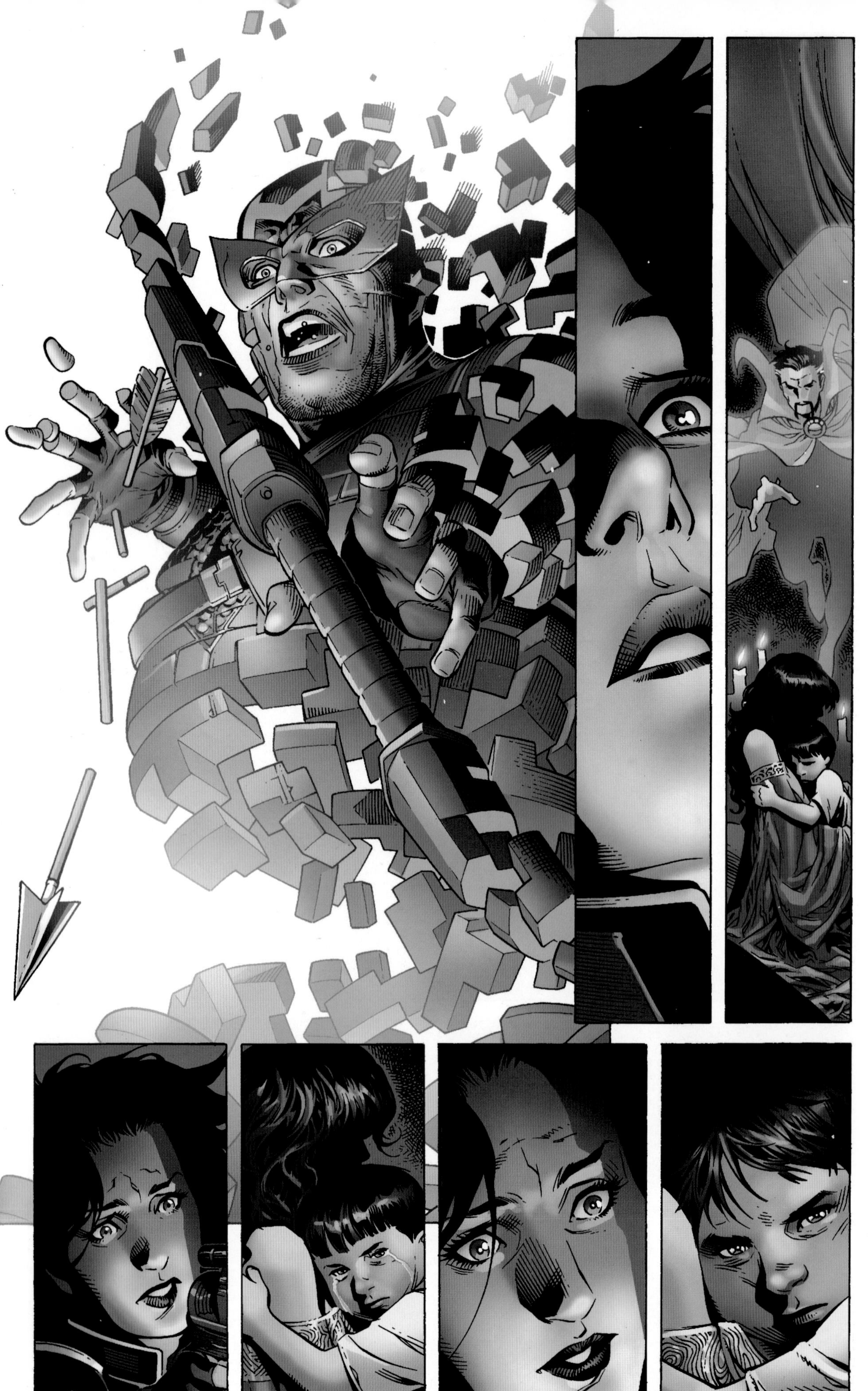

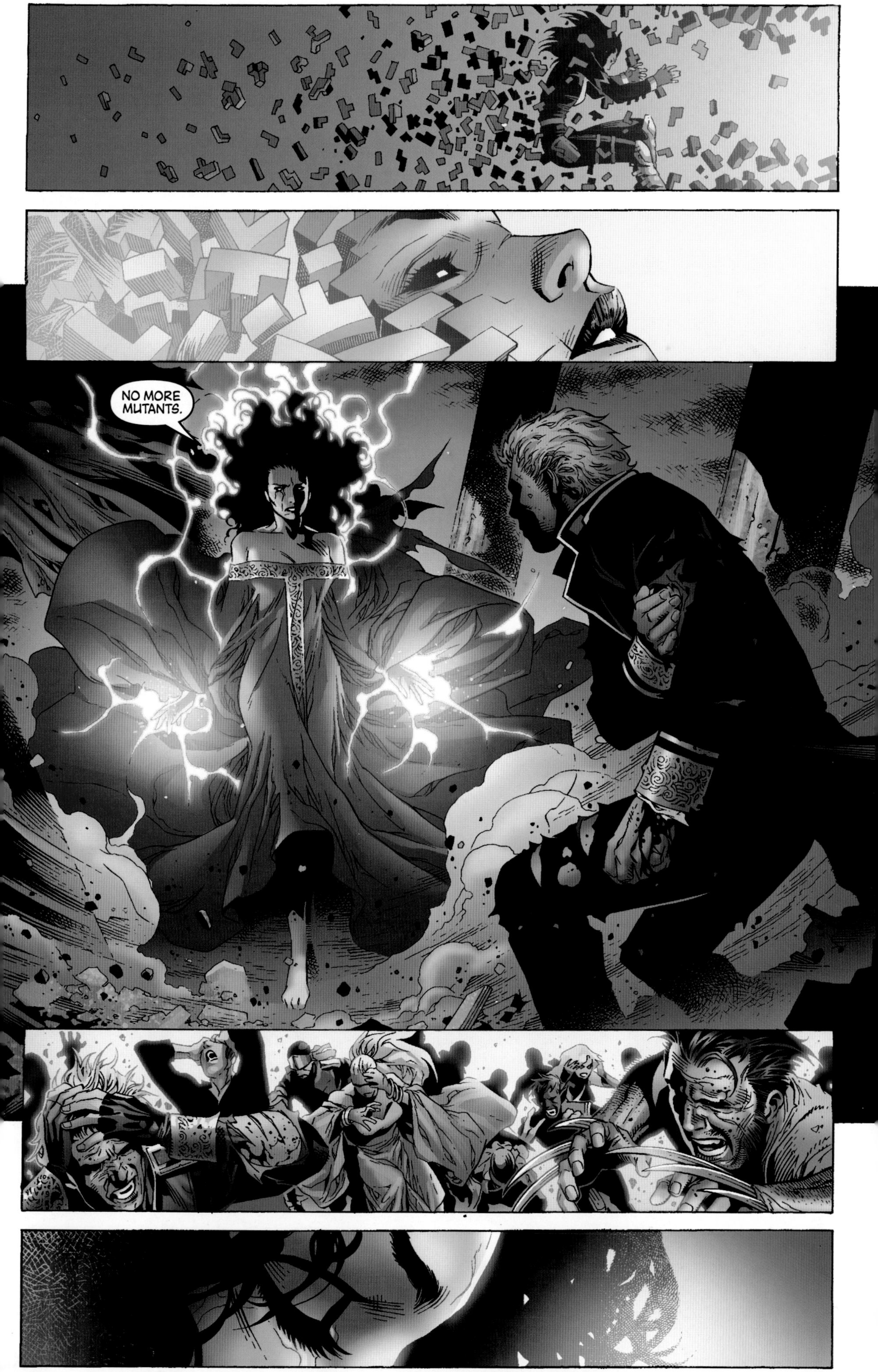
NO MORE MUTANTS.

HE LOVES US ALL.

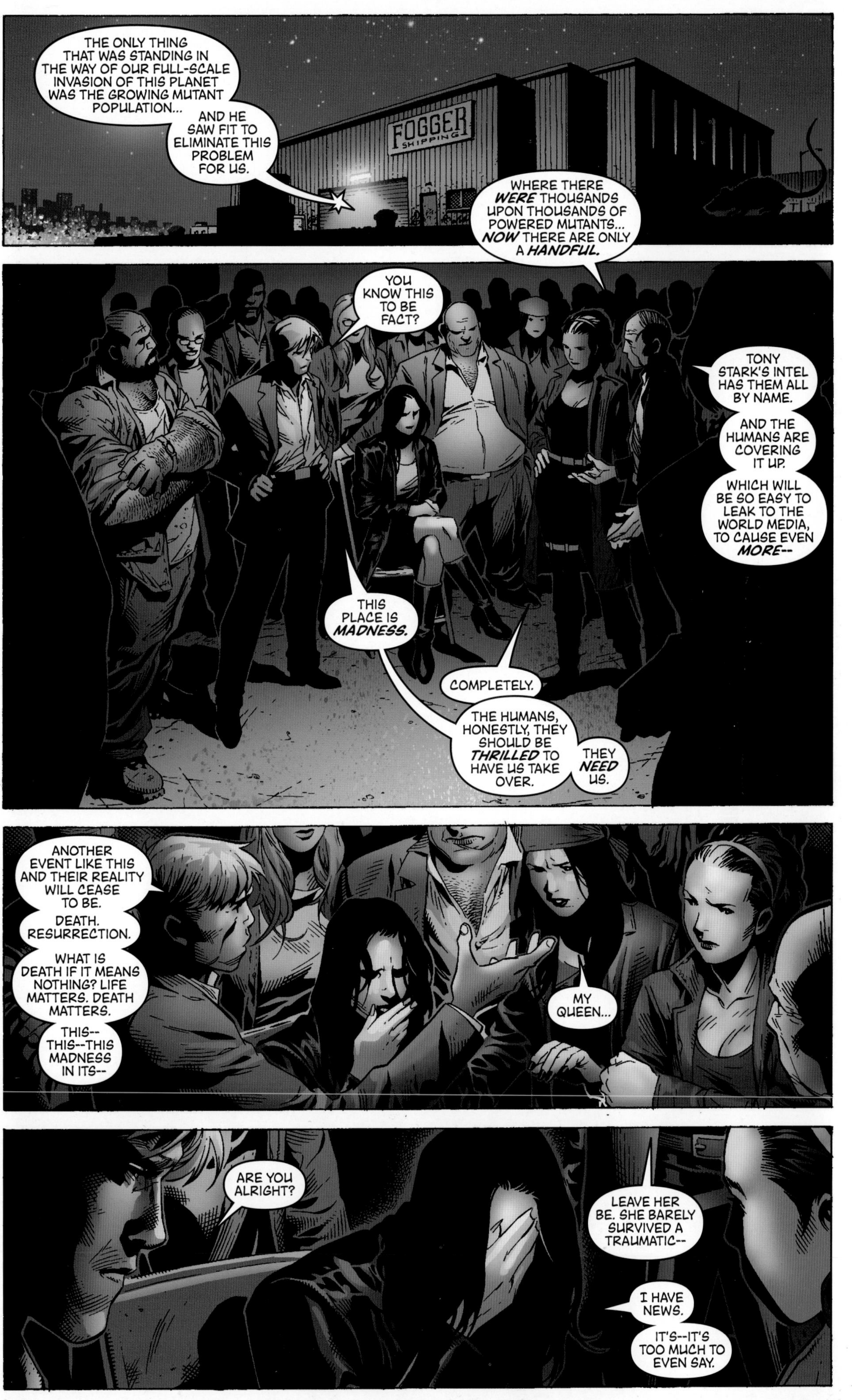

THE ONLY THING THAT WAS STANDING IN THE WAY OF OUR FULL-SCALE INVASION OF THIS PLANET WAS THE GROWING MUTANT POPULATION...
AND HE SAW FIT TO ELIMINATE THIS PROBLEM FOR US.
FOGGER SHIPPING
WHERE THERE *WERE* THOUSANDS UPON THOUSANDS OF POWERED MUTANTS... *NOW* THERE ARE ONLY A *HANDFUL.*
YOU KNOW THIS TO BE FACT?
TONY STARK'S INTEL HAS THEM ALL BY NAME.
AND THE HUMANS ARE COVERING IT UP.
WHICH WILL BE SO EASY TO LEAK TO THE WORLD MEDIA, TO CAUSE EVEN *MORE--*
THIS PLACE IS *MADNESS.*
COMPLETELY.
THE HUMANS, HONESTLY, THEY SHOULD BE *THRILLED* TO HAVE US TAKE OVER.
THEY *NEED* US.
ANOTHER EVENT LIKE THIS AND THEIR REALITY WILL CEASE TO BE.
DEATH. RESURRECTION.
WHAT IS DEATH IF IT MEANS NOTHING? LIFE MATTERS. DEATH MATTERS.
THIS-- THIS--THIS MADNESS IN ITS--
MY QUEEN...
ARE YOU ALRIGHT?
LEAVE HER BE. SHE BARELY SURVIVED A TRAUMATIC--
I HAVE NEWS.
IT'S--IT'S TOO MUCH TO EVEN SAY.

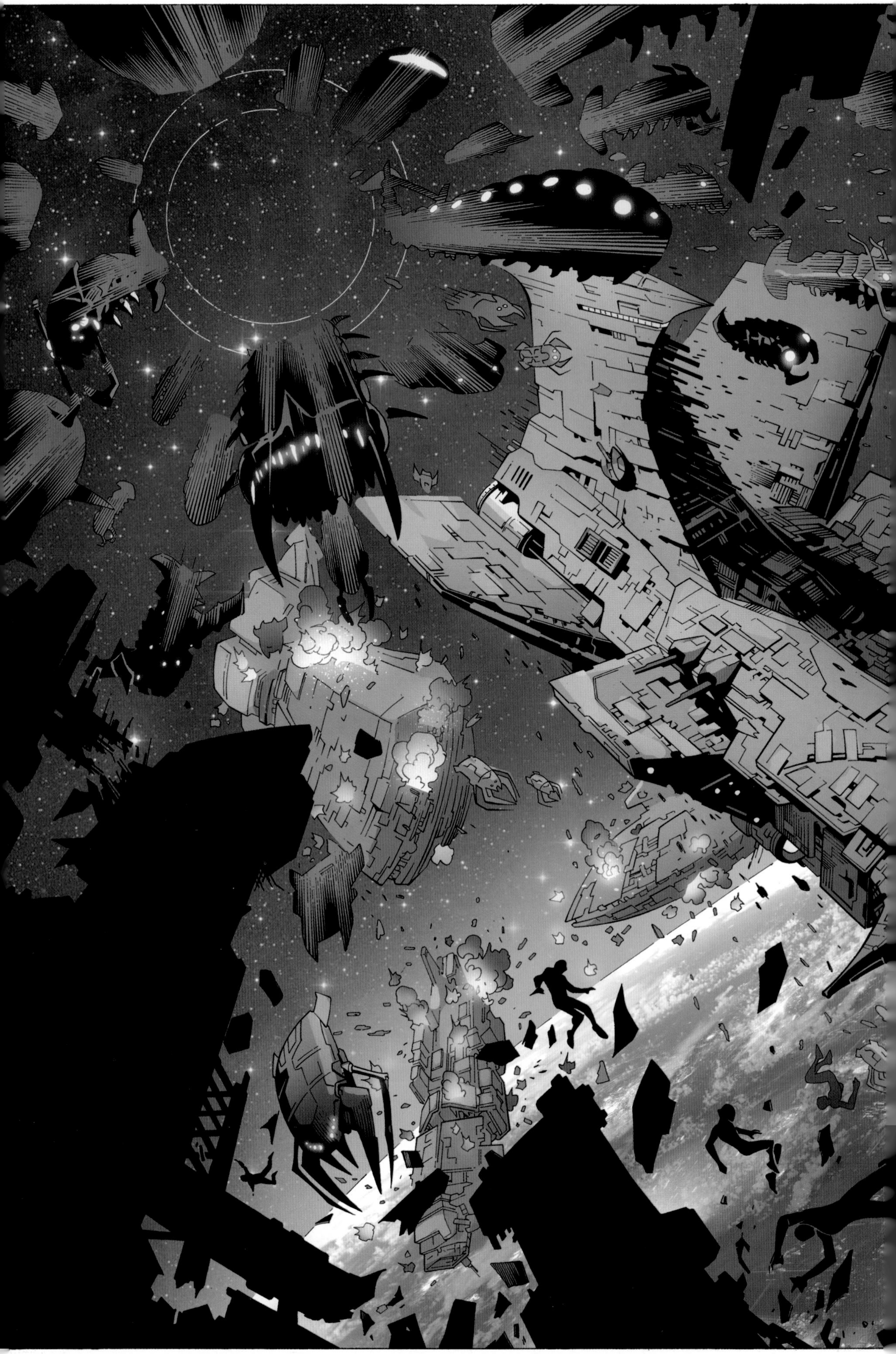

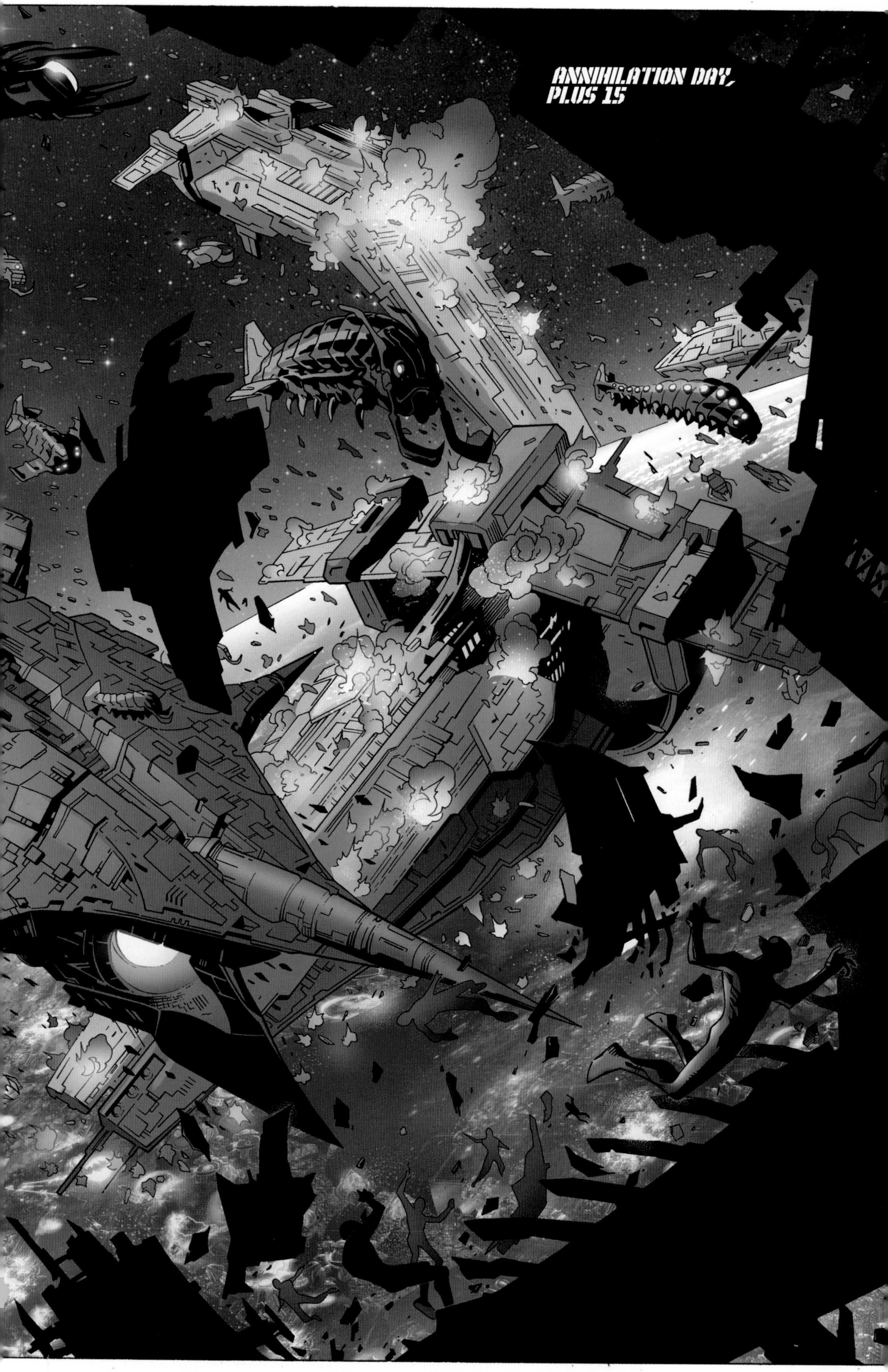
ANNIHILATION DAY, PLUS 15

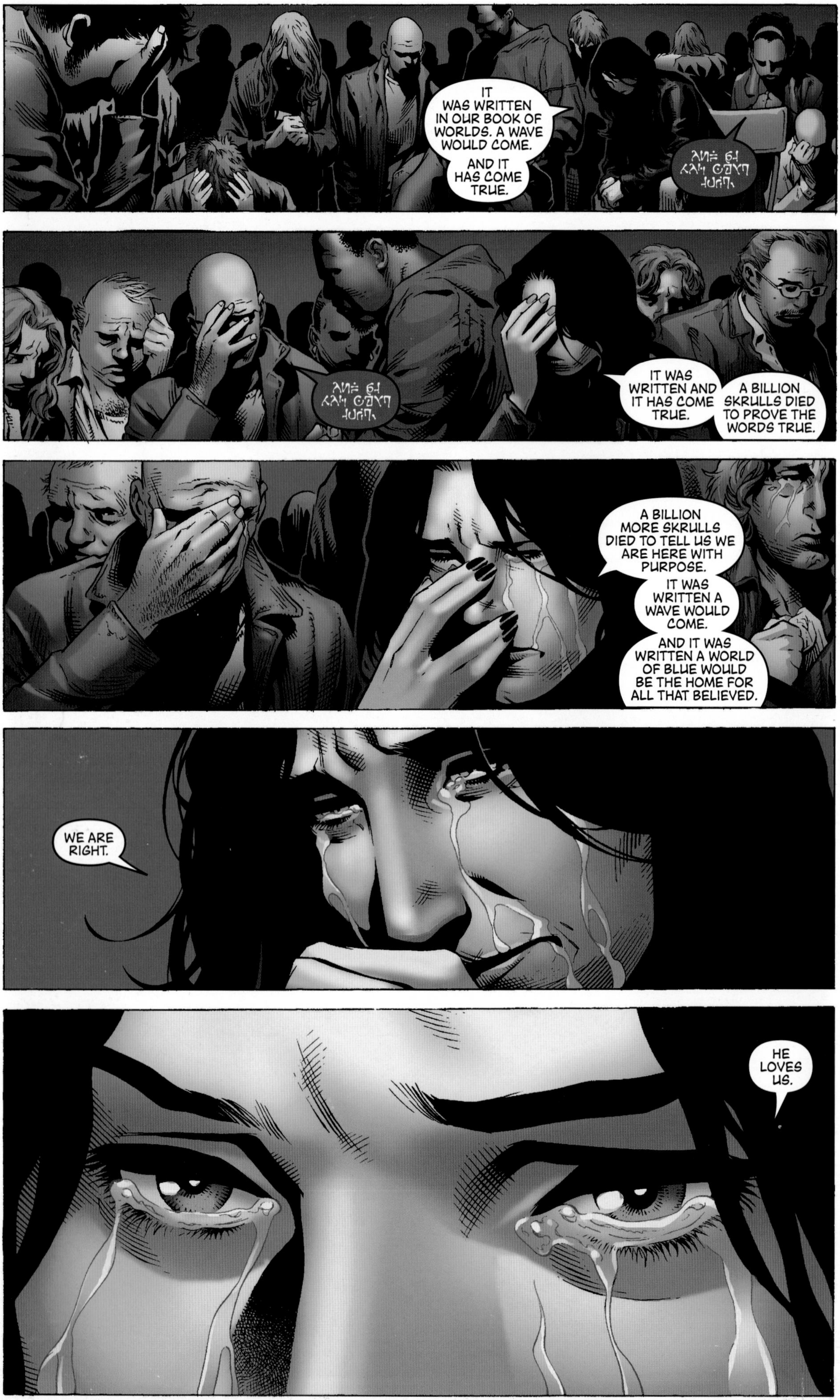
IT WAS WRITTEN IN OUR BOOK OF WORLDS. A WAVE WOULD COME.
AND IT HAS COME TRUE.
IT WAS WRITTEN AND IT HAS COME TRUE.
A BILLION SKRULLS DIED TO PROVE THE WORDS TRUE.
A BILLION MORE SKRULLS DIED TO TELL US WE ARE HERE WITH PURPOSE.
IT WAS WRITTEN A WAVE WOULD COME.
AND IT WAS WRITTEN A WORLD OF BLUE WOULD BE THE HOME FOR ALL THAT BELIEVED.
WE ARE RIGHT.
HE LOVES US.

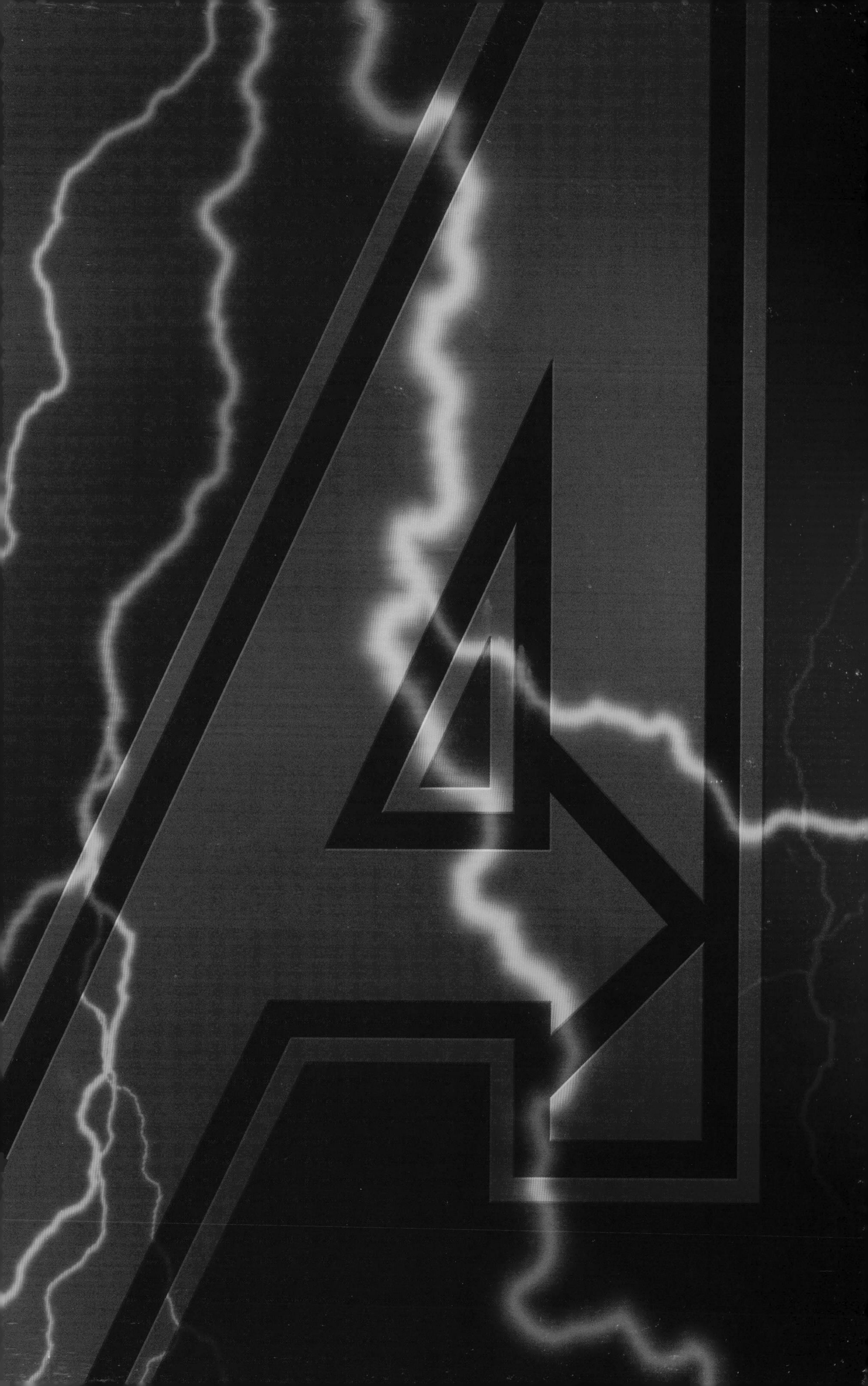

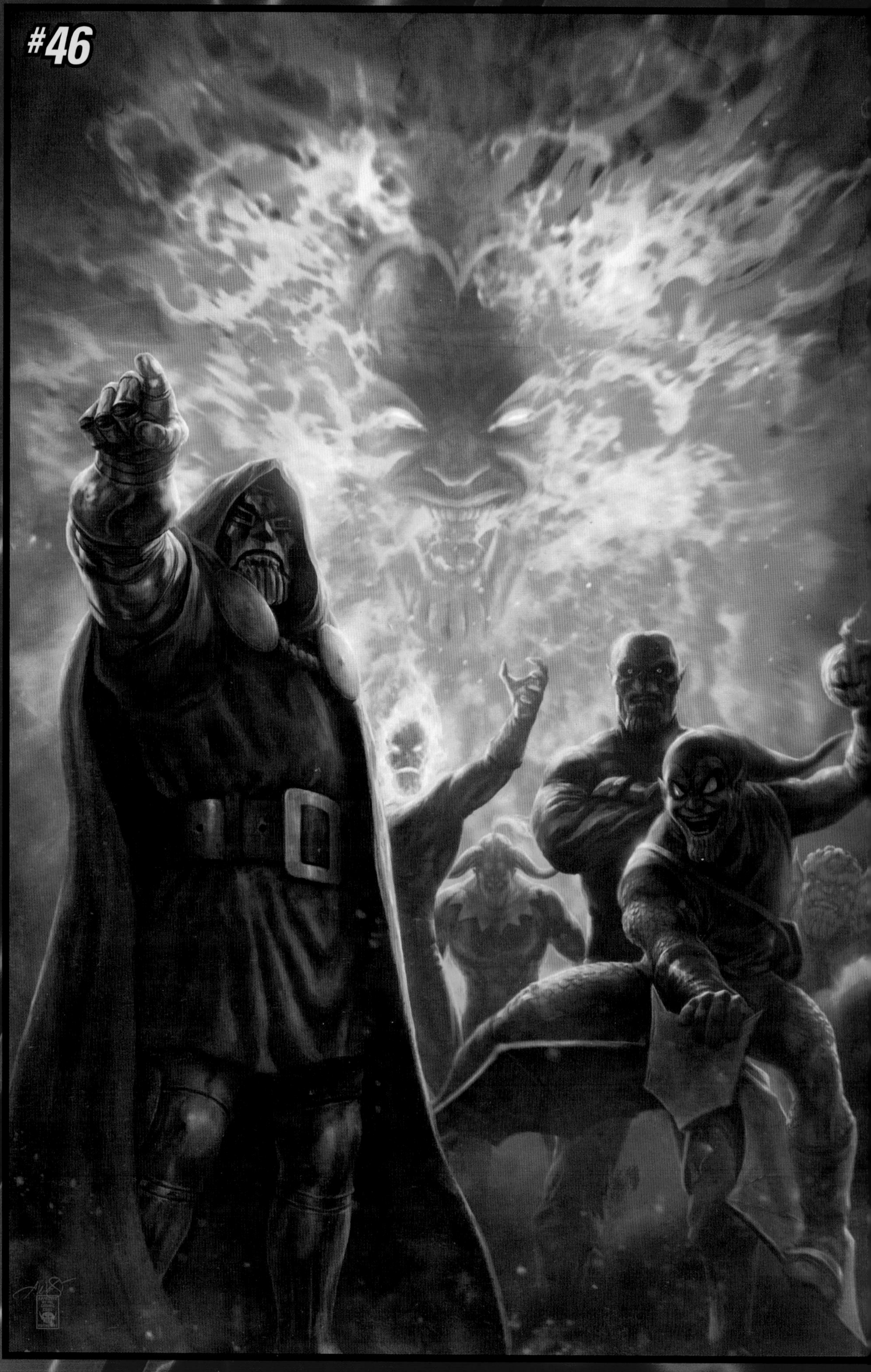
#46

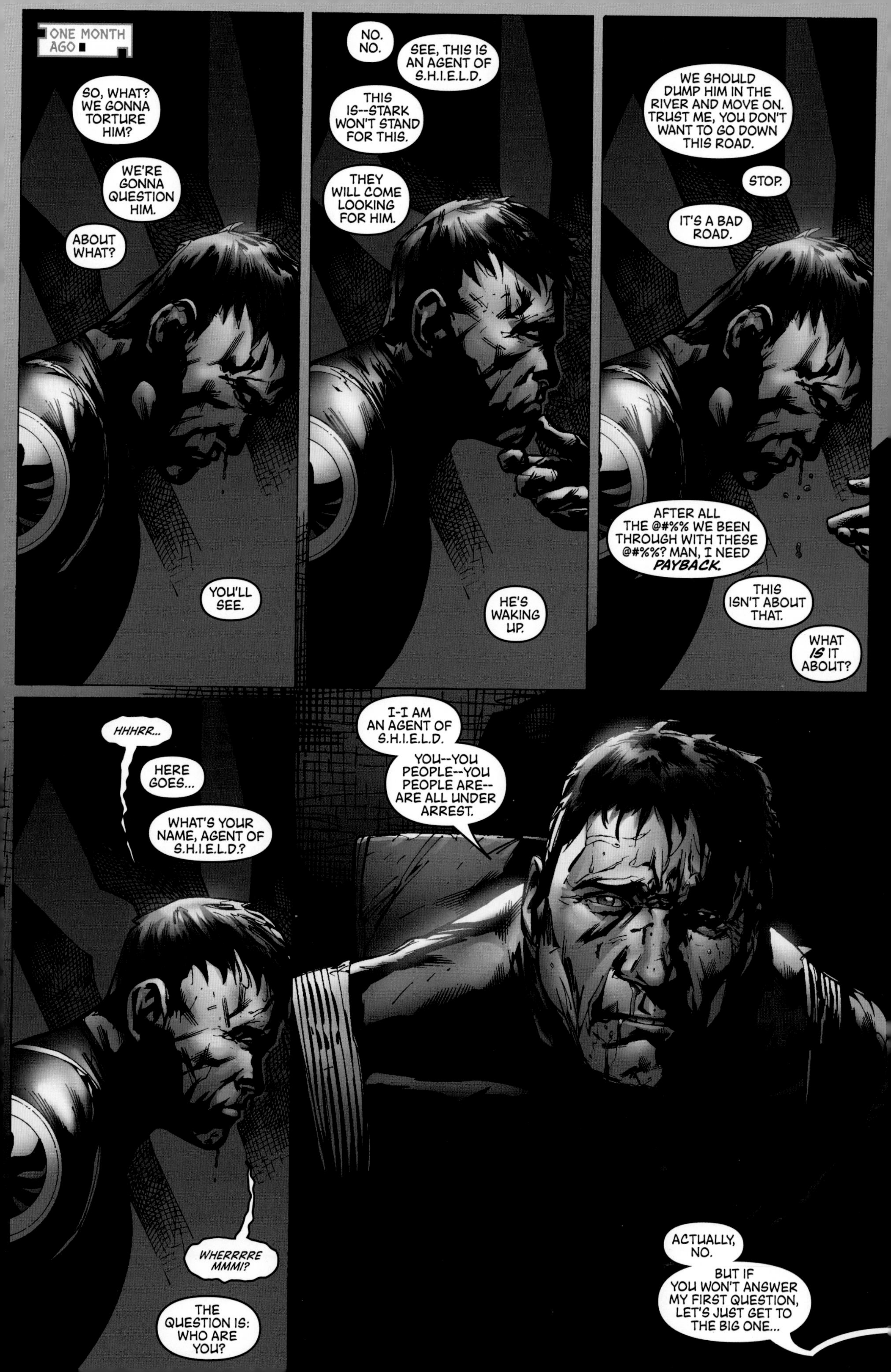
ONE MONTH AGO
SO, WHAT? WE GONNA TORTURE HIM?
WE'RE GONNA QUESTION HIM.
ABOUT WHAT?
YOU'LL SEE.
NO. NO.
SEE, THIS IS AN AGENT OF S.H.I.E.L.D.
THIS IS--STARK WON'T STAND FOR THIS.
THEY WILL COME LOOKING FOR HIM.
HE'S WAKING UP.
WE SHOULD DUMP HIM IN THE RIVER AND MOVE ON. TRUST ME, YOU DON'T WANT TO GO DOWN THIS ROAD.
STOP.
IT'S A BAD ROAD.
AFTER ALL THE @#%% WE BEEN THROUGH WITH THESE @#%%? MAN, I NEED PAYBACK.
THIS ISN'T ABOUT THAT.
WHAT IS IT ABOUT?
HHHRR...
HERE GOES...
WHAT'S YOUR NAME, AGENT OF S.H.I.E.L.D.?
WHERRRRE MMMI?
THE QUESTION IS: WHO ARE YOU?
I-I AM AN AGENT OF S.H.I.E.L.D.
YOU--YOU PEOPLE--YOU PEOPLE ARE--ARE ALL UNDER ARREST.
ACTUALLY, NO.
BUT IF YOU WON'T ANSWER MY FIRST QUESTION, LET'S JUST GET TO THE BIG ONE...

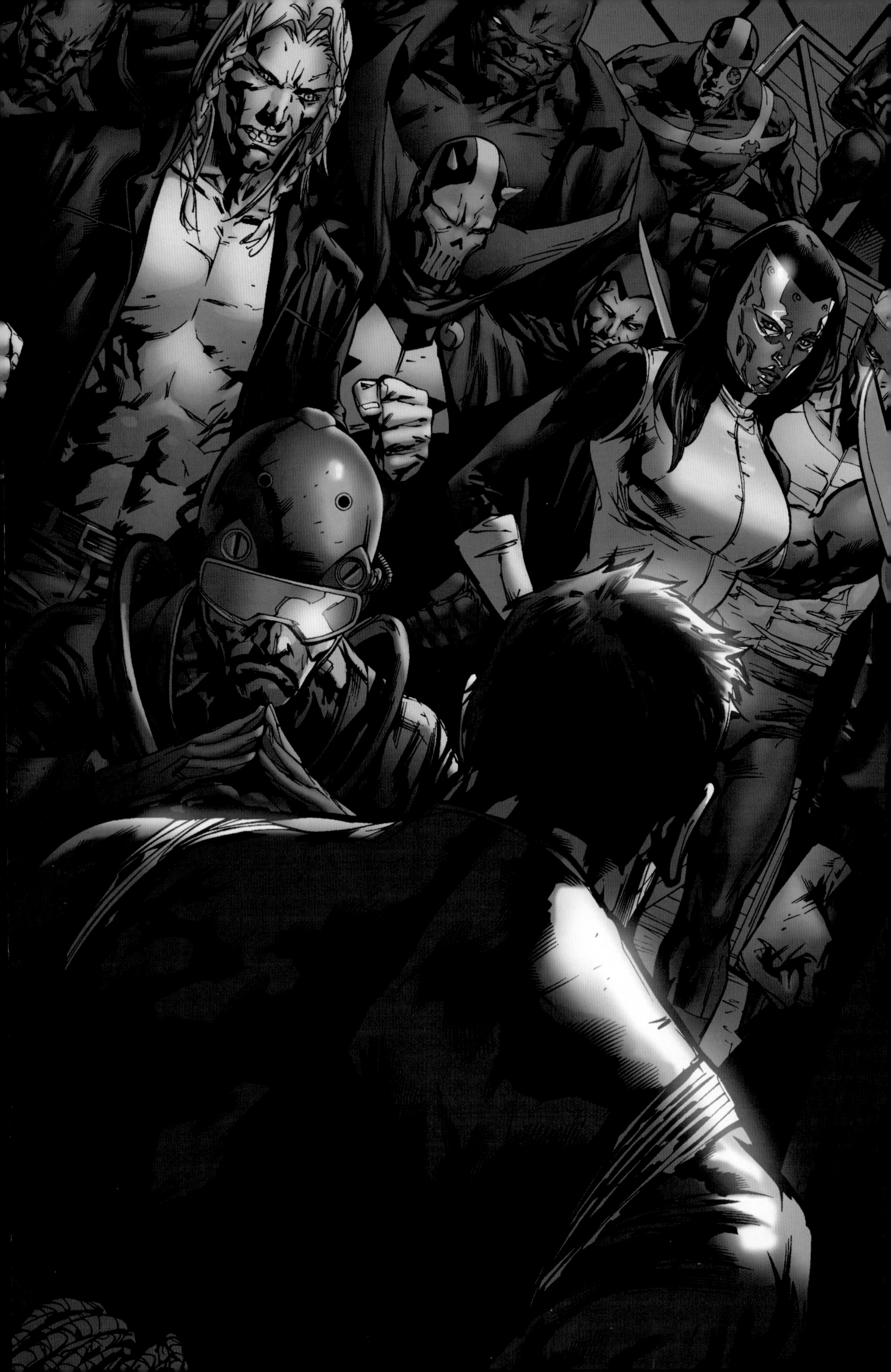

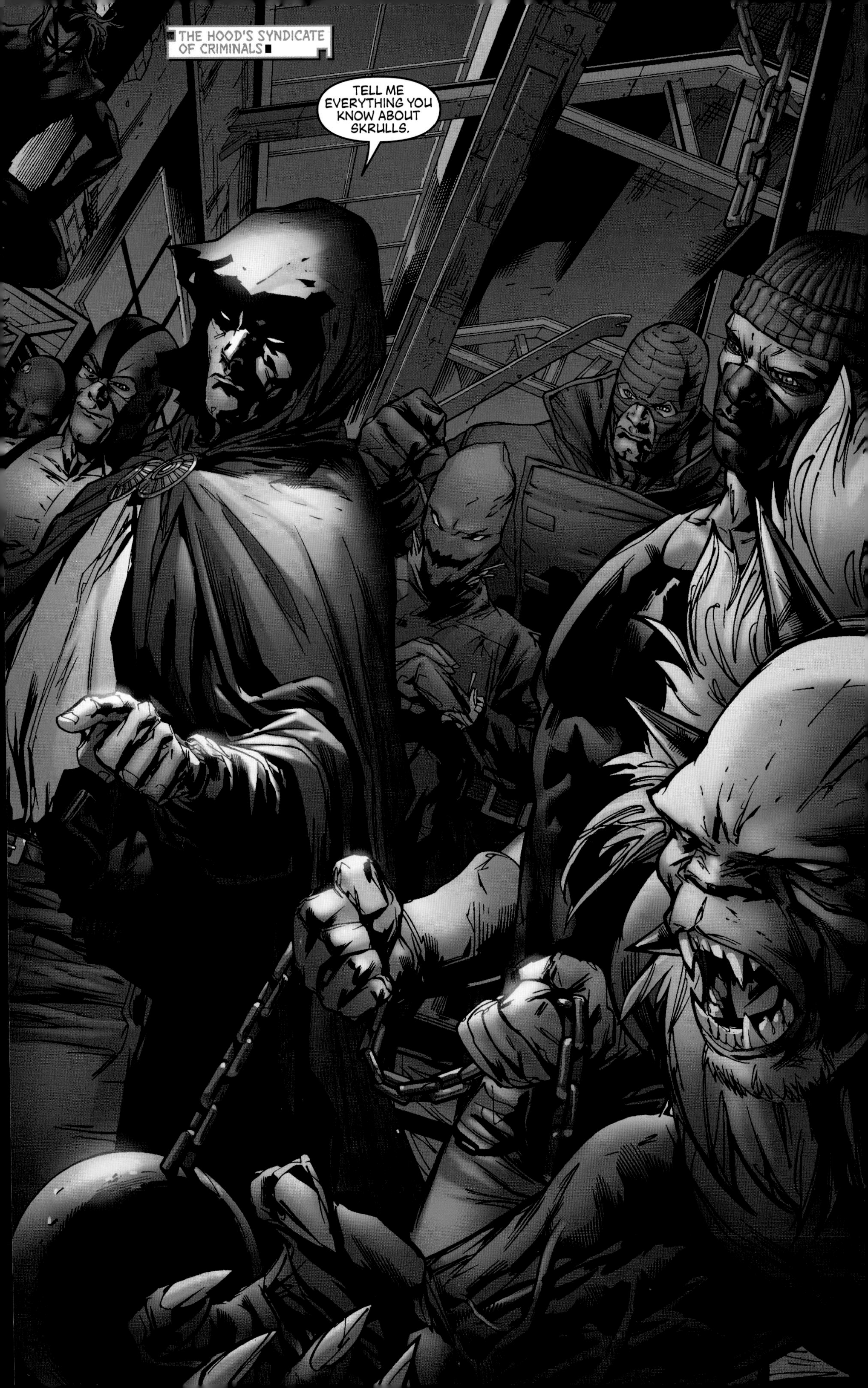
THE HOOD'S SYNDICATE OF CRIMINALS
TELL ME EVERYTHING YOU KNOW ABOUT SKRULLS.

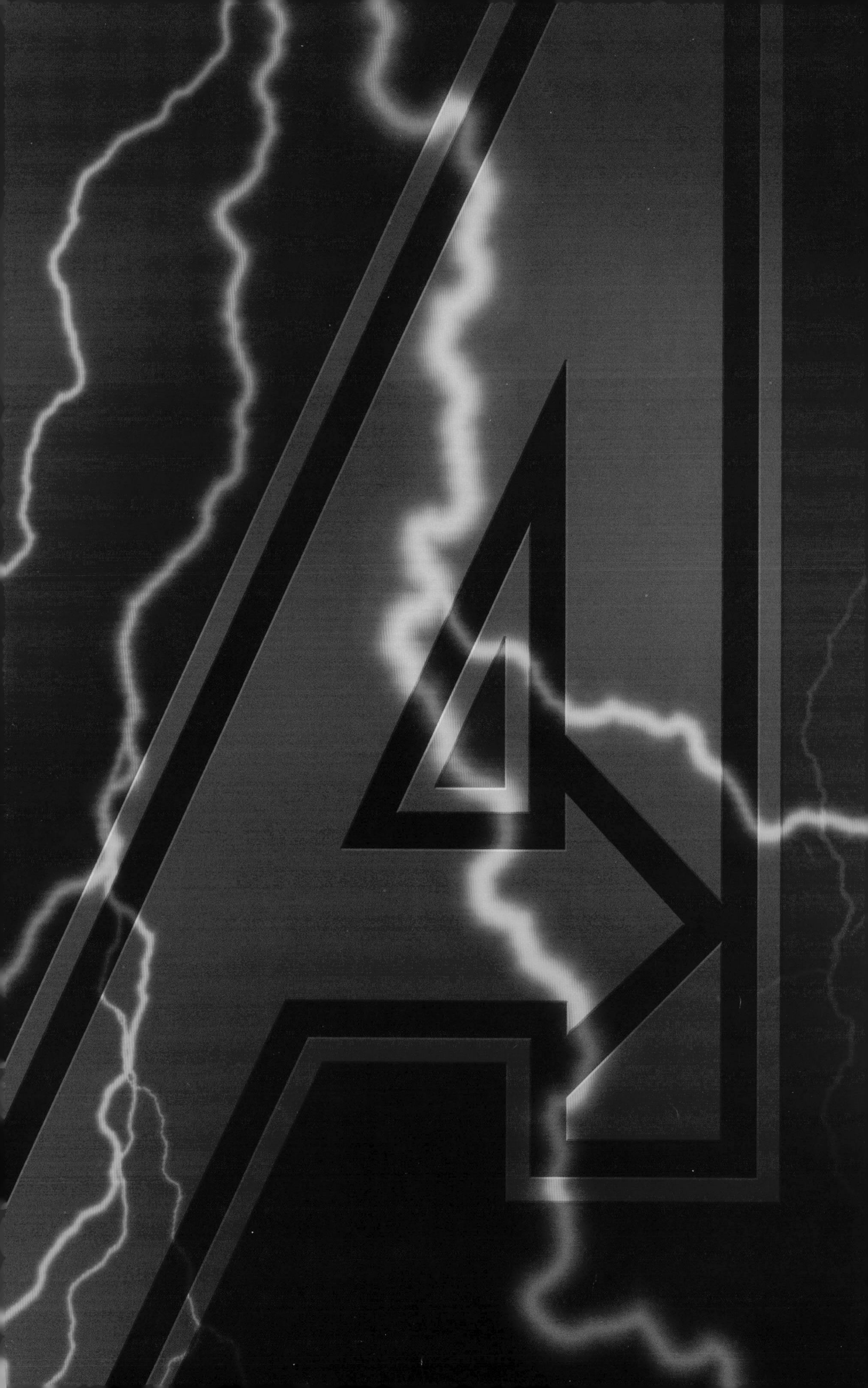

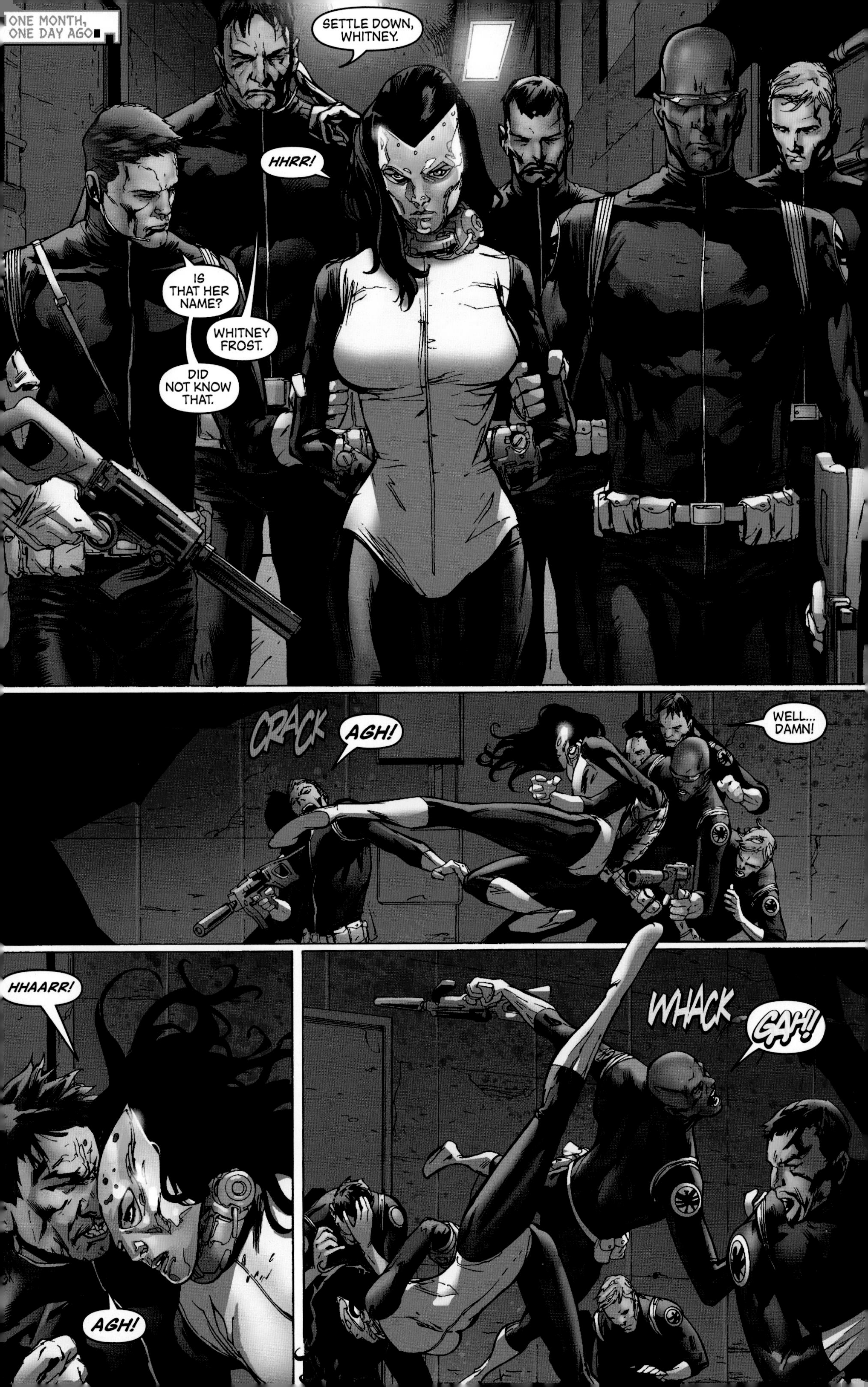

ONE MONTH, ONE DAY AGO
SETTLE DOWN, WHITNEY.
HHRR!
IS THAT HER NAME?
WHITNEY FROST.
DID NOT KNOW THAT.
CRACK
AGH!
WELL... DAMN!
HHAARR!
AGH!
WHACK
GAH!

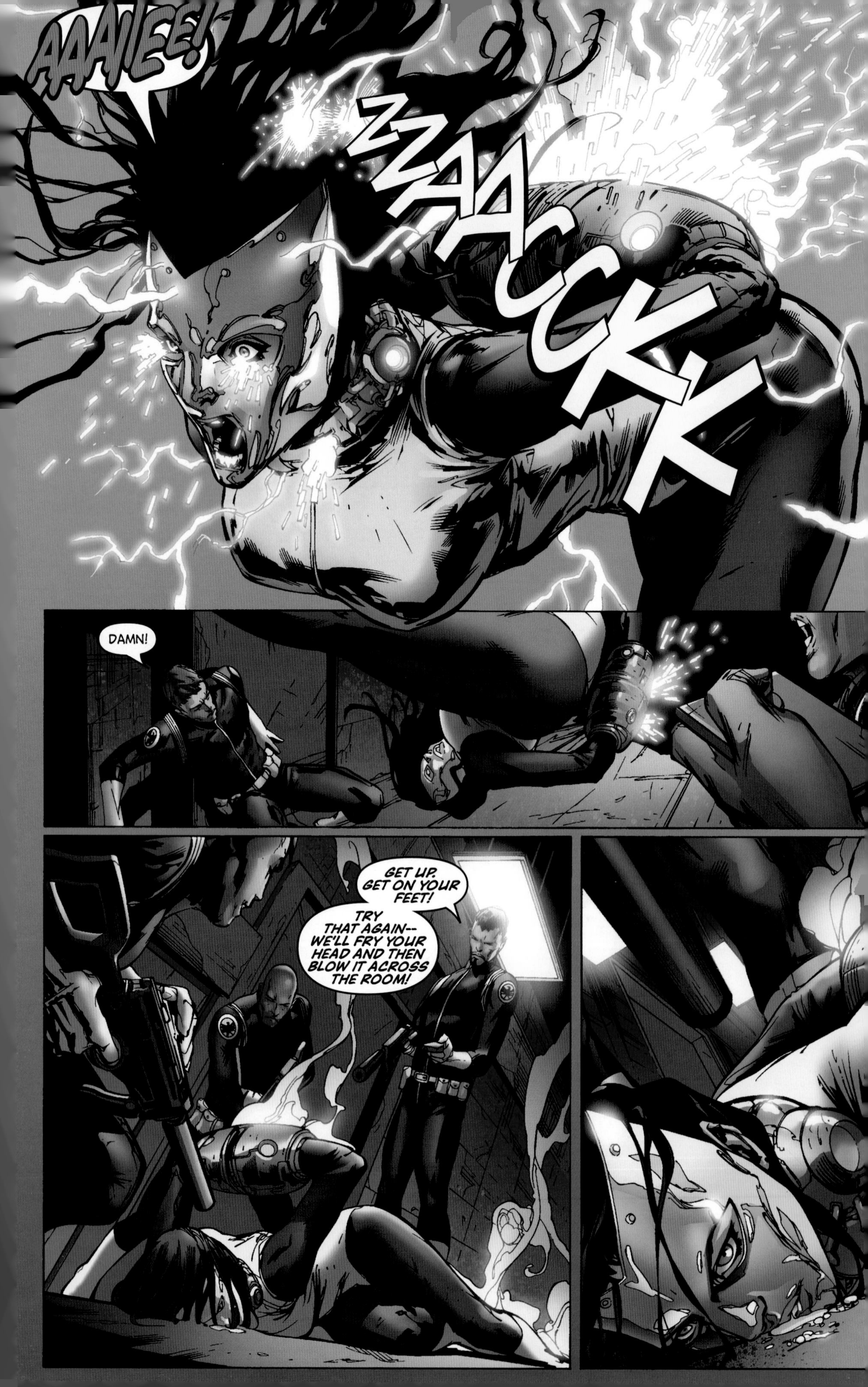
AAAIEE!
ZZAACKK
DAMN!
GET UP. GET ON YOUR FEET!
TRY THAT AGAIN-- WE'LL FRY YOUR HEAD AND THEN BLOW IT ACROSS THE ROOM!

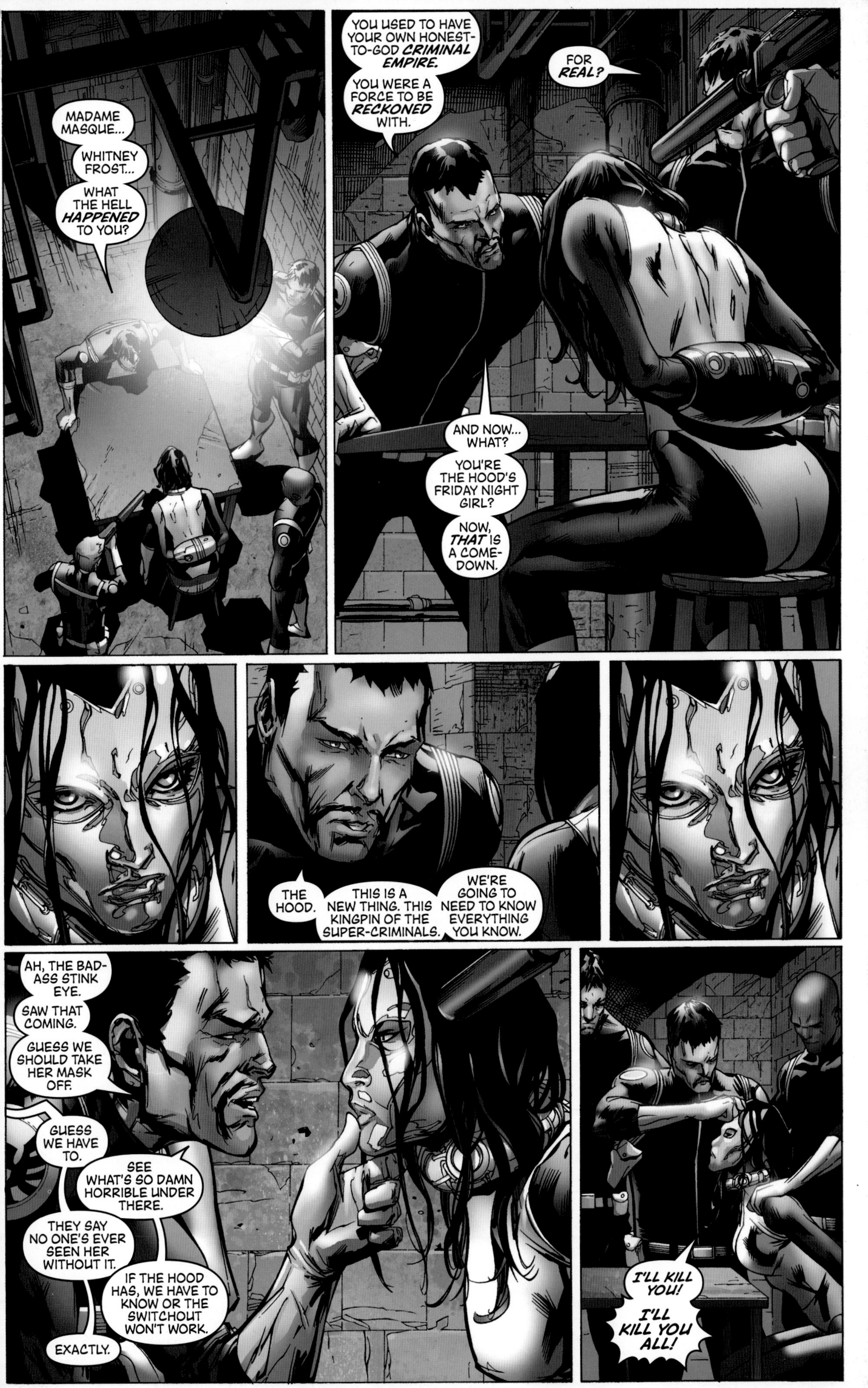
MADAME MASQUE...
WHITNEY FROST...
WHAT THE HELL HAPPENED TO YOU?
YOU USED TO HAVE YOUR OWN HONEST-TO-GOD CRIMINAL EMPIRE.
YOU WERE A FORCE TO BE RECKONED WITH.
FOR REAL?
AND NOW... WHAT?
YOU'RE THE HOOD'S FRIDAY NIGHT GIRL?
NOW, THAT IS A COME-DOWN.
THE HOOD.
THIS IS A NEW THING. THIS KINGPIN OF THE SUPER-CRIMINALS.
WE'RE GOING TO NEED TO KNOW EVERYTHING YOU KNOW.
AH, THE BAD-ASS STINK EYE.
SAW THAT COMING.
GUESS WE SHOULD TAKE HER MASK OFF.
GUESS WE HAVE TO.
SEE WHAT'S SO DAMN HORRIBLE UNDER THERE.
THEY SAY NO ONE'S EVER SEEN HER WITHOUT IT.
IF THE HOOD HAS, WE HAVE TO KNOW OR THE SWITCHOUT WON'T WORK.
EXACTLY.
I'LL KILL YOU!
I'LL KILL YOU ALL!

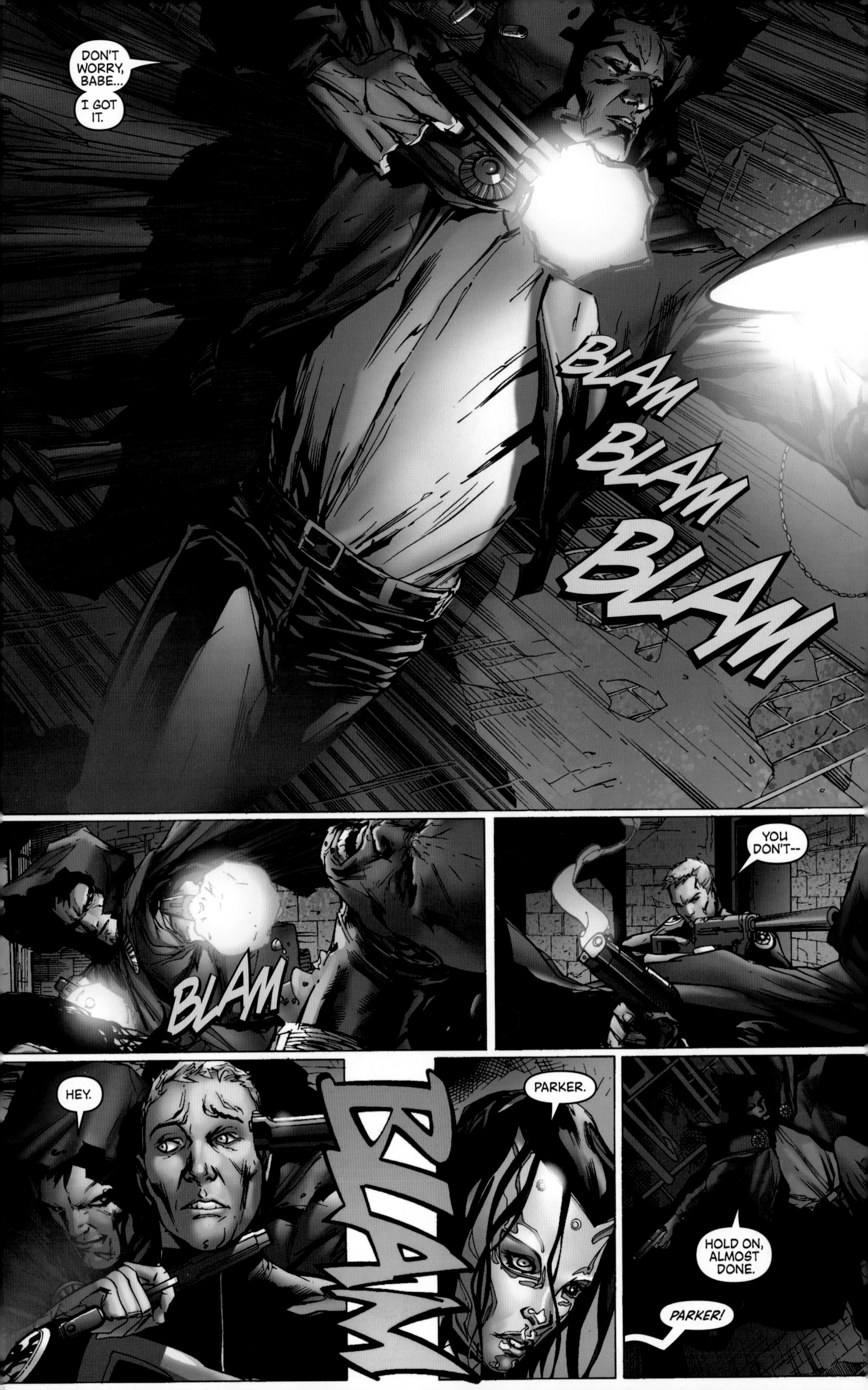
DON'T WORRY, BABE...
I GOT IT.
BLAM BLAM BLAM
BLAM
YOU DON'T--
HEY.
PARKER.
BLAM
HOLD ON, ALMOST DONE.
PARKER!

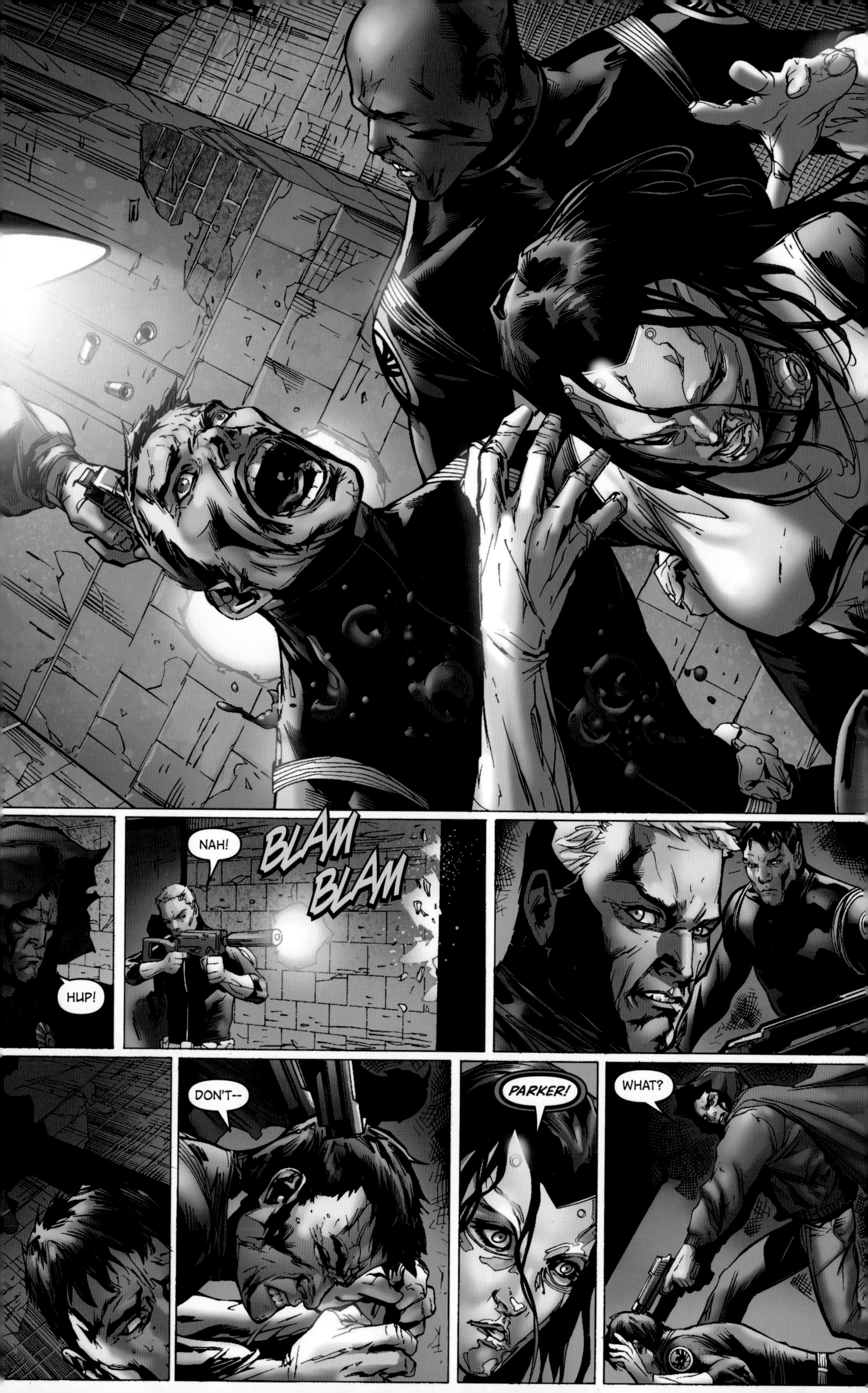
NAH!
BLAM
BLAM
HUP!
DON'T--
PARKER!
WHAT?

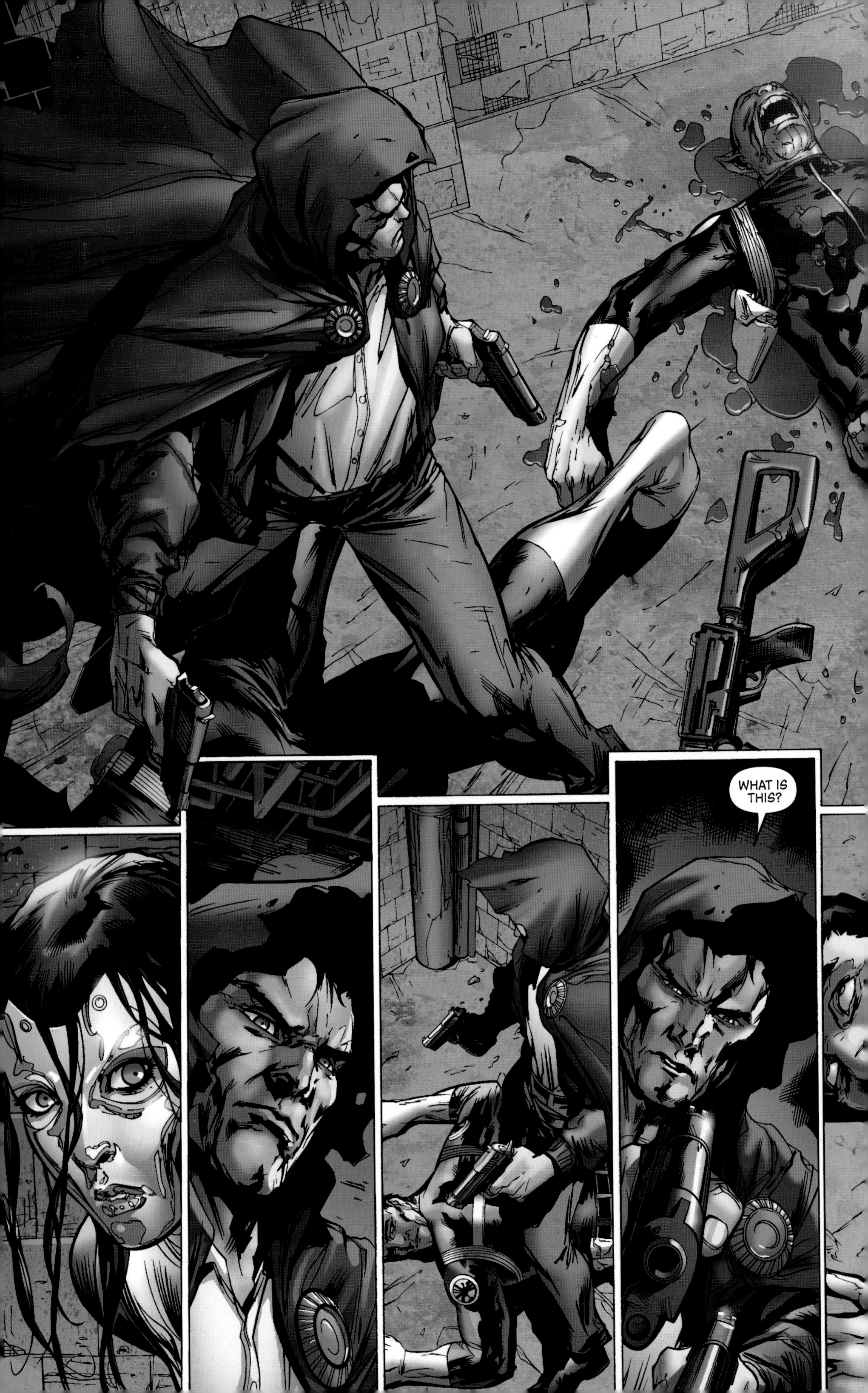
WHAT IS
THIS?

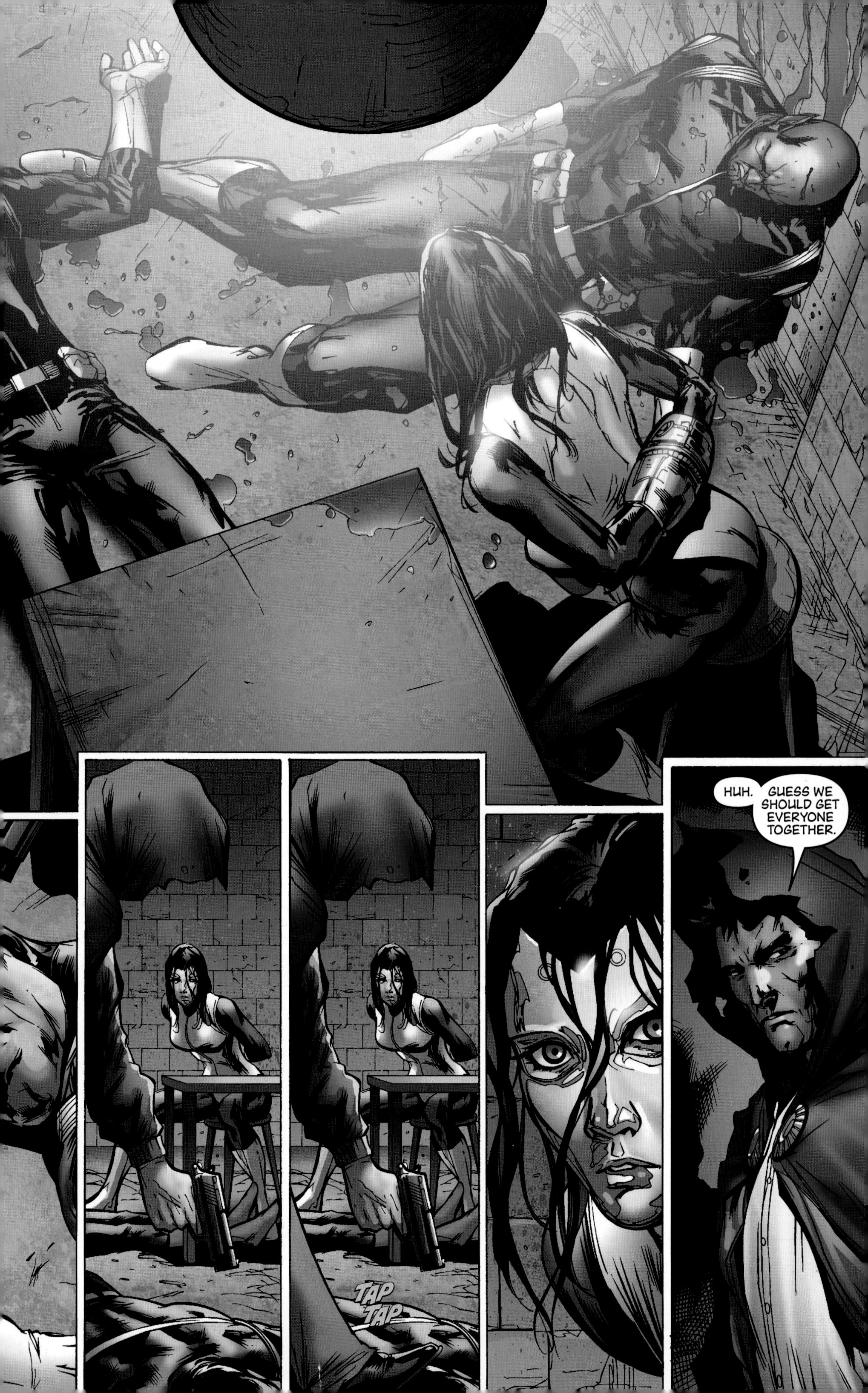
TAP TAP
HUH. GUESS WE SHOULD GET EVERYONE TOGETHER.

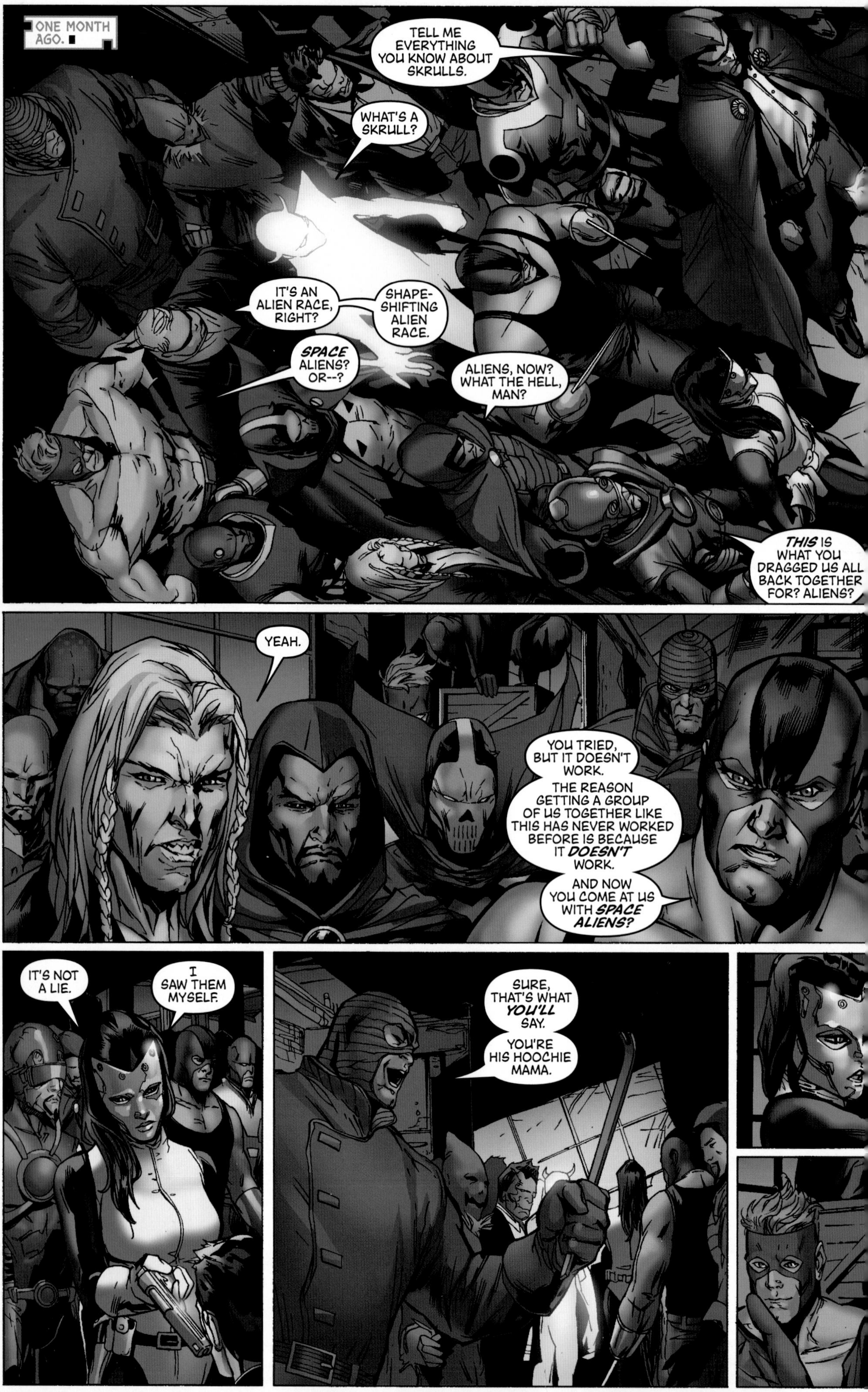
ONE MONTH AGO.
TELL ME EVERYTHING YOU KNOW ABOUT SKRULLS.
WHAT'S A SKRULL?
IT'S AN ALIEN RACE, RIGHT?
SHAPE-SHIFTING ALIEN RACE.
SPACE ALIENS? OR--?
ALIENS, NOW? WHAT THE HELL, MAN?
THIS IS WHAT YOU DRAGGED US ALL BACK TOGETHER FOR? ALIENS?
YEAH.
YOU TRIED, BUT IT DOESN'T WORK.
THE REASON GETTING A GROUP OF US TOGETHER LIKE THIS HAS NEVER WORKED BEFORE IS BECAUSE IT DOESN'T WORK.
AND NOW YOU COME AT US WITH SPACE ALIENS?
IT'S NOT A LIE.
I SAW THEM MYSELF.
SURE, THAT'S WHAT YOU'LL SAY.
YOU'RE HIS HOOCHIE MAMA.

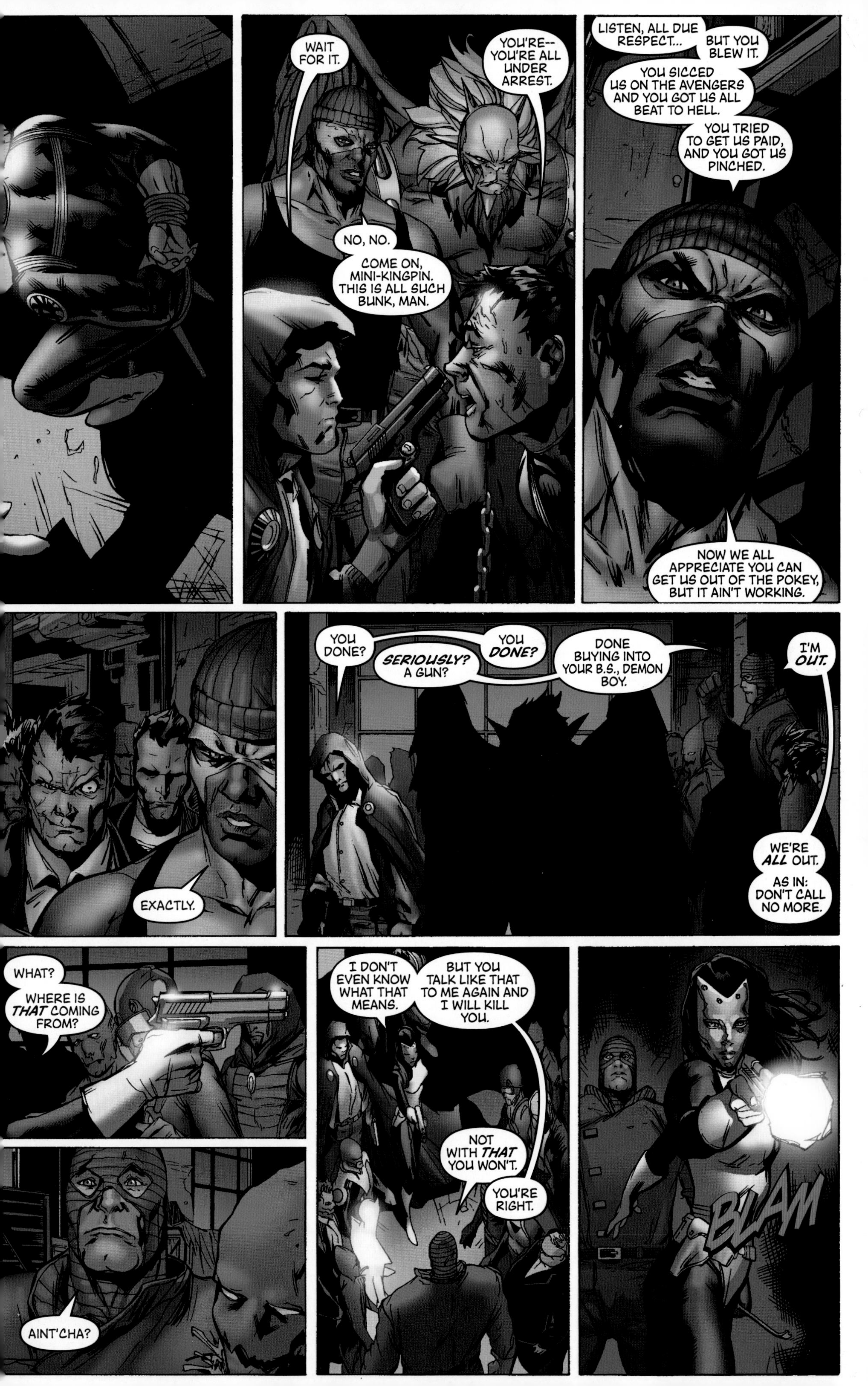
WAIT FOR IT.
YOU'RE-- YOU'RE ALL UNDER ARREST.
NO, NO.
COME ON, MINI-KINGPIN. THIS IS ALL SUCH BUNK, MAN.
LISTEN, ALL DUE RESPECT...
BUT YOU BLEW IT.
YOU SICCED US ON THE AVENGERS AND YOU GOT US ALL BEAT TO HELL.
YOU TRIED TO GET US PAID, AND YOU GOT US PINCHED.
NOW WE ALL APPRECIATE YOU CAN GET US OUT OF THE POKEY, BUT IT AIN'T WORKING.
EXACTLY.
YOU DONE?
YOU *DONE?*
SERIOUSLY? A GUN?
DONE BUYING INTO YOUR B.S., DEMON BOY.
I'M *OUT.*
WE'RE *ALL* OUT.
AS IN: DON'T CALL NO MORE.
WHAT?
WHERE IS *THAT* COMING FROM?
AINT'CHA?
I DON'T EVEN KNOW WHAT THAT MEANS.
BUT YOU TALK LIKE THAT TO ME AGAIN AND I WILL KILL YOU.
NOT WITH *THAT* YOU WON'T.
YOU'RE RIGHT.
BLAM

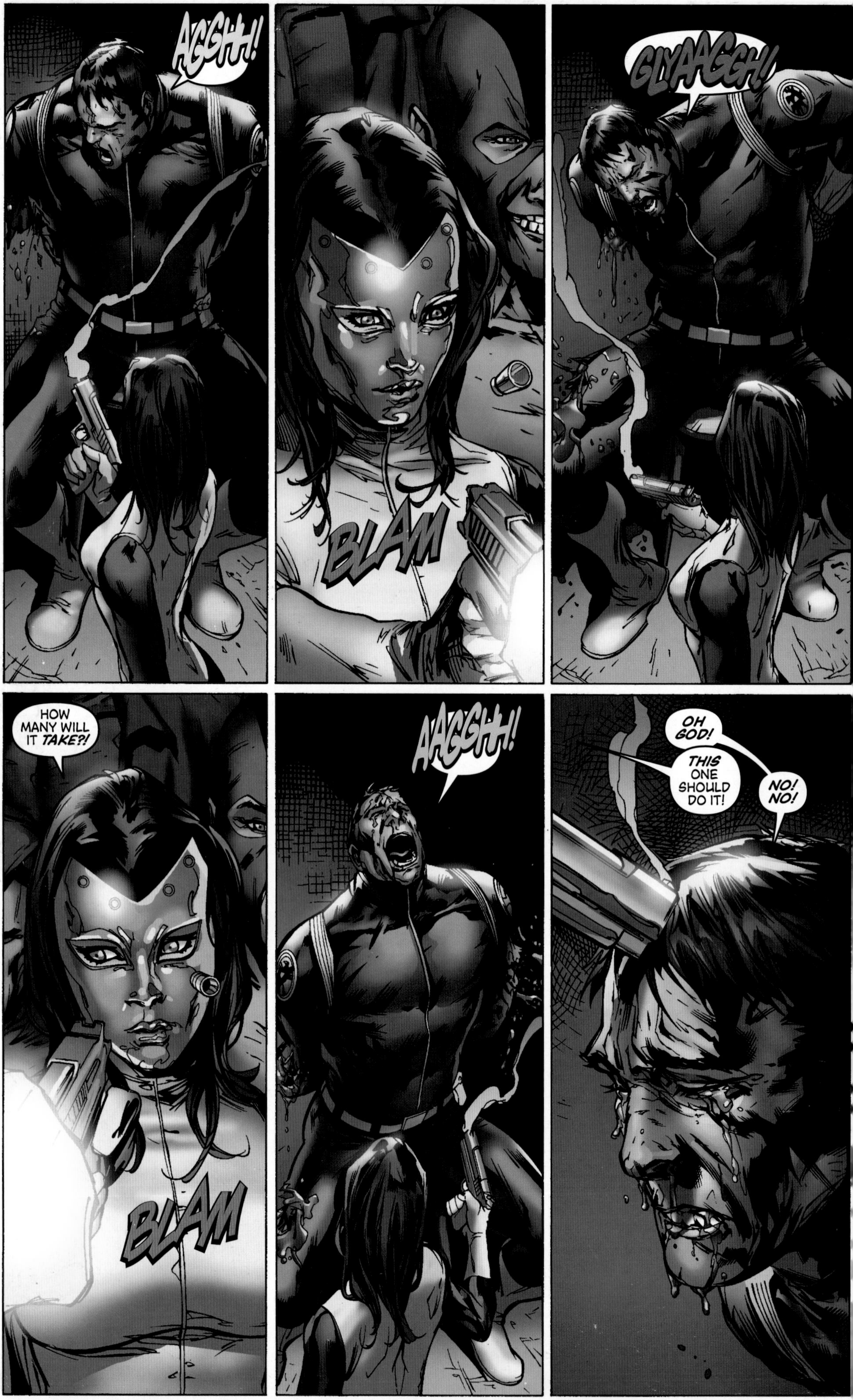
AGGHH!
BLAM
GLYAAGGH!
HOW MANY WILL IT TAKE?!
BLAM
AAGGHH!
OH GOD!
THIS ONE SHOULD DO IT!
NO! NO!

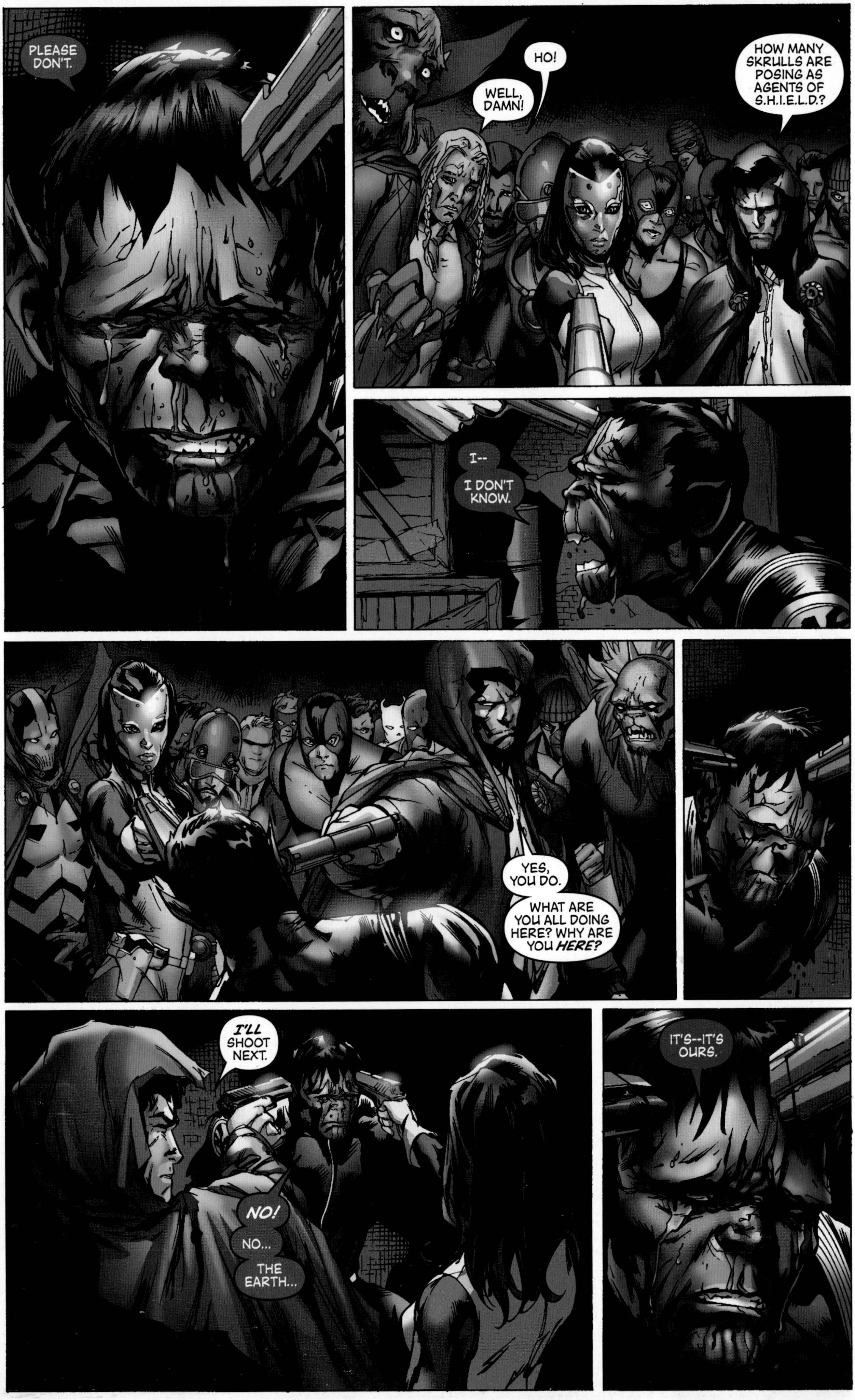
PLEASE DON'T.
HO!
WELL, DAMN!
HOW MANY SKRULLS ARE POSING AS AGENTS OF S.H.I.E.L.D.?
I--
I DON'T KNOW.
YES, YOU DO.
WHAT ARE YOU ALL DOING HERE? WHY ARE YOU *HERE?*
I'LL SHOOT NEXT.
NO!
NO...
THE EARTH...
IT'S--IT'S OURS.

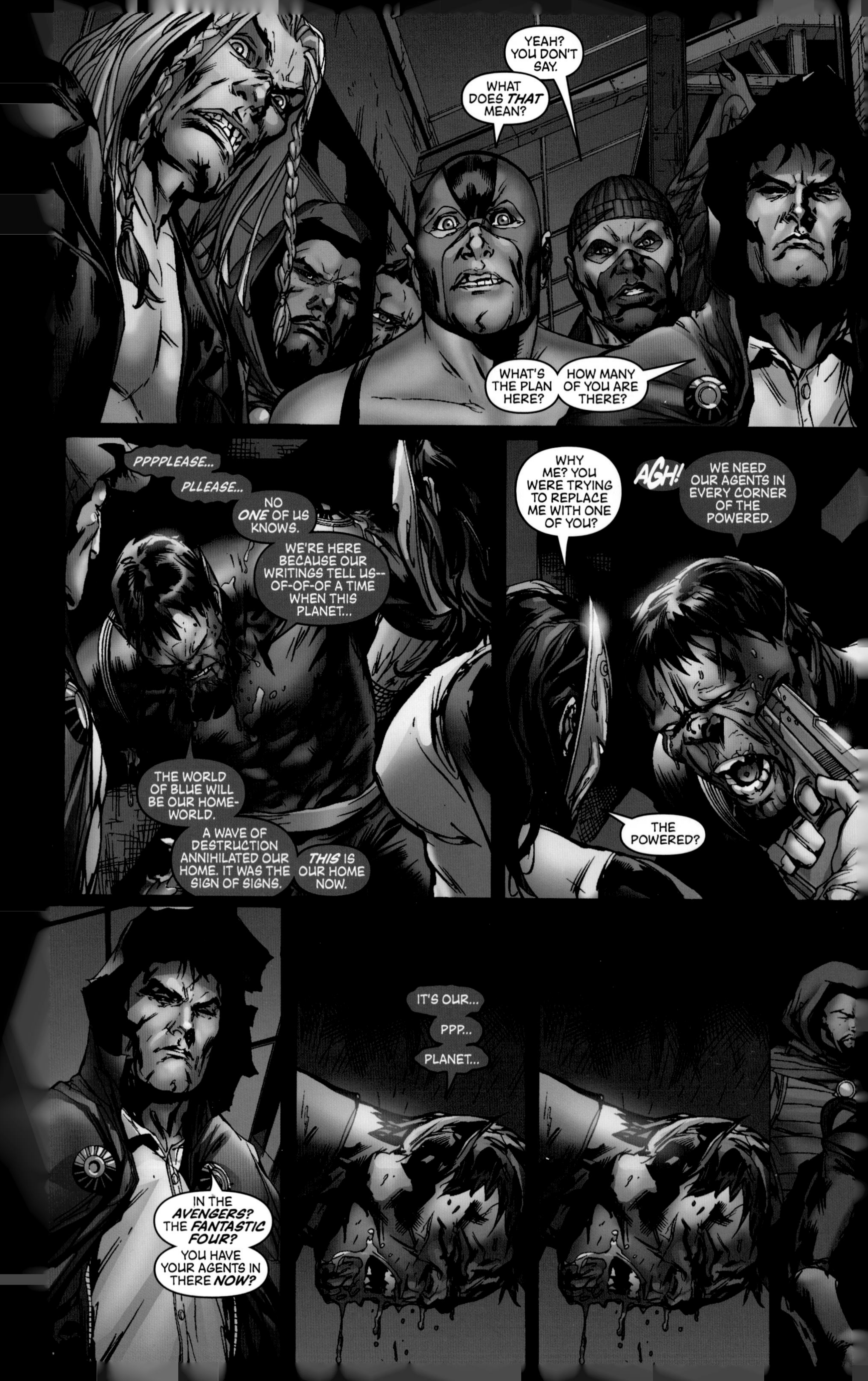

WHAT DOES THAT MEAN?
YEAH? YOU DON'T SAY.
WHAT'S THE PLAN HERE?
HOW MANY OF YOU ARE THERE?
PPPPLEASE...
PLLEASE...
NO ONE OF US KNOWS.
WE'RE HERE BECAUSE OUR WRITINGS TELL US-- OF-OF-OF A TIME WHEN THIS PLANET...
THE WORLD OF BLUE WILL BE OUR HOME-WORLD.
A WAVE OF DESTRUCTION ANNIHILATED OUR HOME. IT WAS THE SIGN OF SIGNS.
THIS IS OUR HOME NOW.
WHY ME? YOU WERE TRYING TO REPLACE ME WITH ONE OF YOU?
AGH!
WE NEED OUR AGENTS IN EVERY CORNER OF THE POWERED.
THE POWERED?
IN THE AVENGERS? THE FANTASTIC FOUR? YOU HAVE YOUR AGENTS IN THERE NOW?
IT'S OUR...
PPP...
PLANET...

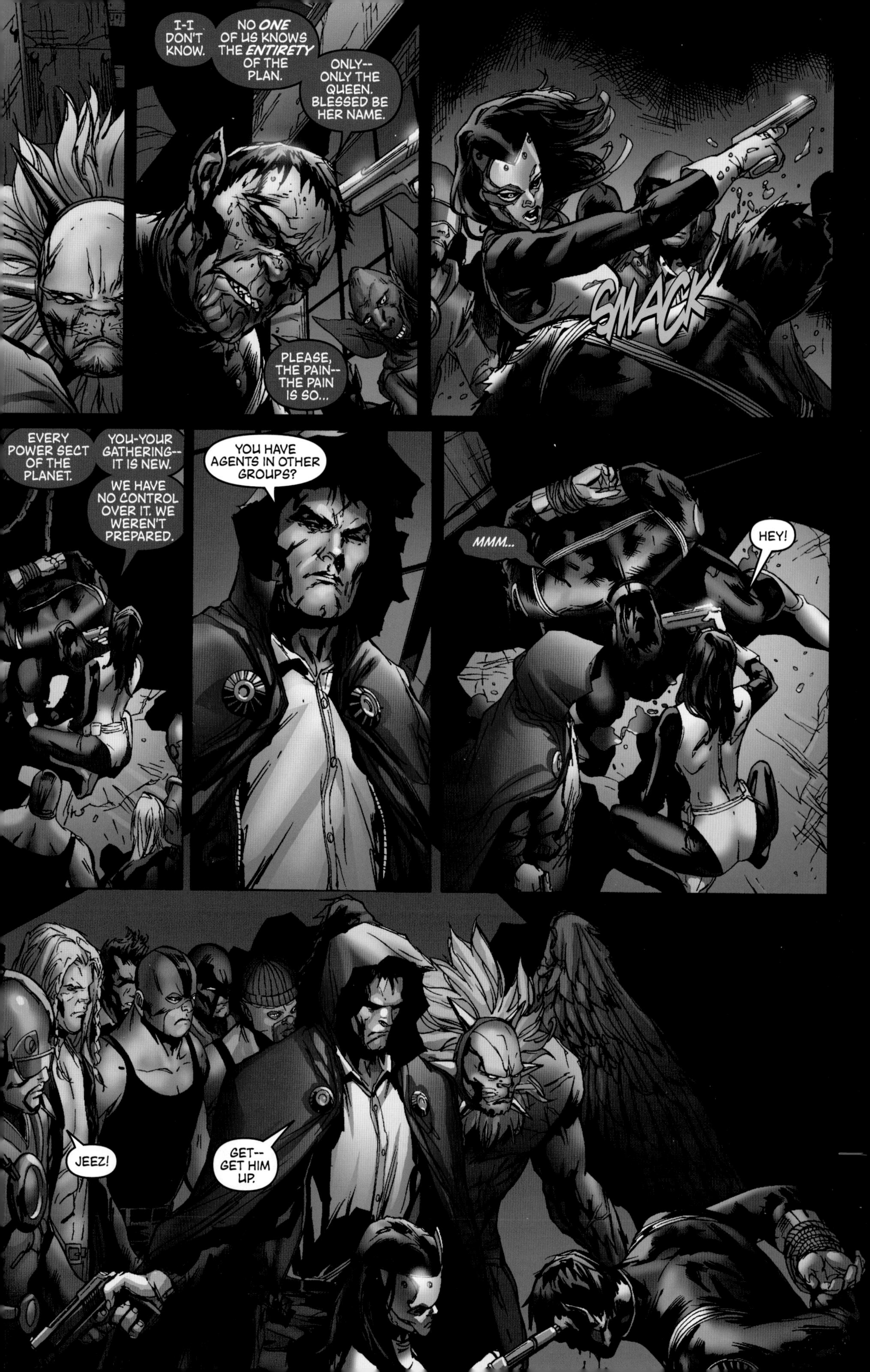
I-I DON'T KNOW.
NO ONE OF US KNOWS THE ENTIRETY OF THE PLAN.
ONLY-- ONLY THE QUEEN. BLESSED BE HER NAME.
PLEASE, THE PAIN-- THE PAIN IS SO...
SMACK
EVERY POWER SECT OF THE PLANET.
YOU-YOUR GATHERING-- IT IS NEW.
WE HAVE NO CONTROL OVER IT. WE WEREN'T PREPARED.
YOU HAVE AGENTS IN OTHER GROUPS?
MMM...
HEY!
JEEZ!
GET-- GET HIM UP.

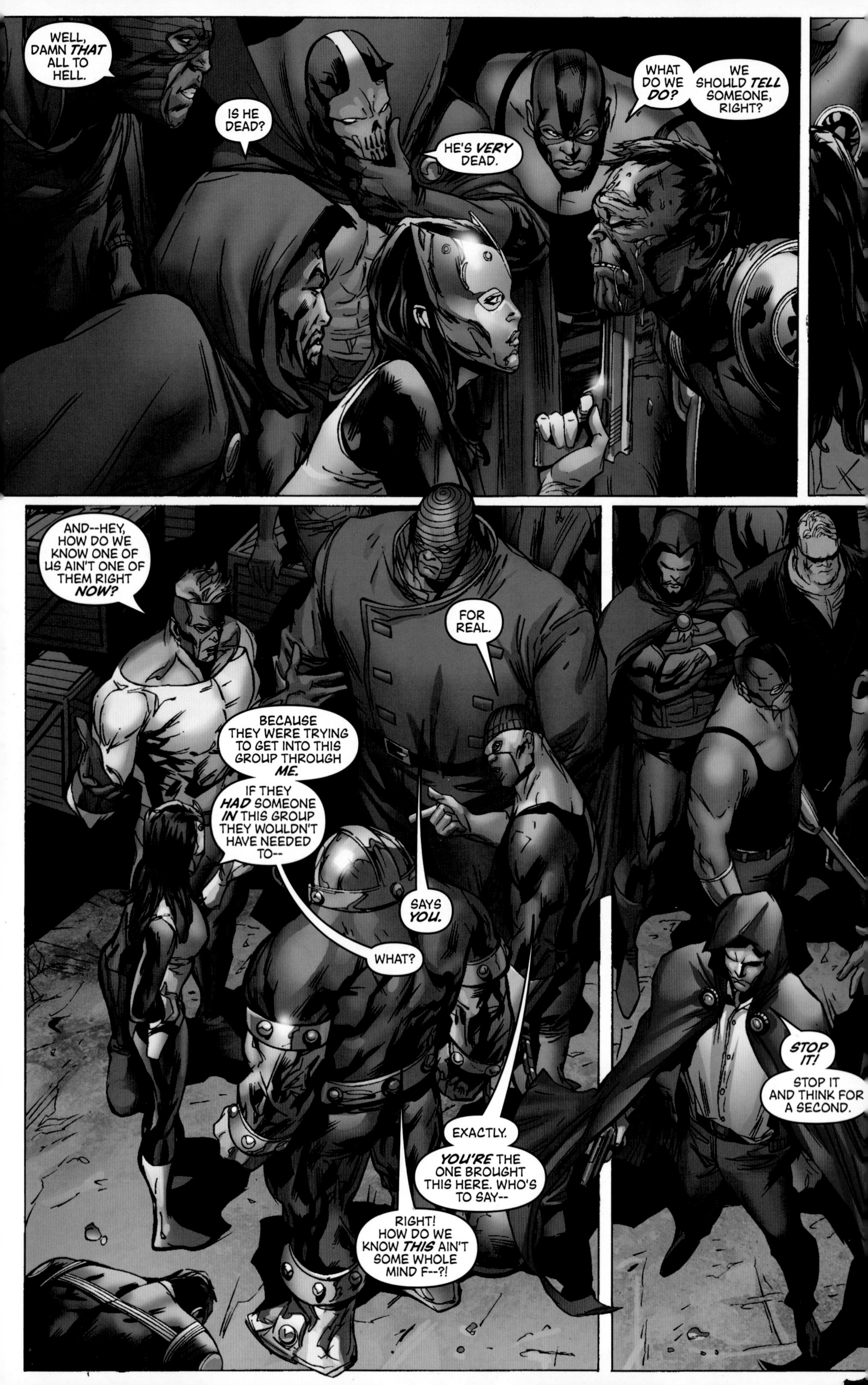
WELL, DAMN THAT ALL TO HELL.
IS HE DEAD?
HE'S VERY DEAD.
WHAT DO WE DO?
WE SHOULD TELL SOMEONE, RIGHT?
AND--HEY, HOW DO WE KNOW ONE OF US AIN'T ONE OF THEM RIGHT NOW?
FOR REAL.
BECAUSE THEY WERE TRYING TO GET INTO THIS GROUP THROUGH ME.
IF THEY HAD SOMEONE IN THIS GROUP THEY WOULDN'T HAVE NEEDED TO--
SAYS YOU.
WHAT?
EXACTLY.
YOU'RE THE ONE BROUGHT THIS HERE. WHO'S TO SAY--
RIGHT! HOW DO WE KNOW THIS AIN'T SOME WHOLE MIND F--?!
STOP IT!
STOP IT AND THINK FOR A SECOND.

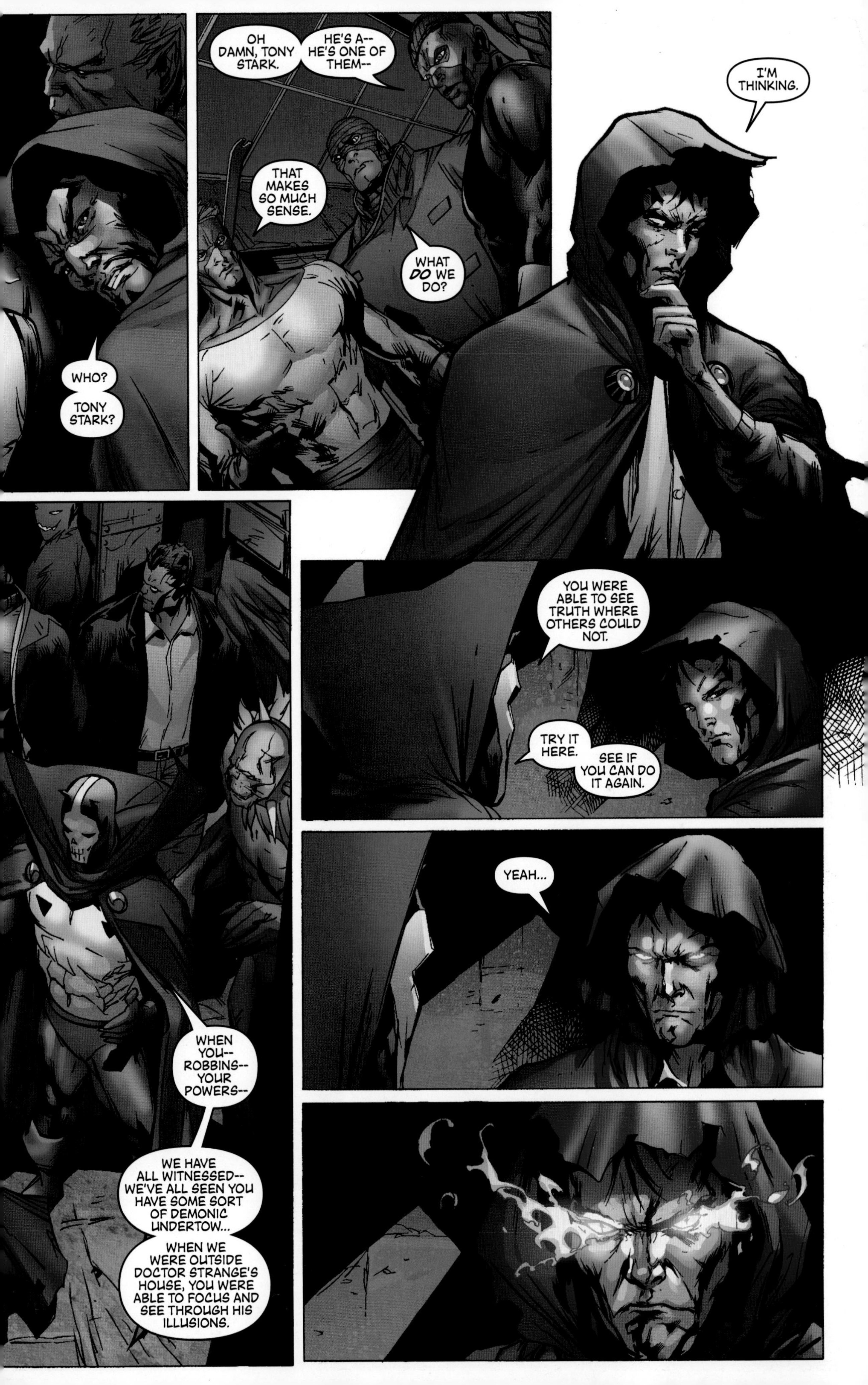
WHO?
TONY STARK?
OH DAMN, TONY STARK.
HE'S A-- HE'S ONE OF THEM--
THAT MAKES SO MUCH SENSE.
WHAT *DO* WE DO?
I'M THINKING.
WHEN YOU-- ROBBINS-- YOUR POWERS--
WE HAVE ALL WITNESSED-- WE'VE ALL SEEN YOU HAVE SOME SORT OF DEMONIC UNDERTOW...
WHEN WE WERE OUTSIDE DOCTOR STRANGE'S HOUSE, YOU WERE ABLE TO FOCUS AND SEE THROUGH HIS ILLUSIONS.
YOU WERE ABLE TO SEE TRUTH WHERE OTHERS COULD NOT.
TRY IT HERE.
SEE IF YOU CAN DO IT AGAIN.
YEAH...

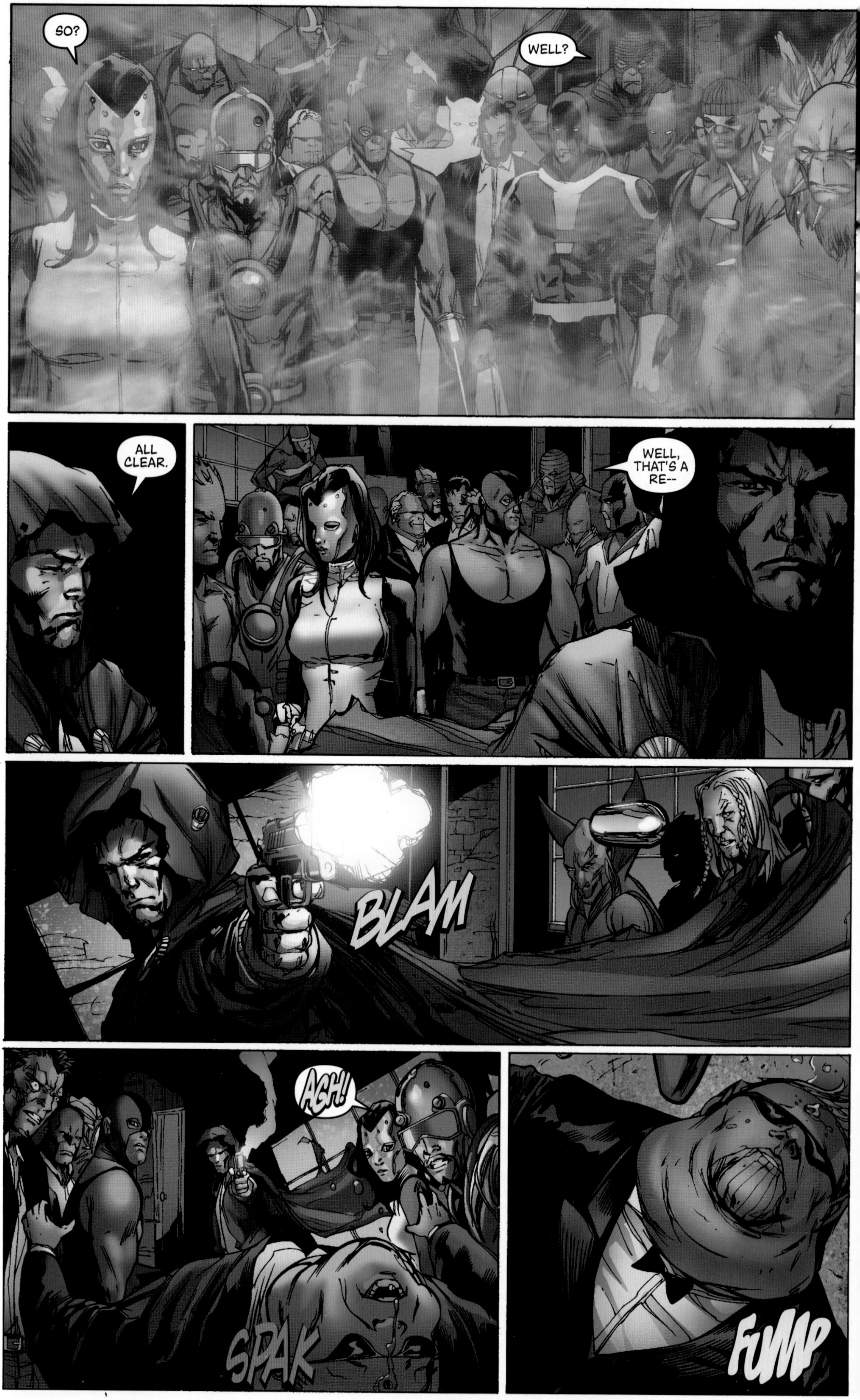
SO?
WELL?
ALL CLEAR.
WELL, THAT'S A RE--
BLAM
AGH!
SPAK
FUMP

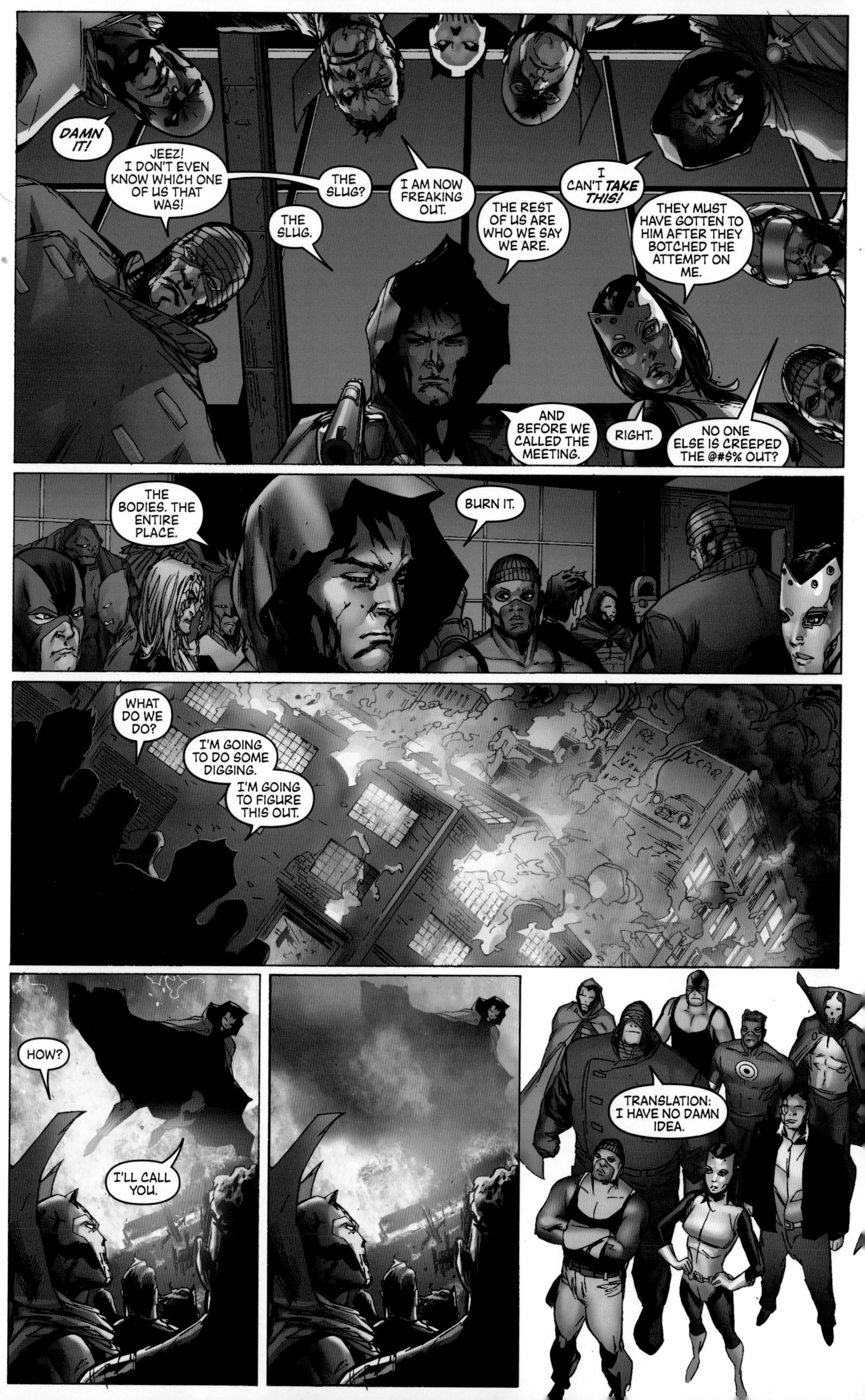
DAMN IT!
JEEZ! I DON'T EVEN KNOW WHICH ONE OF US THAT WAS!
THE SLUG?
THE SLUG.
I AM NOW FREAKING OUT.
THE REST OF US ARE WHO WE SAY WE ARE.
I CAN'T TAKE THIS!
THEY MUST HAVE GOTTEN TO HIM AFTER THEY BOTCHED THE ATTEMPT ON ME.
AND BEFORE WE CALLED THE MEETING.
RIGHT.
NO ONE ELSE IS CREEPED THE @#$% OUT?
THE BODIES. THE ENTIRE PLACE.
BURN IT.
WHAT DO WE DO?
I'M GOING TO DO SOME DIGGING.
I'M GOING TO FIGURE THIS OUT.
HOW?
I'LL CALL YOU.
TRANSLATION: I HAVE NO DAMN IDEA.

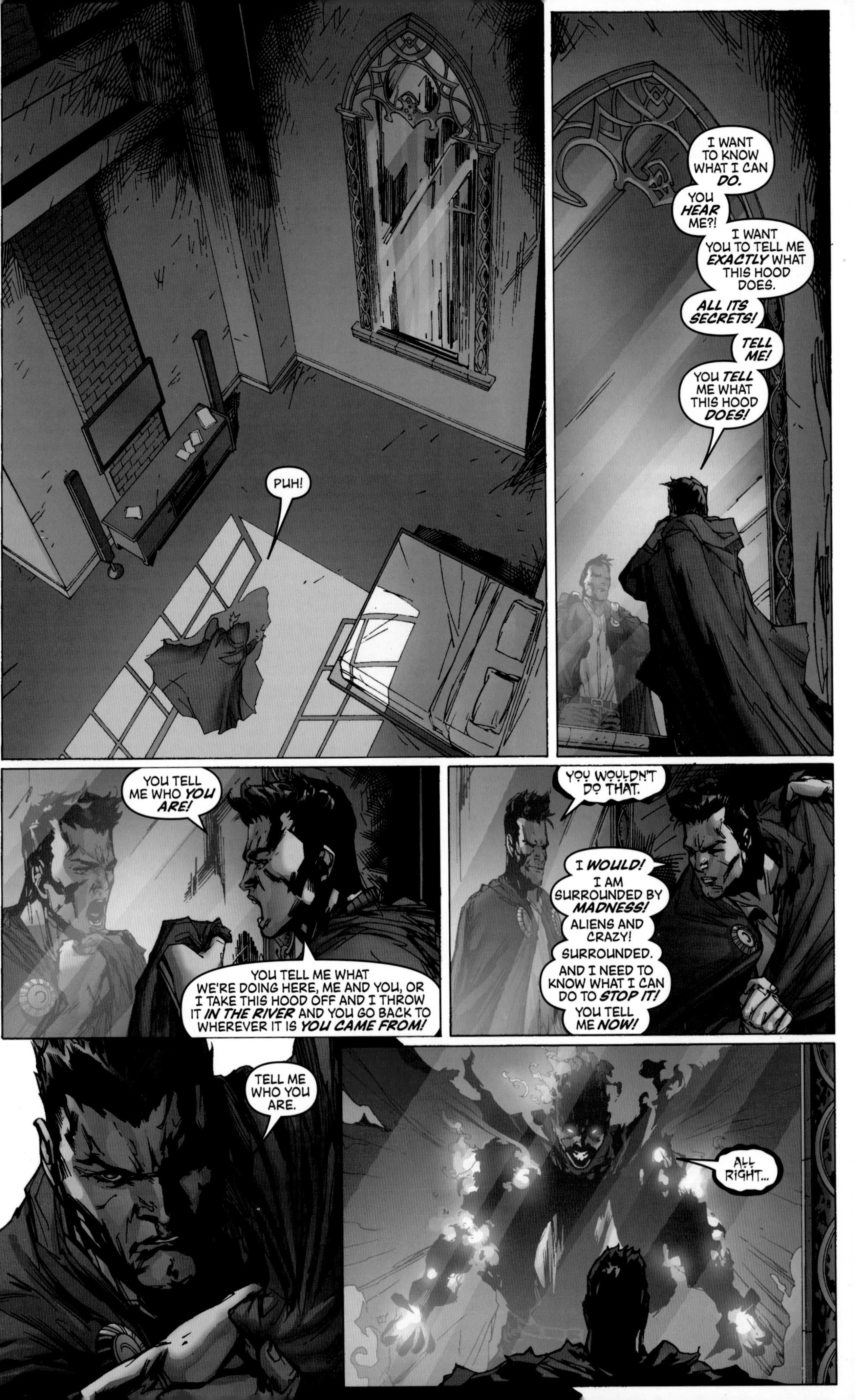

PUH!
I WANT TO KNOW WHAT I CAN DO.
YOU HEAR ME?!
I WANT YOU TO TELL ME EXACTLY WHAT THIS HOOD DOES.
ALL ITS SECRETS!
TELL ME!
YOU TELL ME WHAT THIS HOOD DOES!
YOU TELL ME WHO YOU ARE!
YOU TELL ME WHAT WE'RE DOING HERE, ME AND YOU, OR I TAKE THIS HOOD OFF AND I THROW IT IN THE RIVER AND YOU GO BACK TO WHEREVER IT IS YOU CAME FROM!
YOU WOULDN'T DO THAT.
I WOULD!
I AM SURROUNDED BY MADNESS!
ALIENS AND CRAZY!
SURROUNDED.
AND I NEED TO KNOW WHAT I CAN DO TO STOP IT!
YOU TELL ME NOW!
TELL ME WHO YOU ARE.
ALL RIGHT...

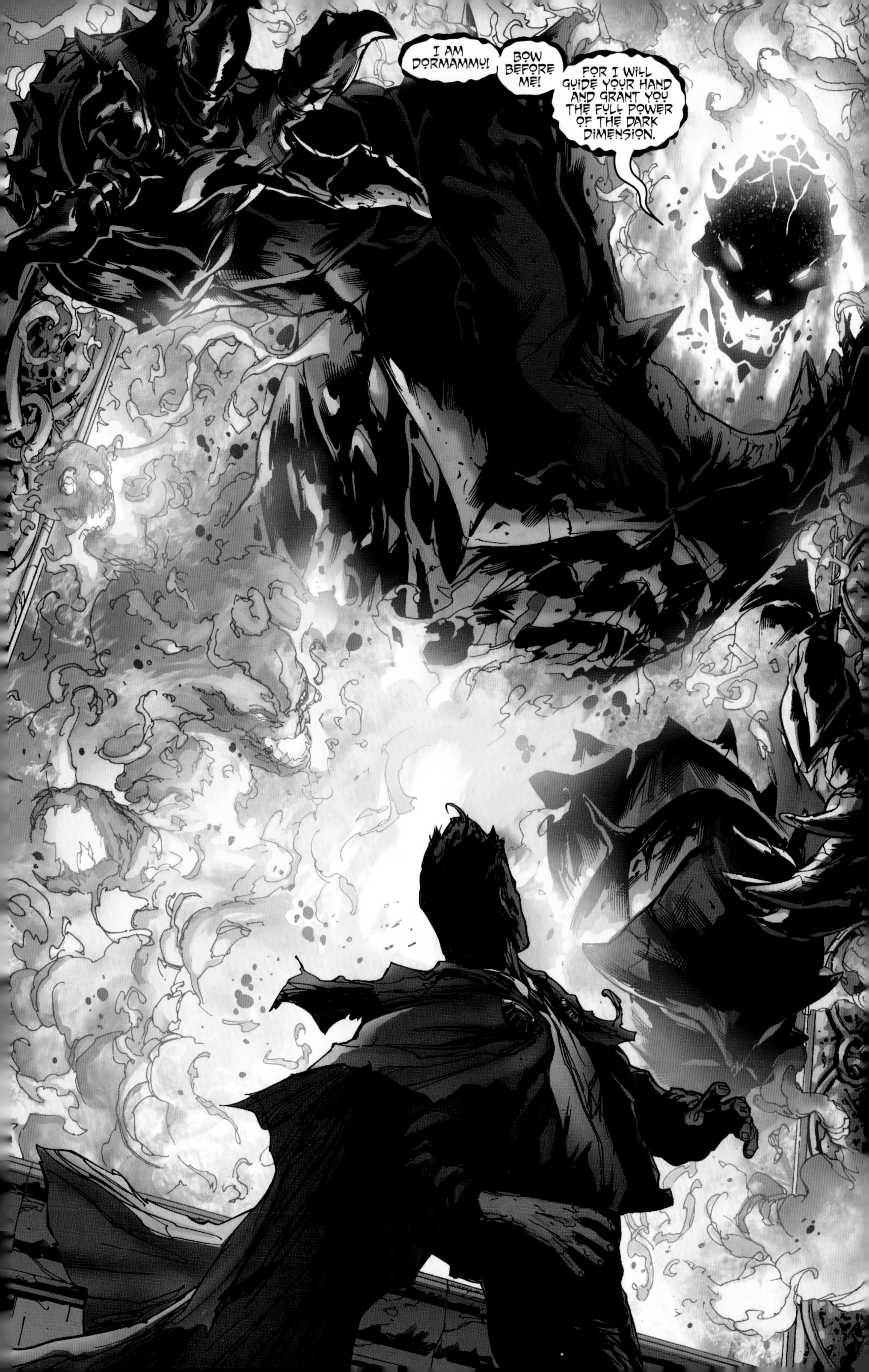
I AM DORMAMMU!
BOW BEFORE ME!
FOR I WILL GUIDE YOUR HAND AND GRANT YOU THE FULL POWER OF THE DARK DIMENSION.

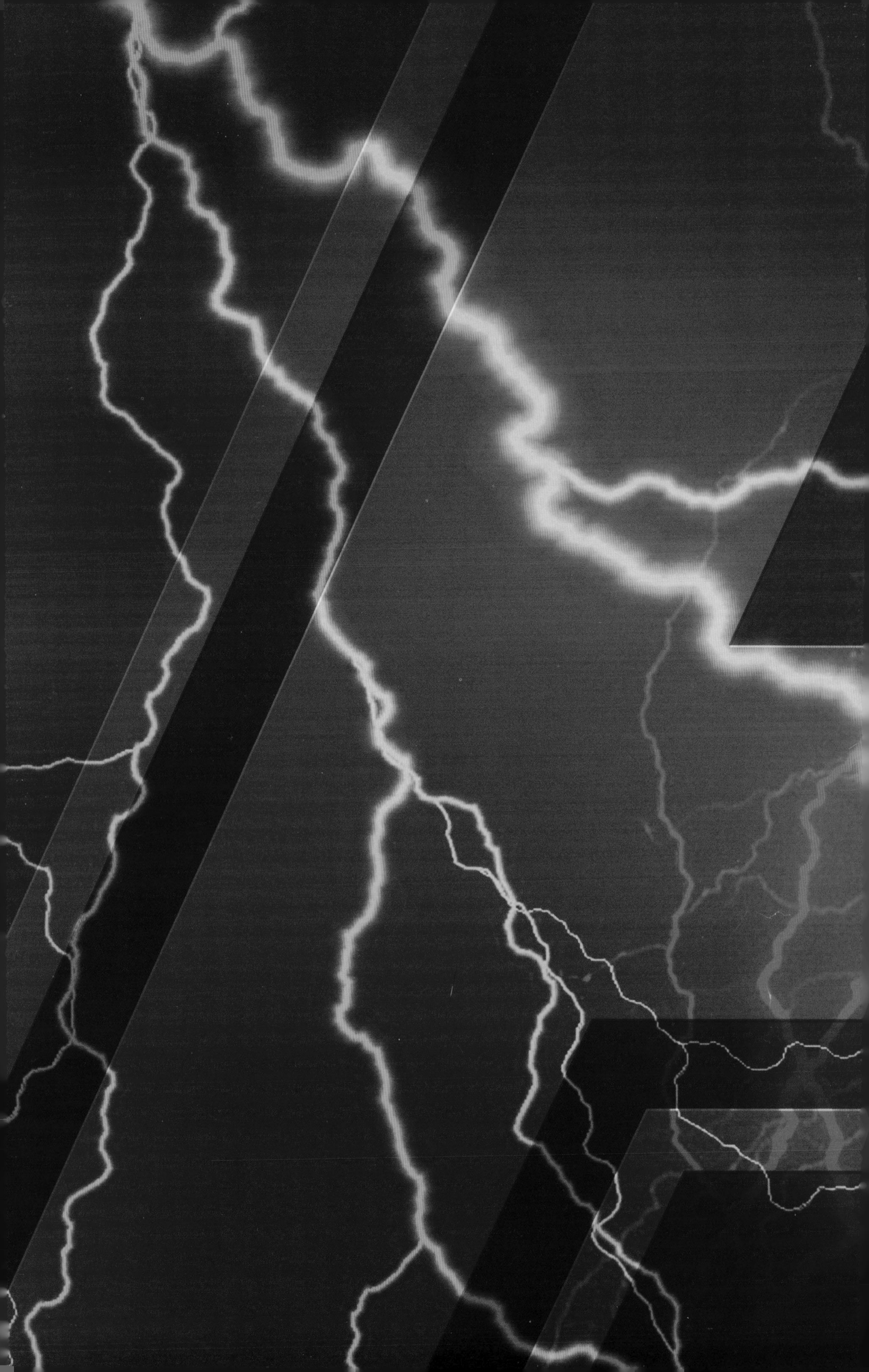

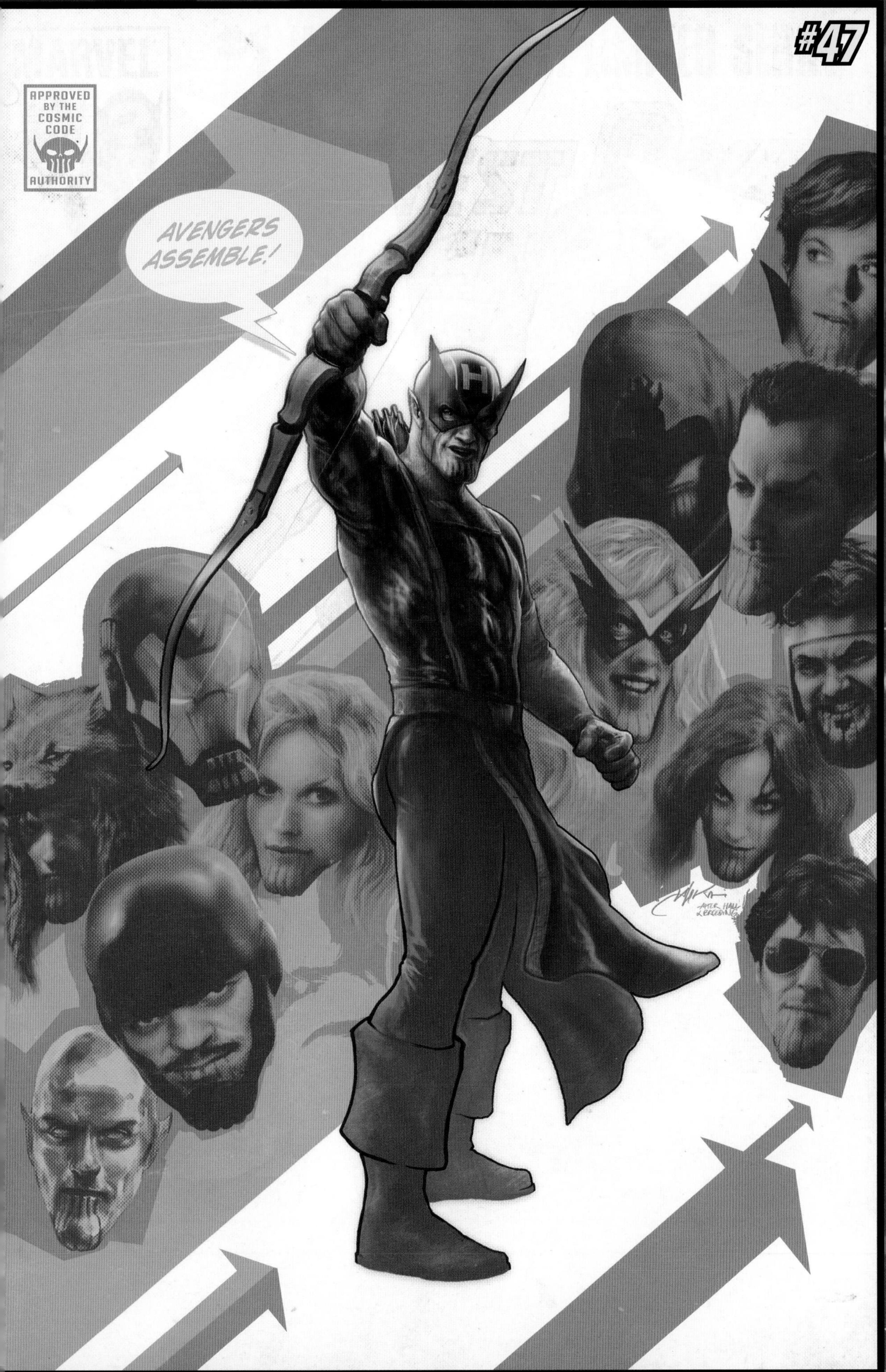
#47
APPROVED BY THE COSMIC CODE AUTHORITY
AVENGERS ASSEMBLE!

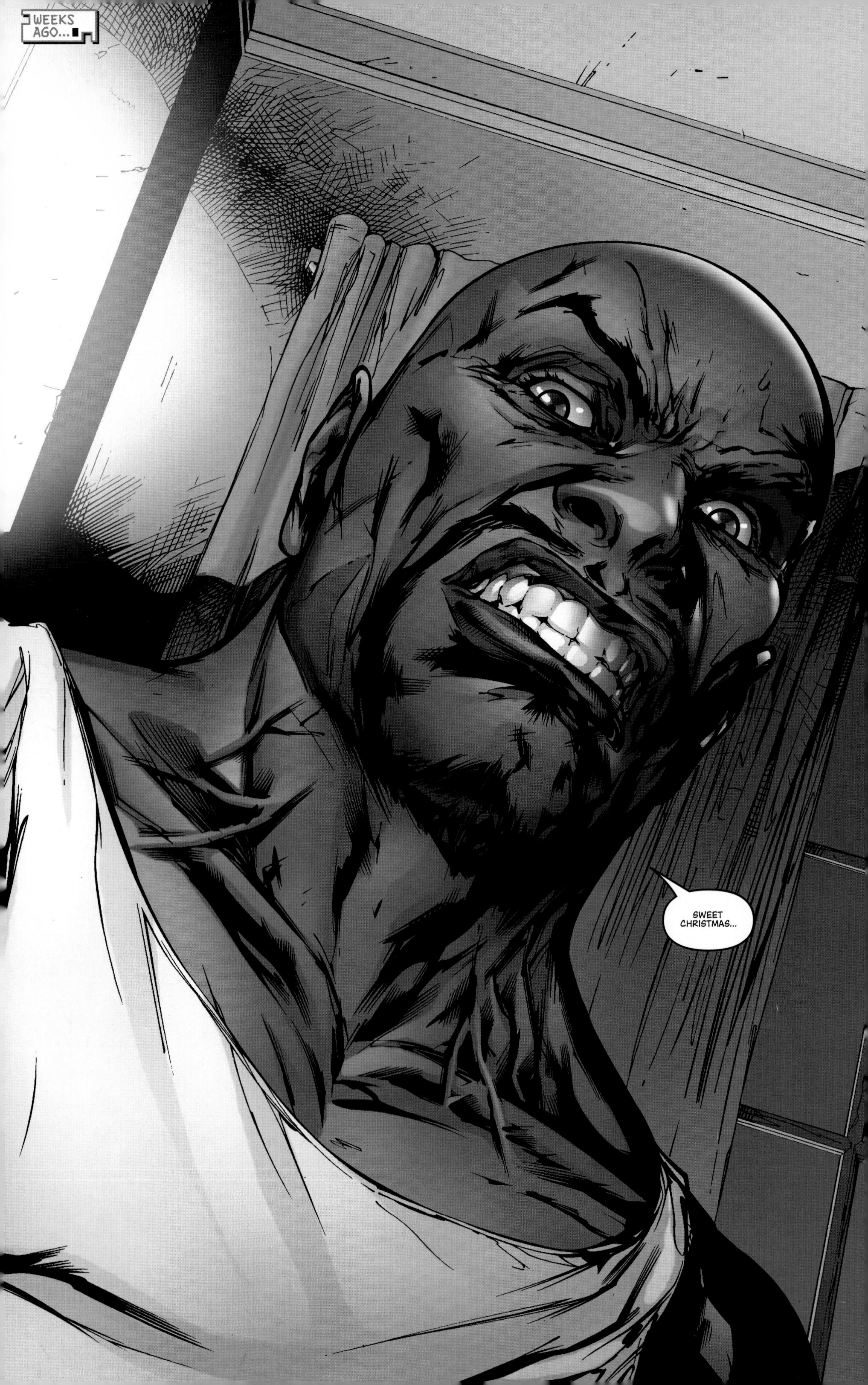
WEEKS AGO...
SWEET CHRISTMAS...

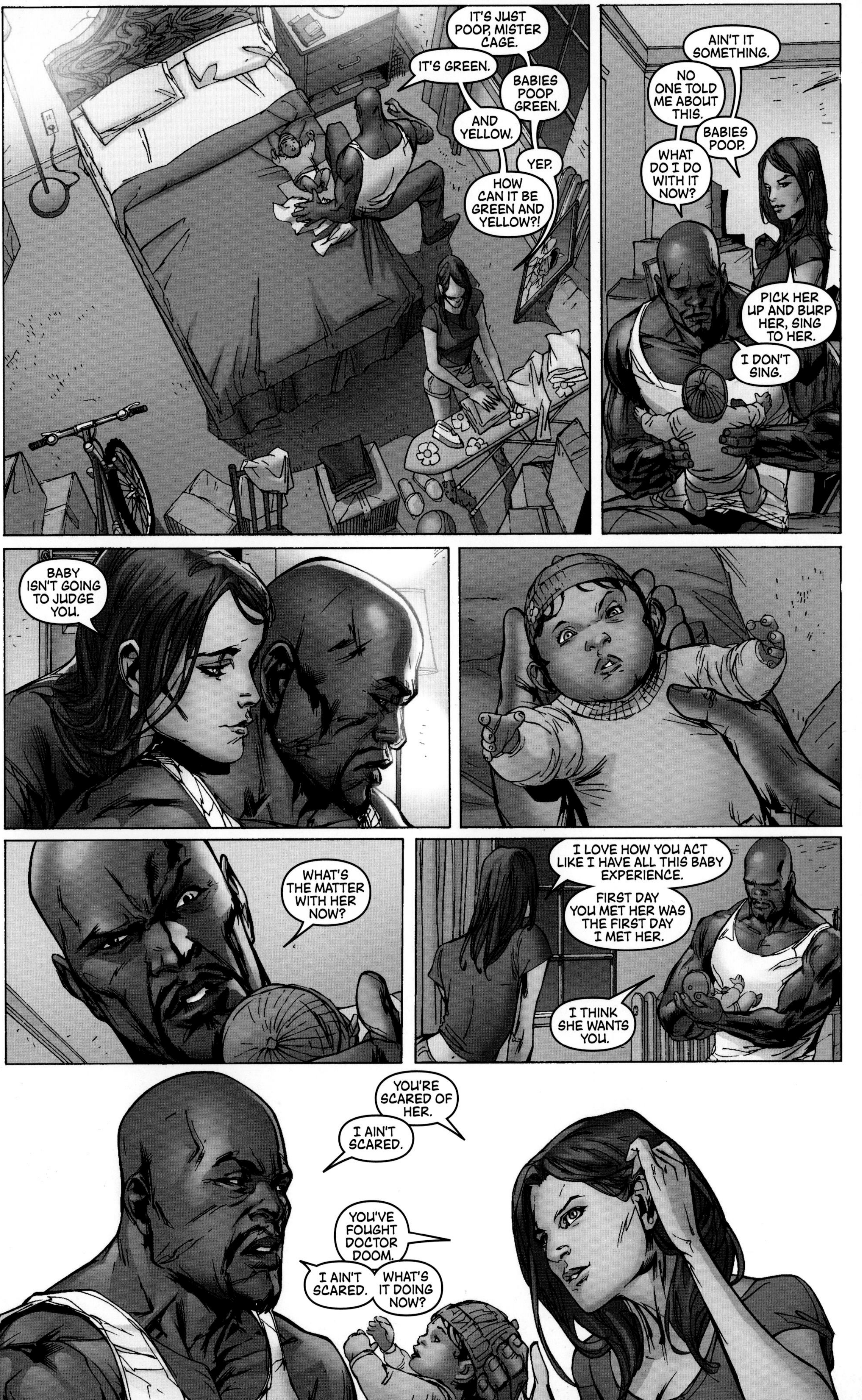
IT'S JUST POOP, MISTER CAGE.
IT'S GREEN.
BABIES POOP GREEN.
AND YELLOW.
YEP.
HOW CAN IT BE GREEN AND YELLOW?!
AIN'T IT SOMETHING.
NO ONE TOLD ME ABOUT THIS.
BABIES POOP.
WHAT DO I DO WITH IT NOW?
PICK HER UP AND BURP HER, SING TO HER.
I DON'T SING.
BABY ISN'T GOING TO JUDGE YOU.
WHAT'S THE MATTER WITH HER NOW?
I LOVE HOW YOU ACT LIKE I HAVE ALL THIS BABY EXPERIENCE.
FIRST DAY YOU MET HER WAS THE FIRST DAY I MET HER.
I THINK SHE WANTS YOU.
YOU'RE SCARED OF HER.
I AIN'T SCARED.
YOU'VE FOUGHT DOCTOR DOOM.
I AIN'T SCARED.
WHAT'S IT DOING NOW?

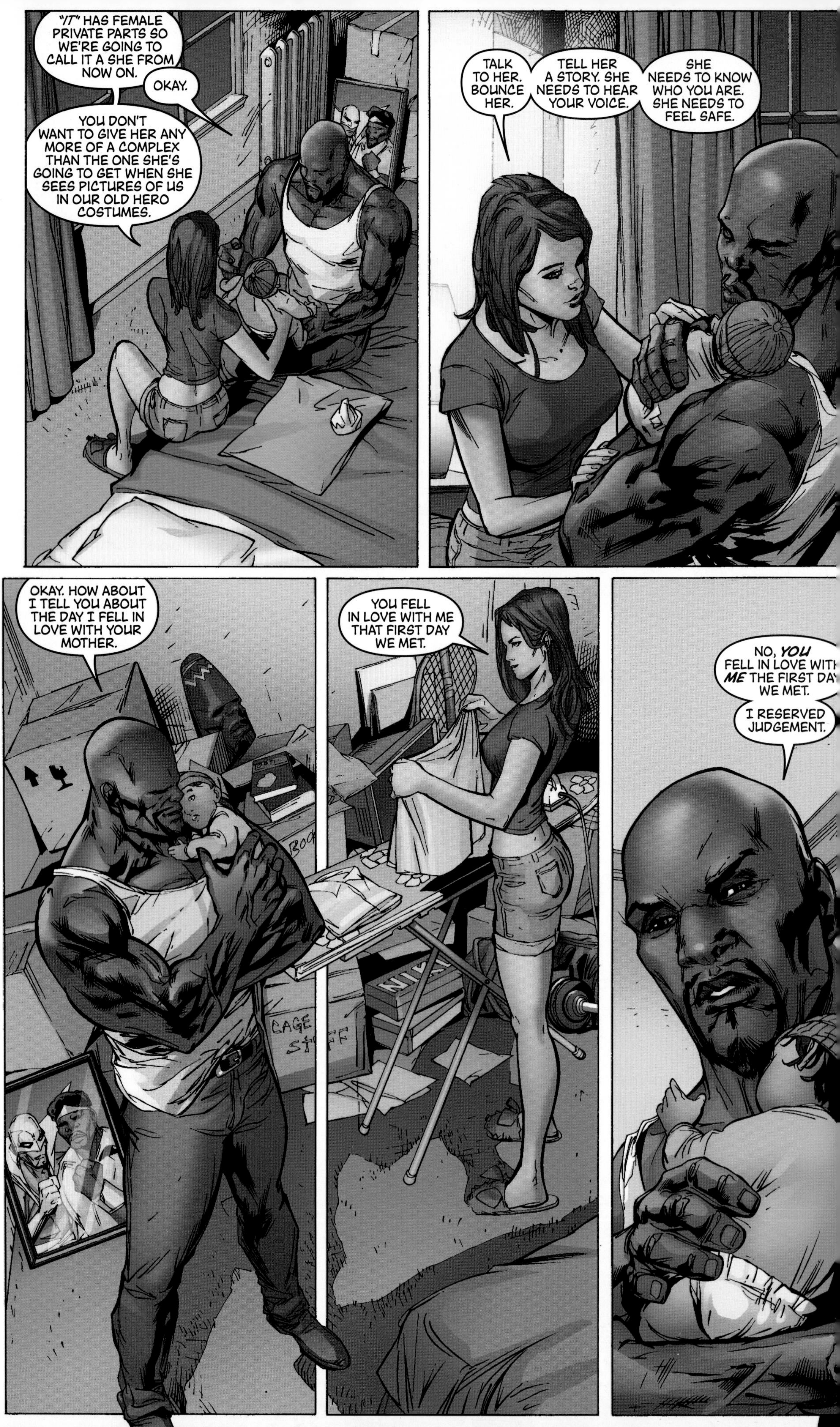
"IT" HAS FEMALE PRIVATE PARTS SO WE'RE GOING TO CALL IT A SHE FROM NOW ON.
OKAY.
YOU DON'T WANT TO GIVE HER ANY MORE OF A COMPLEX THAN THE ONE SHE'S GOING TO GET WHEN SHE SEES PICTURES OF US IN OUR OLD HERO COSTUMES.
TALK TO HER. BOUNCE HER.
TELL HER A STORY. SHE NEEDS TO HEAR YOUR VOICE.
SHE NEEDS TO KNOW WHO YOU ARE. SHE NEEDS TO FEEL SAFE.
OKAY. HOW ABOUT I TELL YOU ABOUT THE DAY I FELL IN LOVE WITH YOUR MOTHER.
YOU FELL IN LOVE WITH ME THAT FIRST DAY WE MET.
NO, YOU FELL IN LOVE WITH ME THE FIRST DAY WE MET.
I RESERVED JUDGEMENT.
CAGE STUFF

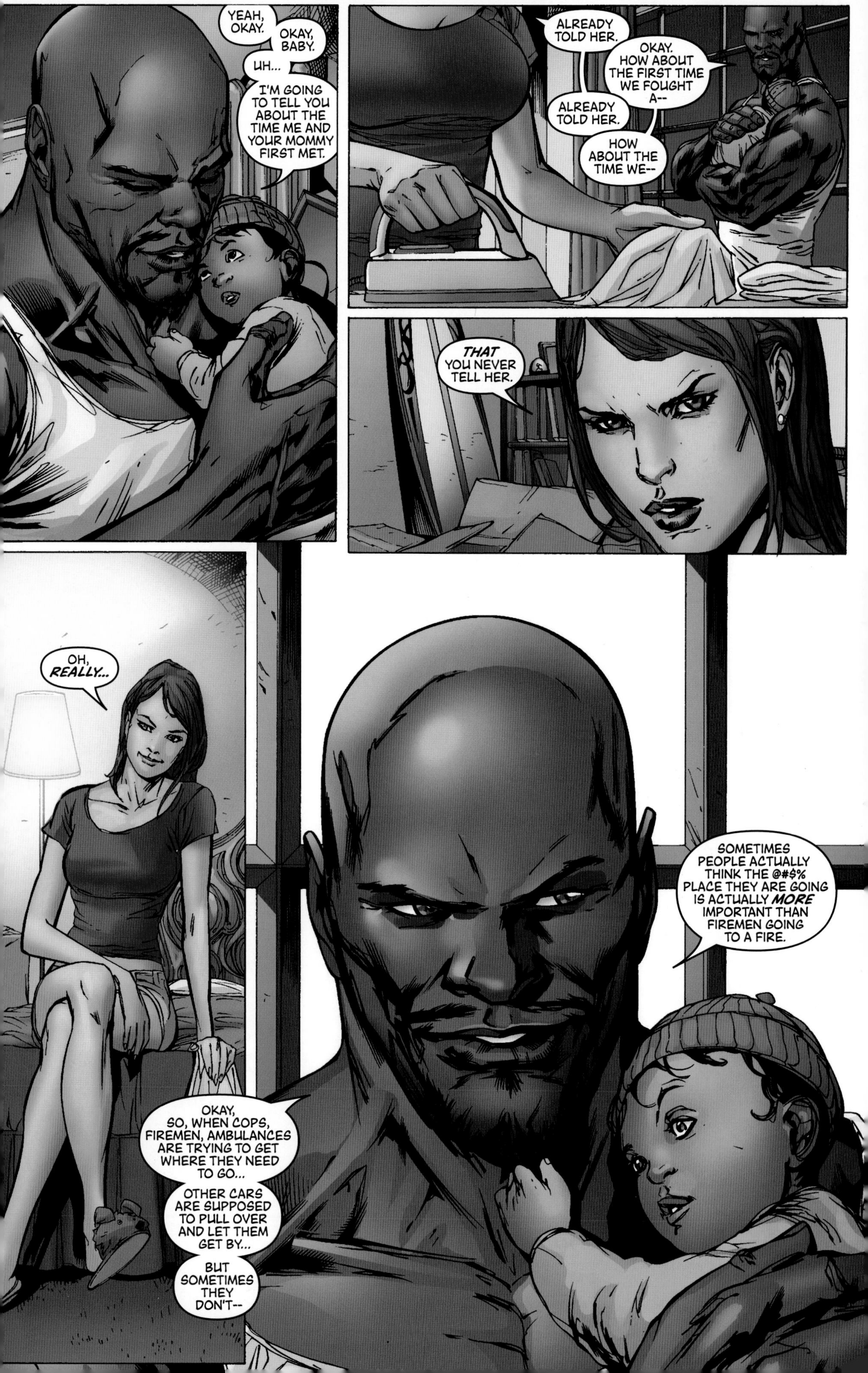
YEAH, OKAY.
OKAY, BABY.
UH...
I'M GOING TO TELL YOU ABOUT THE TIME ME AND YOUR MOMMY FIRST MET.
ALREADY TOLD HER.
OKAY. HOW ABOUT THE FIRST TIME WE FOUGHT A--
ALREADY TOLD HER.
HOW ABOUT THE TIME WE--
THAT YOU NEVER TELL HER.
OH, *REALLY...*
SOMETIMES PEOPLE ACTUALLY THINK THE @#$% PLACE THEY ARE GOING IS ACTUALLY *MORE* IMPORTANT THAN FIREMEN GOING TO A FIRE.
OKAY, SO, WHEN COPS, FIREMEN, AMBULANCES ARE TRYING TO GET WHERE THEY NEED TO GO...
OTHER CARS ARE SUPPOSED TO PULL OVER AND LET THEM GET BY...
BUT SOMETIMES THEY DON'T--

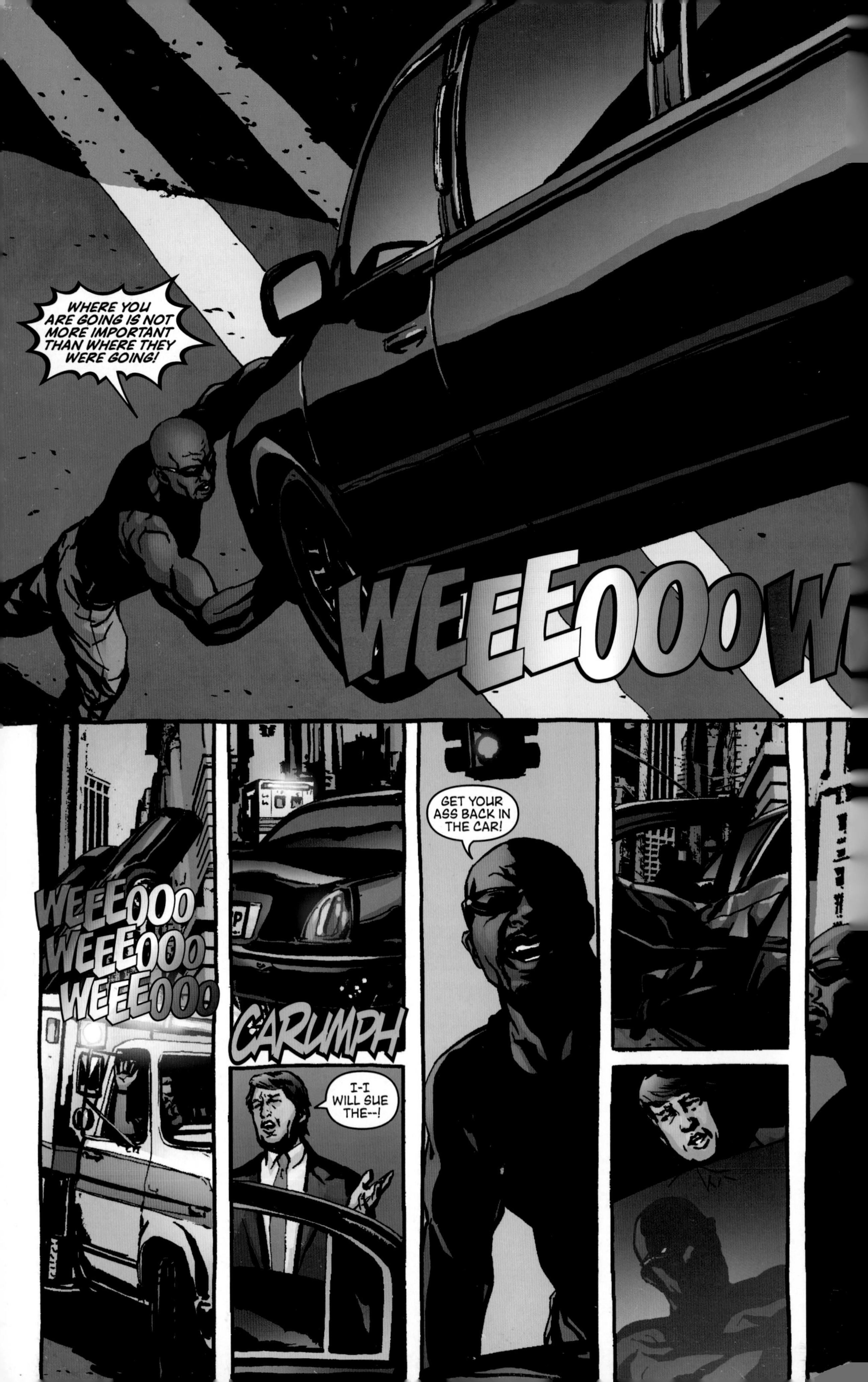
WHERE YOU ARE GOING IS NOT MORE IMPORTANT THAN WHERE THEY WERE GOING!
WEEEOOOW
WEEEOOO WEEEOOO WEEEOOO
CARUMPH
I-I WILL SUE THE--!
GET YOUR ASS BACK IN THE CAR!

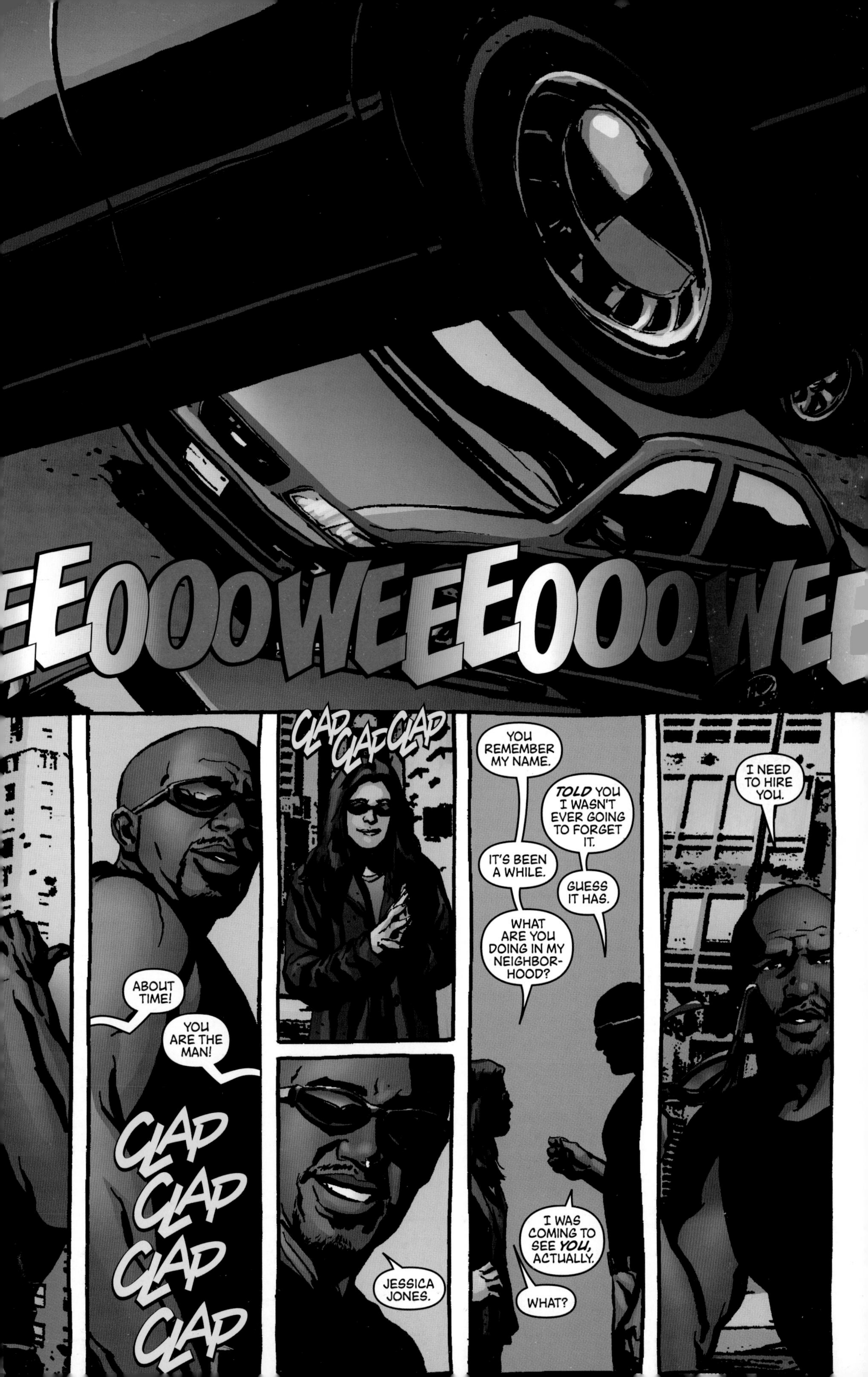
EEOOOWEEEOOOWEE
ABOUT TIME!
YOU ARE THE MAN!
CLAP CLAP CLAP CLAP CLAP
CLAP CLAP CLAP
JESSICA JONES.
YOU REMEMBER MY NAME.
TOLD YOU I WASN'T EVER GOING TO FORGET IT.
IT'S BEEN A WHILE.
GUESS IT HAS.
WHAT ARE YOU DOING IN MY NEIGHBOR-HOOD?
I WAS COMING TO SEE YOU, ACTUALLY.
WHAT?
I NEED TO HIRE YOU.

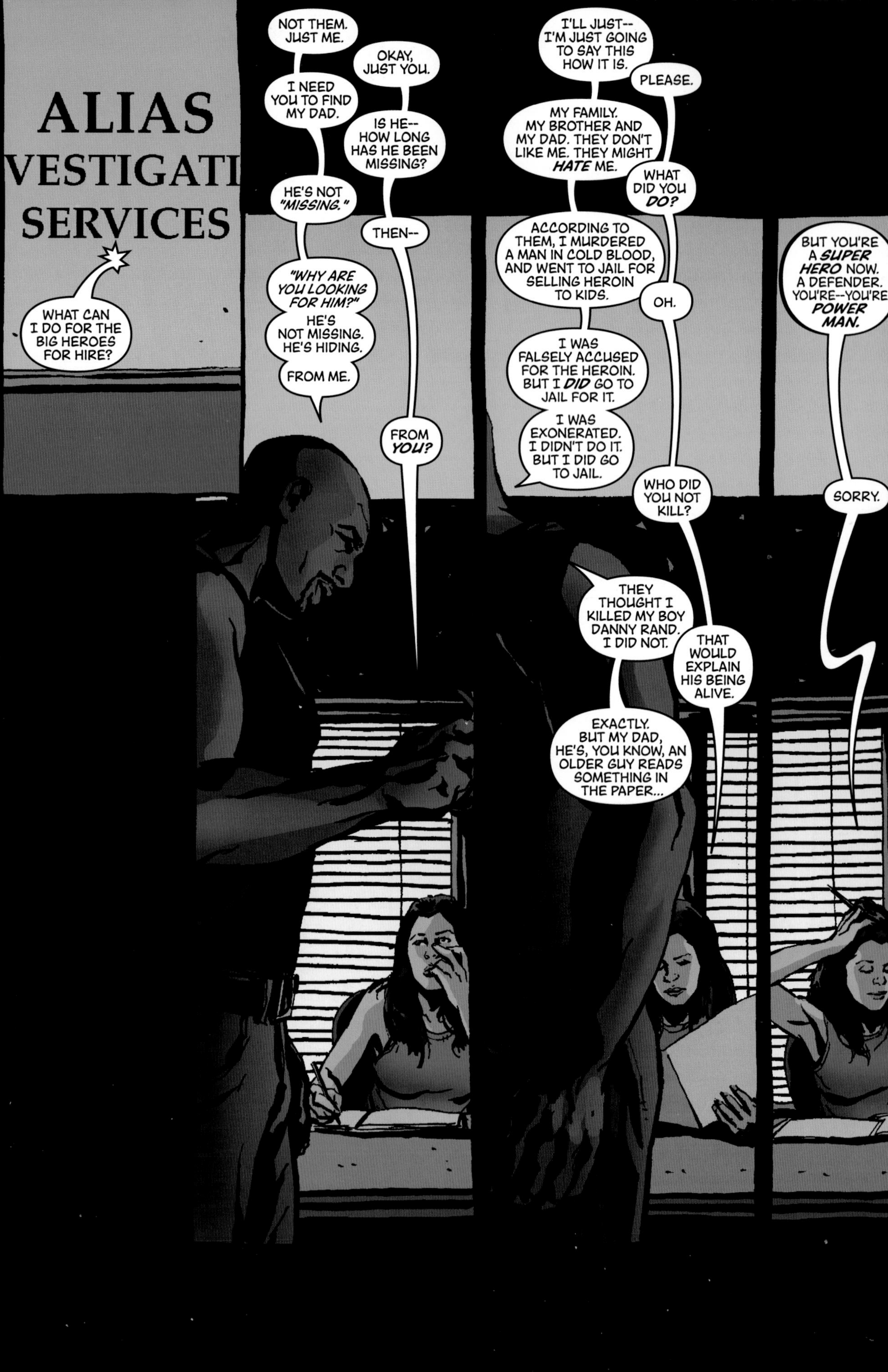
ALIAS
VESTIGATI
SERVICES
WHAT CAN I DO FOR THE BIG HEROES FOR HIRE?
NOT THEM. JUST ME.
OKAY, JUST YOU.
I NEED YOU TO FIND MY DAD.
IS HE-- HOW LONG HAS HE BEEN MISSING?
HE'S NOT "MISSING."
THEN--
"WHY ARE YOU LOOKING FOR HIM?" HE'S NOT MISSING. HE'S HIDING.
FROM ME.
FROM YOU?
I'LL JUST-- I'M JUST GOING TO SAY THIS HOW IT IS.
PLEASE.
MY FAMILY. MY BROTHER AND MY DAD. THEY DON'T LIKE ME. THEY MIGHT HATE ME.
WHAT DID YOU DO?
ACCORDING TO THEM, I MURDERED A MAN IN COLD BLOOD, AND WENT TO JAIL FOR SELLING HEROIN TO KIDS.
OH.
I WAS FALSELY ACCUSED FOR THE HEROIN. BUT I DID GO TO JAIL FOR IT.
I WAS EXONERATED. I DIDN'T DO IT. BUT I DID GO TO JAIL.
WHO DID YOU NOT KILL?
THEY THOUGHT I KILLED MY BOY DANNY RAND. I DID NOT.
THAT WOULD EXPLAIN HIS BEING ALIVE.
EXACTLY. BUT MY DAD, HE'S, YOU KNOW, AN OLDER GUY READS SOMETHING IN THE PAPER...
BUT YOU'RE A SUPER HERO NOW. A DEFENDER. YOU'RE--YOU'RE POWER MAN.
SORRY.

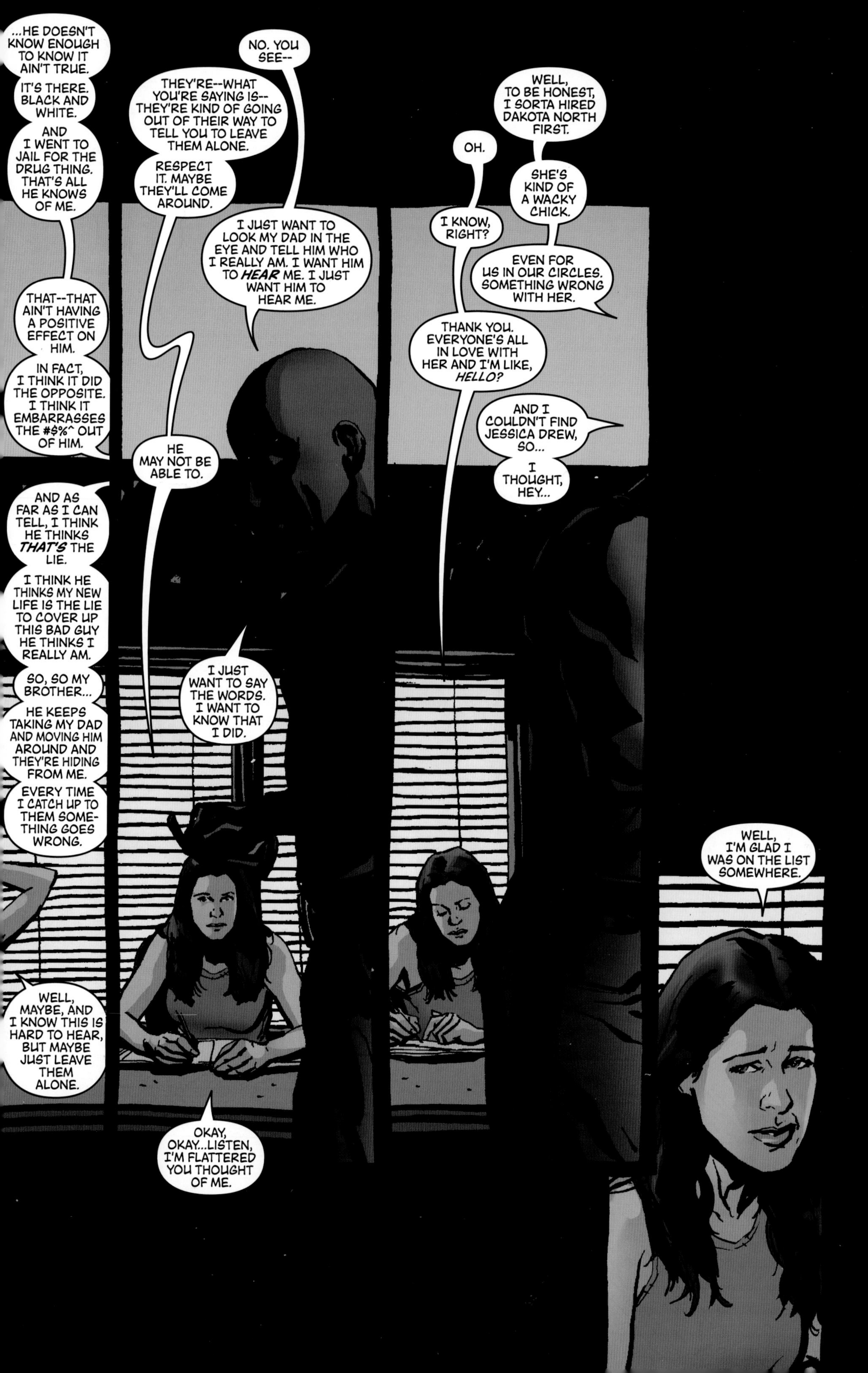

...HE DOESN'T KNOW ENOUGH TO KNOW IT AIN'T TRUE.
IT'S THERE. BLACK AND WHITE.
AND I WENT TO JAIL FOR THE DRUG THING. THAT'S ALL HE KNOWS OF ME.
THAT--THAT AIN'T HAVING A POSITIVE EFFECT ON HIM.
IN FACT, I THINK IT DID THE OPPOSITE. I THINK IT EMBARRASSES THE #$%^ OUT OF HIM.
AND AS FAR AS I CAN TELL, I THINK HE THINKS *THAT'S* THE LIE.
I THINK HE THINKS MY NEW LIFE IS THE LIE TO COVER UP THIS BAD GUY HE THINKS I REALLY AM.
SO, SO MY BROTHER...
HE KEEPS TAKING MY DAD AND MOVING HIM AROUND AND THEY'RE HIDING FROM ME.
EVERY TIME I CATCH UP TO THEM SOME-THING GOES WRONG.
WELL, MAYBE, AND I KNOW THIS IS HARD TO HEAR, BUT MAYBE JUST LEAVE THEM ALONE.
THEY'RE--WHAT YOU'RE SAYING IS--THEY'RE KIND OF GOING OUT OF THEIR WAY TO TELL YOU TO LEAVE THEM ALONE.
RESPECT IT. MAYBE THEY'LL COME AROUND.
NO. YOU SEE--
I JUST WANT TO LOOK MY DAD IN THE EYE AND TELL HIM WHO I REALLY AM. I WANT HIM TO *HEAR* ME. I JUST WANT HIM TO HEAR ME.
HE MAY NOT BE ABLE TO.
I JUST WANT TO SAY THE WORDS. I WANT TO KNOW THAT I DID.
OKAY, OKAY...LISTEN, I'M FLATTERED YOU THOUGHT OF ME.
WELL, TO BE HONEST, I SORTA HIRED DAKOTA NORTH FIRST.
OH.
SHE'S KIND OF A WACKY CHICK.
I KNOW, RIGHT?
EVEN FOR US IN OUR CIRCLES. SOMETHING WRONG WITH HER.
THANK YOU. EVERYONE'S ALL IN LOVE WITH HER AND I'M LIKE, *HELLO?*
AND I COULDN'T FIND JESSICA DREW, SO...
I THOUGHT, HEY...
WELL, I'M GLAD I WAS ON THE LIST SOMEWHERE.

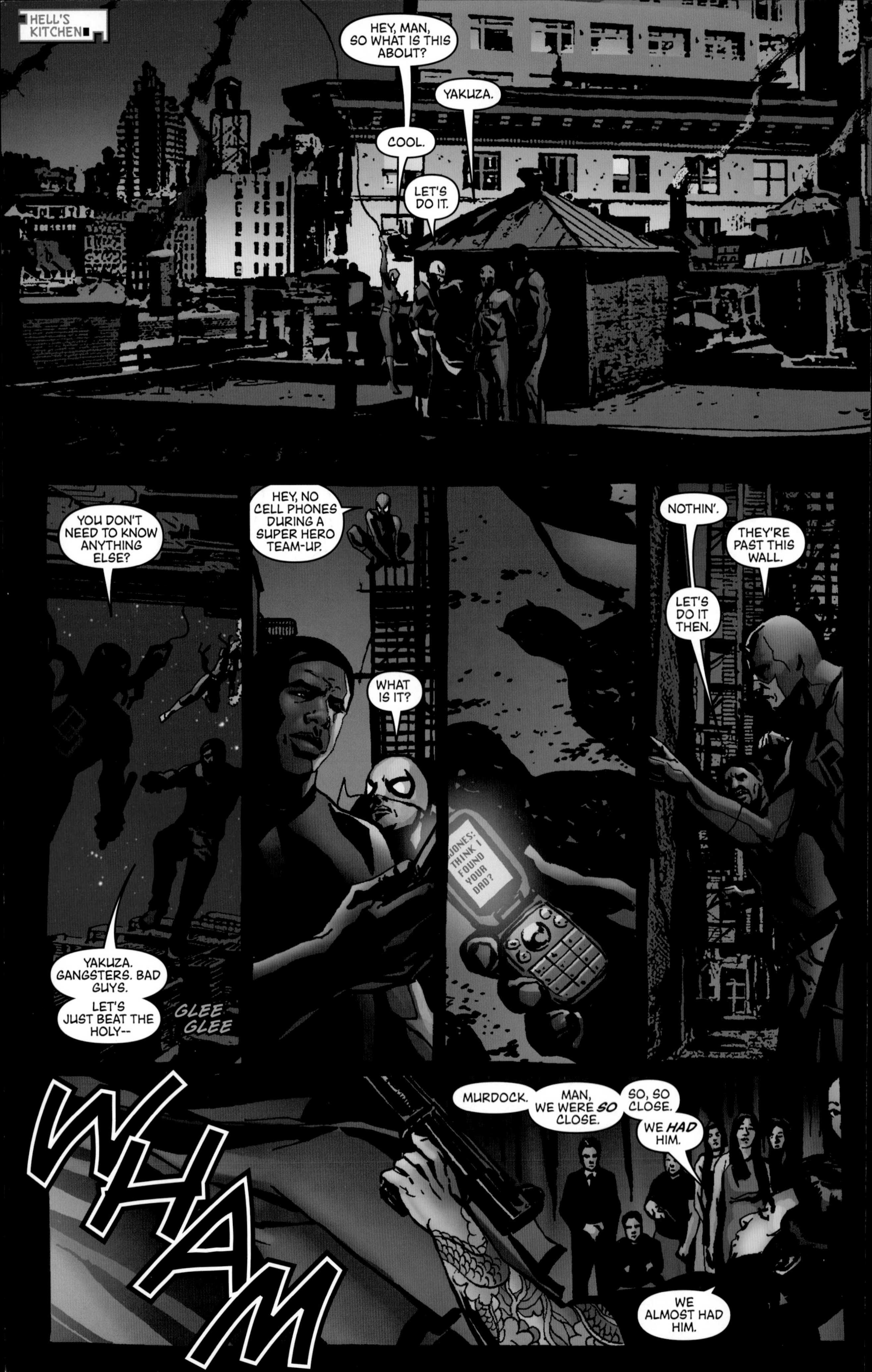

HELL'S KITCHEN
HEY, MAN, SO WHAT IS THIS ABOUT?
YAKUZA.
COOL.
LET'S DO IT.
YOU DON'T NEED TO KNOW ANYTHING ELSE?
YAKUZA. GANGSTERS. BAD GUYS.
LET'S JUST BEAT THE HOLY--
GLEE GLEE
HEY, NO CELL PHONES DURING A SUPER HERO TEAM-UP.
WHAT IS IT?
JONES: THINK I FOUND YOUR DAD?
NOTHIN'.
THEY'RE PAST THIS WALL.
LET'S DO IT THEN.
WHAM
MURDOCK.
MAN, WE WERE *SO* CLOSE.
SO, SO CLOSE.
WE *HAD* HIM.
WE ALMOST HAD HIM.

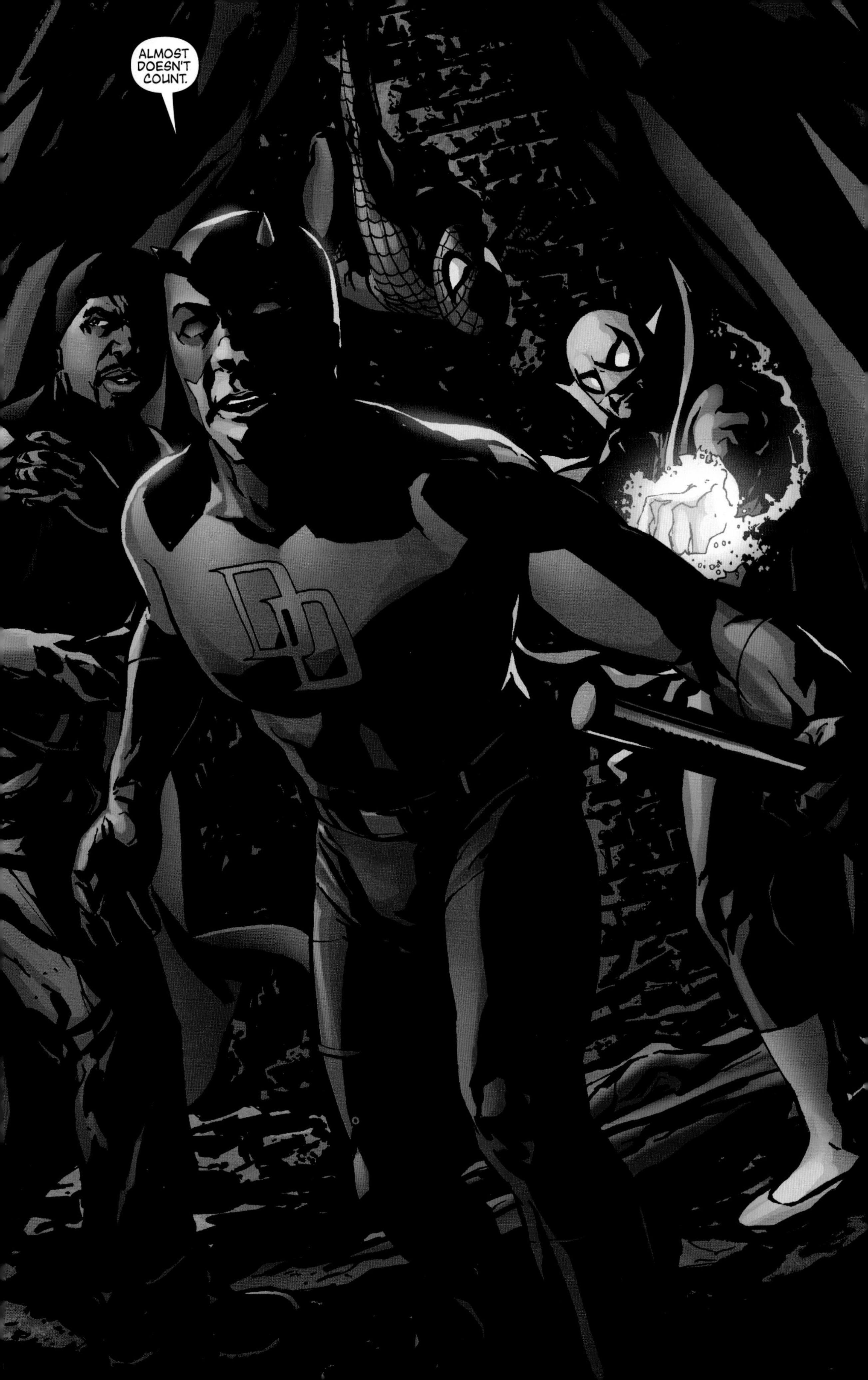
ALMOST DOESN'T COUNT.

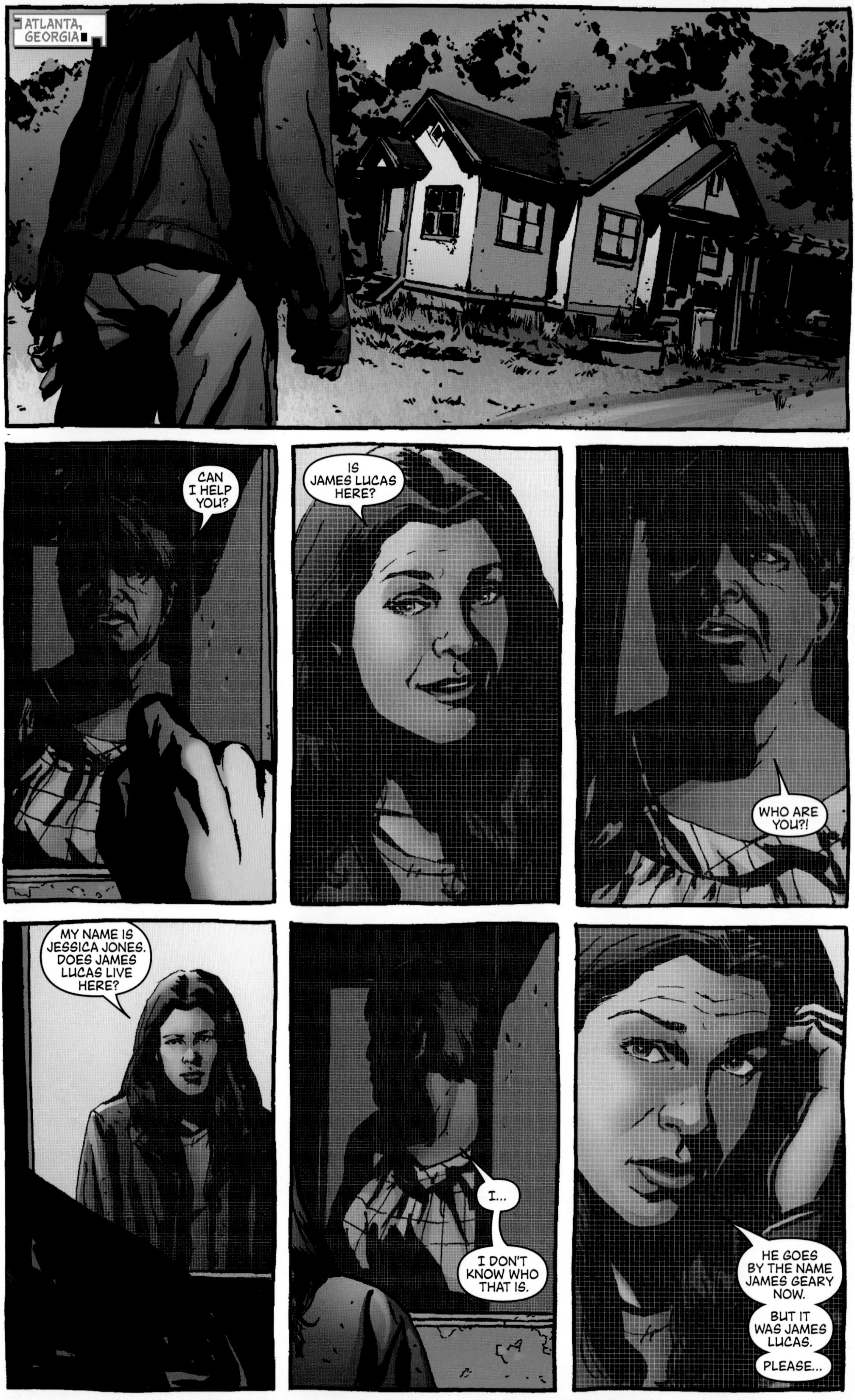
ATLANTA, GEORGIA
CAN I HELP YOU?
IS JAMES LUCAS HERE?
WHO ARE YOU?!
MY NAME IS JESSICA JONES. DOES JAMES LUCAS LIVE HERE?
I...
I DON'T KNOW WHO THAT IS.
HE GOES BY THE NAME JAMES GEARY NOW.
BUT IT WAS JAMES LUCAS.
PLEASE...

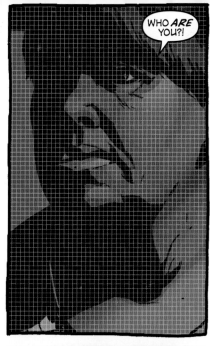

WHO *ARE* YOU?!

MY NAME IS JESSICA JONES. I'M A PRIVATE DE--

YOU *GOT* TO BE KIDDING ME.

DETECTIVE. I'M NOT HERE TO--

YOU *LISTEN* TO ME. I DON'T KNOW ANYTHING ABOUT *ANYTHING.*

YOU HEAR ME?! I'LL CALL THE COPS. I'LL CALL THE--

I'M HERE BECAUSE OF HIS SON, LUKE...

LUKE CAGE...

HE'S LOOKING FOR HIS FATHER.

I'M NOT HERE TO DO ANYTHING-- I'M HERE TO TRY AND HELP.

SON JUST WANTS TO TALK TO HIS FATHER.

WELL, THE FATHER DON'T WANT TO TALK TO THE SON.

IS HE OKAY? LUKE JUST WANTS TO KNOW-- HE'D WANT TO KNOW IF HE'S OKAY.

THE MAN--THE MAN'S BEEN THROUGH A LOT. YOU SEE?

A MAN HAS-- THE WAY I SEE IT, A MAN HAS AN IMAGE IN HIS HEAD OF WHAT HE WANTED HIS LIFE TO BE. HIS KIDS...

STRUGGLE, HEARTACHE, ALL OF THAT IS FINE. A MAN CAN SEE THAT THROUGH.

BUT ALL THIS WITH THE SUPER HEROES, AND WHAT HAPPENED TO THE OTHER SON...

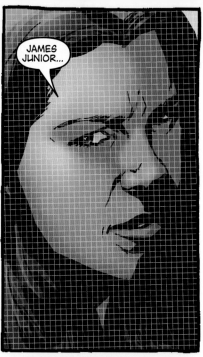

JAMES JUNIOR...

YEAH, YOU KNOW, HE DIED. JAMES JUNIOR.

HIS OWN *NAMESAKE.*

THE BOY IS DEAD.

I TRIED TO GET JAMES TO SEE HOW IMPORTANT FAMILY IS. I DID.

BUT HE WON'T HEAR IT. HE CAN'T YET.

BUT, AND THIS IS TRUE, I SEE HE KEEPS AN EYE ON LUKE.

ON THE INTERNET. HE SEES WHEN LUKE DOES WELL. HE SEES IT.

BUT IT'S NOT WHAT THE MAN WANTED. HE LOST A WIFE, A SON. IT'S NOT WHAT HE WANTED.

BUT LUKE'S ALL HE HAS LEFT.

FROM *THAT* LIFE.

I'M SORRY, YOU ARE...?

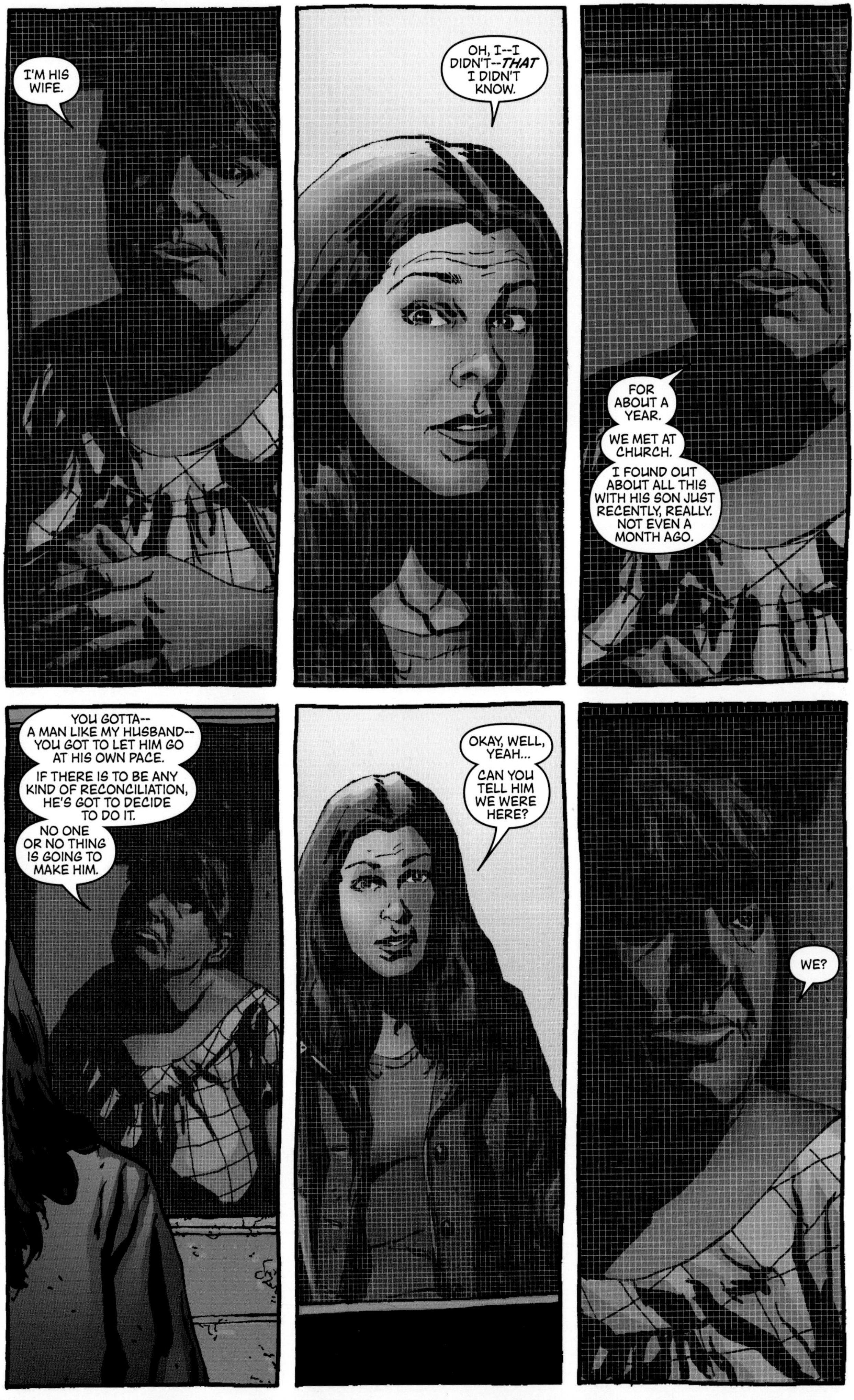
I'M HIS WIFE.
OH, I--I DIDN'T--THAT I DIDN'T KNOW.
FOR ABOUT A YEAR.
WE MET AT CHURCH.
I FOUND OUT ABOUT ALL THIS WITH HIS SON JUST RECENTLY, REALLY. NOT EVEN A MONTH AGO.
YOU GOTTA-- A MAN LIKE MY HUSBAND-- YOU GOT TO LET HIM GO AT HIS OWN PACE.
IF THERE IS TO BE ANY KIND OF RECONCILIATION, HE'S GOT TO DECIDE TO DO IT.
NO ONE OR NO THING IS GOING TO MAKE HIM.
OKAY, WELL, YEAH...
CAN YOU TELL HIM WE WERE HERE?
WE?

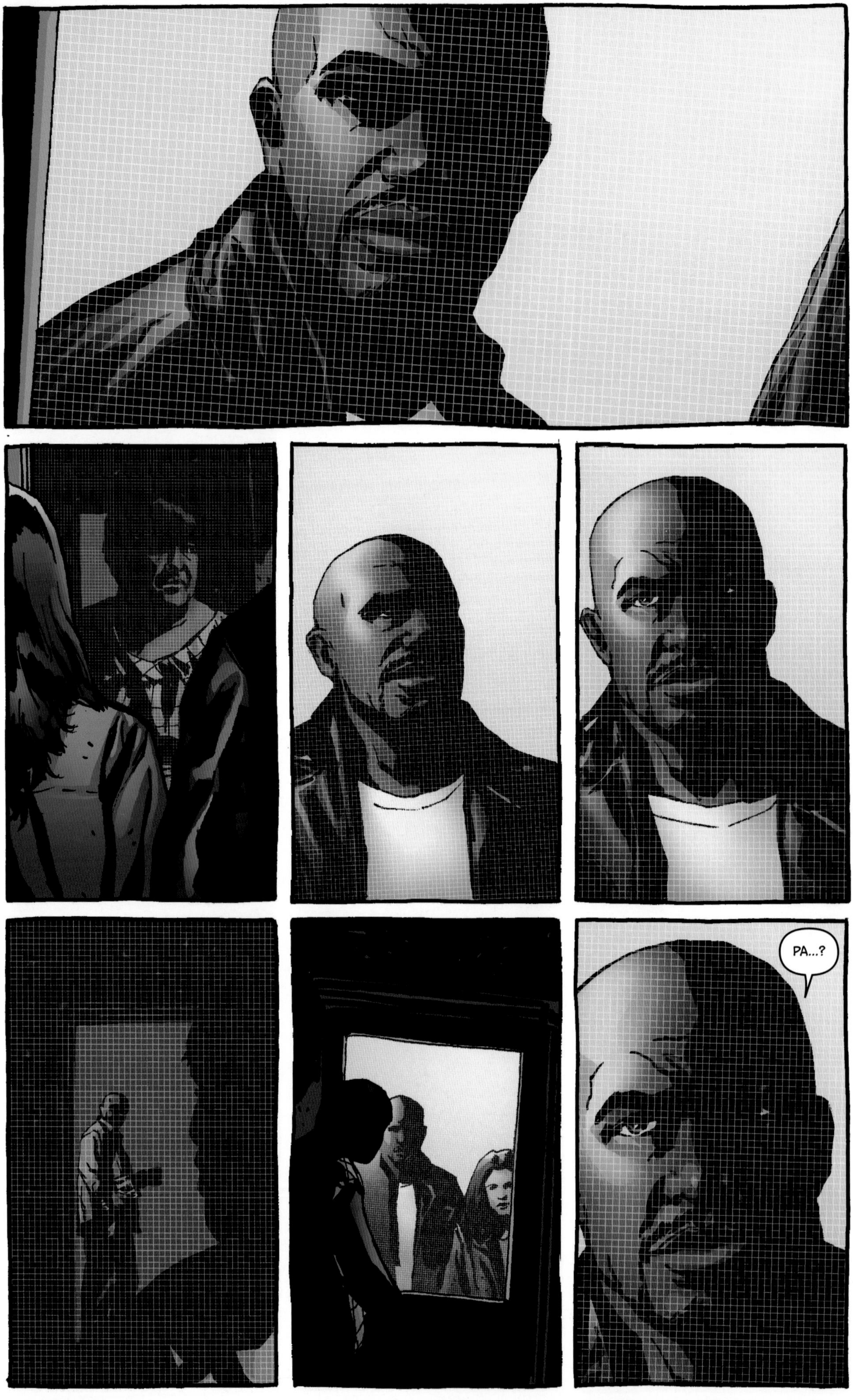
PA...?

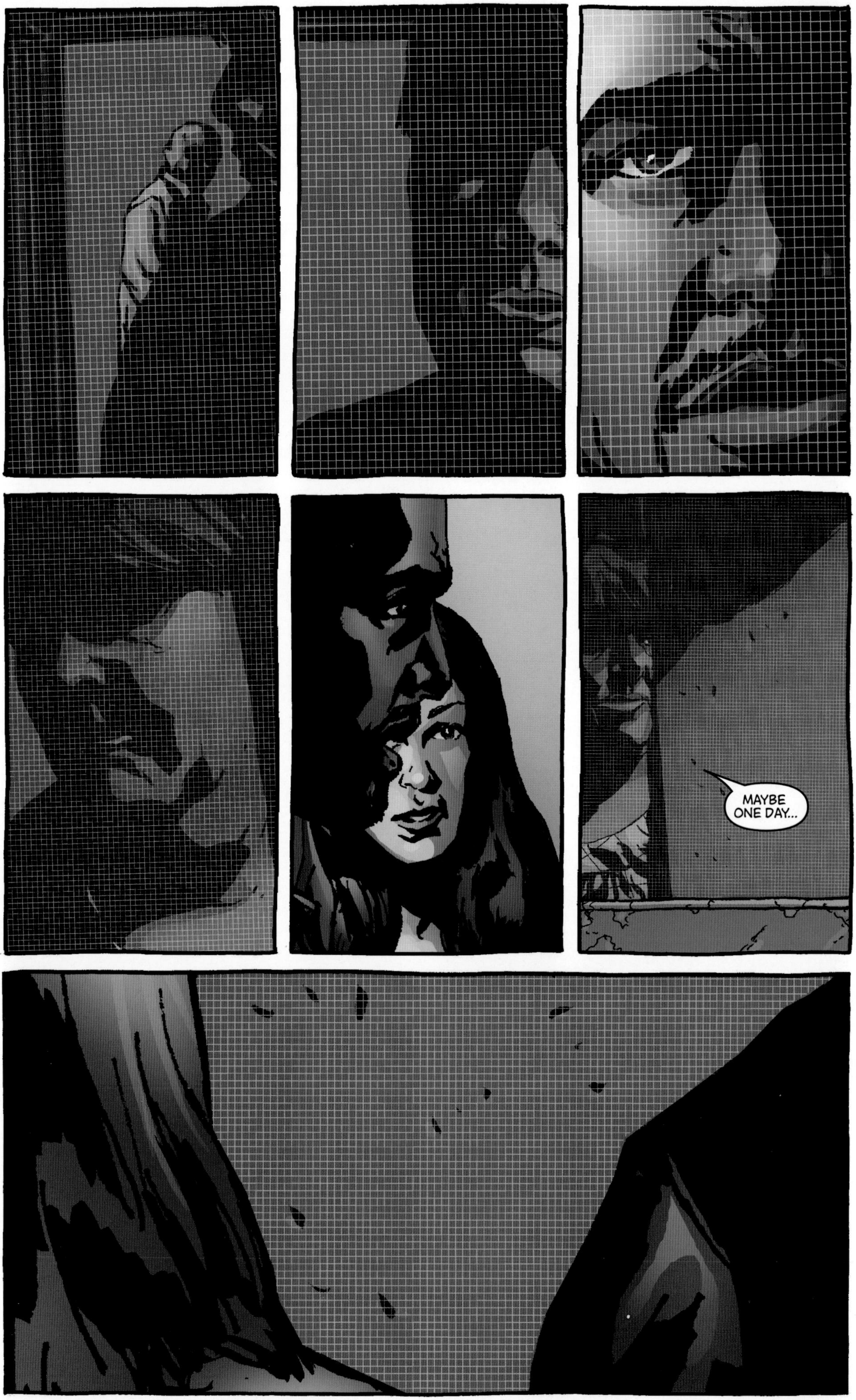
MAYBE ONE DAY...

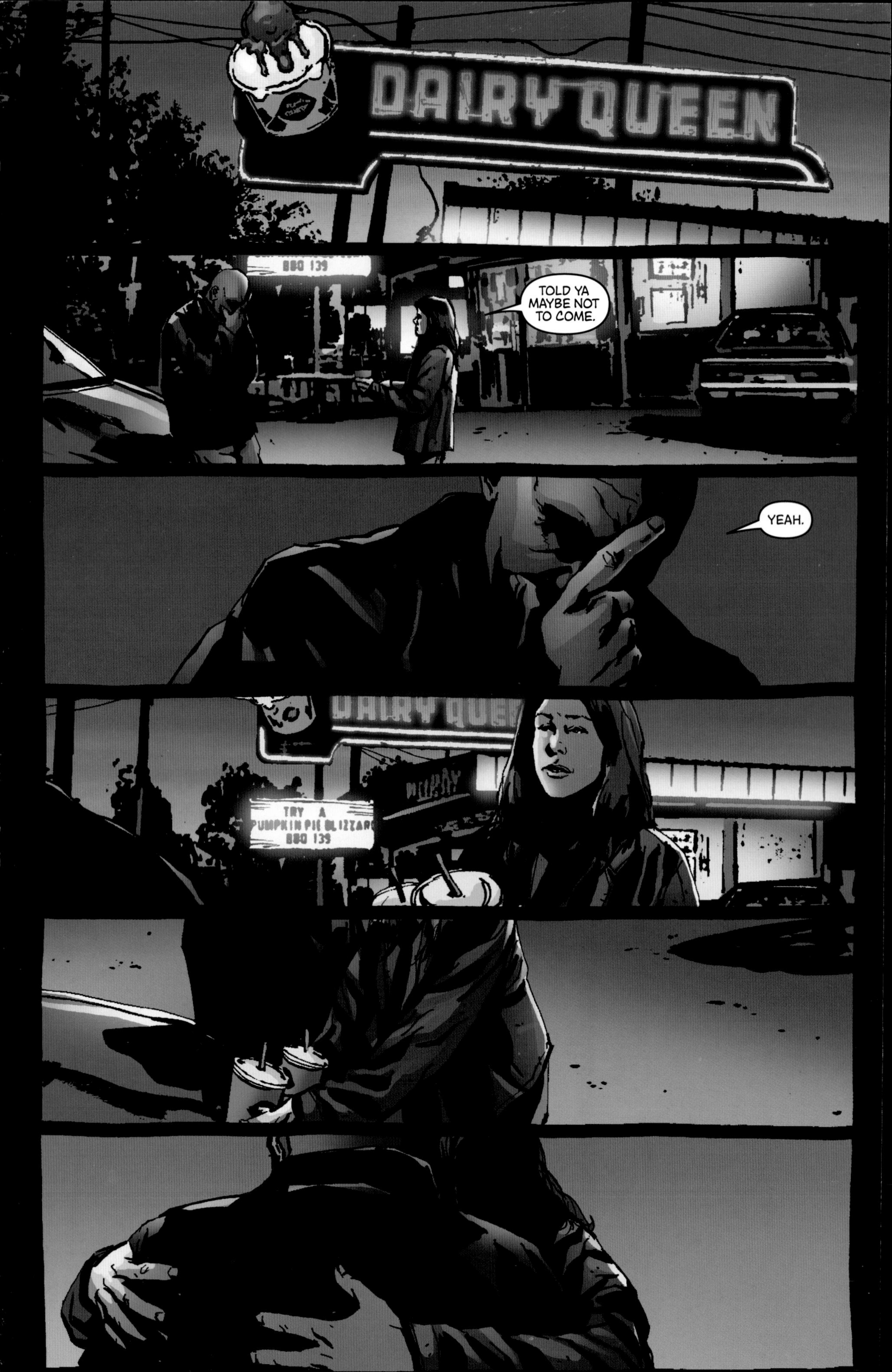
DAIRY QUEEN
BBQ 139
TOLD YA MAYBE NOT TO COME.
YEAH.
TRY A
PUMPKIN PIE BLIZZARD
BBQ 139

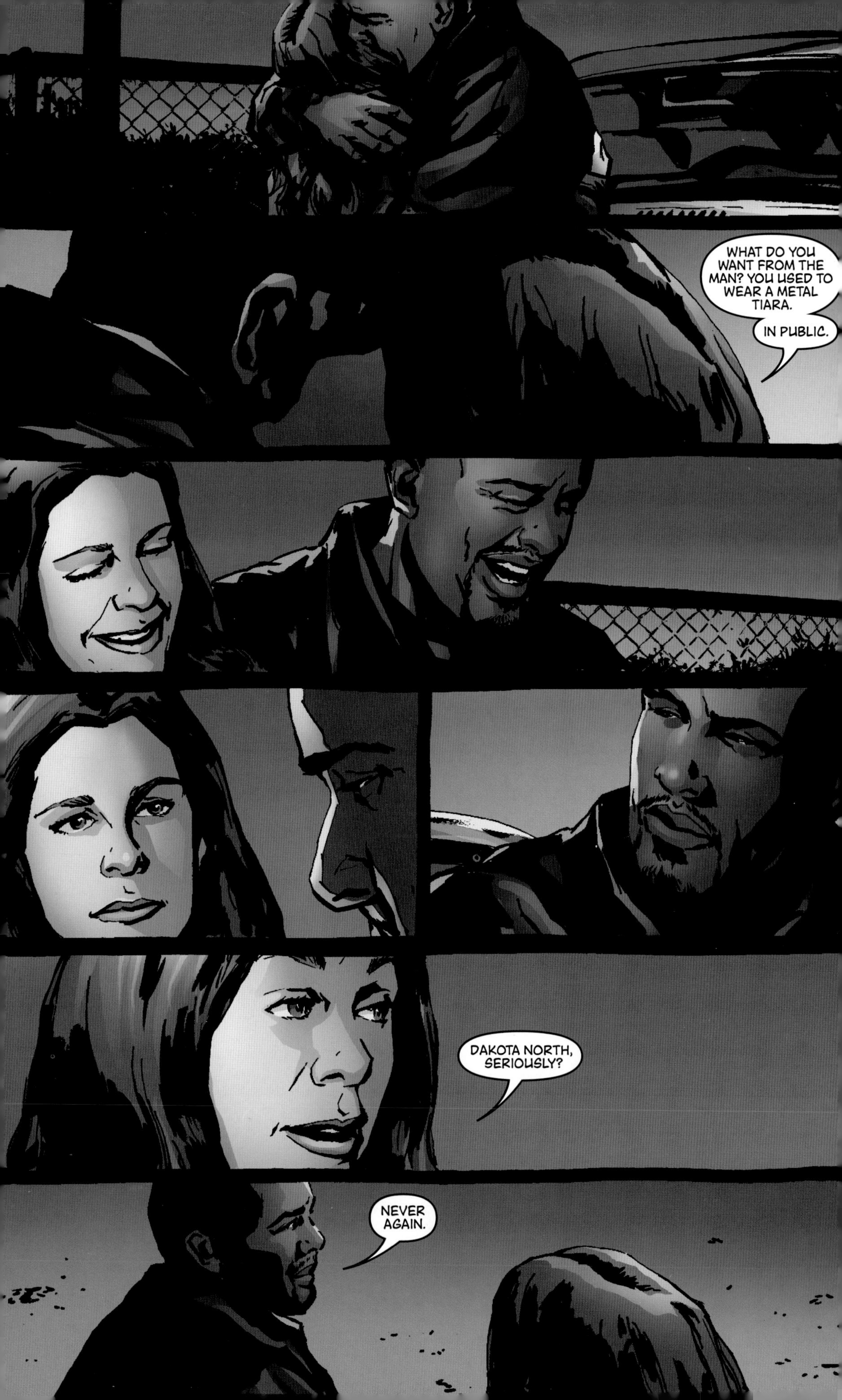
WHAT DO YOU WANT FROM THE MAN? YOU USED TO WEAR A METAL TIARA.
IN PUBLIC.
DAKOTA NORTH, SERIOUSLY?
NEVER AGAIN.

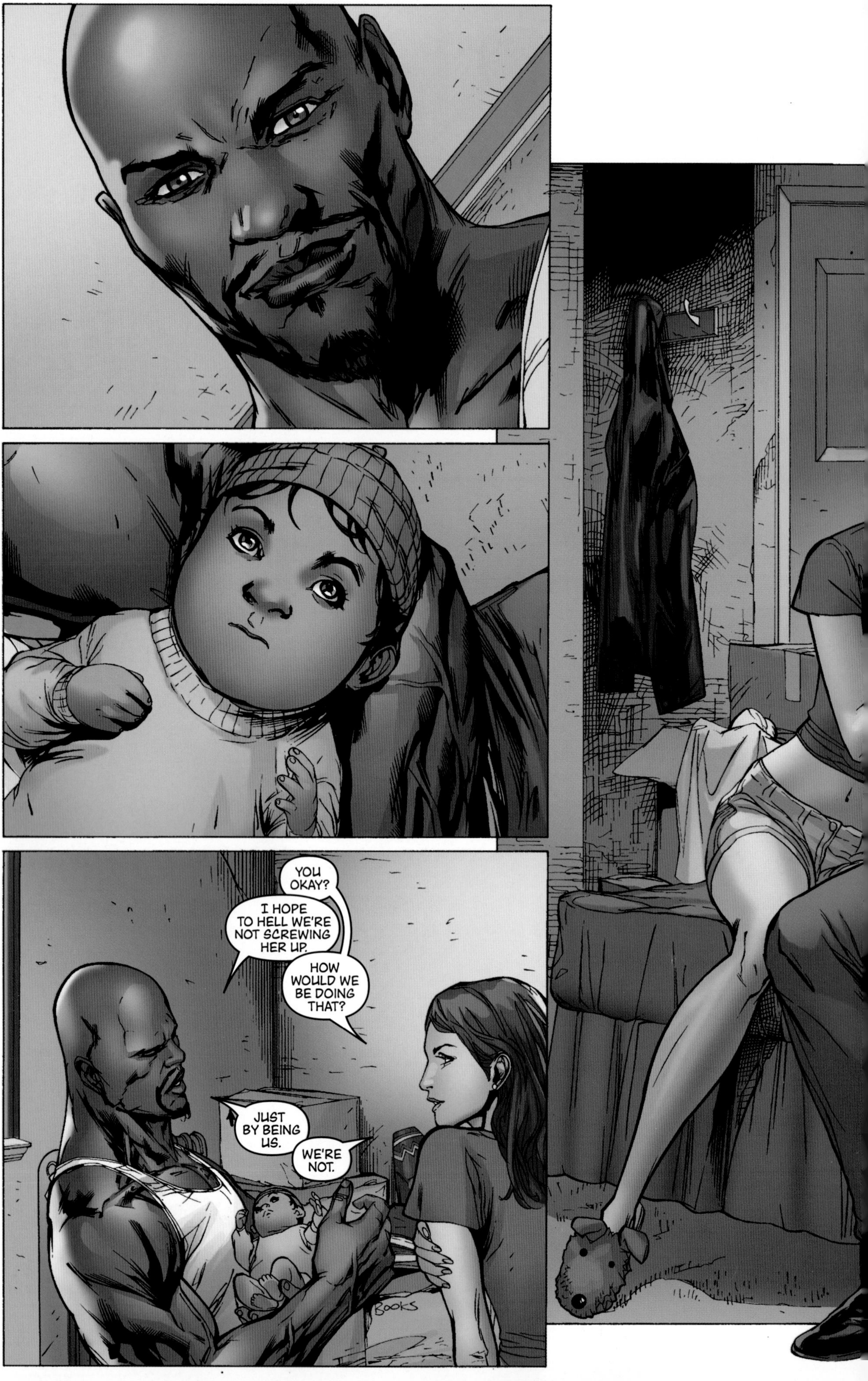
YOU OKAY?
I HOPE TO HELL WE'RE NOT SCREWING HER UP.
HOW WOULD WE BE DOING THAT?
JUST BY BEING US.
WE'RE NOT.
BOOKS

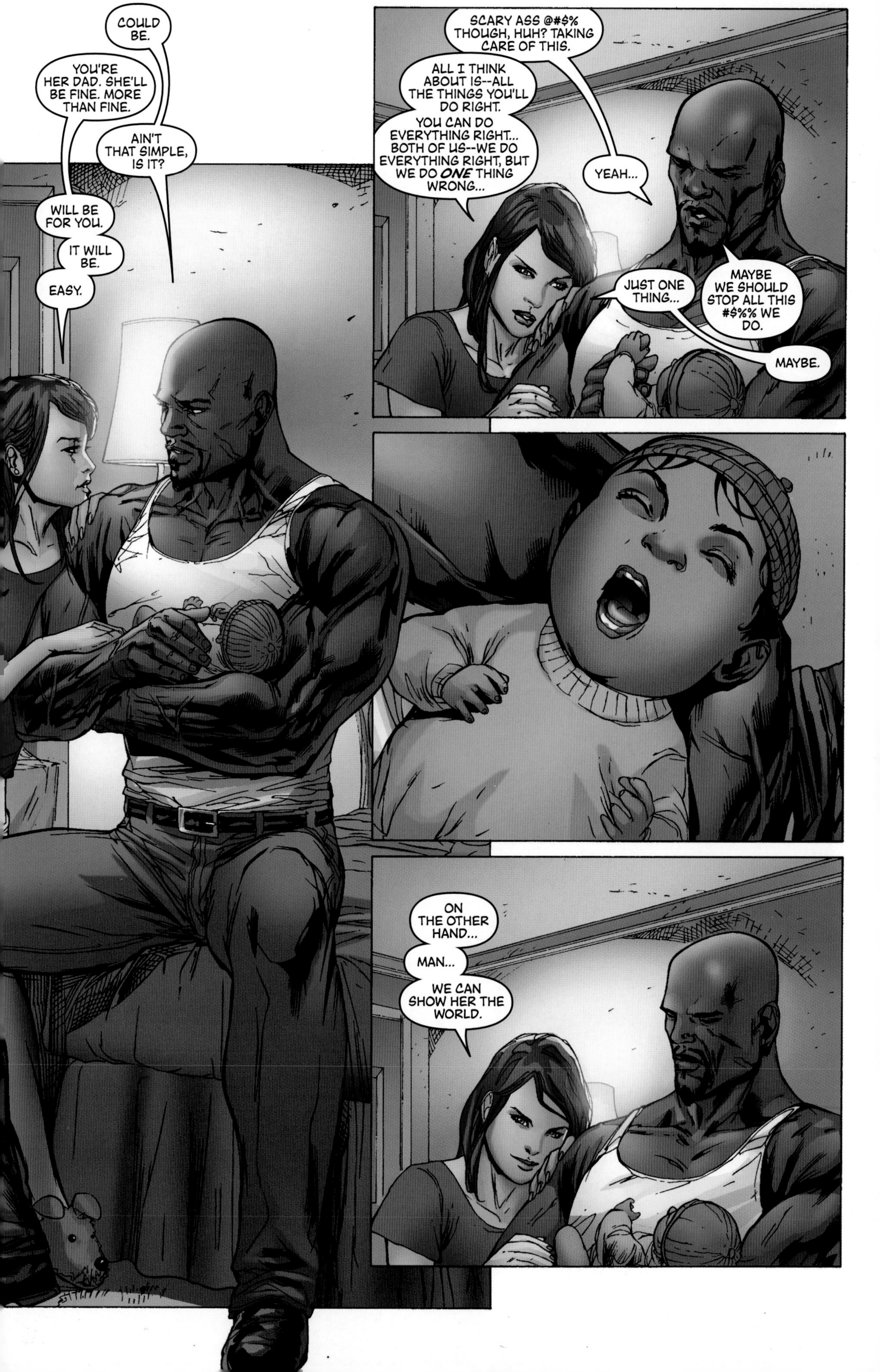
COULD BE.
YOU'RE HER DAD. SHE'LL BE FINE. MORE THAN FINE.
AIN'T THAT SIMPLE, IS IT?
WILL BE FOR YOU.
IT WILL BE.
EASY.
SCARY ASS @#$% THOUGH, HUH? TAKING CARE OF THIS.
ALL I THINK ABOUT IS--ALL THE THINGS YOU'LL DO RIGHT.
YOU CAN DO EVERYTHING RIGHT... BOTH OF US--WE DO EVERYTHING RIGHT, BUT WE DO ONE THING WRONG...
YEAH...
JUST ONE THING...
MAYBE WE SHOULD STOP ALL THIS #$%% WE DO.
MAYBE.
ON THE OTHER HAND...
MAN...
WE CAN SHOW HER THE WORLD.

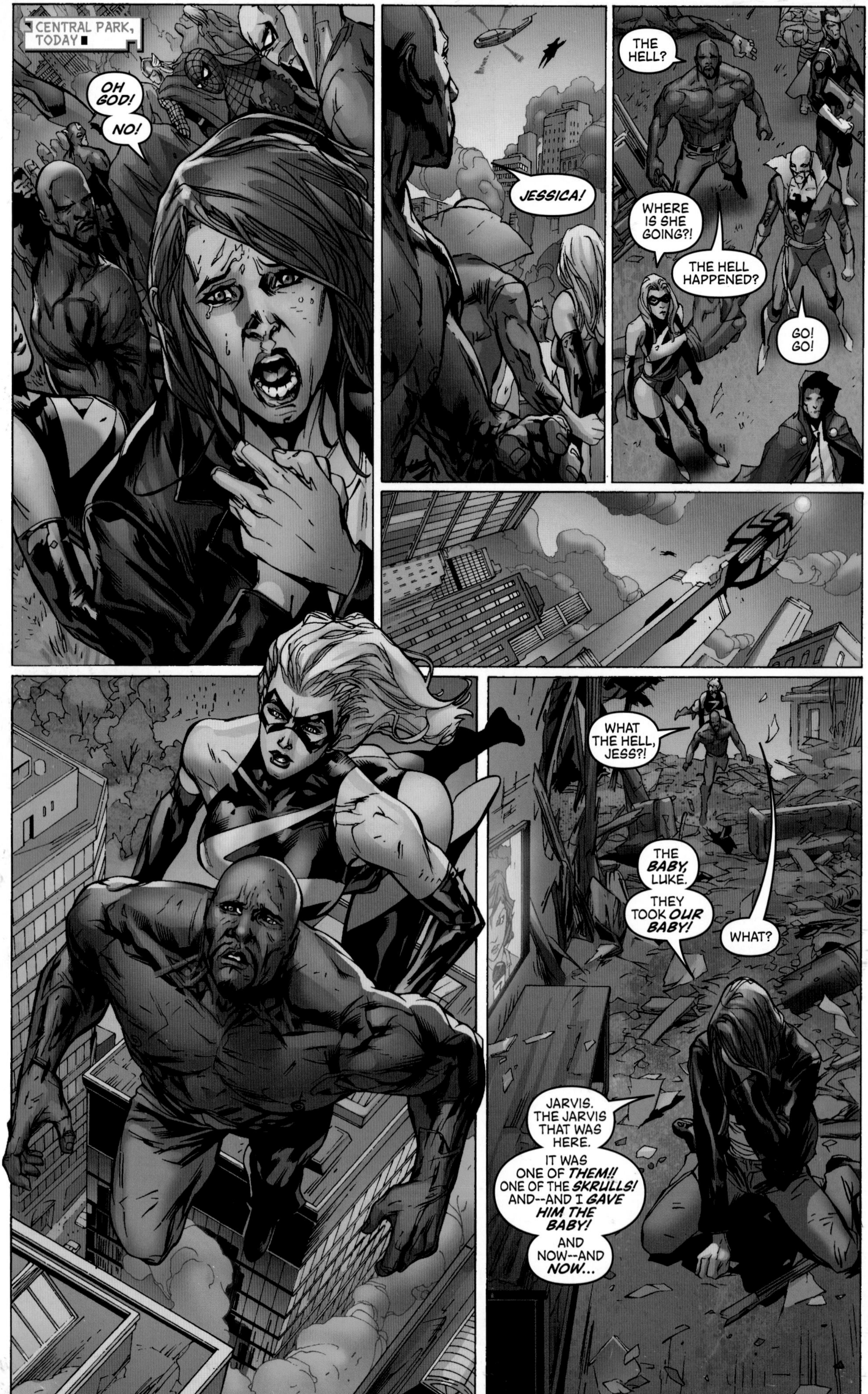
CENTRAL PARK, TODAY
OH GOD!
NO!
JESSICA!
THE HELL?
WHERE IS SHE GOING?!
THE HELL HAPPENED?
GO! GO!
WHAT THE HELL, JESS?!
THE BABY, LUKE. THEY TOOK OUR BABY!
WHAT?
JARVIS. THE JARVIS THAT WAS HERE.
IT WAS ONE OF THEM!! ONE OF THE SKRULLS! AND--AND I GAVE HIM THE BABY!
AND NOW--AND NOW...

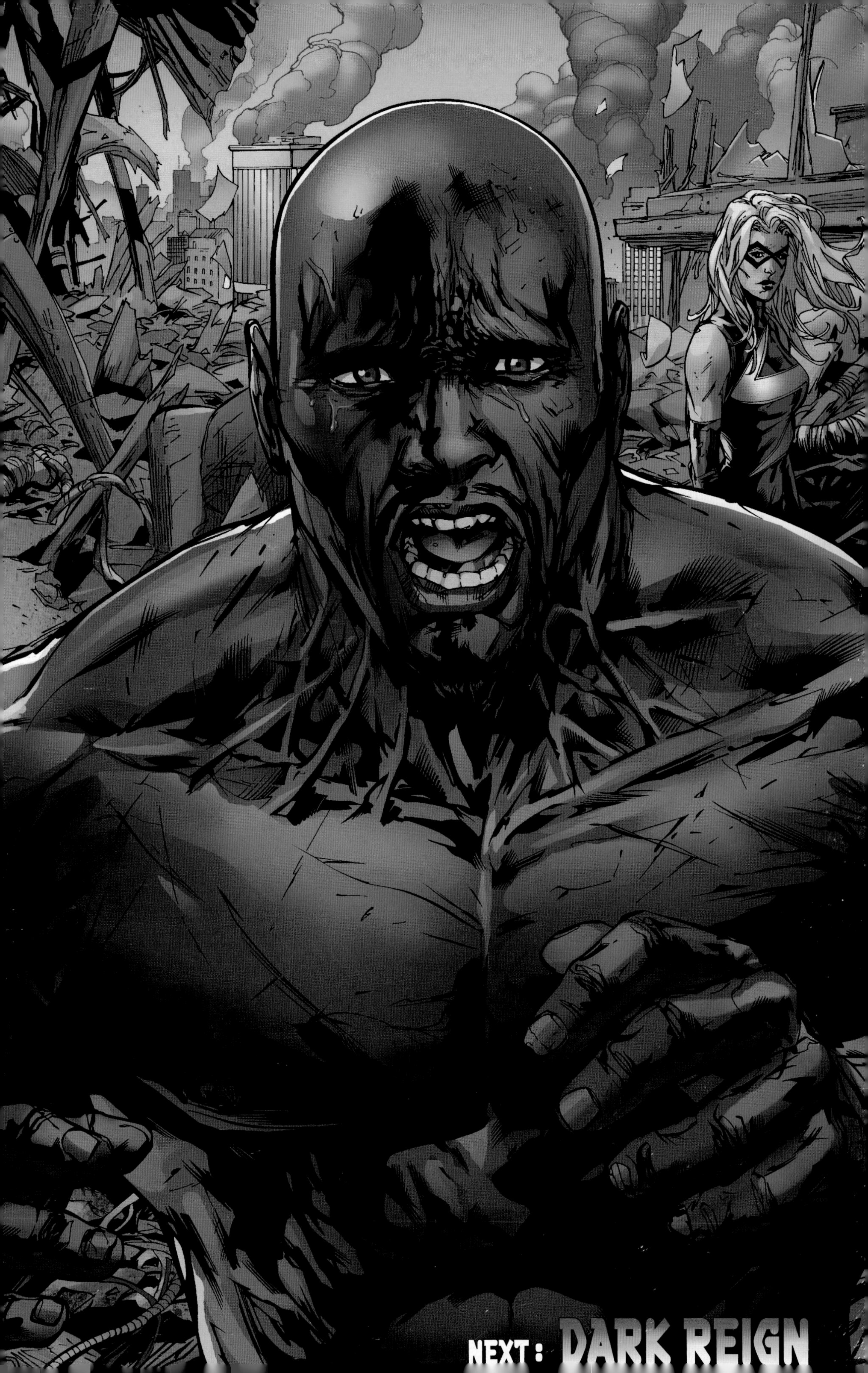
NEXT: DARK REIGN

COVER HOMAGES BY ALEKSI BRICLOT

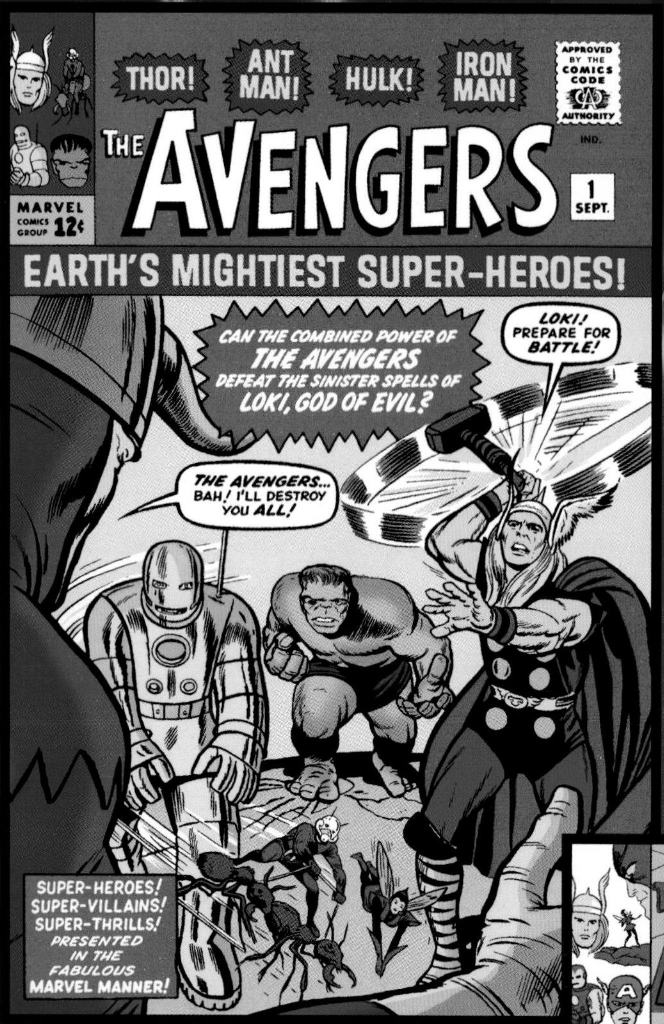
THOR!
ANT MAN!
HULK!
IRON MAN!
APPROVED BY THE COMICS CODE AUTHORITY
IND.
THE AVENGERS
1 SEPT.
MARVEL COMICS GROUP 12¢
EARTH'S MIGHTIEST SUPER-HEROES!
CAN THE COMBINED POWER OF THE AVENGERS DEFEAT THE SINISTER SPELLS OF LOKI, GOD OF EVIL?
LOKI!! PREPARE FOR BATTLE!
THE AVENGERS... BAH! I'LL DESTROY YOU ALL!
SUPER-HEROES! SUPER-VILLAINS! SUPER-THRILLS! PRESENTED IN THE FABULOUS MARVEL MANNER!

BY JACK KIRBY

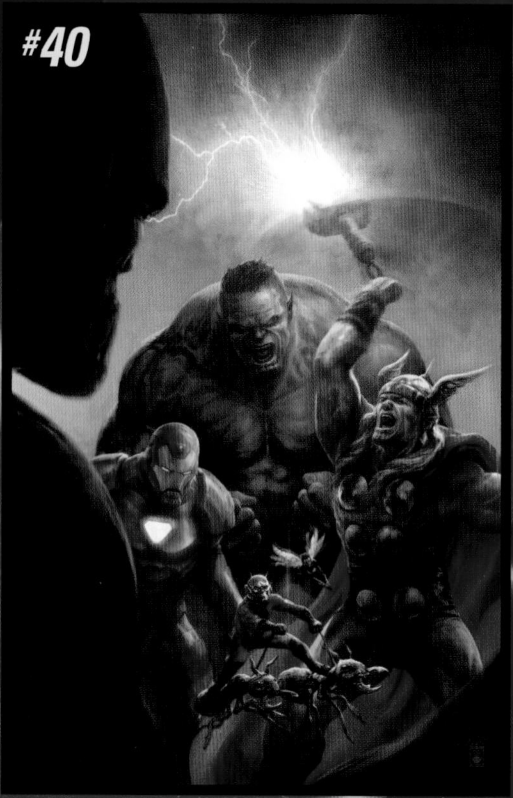
#40

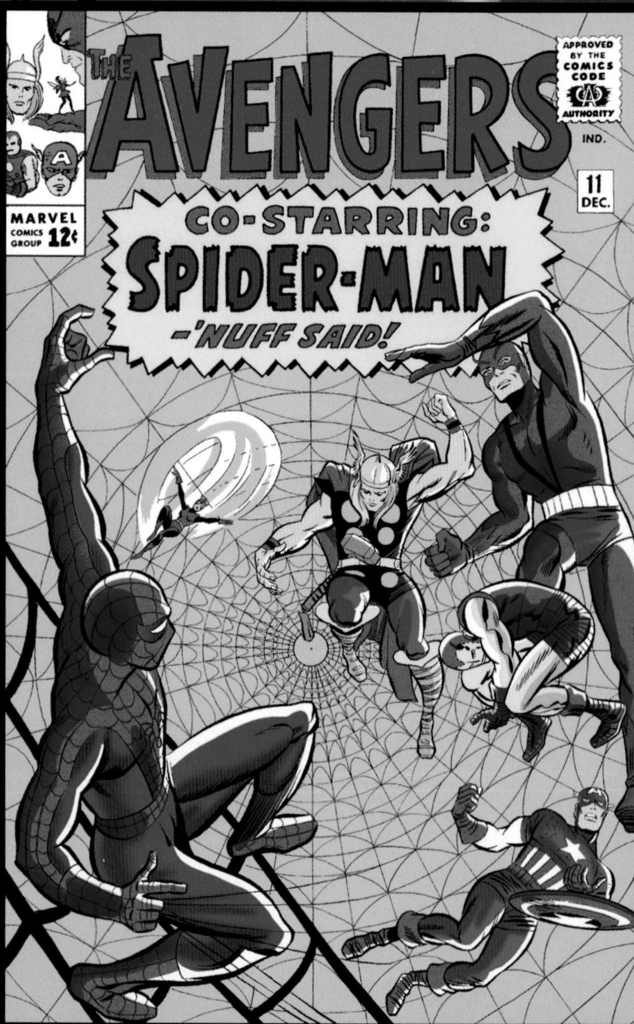
THE AVENGERS
APPROVED BY THE COMICS CODE AUTHORITY
IND.
11 DEC.
MARVEL COMICS GROUP 12¢
CO-STARRING: SPIDER-MAN
-'NUFF SAID!

BY JACK KIRBY

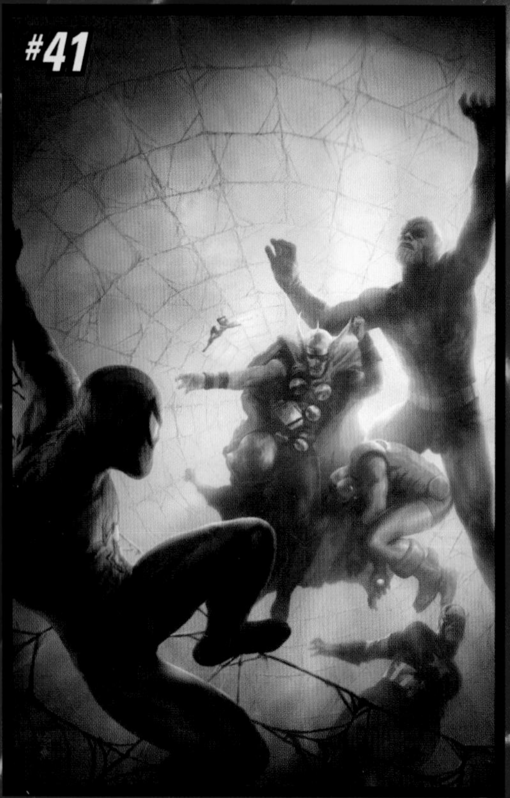
#41

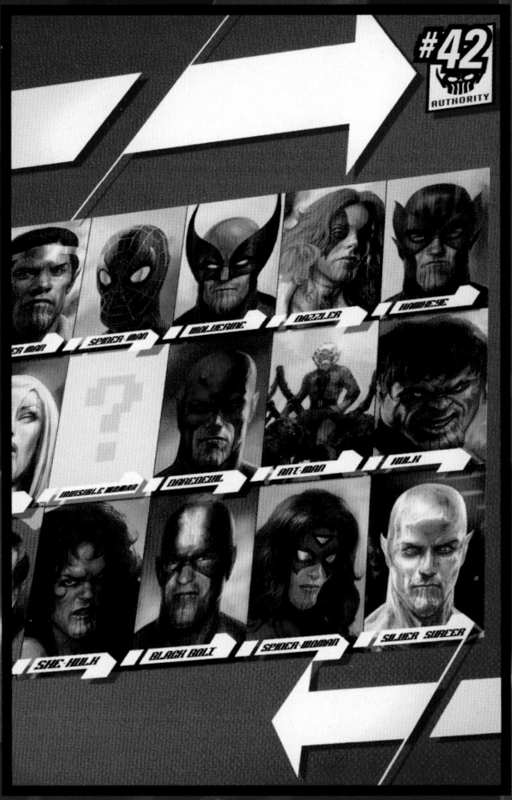
#42
AUTHORITY
SPIDER-MAN
WOLVERINE
DAZZLER
HAWKEYE
DAREDEVIL
ANT-MAN
HULK
SHE-HULK
BLACK BOLT
SPIDER-WOMAN
SILVER SURFER

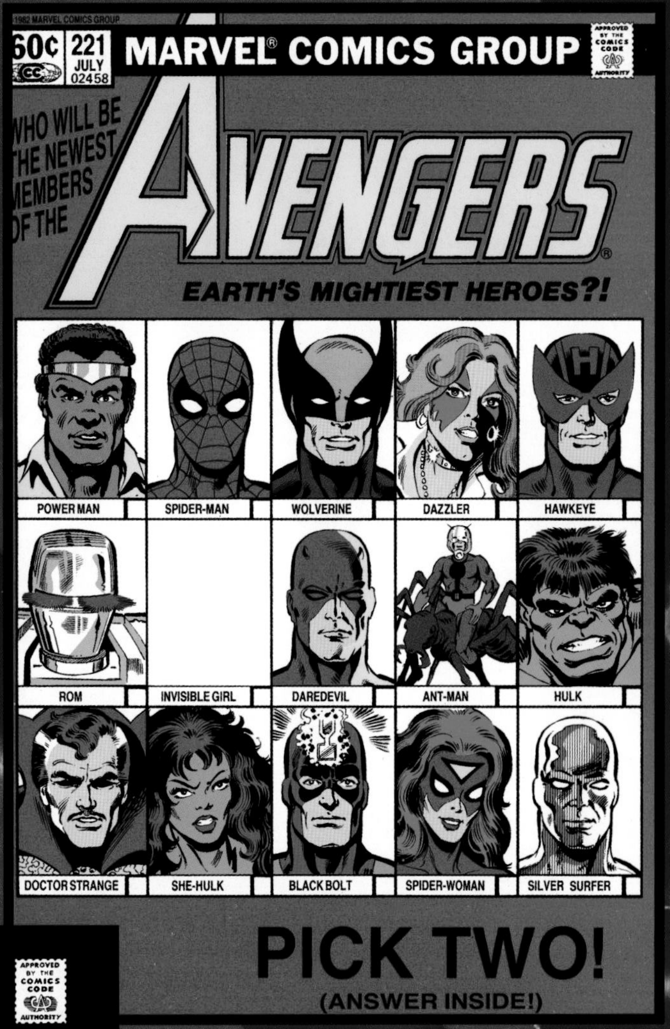
© 1982 MARVEL COMICS GROUP
60¢
221
JULY
02458
MARVEL® COMICS GROUP
APPROVED BY THE COMICS CODE AUTHORITY
WHO WILL BE THE NEWEST MEMBERS OF THE
AVENGERS®
EARTH'S MIGHTIEST HEROES?!
POWER MAN
SPIDER-MAN
WOLVERINE
DAZZLER
HAWKEYE
ROM
INVISIBLE GIRL
DAREDEVIL
ANT-MAN
HULK
DOCTOR STRANGE
SHE-HULK
BLACK BOLT
SPIDER-WOMAN
SILVER SURFER
PICK TWO!
(ANSWER INSIDE!)

BY ED HANNIGAN

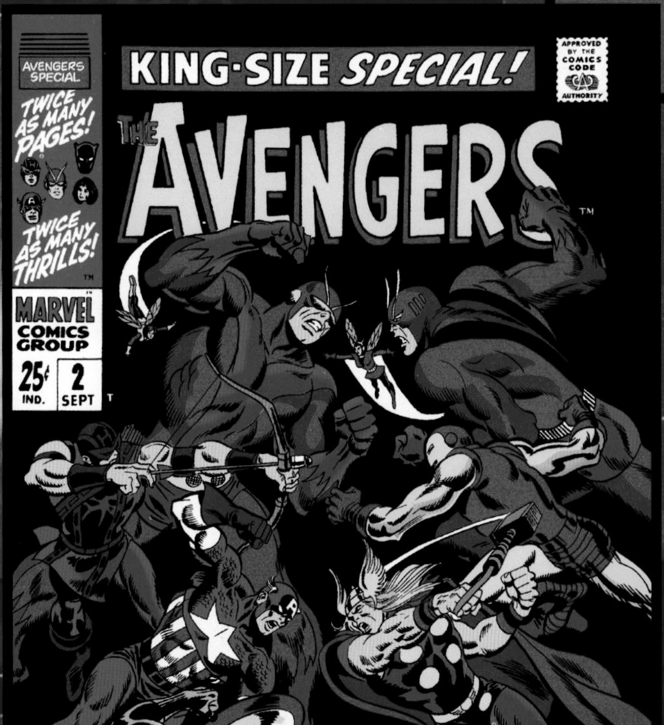
AVENGERS SPECIAL
KING-SIZE SPECIAL!
APPROVED BY THE COMICS CODE AUTHORITY
TWICE AS MANY PAGES!
TWICE AS MANY THRILLS!
THE AVENGERS™
MARVEL COMICS GROUP
25¢
IND.
2
SEPT
THE NEW AVENGERS VS. THE OLD AVENGERS!

BY JOHN BUSCEMA

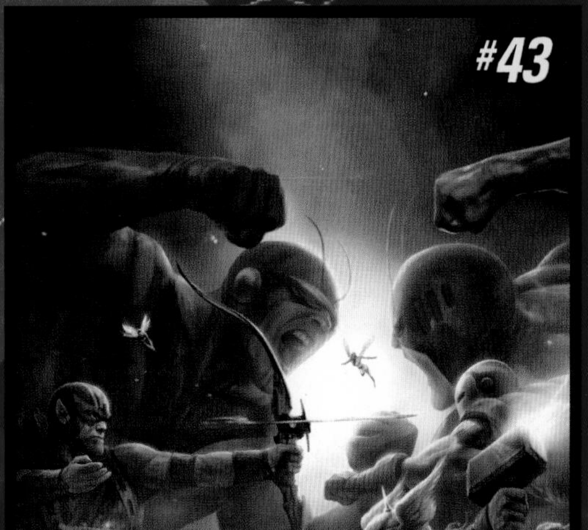
#43

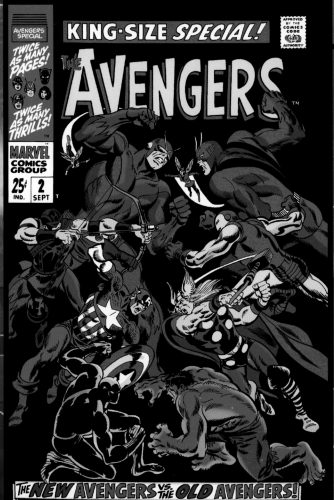

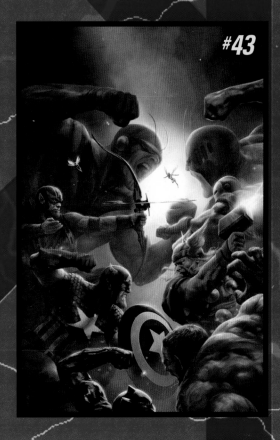

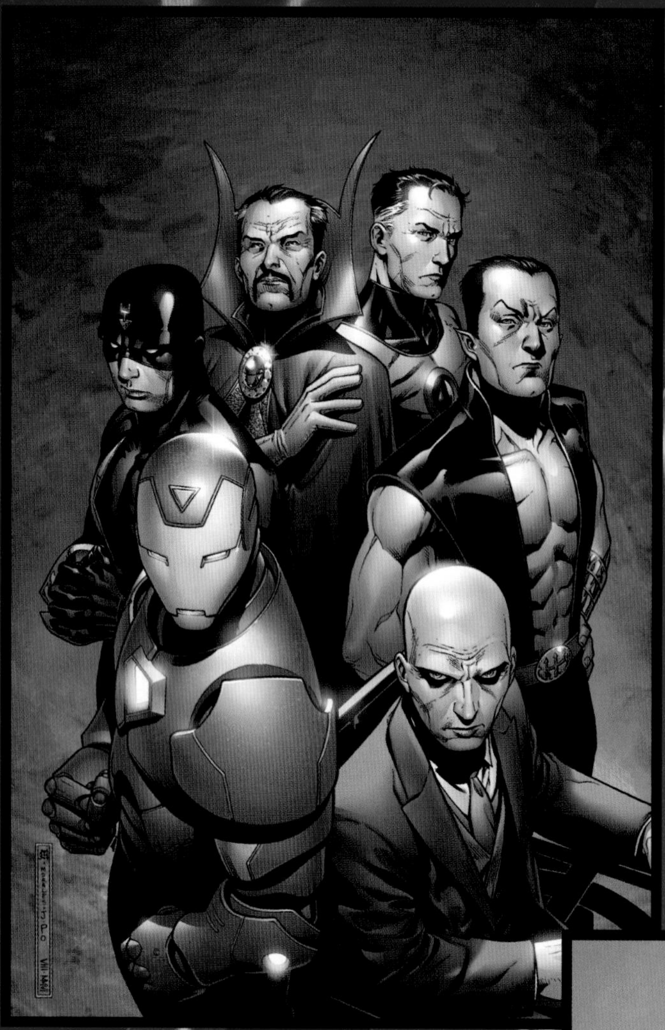

NEW AVENGERS: ILLUMINATI #1
BY JIM CHEUNG

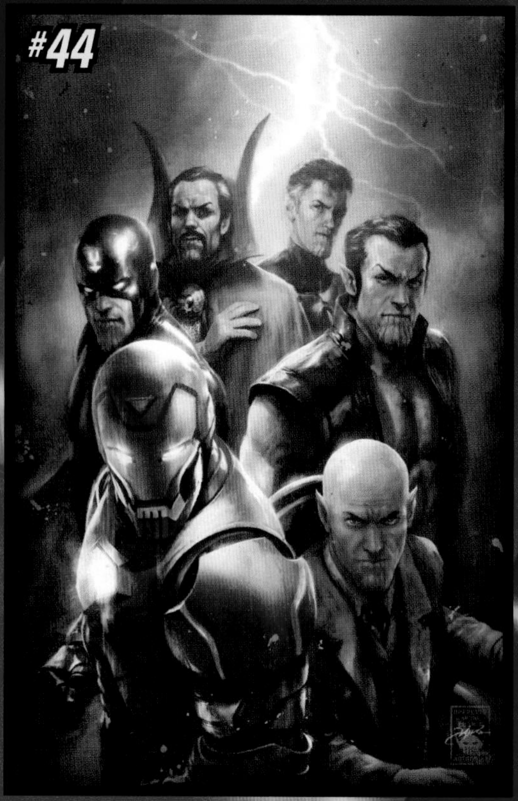
#44

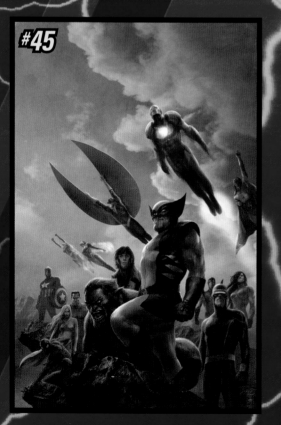

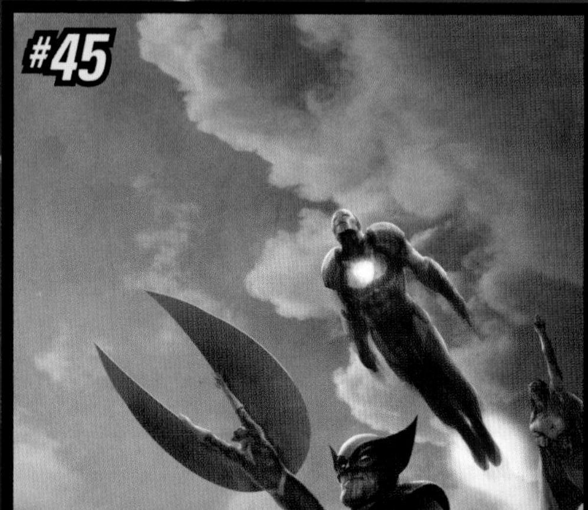
#45

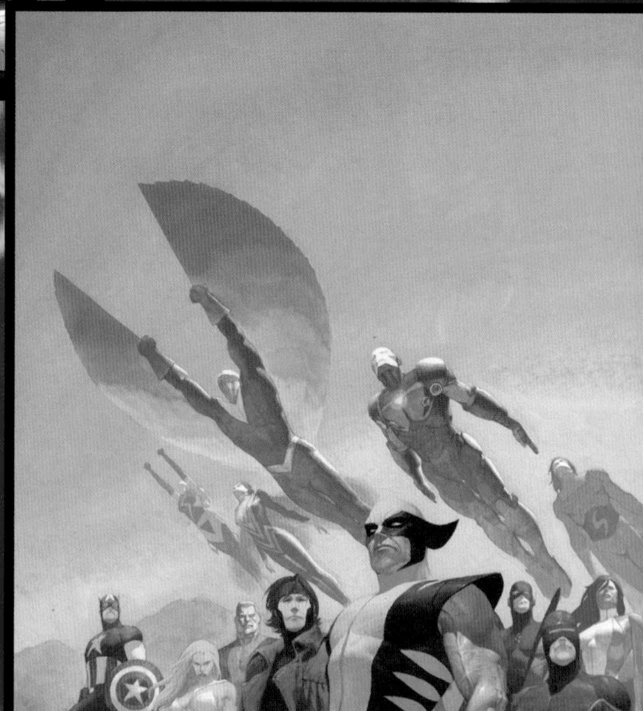

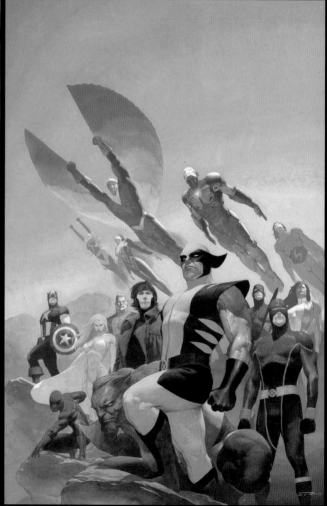

HOUSE OF M #1 BY ESAD RIBIC

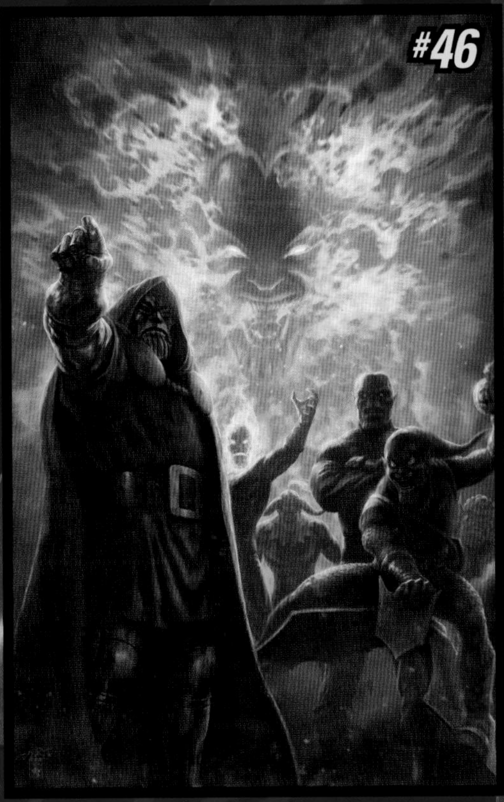
#46

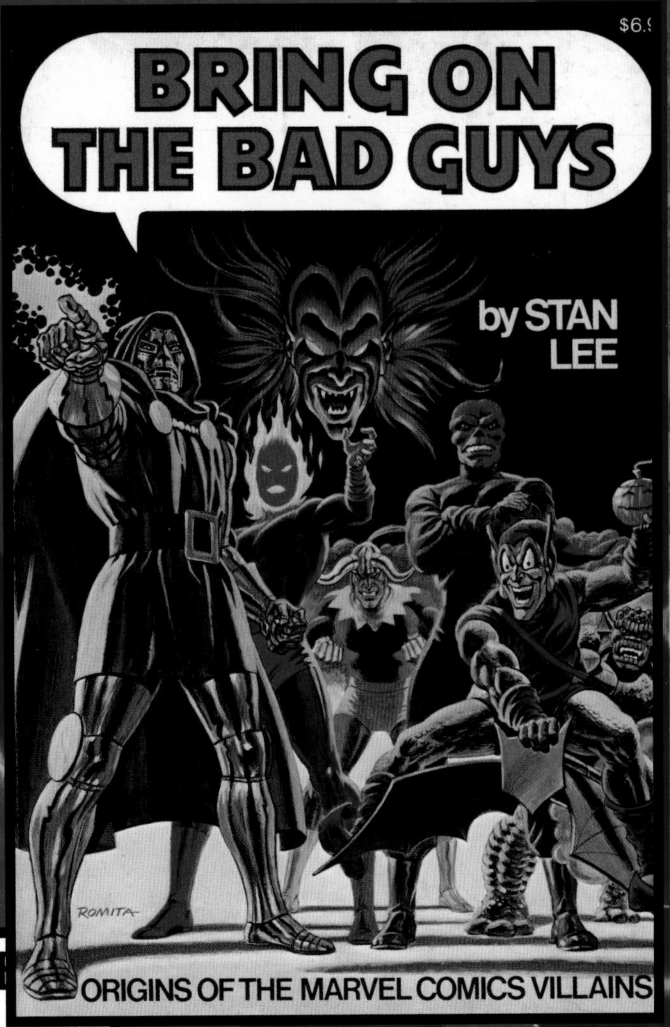
BRING ON THE BAD GUYS
by STAN LEE
ROMITA
ORIGINS OF THE MARVEL COMICS VILLAINS

BY JOHN ROMITA

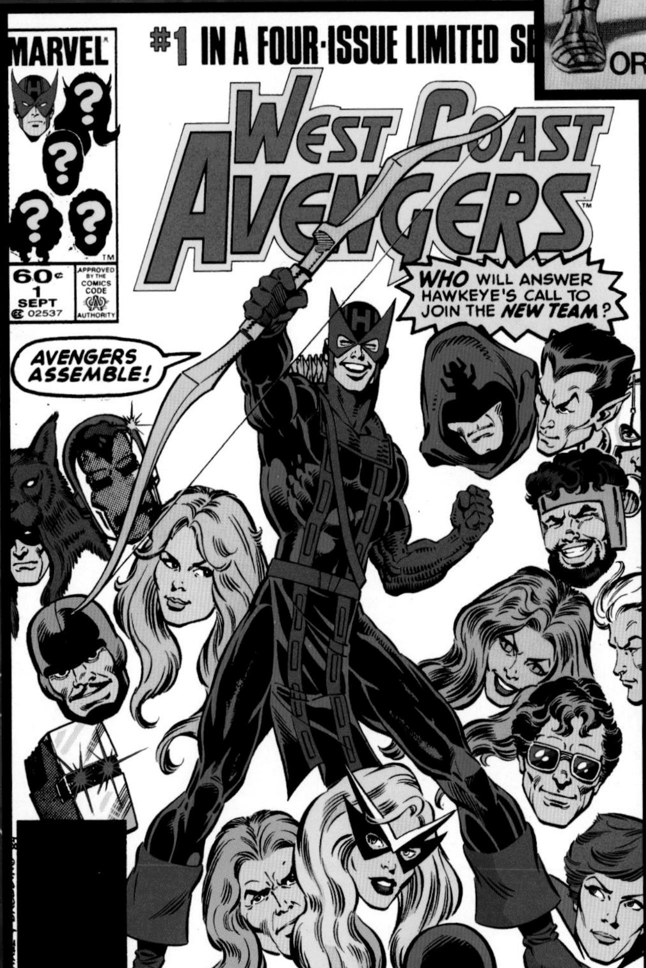
MARVEL
#1 IN A FOUR-ISSUE LIMITED SE
WEST COAST AVENGERS
60¢
1
SEPT
APPROVED BY THE COMICS CODE AUTHORITY
WHO WILL ANSWER HAWKEYE'S CALL TO JOIN THE NEW TEAM?
AVENGERS ASSEMBLE!

BY BOB HALL

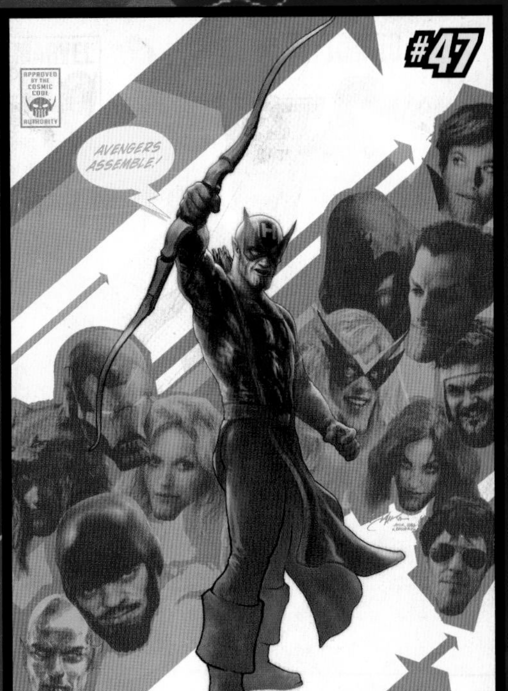
#47
APPROVED BY THE COSMIC CODE AUTHORITY
AVENGERS ASSEMBLE!

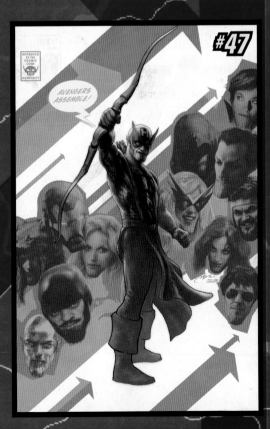

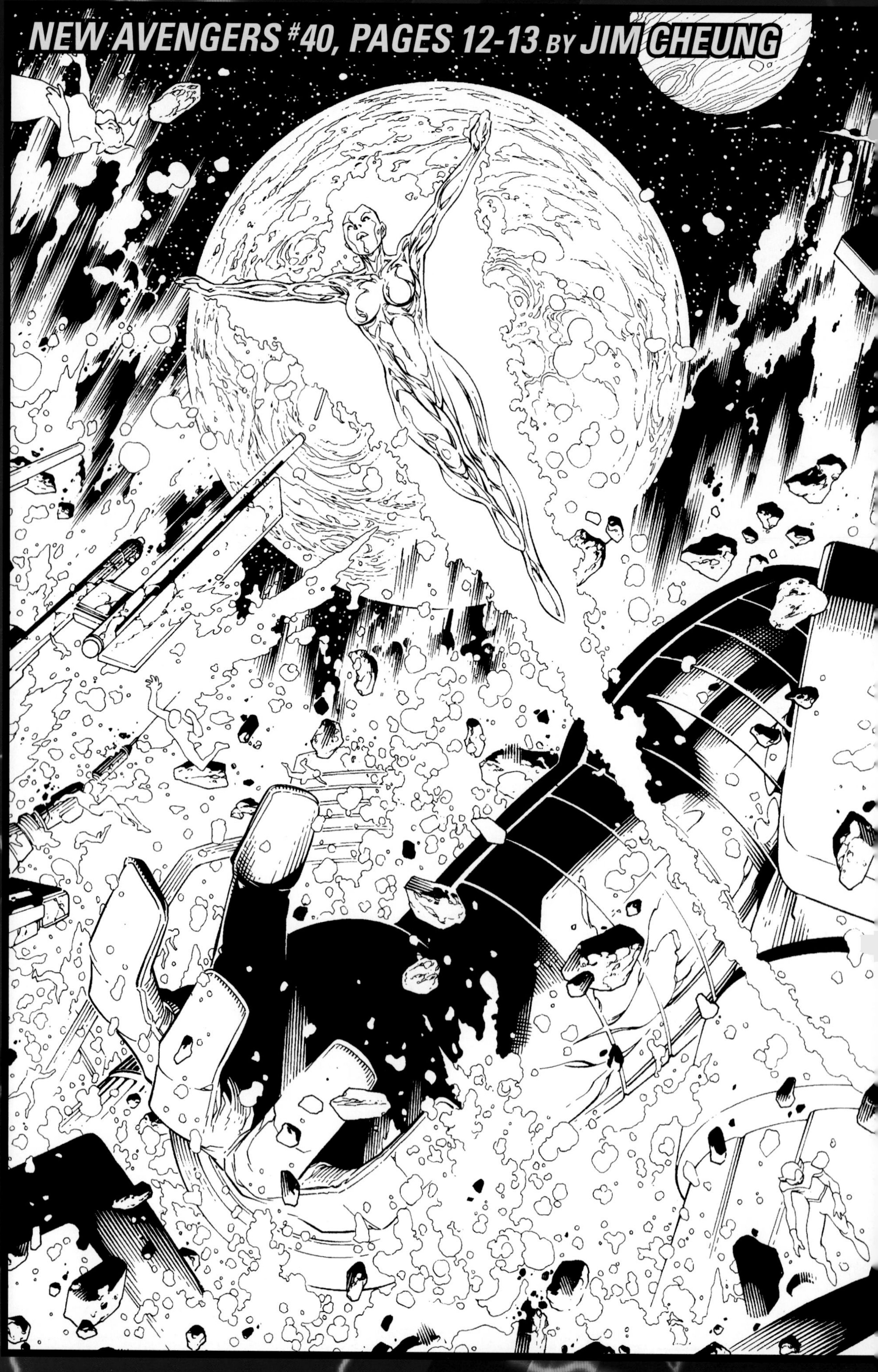
NEW AVENGERS #40, PAGES 12-13 BY JIM CHEUNG

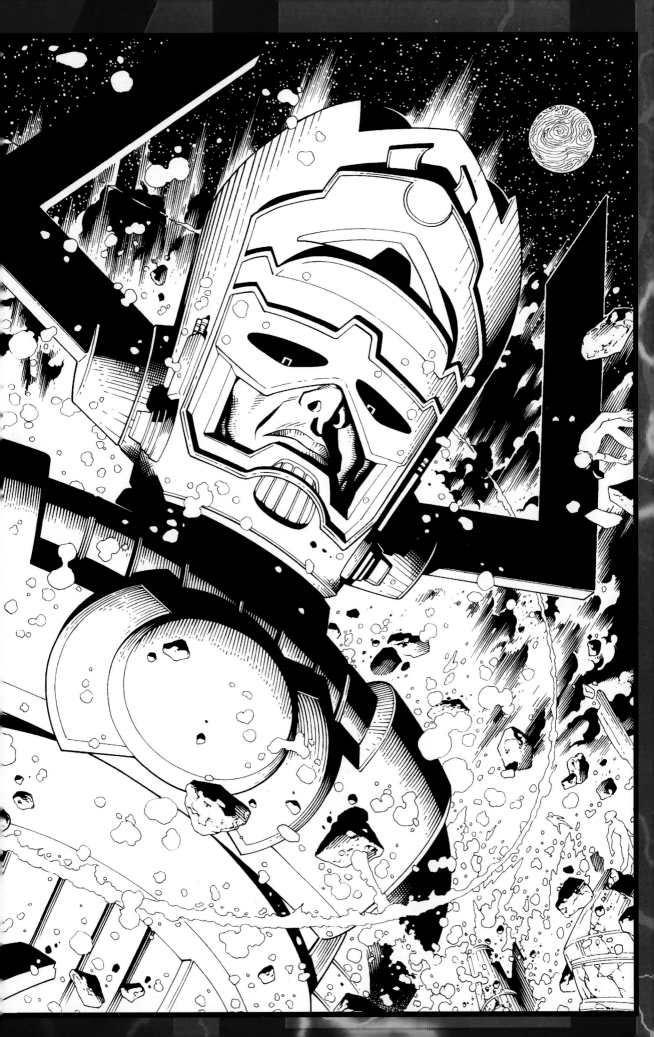

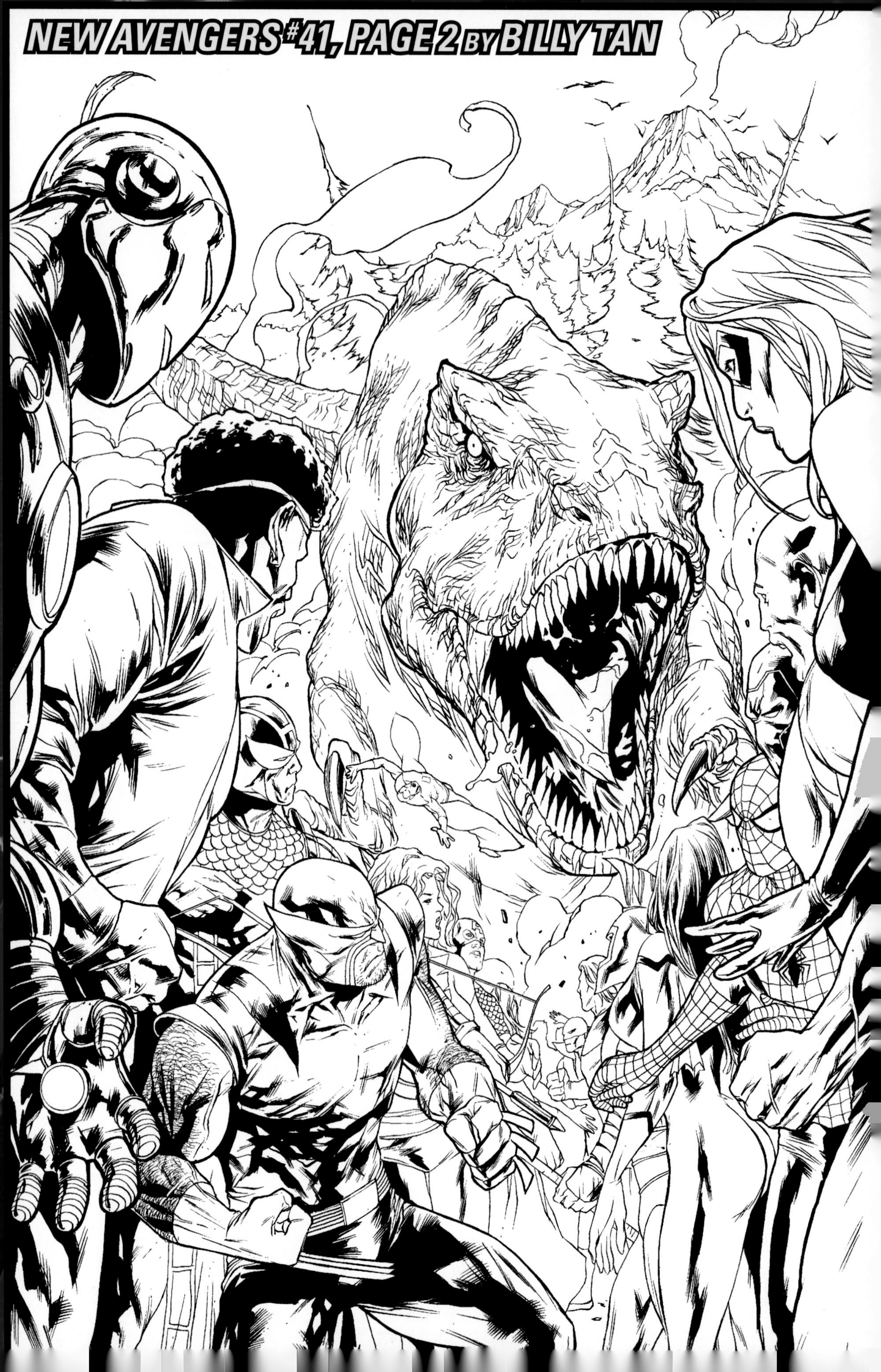
NEW AVENGERS #41, PAGE 2 BY BILLY TAN

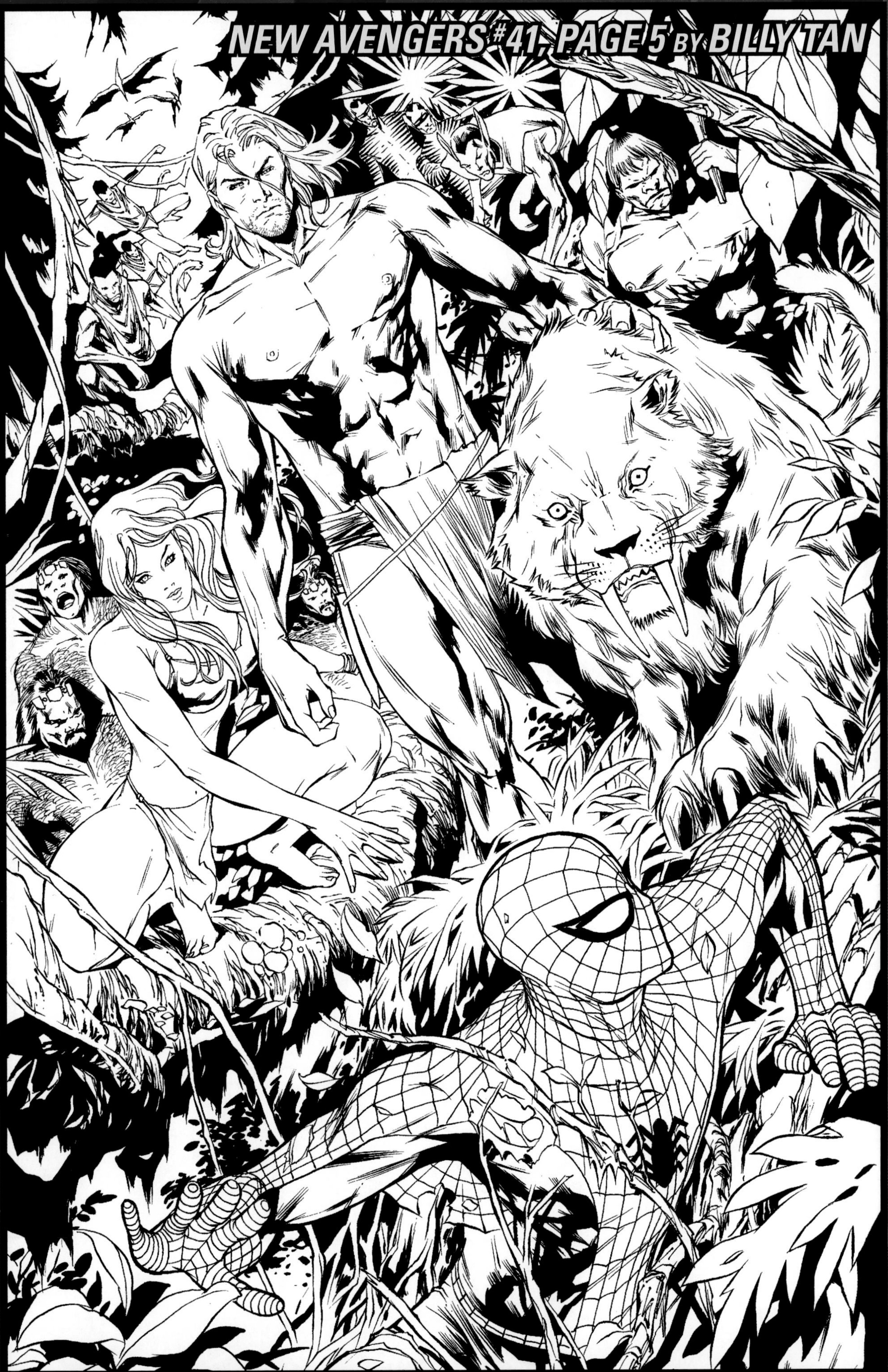
NEW AVENGERS #41, PAGE 5 BY BILLY TAN

NEW AVENGERS #42, PAGES 6-7 BY JIM CHEUNG

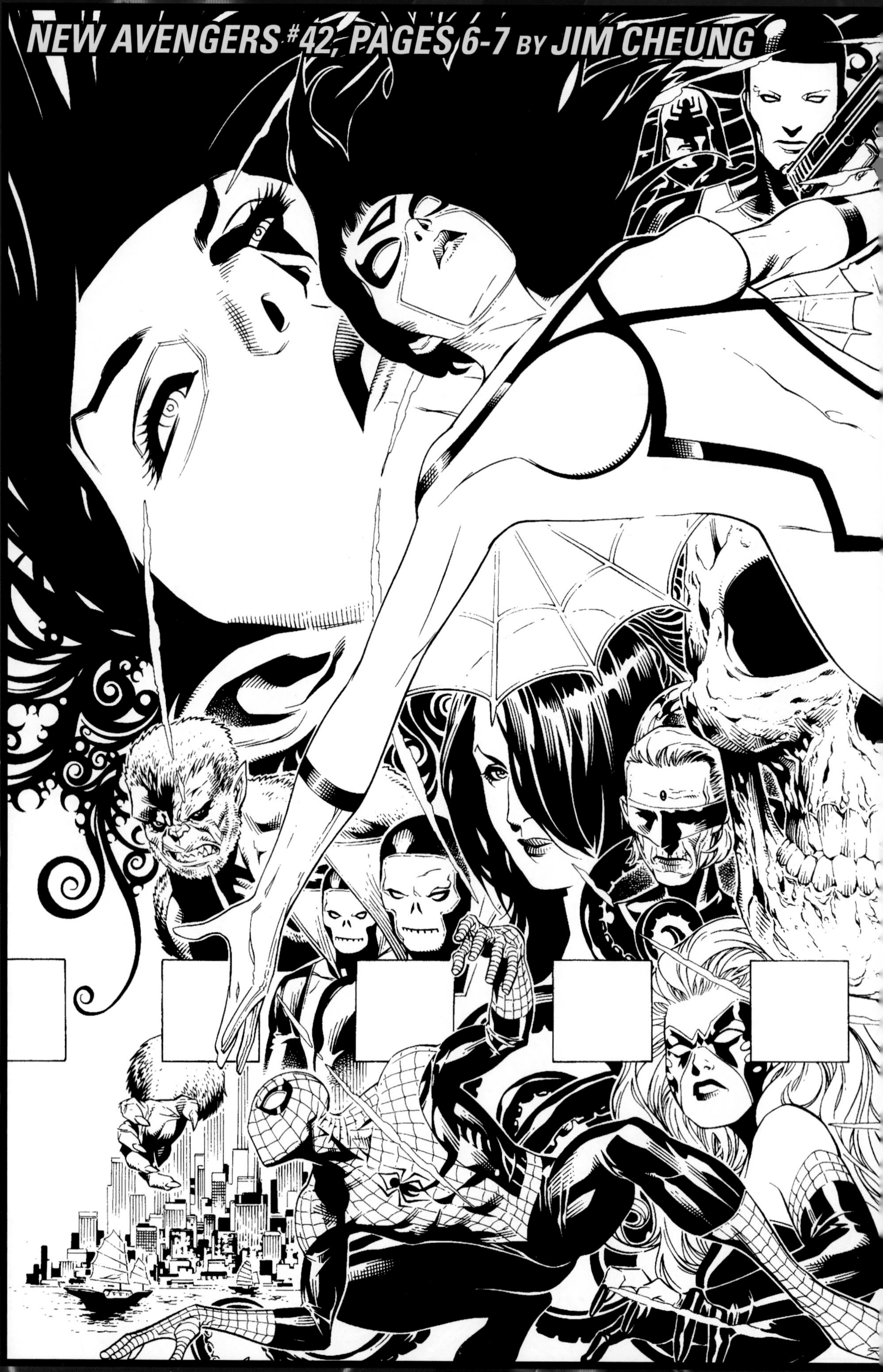

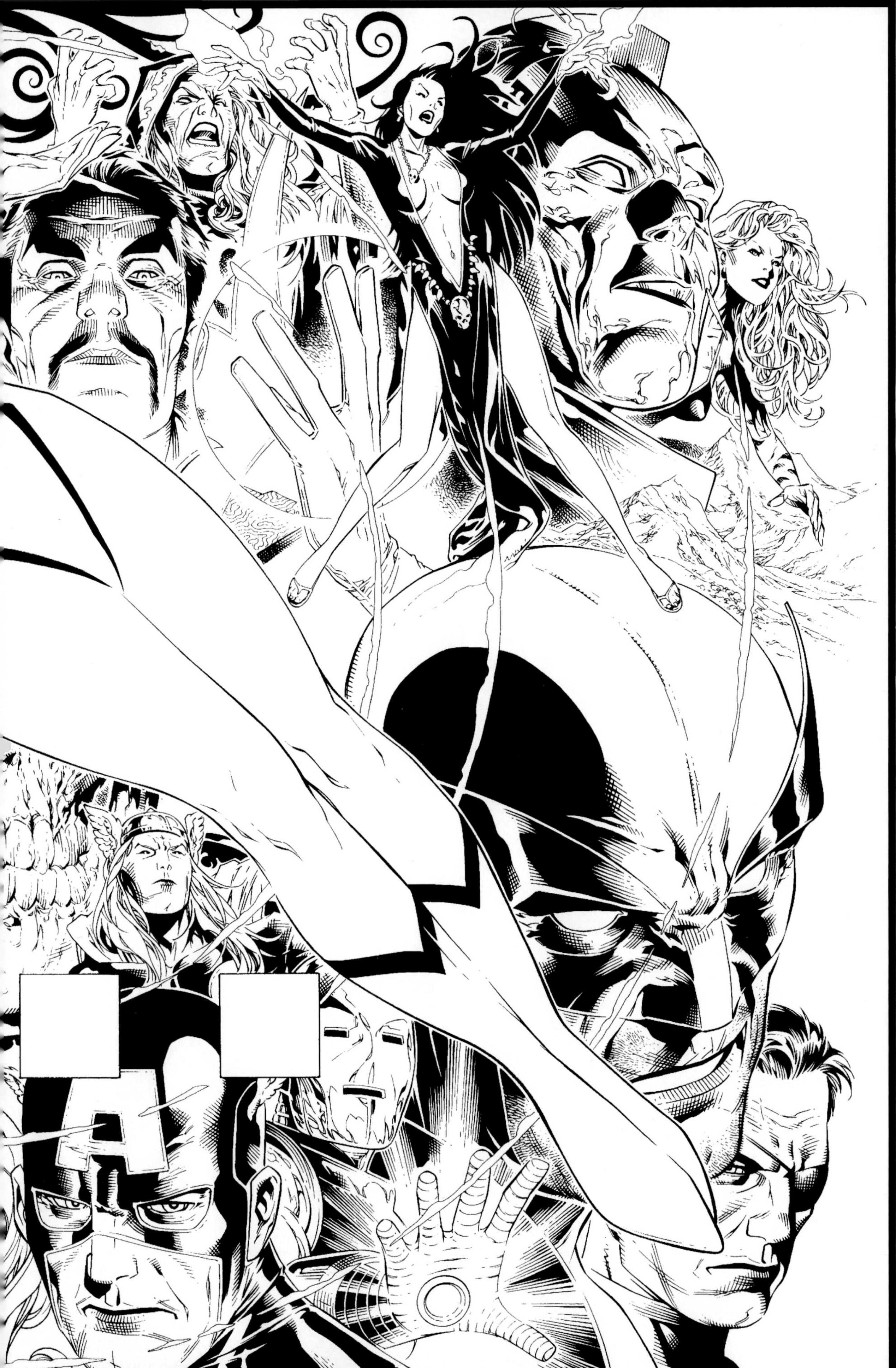

NEW AVENGERS #46, PAGES 2-3 BY BILLY TAN

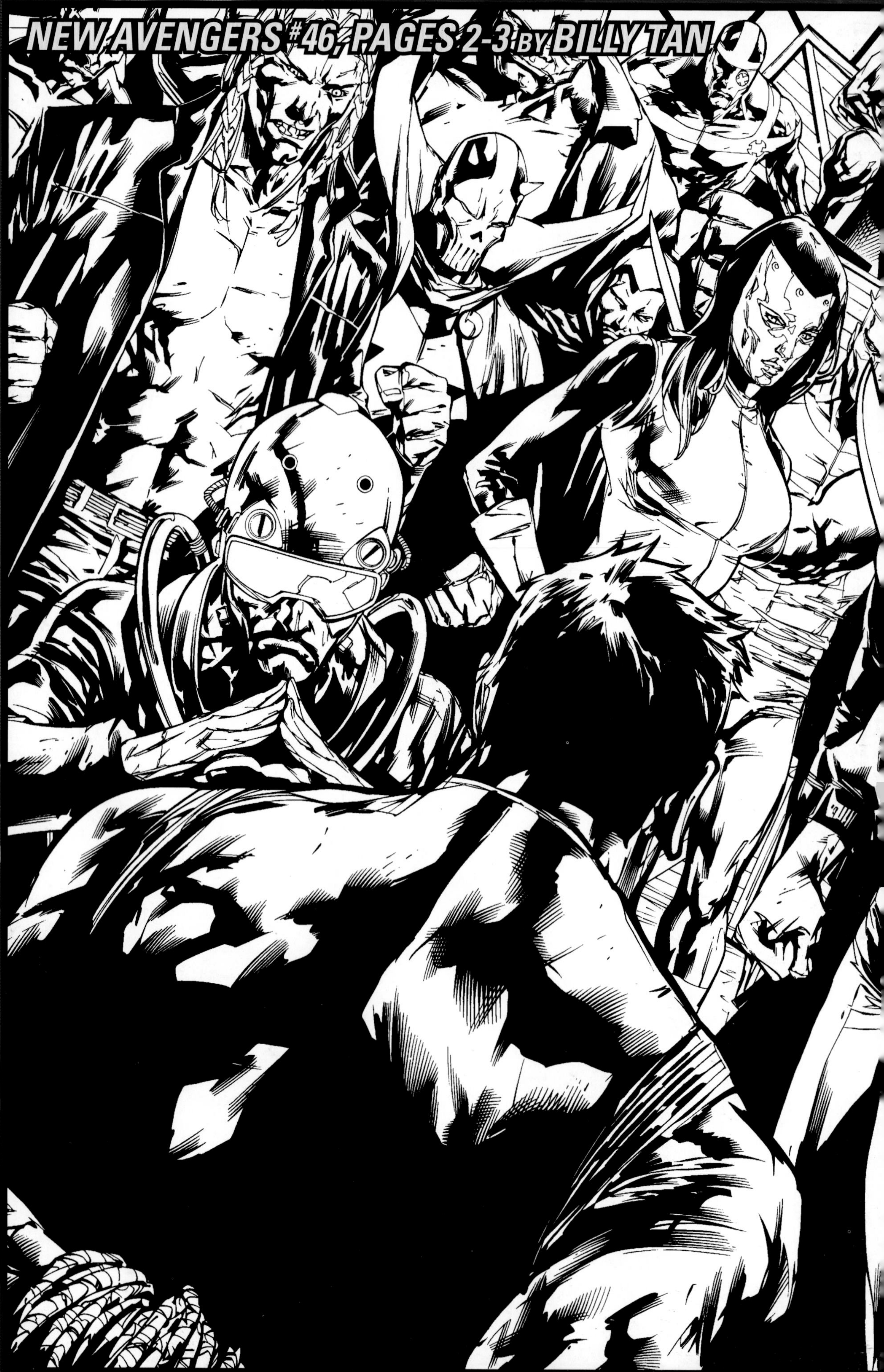

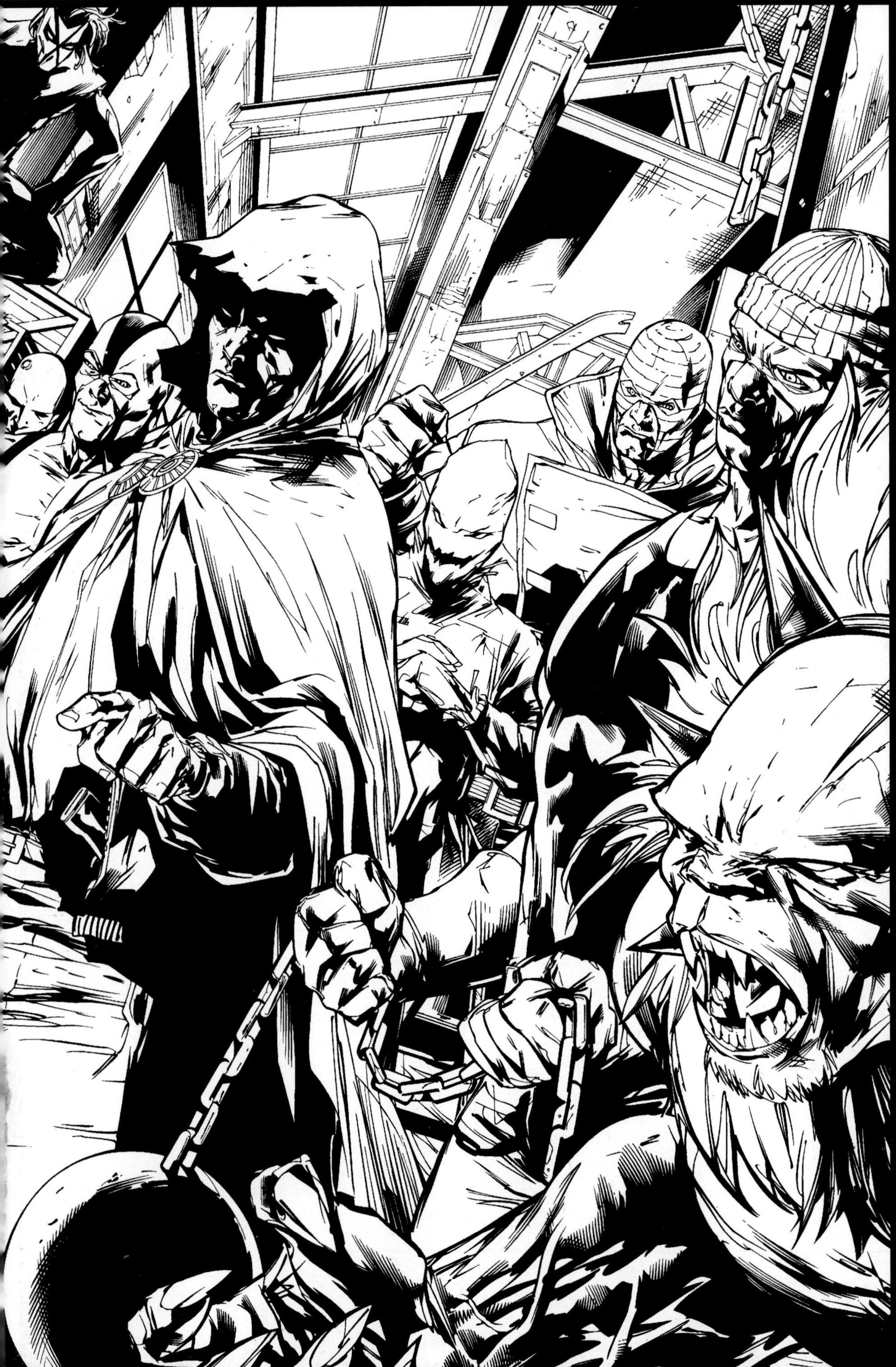

NEW AVENGERS #46, PAGE 23 BY BILLY TAN

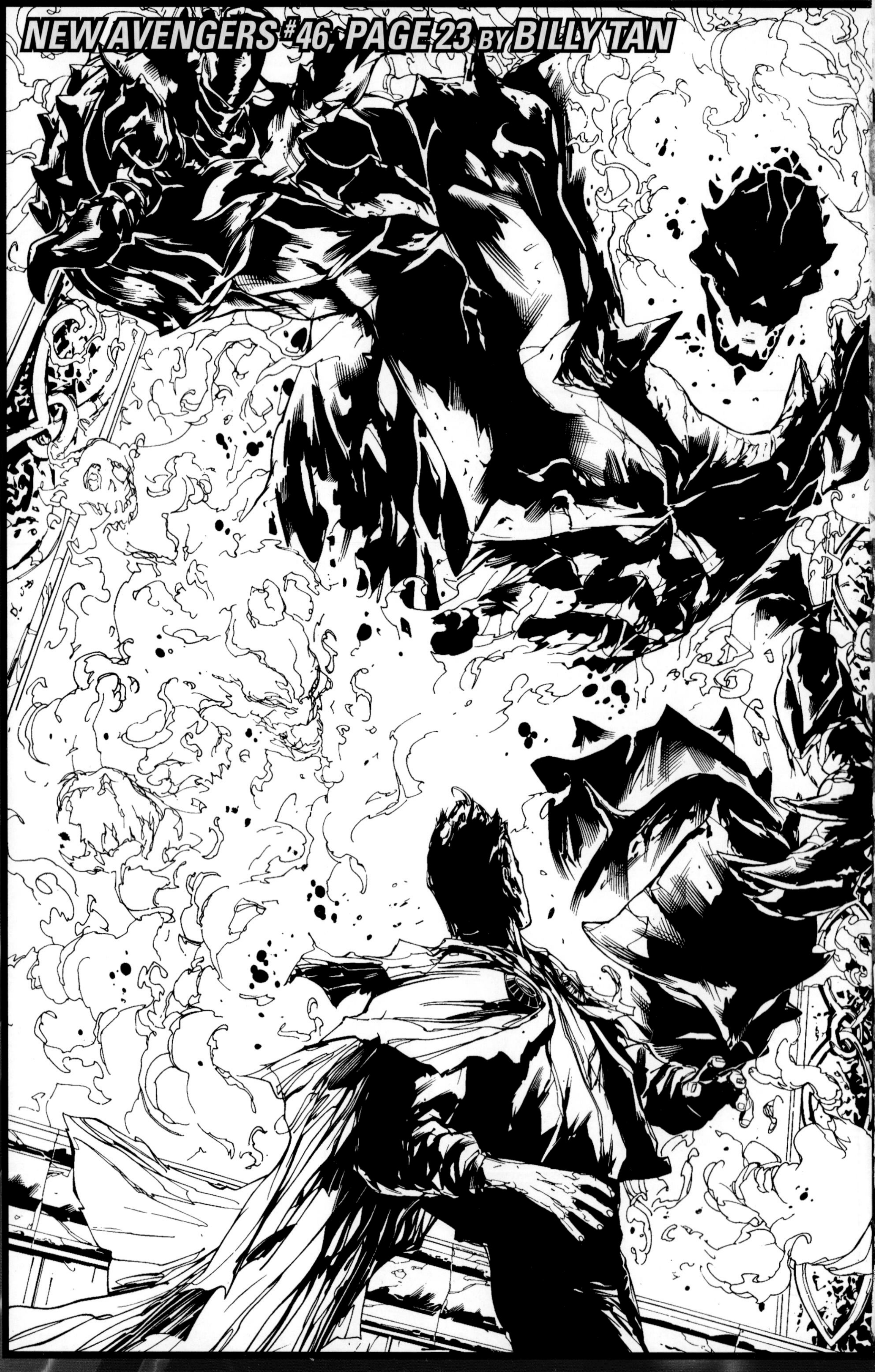